The Basic Writings of
JOSIAH ROYCE

Volume 2

The Basic Writings of
JOSIAH ROYCE

Volume 2:
Logic, Loyalty, and Community

Edited, with a New Introduction, by

John J. McDermott

*Including an Annotated Bibliography of the
Publications of Josiah Royce, Prepared by*
Ignas K. Skrupskelis

Fordham University Press
New York   2005

American Philosophy Series, No. 17
ISSN 1073-2764

Library of Congress Cataloging-in-Publication Data

Royce, Josiah, 1855–1916.
    [Selections. 2005]
    The basic writings of Josiah Royce / edited with an introduction by John J. McDermott ; including an annotated bibliography of the publications of Josiah Royce prepared by Ignas K. Skrupskelis.— 1st Fordham University Press ed.
      p. cm.—(American philosophy series ; no. 17)
    Originally published: Chicago : University of Chicago Press, 1969. With new pref.
    Includes bibliographical references (v. 2, p.) and index.
    Contents: v. 1. Culture, philosophy, and religion—v. 2. Logic, loyalty, and community
    ISBN 0-8232-2483-X (vol. 1)—ISBN 0-8232-2484-8 (vol. 2)
    1. Philosophy, American—20th century. I. McDermott, John J. (John Joseph), 1932– II. Skrupskelis, Ignas K., 1938– III. Title. IV. Series.
B945.R61M3 2005
191—dc22   2005041511

Printed in the United States of America
07 06 05   5 4 3 2 1

First University of Chicago Press edition, 1969

First Fordham University Press edition, 2005

For My Parents

JOHN J. AND HELEN KELLY McDERMOTT

Freedom and loyalty, rarely blended,
is their bequest

After all, however, our lesson is an old and simple one. It is the State, the Social Order, that is divine. We are all but dust, save as this social order gives us life. When we think it our instrument, our plaything, and make our private fortunes the one object, then this social order rapidly becomes vile to us; we call it sordid, degraded, corrupt, unspiritual, and ask how we may escape from it forever. But if we turn again and serve the social order, and not merely ourselves, we soon find that what we are serving is simply our own highest spiritual destiny in bodily form. It is never truly sordid or corrupt or unspiritual; it is only we that are so when we neglect our duty.

Josiah Royce
California

Acknowledgements

My concern for the thought of Josiah Royce dates from lectures given some fifteen years ago by Robert C. Pollock, then professor of philosophy at Fordham University. Robert Pollock was the only person who, in my experience, could make the full case for James and Royce.

Unquestionably, we are of late, witnessing a renascence of interest in the classic American philosophers. Activity in the field of Royce scholarship has generated a small but enthusiastic community of inquiry. In this regard, I am grateful for the generous advice offered by Charles M. Sherover of Hunter College, Robert Neville of Fordham University, Rickard Donovan of Iona College, David Sipfle of Carleton College, Richard Hocking of Emory University, and especially John E. Smith of Yale University. My colleague, Peter T. Manicas of Queens College, was extremely helpful in the preparation of part VI, "Logic and Methodology." Generous secretarial assistance was provided by Mrs. Florence Barry and Mrs. Leona Beck of Queens College.

The man at the center of the contemporary Royce community is Frank M. Oppenheim S.J., of Xavier University. He provided many personal leads as well as considerable advice on the selecting process. I had intended to use his published "Bibliography" but Father Oppenheim selflessly led me to Mr. Ignas Skrupskelis of the University of South Carolina, who had a superior Royce bibliography in preparation. I am happy to report that the bibliography of Mr. Skrupskelis is now included as part IX of volume 2. His work as a bibliographer is outstanding and comes as close to being definitive as is humanly possible. He has spared no effort and left no lead untouched. Mr. Skrupskelis also helped me to

ix

avoid some technical errors in the allocating of correct sources and he clarified some aspects of Royce's career. I am also indebted to the earlier work of Jacob Loewenberg, Daniel Robinson, Stuart Gerry Brown, J. Harry Cotton, John E. Smith, Vincent Buranelli, Peter Fuss, and Thomas F. Powell. My reading of Royce's unpublished papers was enhanced by the efficiency and graciousness of Mr. Kimball C. Elkins and his staff at the Harvard University Archives in Widener Library.

During preparation of the manuscript, I was aided by the encouragement and consideration of Mr. Morris Philipson, director of the University of Chicago Press, and by the care of Mr. Allen Fitchen, humanities editor. I appreciate also some bibliographical assistance from Patrick J. Hill of State University of New York at Stony Brook. Many technical problems and a considerable amount of important detail were handled expertly by my brother Robert A. McDermott of Manhattanville College. He is a man for all seasons, combining enthusiastic responsibility with a respect for another's task.

As always, when the deadline grows near, my wife Virginia generously sets aside massive obligations of her own to help put the manuscript in final shape.

Contents

Preface to the Fordham University Press Edition

It is propitious and gratifying that Fordham University Press has decided to reissue these two volumes of *The Basic Writings of Josiah Royce*. When first published, in 1969, reviewers and commentators were taken with both the sweep and the depth of Royce's thought. After Royce's death on September 14, 1916, his philosophical reputation went into a decline, and he often was represented as being an abstruse acolyte in the Neo-Hegelian tradition. This edition, by contrast, makes crystal-clear that Royce provided us with a thick and expansive philosophical tapestry, including major works in social philosophy, logic, the history of philosophy, and moral philosophy, especially his treatment of loyalty, herein published in full.

Scholarship attendant on Royce's philosophy has developed in quality and quantity since the publication of these volumes in 1969. Of special consideration is the splendid second edition of John Clendenning's *The Life and Thought of Josiah Royce*, in 1999, and the indefatigable, philosophically astute commentaries by Frank Oppenheim, S. J. In March 2003, the Josiah Royce Society was founded; among its tasks will be preparation for a critical edition of Royce's works, published and unpublished. Those of us who recognize the extensive range of his thought believe that, at this time of planetary strife, Royce is among the thinkers who can provide direct and intelligent help as we struggle to ameliorate our condition. Reading Royce is not easy, but then neither are the difficulties we now face.

In addition to the heartfelt acknowledgments found in the original publication of these volumes, I add here gratitude to Scott Pratt, J. Brent Crouch, Kelly Parker, Michael Brodrick, and David Henderson, my research assistant. And I am grateful to Patricia A. McDermott, without whom, for me, nothing would be done.

JOHN J. McDERMOTT

Preface

Few travelers on the heavily used highway from Reno to Sacramento reflect on the names of the small towns as they are quickly passed, one blurring out the other. But one of these towns, Emigrant Gap, California, invites us to travel a bypass, rich with tall pines, clean air, and an invigorating breeze. On that road is the town of Grass Valley, California, where the philosopher Josiah Royce was born in 1855. Now resembling a suburban town, Grass Valley yields little of Royce's memory except for a commemorative plaque in the local library. Slightly to the northeast, however, on Route 20, one finds Nevada City, California. To this day, in Nevada City, we can encounter some of the mining camp atmosphere of Royce's childhood.[1] The saga of the trip west and the early struggles in Grass Valley have been told by Royce's indomitable mother, Sarah Royce.[2] Less than a year before his death Royce recalled these early days and cited their profound impact on his personal and reflective life.

My earliest recollections include a very frequent wonder as to what my elders meant when they said that this was a new community. I frequently looked at the vestiges left by the former diggings of miners, saw that many pine logs were rotten, and that a miner's grave was to be found in a lonely place not far from my own house. Plainly men had lived and died thereabouts. I dimly reflected that this sort of life had

---

[1] Cf. John Steele, *In Camp and Cabin* (New York: Citadel Books, 1962) (1901), for a diary relating mining camp experiences of the early 1850's in Nevada City and the Feather River district.

[2] Sarah Royce, *A Frontier Lady: Recollections of the Gold Rush and Early California*, ed. Ralph Henry Gabriel (New Haven: Yale University Press, 1932); see also Ralph Henry Gabriel, *The Course of American Democratic Thought* (New Haven: Yale University Press, 1956), pp. 303–14.

apparently been going on ever since men dwelt in that land. The logs
and the grave looked old. The sunsets were beautiful. The wide prospects when one looked across the Sacramento Valley were impressive,
and had long interested the people of whose love for my country I
heard much. What was there then in this place that ought to be called
new, or for that matter, crude? I wondered, and gradually came to feel
that part of my life's business was to find out what all this wonder
meant. (*HGC*, pp. 122–23; below, 1:31–32)

In his attempt to realize the meaning of this early wonder Josiah
Royce left no stone unturned. Before his relatively early death
at the age of sixty, Royce had pursued literally every field of
inquiry known to his time. And his creative work shows an unusual
range of genre: literary essays, geographical essays, popular and
rigorously technical philosophical essays, theological treatises,
formal papers in logic and mathematics—even a novel. Although
the selections reprinted in these two volumes are basic to any
understanding of Royce, and in terms of contemporary publishing
practices generously extensive, they constitute only a small part of
his work. An examination of the Bibliography will show this to
be obviously true. It should also be noted that the present edition
does not include selections from *The Problem of Christianity*, for
the entire text is now published as a companion volume by The
University of Chicago Press, with an introduction by John E.
Smith.

The intention of this edition of Royce's writings is threefold:
first, to illustrate the range and quality of his thought; second,
to present a detailed instance of a thinker who forges a viable
relationship between affection for the local experience of community and the demands of a philosophical and scientific version of
the entire human situation; third, to present anew the relevance
of Royce's judgment in matters cultural, moral, and religious.

We are long past the time when the thought of a single philosopher can redirect the historical situation in which we live. But we
cannot afford to ignore any insight however removed from us in
time and style. Royce spent much of his life developing his contention that true individualism is possible only insofar as one
participates in a series of self-sufficient, complete communities. If
true, such an insight is salvific for us in the present situation. We
should pay careful attention Royce's thought on this matter. He
has much to teach us.

JOHN J. McDERMOTT

Chronology

1855   Josiah Royce born in the mining town of Grass Valley, California, November 20.

1866   Attends grade school in San Francisco

1871   Enters the University of California

1875   Receives B.A. degree from the University of California

1875–76 Studies in Germany at Leipzig and Göttingen

1876–78 Completes a Doctorate in Philosophy at Johns Hopkins University

1878   Returns to the University of California as lecturer in the English Department

1880   Marries Katharine Head

1882   Joins faculty at Harvard University as Philosophy instructor

1888   Visits Australia

1890–91 Engages in public, acrimonious controversy with F. E. Abbot and C. S. Peirce

1892   Becomes Professor of the History of Philosophy at Harvard University

1895   Participates in extensive philosophical symposium on the "Conception of God" at the University of California, Berkeley.

1899   Delivers the first half of his Gifford Lectures at the University of Aberdeen. Later published as *The World and the Individual*

1900   Completes Gifford Lectures

1906   Lectures at Johns Hopkins University (lectures published posthumously as *Lectures on Modern Idealism*)

1911   Delivers the Bross Lectures at Lake Forest College in

Illinois (lectures published as *The Sources of Religious Insight*)

1914   Becomes Alford Professor of Natural Religion, Moral Philosophy, and Civil Polity at Harvard University

1916   Dies in Cambridge, Massachusetts, September 14.

Bibliographic Abbreviations

The following is a list of Royce's major publications (excepting articles) and the abbreviations used to designate them in the text and notes. Information concerning Royce's major articles is to be found in the virtually complete Annotated Bibliography at the end of volume 2.

PLA   *Primer of Logical Analysis for the Use of Composition Students.* San Francisco: A. L. Bancroft, 1881.

RAP   *The Religious Aspect of Philosophy.* Boston: Houghton Mifflin Co., 1885.

Cal   *California from the Conquest in 1846 to the Second Vigilance Committee in San Francisco (1856): A Study of American Character.* Boston: Houghton Mifflin Co., 1886.

FOC   *The Feud of Oakfield Creek: A Novel of California Life.* Boston: Houghton Mifflin Co., 1887.

SMP   *The Spirit of Modern Philosophy.* Boston: Houghton Mifflin Co., 1892.

CG   *The Conception of God,* with "Comments" by S. E. Mezes, J. Le Conte, and G. H. Howison. Berkeley: Philosophical Union, 1895. Second Edition, with "Supplementary Essay" by Royce, 1897.

SGE   *Studies of Good and Evil:* A Series of Essays upon Life and Philosophy. New York: Appleton, 1898.

WI   *The World and the Individual.* 2 vols. New York: Macmillan Co., 1899, 1901.

CI   *The Conception of Immortality*. Boston: Houghton Mifflin Co., 1900.

OP   *Outlines of Psychology*. New York, Macmillan Co., 1903.

HS   *Herbert Spencer: An Estimate and a Review*. New York: Fox, Duffield, 1904.

PL   *The Philosophy of Loyalty*. New York: Macmillan Co., 1908.

RQP   *Race Questions, Provincialism, and Other American Problems*. New York: Macmillan Co., 1908.

WJO   *William James and Other Essays on the Philosophy of Life*. New York: Macmillan Co., 1911.

SRI   *The Sources of Religious Insight*. New York: Charles Scribner's Sons, 1912.

PC   *The Problem of Christianity*. 2 vols. New York: Macmillan Co., 1913. Reprinted with new introduction by John E. Smith, in a one volume edition as a companion to the present two volumes. Chicago: University of Chicago Press, 1968.

PrL   "The Principles of Logic." In *Logic (Encyclopedia of the Philosophical Sciences)*. Vol. 1. London: Macmillan Co., 1913: 67–135.

War   *War and Insurance*. New York: Macmillan Co., 1914.

HGC   *The Hope of the Great Community*. New York: Macmillan, 1916.

LMI   *Lectures on Modern Idealism*. Edited by J. Loewenberg. New Haven: Yale University Press, 1919.

FE   *Fugitive Essays by Josiah Royce*. Ed. J. Loewenberg. Cambridge: Harvard University Press, 1920.

RLE   *Royce's Logical Essays*. Ed. Daniel S. Robinson. Dubuque: William C. Brown Co., 1951.

Sem   *Josiah Royce's Seminar, 1913–1914: As Recorded in the Notebooks of Harry T. Costello*. Ed. Grover Smith, with essay on Royce's philosophy by Richard Hocking. New Brunswick: Rutgers University Press, 1963.

Editor's Note on the Text

With the exception of an occasional transition sentence and the concluding acknowledgement paragraph of "The Possibility of International Insurance," I have avoided any internal editing of the text. In only two instances have I broken up an original essay. First, under the chapter title "Types of Order," sections 2 and 3 of *The Principles of Logic* have been reprinted, while section 1 has been omitted. Second, only section 4, which concludes "Some Relations Between Philosophy and Science in the First Half of the Nineteenth Century in Germany," has been reprinted. I have entitled this chapter "The Methodology of Science."

Although the text of *The Philosophy of Loyalty* is reprinted in its entirety, I have eliminated the index, as it no longer serves its original purpose. Where possible, when citing texts from Royce's writings, I have also made reference to their location in the present edition. In my commentary, an asterisk placed after the title of a chapter or essay written by Royce signifies its inclusion in these two volumes. Royce's punctuation, spelling, and frequent use of italics has been retained throughout as have the occasional references of previous editors. The section on Bibliographic Abbreviations and the extended Bibliography will provide maximum information about the sources used throughout these two volumes.

The Basic Writings of
JOSIAH ROYCE

Volume 2

Part VI

Logic and Methodology

Part VI

Logic and Methodology

For his times, Royce was a logician of the first rank. The quality of his work in logic becomes more extraordinary when considered in the context of his multiple achievements in areas of thought quite apart from that effort. Morton White, who is skeptical of Royce's overall achievement, evaluates his contribution in this way.

For Royce was more than a metaphysical soothsayer, more than a philosopher of religion and of loyalty to loyalty: he was also a logician and a philosopher of science. He was one of the first American teachers of philosophy to recognize the importance of research in symbolic logic and to encourage its study both for its own intrinsic intellectual importance and as a tool. Some of his pupils, like C. I. Lewis and H. M. Sheffer, became distinguished Harvard contributors to this subject and founders of one of the most influential centers of logic in the twentieth century.[1]

The partial range of Royce's achievement in logic was made apparent by the publication in 1951 of Daniel S. Robinson's edition of *Royce's Logical Essays.*[2] Still further indication of his interest in the philosophy of science and problems of methodology became manifest with the fortuitous recovery and publication of the notes of Royce's "Seminar of 1913-1914."[3] The often cited influence of

In this section, I am indebted to my colleague at Queens College, Dr. Peter T. Manicas, for sharing his interpretation and evaluation of Royce's work in logic.

[1] "Harvard's Philosophical Heritage," in *Religion, Politics and the Higher Learning* (Cambridge: Harvard University Press, 1959), p. 53.

[2] (Dubuque: Wm. C. Brown Company, 1951).

[3] See Grover Smith, ed., *Josiah Royce's Seminar, 1913-1914: as recorded in the Notebooks of Harry T. Costello* (New Brunswick: Rutgers University Press, 1963). Still another Royce "Seminar" awaits publication, that of 1916, Philosophy 9, devoted to metaphysics. It is being edited by Richard Hocking.

Charles Peirce on Royce is sustained by both of these publications and this influence is obviously a crucial factor in the development of what Royce calls his "Absolute Pragmatism." (*RLE*, p. 364; below 2:813).

Royce's fundamental problem was to account for the existence and knowledge of real individuals, while yet remaining faithful to the accessibility of "absolute truth."[4] In other terms, Royce faced the classical objection to Absolute Idealism, namely, the impossibility of establishing human freedom. As early as 1897, under the press of criticism from G. H. Howison, Royce makes an effort to restate the relationship between the "Absolute and the Individual." (C. G., Supplementary Essay, pp. 135–326). Later he appends to the first volume of the *World and the Individual* another supplementary essay, in order to once again show the plausibility of holding to the view that "an Infinite Multitude, can, without contradiction, be viewed as determinately real. . . ." (*WI*, 1:476)

It is precisely this contention of Royce, which William James rejects in a "Notebook" entry of 1905. "The difficulty for me here is the same that I lay so much stress on in my criticism of Royce's Absolute, only it is inverted. If the whole is all that is experienced, how can the parts be experienced otherwise than as it experiences them? That is Royce's difficulty. *My* difficulty is the opposite: if the parts are all the experience there is, how can the whole be experienced otherwise than as any of them experiences it?"[5]

A third reformulation, by Royce, of this problem occurs in two stages. The first, in 1905, was a continuation of the work of A. B. Kempe, and dealt with the problem of "order," phrased by Royce as the "System Sigma."[6] It was this paper that C. I. Lewis contrasted with the *Principia Mathematica* of Whitehead and Russell, relative to methodological procedure. "By contrast, Professor Royce's is the

---

[4] The persistence of this problem in the thought of Royce is an indication that his early fascination with Spinoza left its mark, perhaps more extensively than that left by the work of Hegel.

[5] Cf. William James, "Unpublished Papers," Houghton Library, Harvard University, box L, n-vii; cited also in Ralph Barton Perry, *The Thought and Character of William James* (Boston: Little, Brown & Co., 1935) 2:751–52.

[6] Josiah Royce, "The Relation of the Principles of Logic to the Foundations of Geometry," *Transactions of the American Mathematical Society*, 24 (July, 1905): 353–415.

method of the path-finder. The prospect of the novel is here much greater. The system may—probably does—contain new continents of order whose existence we do not even suspect."[7] The second stage in this development came in 1913 when Royce published the *Principles of Logic* and attempted to bring together his metaphysical concerns, with his newly developed logic of order. The burden of his argument is found in Sections 2 and 3, reprinted below in their entirety. We, therefore, only isolate out a few texts to show Royce's intention. He insists that the logician, "in considering his order-types, is not abstracting from *all* experience. His world too is, in a perfectly genuine sense, empirical." (*RLE*, p. 338; below, 2:787).

But this tie to experience does not preclude the affirmation of an infinite system.[8] On two separate occasions in the *Principles of Logic*, Royce puts this tension into perspective.

First:

The concept of an individual is thus one whose origin and meaning are due to our will, to our interest, to so-called pragmatic motives. We actively *postulate* individuals and individuality. We do not merely find them. Yet this does not mean that the motives which guide our will in this postulate are wholly arbitrary, or are of *merely* relative value. *There are some active and voluntary attitudes towards our experience which we cannot refuse to take without depriving ourselves of the power to conceive any order whatever as present in our world.*[9] Without objects conceived as unique individuals, we can have *no Classes.*

---

[7] C. I. Lewis, "Types of Order and System," in *Papers in Honor of Josiah Royce on His Sixtieth Birthday*, p. 191. (These papers were originally published in the *Philosophical Review*, 25 [1916], with different pagination. The text from Lewis is found there on p. 419.) See also Smith, *Seminar*, 1913–1914, pp. 178–83, where Royce's critique of Lewis' theory of strict implication is discussed.

[8] For an analysis of Royce's dependence on the shift in emphasis in modern mathematics from quantity to order, see Richard Hocking, "The Influence of Mathematics on Royce's Metaphysics," *Journal of Philosophy*, 53, No. 3 (February, 1956): 77–91. See also the chapter on "Logic as the Science of Order," J. Harry Cotton, *Royce on the Human Self*, pp. 157–89.

[9] This phrasing of Royce seems anticipatory of the notion of posits in the thought of W.V.O. Quine. Cf., e.g., *Word and Object* (Cambridge: The M.I.T. Press, 1960), pp. 21–25. By way of influence, it is perhaps significant that William James mentions the term "posit" as early as 1905. He traced the term to the English philosopher Charles Hinton and considered using it as a name for bits of "pure experience." See William James, "Unpublished Papers," box L, n-vii.

Without classes we can, as we have seen, define *no Relations*, without relations we can have *no Order. But to be reasonable is to conceive of order-systems, real or ideal. Therefore, we have an absolute logical need to conceive of individual objects as the elements of our ideal order systems.* This postulate is the condition of defining clearly any theoretical conception whatever. (*RLE*, p. 350; below 2:799).

Second:

In brief, whatever actions are such, whatever types of action are such, whatever results of activity, whatever conceptual constructions are such, that the very act of getting rid of them, or of thinking them away, logically implies their presence, are known to us indeed both empirically and pragmatically (since we note their presence and learn of them through action); but they are also absolute. And any account which succeeds in telling what they are has absolute truth. Such truth is a "construction" or "creation," for activity determines its nature. It is "found," for we observe it when we act. (*RLE*, p. 365; below 2:813).

As to whether Royce saves his metaphysics by this method is open to debate. But Royce's notion of "interpretation"[10] takes on a clarity when analyzed in the light of his logic, particularly the logic of relations (*RLE*, pp. 338–48; below, pp. 788–97). And, above all, these essays on Logic and Methodology, should put to rest the frequent assertion that Royce's thought was indifferent to the burdens of scientific method. Indeed, Royce evaluated the validity of his metaphysics in relation to the claims of science and logic, as much as did Leibniz and Whitehead.

[10] See Hocking, "Influence of Mathematics," pp. 88–90.

21

Recent Logical Inquiries
and Their
Psychological Bearings

The American Psychological Association has always given a kindly recognition to the general philosophical interests which many of its members represent, as well as to the more distinctively psychological concerns which properly form the center and the main body of its undertakings. In honoring me, by calling me to fill for the year the office of president, my fellow members have well known that they ran the risk of hearing a discussion rather of some philosophical problem than of a distinctively experimental topic. I, in my turn, am quite unwilling to ignore or to neglect the fact that ours is primarily a psychological association, while I am equally aware that the general student of philosophy is at a disadvantage when he tries to discuss with the productive workers in the laboratories the matters which, as their specialty grows, come to be increasingly their own peculiar possession. Yet a presidential address is properly an opportunity for studying the problems suggested by a comparison of various fields and methods of work. And accordingly, upon this occasion, I propose to discuss some questions that lie on the borderland between psychology and the distinctively philosophical disciplines. These questions in part directly touch

[Reprinted from *Psychological Review*, 9 (1902): 105–33.]

undertakings which already occupy a recognized place in the psychological laboratories. In part they seem to me to promise to yield in future still wider opportunities for experimental research than are now open. In any case they are questions of permanent interest, and of increasing importance, which neither the psychologist nor the philosopher can afford to ignore.

I

I have named my paper a discourse upon 'recent logical inquiries and their psychological bearings.' By the term 'recent logical inquiries,' I mean to refer to two decidedly distinct classes of researches, both of which are today receiving much attention. To the first of these two classes belong researches directly bearing upon the psychology of the thinking process, and upon the natural history of logical phenomena in general. Such inquiries may be called logical, since they are sometimes undertaken by logicians for the sake of their own science, and in any case are suggested by the problems of logic. Meanwhile, studies of this class are obviously also, at least in intention, contributions to psychology. But I wish, in addition, before I am done, to call attention to quite another class of researches, whose psychological bearing is not at first sight so evident. This my second class of recent logical inquiries consists of studies in the comparative logic of the various sciences, and of examinations of the first principles of certain special sciences. I refer here especially to such books as Mach's well-known volume on the 'Principles of Mechanics,' and to all the large literature that has grown up about the problems suggested by the fundamental concepts of the different natural sciences. I place in the same class, moreover, the elaborate and fruitful researches into the foundations of arithmetic, of geometry, and of the Theory of Functions, which are due to such mathematicians as Cantor, Dedekind, Peano, Klein, Hilbert. The last three or four decades have seen an enormous extension of the literature of this type. I include, moreover, in the same class, certain more distinctively philosophical treatises such as Russell's 'Essay on the Foundations of Geometry,' and Couturat's volume on the 'Concept of the Infinite,' and these are but specimens of the class of inquiries in question.

I mention this vast collection of significant studies, not because

I am in any sense a master in this field of the comparative logic of the sciences, but because, as a humble learner, I have been trying to make my way in some of the plainer of the paths that these recent studies have been opening, and because I hope, by a few wholly inadequate, but at least timely indications, to show upon this occasion that this relatively new comparative study of the fundamental conceptions of various sciences, is full of promise for the psychologist as well as for the logician.

Of the intrinsic importance of this my second class of 'logical inquiries,' there can be, in many cases, no doubt. From the literature of comparative logic to which I thus refer, there is certain to grow, with time, a new science, which I may venture to call a comparative morphology of concepts. This science will occupy a borderland position. In one respect, it will belong to philosophy properly so called. For it will lead to advances in just that critical consideration of the foundations of knowledge which constitutes one principal division of philosophy. Upon the other hand, the new science will be an empirical as well as a reflective doctrine. It will include a critical examination of the history and evolution of the special sciences. And in this respect it will take its place as a contribution to the general history of culture, and will furnish material for the student of anthropology and of social psychology. And, still further, the new science will contribute to the interests of the student both of general and of experimental psychology. For it will set in a new light the empirical problems of the psychology of the intellect. It will define, in new form, issues which the descriptive psychologist must attempt to reconsider. And, as I am convinced, it will present an ample array of problems for the experimental psychologist,—problems which he alone will be able to pursue into some of their deepest recesses. This new science, then, which you and I can hardly live to see very highly organized, but which the whole century now beginning will greatly advance, will offer large ranges of what one may call neutral ground, where philosopher and psychologist, special student and general inquirer, historian and sociologist, may seek each his own, while a certain truce of God may reign there regarding those boundary feuds which these various types of students are prone to keep alive, whenever they discuss with one another the limits of their various territories, and the relative importance of their different tasks.

II

Two distinct and very large classes of 'logical inquiries' my title is thus intended to bring at once to your attention. My reason for naming them by means of one phrase, and for considering them in one paper, is this: When you examine the first of my two classes of recent inquiries, you find that while much is now doing to advance our knowledge of the psychology of the thinking process, we have to admit that the present state of research in this field is not wholly satisfactory. The general theories about what the place of thought is in the natural history of our minds, and about the special processes of which thinking consists, are numerous; but regarded as psychological theories, they still seem for the most part loose and ill-founded. On the other hand, the special efforts to break paths into the thickets of the psychology of the thinking process by means of experimental research, have so far met with serious obstacles, have often given negative results, and in any case have been confined to the outskirts of the subject. A survey of our first class of recent inquiries will therefore suggest to us the need of looking in new directions for additional sources of aid in the study of the psychology of the higher intellectual processes. In view of this fact it may appear, before we are done, that there is a genuine promise of help towards further advances in this branch of psychology, in case we look for such help to what I have called my second class of recent inquiries in logic. These studies in the comparative logic of the sciences are at once, as I have said, philosophical and empirical studies. They are logical researches regarding the foundations of knowledge. They are also historical reports regarding the way in which our human thinking processes have worked and are working in the world of live thinkers and of socially guided investigations. To call attention, in however feeble or summary a way, to the evidence that is thus attainable regarding the natural history of the thinking process, is a purpose that may justify my necessarily very superficial comments upon this branch of my topic.

III

And so let me next say something about the first of my two classes of recent inquiries, namely, those that are more obviously and explicitly guided by psychological motives.

The psychology of the intellect is one of the oldest branches of psychological inquiry. In Greece it began in pre-Socratic philosophy. It became prominent in Aristotle's doctrine. Both Stoics and Epicureans contributed to it. Scholasticism elaborated and modified Aristotle's theories regarding the whole province. Modern philosophy, and in particular the English psychology, began with renewed interest in the problems of this branch of mind. Thus, the psychology of knowledge was long the favored child of the philosophers, at times when the feelings and the more purely volitional aspects of mental life were comparatively neglected in their researches. In a sense this advantage of the intellectual process has continued in recent times. The psychology of association and that of perception have been steadily advancing. Attention, discrimination, and lately memory, have been experimentally studied. But on the other hand, in recent psychology, just the region where, at the outset, the interest of the philosophers was early centered, namely, the region of study of the higher intellectual processes—conception, judgment and reasoning—is the very province of psychology where progress, in any exact sense, is nowadays so slow. The difficulty of reducing the problems which, for the psychologist, arise in this region, to any form capable of exact experimental inquiry, is notoriously great, and will of course long remain so. Meanwhile, however, the actual importance which psychological methods have won in the esteem of modern writers, have led to repeated attempts to found reforms in logic upon psychological theories. Numerous are the modern works on logic wherein the psychology of the thinking process is expounded at the beginning of the whole research, or at least is made the basis upon which an author's logical doctrines depend. The great influence of Brentano's doctrine of the process of judgment upon one whole series of logical inquiries in Germany is well known, and is an example of what I mean. The earnestness with which the problem of the nature of the 'impersonal' judgments has been discussed by a large number of modern writers on logic is another example of this subordination of logical to psychological issues. For the doctrine of the 'impersonal' forms of expression is a problem of the psychology of language, and to my mind, interests the pure logician hardly at all.

Meanwhile, if psychological doctrines have thus played a large part in the books upon logic, one can hardly feel surprised to find that, in the present state of the psychology of the intellect, the theories about the higher intellectual processes which have been expounded in the logical treatises have been somewhat disheartingly various and capricious. Concerning the processes of abstraction and conception, certain stereotyped formulas were indeed, until quite recently, pretty constantly repeated. But with the doctrine of judgment, chaos in the textbooks of logic began. Judgment was, so one sometimes said, a process of pure association of ideas, wherein the subject idea recalled to mind by contiguity the predicate idea. But no, said others, it was rather a process of Herbartian apperception, wherein the predicate idea assimilated the subject idea and forced it to fuse with itself so that they became but one idea. On the other hand it was often something much nobler; it was an active process of synthesis, not to be confounded either with mere association or with passive fusion—a constructive process wherein subject and predicate idea came to be connected by certain peculiar mental links. Yet not so; on the contrary, it was a process of analysis, whereby a given whole was divided into parts, and the subject and predicate were the products of this sundering. Or, yet again, it was no union and no sundering of ideas at all, but something quite different—an estimate about the objective value of a connection of ideas. But still once more, it was none of all these things, it was an entirely irreducible act of accepting or rejecting an idea or a complex of ideas; and upon this psychologically irreducible and primal act was founded our very conception of any distinction whatever between the objective and the subjective world. All these things judgment has been in the textbooks, and this, as you well know, is not the end. And all these views have been advanced, upon occasion, as psychological theories about the process of judgment, as theories either verifiable by direct introspection or else deducible from more general doctrines about our mental processes.

In presence of such a variety of opinions, many students interested in the theory of the thinking process have tended, in more recent discussion, to choose one of two opposed directions. Either they have been disposed to relieve themselves altogether of any responsibility for settling the psychological problems, by drawing a technically sharp line between Logic and Psychology, by devoting themselves to the former, and by leaving out of the logical inquire all consideration whatever of the descriptive psychology of thinking; or else, choosing rather the psychological road, they have attempted to reduce the problems in question to some shape such as would make possible a more exact introspection of the details of the thinking process by causing these to occur under experimental conditions. The former of these two ways of dealing with the problem of the nature of the thinking process has recently been formally adopted, amongst other writers, by Husserl, in his *Logische Untersuchungen*. Husserl has vigorously protested against all psychologisirende Logik. Logic, he insists, must go its own way, yet Husserl, in his still unfinished and very attractive researches, yet lingers over the problems of what he now calls the 'phenomenological analysis' of the thinking process, and his farewell, as a logician, to psychology proves to be a very long one, wherein the parting is such sweet sorrow that the logician's escape from the presence of psychology is sure to lead to further psychological complications. As a fact, I cordially accept, for myself, the view that the central problems of the logician and of the psychologist are quite distinct, and that the logician is not responsible for, or logically dependent upon a psychological theory of the thinking process. Yet I am unable to doubt that every advance upon one of these two sides of the study of the intellectual life makes possible, under the conditions to which all our human progress is naturally subject, a new advance upon the other side. I believe in not confounding the tasks of these two types of inquiry. But I do believe that a mutual understanding between the workers will be of great importance; and I feel that we need not discuss at very great length, or insist with exaggerated strenuousness upon the mere separation of provinces in a world of inquiry wherein to-day there are rather too many sunderings.

Meanwhile, as to the other ways of approaching the problem of the nature of the thinking processes, namely the way of attacking them from the side of a more careful application of the methods of recent psychology, that at present, as I have said, is beset with well-known difficulties—difficulties upon which I need not dwell long in this presence. The most important thinking processes do not occur under conditions such as either the subject in the laboratory can easily reinstate at will, or the experimenter can determine for the subject while the latter is under observation. The thinking processes upon which experimenters have so far carefully worked are therefore artificially simplified ones—important, but elementary. The numerous investigations regarding the process of the perception of small differences of various types belong here, and constitute, in one aspect, a contribution to the psychology of judgment. The mental reactions upon the presentation of words and phrases, heard or seen by the subject, have been studied by Ribot and by others. Recently Marbe has undertaken to investigate experimentally the psychology of judgment, although under conditions that I have to think by no means very satisfactory. Simple computations, acts of recognition, of estimate, of naming, have also been investigated in various laboratories. But as you know, the positive and assured results of such work have been by no means all that one could wish. Especially notable has been the decidedly negative result of a good deal of this investigation of artificially simplified thinking processes. While, to be sure, the study of the perception of small differences has shown how unexpectedly complex are the psychophysical conditions upon which such judgments depend, the effort in case of even much more complex and intelligent thinking processes to find present in consciousness contents as complex as those of a rational thinker ought to be, has not met, under experimental conditions, with the success that one might have hoped for.

Ribot discovered that in many cases, when one presented to the thoughtful subject a general term whose meaning was somewhat abstract, but nevertheless familiar to him, and when one asked him what mental contents the suddenly presented term directly brought to mind, the answer was simply, 'nothing.' Marbe, dealing with trained subjects, of scientific habits of mind, made them perform and express simple acts of judgment, under experimental conditions, and asked them to observe introspectively the conscious accompaniments of these acts. He found, in general, that the subjective accompaniment of the judgment, apart from the direct consciousness of the very act whereby one gave expression to the judgment, was nothing at all characteristic, and was very often, as in Ribot's subjects, simply nothing at all. The subject in Marbe's experiments was to make a judgment of some intellectual value, but pretty easily accessible to him, regarding a certain presented content; as, for example, he was to choose which one of the two perceived objects had a given character; or he was to answer some other simple question, regarding facts or ideas presented to his attention by the experimenter. He was at once to express this judgment, by word, or by other motor process, as the case might be.

He was then to report what mental accompaniments the act of judging had involved at the critical moment. The result of the experiments was to show that these well-trained thinkers responded to the situation in question in a mainly reflex fashion. They expressed their discriminations, their translations of Latin phrases, or their other simple intellectual processes, with relatively little difficulty; and all that was characteristic of the conscious process at the moment was that they observed, of course, the expressive act itself, which they chose in a conscious sense no more and no less than one chooses any other complicated reflex act of high grade such as comes to consciousness while it is carried out. For the rest, they sometimes observed fleeting states such as doubt or surprise, and various chance associated images, or suggested motor sensations, of no importance for the understanding of what it is to judge. These accompaniments of the act of judgment were merely individual accidents.

Such negative results have appeared, upon second thought, not very surprising either to Ribot or to Marbe. Ribot points out that most of the connected and significant processes of our life have to be largely unconscious, just because we are conscious only from instant to instant, while we live with reference to relatively far-off results, and while the rational connections of life have to do with long periods of time. The organization of our intelligent conduct is necessarily, he thinks, a matter of habit, not of instantaneous insight. And a complex abstract idea, as Ribot points out, is a 'habit in the intellectual order.' "We learn to understand a concept as we learn to walk, dance, fence, or play a musical instrument. . . . General terms cover an organized latent knowledge which is the hidden capital without which we should be in a state of bankruptcy." Marbe comforts himself for his negative results with the reflection that a 'Wissen' can never be, as a content, itself 'im Bewusstsein.' The subject judging knows, as Marbe maintains, what the act means, but no conscious content directly corresponds to or embodies this knowledge. The only necessary conscious content that is present to the subject corresponds to the outward act, the speech or gesture, whereby the subject expresses his meaning, and this, in Marbe's opinion, sufficiently explains the negative result of his own experiments.

No doubt these comments of Marbe and of Ribot have a good deal of justification so far as concerns their own experiments. On the other hand, however, we cannot feel that their experiments were at all well adapted for observing the wealth of our actual thinking processes, because what they studied was not, in most cases, any process by which a thought can come to be built up in our consciousness at all. They could not thus hope to decide how far thought ever can find a peculiar or characteristic place in human consciousness. For what they both examined were relatively reflex processes that express the mere residuum of a mental skill long since acquired by their subjects. Ribot himself thought, and no doubt consciously thought, when he planned his experiments; Marbe thought, when he considered what problem to choose for presentation to his subjects. But the subject (already, in the mentioned cases, a person of relatively high training), had little or no need to think at all in a situation as simple or as familiar in its type as the one in which the experiment placed him. Therefore it was the experimenter and not the subject in whom the process that was to be studied went on. The subject already long since knew how to meet the familiar abstract term, or to translate the simple phrase, or to answer the other plain question. Either this his previous training disposed him to wait passively, upon hearing the well-known word, until he should have some reason to use it himself, or to bring it into connection with his own acts; or else just such training had prepared him (in Marbe's experiments) to accomplish the act whereby one could express a judgment upon the simple problem presented, or could otherwise easily and instantaneously show one's accustomed skill. In no such case was it necessary that any notable intellectual contents of higher grade should come to the subject's consciousness. The mechanism established by long training was ready. It responded as the training determined. Consciousness showed indeed nothing of an abstract thinking process; but then there was no live thought present to show. Ask me "What is the sum of 3 and 2?" or "Who was Washington?" and very probably I shall just then not think at all. If I am disposed, under experimental conditions, to respond to your questions, without knowing beforehand what the question is to be, I shall, upon hearing such an inquiry, respond as smoothly as if I were a wholly reflex mechanism. And very naturally I shall then have nothing to report in the way of introspective facts of a thoughtful sort. For I shall respond much as a baggage clerk at a large station calls out the names of cheques, or as a telegraph operator writes out his messages while listening to the familiar clicks of the instrument.

To say this is not to make light of experimental methods in their application to the psychology of thought, but is to show that if the problems of the psychology of the intellect are to be prepared for more effective and advanced experimental research in future, the thinking process must first, in some measure, be more fruitfully analyzed than has yet been the case, into elementary processes of a type capable of separate experimental study. On the other hand, the way in which these processes are synthesized into the richer life of concrete thinking must be discovered mainly in an indirect fashion, through an examination of the expressions of thought in the various products of the human intellect, as they appear in language, in social institutions, in the mechanical inventions and constructions which human reason has made, and in the constitution of the sciences themselves—those highest expressions of man's ingenuity. Meanwhile, as I think, a preliminary examination of these very larger expressions of the intellect themselves, may also help us to proceed further than we have yet done in the preparatory analysis of the elementary activities upon which our thought depends, and may enable us thus to open the way towards such an experimental investigation of the conscious aspects of live thinking as just now we lack.

What then is the best means to make such a preliminary analysis of the thinking process into its elements? To analyze thought by means of a study of the phenomena of language has so far been, from Plato's time onwards, the principal undertaking of those who have approached the psychological problems of the intellect from the objective side, that is, from the side of the way in which human thought has outwardly expressed itself. The logicians and the psychologists have joined in a frequent examination of the phenomena of speech. Both types of investigators have sought thus to acquire a knowledge of what the thinking process essentially is. And this sort of inquiry still prospers. A recent logician, Benno Erdmann, has undertaken elaborate studies in this field, studies that have combined the analysis of pathological facts with those experimental researches which he and Professor Dodge have made so well known. From the psychological side, and with vast resources in the way of varied materials, Wundt has also lately prepared his really wonderful volumes on language, working with all the equipment of the experimenter, the logician, and the philosopher, but carefully distinguishing the task of this recent book from that of his own earlier treatise on logic. One may say, then, that the psychology of language is indeed in a progressive state. Yet I cannot but hold that the relation of language to the thinking process has been somewhat too exclusively emphasized by many students of the subject. Thought has other modes of expression than through the forms of speech. Language has other business besides the expression of thought. Wundt's book has the merit of emphasizing the close and primary relation of language to the expression of the feelings and to the life of the will. In consequence, Wundt very decidely sets limits to the tendency either to regard the grammatical categories as essentially logical ones, or to use the psychology of language too exclusively as a means for interpreting the psychology of the thinking process. For this very reason his book rather encourages one to look elsewhere for auxiliaries in comprehending the psychology of the intellectual life.

I have thus endeavored to sketch some of the more directly psychological of the recent inquiries into the nature of the thinking process, in order to show why, despite all these various developments, I myself think that the psychologist still has much to learn from researches in other fields than those in which he has so far been most accustomed to seek for help. These other fields are the very ones which are opened by those recent inquiries in the comparative logic of the sciences of which I spoke at the outset.

IV

Some widespread influence, it is hard to tell exactly what, has led, during the last three or four decades, to repeated, and often seemingly independent and spontaneous, efforts on the part of the students of various special sciences to undertake an examination into the first principles of their own branches of inquiry. The mathematicians say that it was the discovery of errors in certain accepted theorems or proofs of theorems which was the principal motive leading to their own modern desire for an increased rigidity of methods, and an increased clearness regarding their fundamental assumptions. A wide extension of some of their earlier conceptions, such as the conception of a function, resulted, during the nineteenth century, from the natural advances of their science. It was found that as such conceptions extended their range of application, theorems to which no exceptions had been known at earlier stages of the science became obviously of restricted application in the new fields thus opened, and often had to be restated altogether. In consequence, proofs of these theorems which had been accepted as valid in earlier stages of the science, were seen, in the light of the enlarged conceptions, to be invalid, or to be capable of rigid statement only through the addition of precise qualifications which had earlier escaped notice. Thus there arose a keenly critical consciousness about what constituted exact statement and rigid proof. Moreover, mathematicians are especially disposed by the work of their science to compare together the results of various and apparently independent sorts of inquiry. Especially is this case when one considers the relations of geometrical and analytical science. At one time geometrical intuition, at another time analytical computation, may lead in the advancement of mathematical knowledge. The question therefore constantly arises, Which of these two sorts of inquiry is the superior in power, or in logical exactness? Such comparisons must lead to constantly renewed self-criticism passed by the science upon itself.

Again, early in the nineteenth century, the constructive imagination of certain geometers of genius initiated an examination of the foundations of Euclidean geometry which has since proved of the utmost importance as a study in the fundamental concepts of all science. Such influences long worked in a comparatively isolated way. Towards the close of the century they combined to bring about a sort of common consciousness on the part of mathematicians regarding the methods that they required of the investigator and of the expounder of mathematical truth. This common consciousness expressed itself not only in the regions where the science was advancing to conquer new territory, but in the study of the oldest, the most fundamental, simple and universally human of mathematical ideas. The concept of number is one of the earliest of human scientific acquisitions; yet it has recently been subjected to a searching logical analysis with decidedly novel and unexpected results, so that nobody can rightly judge what it is to count or to use numbers for purposes of recording measurements, unless he has taken into consideration mathematical discussions that are hardly thirty years old. The various extensions of the number-concept,—the relation between rational and irrational numbers, the relations of number to quantity, the different systems of complex numbers, the conditions logically necessary in order that number systems should be applied to the expression of space-relations,— all these topics have been reviewed from the foundation upwards; and the work still goes on. The various actual or possible conceptions of continuity, the exact meaning to be ascribed to the concepts of numerical and of quantitative infinity, the logical position of the conception of an infinitesimal,—all these matters have been reconsidered with a care and a novelty of results which no one can appreciate who has not come into closer contact with at least a few of these researches. And now what I wish especially to emphasize, is that all these analyses, while their direct purpose is logical, inevitably possess a psychological bearing. For they throw light upon the structure which the universally human processes of counting, measuring, comparing and otherwise dealing with continuous magnitudes have always possessed. They define certain of our most fundamental intellectual interests in our world of experience. They therefore not only logically clarify and in so far transform these interests, but they tend to several otherwise hidden aspects of the natural history of these interests themselves.

For instance, the logical prominence which these modern researches in the logic of arithmetic give to our general concepts of serial order, as contrasted with our more specialized quantitative concepts, involve a generalization about the nature of the thinking process that at once has a psychological application. For we learn hereby to distinguish the activities through which we have formed the conception of any ordered series of facts from the processes whereby we have learned to apply this conception in certain important, but decidedly special, cases to the task of measuring magnitudes. The two processes are different, not only logically, but psychologically. The second is a highly specialized application of the other, which is the more primitive and the simpler. The new problem that arises for the psychologist is that of the psychology of our ideas of serial order. The forms in which this problem is to be attacked with fruitful success by the psychologist must be furnished to him by the logician of mathematics. The latter discovers by analysis what concepts of order are fundamental and what ones, logically speaking, are derived; and how the more complex forms of order are related to the simpler. The solution of this logical question is of course primarily not any decision of a question of genesis. But it is the answer to the question, What forms of order, what types of serial arrangement are of the most importance in human thinking about the world of experience? This answer inevitably tells us, however, something about what is universal in the actual constitution of those habits of our organism upon which our thoughts about order depend. It is true then that to ask, What is logically fundamental in our ideas of order? is to ask not a psychological, but a logical, question. But to discover what is logically universal, as the basis of our exact ideas, is to find out a process that must be very widely represented in those organized modes of action of which our thoughts are an inner expression. Hence the result of the logician's analysis, while it cannot be directly translated into a logical theory, is inevitably the setting of a definite problem for the experimental psychologist.

As a fact, the problems of the psychology of the concept of order form a field for experimental research whose importance the whole modern logic of mathematics makes daily more obvious, while the adaptability of the problems for the labors of the experimenter is so obvious as hardly to need lengthy illustration. Psychologically speaking, the importance of the order in which facts are presented to us is illustrated by every case of an inverted letter, by every disarrangement of a familiar temporal or spatial sequence, by every instance of the illegibility even of our own handwriting when seen in a mirror. One of our earliest and principal mental interests is in the serial order of things and in the weaving of various serial orders into systems. But mathematical science is in large part an analysis of ordinal systems. Hence an advance in our analysis of the logical concept of order, and in our knowledge of its range of application, makes possible a more fruitful study of the natural history of thought than would otherwise lie within our power.

In the modern study of the logic of the space-concept, there is again a rich field where the results of the mathematical logicians suggest problems for the psychologist. I have myself been surprised to see how little interest psychologists have generally taken in the space-theories of modern mathematics. There is a remark of Klein, repeated since by a good many writers, to the effect that modern projective geometry, with its non-metrical methods, is rather a description of the properties that are most prominent in visual space, while ordinary geometry, with its quantitative or metrical concepts, is rather founded upon our experience of the space of our touch and of our bodily movements. This remark emphasizes what is indeed an obvious fact. One may pass lightly over it, and think little of it. But its significance begins to dawn when one learns something of those logical relations between non-metrical and metrical geometry which Cayley, and later Klein himself, first made prominent. Projective geometry, taken in the abstract, can be developed without the use of any conceptions whatever of metrical relations in space. In other words, projective geometry is a science of spatial order, and not at all of spatial quantity. Cayley and Klein showed how, by the use of certain (once more, very abstract and ideal) assumptions, our ordinary metrical geometry can be made to appear as a highly specialized case of this purely ordinal science. In the light of this consideration, Klein's just cited remark about the contrast between visual space and tactual motor space suggests a very interesting, although a very complex psychological problem about the psychology of the concepts of order and of quantity in their application to space. I suppose that no psychologist would admit that visual space is primarily non-metrical; and, of course, Klein did not mean that it was purely so. For the rest, visual space is obviously related to our consciousness of the results of our movements, and cannot be isolated from them, except by a deliberate abstraction. But, on the other hand, visual space certainly does present to us the facts which projective geometry isolates; while our other space experiences do not directly involve these projective facts at all. But the projective facts, as logical analysis shows, are, when taken by themselves, non-metrical, while the laws of the metrical facts regarding space are capable of being conceptually defined as very specialized cases of results, under certain ideal conditions, of the laws of a non-metrical space-world. These considerations may not prove to have important results for the psychology of our concepts of order and of measure; but as they stand, they certainly suggest genuine problems for psychological scrutiny. I wonder, then, to find them so little regarded by the psychological students of the space problems.

In a somewhat different direction various contributions to the questions about our consciousness of space have been made, within the last few years, by M. Poincaré, who has here shown, not only all the knowledge of a great mathematical investigator, but also a decided effort to translate his analysis into psychological terms. These contributions of Poincaré, following the results of Lie and others, have laid stress upon the relation between our general spatial conceptions and the mathematical theory of 'groups'; and they promise in still another way to bring to pass connections between psychological and mathematical investigations. In view of such developments, I feel that the time is approaching when no psychologist will have a right to try to contribute to a knowledge of our space-consciousness, so long as his own geometrical conceptions are still confined to those of the mathematical textbooks of his early youth. Psychological space theories must be brought into explicit relation with mathematical theories.

V

But I must hasten from this mention of the merely mathematical investigations to a still more summary reference to similarly analytic work that has been done in other fields of the logic of science. The books of Mach, whose name I have already mentioned, are surely known to many of you. Dr. Paul Carus has proved, as editor and as director of translations, a beneficent aid to our students in this country by making literature of this type widely accessible amongst us. And you surely know the spirit of much of this modern literature of the logic of science. It is characterized, first, by a certain measure of the same sort of critical skill which has made the modern mathematicians so rigid in their methods of proof, and so critical of their first principles. To be sure, outside of pure mathematics, you seldom meet with the degree of rigidity which that science has of late so carefully cultivated; but still the spirit of watchful self-analysis, the freedom from sacred and unquestionable dogmatic presuppositions of all sorts, the willingness to consider fairly the possibility of the opposite of any once asserted proposition, are the common features which characterize Mach, Pearson, Hertz, and the other typical writers of this recent movement. Even as I have been preparing this discussion there has come into my hands the *Vorlesungen über Naturphilosophie* of Ostwald—a book of whose charm a reading of the first half of the lectures has already convinced me, and whose logical spirit, whatever you may think of its results, is of the most delightful and wholesome. The researches of which such literature is the representative, are characterized by a view of the nature of the thinking process which is closely allied to that which the mathematicians have gradually developed. For one thing, human thought, in the view of such modern writers, is not bound by any one definable collection of unquestionable axioms, nor yet limited in its operation by any mysteriously predetermined set of irreducible primal concepts. It is a variable and progressive process that is concerned with the adjustment of conduct to experience. In place of unquestionable axioms, one has therefore, in any science, only relative first principles, resolutions, so to speak, to treat some portion of the world of experience as describable in certain terms. The immediate purpose of any thinking process in a special science is the description of experience, and is not what used to be meant by the explanation of facts. To describe experience is to construct a conceptual model that corresponds, point for point, so far as desired, with the observed phenomena. In order to construct this conceptual model, one has to set about one's work with a definite plan of action, a plan large enough and coherent enough to cover the intended range. One's provisionally assumed first principles, or, as such writers often say, one's postulates, are therefore chosen simply, as expressions of this coherent plan of action. One constructs one's model according to these postulates, compares the results with the facts, and is judged accordingly. Meanwhile, a paucity of elementary assumptions is to be preferred, because science, as a practical activity, loves economy. Such writers use the older forms of the principle of causation either not at all, or as sparingly as they think possible,—their reason being that they are not quite sure what the principle of causation used to mean, and that they are interested only in finding such relations. But causal explanations, as formerly conceived, seem to them to have supposed the true connections of facts to be founded in something behind the scenes, which no experience could ever bring to light. Such writers therefore seem to themselves to be working in a purely positive spirit, as Auguste Comte long ago, although in a much cruder fashion, advised us work. They often, like Mach and Pearson, call themselves anti-metaphysical. Yet, as a fact, all this analysis of the structure of the thinking processes of the special sciences, and of what I have elsewhere called the world of description, seems to me to be not only in no wise inconsistent with an idealistic philosophy, but to be a most fruitful auxiliary to such an idealistic interpretation of the facts of the universe as, in another place, I have had occasion to maintain. But here is no place for considering the philosophical value of such a view of the logic of science. What I am here concerned to show is that this effort so to expound the principles of science as to make all the assumed relations between the objects of one's thought overt and exact, rather than occult and inscrutable, relations, leads of necessity to an analysis of the process of thinking which is full of psychological suggestiveness. For a similar reason, this effort to justify scientific theories solely by their success in producing conceptual constructions that correspond in definite and controllable fashion with the phenomena, leads to a sort of practical theory of the business of thinking which closely relates the point of view of the logician to that of the psychologist. For the latter must view the thinking process as one of adjustment to the environment; and he must suppose the mental motives which determine the choice of one rather than another way of thinking to be in the long run determined, as to their natural history, by the success of one method of adjustment as compared with that of another.

In consequence, I maintain that the future study of the psychology of the thinking process will have much to gain from a use of such analyses of ideas and processes as this new science of the comparative morphology of concepts will, as it further develops, bring to light.

VI

My hastily-made catalogue of the types of researches which belong to the second of my two classes of recent logical inquiries is thus, within its present very narrow limits, completed. I must still try briefly, however, to lay stress upon a very important general feature of the thinking process which all these recent researches, whether in the specially mathematical field or in the wider field of the logic of the various natural sciences, seem to have brought to clearer light. So long as logicians were largely confined in their researches to results derived from the analysis of language, the problems which they could hand over to the psychologist were principally the classic, but as I think, relatively fruitless problems, to which Ribot's and Marbe's experimental researches have been devoted—such problems as, What has one in mind on hearing an abstract word pronounced? or, What happens in my mind when I judge that A is B? We have already seen that the modern mathematical researches have prepared for the psychologist a large collection of relatively new problems relating to our consciousness of the types of serial order, and relating also to the way in which this consciousness of order is linked to our ideas of quantity, of space and of continuity in general. Many of these problems have assumed, in modern mathematical researches, decidedly instructive forms, which are now nearly if not quite ready for experimental study. But the problems which modern logical research is preparing for the psychologist are by no means limited to these. Let me call attention then to another range of problems of a very complex character, but of a type especially likely to receive, I think, ere long, a form suited to novel experimental researches.

Psychologists have already elaborately studied, in the laboratories, our consciousness of the differences between presented objects of various sorts. But a difference between two sensations, or intervals, or other presented facts, is a matter rather of perception than of more elaborate thought. We judge such a difference indeed; but the judgment occurs as a sort of more or less swift or deliberate reflex, subject to no conscious logical principles, except those implied in every least effort to attend to the facts presented, and to report accordingly. Even in such an effort, however, there appears one element that, in the life of our more familiar and complicated thinking, assumes extremely varied and important forms. The subject in a series of experiments upon just observable differences is obliged to report whether two objects appear to him to differ or not to differ in an assigned respect. Upon this side his act of judgment includes what one may call the 'yes' and 'no' consciousness, the decision as between alternatives, the selection or suppression of a certain possible response to an object. But the 'yes' and 'no' consciousness is one that is of course not limited to the case of observing small differences, but that has applications wherever we are able to judge; and one of its most important applications appears whenever we not only observe the differences of objects, but, in some more elaborate way, classify objects. Two objects, such for instance as a triangle and a circle, are in two such different classes for us (when we do judge them as figures of different classes), not merely because we observe that they are for us different in shape, but because, in the presence of one of them we are disposed, in view of our geometrical training, and even of our purely popular habits of thought and speech, to make certain responses, to perform certain deeds, which, in the presence of the other object we should, if these deeds were suggested, suppress, reject, inhibit, as unfitting, absurd, untrue. In presence of the circle we do not only tend to follow its contour by means of certain eye movements, and to have suggested to us certain names, memories, and aesthetic impressions; but, if we are thinking about circles we consciously accept certain of our suggested motor responses in presence of the circle, as adapted to express what it means for us, and how it is related to the rest of our life. Some of these very responses to which, in presence of a circle, we thus, so to speak, say 'yes' are amongst the ones to which, in presence of a triangle, we say 'no' in case there then arises any suggestion of our making them. Our customary summary expression of the results of many such acceptances and rejections of fitting reactions in the presence of circles and triangles takes the form of saying that 'no circle is a triangle.' This assertion is of course not the same as the assertion that our representative ideas of circle and triangle are different ideas. One's idea of a Frenchman differs from that of a dancing master. But it is absurd to say that because one is a Frenchman he cannot be a dancing master. Our assertion about circle and triangle is that they are not merely different, but belong to mutually exclusive classes. And we define for ourselves this latter fact of the mutual exclusion of the classes by means of a series of processes in which the conciousness of presented or remembered differences is bound up with the 'yes' and 'no' consciousness in a fashion that the logicians and psychologists of all ages have attempted to unravel, and that the psychologists, at least, have failed to discuss with finality, just because they have so little studied the 'yes' and 'no' consciousness, either in itself, or in its relation to our consciousness of difference.

As for the logicians, with their Eulerian diagrams, and their more recent and exact symbolic notations, they have indeed done much to clarify the more formal aspects of the conceptual relations involved in exclusions and negations; but, as Professor Ormond's paper on the place of the negative in logic showed to this association some years since, the questions here involved are amongst the most delicate and fundamental known to thought, and they are not yet closed issues. What, then, is the precise relation of the consciousness of difference to the consciousness of negation, or of mutual exclusion? Both logicians and psychologists need to study this problem more thoroughly.

But now it is just here that the modern reëxamination of the principles of the various sciences has been enlarging our ideas of the importance of the function of what I have called the 'yes' and 'no' consciousness in all our exact thinking. When I first heard about the logic of science, I was told by my teachers that the stage of a science in which it made much of classifications was a relatively imperfect stage. A science, I was told, passed to a higher stage when it learned to substitute explanations for classifications. And its explanations, in their turn, became exact whenever they passed to the highest stage of scientific knowledge, where they became quantitative. Quantity, then, was a concept of a rather mysterious dignity; but it certainly belonged to some very lofty level of thinking, where mere classifications were no longer in question. When one reached this lofty level science became mathematical, and the goal was near.

But nowadays, our new comparative logic of the sciences seems to put this whole matter in a new light. The ideal of exact special science is still mathematical, and will always remain so. But then, for one thing, mathematics, for the enlightened, is no longer merely the science of quantity, but is rather the science of exactly definable relationships of all types. Quantity itself, however, appears, in this new logic, as a conception whose properties and laws, in all the numerous branches of the science of the different kinds of quantity, are definable only in terms of the properties of certain manifolds, or complexes of ideal objects, which are called number-systems. The number-concept, which, as I before pointed out, is for the modern mathematician very prominently an ordinal concept, has become, in its various modern forms, something more general, as well as logically more fundamental, than the concept of quantity. Our exact knowledge of the laws of quantity thus tends, more and more, to appear as founded upon our knowledge of the laws of number, the latter being deeper and more universal. The result is the tendency towards what Klein has called the Arithmetisirung of mathematical methods. Now this Arithmetisirung implies in part, making prominent, as I pointed out earlier in this paper, the ordinal concepts. But it also implies giving a prominence to exactly defined classifications which I suppose has never before been known in the history of science.

Our knowledge of number-system is, in very large measure, a knowledge that there are, in each system, these and these classes of numbers, and that of every number in one of these classes one can assert what one must deny of every other number in the system Dedekind's famous and epoch-making definitions of the irrational numbers as corresponding to the totality of the classifications or *Schnitte* that one can make in the series of rational numbers, is one brilliant instance amongst many of the way in which classifications have become important in modern exact science. Another instance is Georg Cantor's definition of the grades, or dignities, the Machtigkeiten of infinite assemblages of objects. The discovery of this new concept by Cantor seems to me one of the most brilliant feats of constructive imagination in recent times. It has enriched mathematics, and will enrich future philosophy, with wholly new views of the problem of the infinite. Yet it turned upon a beautifully simple application of an exact principle of classification. Modern algebra, in the conception of what are called 'domains of rationality,' has again used an obvious and fundamental principle of classification, whose application to systems of numbers is very vast, and whose value in very various sorts of problems appears to be immeasurable. The most modern researches into the principles of geometry, and of the other exact sciences, in their efforts to find a sufficient and closed system of mutually independent first principles, have shown how much is gained by exactly classifying the ranges, or domains, to which various principles can be said to apply. Even the single principles, taken by themselves, appear, when thus examined, to be simply classifications of facts. Thus the principle that any two points in a space determine one straight line, while two straight lines can have but one point in common, is for certain purposes best stated as a classification of the points of space. The points namely are such that, if you choose at random any two of them, these two determine one class of points such that every point in space either belongs or does not belong to that class, while no two classes so determined have more than one point in common. Thus stated, the principle regarding straight lines and points appears as it ought to appear; namely, it appears as no self-evident axiom, but as a surprising and even baffling property of the points in space, and so as an arbitrary fact of our spatial experience. It is as if you said: "There is a nation of men somewhere such that any two men in that nation belong to one exclusive club, to which every other man either does or does not belong, while no two such clubs have more than a single member in common." Such a nation would have a strange sort of club-life. But just as such an assemblage are the points in space.

Classification from such a point of view reigns then everywhere on the highest level of exact science. Sharp classification is the goal as well as the beginning of the thought that gets embodied in the special sciences. To say 'yes' or 'no' to the question: "Does this object belong or does it not belong, for this purpose, to this collection of objects?" is the last as well as the first task of the human thinker in all his dealing with particular facts. Now the logical interest of this generalization about the nature of science lies in the consideration that, from this modern point of view, for which the special sciences, as you remember, are descriptions of phenomena, all our valid explanation of facts, just so far as they are valid, all our knowledge of the laws of nature, all our quantitative insight into things must be reduced merely to such classifications of facts, and to serially ordered systems of such classifications. Of such materials our conceptions of what I have called our world of description must consist. One modern writer has explicitly made this very generalization. I refer to Mr. A. B. Kempe, in his paper on the 'Theory of Mathematical Form.' Mathematics, according to Mr. Kempe, who illustrates his notion in a very varied way, is purely a science of exact classification, and is nothing else. It defines the relations of objects and systems of objects by classifying certain of these objects, or certain pairs, triads, or other groups of these objects, by placing certain of them together, and by distinguishing them from other objects or assemblages of objects. Thus, according to Mr. Kempe, one studies geometry in a strict logical order by beginning with the conception that the points of space are, as mere points, undistinguished one from another. One then goes further and notes that not only all points, but all pairs of points in space, may be regarded as undistinguished from one another, so long as you ignore the notions of direction and distance. One next observes, however, that if one takes account of triads of points, one has forthwith a classification of such triads, because all collinear triads of points are distinguished from all noncollinear triads. Upon the basis of this primal classification, as Kempe holds, all the rest of geometrical knowledge can be built up by adding further classifications as new principles are introduced. Every new principle means merely a new classification. And this procedure, as Kempe holds, is typical of the processes of exact thought everywhere. Science, then consists altogether of classifications.

Now what I want to point out is the enormous importance that such considerations give to the function which, in the life of our thinking, I have called the 'yes' and 'no' consciousness. This, I have said, is the consciousness wherein we are aware of accepting or inhibiting certain acts—acts through which we treat two or more objects as belonging to one class, or as belonging to classes that exclude each other. The contrast of X and not-X is always a product of the working of such a 'yes' and 'no' consciousness. Now I have said that psychologists have too much neglected the closer study of the 'yes' and 'no' aspect of consciousness. Psychologically speaking, it is that aspect of our mental life which accompanies our attitudes of readiness to perform certain deeds, and of attendant readiness to inhibit other deeds. Here then is a place where the modern logical inquiries counsel the psychologist to undertake a more careful study.

As a fact, classifications depend, for us, upon inhibitions, and upon becoming conscious of our inhibitions, and also upon bringing to notice the positive motor tendencies that are in us correlative to these inhibitions. Those who have studied abstract ideas as Ribot has done, or judgments as Marbe has done, have therefore attacked the problems of the thinking process at the wrong end. They have tried to examine the corpse of a dead thinking process. They have found little left but a reflex act. Live thinking is the process of classifying our objects by suppressing, in their presence, certain of our possible motor acts, by welcoming, emphasizing, or letting go certain of our other acts, by becoming aware, somehow, i.e., in some conscious terms, of these our positive tendencies and inhibitions, and by them regarding the objects in the light of the deeds that thus we welcome or suppress.

The most promising problem about the whole thinking process which is thus suggested to the psychologist may then be defined as this: "In what way, to what extent, and under what conditions, do we become conscious of our inhibitions?" Plainly the negative principle in consciousness, the Geist der stets verneint, is the constant accompaniment of all our higher, our organized, our thoughtful activities. It is the principle which makes exact classifications possible. And descriptive thought, in the light of these modern researches, means exact classification, and means nothing else so much. It is by contrast with our inhibitions that our positive motor processes get their precise conscious definition, as inhibitions of inhibitions, as tendencies to act by means of overcoming opposing considerations, and as assertions that are at once coordinate with, and opposed to, denials. Our abstract ideas are products of such an organized union of negative and positive tendencies. We can therefore understand the psychology of live thinking processes only in case we understand when, how far, and under what conditions, inhibition becomes a conscious process.

But now the psychology of the inhibitory processes—how vast a range of interesting phenomena, and how imperfectly explored a territory, does not this name suggest to us all? The world of the phenomena of primitive tabu, how fascinating it seems! Yet with tabu human thought about certain of the exact classifications, both of conduct and of truth, would seem to have begun. The pathology of our inhibitory consciousness, how interesting its complications—how important clinically—how significant from the humane point of view! Some years since, in a paper on the case of John Bunyan, I tried to present to the members of this Association an instance of the descriptive psychology of an experience largely made up of pathological inhibitions, occurring in the early manhood of a great genius. You all know how rich is the clinical material for the study of such cases. But the experimental psychology of the consciousness inhibition—here surely is another extensive, accessible, and comparatively much neglected, and at the same time perfectly definite and promising field of work. I have now tried to show you that modern logical inquiries, in emphasizing the central significance that the process of classification possesses in all grades of our thought, have made more evident than ever that upon an understanding of the psychology of inhibition must depend a great deal of our further advance in a knowledge of the psychology of the thinking process.

I conclude then by urging upon my fellow members (1) the problem of our inhibitory consciousness and (2) the before-mentioned problem of the psychology of our ordinal concepts, that is, of our consciousness of ordered series of objects, as the two great tasks that are set before the students of the psychology of the thinking process by the results of modern logical inquiry.

If anything that I have said shall tend to further the mutual understanding between workers in psychological and in logical research, I shall be amply repaid for my efforts in trying thus to state to you something of what I see in the present situation of logical inquiry; while you, I hope, may in that case be not wholly unrepaid for the tediously abstract and lengthy road over which, by your kindness, I have been privileged to lead you.

22

The Problem of Truth
in the Light of
Recent Discussion

The question: What is Truth? is a typical philosophical problem. But it has been by no means at all times equally prominent throughout the history of philosophy. The ages in which it has come to the front have been those wherein, as at present, a keenly critical spirit has been predominant. At such times metaphysical interests are more or less subordinated, for a while, to the problems about method, to logical researches, or to the investigations which constitute a Theory of Knowledge.

Such periods, as we know, have recurred more than once since scholastic philosophy declined. And such a period was that which Kant dominated. But the sort of inquiry into the nature of truth which Kant's doctrine initiated quickly led, at the close of the eighteenth century, to a renewed passion for metaphysical construction. The problem regarding the nature of truth still occupied a very notable place in the doctrine of Fichte. It constituted one of the principal concerns, also, of Hegel's so much neglected and ill-understood "Phänomenologie des Geistes." And yet both in the minds of the contemporaries of Fichte and of Hegel, and still

An address delivered before the International Congress of Philosophy at Heidelberg, in September, 1908. [Reprinted from *WJO*, pp. 187–254.]

more in those of their later disciples and opponents, the problem of truth went again into the background when compared with the metaphysical, the ethical, and the theological interests which constructive idealism and its opponents, in those days, came to represent. Hence wherever one looks, in the history of philosophical opinion between 1830 and 1870, one sees how the problem of truth, although never wholly neglected, still remained, for some decades, out of the focus of philosophical interest.

But the scene rapidly changed about and after the year 1870. Both the new psychology and the new logic, which then began to flourish, seemed, erelong, almost equally to emphasize the importance of a reconsideration of the problem as to the nature of truth. These doctrines did this, especially because the question whether logic was henceforth to be viewed as a part of psychology became once more prominent, so soon as the psychological researches then undertaken had attracted the strong interest of the philosophical public. And meanwhile the revived interest in Kant, growing, as it did, side by side with the new psychology, called for a reinterpretation of the problems of the critical philosophy. The reawakening of Idealism, in England and in America, called attention, in its own way, to the same problem. The modern philosophical movement in France,—a movement which was, from the outset, almost equally made up of a devotion to the new psychology and of an interest in the philosophy of the sciences, has coöperated in insisting upon the need of a revision of the theory of truth. And to complete the story of the latest philosophy, recent tendencies in ethics, emphasizing as they have done the problems of individualism, and demanding a far-reaching reconsideration of the whole nature of moral truth, have added the weight of their own, often passionate, interest to the requirements which are here in question.

The total result is that we are just now in the storm and stress of a reëxamination of the whole problem of truth. About this problem the philosophical interest of to-day centers. Consequently, whether you discuss the philosophy of Nietzsche or of mathematics,—whether the *Umwertung aller Werte* or the "class of all classes,"—whether Mr. Russell's "Contradiction" or the *Uebermensch* is in question,—or whether none of these things attract you at all, so that your inquiries relate to psychology, or to evolution, or to the concepts of the historical sciences, or to whatever other region of philosophy you please,—always the same general issue has sooner or later to be faced. You are involved in some phase of the problem about the nature of truth.

So much, then, as a bare indication of the historical process which has led us into our present position. I propose, in the present address, to offer an interpretation of some of the lessons that, as I think, we may learn from the recent discussions of the problem whose place in all our minds I have thus indicated.

I

It seems natural to begin such a discussion by a classification of the main motives which are represented by the principal recent theories regarding the nature of truth. In enumerating these motives I need not dwell, in this company, upon those historical inferences and traditions whose presence in recent thought is most easily and universally recognized. That Empiricism,—due to the whole history of the English school, modified in its later expressions by the Positivism of a former generation, and by the types of Naturalism which have resulted from the recent progress of the special sciences,—that, I say, such empiricism has affected our modern discussion of the nature of truth,—this we all recognize. I need not insist upon this fact. Moreover, the place which Kant occupies in the history of the theory of truth,—that again is something which it is needless here to emphasize. And that the teaching of Fichte and of Hegel, as well as still other idealistic traditions, are also variously represented by present phases of opinion regarding our problem, we shall not now have to rehearse. I presuppose, then, these historical commonplaces. It is not, however, in terms of these that I shall now try to classify the motives to which the latest theories of truth are due.

These recent motives, viewed apart from those unquestionably real influences of the older traditions of the history of philosophy are, to my mind, three in number:

First, there is the motive especially suggested to us modern men by the study of the history of institutions, by our whole interest in what are called evolutionary processes, and by a large part of our recent psychological investigation. This is the motive which leads many of us to describe human life altogether as a more or less progressive adjustment to a natural environment. This motive incites us, therefore, to judge all human products and all human activities as instruments for the preservation and enrichment of man's natural existence. Of late this motive, whose modern forms are extremely familiar, has directly affected the theory of truth. The result appears in a part, although not in the whole, of what the doctrines known as Instrumentalism, Humanism, and Pragmatism have been of late so vigorously teaching, in England, in America, in Italy, in France, and, in still other forms, in Germany.

From the point of view which this motive suggests, human opinions, judgments, ideas, are part of the effort of a live creature to adapt himself to his natural world. Ideas and beliefs are, in a word, organic functions. And truth, in so far as we men can recognize truth at all, is a certain value belonging to such ideas. But this value itself is simply like the value which any natural organic function possesses. Ideas and opinions are instruments whose use lies in the fact that, if they are the right ones, they preserve life and render life stable. Their existence is due to the same natural causes that are represented in our whole organic evolution. Accordingly, assertions or ideas are true in proportion as they accomplish this their biological and psychological function. The value of truth is itself a biological and psychological value. The true ideas are the ones which adapt us for life as human beings. Truth, therefore, grows with our growth, changes with our needs, and is to be estimated in accordance with our success. The result is that all truth is relative as it is instrumental, as human as it is useful.

The motive which recent Instrumentalism or Pragmatism expresses, in so far as it takes this view of the nature of truth, is of course in one sense an ancient motive. Every cultivated nation, upon beginning to think, recognizes in some measure such a motive. The Greeks knew this motive, and deliberately connected both the pursuit and the estimate of truth with the art of life in ways whose problematic aspects the Sophists already illustrated. Socrates and his followers, and later the Stoics as well as the Epicureans, also considered, in their various ways, this instrumental aspect of the nature of truth. And even in the Hindoo Upanishads one can find instances of such humanistic motives influencing the inquiry into the problem of truth. But it is true that the historical science of the nineteenth century, beginning, as it did, with its elaborate study of the history of institutions, and culminating in the general doctrines regarding evolution, has given to this motive an importance and a conscious definiteness such as makes its recent embodiment in Pragmatism a very modern and, in many ways, a novel doctrine about the nature of truth.

II

But closely bound up with this first motive in our recent thinking there is a second motive, which in several ways very strongly contrasts with the first. Yet in many minds these two motives are so interwoven that the writers in question are unaware which motive they are following when they utter their views about the nature of truth. No doubt one may indeed recognize the contrasts between these motives, and may, nevertheless, urge good reasons for following in some measure both of them, each in its own way. Yet whoever blindly confuses them is inevitably led into hopeless contradictions. As a fact, a large number of our recent pragmatists have never learned consciously to distinguish them. Yet they are indeed easy to distinguish, however hard it may be to see how to bring them into a just synthesis.

This second motive is the same as that which, in ethics, is responsible for so many sorts of recent Individualism. It is the motive which in the practical realm Nietzsche glorified. It is the longing to be self-possessed and inwardly free, the determination to submit to no merely external authority. I need not pause to dwell upon the fact that, in its application to the theory of truth, precisely as in its well-known applications to ethics, this motive is Protean. Every one of us is, I suppose, more or less under its influence.

Sometimes, this motive appears mainly as a skeptical motive. Then it criticizes, destructively, traditional truth and thereupon leaves us empty of all assurances. But sometimes it assumes the shape of a sovereign sort of rationalism, whereby the thinking subject, first rebelling against outer authority, creates his own laws, but then insists that all others shall obey these laws. In other cases, however, it takes the form of a purely subjective idealism, confident of its own but claiming no authority. Or again, with still different results, it consciously unites its ethical with its theoretical interests, calls itself "Personal Idealism," and regards as its main purpose, not only the freeing of the individual from all spiritual bondage, theoretical and practical, but also the winning for him of an inner harmony of life. In general, in its highest as in some of its less successful embodiments, when it considers the sort of truth that we ought most to pursue, this motive dwells, as Professor Eucken has so effectively taught it to dwell, upon the importance of a *Lebensanschauung* as against the rigidity and the pretended finality of a mere *Weltanschauung*.

But meanwhile, upon occasion, this same motive embodies itself in various tendencies of the sort known as Irrationalism. In this last case, it points out to us how the intelligence, after all, is but a single and a very narrow function of our nature, which must not be allowed to supersede or even too much to dominate the rest of our complex and essentially obscure, if fascinating, life. Perhaps, on the very highest levels of life, as it hereupon suggests to us: *Gefühl ist alles.* If not, then at all events, we have the alternative formula: *Im Anfang war die Tat.* Or, once again, the solving word of the theory of truth is Voluntarism. Truth is won by willing, by creative activities. The doer, or perhaps the deed, not only finds, but *is*, the truth. Truth is not to be copied, but to be created. It is living truth. And life is action.

I have thus attempted to indicate, by well-known phrases, the nature of this second motive,—one whose presence in our recent theories of truth I believe that you will all recognize. Despite the Protean character and (as you will at once see) the mutually conflicting characters of its expressions, you will observe, I think, its deeper unity, and also its importance as an influence in our age. With us at present it acts as a sort of ferment, and also as an endless source of new enterprises. It awakens us to resist the most various kinds of doctrinal authority,—scientific, clerical, academic, popular. It inspires countless forms of Modernism, both within and without the boundaries of the various confessions of Christendom. As an effective motive, one finds it upon the lowest as also upon the highest levels of our intellectual and moral life. In some sense, as I have said, we all share it. It is the most characteristic and the most problematic of the motives of the modern world. Anarchism often appeals to it; yet the most saintly form of devotion, the most serious efforts for the good of mankind, and our sternest and loftiest spiritual leaders, agree in employing it, and in regarding it as in some sense sacred.

Our age shares this motive with the age of the French Revolution, of the older Idealistic movement, and of the Romantic School. All the more unfortunate, as I think, is the fact that many who glory in the originality of their own recent opinions about the nature of truth, know so little of the earlier history of this motive, read so seldom the lesson of the past, and are thus so ill-prepared to appreciate both the spiritual dignity and the pathetic paradox of this tendency to make the whole problem of truth identical with the problem of the rights and the freedom of the individual.

III

I turn herewith to the third of the motives that I have to enumerate. In its most general form it is a very ancient and familiar motive. It is, indeed, very different from both of the foregoing. Superficially regarded, it seems, at first sight, less an expression of interests that appear ethical. At heart, however, it is quite as deep a motive as either of the others, and it is in fact a profoundly ethical motive as well as a genuinely intellectual one. One may say that, in a sense and to some degree, it pervades the whole modern scientific movement, is present wherever two or three are gathered together for a serious exchange of scientific opinions, and is, in most cases, the one motive that, in scientific assemblies, is more or less consciously in mind whenever somebody present chances to refer to the love of truth, or to the scientific conscience of his hearers.

I have called this third on our list of motives an ancient motive. It is so. Yet in modern times it has assumed very novel forms, and has led to scientific and, in the end, to philosophical enterprises which, until recently, nobody would have thought possible.

It would be unwise at this point to attempt to define this motive in abstract terms. I must first exemplify it. When I say that it is the motive to which the very existence of the exact sciences is due, and when I add the remark that our scientific common sense knows this motive as the fondness for dispassionately weighing evidence, and often simply names it the love of objectivity, I raise more questions in your minds regarding the nature of this motive than at this point I can answer. If, however, anybody suggests, say from the side of some form of recent pragmatism, that I must be referring to the nowadays so deeply discredited motives of a pure "Intellectualism," I repudiate at once the suggestion. The motive to which I refer is intensely practical. Men have lived and died for it, and have found it inestimably precious. I know of no motive purer or sweeter in human life. Meanwhile, it indeed chances to be the motive which has partially embodied itself in Pure Mathematics. And neither the tribe of Nietzsche nor the kindred of the instrumentalists have been able justly to define it.

What I am just now interested to point out is that this motive has entered, in very novel ways, into the formulation of certain modern theories of truth. And when I speak of its most novel forms of expression, the historical process to which I refer is the development of the modern critical study of the foundations of mathematics.

To philosophical students in general the existence of metageo-metrical researches, which began at the outset of the nineteenth century, has now been made fairly familiar. But the non-Euclidean geometry is but a small fragment of that investigation of the foundations of mathematical truth which went on so rapidly during the nineteenth century. Among the most important of the achievements of the century in this direction were the new definitions of continuity and the irrational numbers, the modern exact theory of limits, and the still infant theory of Assemblages. Most important of all, to my mind, were certain discoveries in the field of Logic of which I shall later say a word. I mention these matters here as examples of the influence of a motive whose highly technical applications may make it seem to one at a distance hopelessly intellectualistic, but whose relation to the theory of truth is close, just because, as I think, its relation to truly ethical motives is also extremely intimate.

The motive in question showed itself at the outset of the nineteenth century, and later in the form of an increased conscientiousness regarding what should be henceforth accepted as a rigid proof in the exact sciences. The Greek geometers long ago invented the conception of rigid methods of proof and brought their own methods, in certain cases, very near to perfection. But the methods that they used proved to be inapplicable to many of the problems of modern mathematics. The result was that, in the seventeenth and eighteenth centuries, the mathematical sciences rapidly took possession of new realms of truth, but in doing so sacrificed much of the old classic rigidity. Nevertheless, regarded as the instrumentalists now desire us to regard truth, the mathematical methods of the eighteenth century were indeed incomparably more successful in adjusting the work of the physical sciences to the demands of experience than the methods of the

Greek geometers had ever been. If instrumentalism had been the whole story of man's interest in truth, the later developments would have been impossible. Nevertheless the modern scientific conscience somehow became increasingly dissatisfied with its new mathematical possessions. It regarded them as imperfectly won. It undertook to question, in a thousand ways, its own methods and its own presuppositions. It learned to reject altogether methods of proof which, for a time, had satisfied the greatest constructive geniuses of earlier modern mathematics. The result has been the development of profoundly novel methods, both of research and of instruction in the exact sciences. These methods have in many ways brought to a still higher perfection the Greek ideal of rigid proof. Yet the same methods have shown themselves to be no mere expressions of a pedantic intellectualism. They have meant clearness, self-possession, and a raising of the scientific conscience to higher levels. Meanwhile, they proved potent both in conquering new realms and in discovering the wonderful connections that we now find linking together types of exact truth which at first sight appeared to be hopelessly diverse.

In close union with the development of these new methods in the exact sciences, and, as I may say, in equally close union with this new scientific conscience, there has gradually come into being a reformed Logic,—a logic still very imperfectly expounded in even the best modern textbooks, and as yet hardly grasped, in its unity, by any one investigator,—but a logic which is rapidly progressing, which is full of beauty, and which is destined, I believe, profoundly to influence, in the near future, our whole philosophy of truth. This new logic appears to offer to us an endless realm for detailed researches. As a set of investigations it is as progressive as any instrumentalist can desire. The best names for it, I think, are the names employed by several different thinkers who have contributed to its growth. Our American logician, Mr. Charles Peirce, named it, years ago, the Logic of Relatives. Mr. Russell has called it the Logic, or the Calculus, of Relations. Mr. Kempe has proposed to entitle it the Theory of Mathematical Form. One might also call it a new and general theory of the Categories. Seen from a distance, as I just said, it appears to be a collection of highly technical special researches, interesting only to a few. But when one comes into closer contact with any one of its serious researches, one sees that its main motive is such as to interest every truthful and reflective inquirer who really grasps that motive, while the conception of truth which it forces upon our attention is a conception which neither of the other motives just characterized can be said adequately to express.

In so far as the new logic has up to this time given shape to philosophical theories of truth, it in part appears to tend towards what the pragmatists nowadays denounce as Intellectualism. As a fact Mr. Bertrand Russell, the brilliant and productive leader of this movement in England, and his philosophical friend Mr. George Moore, seem to regard their own researches as founded upon a sort of new Realism, which views truth as a realm wholly independent of the constructive activities by which we ourselves find or pursue truth. But the fact that Mr. Charles Peirce, one of the most inventive of the creators of the new logic, is also viewed by the Pragmatists as the founder of their own method, shows how the relation of the new logic to the theory of truth is something that still needs to be made clear. As a fact, I believe that the outcome of the new logic will be a new synthesis of Voluntarism and Absolutism.

What I just now emphasize is, that this modern revision of the concepts of the exact sciences, and this creation of a new logic, are in any case due to a motive which is at once theoretical and ethical. It is a motive which has defined standards of rigidity in proof such as were, until recently, unknown. In this sense it has meant a deepening and quickening of the scientific conscience. It has also seemed, in so far, to involve a rejection of that love of expediency in thinking which is now a favorite watchword of pragmatists and instrumentalists. And when viewed from this side the new logic obviously tends to emphasize some form of absolutism, to reject relativism in thinking, to make sterner requirements upon our love of truth than can be expressed in terms of instrumentalism or of individualism. And yet the motive which lies beneath this whole movement has been, I insist, no barren intellectualism. The novelty of the constructions to which this motive has led,—the break with tradition which the new geometry (for instance) has involved,—such things have even attracted, from a distance, the attention of some of the least exactly trained of the pragmatist thinkers, and have aroused their hasty and uncomprehending sympathy. "This non-Euclidean geometry," they have said, "these novel postulates, these *'freie Schöpfungen des menschlichen*

Geistes' (as Dedekind, himself one of the great creative minds of the new logical movement, has called the numbers),—well, surely these must be instances in favor of *our* theory of truth. Thus, as we should have predicted, novelties appear in what was supposed to be an absolutely fixed region. Thus (as Professor James words the matter), human thought 'boils over,' and ancient truths alter, grow, or decay." Yet when modern pragmatists and relationists use such expressions, they fail to comprehend the fact that the new discoveries in these logical and mathematical fields simply exemplify a *more* rigid concept of truth than ever, before the new movement began, had been defined in the minds of the mathematicians themselves. The non-Euclidean geometry, strange to say, is not a discovery that we are any freer than we were before to think as we like regarding the system of geometrical truth. It is one part only of what Hilbert has called the "logical analysis" of our concept of space. When we take this analysis as a whole, it involves a deeper insight than Euclid could possibly possess into the unchangeable necessities which bind together the system of logical relationships that the space of our experience merely exemplifies. Nothing could be more fixed than are these necessities. As for the numbers, which Dedekind called *"freie Schöpfungen,"*—well, his own masterpiece of logical theory is a discovery and a rigid demonstration of a very remarkable and thoroughly objective truth about the fundamental relations in terms of which we all of us do our thinking. His proof that all of the endless wealth of the properties of the ordinal numbers follows from a certain synthesis of two of the simplest of our logical conceptions, neither one of which, when taken alone, seems to have anything to do with the conception of order or of number,—this proof, I say, is a direct contribution to a systematic theory of the categories, and, as such, is, to the logical inquirer, a dramatically surprising discovery of a realm of objective truth, which nobody is free to construct or to abandon at his pleasure. If this be relativism, it is the relativism of an eternal system of relations. If this be freedom, it is the divine freedom of a self-determined, but, for that very reason, absolutely necessary fashion of thought and of activity.

Well,—to sum up,—this third motive in modern inquiry has already led us to the discovery of what are, for us, novel truths regarding the fundamental relations upon which all of our thought and all of our activity rest. These newly discovered truths possess an absoluteness which simply sets at naught the empty trivialities of current relativism. Such truth has, in fact, the same sort of relation to the biologically "instrumental" value of our thinking processes as the Theory of Numbers (that "divine science," as Gauss called it) has to the account books of the shopkeeper.

And yet, as I must insist, the motive that has led us to this type of absolutism is no pure intellectualism. And the truth in question is as much a truth about our modes of activity as the purest voluntarism could desire it to be. In brief, there is, I believe, an absolute voluntarism, a theory of the way in which activities must go on if they go on at all. And, as I believe, just such a theory is that which in future is to solve for us the problem of the nature of truth.

I have illustrated our third motive at length. Shall I now try to name it? Well, I should say that it is at bottom the same motive that lay at the basis of Kant's Critical Philosophy; but it is this motive altered by the influence of the modern spirit. It is the motive which leads us to seek for clear and exact self-consciousness regarding the principles both of our belief and of our conduct. This motive leads us to be content only in case we can indeed find principles of knowledge and of action,—principles, not mere transient expediences, and not mere caprices. On the other hand, this motive bids us decline to accept mere authority regarding our principles. It requires of us freedom along with insight, exactness side by side with assurance, and self-criticism as well as search for the ultimate.

IV

In thus sketching for you these three motives, I have been obliged to suggest my estimate of their significance. But this estimate has so far been wholly fragmentary. Let me next indicate the sense in which I believe that each of these three motives tends, in a very important sense, to throw light upon the genuine theory of truth.

I begin here with the first of the three motives,—namely, with the motive embodied in recent instrumentalism. Instrumentalism views truth as simply the value belonging to certain ideas in so far as these ideas are biological functions of our organisms, and psychological functions whereby we direct our choices and attain our successes.

Wide and manifold are the inductive evidences which the partisans of such theories of truth adduce in support of their theory. There is the evidence of introspection and of the modern psychological theory of the understanding. Opinions, beliefs, ideas,—what are they all but accompaniments of the motor processes whereby, as a fact, our organisms are adjusted to their environment? To discover the truth of an idea, what is that for any one of us to observe our success in our adjustment to our situation? Knowledge is power. Common sense long ago noted this fact. Empiricism has also since taught us that we deal only with objects of experience. The new instrumentalism adds to the old empiricism simply the remark that we possess truth in so far as we learn how to control these objects of experience. And to this more direct evidence for the instrumental theory of truth is added the evidence derived from the whole work of the modern sciences. In what sense are scientific hypotheses and theories found to be true? Only in this sense, says the instrumentalist,—only in this sense, that through these hypotheses we acquire constantly new sorts of control over the course of our experience. If we turn from scientific to moral truth, we find a similar result. The moral ideas of any social order are practical plans and practical demands in terms of which this social order endeavors, by controlling the activities of its members, to win general peace and prosperity. The truth of moral ideas lies solely in this their empirical value in adjusting individual activities to social demands, and in thus winning general success for all concerned.

Such are mere hints of the evidences that can be massed to illustrate the view that the truth of ideas is actually tested, and is to be tested, by their experienced workings, by their usefulness in enabling man to control his empirically given situation. If this be the case, then truth is always relative to the men concerned, to their experience, and to their situations. Truth grows, changes, and refuses to be tested by absolute standards. It *happens* to ideas, in so far as they *work*. It belongs to them when one views them as instruments to an end. The result of all this is a relativistic, an evolutionary, theory of truth. For such a view logic is a part of psychology,—a series of comments upon certain common characteristics of usefully working ideas and opinions. Ethical theory is a branch of evolutionary sociology. And in general, if you want to test the truth of ideas and opinions, you must look forward to their workings, not backward to the principles from which they might be supposed to follow, nor yet upwards to any absolute standards which may be supposed to guide them, and least of all to any realm of fixed facts that they are supposed to be required, willy nilly, to copy. Truth is no barren repetition of a dead reality, but belongs, as a quality, to the successful deeds by which we produce for ourselves the empirical realities that we want.

Such is the sort of evidence which my friends, Professor James and Professor Dewey, and their numerous followers, in recent discussion, have advanced in favor of this instrumental, practical, and evolutionary theory of truth. Such are the considerations which, in other forms, Mach has illustrated by means of his history and analyses of the work of modern science.

Our present comment upon this theory must be given in a word. It contains indeed a report of the truth about our actual human life, and about the sense in which we all seek and test and strive for truth, precisely in so far as truth-seeking is indeed a part of our present organic activities. But the sense in which this theory is thus indeed a true account of a vast range of the phenomena of human life is not reducible to the sense which the theory itself ascribes to the term "truth."

For suppose I say, reporting the facts of the history of science: "Newton's theory of gravitation proved to be true, and its truth lay in this: The definition and the original testing of the theory consisted in a series of the organic and psychological functions of the live creature Newton. His theories were for him true in so far as, after hard work, to be sure, and long waiting, they enabled him to control and to predict certain of his own experiences of the facts of nature. The same theories are still true for us because they have successfully guided, and still guide, certain observations and experiences of the men of to-day." This statement reduces the truth of Newton's theory to the type of truth which instrumentalism demands. But in what sense is my account of this matter itself a true account of the facts of human life? Newton is dead. As mortal man he succeeds no longer. His ideas, as psychological functions, died with him. His earthly experiences ceased when death shut his eyes. Wherein consists to-day, then, the historical truth that Newton ever existed at all, or that the countless other men whom his theories are said to have guided ever lived, or experienced, or succeeded? And if I speak of the men of to-day, in what sense is the statement true that they now live, or have experience, or use Newton's theory, or succeed with it as an instrument? No doubt all these historical and socially significant statements of mine are indeed substantially true. But does their truth consist in my success in using the ideal instruments that I use when I utter these assertions? Evidently I mean, by calling these my own assertions true, much more than I can interpret in terms of my experience of their success in guiding my act.

In brief, the truth that historical events ever happened at all; the truth that there ever was a past time, or that there ever will be a future time; the truth that anybody ever succeeds, except in so far as I myself, just now, in the use of these my present instruments for the transient control of my passing experience chance to succeed; the truth that there is any extended course of human experience at all, or any permanence, or any long-lasting success,—well, all such truths, they are indeed true, but their truth cannot possibly consist in the instrumental value which any man ever experiences as belonging to any of his own personal ideas or acts. Nor can this truth consist in anything that even a thousand or a million men can separately experience, each as the success of his own ideal instruments. For no one man experiences the success of any man but himself, or of any instruments but his own; and the truth, say, of Newton's theory consists, by hypothesis, in the perfectly objective fact that generations of men have really succeeded in guiding their experience by this theory. But that this is the fact no man, as an individual man, ever has experienced or will experience under human conditions.

When an instrumentalist, then, gives to us his account of the empirical truth that men obtain through using their ideas as instruments to guide and to control their own experience, his account of human organic and psychological functions may be,—yes, is,—as far as it goes, true. But if it is true at all, then it is true as an account of the characters actually common to the experience of a vast number of men. It is true, if at all, as a report of the objective constitution of a certain totality of facts which we call human experience. It is, then, true in a sense which no man can ever test by the empirical success of his own ideas as his means of controlling his own experiences. Therefore the truth which we must ascribe to instrumentalism, if we regard it as a true doctrine at all, is precisely a truth, not in so far as instrumentalism is itself an instrument for helping on this man's or that man's way of controlling his experience. If instrumentalism is true, it is true as a report of facts about the general course of history, of evolution, and of human experience,—facts which transcend every individual man's experience, verifications, and successes. To make its truth consist in the mere sum of the various individual successes is equally vain, unless indeed that sum is a fact. But no individual man ever experiences that fact.

Instrumentalism, consequently, express no motive which by itself alone is adequate to constitute any theory of truth. And yet, as I have pointed out, I doubt not that instrumentalism gives such a substantially true account of man's natural functions as a truth seeker. Only the sense in which instrumentalism is a true account of human life is opposed to the adequacy of its own definition of truth. The first of our three motives is, therefore, useful only if we can bring it into synthesis with other motives. In fact it is useless to talk of the success of the human spirit in its efforts to win control over experience, unless there is indeed a human spirit which is more than any man's transient consciousness of his own efforts, and unless there is an unity of experience, and unity objective, real, and supratemporal in its significance.

V

Our result so far is that man indeed uses his ideas as means of controlling his experience, and that truth involves such control, but that truth cannot be defined solely in terms of our personal experience of our own success in obtaining this control.

Hereupon the second of the motives which we have found influencing the recent theories of truth comes to our aid. If instrumentalism needs a supplement, where are we, the individual thinkers, to look for that supplement, except in those inner personal grounds which incline each of us to make his own best interpretation of life precisely as he can, in accordance with his own will to succeed, and in accordance with his individual needs?

To be sure, as one may still insist, we are always dealing with live human experience, and with its endless constraints and limitations. And when we accept or reject opinions, we do so because, at the time, these opinions seem to us to promise a future empirical "working," a successful "control" over experience,—in brief, a success such as appeals to live human beings. Instrumentalism in so far correctly defines the nature which truth possesses in so far as we ever actually verify truth. And of course we always believe as we do because we are subject to the constraint of our present experience. But since we are social beings, and beings with countless and varied intelligent needs, we constantly define and accept as valid very numerous ideas and opinions whose truth we do not hope personally to verify. Our act in accepting such unverified truths is (as Professor James states the case) essentially similar to the act of the banker in accepting credit values instead of cash. A note or other evidence of value is good if it *can* be turned into cash at some agreed time, or under specified conditions. Just so, an idea is true, not merely at the moment when it enables somebody to control his own experience. It is true if, under definable conditions which, as a fact, you or I may never verify, it *would* enable some human being whose purposes agree with ours to control his own experience. If we personally do not verify a given idea, we can still accept it then upon its credit value. We can accept it precisely as paper, which cannot now be cashed, is accepted by one who regards that paper as, for a given purpose, or to a given extent, equivalent to cash. A bond, issued by a government, may promise payment after fifty years. The banker may today accept such a bond as good, and may pay cash for it, although he feels sure that he personally will never live to see the principal repaid by the borrower.

Now, as Professor James would say, it is in this sense that our ideas about past time, and about the content of other men's minds, and about the vast physical world, "with all its stars and milky ways," are accepted as true. Such ideas have for us credit values. We accept these ideas as true because we need to trade on credits. Borrowed truth is as valuable in the spiritual realm as borrowed money is in the commercial realm. To believe a now unverified truth is simply to say: "I accept that idea, upon credit, as equivalent to the cash payments in terms of live experience which, as I assert, I could get in case I had the opportunity."

And so much it is indeed easy to make out about countless assertions which we all accept. They are assertions about experience, but not about our present experience. They are made under various constraints of convention, habit, desire, and private conviction, but they are opinions whose truth is for us dependent upon our personal assent and acquiescence.

Herewith, however, we face what is, for more than one modern theory of truth, a very critical question. Apparently it is one thing to say: "I accept this opinion upon credit," and quite another thing to say: "The truth of this opinion consists, solely and essentially, in the fact that it is credited by me." In seeming, at least, it is one thing to assert: "We trade upon credit; we deal in credits," and quite another thing to say: "There is no value behind this bond or behind this bit of irredeemable paper currency, except its credit value." But perhaps a modern theory of truth may decline to accept such a difference as ultimate. Perhaps this theory may say: The truth *is* the credit. As a fact, a vast number of our human opinions—those, for instance, which relate to the past, or to the contents of other men's minds—appear, within the range of our personal experience, as credits whose value we, who believe the opinions, cannot hope ever to convert into the cash of experience. The banker who holds the bond not maturing within his own lifetime can, after all, if the bond is good, sell it to-day for cash. And that truth which he can personally and empirically test whenever he wants to test, is enough to warrant his act in accepting the credit. But I, who am confident of the truths of history, or of geology, or of physics, and who believe in the minds of other men, —I accept as valid countless opinions that are for me, in my private capacity and from an empirical point of view, nothing but irredeemable currency. In vain do I say: "I *could* convert these ideas into the cash of experience *if* I were some other man, or *if* I were living centuries ago instead of to-day." For the question simply recurs: In what sense are these propositions about my own possible experience true when I do not test their truth,—yes, true although I, personally, *cannot* test their truth? These credits, irredeemable in terms of the cash of my experience,—wherein consists their true credit value?

Here one apparently stands at the parting of the ways. One can answer this question by saying: "The truth of these assertions (or their falsity, if they are false) belongs to them whether I credit them or no, whether I verify them or not. Their truth or their falsity is their own character and is independent of my credit and my verification." But to say this appears to be, after all, just the intellectualism which so many of our modern pragmatists condemn. There remains, however, one other way. One can say: "The truth of the unverified assertions *consists simply in the fact that,* for our own private and individual ends, *they are credited.* Credit is relative to the creditor. If he finds that, on the whole, it meets his purpose to credit, he credits. And there is no truth, apart from present verifications, except this truth of credit." In other words, that is true for me which I find myself accepting as my way of reacting to my situation.

This, I say, is a theory of truth which can be attempted. Consider what a magnificent freedom such a theory gives to all of us. Credit is relative to the creditor. To be sure, if ever the day of reckoning should come, one would be subject, at the moment of verification, to the constraints of experience. At such times, one would either get the cash or would not get it. But after all very few of our ideas about this great and wonderful world of ours ever are submitted to any such sharp tests. History and the minds of other men, —well, our personal opinions about these remain credits that no individual amongst us can ever test for himself. As your world is mainly made up of such things, your view of your world remains, then, subject to your own needs. It ought to be thus subject. There is no absolute truth. There is only the truth that you need. Enter into the possession of your spiritual right. Borrow Nietzsche's phraseology. Call the truth of ordinary intellectualism mere *Sklavenwahrheit*. It pretends to be absolute; but only the slaves believe in it. "Henceforth," so some Zarathustra of a new theory of truth may say, "I teach you *Herrenwahrheit*." Credit what you choose to credit. Truth is made for man, not man for truth. Let your life "boil over" into new truth as much as you find such effervescence convenient. When, apart from the constraints of present verification, and apart from mere convention, I say: "This opinion of mine is true," I mean simply: "To my mind, lord over its own needs, this assertion now appears expedient." Whenever my expediency changes, my truth will change.

But does anybody to-day hold just *this* theory of truth? I hesitate to make accusations which some of my nearest and dearest friends may repudiate as personally injurious. But this I can say: I find a great many recent theorists about truth talking in just this spirit so long as they feel free to glorify their spiritual liberty, to amuse their readers with clever assaults upon absolutism, and to arouse sympathy by insistence upon the human and the democratic attractiveness of the novel views of truth that they have to advance. Such individualism, such capriciousness, is in the air. Our modern theorists of truth frequently speak in this way. When their expressions of such views are criticized, they usually modify and perhaps withdraw them. What, as individuals, such teachers really mean, I have no right to say. Nobody but themselves can say; and some of them seem to say whatever they please. But this I know; Whoever identifies the truth of an assertion with his own individual interest in making that assertion may be left to bite the dust of his own confusion in his own way and time. The outcome of such essential waywardness is not something that you need try to determine through controversy. It is self-determined. For in case I say to you: "The sole ground for my assertions is this, that I please to make them,"—well, at once I am defining exactly the attitude which we all alike regard as the attitude of one who chooses *not* to tell the truth. And if, hereupon, I found a theory of truth upon generalizing such an assertion,—well, I am defining as truth-telling precisely that well-known practical attitude which is the contradictory of the truth-telling attitude. The contrast is not one between intellectualism and pragmatism. It is the contrast between two well-known attitudes of will,—the will that is loyal to truth as an universal ideal, and the will that is concerned with its own passing caprices. If I talk of truth, I refer to what the truth-loving sort of will seeks. If hereupon I define the true as that which the individual personally views as expedient in opinion or in assertion, I contradict myself, and may be left to my own confutation. For the position in which I put myself, by this individualistic theory of truth, is closely analogous to the position in which Epimenides the Cretan, the hero of the fallacy of the liar, was placed by his own so famous thesis.

VI

And yet, despite all this, the modern assault upon mere intellectualism is well founded. The truth of our assertions is indeed definable only by taking account of the meaning of our own individual attitudes of will, and the truth, whatever else it is, is at least instrumental in helping us towards the goal of all human volition. The only question is whether the will really means to aim at doing something that has a final and eternal meaning.

Herewith I suggest a theory of truth which we can understand only in case we follow the expressions of the third of the three modern motives to which I have referred. I have said that the new logic and the new methods of reasoning in the exact sciences are just now bringing us to a novel comprehension of our relation to absolute truth. I must attempt a very brief indication as to how this is indeed the case.

I have myself long since maintained that there is indeed a logic of the will, just as truly as there is a logic of the intellect. Personally, I go further still. I assert: all logic is the logic of the will. There is no pure intellect. Thought is a mode of action, a mode of action distinguished from other modes mainly by its internal clearness of self-consciousness, by its relatively free control of its own procedure, and by the universality, the impersonal fairness and obviousness of its aims and of its motives. An idea in the consciousness of a thinker is simply a present consciousness of some expression of purpose,—a plan of action. A judgment is an act of a reflective and self-conscious character, an act whereby one accepts or rejects an idea as a sufficient expression of the very purpose that is each time in question. Our whole objective world is meanwhile defined for each of us in terms of our ideas. General assertions about the meaning of our ideas are reflective acts whereby we acknowledge and accept certain ruling principles of action. And in respect of all these aspects of doctrine I find myself at one with recent voluntarism, whether the latter takes the form of instrumentalism, or insists upon some more individualistic theory of truth. But for my part, in spite, or in fact because of this my voluntarism, I cannot rest in any mere relativism. Individualism is right in saying, "I will to credit this or that opinion." But individualism is wrong in supposing that I can ever be content with my own will in as far as it is merely an individual will. The will to my mind is to all of us nothing but a thirst for complete and conscious self-possession, for fullness of life. And in terms of this its central motive, the will defines the truth that it endlessly seeks as a truth that possesses completeness, totality, self-possession, and therefore absoluteness. The fact that, in our human experience, we never meet with any truths such as completely satisfy our longing for insight, this fact we therefore inevitably interpret, not as any defect in the truth, but as a defect in our present state of knowledge, a limitation due to our present type of individuality. Hence we acknowledge a truth which transcends our individual life. Our concepts of the objectively real world, our ethical ideals of conduct, our estimates of what constitutes the genuine worth of life,—all these constructions of ours are therefore determined by the purpose to conform our selves to absolute standards. We will the eternal. We define the eternal. And this we do whenever we talk of what we call genuine facts or actualities, or of the historical content of human experience, or of the physical world that our sciences investigate. If we try to escape this inner necessity of our whole voluntary and self-conscious life, we simply contradict ourselves. We can define the truth even of relativism only by asserting that relativism is after all absolutely true. We can admit our ignorance of truth only by acknowledging the absoluteness of that truth of which we are ignorant. And all this is no caprice of ours. All this results from a certain necessary nature of our will which we can test as often as we please by means of the experiment of trying to get rid of the postulate of an absolute truth. We shall find that, however often we try this experiment, the denial that there is any absolute truth simply leads to its own denial, and reinstates what it denies.

The reference that I a little while since made to our assertions regarding the past, and regarding the minds of other men, has already suggested to us how stubbornly we all assert certain truths which, for every one of us, transcend empirical verification, but which we none the less regard as absolutely true. If I say: "There never was a past," I contradict myself, since I assume the past even in asserting that a past never was. As a fact our whole interpretation of our experience is determined, in a sense akin to that which Kant defined, by certain modes of our own activity, whose significance is transcendental, even while their whole application is empirical. These modes of our activity make all our empirical sciences logically possible. Meanwhile it need not surprise us to find that Kant's method of defining these modes of our activity was not adequate, and that a new logic is giving us, in this field, new light. The true nature of these necessary modes of our activity becomes most readily observable to us in case we rightly analyze the methods and concepts, not of our own empirical, but rather of our mathematical sciences. For in these sciences our will finds its freest expression. And yet for that very reason in these sciences the absoluteness of the truth which the will defines is most obvious. The new logic to which I refer is especially a study of the logic of mathematics.

VII

That there are absolutely true propositions, the existence of the science of pure mathematics proves. It is indeed the case that, as Russell insists, the propositions of pure mathematics are (at least in general) hypothetical propositions. But the hypothetical character of the propositions of pure mathematics does not make the truth that a certain mathematically interesting consequent follows from a certain antecedent, in any way less than absolutely true. The assertion, "*a* implies *b*," where *a* and *b* are propositions, may be an absolutely true assertion; and, as a fact, the hypothetical assertions of pure mathematics possess this absolutely true character. Now it is precisely the nature and ground of this absoluteness of purely mathematical truth upon which recent research seems to me to have thrown a novel light. And the light which has appeared in this region seems to me to be destined to reflect itself anew upon all regions and types of truth, so that empirical and contingent, and historical and psychological and ethical truth, different as such other types of truth may be from mathematical truth, will nevertheless be better understood, in future, in the light of the newer researches into the logic of pure mathematics. I can only indicate, in the most general way, the considerations which I here have in mind.

At the basis of every mathematical theory,—as, for instance, at the basis of pure geometry, or pure number theory,—one finds a set of fundamental concepts, the so-called "indefinables" of the theory in question, and a set of fundamental "propositions," the so-called "axioms" of this theory. Modern study of the logic of pure mathematics has set in a decidedly novel light the question: What is the rational source, and what is the logical basis of these primal concepts and of these primal propositions of mathematical theory? I have no time here to deal with the complications of the recent discussion of this question. But so much I can at once point out: there are certain concepts and certain propositions which possess the character of constituting the doctrine which may be called, in the modern sense, Pure Logic. Some of these concepts and propositions were long ago noted by Aristotle. But the Aristotelian logic actually took account of only a portion of the concepts of pure logic, and was able to give, of these concepts, only a very insufficient analysis. There is a similar inadequacy about the much later analysis of the presuppositions of logic which Kant attempted. The theory of the categories is in fact undergoing, at present, a very important process of reconstruction. And this process is possible just because we have at present discovered wholly new means of analyzing the concepts and propositions in question. I refer (as I may in passing state) to the means supplied by modern Symbolic Logic.

Well, the concepts of pure logic, when once defined, constitute an inexhaustible source for the constructions and theories of pure mathematics. A set of concepts and of propositions such as can be made the basis of a mathematical theory is a set possessing a genuine and unquestionable significance if, and only if, these concepts and these propositions can be brought into a certain definite relation with the concepts and propositions of pure logic. This relation may be expressed by saying that if the conditions of general logical theory are such as to imply the valid possibility of the mathematical definitions and constructions in question, then—but only then—are the corresponding mathematical theories at once absolutely valid and significant. In brief, pure mathematics consists of constructions and theories based wholly upon the conceptions and propositions of pure logic.

The question as to the absoluteness of mathematical truth hereupon reduces itself to the question as to the absolutenesss of the truths of pure logic.

Wherein, however, consists this truth of pure logic? I answer, at once, in my own way. Pure logic is the theory of the mere form of thinking. But what is thinking? Thinking, I repeat, is simply our activity of willing precisely in so far as we are clearly conscious of what we do and why we do it. And thinking is found by us to possess an absolute form precisely in so far as we find that there are certain aspects of our activity which sustain themselves even in and through the very effort to inhibit them. One who says: "I do not admit that for me there is any difference between saying yes and saying no,"—says "no," and distinguishes negation from affirmation, even in the very act of denying this distinction. Well, affirmation and negation are such self-sustaining forms of our will activity and of our thought activity. And such self-sustaining forms of activity determine absolute truths. For instance, it is an absolute truth that there is a determinate difference between the assertion and the denial of a given proposition, and between the doing and the not doing of a given deed. Such absolute truths may appear trival enough. Modern logical theory is for the first time making clear to us how endlessly wealthy in consequences such seemingly trivial assertions are.

The absoluteness of the truths of pure logic is shown through the fact that you can test these logical truths in this reflective way. They are truths such that to deny them is simply to reassert them under a new form. I fully agree, for my own part, that absolute truths are known to us only in such cases as those which can be tested in this way. I contend only that recent logical analysis has given to us a wholly new insight as to the fruitfulness of such truths.

VIII

An ancient example of a use of that way of testing the absoluteness of truth which is here in question is furnished by a famous proof which Euclid gave of the theorem, according to which there exists no last prime number in the ordinal sequence of the whole numbers. Euclid, namely, proved this theorem by what I suppose to be one device whereby individual instances of absolute truths are accessible to us men. He proved the theorem by showing that the denial of the theorem implies the truth of the theorem. That is, if I suppose that there is a last prime number, I even thereby provide myself with the means of constructing a prime number, which comes later in the series of whole numbers than the supposed "last" prime, and which certainly exists just as truly as the whole numbers themselves exist. Here, then, is one classic instance of an absolute truth.

To be sure Euclid's theorem about the prime numbers is a hypothetical proposition. It depends upon certain concepts and propositions about the whole numbers. But the equally absolute truth that the whole numbers themselves form an endless series, with no last term, has been subjected, in recent times, to wholly new forms of reëxamination by Dedekind, by Frege, and by Russell. The various methods used by these different writers involve substantially the same sort of consideration as that which Euclid already applied to the prime numbers. There are certain truths which you cannot deny without denying the truth of the first principles of pure logic. But to deny these latter principles is to reassert them under some other and equivalent form. Such is the common principle at the basis of the recent reëxamination of the concept of the whole numbers. Dedekind, in showing that the existence of the dense ordinal series of the rational numbers implies the existence of the Dedekind *Schnitte* of this series, discovered still another absolute, although of course hypothetical, truth which itself implies the truth of the whole theory of the so-called real numbers. Now all such discoveries are indeed revelations of absolute truth in precisely this sense, that at the basis of all the concepts and propositions about number there are concepts and propositions belonging to pure logic; while if you deny these propositions of pure logic, you imply, by this very denial, the reassertion of what you deny. To discover this fact, to see that the denial of a given proposition implies the reassertion of that proposition, is not, as Kant supposed, something that you can accomplish, if at all, then only by a process of mere "analysis." On the contrary, Euclid's proof as to the prime numbers, and the modern exact proofs of the fundamental theorems of mathematics, involve, in general, a very difficult synthetic process,—a construction which is by no means at first easy to follow. And the same highly synthetic constructions run through the whole of modern logic.

Now once again what does one discover when he finds out such absolute truths? I do not believe, as Russell believes, that one in such cases discovers truths which are simply and wholly independent of our constructive processes. On the contrary, what one discovers is distinctly what I must call a voluntaristic truth,—a truth about the creative will that thinks the *truth*. One discovers, namely, that our constructive processes, viewed just as activities, possess a certain absolute nature and conform to their own self-determined but, for that very reason, absolute laws. One finds out in such cases what one must still, with absolute necessity, do under the presupposition that one is no longer bound by the constraints of ordinary experience, but is free, as one is in pure mathematics free, to construct whatever one can construct. The more, in such cases, one deals with what indeed appear to be, in one aspect, "*freie Schöpfungen des menschlichen Geistes,*" the more one discovers that their laws, which are the fundamental and immanent laws of the will itself, are absolute. For one finds what it is that one must construct even if one denies that, in the ideal world of free construction which one is seeking to define, that construction has a place. In brief, all such researches illustrate the fact that while the truth which we acknowledge is indeed relative to the will which acknowledges that truth, still what one may call the pure form of willing is an absolute form, a form which sustains itself in the very effort to violate its own laws. We thus find out absolute truth, but it is absolute truth about the nature of the creative will in terms of which we conceive all truths.

Now it is perfectly true that such absolute truth is not accessible to us in the empirical world, in so far as we deal with individual phenomena. But it is also true that we all of us conceive the unity of the world of experience—the meaning, the sense, the connection of its facts—in terms of those categories which express precisely this very form of our creative activity. Hence, although every empirical truth is relative, all relative truth is inevitably defined by us as subject to conditions which themselves are absolute. This, which Kant long ago maintained, gets a very new meaning in the light of recent logic,—a far deeper meaning, I think, than Kant could conceive.

In any case, the new logic, and the new mathematics, are making us acquainted with absolute truth, and are giving to our knowledge of this truth a clearness never before accessible to human thinking. And yet the new logic is doing all this in a way that to my mind is in no wise a justification of the intellectualism which the modern instrumentalists condemn. For what we hereby learn is that all truth is indeed relative to the expression of our will, but that the will inevitably determines for itself forms of activity which are objectively valid and absolute, just because to attempt to inhibit these forms is once more to act, and is to act in accordance with them. These forms are the categories both of our thought and of our action. We recognize them equally whether we consider, as in ethics, the nature of reasonable conduct, or, as in logic, the forms of conceptual construction, or, as in mathematics, the ideal types of objects that we can define by constructing, as freely as possible, in conformity with these forms. When we turn back to the world of experience, we inevitably conceive the objects of experience in terms of our categories. Hence the unity and the transindividual character which rightly we assign to the objects of experience. What we know about these objects is always relative to our human needs and activities. But all of this relative knowledge is—however provisionally—defined in terms of absolute principles. And that is why the scientific spirit and the scientific conscience are indeed the expression of motives, which you can never reduce to mere instrumentalism, and can never express in terms of any individualism. And that is why, wherever two or three are gathered together in any serious moral or scientific enterprise, they believe in a truth which is far more than the mere working of any man's ephemeral assertions.

In sum, an absolute truth is one whose denial implies the reassertion of that same truth. To us men, such truths are accessible only in the realm of our knowledge of the forms that predetermine all of our concrete activities. Such knowledge we can obtain regarding the categories of pure logic and also regarding the constructions of pure mathematics. In dealing, on the other hand, with the concrete objects of experience, we are what the instrumentalists suppose us to be, namely, seekers for a successful control over this experience. And as the voluntarists also correctly emphasize, in all our empirical constructions, scientific and practical, we express our own individual wills and seek such success as we can get. But there remains the fact that in all these constructions we are expressing a will which, as logic and pure mathematics teach us, has an universal absolute nature,—the same in all of us. And it is for the sake of winning some adequate expression of this our absolute nature, that we are constantly striving in our empirical world for a success which we never can obtain at any instant, and can never adequately define in any merely relative terms. The result appears in our ethical search for absolute standards, and in our metaphysical thirst for an absolute interpretation of the universe,— a thirst as unquenchable as the over-individual will that expresses itself through all our individual activities is itself world-wide, active, and in its essence absolute.

In recognizing that all truth is relative to the will, the three motives of the modern theories of truth are at one. To my mind they, therefore, need not remain opposed motives. Let us observe their deeper harmony, and bring them into synthesis. And then what I have called the trivialities of mere instrumentalism will appear as what what they are,—fragmentary hints, and transient expressions, of that will whose life is universal, whose form is absolute, and whose laws are at once those of logic, of ethics, of the unity of experience, and of whatever gives sense to life.

Tennyson, in a well-known passage of his "In Memoriam," cries:

> Oh living Will that shalt endure
>   When all that seems shall suffer shock,
>   Rise in the spiritual rock,
> Flow through our deeds and make them pure.

That cry of the poet was an expression of moral and religious sentiment and aspiration; but he might have said essentially the same thing if he had chosen the form of praying: Make our deeds logical. Give our thoughts sense and unity. Give our Instrumentalism some serious unity of eternal purpose. Make our Pragmatism more than the mere passing froth of waves that break upon the beach of triviality. In any case, the poet's cry is an expression of that Absolute Pragmatism, of that Voluntarism, which recognizes all truth as the essentially eternal creation of the Will. What the poet utters is that form of Idealism which seems to me to be indicated as the common outcome of all the three motives that underlie the modern theory of truth.

23

The Mechanical,
the Historical,
and the Statistical

I *Practical Purposes of This Meeting*

This meeting is the outcome of conversations which resulted from the recent book of Dr. Henderson on "The Fitness of the Environment." Yet this company is not called for the sake of discussing, on the present occasion, that book, or any of the scientific problems which it more directly considers. The connection, then, between Dr. Henderson's book and this evening's undertaking needs some explanation. As you know from the wording of the call to which you have so kindly responded, one principal purpose which I have in mind as I address you is practical. I shall ask you, before the evening is done, to give some thought to the question: Is it advisable for us to meet again occasionally, as opportunity offers, in order to discuss some questions of common scientific interest? You represent various departments of research. Is it worth while for you, or some of you, at your own pleasure, to come together in such a way as the present one, in order to take counsel about different problems which belong, not only to a single science, and not only to some special group of sciences, but also to the realm

[Reprinted from *Science*, n.s. (1914) 39:551–66.]

which is common to a decidedly wide and varied range of scientific inquiries?

My part in this evening's discussion is determined by this practical question. I can not come here as a representative of any one department of research in natural science. I am limited in my present undertaking to such an appeal as a student of philosophy may have a right to address to a company of scientific men, when he wishes to ask them a practical question whose answer concerns them all.

The only justification which I have for addressing you is that the habits of a student of philosophy, and, in particular, of a student of logic, makes him sensitive to the value of a comparative scrutiny of the methods, the conceptions and the problems of various sciences.

If the main topic of the evening is a question relating to the practical value of some new mode of cooperation, in which a number of representatives of different departments of scientific research are to be asked to take part, the student of philosophy may possibly serve as a sort of travelling agent. For the kind of cooperation to which I have been asked to invite your attention would involve, if it succeeded, certain journeys which some of you might thereby be induced to make into the provinces of your colleagues. Widely traveled though all of you are, these journeys may lead occasionally to novel incidents, and may please or arouse you in new ways. My business, I say, is to act this evening merely as such a tourist agent, describing and praising as I can the new kind and combination of journeys to which my agency proposes to invite you.

Philosophy itself, in so far as it is a legitimate calling at all, may in fact be compared to a sort of Cook's bureau. Its servants are taught to speak various languages—all of them ill—and to know little of the inner life of the numerous foreign lands to which they guide the feet, or check the luggage of their fellow-men.

But if new comparative studies of the ideas of various and widely sundered provinces of research are to be carried out at all, Cook's agents, tedious as they often are, have their part to play. Regard me, then, if you wish to vary the name, as representing this evening some bureau of university travel.

II *Preliminary View of the Theoretical
Problem of This Paper*

Speaking seriously, let me say that my task, upon its theoretical
side, involves undertaking to present to you, in a perspective which
may prove to be not wholly familiar, an outline sketch of certain
conceptions and methods which actually belong to widely various
sciences. These conceptions and methods in some measure concern you all, and, in our day, they are undergoing various changes,
and are being applied to new problems.

The problems of each science are its own affair; but they also
concern the whole body of scientific workers. To look over a
somewhat wide range of scientific work, not for the sake of con-
tributing to the researches of any one special science or group of
special sciences, but for the sake of studying for their own sake
some of the most general ideas and methods that are used by various scientific workers—this is, at the present time, a legitimate undertaking, and, in view of what has already been done, and is now
under way, is not a hopeless undertaking.

The perspective in which such a study may place the problems
of other people may help them to understand one another better.
My task on its theoretical side is limited this evening to a few such
general methodological remarks. These remarks may then lead us
back to our practical question.

III *The Problem of Vitalism*

The name vitalism is often given to those doctrines which have
used the hypothesis that the phenomena of living organisms are
due to some process which is essentially identical in its nature
with the process exemplified by our own conscious voluntary activities. We deliberate, plan and choose. It seems to us as if certain
things and occurrences in the world are due to these our plans and
choices, and are different from what they would be were our will
not a factor in the world-process. On the other hand, some things
and events in the natural world—notably the recurrent movements
of the heavenly bodies, and the processes which attend the workings of machines, seem to us to be, in some or in many respects
essentially different from the processes which result from our

plans, our choices and our voluntary deeds. What is called a mechanical theory of nature, or, more generally still, materialism, undertakes to account for the vital processes, for the activities of organisms, by supposing that they too are not essentially different from the other material processes, and that they really exemplify the same natural laws which the movements of the heavenly bodies and the workings of machines illustrate.

The contrast between vitalism and materialism is, in the history of science and of philosophy, very ancient. The Greeks began with doctrines which were, in a somewhat confused way, both materialistic and vitalistic. The natural world was viewed as, in one of its aspects, a sort of machine, a chariot whose mechanical movement was an essential feature of its very being. The natural world was also regarded as through and through alive—a world of love and strife, of mixing and of sundering, of wisdom and of something resembling contrivance.

To this early Greek vitalism, which had various forms, the materialism of Democritus opposed a mechanical theory of nature which was much more ingenious and considerate than were the earliest forms in which the machine-like aspect of nature was described. On the whole, however, vitalism, the doctrine that nature acts not in vain, but in an essentially planful and designing way, was predominant in Greek thought.

The greatest Greek vitalist was Aristotle. Materialism remained in the background of ancient thought, and was destined to be revived, and to take on the form of the modern mechanical theory of nature, only after the beginnings of the new science in the seventeenth century of our era.

These ancient problems as to whether nature is rather a mechanism or an expression of something which essentially involves or resembles wisdom and contrivance, are certainly not questions which belong to any one natural science or group of natural sciences. From time to time, however, they come nearer to the surface of popular or of scientific discussion. The present is a moment when a certain interest in various forms of vitalism has once more become prominent in the discussions not only of philosophers and of leaders in popular inquiry, but of some professional students of the natural sciences of life as well.

I do not know how far it will prove to be interesting or profitable for you, as scientific men, to discuss, in your future meetings, if you have any future meetings, problems directly connected with vitalism, or with its old opponent, the mechanistic theory of the nature of life. I know only that when we mention such problems we call attention to one of the ancient boundary lines, or, as one may say, to one of the beaches where, in the realms of inquiry, sea and land come face to face with each other; so that two widely constrasting realms of nature here seem to clash. Here, then, the waves of experience tumble, and the tides of opinion rise and fall. Here, then, for that very reason, and especially at this very time, new discoveries are likely to be made in especially impressive ways.

If you are to compare notes, it will therefore not be surprising to find that questions about the relations, the contrasts and the connections of life and of mechanism will become prominent in your discussions. My own preliminary remarks on the classification of scientific methods may well be guided, then, by some interest in the scientific processes which go on upon this old boundary line— this sea-beach—of opinion and of investigation, where the vast and doubtful seas of inquiry into the phenomena of life encounter, as it were, the firm land where the mechanical view of nature finds its best known illustrations.

IV *The Vitalism of Aristotle*

It will help us in our survey of our problems about the contrasting ideas and methods followed by the inorganic sciences on the one hand and the sciences of life on the other hand, if we next say a word about one aspect of Greek vitalism which is frequently neglected.

Life-processes in general resemble our own voluntary human processes, as we have said, in so far as any living organism seems to us as if it were guided by some sort of design, and as if, through a kind of wisdom or contrivance it adjusted means to ends. To say this, however, and even to believe that this seeming is well founded, and that, in some wise living nature really is planful, and does embody something of the nature of will, or of purpose—to assert all this is not yet to decide how close the real resemblance is between the teleology of nature and the choices and contrivances of a man who is planning and who is exerting his will.

As a fact there have been many vitalists who thought nature, and in particular organic nature, to be purposive, but who did not believe that nature is clearly aware of her own designs.

There have been many vitalists who conceived of nature as in some sense even divine in its skill, but who did not accept theism either in its primitive or in its more cultivated forms. The design argument in its later theological formulations is not any classic argument for vitalism. All this becomes manifest if you look for a moment at Greek vitalism, and, in particular, at the vitalism of Aristotle.

The Greek vitalists well knew that nature, however wise she seems to be, does not show signs of deliberating like an architect before he builds a house, or of piecing together her works as a carpenter devises a chest or a bed. For the Greek vitalist, and, in particular, for Asistotle, nature fashions, but not as a human mechanic fashions—piecemeal and by trial and error.

Nature's skill is (so such vitalists think) more like that of a creative artist, who does not pause to know how he creates. If ideas inspire the artist, he does not reflect upon what they are. Just so, while the being whom Aristotle calls God, who is conceived to exist quite apart from the world, is indeed self-knowing and is wisely self-observant, Aristotle's God is not the God of the later design argument. For he neither creates nor fashions the natural world. Nature, in Aristotle's opinion, is not God and is not God's handiwork, but is, with a certain instinctive and unconscious wisdom, a sort of artistic imitator of God's wisdom. And this natural process of imitating the divine perfection by quickening a material world with a tendency to be fashioned after a divine pattern—this process constitutes the life of the natural world.

The designs which nature expresses are therefore for Greek vitalism not the conscious designs of anybody—either God or man. They are the creative tendencies which embody themselves in the material world, by a process which we can best compare with the workings of instinct or genius.

Now modern vitalism is far away from its Greek forerunners, but whenever, for any reason, vitalism becomes afresh interesting to any group either of philosophers or of scientific workers, it is well to remember that the contrast and the conflict between a mechanical view of nature and vitalistic view has hardly ever been limited to the decidedly special and artificial antithesis between blind mechanism, on the one hand, and conscious or deliberative design, on the other hand. For even our human art is, as Aristotle remarks, partly guided by a skill which is not conscious and is not deliberate. That which, in recent years, Bergson has called élan vital—the creative vital power, was well known, in their own way, to the Greeks.

Different as Bergson's vitalism is from that of Aristotle, the ancient view and Bergson's vitalism have in common the belief that life means a process of which the instinctive skill and the artistic genius of man give examples. The problem of vitalism is always the problem as to how such unconsicous skill, such undeliberative art is made possible.

And so, even in this sketch of the varieties of scientific method, I shall in passing name to you one way in which some of the newest hypotheses may enable us to face, and perhaps in some measure to clarify, the problem as to how this stimulation of conscious designs by processes which are themselves unconsciously or, so to speak, blindly wise, is a possibility in the natural world.

V   *Three Types of Knowledge: The Historical,*
  the Mechanical and the Statistical

So much must suffice as an introductory word regarding those problems about vitalism and mechanism which have recently been revived, and have brought us together. Herewith we are ready to proceed to our classification of the conceptions and the methods which may be used in dealing with such a range of problems as is this.

The attempt to sketch in a preliminary way what these conceptions and methods are can be preserved, I think, from vagueness, if I begin by using the guidance of a man of whom you all are accustomed to think as a true natural philosopher—one who was possessed of a very exact sort of scientific knowledge, and who was a great scientific discoverer. He was also very fond of a comparative study whereby he lighted up his own researches through thoughts that came to him from far-off fields. I refer to Clerk Maxwell. In a paper whereof some fragments are printed in his biography, as well as in various remarks in his published writings, Clerk Maxwell more than once used the classification of scientific knowledge which I shall here employ for our present purpose. Natural science, in so far as it studies the processes of the natural world, has three kinds of objects with which it deals. And it adjusts itself to these three kinds of objects by methods which, in each of three fields thus defined, vary widely from one another; while in each of the three fields both the conceptions and the methods used have much in common, and much too whereby each of the three fields differs from the others. The three sorts of objects are: (1) Historical objects, (2) mechanisms, and (3) statistically defined assemblages. The three sorts of methods are: The historical, the mechanical and the statistical.

Clerk Maxwell's few but momentous observations upon these three fields of scientific knowledge have a beautiful brevity, and show a fairly poetical skill of imagination whereby he finds and expresses his illustrations both of scientific ideas and of methods. I can not follow the master in his own skill. And I shall be unable to use his language. I must portray his classification in my own way, and must use my own illustrations.

If you wish to come into closer touch with this aspect of the master's thought, you may use the concluding passage of his famous elementary treatise on the "Theory of Heat," and several remarks in his article on "Atoms" in the ninth edition of the Encyclopedia Britannica. In addition I may refer you to the citations made by Theodore Merz in the eleventh chapter of Volume II of his "History of European Thought in the Nineteenth Century" (pp. 599, 601 and 603).

Let me briefly review, with a few illustrations, this classification of the three fields and the three methods of natural science.

Science deals either with substantial things (such as atoms or organisms) or else with events. Let us confine ourselves here to the works of science in its dealings with natural events and processes. Science deals with the historical when its objects are individual events or complexes of events, such as is a single solar eclipse, or such as is the birth or the death of this man, or the performance of just this act of choice by this individual voluntary agent.

Science deals with the mechanical when its objects are the invariant laws to which all the individual events of some field of inquiry are subject, and when such invariant laws actually exist, and can be used to compute and to predict actual events. Thus, if the acceleration which every individual body belonging to a system of material bodies undergoes depends at every instant, in an invariant way, upon the spatial configuration of the system of bodies at just that moment, the system is a mechanical system—such, for instance, as a system of bodies moving in accordance with the Newtonian law of gravitation.

Science deals, in the third place, with the statistical, when it studies the averages in terms of which aggregates or collections of events can be characterized, and when it considers not the invariant laws, but the always variable possibilities that these averages will be subject to certain uniformities, and will undergo definable changes.

In brief, the object of historical knowledge is the single event, occurring, in the ideally simple case, to an individual thing. A free-will act or an observed eclipse serves as an example. The object of mechanical knowledge is the unchanging natural law under which every event of some type can be subsumed. Sometimes the object of mechanical science may be an individual event, but only in so far as, like the eclipse, it can be predicted by means of such an invariant law. The object of statistical knowledge is not the single event and is not the invariant law but is the relatively uniform behavior of some average constitution, belonging to an aggregate of things and events, and the probability that this average behavior will remain, within limits, approximately, although always imperfectly uniform.

VI *Applications of This Classification*

In view of this classification of the objects of scientific knowledge, you may see at once that the issues between such doctrines as vitalism and a mechanistic account of nature appear, from the point of view of Maxwell's classification, in a somewhat unfamiliar perspective. For one need no longer merely contrast two views, the mechanical and the vitalistic. One now has a third and a mediating point of view to compare with both of them. The result is instructive.

Vitalism, whatever else it involves, always makes prominent some aspect of nature, and in particular some aspect of organic nature, such that this aspect is supposed to be, in some individual case, strictly historical. If an organism is due to a purposive process, if the reactions of an organism are, in any instance, events of the nature of conscious or of subconscious deeds—then something unique, historical and novel occurs whenever one of these vital processes is exemplified by an individual event.

On the other hand, if the mechanistic view of nature can exhaustively express the real facts, then the only natural events are of the type which the eclipses exemplify. The single events are, so to speak, points on a curve, selections from an ideal continuum whose constitution is definable in terms of an invariant differential equation.

But the third or statistical mode of viewing nature takes account of another aspect of the processes of nature. The world of the statistical view still contains events supposed to be unique and individual; but from the statistical point of view the main interest lies no longer in each event as it occurs, nor yet in its unique character. The statistical interest is directly concerned with a set or aggregate of events, with a discrete multitude of occurrences. These occurrences may prove to be examples of law. The statistical view is deeply interested in finding that they are examples of law. But the law for which the statistical method seeks is no longer a law that is ideally stable in terms of an invariant differential equation or in terms of any other timeless invariant. When found, the statistical law is an account of a collection of facts in terms of averages involving many events.

This account takes some such form as saying: "The average magnitude or velocity or size or range of the events of the class C is approximately V." Or, again, the statistical view succeeds when we can say: "A proportion which is approximately p of the events of the class a have the character b." Or finally, one expresses the statistical view when one is able to assert: "There is a probability q that c differs from d by not more than such and such an amount, —say X." All such generalizations, where the objects in question are living organisms, relate to events, but neither to merely historical single events nor to events subject to fixed laws. The statistical laws are probable and approximate laws about numbers of events.

Laws and probabilities, stated in some such form as the one just suggested, constitute the characteristic formulas of the statistical view of nature.

It is easy to illustrate how the statistical view contrasts with both the mechanical and the historical point of view by considering how each point of view applies to an event such as is expressed by the assertion: "A killed B."

For a strictly historical point of view this event, this homicide, is an unique occurrence—possibly a free-will act. It falls under moral and criminal laws, but these relate only to its value and its legal consequences. The interest of the case for a judge or a jury lies in its novelty—and in its uniqueness. For a strictly mechanical view of things the killing resembles an eclipse. Unique as it is, it is supposed to have been essentially predictable. Perhaps if you had known the precise configuration and the accelerations of all the physical particles in the world at some appropriate moment, then this killing could have been calculated in advance. It is a mere case of a law—an eclipse, so to speak, of some sun—a point on some curve.

But for a statistical view the single killing of B by A is an event against which an insurance provision could have been made in advance—not because any mortal could have predicted whether or no A would kill B, but because the death-rate of men of B's age and occupation can be statistically known with an approximate and probable accuracy, so as to make a policy insuring B's life a contract whose value is calculable, not on mechanical but upon statistical grounds.

Now you will easily recognize that the actual knowledge of vital phenomena which science possesses is, in the main, a statistical knowledge. It is the sort of knowledge which the mortality tables of the insurance companies exemplify. We know little of the history of individual organisms, and less of their mechanism, but we can and do study the statistics of groups of organisms. In such statistical terms heredity and variation are now constantly investigated. In such terms growth and disease, as well as death, economic prosperity and social transformations, financial and political processes, the geographical distribution of organisms and the gradual accumulation and change of the material as well as the mental products of civilization—in such statistical terms, I say, all such things come to be the objects of scientific description and explanation. To give an account of the special phenomena of life in terms of mechanism remains in practise a remote ideal, despite all the proofs that the vital processes, being subject to physical and chemical laws, must be, in some sense, if not wholly, then very largely mechanical in their nature. Life may be a case of mechanism; but its phenomena are best known to science in terms of statistical averages, of laws which hold approximately true regarding these averages, and of probabilities which are definable in such terms as are used when the insurance value of a life-policy is computed. The logic of the insurance actuary is essentially the same as the logic which is consciously or unconsciously used in dealing with all forms and grades of vital processes.

This general rule regarding the methods of the sciences of life is well known to you. For it is also known that, just as a mechanical theory of the details of the phenomena of life still remains a remote ideal, so too an historical knowledge of the individual events of the life of an organism is something which may possess upon occasion great moral or social or perhaps clinical interest, but can occupy but a part, and usually a very small part, of the interest of the sciences of life.

Into the study of human history itself, devoted as such a study naturally is to the sequences of individual events, natural science enters in so far as something of the nature of statistical knowledge is acquired. And therefore the use of deliberately statistical methods in historical study, the use which Dr. Woods has recently proposed—such a use, I say, is in principle nothing essentially opposed to methods long since inexactly and unconsciously employed. For the historiometry of Dr. Woods is in principle a legitimate extension and a logically legitimate refinement of the long since well-known disposition to explain human history in terms of "historical tendencies" and of "historical forces."

In fact, the term *tendency* is, in every exact usage which you can give it, an essentially statistical term. To say that *a* has a tendency to lead to *b* is to declare that a more or less certainly and definitely known proportion of events of the class *a* are followed by events of the class *b*.

To introduce statistics into historical study is simply to try to make some such assertions about tendencies exact.

The constant extension of the use of statistical methods in all the sciences of life is something as familiar as it is momentous. Its very familiarity, in fact, tends to blind the minds of many to its real importance. In truth, the statistical view of nature has a logic of its own. Its three fundamental conceptions, that of an average, that of approximation and that of probability, are indeed not the only fundamental categories of our thought, but they are conceptions which go down to the very roots of our own intelligence as well as of our voluntary activity. It seems increasingly plausible to assert that these three conceptions, while they certainly have their special province, still, within that province go down to the roots of that nature of things which our sciences are studying. At all events, I find it hard to exaggerate the importance of those methods and of these ideas of natural science which are definable in terms of approximation and of probability, in the modern sense of those terms.

When Clerk Maxwell made his threefold classification of scientific methods, he did so with his eyes well open to the fact that by the statistical view of nature, and by statistical methods in science he meant something much wider and deeper than is the mere commonplace that statistical tables can be made by the census bureaus, and can be used by the insurance companies, or applied to the discovering of various special laws of nature. Let me remind you of what Maxwell had in mind.

VII   *The Statistical View in Physics*

Clerk Maxwell was a physicist. His greatest treatise was that upon electricity and magnetism. The theory of electricity and magnetism follows methods which illustrate the mechanistic way of dealing with the problems of nature. Maxwell defined a system of differential equations in terms of which certain elementary electro-magnetic processes can be expressed. Assuming these equations to be true, one can compute the consequences of one's hypotheses, as Newton computed the consequences of supposing the law of the inverse squares to be true for a field of gravitative force. One can then compare the computed results with experience, and upon such computation and comparison with experiment one's method in this case depends. Such is an example of the essentially mechanical view of nature.

But Clerk Maxwell, working as he did at a time when the general theory of energy was in its period of most rapid development, was not content to confine himself to problems of the type of the theory of electricity. He also had his attention especially directed to those physical processes which are illustrated by the diffusion of gases, by the irreversible tendency of energy to pass over from available to unavailable forms, and by various analogous phenomena which can not be expressed in terms of the classic types of mechanical theories.

Following the initiative of Clausius, but developing along lines of his own, Maxwell thereupon worked out his kinetic theory of gases. It is that theory of which he is thinking when he distinguishes the statistical way of viewing nature both from the historical and from the mechanical view.

In fact, when the kinetic theory of gases first defines its swarms of molecules, with their countless paths and collisions, it appears to be viewing a gas simply as a complex mechanism; and in certain respects this seeming is well founded. But the logic of the theory of probabilities, which the kinetic theory uses in deducing the physical properties of gases from the statistical averages of collisions, and free paths of the hypothetical molecules, is no longer reducible to the logic of mechanics. For the velocity, the path, and the collision of each individual molecule are all indifferent facts for this kinetic theory of gases; which devotes itself to the study of probabilities and of tendencies. And its methods are in part those which the procedure of the insurance actuaries exemplifies. The logic in question is one which in some respects still needs further elucidation. For even up to the present time the logic of the theory of probabilities is a controverted topic. But there are a few features of the situation about which nobody who looks carefully into the subject can retain, I think, any serious doubt.

First, then, the average behavior of a very large collection of irregularly moving objects has characters which are decidedly lawful, even although the laws in question are what may be called laws of chance.

The recent familiar use of statistical diagrams for illustrative purposes has made this law of chance more familiar to many classes of students than it was in the day when Maxwell wrote certain words which you will find in his "Theory of Heat."[1] These words give you the very heart of the statistical aspect of nature.

The distribution of the molecules according to their velocities is found to be of exactly the same mathematical form as the distribution of observations according to the magnitude of their errors, as described in the theory of errors of observation. . . . Whenever in physical phenomena some cause exists over which we have no control, and which produces a scattering of the particles of matter, a deviation of observations from the truth, or a diffusion of velocity or of heat, mathematical expressions of this exponential form are sure to make their appearance.

[1] Page 309 of the Appleton edition of 1875.

This, then, is in concrete form the law of random distribution, the form of iron necessity which one finds in the realm of chance.

All this law of chance variation was, of course, at that time no novelty, although the popular use of statistics has since made it more familiar. What was new, however, was the fact that when Maxwell computed the consequences which followed from supposing the existence of his swarm of colliding molecules with their chance distribution of velocities, he was able to deduce not only the principal physical properties of gases, but in particular those properties which, like all the phenomena which illustrate the second law of the theory of energy, are not expressible in terms of merely mechanical laws, unless these laws are applied to the case of a system complex enough to ensure that the velocities of its molecules shall approximate closely to this chance distribution.

Since Maxwell's time, the same theoretical methods have been applied to a vast range of physical phenomena, with the general result that the second law of the theory of energy is now generally regarded, by all except the extreme *Energetiker*, as essentially a statistical law. So viewed, the second law of energy becomes a principle stated wholly in terms of the theory of probability. It is the law that the physical world tends, in each of its parts, to pass from certain less probable to certain more probable configurations of its moving particles. As thus stated the second principle not only becomes a law of evolution, an historical principle, but also ceases to be viewed as any mechanically demonstrable or fundamentally necessary law of nature. Whether nature is a mechanism or not, energy, according to the kinetic theory, runs down hill as it does for statistical and not for mechanical reasons. Energy need not always run down hill; and in fact would not do so if there were present in nature any persistent tendency, however imperfect, towards a suitable sorting of molecules. Maxwell suggested in his image of the demons sorting the atoms of a gas, how such a tendency might make energy run up hill instead of down, without the violation of any mechanical principle.

More recently Boltzmann, in his further development of Maxwell's hypothesis, pointed out how the theory of probability itself requires that, in the course of very vast intervals of time, there must occur some occasional concentrations of energy and some sensible unmixings—some reversals of the diffusion of gases, in case indeed the kinetic theories are themselves true. And still more recently Arrhenius has suggested that the nebulae may furnish the conditions for the occasional if not the general reversal of the second law of the theory of energy. Of such speculations I can of course form no judgment. They interest us here only as examples of the logic of the statistical view of nature.

In sum, all these investigations have tended to this general result: If a law of the physical world does not appear consistent with the mechanical view of nature so long as you confine your attention to a single system of bodies, whose individual movements you follow and compute, this law may still become perfectly intelligible when viewed as the expression of the average behavior of a kinetic system complex enough to give an opportunity for the application of statistical laws, and for the use of the conception of probability.

VIII *The Canonical Form of Scientific Theories*

All the foregoing instances may appear to you merely to suggest that, in dealing with mechanisms too complicated to be the object of a direct computation, our ignorance may force us to make use of statistical modes of computation. These statistical methods, you may say, are convenient devices whereby we neutralize, for certain special purposes, the defects of our mechanical knowledge.

If the insurance actuaries—so you may say—could use a sufficient knowledge of the world's mechanism, they would compute the precise time when each individual man is to die, just as the astronomers compute the eclipses. An almanac of mortality would take the place of the present nautical almanac. Everybody's funeral would be announced, if that were convenient, years in advance; and life insurance would appear to be a blundering and an awkward substitute for scientific prediction. Because and only because, as a fact, no knowledge of the differential equations of the precise movements of matter, and no exact measurements of the accelerations or of the other rates of change in these movements gives us the power to predict the phenomena of nature in their detail, including the movements which determine life and death, we are obliged to substitute a statistical definition of the probable tendencies of a definable proportion of great numbers of men to die, in a way which varies with their numbers and their ages, for the precise knowledge of the hour of each man's death which we should all regard as a scientific ideal, if we could know the mechanism of life and death. The statistical view is a mere substitute for a mechanical view which our ignorance makes us unable to use, in the individual case, with sufficient accuracy. Such may be your comment. The nautical almanac (so you may say) is the model of what applied science ought to be. The mortality table is the convenient summary due to a necessary scientific evil. It is a device for recording our ignorance of the details of the world's mechanism along with our imperfect knowledge of certain probable and approximate tendencies to which the averages of many human lives are subject.

In other words, you may be disposed to insist: "Mechanical theories are the canonical forms towards which a growing scientific knowledge guides our way. Computations of individual events in terms of invariant laws whose validity is independent of time, are the models of what our scientific ideals seek. The statistical view of very complex mechanisms is an asylum in which our ignorance, perforce, has to find its refuge whenever, as in the case of the swarms of molecules and the labyrinthine complications of organisms, the mechanical view of nature, as applied by us, loses its way."

In answer to this very natural comment, I am next led to say that, whether the natural world is a mechanism or not, the statistical view of nature would be, and so far as we know the facts is, applicable to sufficiently complicated systems of things and events, not as a mere substitute for these more exact computations which our ignorance of mechanical laws makes necessary, but as an expression of a very positive, although only probable and approximate, knowledge, whose type all of the organic and social sciences, as well as most aspects of the inorganic sciences, illustrate. There is therefore good reason to say that not the mechanical but the statistical form is the canonical form of scientific theory, and that if we knew the natural world millions of times more widely and minutely than we do, the mortality tables and the computations based upon a knowledge of averages would express our scientific knowledge about individual events much better than the nautical almanac would do. For our mechanical theories are in their essence too exact for precise verification. They are verifiable only approximately. Hence, since they demand precise verification, we never know them to be literally true.

But statistical theories, just because they are deliberate approximations, are often as verifiable as their own logical structure permits. They often can be known to be literally, although only approximately, true.

This assertion is, in its very nature, a logical assertion. It is not any result of any special science, or of any one group of sciences. It solves no one problem about vitalism. It is a general comment on the value of the statistical point of view.

But, if the assertion is true, it tends to relieve us of a certain unnecessary reverence for the mechanical form of scientific theory —a reverence whose motives are neither rationally nor empirically well founded. It is the merit of Charles Peirce to have emphasized these logical considerations. Their importance for the study of scientific methods has grown greater with every year since 1891, when he began the publication of his remarkable papers in the *Monist*, entitled: "The Architecture of Theories," "The Doctrine of Necessity Examined" and "The Law of Mind." These papers are fragmentary; and yet in their way they are classical statements of the limitations of the mechanical view of nature, and of the significance of the statistical view of nature.

As I close, let me merely outline some aspects of Peirce's extension of the statistical view of nature beyond the range which Maxwell's and Boltzmann's study of the theory of gases directly exemplified.

IX   *Application of the Statistical View to Theories of Non-Mechanical Systems. Aggregation and Assimilation as Statistical Tendencies*

It at first seems, I have said, as if the statistical methods of the kinetic theory were applicable only to mechanisms whose complications were too vast to make it possible to follow in individual detail their necessary sequences of movements.

But this seeming is unfounded. Let me summarize in my own words a few considerations which Peirce summarily states, and which, to my mind, get a constantly increasing importance as the statistical view of nature comes to be applied to wider and wider fields of research.

Suppose an aggregate of natural objects which contains a very great number of members, each one of which is subject to some more or less exhaustively definable range of possible variations. These objects may be things or events, at your pleasure. They may be molecules or stars or cells or multicellular organisms or members of a society or observations of a physical quantity or proposals of marriage or homicides or literary compositions or moral agents or whatever else you will. The essential basis which is needed for a statistical view of such an aggregate is this:

First, the members of each aggregate must actually form a collection which is, for some physical or moral reason, a genuine and therefore in some way a definable whole.

Next, some more or less systematic tendency towards a mutual assimilation of the fortunes, the characters or the mutual relations of the members of this aggregate must exist. This tendency toward mutual assimilation may be of very various sorts.

The policyholders of an insurance company tend to assimilate the fortunes of their various investments when they all of them pay their premiums to the same company. The stars tend to a certain assimilation of the mutual relations amongst those photographs of their various spectra which chance to get collected on the photographic plates of the same astronomical observatory. For, as a consequence of this aggregation of photographs, the stellar spectra in question may tend to be classified; and the logical, as well as the other socially important, and the physical fortunes of objects which are once viewed or arranged or tabulated as objects belonging to the same class, tend, in general, to a further mutual assimilation.

Birds of a feather not only flock together, but tend to get statistically similar fortunes, when they come into chance contact with other birds or with breeders, with hunters or with biometrical statisticians.

All objectively well-founded classification is not only founded upon real similarities amongst the objects which belong to an aggregate, but tend to some increase of these similarities, in so far as these objects are not changeless mathematical entities, but are natural objects, whose fortunes are subject to change.

One of the most widely applicable laws of nature is, in fact, the law, wholly indefinable in mechanical terms, but always expressible in terms of statistical tendencies—the law that aggregation tends to result in some further and increasing mutual assimilation of the members of the aggregate. This assimilation may express itself in the fact that one classification or aggregation leads both logically and physically to another and deeper and also wider aggregation.

If the stars are already physically classified into two distinct drifts, which move through each other in two different directions, and if the stars in question tend to get the photographs of their spectra assembled in the same observatory, then the classes into which the photographs tend in the long run to be grouped also tend to be such that, at least for some one resulting classification or aggregation of the photographs, the photographs of the spectra of the stars of one of the star drifts are grouped together, not only in the ideas which the astronomers form, but in the physical arrangements towards which certain groups of photographs, of symbols and of statistical tables, persistently tend.

The principles here involved depend upon the sorts of assimilation which the radiant phenomena of light make possible. For a photograph is a physical expression of a certain tendency whereby the structure of a photographic plate tends to be assimilated to the molecular structure and state of a radiating object—say a star. When the photographs of stellar spectra are grouped in classes, a secondary assimilation tends to take place, since similar spectra tend to get either placed or tabulated in similar ways. When this secondary assimilation of the photographs leads to an indirect discovery of the existence of the two star drifts themselves, a tertiary assimilation of the fortunes of those stars whose proper motions are sufficiently similar takes place, and tends to get represented in the knowledge of different astronomers.

The ideas of these various astronomers tend to further assimilation through the means used in scientific communication. The radiation of scientific knowledge continues the natural process which the radiation of light and the making of photographs of stellar spectra have already illustrated, and the rule continues to be illustrated that mutual assimilation is one aspect of classification and aggregation, and is a cumulative statistical tendency which accompanies them both.

The insurance companies and the transformation of modern civilization through the extension and aggregation of modes and devices whereby insurance is accomplished, furnish numerous other examples of this law of the fecundity of aggregation. The law, as I have said, holds in general for non-mechanical systems, although, as stellar evolution seems to indicate, it can also hold for mechanical systems. It may hold, in fact, for all natural processes which involve evolution.

Clerk Maxwell himself believed that the sharp distinction which separate the different classes of elementary atoms, and the different types of molecular structure which determine the spectra of the molecules of different elements, are signs that no kinetic theory of the evolution of the chemical elements would ever be possible. It is precisely here that the latest advances, on the still so imperfectly defined outlying boundaries of physical and of chemical research, give a new significance to the statistical view of nature, by showing that if we take account of sufficiently large aggregates of things and of events, a kinetic theory of the evolution of chemical elements becomes a possibility worthy of future investigation, and certain to receive, in connection with the phenomena of radioactivity, further investigation upon statistical lines, whatever be the further fortunes of the mechanical view of nature, or of this problem about the evolution of the elements.

Of such speculations one can say that, if ever a theory of the evolution of the chemical elements becomes feasible, it will be, in part at least, a statistical theory, and will illustrate in new ways how widespread in material nature is the tendency to that mutual assimilation which all the phenomena of radiant energy illustrate, and of which the relatively uniform constitution and distribution of each one of the various chemical elements through vast ranges of the physical universe may well be the result.

In brief, the evolution of stars, of elements, of social orders, of minds and of moral processes, apparently illustrates the statistical fecundity of nature's principal tendency—the tendency to that mutual assimilation which both defines aggregates, that is, real classes of natural objects, and tends to keep these classes or aggregates permanent in the world and to increase both their wealth of constitution and their extent.

Now it is this principle of the fecundity of aggregation which seems to be the natural expression, in statistical terms, for the tendency of nature towards what seems to be a sort of unconscious teleology—towards a purposiveness whose precise outcome no finite being seems precisely to intend. It is a statistically definable rule that changeable aggregates, when they are real at all, result from likenesses which their very existence tends both to increase and to diversify. The social fecundity of the principle of insurance

illustrates this natural tendency. That marvelous result of the
aggregation of scientific observers, of tabulations and of photographs, of the radiant phenomena which makes the stars visible
and of the microscopic phenomena and the logical interests which
make probability definable—that marvelous result of these various
aggregations which constitutes the whole procedure and outcome
of modern inductive science itself, is an expression of this same
general tendency—apparently the most vital and the most vitalizing
tendency both of the physical and of the spiritual world—the tendency of aggregation and of classification to be fruitful both of
new aggregations and of the orderly array of natural classes and of
natural laws.

In the purely logical and mathematical worlds this tendency
can get, and does get, precise description in terms of the pure logic
of number and of order. In the physical world, in the world of
time and change, this principle gets further expressed as a statistical
rather than a mechanical law—the law that classes, aggregations
and organizations tend towards a definable sort of evolution.

As Charles Peirce pointed out, you need not suppose the real
world to be mechanical in order to define and to conceive this sort
of evolution. You need only suppose (1) the presence of the just-
mentioned tendency to form aggregates, and of the mutual assimilation of the various parts of nature; (2) the statistically definable
tendency to some sort of sorting or selection of the probable results to which any definable average constitution of the natural
world at any moment leads; and (3) a tendency—and once more,
a statistical and non-mechanical tendency, towards a formation of
habits, and towards a repetition of such types of movement as have
once appeared. Suppose these three tendencies (aggregation, selection and habit—and the statistical method shows these three to
be widespread in the physical world); suppose these three, and
you can define a process of evolution, never mechanical and never
merely expressive of any previously settled designs, either of gods
or of men. This process of evolution will then lead from mere
chance towards the similation of mechanism, from disorderly to
a more orderly arrangement, not only of things and of individual
events, but of the statistically definable laws of nature; that is, of
the habits which nature gathers as she matures. The philosophy of
nature which will result will show how nature may well tend to
appear in certain aspects more and more teleological, and to mani-

fest what Greek vitalism found in nature. Whether the whole world is ultimately and consciously teleological or not, this view of nature would of course be unable to decide. But it would lay stress upon the thought that what is indeed most vital about the world is that which also characterizes the highest life of the spirit, namely, the fecundity of whatever unites either electrons or souls or stars into streams or into other aggregations that, amid all chances, illustrate some tendency to orderly cooperation.

If this view of nature has any foundation, gentlemen, then, as the whole progress of inductive science illustrates, the way to further such scientific evolution is to get together, and to leave the rest to the statistically definable tendencies of nature. These are tendencies away from the chance distributions which the bell-shaped curve of random distribution illustrates, towards the orderliness of which the mechanical view of nature gives us one illustration, and by no means the most probably true illustration.

I should suppose, then, that whatever notes you may compare in these meetings, you will probably frequently and variously illustrate the statistical view of nature. This view is ill understood by those who think only how dry statistical tables and averages may seem. Mechanism is rigid, but probably never exactly realized in nature. But life, although it has its history, has also its statistics. And averages cease to be dry when they are averages that express the unities and the mutual assimilations in which the common ideals and interests, the common hopes and destinies of the men, of the social orders, of the deeds—yes, and perhaps of the stars and of all the spiritual world are bound up and are expressed.

Do you wish to experiment upon some new processes of social aggregation, of mutual assimilation, and of the study of photographs of your various spiritual spectra?

This practical question is for you to consider.

24

Mind

The present article must be limited to a discussion of the metaphysical theories of mind. Owing to the peculiar position which these problems occupy in philosophy, as well as in the study of ethical and religious problems, it is advisable, first of all, to make explicit some of the epistemological problems which especially confront the student of the nature of mind; and in order to do this, we must, in view of numerous traditional complications which beset the theory of the knowledge of mind, open our discussion with some general statements concerning the nature of problems of knowledge.

The history of epistemology has been dominated by a well-known contrast between two kinds of knowledge, namely, perceptual knowledge and conceptual knowledge. This dual contrast seems insufficient to supply us with a basis for a really adequate classification of the fundamental types of knowledge. It is proposed in the present article to base the whole discussion upon a threefold classification of knowledge. Having begun with this threefold classification and briefly illustrated it, we shall go on to apply it to the special problems which we have to face in dealing with mind. We shall then consider in some detail what kinds of mental facts correspond to the three different kinds of knowledge thus defined. In conclusion, we shall deal with some problems of

[Reprinted from *Encyclopedia of Religion and Ethics* (New York: Charles Scribner's Sons, 1916), 8:649–57.]

the philosophy of mind in the light of the previous discussion.

1. *Perception and conception as fundamental cognitive processes.*—A careful study of the processes of knowledge, whether these occur in the work of science or in the efforts of common sense to obtain knowledge, shows us three, and only three, fundamental processes which are present in every developed cognitive activity and interwoven in more or less complicated fashion. Of these two have been recognized throughout the history of science and philosophy, and their familiar contrast has dominated epistemology. The third, although familiar and often more or less explicitly mentioned, was first distinguished with sharpness, for epistemological purposes, by the American logician, Charles Peirce. We shall speak first of the two well-known types of cognitive process, perception and conception.

The name 'perception' is used in psychology with special reference to the perceptions of the various senses. We are here interested only in the most general characteristics of perception. William James has used, for what is here called perception, the term 'knowledge of acquaintance.' He distinguishes 'knowledge of acquaintance' from 'knowledge about.' In the simplest possible case one who listens to music has 'knowledge of acquaintance' with the music; the musician who listens in the light of his professional knowledge has not only 'knowledge of acquaintance,' but also 'knowledge about'; he recognizes what changes of key take place and what rules of harmony are illustrated. A deaf man who has learned about the nature of music through other people, in so far as they can tell him about it, but who has never heard music, has no 'knowledge of acquaintance,' but is limited to 'knowledge about.' 'Knowledge of acquaintance' is also sometimes called 'immediate knowledge.' In the actual cognitive process of the individual human being it never occurs quite alone, since, when we know something perceptually or by acquaintance, we also always have more or less 'mediate' knowledge, *i.e.*, one who listens to music, but who also considers the person of the artist, the relation of the music to the programme, the name of the composer, or the place of this experience in his own life, has in his knowledge that which is more than the immediate hearing of the music.

'Knowledge about' includes, on occasion, mental processes which may vary very widely and which may be mingled with 'knowledge of acquaintance' in ways which are far too complex to analyze here. But 'knowledge about' is especially opposed to 'knowledge of acquaintance' in one class of cases which need to be emphasized through the use of a special name. We may name that class by calling the kind of knowledge involved in it by the name already used, 'conceptual knowledge.' Conceptual knowledge is knowledge of universals, or relations, or of other such 'abstract' objects. The Socratic-Platonic theory of knowledge called attention from its very beginning to universals and relations, and consequently made this type of knowledge specially prominent.

No doubt, even if one is disposed to cling to this merely dual classification of knowledge, one may well question whether all knowledge which is not merely 'knowledge of acquaintance' is of the grade of conceptual knowledge. For there is much 'knowledge about' concerning which we should all hesitate to say that it is knowledge of universals. Socrates himself, in his effort to define the knowledge of universals, met at the start with the fact that much of our knowledge of universals is confused and inarticulate. But if, for the moment, we neglect the intermediate cognitive states in which we more or less mingle 'knowledge of acquaintance' and conceptual knowledge, or possess conceptual knowledge in imperfect degrees of development, we may readily admit that this traditional dual classification of cognitive states is sufficient to call attention to a distinction which is of the utmost importance, both for empirical science and for metaphysics.

While the distinction between perceptual and conceptual knowledge is of great importance in determining the distinction between the deductive and the inductive methods in the sciences, the classification of these two modes of cognition does not of itself suffice to determine what constitutes the difference between inductive and deductive science. When we have clear and accurate conceptual knowledge, we are in general prepared to undertake scientific processes that in the case of further development will involve deductive methods. Thus, in particular, a conceptual knowledge of universals leads, in the mathematical sciences, to the assertion of propositions. Some of these propositions may appear at the outset of a science as axioms. Whether accepted as necessarily true or used merely as hypotheses, these propositions, either alone or in combination, may, and in the mathematical sciences do, form the starting-point for a system of rational deductions. The type of knowledge involved in this deductive process will be, in the main, the conceptual type. In what sense and to what degree a 'knowledge of acquaintance' enters into a process of mathematical reasoning we have not here to consider. All will admit that the sort of knowledge which dominates such a deductive process is 'abstract,' is concerned in reaching results which are true about the propositions that themselves form the premisses of the deduction. And so our knowledge concerning numbers, the operations of a mathematical science, and similar cases form exceptionally good instances of what characterizes conceptual knowledge in its exact and developed form.

In the inductive use of scientific methods we find a more complicated union of the perceptual and the conceptual types of knowledge. When a hypothesis, such as Newton's formula for gravitation, or Galileo's hypothesis concerning the laws of falling bodies, is stated, the type of knowledge involved in formulating and in understanding the hypothesis is prevailingly conceptual. When the hypothesis is tested by comparing the predictions based upon it with experience, the test involves appealing at some point to perceptual knowledge, or 'knowledge of acquaintance.' The processes of experiment used in an inductive science might seem to be typical cases of processes involving perceptual knowledge. And experiments unquestionably do involve such knowledge. But an experiment reveals a truth, because it brings concepts and percepts into some sort of active synthesis. Upon such active synthesis depends the process of validation which is used as the basis for the definition of truth used by recent pragmatists.

In so far as we insist upon this dual classification of fundamental processes of cognition, the questions which most come to our notice, regarding both knowledge and its objects, concern (1) the relative value of these two cognitive processes, and (2) the degree to which, in our actual cognitive processes, or in ideal cognitive processes (such as we may ascribe to beings of some higher order than ours), the two can ever be separated. These two questions have proved especially momentous for the theory both of knowledge and of reality.

(1) Regarding the relative value of the two fundamental types of cognition, Plato, as is well known, held that conceptual knowledge is the ideal type, the right result an expression of reason. Conceptual knowledge gives truth; perceptual knowledge gives illusion or appearance—such is, on the whole, the Platonic doctrine.

In recent discussion the pragmatists—and still more emphatically Bergson—have insisted upon the relative superiority of the perceptual type of knowledge. The familiar expression of this view is the thesis of recent pragmatism that conceptual knowledge has only a sort of 'credit value'; perceptual knowledge furnishes the 'cash of experience'; conceptions are 'bank notes'; perceptions, and perceptions only, are 'cash.' The statement of Bergson goes further, and declares that, if we had unlimited perceptual knowledge, *i.e.* 'knowledge of acquaintance' whose limits and imperfections we had no occasion to feel, because it had no limits and no imperfections, then conceptions could have no possible interest for us as cognitive beings. In other words, we use concepts, *i.e.*, we seek for a knowledge of universals, only when our perceptions in some way fail us. Conceptual knowledge is in its very essence a substitute for failing perceptual knowledge. The opposition between Plato and Bergson regarding this estimate of the relative significance and truthfulness of the two kinds of cognitive processes is thus characteristic of the contrast which is here in question. Of course all the philosophers admit that, in practice, our knowledge makes use of, and from moment to moment consists in, a union which involves both conceptual and perceptual processes.

(2) On the question whether the two foregoing types of knowledge, however closely linked in our normal human experience, can, at least in ideal, be separated—*i.e.*, whether a knowledge by 'pure reason' is possible on the one hand, or a knowledge of 'pure experience' is ever attainable on the other hand—the historical differences of opinion are closely related to well-known metaphysical controversies. For Plato, as (in another age, and in a largely different metaphysical context) for Spinoza, it is at least in ideal possible for philosophy, or for the individual philosopher, to attain a purely intellectual insight into the realm of 'ideas' or into the nature of the 'substance.' For various forms of mysticism, as well as for theories such as the one set forth in the *Kritik der reinen Erfahrung* (Leipzig, 1888-90) of R. H. L. Avenarius, a mental transformation may be brought about through a process which involves either a practical or a scientific correction and gradual suppression of erroneous intellectual illusion; and, at the limit of this process, reality becomes immediately and perceptually known, without confusion through abstractions.

The 'radical empiricism' of James's later essays makes use of a theory of knowledge which attempts, as far as possible, to report, apart from conceptual constructions, the data of pure experience.

2. *Interpretation through comparison of ideas as a third fundamental cognitive process.*—It is an extraordinary example of a failure to reflect in a thoroughgoing way upon the process of knowledge that until recently the third type of cognitive process to which we must next refer has been neglected, although every one is constantly engaged in using and in exemplifying it.

When a man understands a spoken or written word or sentence, what he perceives is some sign, or expression of an idea or meaning, which in general belong to the mind of some fellow-man. When this sign or expression is understood by the one who hears or who reads, what is made present to the consciousness of the reader or hearer may be any combination of perceptual or conceptual knowledge that chances to be in question. But, if any one cries 'Fire!', the sort of knowledge which takes place in my mind when I hear and understand this cry essentially depends upon this fact; I regard my fellow's cry as a sign or expression of the fact either that he himself sees a fire or that he believes that there is a fire, or that, at the very least, he intends me to understand him as asserting that there is a fire, or as taking an interest of his own in what he calls a fire. Thus, while I cannot understand my fellow's cry unless I hear it, unless I have at least some perceptual knowledge, and while I equally shall not have a 'knowledge about' the nature of fire, and so a 'knowledge about' the object to which the cry refers, unless I am possessed of something which tends to be conceptual knowledge of his object, my knowledge of my fellow's meaning, my 'grasping of his idea,' consists neither in the percept of the sign nor in a concept of its object which the sign arouses, but in my *interpretation* of the sign as an indication of an idea which is distinct from any idea of mine, and which I refer to a mind not my own, or in some wise distinct from mine.

It is to be noted that, however we reach the belief in the existence of minds distinct from our own, we do not regard these minds, at least in ordinary conditions, as objects of our own perceptual knowledge. For the very motives, whatever they are, which lead me to regard my perceptions as my own even thereby lead me to regard my fellows' perceptions as never present within my own field of awareness. My knowledge of my own physical pains, of the colours that I see, or of the sounds that I hear is knowledge that may be called, in general terms, perceptual. That is, these are objects with which I am, or upon occasion could be, acquainted. But with my fellow's pains I am not acquainted. To say this is merely to say that, whatever I mean by 'myself' and by 'the Alter,' the very distinction between the two is so bound up with the type of cognition that is in question that whatever I am acquainted with through my own perception is *ipso facto* my own object of acquaintance. Thus, then, in general, perceptual knowledge has not as its object what is at the same time regarded as the state of another mind than my own.

But, if the mind of my fellow, in particular his ideas, his feelings, his intentions, are never objects of perceptual knowledge for me, so that I am not directly acquainted with any of these states, must we regard our knowledge of the mind, or the ideas, of the intents, purposes, feelings, interests of our fellow-man as a conceptual knowledge? Is our fellow-man's mind the object of a concept of our own? Is the fellow-man a universal, or a relation, or a Platonic idea? Wherein does he differ from a mathematical entity or a law of nature? Unquestionably we regard him as possessing conceptual knowledge of his own, and also as engaged in processes of knowledge which may be conceptual, or which may involve any union of percept and concept. But the fact remains that neither by our own perceptions can we become acquainted with his states of mind, nor yet by our own conceptions can we become able to know the objects which constitute his mental process. In fact, we come to know that there are in the world minds not our own by interpreting the signs that these minds give us of their presence. This interpretation is a third type of knowledge which is closely interwoven with perceptual and conceptual knowledge, very much as they in turn are bound up with it, but which is not reducible to any complex or combination consisting of elements which are merely perceptual or merely conceptual.

Every case of social intercourse between man and man, or (what is still more important) every process of inner self-comprehension carried on when a man endeavours to 'make up his own mind' or 'to understand what he is about,' involves this third type of cognition, which cannot be reduced to perception or to conception. It is to this third cognitive process that, following the terminology which Peirce proposed, we here apply the name 'interpretation.'

In order to distinguish more clearly the three types of cognition, we may say that the natural object of perception is some inner or outer datum of sense or feeling, such as a musical tone, a colour, an emotional state, or the continual flow of the inner life upon which Bergson so much insists. For these are typical objects of perceptual knowledge, *i.e.* of 'knowledge of acquaintance.' The typical objects of conceptual knowledge are such objects as numbers, and relations such as identity and difference, equality, and so on. But typical objects of interpretation are signs which express the meaning of some mind. These signs may be expressions of the meaning of the very mind which also interprets them. This is actually the case whenever in memory we review our own past, when we reflect upon our own meaning, when we form a plan, or when we ask ourselves what we mean or engage in any of the inner conversation which forms the commonest expression of the activity whereby an individual man attains some sort of explicit knowledge of himself.

The form of cognitive process involved in the social relations between man and man is essentially the same as that involved in the cognitive process by which a man makes clear to himself his own intent and meaning. For, despite well-known assertions to the contrary on the part of Bergson, nobody has any adequate intuitive 'knowledge of acquaintance' with himself. If such perceptual or intuitive knowledge of the self by the self were possible, we should not be obliged to acknowledge that the world of human beings is dominated by such colossal and often disastrous ignorance of every man regarding himself, his true interests, his real happiness, his moral and personal value, his intents, and his powers, as we actually find characterizing our human world. In brief, man's knowledge, both of himself and of his neighbour, is a knowledge which involves an interpretation of signs. This thesis, very ably maintained by Peirce in some of his early essays, involves consequences which are at once familiar and momentous for the theory of knowledge.

That the type of knowledge involved whenever signs are interpreted is a fundamental type of knowledge which cannot be represented either to perception or to conception can be exemplified in most manifold ways, and will appear somewhat more clearly through the illustrations given below. It may be useful to point out here that, while all our interpretations, like all our perceptual and conceptual knowledge, are subject to the most manifold illusions in detail, it still remains the case that, whenever one is led to attempt, propose, or believe an interpretation of a sign, he has actually become aware, at the moment of his interpretation, that there is present in his world some meaning, some significant idea, plan, purpose, undertaking, or intent, which, at the moment when he discovers its presence, is from his point of view not identical with whatever idea or meaning is then his own.

If somebody speaking to me uses words which I had not intended to use, I may misunderstand the words, or I may not understand them at all. But, in so far as I take these words to be the expression of a meaning, this meaning is one that just then I cannot find to be my own—*i.e.*, these words do not express my ideas, in so far as these ideas are by me interpreted as my own. The cognitive process here in question divides, or at least distinguishes, that part of the objects, ideas, or meanings in question into two distinct regions, provinces, or modes of mental activity. One of these regions is interpreted at the moment as 'my own present idea,' 'my own purpose,' 'my own meaning'; the other is interpreted as 'some meaning not just now my own,' or as 'some idea or meaning that was once my own'—*i.e.*, as 'my own past idea,' or as 'my neighbour's meaning,' or perhaps as 'a meaning that belongs to my social order,' or 'to the world,' or, if I am religiously minded, 'to God.' In each case the interpretation that is asserted may prove to be a wrong one. Interpretation is fallible. So, too, is conception, when viewed as a cognitive process, and so is perception, whose character as 'acquaintance with' is no guarantee of its accuracy, whether mystical apprehension or ordinary observation is in question. The fact for our present purpose is not that our human knowledge is at any point infallible, but that there is the mode or type of cognition here defined as interpretation. Interpretation is the knowledge of the meaning of a sign. Such a knowledge is not a merely immediate apprehension, nor yet a merely conceptual process; it is the essentially social process whereby the knower at once distinguishes himself, with his own meanings, ideas, and expressions, from some other self, and at the same time knows that these selves have their contrasted meanings, while one of them at the moment is expressing its meaning to the other. Knowledge by interpretation is, therefore, in its essence neither mere 'acquaintance' nor yet 'knowledge about.'

There is another way of expressing the distinction of these

three kinds of knowledge which proves useful for many purposes. Knowledge of the first kind, 'knowledge of acquaintance,' may for certain purposes be characterized as 'appreciation.' Conceptual knowledge, owing to the means often employed in making a concept explicit, may be for many purposes called 'description.' In each case, as will be noted, the main character of the type of knowledge in question can be designated by a single term, namely, appreciation or description, just as in the foregoing these two types of knowledge have been designated each by a single term, acquaintance in one case and conception in the other.

In designating the instances of interpretation it is well to note that every interpretation has three aspects. For the one who interprets it is an expression of his own meaning. With reference to the object, *i.e.* to the sign, or to the mind whose sign this is, the interpretation is the reading or rendering of the meaning of this mind by another mind. In other words, every interpretation has so far a dual aspect: it at once brings two minds into quasi-social contact and distinguishes between them or contrasts them. In the light of this contrast and with reference to the direction in which it is read, the two minds are known each in the light of the other. As has already been said, the two minds in question may be related as a man's own past self is related to his present or future self. And in fact, as Peirce has pointed out, every act of interpretation has also a triadic character. For the cognitive process in question has not only a social character, but what one may call a directed 'sense.' In general, when an interpretation takes place, there is an act B wherein a mental process A is interpreted, read, or rendered *to* a third mind. That the whole process can take place within what, from some larger point of view, is also a single mind with a threefold process going on within it has already been pointed out. Thus, when a man reflects on his plans, purposes, intents, and meanings, his present self, using the signs which memory offers as guides, interprets his past self to his future self, the cognitive process being well exemplified when a man reminds himself of his own intents and purposes by consulting a memorandum made yesterday for the sake of guiding his acts to-day. Every explicit process involving self-consciousness, involving a definite sequence of plans of action, and dealing with long stretches of time, has this threefold character. The present self interprets the past self to the future self; or some generally still more explicit social process takes place whereby one self or quasi-self has its meanings stated by an interpreter for the sake of some third self.

Thus, in brief, knowledge by interpretation is (1) an expression (by an 'interpreter') of (2) the idea or meaning whereof some other mind gives a sign, and (3) such an expression as is addressed to some third mind, to which the interpreter thus reads or construes the sign.

3. *Self-interpretation, comparison of one's own ideas, and knowledge of time.*—When such interpretation goes on within the mind of an individual man, it constitutes the very process whereby, as is sometimes said, he 'finds himself,' 'comes to himself,' 'directs himself,' or 'gets his bearings,' especially with reference to time, present, past, and future. In the inner life of an individual man this third mode of cognition, therefore, appears at once in its most fundamental and simplest form as the cognitive process whose being consists in a *comparison of ideas.* The ideas compared here belong in one sense to the 'same self'; but they differ as the ideas of 'past self' and 'future self'; or, in various other ways, they belong to different 'quasi-minds.'

That such a process is, indeed, irreducible to pure perception, to pure conception, or to that active synthesis of the two which James has in mind when he uses the term 'idea,' readily becomes manifest if we consider what takes place when two 'ideas' are 'compared,' whether these two belong to men who are 'different individuals' or to the past, present, or future selves of one who is, from another point of view, the same man.

An 'idea,' when the term is used in the sense which recent pragmatism[1] has made familiar and prominent, is not a mere perception, nor a mere collection or synthesis of various perceptions, images, and other immediate data; nor yet is it a mere conception, whether simple or complex. It is, for James and his allies, a 'leading,' an 'active tendency,' 'a fulfilment of purpose,' or an effort towards such a fulfilment, an 'adjustment to a situation,' a seeking for the 'cash,' in the form of sense-data, such as may, when found, meet the requirements, or 'calls,' made by the conceptual aspect of the very idea which is in question. This concept has, in Bergson's phrase, its 'credit value.' Eventual sense-data may furnish the corresponding 'cash.' The idea is the seeking for this 'cash.'

---

[1] See W. James, *Pragmatism*, London, 1907.

LOGIC AND METHODOLOGY

When the wanderer in the woods decides to adopt the idea that 'yonder path leads me home,' he makes an active synthesis of his concept of home and of his present sense-data. This active synthesis expressed in his idea, 'I am homeward bound,' is a 'leading,' which, if he is successful, will result in furnishing to him, when his wanderings cease, the perceptions of home which constitute the goal of his quest. This, then, is what is meant by the term 'idea' in that one of its senses which pragmatism has recently most emphasized.

In this way we may also illustrate how the cognitive process possesses the two forms or aspects which have usually been regarded as the only fundamentally distinct aspects of knowledge: perception and conception. We meanwhile illustrate that active *union* of these two which constitutes the 'idea' as defined by recent pragmatism. But we do not thus illustrate an aspect of cognition which is equally pervasive and significant, and which consists in the *comparison of ideas*. It is just this aspect of cognition upon which our present theory most insists. For by what process does the wanderer, when he reaches home, recognize that this home which he finds is the very home that he had sought? Not by the mere presence of a 'home-feeling,' not by a perception which, merely at the moment of home-coming, pays the 'cash' then required by some then present conception of home, but by a process involving a comparison of his ideas about his home, at the moment when reaches home, with his memories of what his ideas were while he was lost in the woods and while he still inquired or sought the way home.

In order to consider what such a comparison essentially involves, it is not necessary to suppose that the act of comparison must take place in a form involving any high grade of self-consciousness, or depending upon a previous formation of an elaborate system of ideas about the self, the past, and similar objects. The essentially important fact is that whoever begins, even in the most rudimentary way, to take account of what seems to him as if it were his own past, whoever is even vaguely aware that what he has been seeking is the very object which now he finds, is not merely perceiving the present, and is not conceiving the past, and is not simply becoming aware of his present successes and disappointments as present facts—he is comparing his ideas of present success and failure with his ideas of his past efforts. This comparison is essentially an interpretation of some portion of his own past life, as he remembers that life, in the light of his present successes or disappointments, as he now experiences them. A third cognitive process is then involved. This interpretation compares at least two ideas: (1) the past idea or 'leading' (*e.g.*, the past search for home by the path through the woods); (2) the present success or failure (*e.g.*, the reaching home itself, or getting to the close of some stage of the wandering); and, in making this comparison, this interpretation estimates the result, perhaps in the light of one's idea of one's own future ('and henceforth I need search no more'), or perhaps in the light of one's idea of one's entire self ('I have succeeded,' or 'I am a knower of the truth,' or 'So much of the world of reality is mine'). In any case two comments may be made upon every such act of comparing two ideas and interpreting one in the light of the other.

(1) Unless such processes of comparing ideas were possible, and unless, in at least some rudimentary form, it took place, we could never make even a beginning in forming a coherent view of our own past and future, of our own selves as individuals, or of selves not our own. Our ideas both of the Ego and of the Alter depend upon an explicit process of comparing ideas. The simplest comparison of ideas—such as the case upon which recent pragmatism lays so much stress—the comparison upon which the very idea 'my success' also depends, the comparison, namely, which is expressed by saying, 'What I sought at a past moment is the very same as what, at the present moment, I now find,' is an instance of an act of interpretation, and is not reducible to the two other types of knowledge.

(2) All such processes of comparison are equally characteristic of the cognitive activity which goes on during our explicitly and literally social life and of the cognitive activity which is needed when we think about our relations to our own individual past and future. In brief, neither the individual Ego nor the Alter of the literal social life, neither past nor future time can be known to us through a cognitive process which may be defined exclusively in terms of perception, of conception, and of the ideal 'leadings' of the pragmatists. The self, the neighbour, the past, the future, and the temporal order in general become known to us through a third type of cognition which consists of a comparison of ideas—a process wherein some self, or quasi-self, or idea interprets another

idea, by means of a comparison which, in general, has reference to, and is more or less explicitly addressed to, some third self or idea.

4. *The relation of the three cognitive processes to our knowledge that various minds exist and to our views about what sorts of beings minds are.*—The use of the foregoing classification of the types of cognitive processes appears of special importance as soon as we turn to a brief outline of some of the principal theories about the nature of mind which have played a part in the history of philosophy. Nowhere does the theory of knowledge show itself of more importance in preparing the way for an understanding of metaphysical problems than in the case of the metaphysics of mind. No attentive student of the problem of mind can easily fail at least to feel, even if he does not very explicitly define his feeling, that in dealing with the philosophy of mind both common sense and the philosophers are accustomed to combine, sometimes in a very confused way, a reference to different more or less hypothetical beings, while the ideas that are proposed with regard to the nature of these beings are of profoundly different types.

Thus it may be a question for common sense or for a given metaphysical doctrine as to whether or not there exists a so-called soul. Now it makes a great difference for the theory of the soul whether the kind of soul which is in question is viewed as in its essence an object of a possible immediate acquaintance or perception, as an object of a possible adequate conception, or as an object whose being consists in the fact that it is to be interpreted thus or so. Unless the three kinds of cognition are clearly distinguished, the one who advances or tests a given theory of the soul does so without observing whether he himself is speaking of the soul as a possible perception, or is treating it as if it were, in its inmost nature, an object which can be known only through some adequate conception. If one has called to his attention the fact that he is speaking now in perceptual and now in conceptual terms of the mind or soul which his theory asserts to be real, he may then attempt to solve his difficulties in the way which recent pragmatism has emphasized, *i.e.,* he may declare that his doctrine is of necessity a 'working hypothesis' about the nature of the soul, that it is, of course, in part stated in conceptual terms, but that the concepts are true only in so far as they prove to be somewhere directly verifiable in terms of immediate percepts.

Yet nowhere does recent pragmatism, in the form in which

William James left it, more display its inadequacy as a theory of knowledge than in the case where it is applied to an effort to define the truth of hypotheses concerning mind, or to test such truth. For, as a fact, nobody who clearly distinguishes his neighbour's individual mind from his own expects, or can consistently anticipate, that his neighbour's mental states, or that anything which essentially belongs to the inner life or to the distinct mind of his neighbour, can ever become, under any circumstances, a direct perception of his own. For, if my neighbour's physical pains ever became mine, I should know them by immediate acquaintance only in so far as they were mine and not my neighbour's. And the same holds true of anything else which is supposed to be a fact essentially belonging to the individual mind of my neighbour. At best I can hope, with greater or less probability, to *interpret* correctly the meaning, the plan, or some other inner idea of the mind of my neighbour; but I cannot hope to go beyond such correct interpretation so far as to perceive my neighbour's mental states. For, if my neighbour's mental states become the immediate object of my own acquaintance, my neighbour and I would so far simply melt together, like drops in the ocean or small pools in a greater pool. The immediate acquaintance with my neighbour's states of mind would be a knowledge neither of himself as he is in distinction from me nor of myself as I am in distinction from him. For this general reason 'working hypotheses' about the interior reality which belongs to the mind of my neighbour can never be 'converted into the cash of experience.' My neighbour's mind is never a verifiable object of immediate acquaintance, precisely as it is never an abstract and universal idea. The one sort of knowledge for which recent pragmatism has no kind of place whatever is a knowledge, statable in pragmatistic terms, concerning my neighbour's mind.

James himself follows a well-known and ancient philosophical tradition by declaring that our assertion of the existence of our neighbour's mind depends upon the argument from analogy. Because of similar behaviours of our organism we regard it as by analogy probable that both our neighbour's organism and our own are vivified by more or less similar mental lives, so that we have similar experiences. But to regard or to believe in the mind of our neighbour as an object whose existence is to be proved through an argument from analogy raises a question whose answer is simply fatal to the whole pragmatistic theory of knowledge. Surely an argument from analogy is not its own verification. For pragmatism the truth of a hypothesis depends upon the fact that its conceptual constructions are capable of immediate verification in terms of certain facts of immediate experience. But my neighbour's inner states of mind can never become for me objects of immediate acquaintance, unless they become my states of mind and not his, precisely in so far as he and I are distinct selves.

The hypothesis that our mental lives are similar may thus be suggested by analogy or may be stated in terms of analogy; but the analogy in question is essentially unverifiable in the required terms, *i.e.*, in terms of immediate perceptions. For my neighbour can immediately perceive only his own states, while I, in so far as I am not my neighbour, can verify only my own states. From the point of view, then, of the argument from analogy, my neighbour, in observing his own states, does *not* verify my hypothesis in the sense in which my hypothesis about him demands verification, namely in terms of the experience of the self who makes the hypothesis. From this point of view, the problem of the mind of my neighbour remains hopeless.

It is possible, of course, to say of the foregoing argument from analogy what is also said both by common sense and by science, on the basis of a theory of truth which is in its essence conceptual and realistic. One can, of course, assert that in actual fact the mental states of my neighbour really exist and are in a certain relation which makes it true to say that they are analogous to mine. This real relation may be asserted to be as much a fact as any other fact in the universe. If this fact of the real analogy is granted, then it may be declared that my hypothesis to the effect that my neighbour's mind is a reality is actually true. This, however, is precisely the type of truth which William James's pragmatism undertakes to reject.

A very different appearance is assumed by the whole matter if we recognize that there is a third kind of knowledge, which is neither conceptual nor perceptual, and which is also not the sort of union of conception and perception which is completely expressible in terms of the favorite metaphor of Bergson and the pragmatists, namely, the metaphor of the conversion of conceptual credits or bank-notes into perceptual cash, *i.e.*, into immediate data of experience. For interpretations are never verified merely through immediate data, nor through the analysis of conceptions. This is true whether I myself am the object of my own interpretation or my neighbour is in question. If we seek for metaphors, the metaphor of the conversation, already used, furnishes the best means of indicating wherein consists the relative, but never immediate, verifiability of the truth of an interpretation.

When I interpret (whether my own purposes or intents or the ideas of another man are the objects which I seek to interpret), what I first meet in experience is neither a matter of acquaintance nor a mere 'knowledge about.' What I meet is the fact that, in so far as I now understand or interpret what I call myself, I have also become aware, not immediately but in the temporal process of my mental life, that ideas have come to me which are not now my own, and which need further expression and interpretation, but which are already partially expressed through signs. Under these circumstances, what happens is that, as interpreter of these signs, I offer a further expression of what to me they seem to mean, and I make the further hypothesis that this expression makes more manifest to me both the meaning of this sign and the idea of the mind or self whereof this sign gave partial expression. It is of the essence of an expression which undertakes to interpret a sign that it occurs because the sign already expresses a meaning which is not just at the present moment our own, and which, therefore, needs for us some interpretation, while the interpretation which at the moment we offer is itself not complete, but requires further interpretation.

In literal conversation our neighbour utters words which already express to us ideas. These ideas so contrast with our own present ideas that, while we find the new ideas intelligible, and, therefore, view them as expressions of a mind, we do not fully know what they mean. Hence, in general, our neighbour having addressed us, we in reply ask him, more or less incidentally or persistently, whether or not this is what he means—*i.e.*, we give him back our interpretation of his meaning, in order to see whether this interpretation elicits a new expression which is in substantial agreement with the expression which we expected from him. Our method in a conversation is, therefore, unquestionably the method of a 'working hypothesis.' But since this 'working hypothesis' refers to our neighbour's state of mind, it is never conceivably capable of direct verification.

Nor does what the pragmatists are accustomed to call the successful 'working' of this hypothesis consist in the discovery of any perceptible fact with which we get into merely immediate relation. Our interpretation of our neighbour satisfies our demands, precisely in so far as our interpretations which are never complete, and which always call for new expressions and for further interpretations, lead to a conversation which remains, as a whole, essentially 'coherent,' despite its endless novelties and unexpected incidents.

Our whole knowledge of mind, in so far as by this term we mean intelligent mind, not only depends upon, but consists in, this experience of a consistent series of interpretations, which we obtain, not merely by turning conceptual 'credits' into the 'cash of immediate acquaintance,' but by seeking and finding endlessly new series of ideas, endlessly new experiences and interpretations. This never-ended series of ideas, in so far as we can hold them before our minds, tends to constitute a connected, a reasonable, a comprehensible system of ideal activities and meanings. The essence of mental intercourse—we may at once say the essence of intelligent mental life and of all spiritual relations—not only depends upon, but consists in, this coherent process of interpretation.

Or, again, an interpretation is not a conceptual hypothesis which can be converted into 'perceptual knowledge'; it is a hypothesis which leads us to anticipate further interpretations, further expressions of ideas, novel bits of information, further ideas not our own, which shall simply stand in a coherent connexion with one another and with what the original interpretation, as a hypothesis, had led us to expect. When I deal with inanimate nature, I may anticipate facts of perception, and then my hypothesis about these facts 'work,' in so far as the expected perceptions come to pass. But, when I deal with another mind, I do not merely expect to get definable perceptions from that mind; I expect that mind to give me new ideas, new meanings, new plans, which by contrast are known at each new stage of social experience to be not my own, and which may be opposed to my own and in many respects repellent to me.

But it is essential to the social intercourse between minds that these endlessly novel ideas and meanings should, through all conflicts and novelties and surprises, retain genuine coherence. Thus, in dealing with other minds, I am constantly enlarging my own mind by getting new interpretations, both of myself and of my neighbour's life. The contrasts, surprises, conflicts, and puzzles which these new ideas present to me show me that in dealing with them I am dealing with what in some respects is not my own mind. The coherence of the whole system of interpretations, ideas, plans, and purposes shows me just as positively that I am dealing with a mind, *i.e.*, with something which through these expressions constantly interprets itself, while, as I deal with it, I in turn constantly interpret it, and even in and through this very process interpret myself. It will and must be observed that this Alter, with which I have to deal, both in reflecting on my own mind and in seeking for new light from my neighbour, is never a merely single or separable or merely detached or isolated individual, but is always a being which is of the nature of a community, a 'many in one' and a 'one in many.' A mind knowable through interpretation is never merely a 'monad,' a single detached self; its unity, in so far as it possesses genuine and coherent unity, tends, in the most significant cases, to become essentially such as the unity which the apostle Paul attributes to the ideal Church: many members, but one body; many gifts, but one spirit (Ro 12 4ff.)—an essentially social unity, never to be adequately conceived or felt, but properly the object of what the Apostle viewed, in its practical and religious aspect, as the spiritual gift of charity, in its cognitive aspect as interpretation: pray rather that ye may interpret (1 Co 14 13).

5. *Metaphysical theories of the nature of mind.*—(a) *Predominantly perceptual theories*—The nature of mind may be defined by a given metaphysical theory mainly in terms which regard mind as best or most known through possible 'perceptions' or through possible 'acquaintance' with its nature. Such theories have been prominent throughout the whole history of human thought. They depend, first, upon ignoring the fact that what is most essential in the mind is known through the cognitive process of interpretation. They depend, further, upon making comparatively light of the effort to give any abstract conceptual description of what constitutes the essence of mind. They depend upon turning to what is sometimes called 'introspection,' or again, 'intuition,' to bring about an immediate acquaintance with mind.

Since, in general, any one who forms a predominantly perceptual idea of what mind is very naturally is not depending solely upon his own personal experience, but upon the experiences which he supposes other minds to possess, these perceptual theories of the nature of mind actually make a wide use of the reports of other people and so, more or less consciously, of arguments from analogy.

The simplest and vaguest, but in some respects the most persistent, of all theories of mental life appears, upon a largely perceptual basis, and also upon a basis of an argument from analogy, in countless forms of so-called 'animism.' Leaving aside all the historical complications, we may sum up the animistic theory of mind thus. We perceive, within ourselves, certain interesting processes which include many of our feelings, embody many of our interests, and characterize many of our activities. These activities, which in ourselves we more or less directly observe, are closely connected with the whole process of the life of the organism, *i.e.*, of the body in whose fortunes each one of us is so interested. That which produces all these feelings, awakens in us all these interests, vitalizes our own body, and forms for each of us a centre of his own apparent world—this is the mind. The mind, then, strives and longs. It feels pain and pleasure. It prospers as the body prospers, and suffers as the body suffers.

Analogy shows that other people have such minds. These minds are as numerous as the organisms in question. They resemble one another and differ from one another, much as the organisms resemble and differ from each other. An extension of this analogy, on the basis of many motives, leads us to regard the world about us as containing many minds which are not connected with human bodies—at least in precisely the same way in which our minds are connected with our bodies. When the vast mass of superstitious beliefs which have made use of such analogies and such experiences can be more effectively controlled through the advances of the human intelligence, this primitive animism tends to pass over into theories of which we find some well-known examples in early Greek philosophies. These early Greek theories of mind appear, on a somewhat primitive and already philosophical level, as 'hypozoistic.' The world or at all events, the organic world, has life principles in it which vary as the organisms vary, and which are also of a nature that feeling and desire reveal to our relatively immediate 'knowledge of acquaintance' with our own minds.

The theories of mind of this type have played a great part in the life both of philosophy and of religion. As a general theory, animism has proved very persistent, and that for obvious reasons.

One of the Hindu *Upanishads*[2] well suggests both the origin and the logical basis—such as it is—of these theories when, in an allegory, it represents the question arising within the body as to where and what the soul most is. The question is disputed amongst the various bodily organs, each asserting itself to be the principal seat of life and also of mind. To discover which view is true, the members of the body take turns in leaving the organism. When the eyes go, blindness ensues, but life and mind continue, and so on with various other members. But when the breath starts to leave the body, all the other members together cry, 'Stay with us! You are the life, you are the soul, you are the self or Atman.' This allegory sufficiently indicates how primitive, how vague, and how stubborn is such a perceptual theory of mind when defined in terms of immediate intuition, and of a more or less pragmatic testing of various views about the physical organism.

Later in its origin, but continuing in its influence to the present day, is another perceptual theory of mind, which the later *Upanishads* present at length, and which, in another form, is exemplified by a notable assertion of H. Bergson in his *Introduction to Metaphysics*[3]—namely, that of one object at least we all have intuitive knowledge, this object being the self. The entire history of mysticism, the history also of the efforts to discover the nature of mind through introspection, can be summarized by means of these instances in the Hindu *Upanishads* that discover the true self through the experiment with breathing, and of the latest vision of Bergson, who defines the nature of mind, and also its contrast with body, in terms of the *élan vital;* for all these views emphasize, in various more or less primitive, or in more or less modern, forms, essentially the same theory of mind: the essence of the mind is to be known through immediate acquaintance. That which Schopenhauer calls the will to live, that which Bergson characterizes in the terms just mentioned, that which the shamans and medicine-men of all the more intelligent tribes have sought to know, is, in every case, mind viewed as an object of possible perception.

In the history of thought such perceptual theories of mind have

---

[2] *Brhada-ranyaka Upanishad*, vol. i. 7–14, tr. in P. Duessen, *Sechzig Upanishad's des Veda*, Leipzig, 1897, p. 503.

[3] Eng. tr., London, 1913.

become more highly developed and diversified, and have assumed other and very widely influential forms, by virtue of an insistence that we have an immediate perception of what is variously called 'mental activity,' 'the active soul,' or 'the principle of individual self-hood.' Motives which as a fact are not stable in purely perceptual terms have joined with this fondness for defining mind in perceptual terms to make emphatic the assertion that this theory of mind ought to be stated in expressly 'pluralistic' terms. It has, consequently, been freely asserted that we 'immediately know' our own self to be independent, to be distinct from all other selves, and thus to be unique. Since it is also sometimes asserted that we know, or that we 'know intuitively,' upon occasion, the fact that we can never be directly acquainted with the conditions of our neighbour's mind, such perceptual theories have given rise to the so-called problem of 'Solipsism.' For, if we know mind by perception only, and if we are sure of it only when we perceive it, and if each of us can perceive only his own mind, then what proves for any one of us that there is any mind but his own? The analogy which primitive animism so freely and so vaguely used becomes, for the critical consciousness questionable. In consequence, the problem of Solipsism has remained in modern times a sort of scandal of the philosophy of the mind.

The solution of the problem of Solipsism lies in the fact, upon which Peirce so well insisted,[4] that no one of us has any purely perceptual knowledge of his own mind. The knowledge of mind is not statable, in the case either of the self or of the neighbour, in terms of merely immediate acquaintance. If the truth of this proposition is once understood, the entire theory of mind, whether for metaphysics or for empirical psychology, is profoundly altered. Until this inadequacy of knowledge through acquaintance to meet the real end of human knowledge is fully grasped, it is impossible to define with success either the mind or the world, either the individual self or the neighbour.

(b) *Predominantly conceptual theories.*—As is the case with every highly developed doctrine, the conceptual form is very naturally assumed by any philosophical theory of mind which seeks for theoretical completeness. The conceptual theories of mind have been in history of two general types: (1) the purely

---

[4] See Royce, *Problem of Christianity*, ii.

conceptual, *i.e.* 'the abstractly rational' metaphysical theories; and (2) the more inductive conceptual theories based upon the more or less highly developed 'empirical psychologies' of the period in which these theories have flourished. We need not enumerate these theories or give their history.

Of principal importance in their history have been (1) that type of vitalism whose most classical representative is the Aristotelian theory of mind; (2) the monistic theory of mind, which often depends not so much upon the general metaphysical tendency to define the whole universe as One, but rather upon the effort to conceive mind and matter by regarding them both as the same in substance; and (3) the various types of monadology, which are characterized by the assertion of the existence of many real and more or less completely independent minds or selves, whose nature it is either to be themselves persons or to be beings which under certain conditions can assume the form of persons.

Of those various important theories which are expressed in the predominantly conceptual form that of Aristotle is very deeply and interestingly related to primitive animism on the one hand, while, on the other hand, it looks towards that development of the idea of the distinct individual self upon which more modern forms of monadology have depended.

Whatever special forms the conceptual theories of mind may assume, the well-known problem remains: How are these conceptions of the various mental substances, or principles, or monads, which are each time in question related to the sorts of experience which the psychologists, the students of the natural history of mind, have at any stage of knowledge discovered or may yet hope to discover? From the point of view of modern pragmatism, conceptual theories of mind might be entertained as 'working hypotheses' if they led to verification in perceptual terms.

In fact, the modern physical sciences, in conceiving the nature of matter, deal with manifold problems, but use conceptual hypotheses regarding the nature of matter which are, in a large measure, subject to pragmatic tests. Molecules and atoms and, of late, various other types of conceptual physical entities, which were formerly supposed to be incapable of becoming objects of physical experience, now appear to come within the range of the experimenter's verifications. Therefore the processes of the experimental verification of physical hypotheses have, on the whole, a direct relation to the sort of knowledge upon which the pragmatists so much insist. The 'conceptual credits' of physical hypotheses are, on the whole, verifiable in terms of the 'perceptual cash' of laboratory experience. When this is not the case, there is a tendency towards such direct verification. Hence physical hypotheses, at least regarding what is generally called the phenomenal nature of matter, have generally proved to be topics for an inquiry within the strict realm of inductive science.

But it has been, in the past, the reproach of the conceptual theories about the nature of mind that no pragmatic test can be discovered by which one might learn what difference it would make to an observer of mental processes and, in particular, of his own mental processes whether minds are 'soul substances,' or Leibnizean monads, or not, or whether the introspective observer of his own sensations or feelings is or is not himself a Leibnizean monad or Aristotelian 'entelechy'; or again, whether he is essentially persistent and indestructible. Thus, from the pragmatic point of view, the majority of these conceptual hypotheses regarding the nature of mind show little sign of promising to prove more verifiable than they thus far have been. In consequence, the outcome of conceptual views regarding the real nature of mind has been, for many reasons, on the whole sceptical. In fact, the whole nature of mind cannot be adequately conceived, and could not be so conceived even if one's power to perceive mental processes were increased indefinitely, unless another type of cognitive processes were concerned in such an enlargement. For a mind is essentially a being that manifests itself through signs. The very being of signs consists in their demanding interpretation. The relations of minds are essentially social; so that a world without at least three minds in it—one to be interpreted, one the interpreter, and the third the one for whom or to whom the first is interpreted—would be a world without any real mind in it at all. This being the case, it might well be expected that a conceptual theory of mind would fail precisely as a perceptual theory fails. Such theories would fail because they do not view the cognitive process as it is and do not take account of that which is most of all needed in order even in the most rudimentary fashion to grasp the nature of an intelligent mind.

(c) *Theories making use of the cognitive process of the interpretation.*—Despite the inadequate development of the doctrine of interpretation thus far in the history of epistemology, there have not been lacking theories regarding the nature of mind according to which mind is an object to be known through interpretation, while its manifestations lie not merely in the fact that it possesses or controls an organism, but in the fact that, whether through or apart from an organism, it expresses its purposes to other minds, so that it not merely has or is a will, but manifests or makes comprehensible its will, and not merely lives in and through itself, as a monad or a substance, but is in essence a mode of self-expression which progressively makes itself known either to its fellows or to minds above or below its own grade.

That theories of mind which are based on such a view have existed, even from very primitive times, is manifest wherever in the history of religion a consultation of oracles, discovery of the future or of the will of the gods through divination, or, in fact, any such more or less superstitious appeals to other minds, and readings or interpretations of these appeals have taken place. Primitive belief in magic arts has apparently, on the whole, a conceptual type of formulation. Therefore magic has been called the physics of primitive man. It depends upon the view that man is subject to laws which, if he could discover them, he could use for his purposes, just as we now make use of the known laws of physics for industrial purposes. The supposed realm of magic arts is thus analogous to our present realm of industrial arts. The view of pragmatism—that primitive magic is not true merely because its hypotheses regarding how to cause rain or how to cure diseases do not 'work'—is in this case fairly adequate to express the situation both epistemologically and metaphysically.

Moreover, as we have seen, animism, in its more primitive forms, expresses a predominantly perceptual theory of mind, and whether such a theory, either of mind or of the relations between mind and the physical world, is held in some simple form by the medicineman of an obscure tribe or is impressively reiterated in a Hindu *Upanishad*, or is fascinatingly placed in the setting of a modern evolutionary theory by Bergson, makes comparatively little difference to the essential views of the philosophy of mind which are in question. But that view of the nature of mind which gained, apparently, its earliest type of expression when men first consulted, and hereupon more or less cautiously interpreted, the oracles of their gods has (as befits a theory of mind which is founded upon a fundamental cognitive process) persisted throughout the history of human thought. This way of viewing mind has, in fact, persisted in a fashion which enables us to distinguish its expressions with sufficient clearness from those which have had their origin either in the conceptions of primitive magic or in the perceptions which guided primitive animism.

From the point of view of the cognitive process of interpretation mind is, in all cases where it reaches a relatively full and explicit expression, equally definable in terms of two ideas—the idea of the self, and the idea of the community of selves. To an explicit recognition of what these two ideas involve a great part of the history of the philosophy of mind has been devoted. Both ideas have been subject to the misfortune of being too often viewed as reducible either to purely conceptual terms or to purely perceptual terms. If the self was defined in predominantly conceptual terms, it tended to degenerate into a substance, a monad, or a mere thing of some sort. Under the influence of a too abstract epistemology (such as the Kantian) the self also appeared as the 'logical ego,' or else as the 'pure subject.'

The fortunes of the idea of the community have been analogous. In religion this idea has proved one of the most inspiring of the ideas which have gradually transformed tribal cults into the two greatest religions which humanity possesses—Buddhism and Christianity. In ancient philosophy the community, viewed as the soul 'writ large,' inspired some of the most fruitful philosophical interpretations of Plato, Aristotle, and the Stoics. In the general history of civilization loyalty, which is identical with the practically effective love of communities as persons that represent mind on a level higher than that of the individual, is, like the Pauline charity (which is explicitly a love for the Church universal and for its spirit), the chief and the soul of the humanizing virtues—that virtue without which all the others are but 'sounding brass or a tinkling cymbal.' Yet, in the history of thought the idea of the community has greatly suffered, less frequently from the attempt to view it as the proper object of a direct mystical perception than from the tendency to reduce it to a purely conceptual form. As a conceptual object the 'mind of the community,' the 'corporate mind,' has tended to be thought of as an entity possibly significant in a legal or in a sociological sense, but difficult and perhaps unreal, in a metaphysical sense.

Experience shows, however, that the two ideas—the idea of the individual self and that of the community—are peculiarly adapted to interpret each the other, both to itself and to the other, when such interpretation is carried on in the spirit which the religion of Israel first made central in what undertook to be a world religion, and which the apostle Paul laid at the basis both of his philosophy of human history and of his Christology.

Modern idealism, both in the more vital and less formal expressions of Hegel's doctrine and in its recent efforts at a social interpretation of the self, of the course of human evolution, and of the problems of metaphysics, has already given a partial expression to a theory of which we tend to become clearly aware in proportion as we recognize what the cognitive process of interpretation is and how it contrasts with, and is auxiliary to, the processes of conception and perception. Only in terms of a theory of the threefold process of knowledge can we hope fully to express what is meant by that form of idealism which views the world as the 'process of spirit' and as containing its own interpretation and its own interpreter.

25

[*The Methodology of Science*]

Inductive scientific generalizations, in the logically simplest cases, depend upon what Mr. Charles Peirce has defined as the method of taking a "fair sample" of a chosen type of facts. Thus one who samples, to use Mr. Peirce's typical example, a cargo of wheat, by taking samples from various parts of the cargo, carefully selecting the samples so that they shall not tend to represent one part of the cargo only, but any part chosen at random, employs essentially the same inductive method which, as I gather from inquiry, Virchow used in reaching the main fundamental generalizations of his cellular pathology. Samples chosen from investigation from a great variety of growths show, both in the case of normal and in the case of morbid tissues, that in the observed samples there is sufficient evidence of the origin of each cell from a previous cell, and evidence too that the tissue is formed of generations of cells whose beginnings, both in the normal and in the morbid growths, lead back to parent cells of certain definable types. This outcome of observation, repeatedly confirmed by samples fairly chosen, that is, by samples chosen from various organisms, from various tissues, and chosen not merely to illustrate the theory, but to represent as well as may be all sorts of growth—this, I say, leads to the

|Reprinted from "Some Relations Between Philosophy and Science in the First Half of the Nineteenth Century," *Science*, n.s., 38 (1913):567-84. Only section 4 is reprinted here. This section was reprinted by Daniel S. Robinson as "Hypotheses and Leading Ideas," in *Royce's Logical Essays* (Dubuque: Wm. C. Brown, 1951), pp. 260-67.|

probable assertion that this kind of origin of tissues is universal, and that one is dealing with a genuine law of nature. The probability of such a generalization can be tested in a more or less exact way, as Peirce has shown, by the principles of the mathematical theory of probabilities. Inductions of this type we may call statistical inductions. They presuppose nothing at the outset as to what laws are present in the world of the facts which are to be sampled. The technique of induction here consists wholly in learning, (1) how to take fair samples of the facts in question, and (2) how to observe these facts accurately and adequately. This kind of induction seems to be especially prominent in the organic sciences. Its logical theory is reducible to the general theory of probability, since fair samples, chosen at random from a collection of objects, tend to agree in their constitution with the average constitution of the whole collection.

But now, as you well know, a great deal of scientific work consists of the forming and testing of hypotheses. In such cases the inductive process is more complex. Peirce defines it first as the process of taking a fair sample from amongst the totality of those consequences which will be true if the hypothesis to be tested is true, and secondly as the process of observing how far these chosen consequences agree with experience. If a given hypothesis, in case it is true, demands, as often happens, countless consequences, you of course can not test all of these consequences, to see if every one of them is true. But you select a fair sample from amongst these consequences, and test each of these selected consequences of the hypothesis. If they agree with experience, the hypothesis is thereby rendered in some degree probable. The technique of induction now involves at least four distinct processes: (1) The choice of a good hypothesis; (2) the computation of certain consequences, all of which must be true if the hypothesis is true; (3) the choice of a fair sample of these consequences for a test; and (4) the actual test of each of these chosen consequences. So far as you make use of this method of induction, you need what is called training in the theory of your topic, that is, training in the art of deducing the consequences of a given hypothesis. This may involve computations of all degrees of complexity. You also need training in the art of taking a fair sample of consequences for your test; for a given hypothesis may involve numerous consequences that are already known, from previous experience, to be true. And such consequences furnish you with no crucial tests. In case of success, your hypothesis may become very highly probable. But induction never renders it altogether certain.

Classic instances of this method of induction exist in the physical sciences. In the organic sciences the process of testing hypotheses is frequent, but is less highly organized, and generally less exact than in the great cases that occur in the inorganic sciences. No theory of the consequences of any hypothesis in the organic sciences has ever yet reached the degree of precision attained by the kinetic theory of gases, or by the theory of gravitation.

So much for the two great inductive methods, as Peirce defines them. But now does successful scientific method wholly reduce to these two processes, viz., (1) sampling the constitution of classes of phenomena; and (2) sampling the theoretical consequences of hypotheses? Many students of the subject seem to think so. I think that the history of science shows us otherwise.

As a fact, I think that the progress of science largely depends upon still another factor, viz., upon the more or less provisional choice and use of what I have already called, in this paper, leading *ideas*.

A leading idea is, of course, in any given natural science, an hypothesis. But it is an hypothesis which decidedly differs from those hypotheses that you directly test by the observations and experiments of the particular research wherein you are engaged. Unlike them, it is an hypothesis that you use as a guide, or in Kant's phrase, as a regulative principle of your research, even although you do not in general intend directly to test it by your present scientific work. It is usually of too general a nature to be tested by the means at the disposal of your special investigation. Yet it does determine the direction of your labors, and may be highly momentous for you.

Such a leading idea, for instance, is the ordinary hypothesis that even in the most confused or puzzling regions of the natural world law actually reigns, and awaits the coming of the discoverer. We can not say that our science has already so fairly sampled natural phenomena as to have empirically verified this assumption, so as to give it a definite inductive probability. For as a fact, science usually pays small attention to phenomena unless there appears to be a definable prospect of reducing them to some sort of law within a reasonable time; and chaotic natural facts, if there were such, would probably be pretty stubbornly neglected by science, so far as such neglect was possible. On the other hand, the leading idea that law is to be found if you look for it long enough and carefully enough is one of the great motive powers not only of science but of civilization.

It may interest you to know that the modern study of the so-called axioms of geometry, as pursued by the mathematicians themselves, has shown that such principles as the ordinary postulate about the properties of parallel lines (as Euclid defines that postulate) are simply leading ideas. What the text-books of geometry usually assert to be true about the fundamental properties of parallel lines is a principle that is neither self-evident, nor necessarily true, nor even an inductively assured truth of experience. It turns out, in the light of modern logical mathematical analysis, to be, I say, simply a leading idea,—that is, a principle which we can neither confirm nor refute by any experience now within our range, but which we use and need in geometry precisely because it is so serviceable in simplifying the geometry of the plane.

If I may venture to cite an example from your own science, I should suggest the following: That fundamental principle of Virchow's "Cellular Pathology" which asserted the origin of every cell from a cell was, as I already said, a perfectly straightforward induction, of Peirce's first type, that is, it was a probable assertion of a certain constitution as holding for a whole type of cases—an assertion made simply because this constitution had been observed to hold for a sufficient number of fairly selected samples of the type. But, on the other hand, consider another principle which Virchow asserted already in 1847 or earlier, and which, as I have long been told, has been of the first importance for the whole later development of your science: "We have learned to recognize," says Virchow, "that diseases are not autonomous organisms, that they are no entities that have entered into the body, that they are no parasites which take root in the body, but that they merely show us the course of the vital processes under altered conditions" ("*das sie nur den Ablauf der Lebenserscheinungen unter veränderten Bedingungen darstellen*").

Now of course I have nothing to suggest regarding the objective truth of this assertion. But I venture to point out that, logically regarded, it is not an hypothesis to be definitely tested by any observation, but is rather an hypothesis of the type of Euclid's postulate about the parallel lines, that is, it is a leading idea. For, on the one hand, how could Virchow regard this principle as one that had been definitely tested, and already confirmed by direct observation and experience at a time when, as in 1847, he was not yet possessed even of his own general principle of a cellular pathology, and when he regarded the whole science of pathology as in its infancy, and the causation of disease as very largely unknown? On the other hand, what experience could one look for that would definitely refute the principle if it were false? Would the experience of such facts as those of your modern bacteriology refute that principle? No, at least so far as I understand the sense of the principle as Virchow stated it in 1847. For when bacteria, or when any of their products or accompaniments came to be recognized either as causing disease, or as affecting the course of disease in any way, it was still open to Virchow to say that the causes thus defined simply constitute these very *veränderte Bedingungen* under which the *Ablauf der Lebenserscheinungen* takes place. In other words, the principle, if understood with sufficient generality, simply asserts that a disease can not occur in an organism without the processes of the disease being themselves alterations of the processes of the organism, and such alterations as the altered conditions, whatever they are, determine. Such a principle, so understood, seems tolerably safe from empirical refutation. It would remain unrefuted, and empirically irrefutable, so far as I can see, even if the devil caused disease. For the devil would then simply be one of the *veränderte Bedingungen*. Thus when the devils on a famous occasion entered, in the tale, into the Gaderene swine, the *Ablauf* of the *Lebenserscheinungen* of the swine was such, under the *veränderte Bedingungen*, that, as we are told, they ran down a steep place into the sea. But I do not see that this just stated pathological postulate of Virchow's need have suffered shipwreck, or need even have received any damage, even on this occasion. The devils are indeed represented in the tale as entities that from without entered into the swine, as bullets might have done. But the running down into the sea is *nur der Ablauf der Lebenserscheinungen* of the swine themselves. Let bullets or bacteria, poisons or compressed air, be the *Bedingungen*, the postulate that Virchow states will remain irrefutable, if only it be interpreted to meet the case. For the principle merely says that whatever entity it may be, fire or air or bullet or poison or devil, that effects the organism, the disease is not that entity, but is the changed process of the organism. What then is this hypothesis, this rejection of every external-entity-theory of disease, as the hypothesis appears when Virchow writes these words in 1847? I reply, this is no hypothesis in the stricter sense; that is, it is no trial proposition to be submitted to precise empirical tests. It is, on the contrary, a very precious leading idea. It is equivalent to a resolution to search for the concrete connection between the processes of any disease and the normal process of the organism, so as to find the true unity of the pathological and the normal process through such a search. Without some such leading idea, the cellular pathology itself could never have resulted; because the facts in question would never have been observed. And I suppose that some equivalent leading idea, if not precisely that which Virchow stated in 1847, is just as precious to you to-day in your own pathological work.

The value of such leading ideas for a science lies in the sorts of research that they lead men to undertake, and also in the sorts of work that they discourage. They are, I repeat, regulative principles. Observation does not, at least for the time, either confirm or refute them. But, on the other hand, they awaken interest in vast ranges of observation and experiment, and sustain the patience and enthusiasm of workers through long and baffling investigations. They organize science, keep it in touch with the spirit of the age, keep alive in it the sense of the universal, and assure its service to humanity. Specialism, without leading ideas, remains but a sounding brass and a tinkling cymbal.

The sources of useful leading ideas seem to me to be various. Social, and in particular industrial interests, suggest some of them, as the perennial need of paying the coal-bills for the steam engines suggested, as we have seen, one of the leading ideas which pointed the way towards the modern theory of energy. The comparison of the results of various sciences awakens such leading ideas in various minds. Schleiden set Schwamm searching for the basis of the cell theory in animal tissues. That was the suggestion of an hypothesis in the narrower sense, to be tested. But when the physical sciences set the students of organic science to the work of conceiving organic processes as mechanical in their inmost nature, that was the suggestion of a leading idea.

But another source of such leading ideas has been, upon occasion, philosophy. Philosophy itself might be defined as a systematic scrutiny of leading ideas. It has also proved to be often an inventory and interpreter of such ideas.

26

Introduction to Poincaré's
Science and Hypothesis

I

The branches of inquiry collectively known as the Philosophy of Science have undergone great changes since the appearance of Herbert Spencer's *First Principles,* that volume which a large part of the general public in this country used to regard as the representative compend of all modern wisdom relating to the foundations of scientific knowledge. The summary which M. Poincaré gives, at the outset of his own introduction to the present work, where he states the view which the 'superficial observer' takes of scientific truth, suggests, not indeed Spencer's own most characteristic theories, but something of the spirit in which many disciples of Spencer interpreting their master's formulas used to conceive the position which science occupies in dealing with experience. It was well known to them, indeed, that experience is a constant guide, and an inexhaustible source both of novel scientific results and of unsolved problems; but the fundamental Spencerian principles of science, such as 'the persistence of force,' the 'rhythm of motion' and the rest, were treated by Spencer himself as demonstrably objective, although indeed 'relative' truths, capable of being tested once for all by the 'inconceivability of the opposite,' and certain

|Reprinted from the Introduction to Henri Poincaré, *Science and Hypothesis,* trans. G. B. Halsted (New York: Science Press, 1905), pp. xv–xxxi.]

to hold true for the whole 'knowable' universe. Thus, whether one dwelt upon the results of such a mathematical procedure as that to which M. Poincaré refers in his opening paragraphs, or whether, like Spencer himself, one applied the 'first principles' to regions of less exact science, this confidence that a certain orthodoxy regarding the principles of science was established forever was characteristic of the followers of the movement in question. Experience, lighted up by reason, seemed to them to have predetermined for all future time certain great theoretical results regarding the real constitution of the 'knowable' cosmos. Whoever doubted this doubted 'the verdict of science.'

Some of us well remember how, when Stallo's 'Principles and Theories of Modern Physics' first appeared, this sense of scientific orthodoxy was shocked amongst many of our American readers and teachers of science. I myself can recall to mind some highly authoritative reviews of that work in which the author was more or less sharply taken to task for his ignorant presumption in speaking with the freedom that he there used regarding such sacred possessions of humanity as the fundamental concepts of physics. That very book, however, has quite lately been translated into German as a valuable contribution to some of the most recent efforts to reconstitute a modern 'philosophy of nature.' And whatever may be otherwise thought of Stallo's critical methods, or of his results, there can be no doubt that, at the present moment, if his book were to appear for the first time, nobody would attempt to discredit the work merely on account of its disposition to be agnostic regarding the objective reality of the concepts of the kinetic theory of gases, or on account of its call for a logical rearrangement of the fundamental concepts of the theory of energy. We are no longer able so easily to know heretics at first sight.

For we now appear to stand in this position: The control of natural phenomena, which through the sciences men have attained, grows daily vaster and more detailed, and in its details more assured. Phenomena men know and predict better than ever. But regarding the most general theories, and the most fundamental, of science, there is no longer any notable scientific orthodoxy. Thus, as knowledge grows firmer and wider, conceptual construction becomes less rigid. The field of the theoretical philosophy of nature—yes, the field of the logic of science—this whole region is today an open one. Whoever will work there must indeed accept the verdict of experience regarding what happens in the natural world. So far he is indeed bound. But he may undertake without hindrance from mere tradition the task of trying afresh to reduce what happens to conceptual unity. The circle-squarers and the inventors of devices for perpetual motion are indeed still as unwelcome in scientific company as they were in the days when scientific orthodoxy was rigidly defined; but that is not because the foundations of geometry are now viewed as completely settled, beyond controversy, nor yet because the 'persistence of force' has been finally so defined as to make the 'opposite inconceivable' and the doctrine of energy beyond the reach of novel formulations. No, the circle-squarers and the inventors of devices for perpetual motion are to-day discredited, not because of any unorthodoxy of their general philosophy of nature, but because their views regarding special facts and processes stand in conflict with certain equally special results of science which themselves admit of very various general theoretical interpretations. Certain properties of the irrational number π are known, in sufficient multitude to justify the mathematician in declining to listen to the arguments of the circle-squarer; but, despite great advances, and despite the assured results of Dedekind, of Cantor, of Weierstrass and of various others, the general theory of the logic of the numbers, rational and irrational, still presents several important features of great obscurity; and the philosophy of the concepts of geometry yet remains, in several very notable respects, unconquered territory, despite the work of Hilbert and of Pieri, and of our author himself. The ordinary inventors of the perpetual motion machines still stand in conflict with accepted generalizations; but nobody knows as yet what the final form of the theory of energy will be, nor can any one say precisely what place the phenomena of the radioactive bodies will occupy in that theory. The alchemists would not be welcome workers in modern laboratories; yet some sorts of transformation and of evolution of the elements are to-day matters which theory can find it convenient, upon occasion, to treat as more or less exactly definable possibilities; while some newly observed phenomena tend to indicate, not indeed that the ancient hopes of the alchemists were well founded, but that the ultimate constitution of matter is something more fluent, less invariant, than the theoretical orthodoxy of a recent period supposed. Again, regarding the foundations of biology, a theoretical orthodoxy grows less possible, less definable, less conceivable (even as a hope) the more knowledge advances. Once 'mechanism' and 'vitalism' were mutually contradictory theories regarding the ultimate constitution of living bodies. Now they are obviously becoming more and more 'points of view,' diverse but not necessarily conflicting. So far as you find it convenient to limit your study of vital processes to those phenomena which distinguish living matter from all other natural objects, you may assume, in the modern 'pragmatic' sense, the attitude of a 'neo-vitalist.' So far, however, as you are able to lay stress, with good results, upon the many ways in which the life processes can be assimilated to those studied in physics and in chemistry, you work as if you were a partisan of 'mechanics.' In any case, your special science prospers by reason of the empirical discoveries that you make. And your theories, whatever they are, must not run counter to any positive empirical results. But otherwise, scientific orthodoxy no longer predetermines what alone it is respectable for you to think about the nature of living substance.

This gain in the freedom of theory, coming, as it does, side by side with a constant increase of a positive knowledge of nature, lends itself to various interpretations, and raises various obvious questions.

II

One of the most natural of these interpretations, one of the most obvious of these questions, may be readily stated. Is not the lesson of all these recent discussions simply this, that general theories are simply vain, that a philosophy of nature is an idle dream, and that the results of science are coextensive with the range of actual empirical observation and of successful prediction? If this is indeed the lesson, then the decline of theoretical orthodoxy in science is— like the eclipse of dogma in religion—merely a further lesson in pure positivism, another proof that man does best when he limits himself to thinking about what can be found in human experience, and in trying to plan what can be done to make human life more controllable and more reasonable. What we are free to do as we please—is it any longer a serious business? What we are free to think as we please—is it of any further interest to one who is in search of truth? If certain general theories are mere conceptual constructions, which to-day are, and to-morrow are cast into the oven, why dignify them by the name of philosophy? Has science any place for such theories? Why be a 'neo-vitalist,' or an 'evolutionist,' or an 'atomist,' or an 'Energetiker'? Why not say, plainly: "Such and such phenomena, thus and thus described, have been observed; such and such experiences are to be expected, since the hypotheses by the terms of which we are required to expect them have been verified too often to let us regard the agreement with experience as due merely to chance; so much then with reasonable assurance we know; all else is silence—or else is some matter to be tested by another experiment?" Why not limit our philosophy of science strictly to such a counsel of resignation? Why not substitute, for the old scientific orthodoxy, simply a confession of ignorance, and a resolution to devote ourselves to the business of enlarging the bounds of actual empirical knowledge?

Such comments upon the situation just characterized are frequently made. Unfortunately, they seem not to content the very age whose revolt from the orthodoxy of traditional theory, whose uncertainty about all theoretical formulations, and whose vast wealth of empirical discoveries and of rapidly advancing special researches, would seem most to justify these very comments. Never has there been better reason than there is to-day to be content, if rational man could be content, with a pure positivism. The splendid triumphs of special research in the most various fields, the constant increase in our practical control over nature—these, our positive and growing possessions, stand in glaring contrast to the failure of the scientific orthodoxy of a former period to fix the outlines of an ultimate creed about the nature of the knowable universe. Why not 'take the cash and let the credit go'? Why pursue the elusive theoretical 'unification' any further, when what we daily get from our sciences is an increasing wealth of detailed information and of practical guidance?

As a fact, however, the known answer of our own age to these very obvious comments is a constant multiplication of new efforts towards large and unifying theories. If theoretical orthodoxy is no longer clearly definable, theoretical construction was never more rife. The history of the doctrine of evolution, even in its most recent phases, when the theoretical uncertainties regarding the 'factors of evolution' are most insisted upon, is full of illustrations of this remarkable union of scepticism in critical work with

774 LOGIC AND METHODOLOGY

courage regarding the use of the scientific imagination. The history of those controversies regarding theoretical physics, some of whose principal phases M. Poincaré, in his book, sketches with the hand of the master, is another illustration of the consciousness of the time. Men have their freedom of thought in these regions; and they feel the need of making constant and constructive use of this freedom. And the men who most feel this need are by no means in the majority of cases professional metaphysicians—or students who, like myself, have to view all these controversies among the scientific theoreticians from without as learners. These large theoretical constructions are due, on the contrary, in a great many cases to special workers, who have been driven to the freedom of philosophy by the oppression of experience, and who have learned in the conflict with special problems the lesson that they now teach in the form of general ideas regarding the philosophical aspects of science.

Why, then, does science actually need general theories, despite the fact that these theories inevitably alter and pass away? What is the service of a philosophy of science, when it is certain that the philosophy of science which is best suited to the needs of one generation must be superseded by the advancing insight of the next generation? Why must that which endlessly grows, namely, man's knowledge of the phenomenal order of nature, be constantly united in men's minds with that which is certain to decay, namely, the theoretical formulation of special knowledge in more or less completely unified systems of doctrine?

I understand our author's volume to be in the main an answer to this question. To be sure, the compact and manifold teachings which this text contains relate to a great many different special issues. A student interested in the problems of the philosophy of mathematics, or in the theory of probabilities, or in the nature and office of mathematical physics, or in still other problems belonging to the wide field here discussed, may find what he wants here and there in the text, even in case the general issues which give the volume its unity mean little to him, or even if he differs from the author's views regarding the principal issues of the book. But in the main, this volume must be regarded as what its title indicates—a critique of the nature and place of hypothesis in the work of science and a study of the logical relations of theory and fact. The result of the book is a substantial justification of the scientific utility of theoretical construction—an abandonment of dogma, but a vindication of the rights of the constructive reason.

III

The most notable of the results of our author's investigation of the logic of scientific theories relates, as I understand his work, to a topic which the present state of logical investigation, just summarized, makes especially important, but which has thus far been very inadequately treated in the text-books of inductive logic. The useful hypotheses of science are of two kinds:

1. The hypotheses which are valuable *precisely* because they are either verifiable or else refutable through a definite appeal to the tests furnished by experience; and

2. The hypotheses which, despite the fact that experience suggests them, are valuable *despite*, or even *because*, of the fact that experience can *neither* confirm nor refute them. The contrast between these two kinds of hypotheses is a prominent topic of our author's discussion.

Hypotheses of the general type which I have here placed first in order are the ones which the text-books of inductive logic and those summaries of scientific method which are customary in the course of the elementary treatises upon physical science are already accustomed to recognize and to characterize. The value of such hypotheses is indeed undoubted. But hypotheses of the type which I have here named in the second place are far less frequently recognized in a perfectly explicit way as useful aids in the work of special science. One usually either fails to admit their presence in scientific work, or else remains silent as to the reasons of their usefulness. Our author's treatment of the work of science is therefore especially marked by the fact that he explicitly makes prominent both the existence and the scientific importance of hypotheses of this second type. They occupy in his discussion a place somewhat analogous to each of the two distinct positions occupied by the 'categories' and the 'forms of sensibility,' on the one hand, and by the 'regulative principles of the reason,' on the other hand, in the Kantian theory of our knowledge of nature. That is, these hypotheses which can neither be confirmed nor refuted by experience appear, in M. Poincaré's account, partly (like the conception of 'continuous quantity') as devices of the understanding whereby we give conceptual unity and an invisible connectedness to certain types of phenomenal facts which come to us in a discrete form and in a confused variety; and partly (like the larger organizing concepts of science) as principles regarding the structure of the world in its wholeness; i. e., as principles in the light of which we try to interpret our experience, so as to give to it a totality and an inclusive unity such as Euclidean space, or such as the world of the theory of energy is conceived to possess. Thus viewed, M. Poincaré's logical theory of this second class of hypotheses undertakes to accomplish, with modern means and in the light of to-day's issues, a part of what Kant endeavored to accomplish in his theory of scientific knowledge with the limited means which were at his disposal. Those aspects of science which are determined by the use of the hypotheses of this second kind appear in our author's account as constituting an essential human way of viewing nature, an interpretation rather than a portrayal or a prediction of the objective facts of nature, an adjustment of our conceptions of things to the internal needs of our intelligence, rather than a grasping of things as they are in themselves.

To be sure, M. Poincaré's view, in this portion of his work, obviously differs, meanwhile, from that of Kant, as well as this agrees, in a measure, with the spirit of the Kantian epistemology. I do not mean therefore to class our author as a Kantian. For Kant, the interpretations imposed by the 'forms of sensibility,' and by the 'categories of the understanding,' upon our doctrine of nature are rigidly predetermined by the unalterable 'form' of our intellectual powers. We 'must' thus view facts, whatever the data of sense must be. This, of course, is not M. Poincaré's view. A similarly rigid predetermination also limits the Kantian 'ideas of the reason' to a certain set of principles whose guidance of the course of our theoretical investigations is indeed only "regulative,' but is a 'a priori,' and so unchangeable. For M. Poincaré, on the contrary, all this adjustment of our interpretations of experience to the needs of our intellect is something far less rigid and unalterable, and is constantly subject to the suggestions of experience. We must indeed interpret in our own way; but our way is itself only relatively determinate; it is essentially more or less plastic; other interpretations of experience are conceivable. Those that we use are merely the ones found to be most convenient. But this convenience is not absolute necessity. Unverifiable and irrefutable hypotheses in science are indeed, in general, indispensable aids to the organization and to the guidance of our interpretation of experience. But it is experience itself which points out to us what lines of interpretation will prove most convenient. Instead of Kant's rigid list of *a priori* 'forms,' we consequently have in M. Poincaré's account a set of conventions, neither wholly subjective and arbitrary, nor yet imposed upon us unambiguously by the external compulsion of experience. The organization of science, so far as this organization is due to hypotheses of the kind here in question, thus resembles that of a constitutional government—neither absolutely necessary, nor yet determined apart from the will of the subjects, nor yet accidental —a free, yet not a capricious establishment of good order, in conformity with empirical needs.

Characteristic remains, however, for our author, as, in his decidedly contrasting way, for Kant, the thought that *without principles which at every stage transcend precise confirmation through such experience as is then accessible the organization of experience is impossible.* Whether one views these principles as conventions or as *a priori* 'forms,' they may therefore be described as hypotheses, but as hypotheses that, while lying at the basis of our actual physical sciences, at once refer to experience and help us in dealing with experience, and are yet neither confirmed nor refuted by the experiences which we possess or which we can hope to attain.

Three special instances or classes of instances, according to our author's account, may be used as illustrations of this general type of hypotheses. They are: (1) The hypothesis of the existence of continuous extensive *quanta* in nature; (2) The principles of geometry; (3) The principles of mechanics and of the general theory of energy. In case of each of these special types of hypotheses we are at first disposed, apart from reflection, to say that we *find* the world to be thus or thus, so that, for instance, we can confirm the thesis according to which nature contains continuous magnitudes; or can prove or disprove the physical truth of the postulates of Euclidean geometry; or can confirm by definite experience the objective validity of the principles of mechanics. A closer examination reveals, according to our author, the incorrectness of all such opinions. Hypotheses of these various special types are needed; and their usefulness can be empirically shown. They are in touch with experience; and that they are not merely arbitrary conventions is also verifiable. They are not *a priori* necessities; and we can easily conceive intelligent beings whose experience could be best interpreted without using these hypotheses. Yet these hypotheses are *not* subject to direct confirmation or refutation by experience. They stand then in sharp contrast to the scientific hypotheses of the other, and more frequently recognized, type, *i. e.*, to the hypotheses which *can* be tested by a definite appeal to experience. To these other hypotheses our author attaches, of course, great importance. His treatment of them is full of a living appreciation of the significance of empirical investigation. But the central problem of the logic of science thus becomes the problem of the relation between the two fundamentally distinct types of hypotheses, *i. e.*, between those which can not be verified or refuted through experience, and those which can be empirically tested.

IV

The detailed treatment which M. Poincaré gives to the problem thus defined must be learned from his text. It is no part of my purpose to expound, to defend or to traverse any of his special conclusions regarding this matter. Yet I can not avoid observing that, while M. Poincaré strictly confines his illustrations and his expressions of opinion to those regions of science wherein, as special investigator, he is himself most at home, the issues which he thus raises regarding the logic of science are of even more critical importance and of more impressive interest when one applies M. Poincaré's methods to the study of the concepts and presuppositions of the organic and of the historical and social sciences, than when one confines one's attention, as our author here does, to the physical sciences. It belongs to the province of an introduction like the present to point out, however briefly and inadequately, that the significance of our author's ideas extends far beyond the scope to which he chooses to confine their discussion.

The historical sciences, and in fact all those sciences such as geology, and such as the evolutionary sciences in general, undertake theoretical constructions which relate to past time. Hypotheses relating to the more or less remote past stand, however, in a position which is very interesting from the point of view of the logic of science. Directly speaking, no such hypothesis is capable of confirmation or of refutation, because we can not return into the past to verify by our own experience what then happened. Yet indirectly, such hypotheses may lead to predictions of coming experience. These latter will be subject to control. Thus, Schliemann's confidence that the legend of Troy had a definite historical foundation led to predictions regarding what certain excavations would reveal. In a sense somewhat different from that which filled Schliemann's enthusiastic mind, these predictions proved verifiable. The result has been a considerable change in the attitude of historians toward the legend of Troy. Geological investigation leads to predictions regarding the order of the strata or the course of mineral veins in a district, regarding the fossils which may be discovered in given formations, and so on. These hypotheses are subject to the control of experience. The various theories of evolutionary doctrine include many hypotheses capable of confirmation and of refutation by empirical tests. Yet, despite all such empirical control, it still remains true that whenever a science is mainly concerned with the remote past, whether this science be archeology, or geology, or anthropology, or Old Testament history, the principal theoretical constructions always include features which no appeal to present or to accessible future experience can ever definitely test. Hence the suspicion with which students of experimental science often regard the theoretical constructions of their confrères of the sciences that deal with the past. The origin of the races of men, of man himself, of life, of species, of the planet; the hypotheses of anthropologists, of archeologists, of students of 'higher criticism'—all these are matters which the men of the laboratory often regard with a general incredulity as belonging not at all to the domain of true science. Yet no one can doubt the importance and the inevitableness of endeavoring to apply scientific method to these regions also. Science needs theories regarding the past history of the world. And no one who looks closer into the methods of these sciences of past time can doubt that verifiable and unverifiable hypotheses are in all these regions inevitably interwoven; so that, while experience is always the guide, the attitude of the investigator towards experience is determined by interests which have to be partially due to what I should call that 'internal meaning,' that human interest in rational theoretical construction

which inspires the scientific inquiry; and the theoretical constructions which prevail in such sciences are neither unbiased reports of
the actual constitution of an external reality, nor yet arbitrary
constructions of fancy. These constructions in fact resemble in a
measure those which M. Poincaré in this book has analyzed in the
case of geometry. They are constructions molded, but *not* predetermined in their details, by experience. We report facts; we
let the facts speak; but we, as we investigate, in the popular phrase,
'talk back' to the facts. We interpret as well as report. Man is not
merely made for science, but science is made for man. It expresses
his deepest intellectual needs, as well as his careful observations.
It is an effort to bring internal meanings into harmony with external verifications. It attempts therefore to control, as well as to
submit, to conceive with rational unity, as well as to accept data.
Its arts are those directed towards self-possession as well as towards
an imitation of the outer reality which we find. It seeks therefore
a disciplined freedom of thought. The discipline is as essential as
the freedom; but the latter has also its place. The theories of science
are human, as well as objective, internally rational, as well as
(when that is possible) subject to external tests.

In a field very different from that of the historical sciences,
namely, in a science of observation and of experiment, which is
at the same time an organic science, I have been led in the course
of some study of the history of certain researches to notice the
existence of a theoretical conception which has proved extremely
fruitful in guiding research, but which apparently resembles in a
measure the type of hypotheses of which M. Poincaré speaks when
he characterizes the principles of mechanics and of the theory of
energy. I venture to call attention here to this conception, which
seems to me to illustrate M. Poincaré's view of the functions of
hypothesis in scientific work.

The modern science of pathology is usually regarded as dating
from the earlier researches of Virchow, whose 'Cellular Pathology'
was the outcome of a very careful and elaborate induction. Virchow, himself, felt a strong aversion to mere speculation. He
endeavored to keep close to observation, and to relieve medical
science from the control of fantastic theories, such as those of the
Naturphilosophen had been. Yet Virchow's researches were, as
early as 1847, or still earlier, already under the guidance of a
theoretical presupposition which he himself states as follows: "We

have learned to recognize," he says, "that diseases are not autonomous organisms, that they are no entities that have entered into
the body, that they are no parasites which take root in the body,
but *that they merely show us the course of the vital processes under
altered conditions*" ('dass sie nur Ablauf der Lebenserscheinungen
unter veränderten Bedingungen darstellen').

The enormous importance of this theoretical presupposition for
all the early successes of modern pathological investigation is
generally recognized by the experts. I do not doubt this opinion.
It appears to be a commonplace of the history of this science.
But in Virchow's later years this very presupposition seemed to
some of his contemporaries to be called in question by the successes
of recent bacteriology. The question arose whether the theoretical
foundations of Virchow's pathology had not been set aside. And
in fact the theory of the parasitical origin of a vast number of
diseased conditions has indeed come upon an empirical basis to
be generally recognized. Yet to the end of his own career Virchow
stoutly maintained that in all its essential significance his own
fundamental principle remained quite untouched by the newer
discoveries. And, as a fact, this view could indeed be maintained.
For if diseases proved to be the consequences of the presence of
parasites, the diseases themselves, so far as they belonged to the
diseased organism, were still not the parasites, but were, as before,
the reaction of the organism to the *veränderte Bedingungen* which
the presence of the parasites entailed. So Virchow could well insist.
And if the famous principle in question is only stated with sufficient generality, it amounts simply to saying that if a disease
involves a change in an organism, and if this change is subject to
law at all, then the nature of the organism and the reaction of the
organism to whatever it is which causes the disease must be understood in case the disease is to be understood.

For this very reason, however, Virchow's theoretical principle
in its most general form *could be neither confirmed nor refuted
by experience*. It would remain empirically irrefutable, so far as
I can see, even if we should learn that the devil was the true cause
of all diseases. For the devil himself would then simply predetermine the *veränderte Bedingungen* to which the diseased organism
would be reacting. Let bullets or bacteria, poisons or compressed
air, or the devil be the *Bedingungen* to which a diseased organism
reacts, the postulate that Virchow states in the passage just quoted

will remain irrefutable, if only this postulate be interpreted to meet the case. For the principle in question merely says that whatever entity it may be, bullet, or poison, or devil, that affects the organism, the disease is not that entity, but is the resulting alteration in the process of the organism.

I insist, then, that this principle of Virchow's is no trial supposition, no scientific hypothesis in the narrower sense—capable of being submitted to precise empirical tests. It is, on the contrary, a very precious *leading idea*, a theoretical interpretation of phenomena, in the light of which observations are to be made—'a regulative principle' of research. It is equivalent to a resolution to search for those detailed connections which link the processes of disease to the normal process of the organism. Such a search undertakes to find the true unity, whatever that may prove to be, wherein the pathological and the normal processes are linked. Now without some such leading idea, the cellular pathology itself could never have been reached; because the empirical facts in question would never have been observed. Hence this principle of Virchow's was indispensable to the growth of his science. Yet it was not a verifiable and not a refutable hypothesis. One value of unverifiable and irrefutable hypotheses of this type lies, then, in the sort of empirical inquires which they initiate, inspire, organize and guide. In these inquiries hypotheses in the narrower sense, that is, trial propositions which are to be submitted to definite empirical control, are indeed everywhere present. And the use of the other sort of principles lies wholly in their application to experience. Yet without what I have just proposed to call the 'leading ideas' of a science, that is, its principles of an unverifiable and irrefutable character, suggested, but not to be finally tested, by experience, the hypotheses in the narrower sense would lack that guidance which, as M. Poincaré has shown, the larger ideas of science give to empirical investigation.

V

I have dwelt, no doubt, at too great length upon one aspect only of our author's varied and well-balanced discussion of the problems and concepts of scientific theory. Of the hypotheses in the narrower sense and of the value of direct empirical control, he has also spoken with the authority and the originality which belong to his position. And in dealing with the foundations of mathematics he has raised one or two questions of great philosophical import into which I have no time, even if I had the right, to enter here. In particular, in speaking of the essence of mathematical reasoning, and of the difficult problem of what makes possible novel results in the field of pure mathematics, M. Poincaré defends a thesis regarding the office of 'demonstration by recurrence'—a thesis which is indeed disputable, which has been disputed and which I myself should be disposed, so far as I at present understand the matter, to modify in some respects, even in accepting the spirit of our author's assertion. Yet there can be no doubt of the importance of this thesis, and of the fact that it defines a characteristic that is indeed fundamental in a wide range of mathematical research. The philosophical problems that lie at the basis of recurrent proofs and processes are, as I have elsewhere argued, of the most fundamental importance.

These, then, are a few hints relating to the significance of our author's discussion, and a few reasons for hoping that our own students will profit by the reading of the book as those of other nations have already done.

Of the person and of the life-work of our author a few words are here, in conclusion, still in place, addressed, not to the students of his own science, to whom his position is well known, but to the general reader who may seek guidance in these pages.

Jules Henri Poincaré was born at Nancy, in 1854, the son of a professor in the Faculty of Medicine at Nancy. He studied at the École Polytechnique and at the École des Mines, and later received his doctorate in mathematics in 1879. In 1883 he began courses of instruction in mathematics at the École Polytechnique; in 1886 received a professorship of mathematical physics in the Faculty of Sciences at Paris; then became member of the Academy of Sciences at Paris, in 1887, and devoted his life to instruction and investigation in the regions of pure mathematics, of mathematical physics and of celestial mechanics. His list of published treatises relating to various branches of his chosen sciences is long; and his original memoirs have included several momentous investigations, which have gone far to transform more than one branch of research. His presence at the International Congress of Arts and Science in St. Louis was one of the most noticeable features of that remarkable gathering of distinguished foreign guests. In Poincaré the reader meets, then, not one who is primarily a speculative student of general problems for their own sake, but an original investigator of the highest rank in several distinct, although interrelated, branches of modern research. The theory of functions—a highly recondite region of pure mathematics—owes to him advances of the first importance, for instance, the definition of a new type of functions. The 'problem of the three bodies,' a famous and fundamental problem of celestial mechanics, has received from his studies a treatment whose significance has been recognized by the highest authorities. His international reputation has been confirmed by the conferring of more than one important prize for his researches. His membership in the most eminent learned societies of various nations is widely extended; his volumes bearing upon various branches of mathematics and of mathematical physics are used by special students in all parts of the learned world; in brief, he is, as geometer, as analyst and as a theoretical physicist, a leader of his age.

Meanwhile, as contributor to the philosophical discussion of the bases and methods of science, M. Poincaré has long been active. When, in 1893, the admirable *Revue de Métaphysique et de Morale* began to appear, M. Poincaré was soon found amongst the most satisfactory of the contributors to the work of that journal, whose office it has especially been to bring philosophy and the various special sciences (both natural and moral) into a closer mutual understanding. The discussions brought together in the present volume are in large part the outcome of M. Poincaré's contributions to the *Revue de Métaphysique et de Morale*. The reader of M. Poincaré's book is in presence, then, of a great special investigator who is also a philosopher.

27

[*Types of Order*]

General Survey of the Types of Order

§ 15. When the methodical procedure of any more exact physical science has led to success, the result is one which the well known definition that Kirchhoff gave of the science of Mechanics exemplifies. The facts of such a science, namely, are *"described"* with a certain completeness, and in as "simple," that is, in as *orderly* a fashion as possible. The *types of order* used in such a description are at once "forms of thought," as we shall soon see when we enumerate them, and forms of the world of our physical experiences in so far, but *only* in so far as, "approximately" and "probably," our descriptions of the world of the facts of "possible physical experience" in these terms are accurate. The philosophical problem as to *how and why the given facts of physical experience conform as nearly as they do to the forms of our thought*, is a question that can be fairly considered only when the types of order themselves have been discussed precisely *as* forms of thought, that is as "constructions" or "inventions," or "creations," or otherwise stated, as "logical entities," which our processes of thinking can either be said to "construct" or else be said to "find" when we consider, not the physical, but the logical realm itself, studying the order-types without regard to the question whether or no the physical world exemplifies them.

[Reprinted from PrL., secs. 2 and 3, pp. 92–135.]

That this mode of procedure, namely the study of the order-types apart from our physical experience, is important for our whole understanding of our logical situation (as beings whose scientific or thoughtful interpretation of nature is in question), is especially shown by the considerations with which our sketch of Methodology has just closed. For it is notable that *all highly developed scientific theories make use of concepts,*—such for instance as the quantitative concepts,—*whose logical exactness is of a grade that simply defies absolutely precise verification in physical terms.* The Newtonian theory of gravitation, for instance, can never be precisely verified. For the conception of a force varying inversely with the square of the distance, with its use of the concept of a material particle, involves consequences whose precise computation (even if the theory itself did not also involve the well known, still insurmountable, deductive difficulties of the problem of the gravitative behaviour of three or more mutually attracting bodies), would result in the definition of physical quantities that, according to the theory, would have to be expressed, in general, by irrational numbers. But actual physical measurements can never even appear to verify any values but those expressed in rational numbers. Theory, in a word, demands, in such cases, an absolute precision in the definition of certain ideal entities. Measurement, in its empirical sense, never is otherwise than an approximation, and at best, when absolutely compared with the ideal, a rough one.

Why such concepts, which can never be shown to represent with exactness any physical fact, are nevertheless of such value for physical science, our methodological study has now shown us. *Their very unverifiability, as exactly defined concepts about the physical world, is the source of their fecundity as guides to approximate physical verification.* For what the observers verify are the detailed, even if but approximate correspondences between very large samples of empirical data, and samples of the consequences of hypotheses. The exactness of the theoretical concepts enables the consequences of hypotheses to be computed, that is, deductively predetermined, with a wealth and variety which far transcend precise physical verification, but which, for that very reason, constantly call for and anticipate larger and larger samples of facts of experience such as can furnish the relative and approximate verifications. *It is with theoretical science as it is with con-*

duct. *The more unattainable the ideals by which it is rationally guided, the more work can be done to bring what we so far possess or control into conformity with the ideal.*

The order-systems, viewed as ideals that our thought at once, in a sense "creates," and, in a sense "finds" as the facts or "entities" of a purely logical (and not of a physical) world, are therefore to be studied with a true understanding, only when one considers them in abstraction from the "probable" and "approximate" exemplifications which they get in the physical world.

§ 16. Yet the logician also, in considering his order-types, is not abstracting from *all* experience. His world too is, in a perfectly genuine sense, empirical. We have intentionally used ambiguous language in speaking of his facts as *either* his "creations" *or* his "data." For if we say that, in one sense, he seems to "create" his order-types (just as Dedekind, for instance, calls the whole numbers "*freie Schöpfungen des menschlichen Geistes*"), his so-called "creation" is, in this case, *an experience of the way in which his own rational will, when he thinks, expresses itself.* His so-called "creation" of his order-types is in fact a finding of the forms that *characterize all orderly activity, just in so far as it is orderly,* and is therefore no capricious creation of his private and personal whim or desire. In his study of the Science of Order, the logician *experiences the fact that these forms are present in his logical world, and constitute it, just because they are, in fact, the forms of all rational activity.* This synthetic union of "creation" and "discovery" is, as we shall see, the central character of the world of the "Pure Forms."

A survey of the forms of order may therefore well begin by viewing them *empirically*, as a set of phenomena presented to the logician by the experience which the theoretical or deductive aspect of science furnishes to any one who considers what human thought has done. The most notable source of such an experience is of course furnished by the realm of the mathematical sciences, whose general business it is *to draw exact deductive conclusions from any set of sufficiently* precise hypotheses. If one considers the work of Mathematics,—analyzing that work as, for instance, the Italian school of Peano and his fellow workers have in recent years been doing,—one finds that the various Mathematical Sciences use certain fundamental concepts and order-systems, and

788   LOGIC AND METHODOLOGY

that they depend for their results upon the properties of these concepts and order-systems. Let us next simply report, in an outline sketch, what some of these concepts and systems are.

§ 17. *Relations.* One "concept," one "logical entity," or (to use Mr. Bertrand Russell's term, employed in his *Principles of Mathematics*) one "logical constant," which is of the utmost importance in the whole Theory of Order, is expressed by the term *Relation*. Without this concept we can make no advance in the subject. Yet there is no way of defining this term *relation* without using other terms that, in their turn, must presuppose for their definition a knowledge of what a relation is. In order, then, not endlessly to wait outside the gate of the Science of Order, for some "presuppositionless" concept that can show us the way in, we may well begin with some observation that can help us to grasp what is meant when we speak of a relation. A formal definition "without presuppositions" is impossible, whenever we deal with any terms that are of fundamental significance in philosophy.

Any object, physical or psychical or logical, whereof we can think at all, possesses *characters, traits, features,* whereby we distinguish it from other objects. Of these characters, some are *qualities,* such as we ordinarily express by *adjectives.* Examples are *hard, sweet, bitter,* etc. These qualities, as we usually conceive of them, often seem to belong to their object without explicit reference to other objects. At all events they may be so viewed. When we think of qualities, as such, we abstract from other things than the possessors of the qualities, and the qualities themselves. But, in contrast with *qualities,* the *relations* in which any object stands are *characters that are viewed as belonging to it when it is considered with explicit reference to, that is, as in ideal or real company with another object, or with several other objects.* To be viewed as a *father* is to be viewed with explicit reference to a child of whom one is father. To be an *equal* is to possess a character that belongs to an object only when it exists along with another object to which it is equal: and so on.

In brief, *a relation is a character that an object possesses as a member of a collection* (a pair, a triad, an *n*-ad, a club, a family, a nation, etc.), and which (as one may conceive), would *not* belong to that object, were it not such a member. One can extend this definition from any one object to any set of objects by saying that a relation is a character belonging to such a set when the members of the set are either taken together, or are considered along with the members of still other sets.

It is often assumed that relations are essentially *dyadic* in their nature; that is, are characters which belong to a member of a pair *as* such a member, or to the pair itself as a pair. The relation of a *father*, or that of an *equal*, or that of a *pair of equals*, may be viewed as such a dyadic relation. But, as fact, there are countless relations which are *triadic, tetradic,—polyadic*, in any possible way. When, for instance, is an object a *gift*? When, and only when there exists the triad: *giver, person or other entity whereto* something is *given*, and *object given*. When is an object a legal debt? Only, in general, when *creditor, debtor, debt*, and *consideration* or other *ground* for which or by virtue of which the debt has been incurred, exist. So that the *debtor*-relation: "*a* owes *b*, to *c*, for *d*," is in general a *tetradic* relation. Relations involving still more numerous related objects or terms are frequent throughout the exact sciences.

If a relation is dyadic, we can readily express the proposition which asserts this relation by using the symbol (a R b), meaning: "The entity a stands in the relation R to b." Whenever the proposition (a R b) is true, there is always also a relation, often symbolized by Ř, in which b stands to a. This may be called the inverse relation of the relation R. Thus if: "*a* is father of b," "b is child of a;" and if one hereby means "child of a father" the relation *child of* is, in so far, the inverse of the relation *father of*.

If a relation is polyadic, then such symbols as R(a b c d . . .), meaning "*a, b, c, d*, etc. (taken in a determinate order or way which indicates the place of each in the relational *n*-ad in question), stand in the (polyadic) relation *R*." Thus, with due definition of terms R (a b c d) may be used to symbolize the assertion: "*a* owes *b* to *c* for (or in consideration of) *d*;" and so on.

§ 18. *Logical Properties of Relations*. Relations are of such importance as they are for the theory of order, mainly because, in certain cases, they are subject to exact laws which permit of a wide range of deductive inference. To some of these laws attention must be at once directed. They enable us to classify relations according to various *logical properties. Upon such properties of relations all deductive science depends. The doctrine of the Norms of deductive reasoning is simply the doctrine of these relational properties when they are viewed as lawful characteristics of rela-*

tions which can guide us in making inferences, and thus Logic as the "Normative Science" of deductive inference is merely an incidental part of the Theory of Order.

Dyadic relations may be classified, first, as *Symmetrical* and *Non-symmetrical* relations. A symmetrical dyadic relation is sometimes defined as one that is *identical with its own inverse relation.* Or again, if S is a symmetrical relation, then, whenever the assertion $(a\ S\ b)$ is true, the assertion $(b\ S\ a)$ is true, whatever objects a and b may be. The relation of *equality*, symbolized by $=$, is a relation of this nature, for if $(a = b)$, then always $(b = a)$.

If a relation is *non*-symmetrical, various possibilities are still open. Thus, if R be a non-symmetrical relation, and if $(c\ R\ d)$, the relation R may be such that the assertion $(d\ R\ c)$ is *always excluded* by the proposition $(c\ R\ d)$, so that both cannot be true at one of whatever (c, d) one may use as the "terms" of the relation, then, in this case, the relation R is *totally* non-symmetrical. Russell proposes to call such relation Asymmetrical. The relation "greater than" is of this type in the world of quantities. But in other cases the relation R may be such that $(c\ R\ d)$ does not exclude $(d\ R\ c)$ in *every* instance, but only in certain instances. In the case of different relations, the exceptional instances may be for a given R, unique, or may be many, and may be in certain cases determined by precise subordinate laws of their own. Thus it may be the law that $(c\ R\ d)$ excludes $(d\ R\ c)$, unless some other relational proposition $(e\ R'\ f)$ is true; while if $(e\ R'\ f)$ is true, then $(c\ R'\ d)$ necessitates $(d\ R\ c)$; and so on.

Without reference to the foregoing concept of symmetry, the dyadic relations may be classified afresh, by another and independent principle, which divides them into Transitive and Non-Transitive relations. This new division is based upon considerations which arise when we consider *various pairs* of objects with reference to some one relation R. If, in particular, $(a\ R\ b)$ and $(b\ R\ c)$, the relation R may be such that $(a\ R\ c)$ is, under the supposed conditions *always* true, whatever the objects (a, b, c) may be, then in this case the relation R is *transitive*. If such a law does *not* universally hold, the relation R is non-transitive. The relation, *equal to*, is a transitive relation, according to all the various definitions of equality which are used in the different exact sciences. The so-called "axiom" that "Things equal to the same thing are equal to each other" is, in fact, a somewhat awkward expression of this transitivity, which, by definition, is always assigned, in any exact science to the relation =. The expression is awkward, because, by the use of "each other" in the so-called "axiom," the *transitivity* of the relation =, is so stated as not to be clearly distinguished from the *symmetry* which also belongs to the same relation. Yet *transitivity and symmetry are mutually independent relational characters.* The relations, "*greater than,*" "*superior to,*" etc., are, like the relation =, transitive, but they are *totally non-symmetrical.* The relations "*opposed to,*" and "*contradictory of*" are both of them *symmetrical,* but are also *non-transitive.*

Fewer formulations of this general type have done more to confuse untrained minds than the familiar "axiom": "Things equal to the same thing are equal to each other," because the form of expression used suggests that the relation, =, *possesses* its transitivity *because of* its symmetry. Everybody easily feels the symmetry of the relation =. Everyone admits (although usually without knowing whether the matter is one of definition, or is one of some objectively necessary law of reality, true apart from our definitions), that the relation = is transitive. The "axiom" suggests by its mode of expression that this symmetry and this transitivity are at least in this case, necessarily united. The result is a widespread impression that the symmetry of a relation always implies some sort of transitivity of this same relation,—an impression which has occasionally appeared in philosophical discussions. But nowhere is a sharp distinction between two characters more needed than when we are to conceive them as, in some special type of cases necessarily united, whether by arbitrary definition or by the nature of things.

If some dyadic relation, say X, is *non-transitive,* then there is at least one instance in which the propositions $(d \; X \; e)$ and $(e \; X \; f)$ are both of them true of some objects (d, e, f), while $(d \; X \; f)$ is false. As in the case of the non-symmetrical relations, so in the case of the non-transitive relations, this *non-transitivity,* like the before mentioned *non-symmetry,* may appear in the form of an universal law, forbidding for a given relation R *all* transitivity; or else in the form of one or more special cases where a given relation does not conform to the law that the principle of transitivity would require. These special cases may be themselves subject to special laws. A relation, T, is *totally non-transitive,* in case the two assertions $(a \; T \; b)$ and $(b \; T \; c)$ if both at once true, exclude the

792 LOGIC AND METHODOLOGY

possibility that (a T c) is true. Thus if "*a* is father of *b*" and "*b* is father of *c*," it is impossible that "*a* is father of *c*" should be true. The relation *father of*, is both totally non-symmetrical and also totally non-transitive. That relation between propositions which is expressed by the verb "contradicts," or by the expression "is contradictory of," is symmetrical, but totally non-transitive. For propositions which contradict the same proposition are mutually equivalent propositions. The relation "*greater than*," as we have seen, is transitive, but totally non-symmetrical. The relation = is both transitive and symmetrical. And thus the mutual independence of transitivity and symmetry, as relational properties, becomes sufficiently obvious.

Still a third, and again an independent classification of dyadic relations appears, when we consider the *number of* objects to which one of two related terms can stand, or does stand, in a given relation R, or in the inverse relation Ř. If "a is father of b," it is possible and frequent that there should be several other beings, *c*, *d*, etc., to whom *a* is also father. If "*m* is twin-brother of *n*," then, by the very definition of the relation, there is but *one* being, viz. *n*, to whom *m* can stand in this relation. If "*e* is child of *f*," there are *two* beings, namely the father and the mother, to whom *e* stands in this relation. In a case where the estate of an insolvent debtor is to be settled, and where the debtor is a single person (not a partnership nor yet a corporation), then the transactions to be considered in this one settlement may involve many creditors, but, by hypothesis, only one debtor, so far as this insolvent's estate alone is in question. Here, there are then several beings, (p, q, r, etc.), of each of whom the assertion can be made:—"*p* is creditor of *x*." But so far as this one case of insolvency alone is concerned, all the creditors in question are viewed as a *many* to whom only *one* debtor corresponds, as *the* debtor here in question.

The questions suggested by such cases are obviously capable of very variously multiplex answers, according to the relational systems concerned. Of most importance are the instances where some general law characterizes a given relation *R*, in such wise that such questions as the foregoing cases raise can be answered in universal terms. The principal forms which such laws can take are sufficiently indicated by the three following classes of cases:—

    1. The relation *R* may be such that, if (*a* R *b*) is true of some pair of individual objects (a, b), then, in case we consider one of

these objects, *b*, there are or are possible *other* objects, besides *a*,—objects *m*, *n*, etc.,—of which the assertions (m R b), (n R b), etc., are true; while at the same time, if we fix our attention upon the other member of the pair, *a*, there are other objects (*p*, *q*, *r*) either actual, or, from the nature of the relation *R*, possible, such that (a R p), (a R q), etc., are true propositions. Such a relation *R* is called by Russell and others a "*many-many*" relation. The laws that make it such may be more or less exact, general and important. Thus the relation "*1° of latitude south of*" is such a "many-many" relation, subject to exact general laws.

2. The relation *R* may be such that, when (a R b) is true of some pair (a, b), the selection of *a* is uniquely determined by the selection of *b* while, given *a*, then, in place of *b*, any one of some more or less precisely determined set of objects could be placed. Thus if "*a is sovereign of b*," where the pair (*a*, *b*) is a pair of persons, and where the relation *sovereign of* is that of some one wholly independent kingdom (whose king's soverign rights are untramelled by feudal or federal or imperial relationships to other sovereigns),—then, by law, there is only *one a* whereof the assertion: "*a* is sovereign of *b*" is true. But if we first choose *a*, there will be many beings that could be chosen in place of *b*, without altering the truth of the assertion. A case of such a relation in the exact sciences is the case "*a* is centre of the circle *b*." Here, given the circle *b*, its centre is uniquely determined. But any one point may be the centre of any one of an infinite number of circles. Such a relation *R* is called a "one-many" relation. Its inverse Ř would be called a "many-one" relation.

3. A relation *R* may be such that (whether or no there are many different pairs that exemplify it), in case (*a R b*) is true of any pair whatever, the selection of *a* uniquely determines what *one b* it is of which (*a R b*) is true, while the selection of *b* uniquely determines what *a* it is of which (*a R b*) is true. Such a relation is called a "one-one" relation. Couturat prefers the name "bi-univocal" relation in this case. The "one-one" relations, or, as they are often called "one-one correspondences," are of inestimable value in the order systems of the exact sciences. They make possible extremely important deductive inferences, for example those upon which a great part of the modern "Theory of Assemblages" depends.

The various classifications of dyadic relationships that have now been defined, may be applied, with suitable modifications, to triadic, tetradic, and other polyadic relations. Only, as the sets of related terms are increased, the possible classifications become, in general, more varied and complicated. A few remarks must here suffice to indicate the way in which such classifications of the polyadic relations would be possible.

If the symbol S (*a b c d* . . .) means: "The objects *a, b, c, d*, etc., stand in the symmetrical polyadic relation S," then the objects in question can be mutually substituted one for another, *i.e.* the symbols *a, b, c*, etc., can be interchanged in the foregoing expression, without altering the relation that is in question, and without affecting the truth of the assertion in question. This is for instance the case if S (*a b c d* . . .) means: "*a, b, c, d*, . . . are fellow-members of a certain club," or: "are points on the same straight line," so long as no *other* relation of the "fellow-members" or of the "points" is in question except the one thus asserted. In such cases S (*a b c d* . . .), S (*b c d a* . . .), etc., are equivalent propositions. Such a relation S is polyadic and symmetrical. The relation R, expressed by the symbol R (*a b c d*), is non-symmetrical (partially or totally) if in one, in many, or in all cases where this relation is thus asserted there is some interchanging of the terms or of the objects,—some substituting of one for another,—which is not permitted without an alteration of the relation R, or a possible destruction of the truth of the relational proposition first asserted. This is the case if R (*a b c d*) means: "*a* owes *b* to *c* for, or in consideration of *d*;" or, in a special case "*a* owes *ten dollars* to *c* for *one week's wages*." Such a relation is non-symmetrical. The number of terms used greatly increases the range of possibilities regarding what sorts of non-symmetry are each time in question; since, in some cases, *certain* of the terms of a given polyadic relational assertion can be interchanged, while others cannot be interchanged without an alteration of meaning or the change of a true into a false assertion. Thus if the assertion R (*a b c d*) means "*a* and *b* are points lying on a certain segment of a straight line whose extremities are *c* and *d*,"—then *a* and *b* can be interchanged, and *c* and *d* can be interchanged, without altering the truth or falsity of the assertion; but if the pair (*a, b*) is substituted for the pair (*c, d*), and conversely, the assertion would *in general* be changed in its meaning, and might be true in one form, but false when the interchange was made. Consequently we have to say, in general, that a given polyadic relation, *R*, is symmetrical or non-symmetrical

with reference to this or that pair or triad or other partial set
of its terms, or with reference to this or that *pair of pairs*, or *pair
of triads*, of its terms; and so on. In case of complicated order-
systems, such as those of *functions* in various branches of mathematics, or of *sets of points, of lines*, etc., in geometry, the resulting
complications may be at once extremely exact and definable, and
very elaborate, and may permit most notable systems of deductive
inferences.

In place of the more elementary concept of transitivity, a
more general, but at the same time more plastic concept, in terms
of which certain properties of polyadic relations can be defined,
is suggested by the process of *elimination*, so familiar in the deductive inferences of the mathematical sciences. Suppose R ($a\ b\ c\ d$)
is a tetradic relation, symmetrical or non-symmetrical; suppose
that the relation is such that if the propositions R ($a\ b\ c\ d$) and
R ($c\ d\ e\ f$) are at once true, then R ($a\ b\ e\ f$) necessarily follows.
A very notable instance of such a relation exists in the case of the
"entities of Pure Logic" of which we shall speak later. We could
here easily generalize the concept of transitivity so as to say that
this relation R is "transitive by pairs." But such transitivity, as
well as the transitivity of a dyadic relation, is a special instance
of a general relational property which *permits the elimination of
certain terms that are common to two or more relational propositions, in such wise that a determinate relational proposition concerning the remaining terms can be asserted to be true in case* the
propositions with which we began are true. Let the symbol a
represent, not necessarily a single object, but any determinate
pair, triad, or n-ad of objects. Let β represent another such determinate set of objects, and γ a third set. Let R and R' be polyadic
relations such that R ($a\ \beta$) and R' ($\beta\ \gamma$). The first of these symbols
means the assertion: "The set of objects consisting of the combination of the sets a and β (taken in some determinate mode or
sequence), is a set of objects standing in the relation R." The
second symbol, viz. R' ($\beta\ \gamma$) is to be interpreted in an analogous
way. Hereupon, suppose that either always, or in some definable
set of cases, the proposition R ($a\ \beta$) and R' ($\beta\ \gamma$), if true together,
imply that R'' ($a\ \gamma$), where R'' is some third polyadic relation,
which may be, upon occasion, identical with either or both of the
foregoing relations, R' and R. In such a case, the information
expressed in R ($a\ \beta$) and R' ($\beta\ \gamma$), is *such as to permit the elimina-*

tion of the set or collection β, so that a determinate relational proposition, results from this elimination. It is plain that transitivity, as above defined, is a special instance where such an elimination is possible.[1]

With regard to the "one-one," "many-one" and "many-many" classification of dyadic relations, we may here finally point out that a vast range for generalizations and variations of the concepts in question is presented, in case of triadic, and, in general, of polyadic relations, by the "operations" of the exact sciences,— operations which have their numerous more or less "approximate" analogues in the realm of ordinary experience. These operations make possible deductive inferences whose range of application is inexhaustible.

An "operation," such as "addition" or "multiplication," is (in the most familiar cases that are used in the exact sciences) founded upon a *triadic* relation. If R ($a\ b\ c$) means "The sum of a and b is c," or in the usual symbolic form, $a + b = c$, then the triadic relation in question is that of two numbers or quantities to a *third* number or quantity called their "sum." As is well known, the choice of two of these elements, namely the choice of the a and b that are to be added together (the "summands"), determines c uniquely, in ordinary addition. That is, to the pair (a, b) the third element of the triad (a, b, c) *uniquely corresponds*, in case R (a b c) is to be true. On the other hand, given c, the "sum," there are in general, various, often infinitely numerous, pairs (d, e), (f, g), etc., of which the propositions, $d + e = c$, $f + g = c$, etc., may be true. But in case of ordinary addition if c, the "sum," is first given, and if then *one* of the "summands," say a, is given, the other, say b, can always be found (if the use of "negative"

---

[1] In the closing chapter of his *Psychology*, in a beautiful sketch of the psychological aspects of scientific thinking, Professor Wm. James characterizes the transitivity of those dyadic relations, which are so often used in the natural sciences, by saying that the objects whose relations are of this transitive type follow what he calls "The axiom of skipped intermediaries." This is a characteristically concrete way of stating the fact that *one* main deductive use of transitivity, as a relational property, lies in the fact that it permits certain familiar *eliminations*. If, namely: "*a* is greater than *b*, and *b* is greater than *c*," *we may eliminate the intermediary b*, and conclude deductively that *a* is greater than *c*. We are here concerned, in our text, with the fact that dyadic transitivity is only a special instance of the conditions that make elimination in general possible, and that determine a whole class of Norms of deductive inference.

numbers or quantities is indeed permitted in the system with which we are dealing), and, when found, is then uniquely determined. Triadic relations, such as that which characterizes addition, may therefore be subject to precise laws whereby, to one element, or to two elements which are to enter into a triad, either one or many ways of completing the triad may correspond, these possible ways varying with the relational proposition whose truth is to be, in a given case, asserted or denied, or is to remain unchanged through the substitution of various new objects for those already present in a given triad.

The "operations" of the exact sciences are of inestimable importance for all the order-systems in terms of which precise theories are defined and facts are described. It is not necessary that they should precisely resemble, in their relational properties, either the "multiplication" or the "addition" of the ordinary numbers and quantities. A glance at their possible varieties (as these are discussed in connection with modern "group-theory," or as a part of the treatment of the various "algebras" which newer mathematics has frequent occasion to develop), will readily show to any thoughtful observer the absurdity of the popular opinion, still often entertained by certain philosophical students, that "mathematics is the science of quantity." The "quantities" are objects that are indeed vastly important. Their "order-system" is definable in terms of a few important properties of certain dyadic and triadic relations. *All our power to reason deductively about quantity depends upon these few relational properties,* whose consequences are nevertheless inexhaustibly wealthy. But the algebra of quantity is *one* only of infinitely numerous algebras whose operations are definable in terms of triadic relations. And there is no reason why other operations should not be defined in terms of tetradic, and, in fact of *n*-adic relations. The "Algebra of Pure Logic" is, in fact, as Mr. Kempe has shown, the symbolism of a system whose "operations" are superficially viewed, triadic, but are really founded upon tetradic relations (see § 24, below). And mathematical science includes within its scope the deductive reasonings possible in case of all these order-systems, and capable of being symbolized by all these algebras.

§ 19. *Classes.* In describing relations and their properties, we have inevitably presupposed the familiar concept of a *set* or *collection, i.e.* of a *class* of objects as already known. *Relations are impossible unless there are also classes.* Yet if we attempt to define this latter concept, we can do so only by presupposing the conception of *Relation* as one already understood. As we have already pointed out, such a "circle in definition" is inevitable in dealing with all philosophical concepts of a fundamental nature.

The concept of a Class or Set or Collection or Assemblage (*Menge*) of objects, is at once one of the most elementary and one of the most complex and difficult of human constructions. The apparent commonplaces of the Socratic-Platonic Methodology, and their intimate relation to the profound problems of the Platonic Metaphysic, which we touched upon in § 3, have shown us from the outset how the most obvious and the deepest considerations are united in this problem. The "burning questions" of the new "Theory of Assemblages" as they appear in the latest logical-mathematical investigations of our days, illustrate surprisingly novel aspects of the same ancient topic.

The concept of a Class, in the logical sense, depends (1) Upon the concept of an *Object*, or *Element* or *Individual*, which *does or does not belong to a given class;* (2) Upon the concept of the *relation* of *belonging to,* i.e. *being a member of* a class, or of *not so belonging;* (3) Upon the concept of *assertions,* true or false, which *declare that* an object is or is not a *member of* a given class; (4) Upon the concept of a Principle, Norm, or Universal which enables us to decide which of these assertions are true and which are false.

The *first* of these concepts is in many ways the most problematic of all the concepts used in the exact sciences. What constitutes an Individual, what is the "principle of individuation," how are individuals known to exist at all, how are they related to universal types, how they can be identified in our investigations, or how they can be distinguished from one another, whether they can be "numerically distinct" and yet wholly or partially similar or identical,—these are central problems of philosophy, which we in vain endeavour to escape by asserting in the usual way that "individuals are presented to us as empirical objects, by our senses." Whoever has had occasion to study any problem involving the doubtful or disputed *identity* of any individual object, knows that *no* direct sense-experience ever merely presents to us an individual object such as we conceive of, where we subject our processes of identification to exact rules and tests.

For *logical* purposes, an Individual Object is one that we *propose to regard at once as recognizable* or *identifiable throughout some process of investigation, and as unique within the range of that investigation, so that no other instance of any mere kind of object suggested by experience, can take the precise place of any one individual,* when we view ourselves as having found any individual object. Thus *to propose to treat* an object as always *recognizable* under certain conditions, and as such that no *substitute* for it is possible, in so far as we treat it as *this* individual,—all this involves an *attitude of will* which our sense-experience can illustrate and more or less sustain, but *can never prove to be necessary,* or present to us as successfully and finally warranted by mere data.

The concept of an individual is thus one whose origin and meaning are due to our will, to our interest, to so-called pragmatic motives. We actively *postulate* individuals and individuality. We do not merely find them. Yet this does not mean that the motives which guide our will in this postulate are wholly arbitrary, or are of *merely* relative value. *There are some active and voluntary attitudes towards our experience which we cannot refuse to take without depriving ourselves of the power to conceive any order whatever as present in our world.* Without objects conceived as unique individuals, we can have *no Classes.* Without classes we can, as we have seen, define *no Relations,* without relations we can have *no Order. But to be reasonable is to conceive of order-systems, real or ideal. Therefore, we have an absolute logical need to conceive of individual objects as the elements of our ideal order systems.* This postulate is the condition of defining clearly any theoretical conception whatever. The further metaphysical aspects of the concept of an individual we may here ignore. *To conceive of individual objects is a necessary presupposition of all orderly activity.*

An individual once postulated as present may be *classed with* other individuals. If the various individuals in question are *viewed as if they were* already given, the act of *classing them thus,* that is of asserting that these individuals belong in the same class, is again an act of will. Its value is so far *pragmatic.* We accomplish in this way some *purpose* of our own, some purpose of treating things as for some special reason distinguished or, on the other hand, undistinguished. In this sense, *all classes are subjectively distinguished from other classes by the voluntarily selected Norms, or principles of classification which we use. Apart from some classify-*

*ing will, our world contains no classes. Yet without classifications
we can carry on no process of rational activity, can define no orderly realm whatever, real or ideal. In this sense, the act of defining at least some norms or principles of classification is an act whose
logical value is not only pragmatic, but also absolute.* For a world
that we might conceive as wholly *without* classes, would be simply
no world at all. We could do nothing with it or in it. For to act,
consciously and voluntarily, in any way whatever is to classify
individuals into the objects that *do* and into those that *do not* concern, meet, serve, correspond to, stimulate or result from each sort
of activity. Thus classes are in one sense "creations," in another
sense absolute presuppositions of all our voluntary activity, and
so of all our theories.

If we have in mind some norm of principle of classification, this
norm inevitably defines at least one pair of classes, namely a given
class and its *negative* or *contradictory* class. For if the class x is
defined by a given norm, then the same norm defines the class
consisting of whatever objects are not x, a class here to be symbolized by $\bar{x}$.

Whenever we set out to classify any region of our world, real
or ideal, we of course always do so because we know, or at least
postulate, that there are *some* individuals in that region to be classified. And considered with reference to a given norm, which defines
a class x, these individuals will belong *either to x or else to $\bar{x}$*. But
of course our norm does not of itself tell us whether there are any
individuals, in the region to be classified, which *are* of the class x.
We can, then, define a norm for a class x, and later discover that
"Everything is $\bar{x}$," so that "There are no x's." In general, then,
when we define by its norm the class x, either one of two assertions
may turn out to be true about x. Either (1) "x has *no* member," or
(2) "x has at least one member." Of these two assertions *one* is true,
the other false, when uttered about any determinate class x. That
is, these assertions are *mutually contradictory*.

A very vast range of the assertions of the exact sciences can be
said to be of one or the other of these two comparatively simple
types. A class that has *no* members, a "nothing-class," an "empty
class," or "zero-class" may be symbolized by o. It is in that case a
class sharply defined by its norm, but known *not* to contain any
of the objects that we have chosen to regard or to define as the

individuals of the world (real or ideal) with which we are dealing. If a class *x* has *no* members, its negative, viz. $\bar{x}$, comprises *everything* that belongs to the realm or (in the phrase of the English logician, De Morgan) to the "universe of discourse" with which we are dealing. The class *everything* can be symbolized by 1. Regarding 0 and 1 as classes, and using = as the symbol, in the present case, of the relation of logical *equivalence* or *identity* between any two classes, we can assert, as formally true of any world, which for any reason, we can classify, that:—

$$\text{(1)} \quad 0 = \bar{1}; \quad \text{(2)} \quad \bar{0} = 1.$$

That is, the class *nothing* and the class *everything* are negatives each of the other, whenever these terms are used of any one "universe of discourse" into which a definite classification has been introduced.

Given any two distinct classes, *x* and *y*, defined by different norms or principles of classification, then inevitably, and without regard to whether *x* and *y* are, either or both of them "zero," that is "empty" classes, the very definitions of *x* and of *y* require that two new *resulting* classes should be present, as classes that may or may not have members, in our classified world. These new classes are: (1) The "Logical Product" of the classes *x* and *y*, that is, the class of those objects in our "universe of discourse" that conform *at once* to the norm of *x* and to the norm of *y*, and that, therefore belong at once to both the classes *x* and *y*; (2) The Logical Sum of the classes *x* and *y*, that is, the class of those objects that conform *either* to the norm of *x* *or* to the norm of *y*, and that therefore belong to *one at least* of the two classes (x, y). We symbolize by *xy* the logical product of *x* and *y*, and by $x + y$, their logical sum. In every extended discussion of classes logical sums and products are sure to occur.

Between two classes, *p* and *q*, there may or may not exist a certain relation which is of fundamental importance for all study of classes, and so for all exact science. This is the relation of *subsumption*. It is a relation non-symmetrical, but *not totally* non-symmetrical. We may symbolize this relation by $-\!\!\prec$. If $p -\!\!\prec q$, then whatever conforms to the norm of *p* conforms to the norm of *q*; or, as we also may say, the class p is *included in* the class q. If $(p-\!\!\prec q)$ and $(q-\!\!\prec p)$ are at once true, then $(p = q)$. In case the relation $(p-\!\!\prec q)$ holds true, the logical product of p and $\bar{q}$ has *no* members, or in symbols, $p\bar{q} = 0$. The *subsumption* relation is transitive, that is:—

"If $(p\!\!-\!\!<\!q)$ and $(q\!\!-\!\!<\!r)$ then $(p\!\!-\!\!<\!r)$."

As the modern study of the topic has shown, *the entire traditional "theory of the syllogism" can be expressed as a sort of comment upon, and relatively simple application of, this transitivity of the subsumption-relation.* Thus does the theory of the "norms of thought" form merely a subordinate part of the theory of Logical Order.

One relation remains here to be explicitly characterized,—a relation often confounded with the subsumption relation, but carefully distinguished therefrom, in recent times by Frege, Peano, and Russell. It is *the relation in which an individual stands* to the class to which it belongs, and of which it is a member. The school of Peano symbolize this relation by ϵ. Thus, supposing i to be the name of an individual object, the symbol $(i \,\epsilon\, x)$ means: "i is a member of, that is, belongs to the class x." Since a class itself can be and sometimes is treated logically as an individual, in case this class is taken *as* one member of a *set of classes* (as, for instance, when one says: "The powers of 2, such as 2^2, 2^3, etc., form a class that is one of the classes of whole numbers"), we can suppose the proposition $x \,\epsilon\, y$ to be true of some class x, y being a class of classes. But in such a case, if $(i \,\epsilon\, x)$ and $(x \,\epsilon\, y)$, then the assertion $(i \,\epsilon\, y)$ is, in general, false. So that the ϵ-relation is *non-transitive*, while the relation $—\!<$, the subsumption relation is transitive. They are, then, quite different relations.

Any class, x, consists of the individuals, i, i', i'' . . ., whereof the corresponding assertions $(i \,\epsilon\, x)$, $(i' \,\epsilon\, x)$, etc., are true. From the formal point of view it is thus possible, and in fact, for certain logical purposes necessary, to develop the "Theory of Classes" upon the basis of the "Theory of Propositions." Propositions, themselves, have certain characteristic logical relations, of *contradiction, implication,* and so on. To these relations of propositions those relations of classes which we have named, viz. *negation, subsumption,* etc., correspond in certain exact ways. There is therefore possible a "calculus of classes"; although the two doctrines have certain notable differences regarding the principles available for deductive purposes in each of them.

The assertions of the type $(i \,\epsilon\, x)$ upon which classifications may be said to rest, have the aforesaid paradoxical character. They are, namely, the expressions of *postulates*, or voluntary acts, since all classification involves a more or less arbitrary norm or principle of classification. Yet the *laws* to which such propositions, as well as any logical system of classes are subject, are nevertheless exact, are definable (as we have seen) in terms of precise dyadic, triadic and tetradic relations, and *are not in the least arbitrary*. In fact, despite the arbitrariness of each individual classification, the general laws of logic possess an absoluteness which cannot conceivably be surpassed, and lie at the basis of all order-system and of all theory.

The only possible answer to the question as to *how* the absoluteness of the logical principles is thus consistent with the arbitrariness of each of the classifications which we make, lies in saying that the logical principles define precisely the nature of the "Will to act in an orderly fashion" or in other words of the "Will to be rational."

§ 20. *The Types of Order*. The foregoing concepts of Relation, of Relational Properties, and of Classes, have enabled modern mathematicians, and other students of logic, to define in exact terms a surprisingly vast range of order-systems. With almost dramatic suddenness the considerations which may have seemed so varied, disunited and abstract in the foregoing sketch, suddenly give us, when they are once properly combined, an insight into precisely what is most momentous about the order present in the worlds of Number, of Quantity, of Geometry, and of Theoretical Natural Science generally.

For, in the first place, what order-type is universally present wherever there is *any* order in the world? The answer is, *Serial Order*. What is a *Series*? Any row, array, rank, order of precedence, numerical or quantitative set of values, any straight line, any geometrical figure employing straight lines, yes all space, all time,— any such object involves serial order. Serial order may exist in two principal types, the *"open"* series, and the *"closed"* series or *cycle*. Since the latter type of order may be reduced to the former by certain well-known devices, it suffices here to characterize any serial order that is "open," *i.e.* that does not return into itself. So viewed, a *Series* is:—*A class of individuals or elements such that there exists a single relation R, dyadic, transitive, and totally non-symmetrical, while this relation R is of such a nature that, whatever pair (a,b) of distinct elements of the class in question be chosen, either (a R b) or else (b R a) is true.* Since the relation R is by definition totally non-symmetrical, $(a\,R\,b)$ and $(b\,R\,a)$ cannot be true at once of any chosen pair of objects belonging to the series defined in terms of R. If we begin with any pair (c, h), of elements of a given series, the "place" of any other element a or g is determined with reference to c and h by such assertions as $(a\,R\,c)$ and $(c\,R\,g)$, $(g\,R\,h)$, etc., while the transitivity of the relation R *enables us to use such assertions as a basis for deductive inferences whenever two pairs with a common element appear in the course of our determinations.* Chains of inference, eliminations, etc., result. Thus, once more, certain norms of deductive inference are determined by relational properties.

Now in terms of the variations which this definition of *series* permits to be present in the classes and sub-classes of which a series may consist, an infinite variety of distinct serial types can be defined upon the basis of the single definition just stated, and of the logical properties of classes.[2]

The series of the positive whole numbers, for instance, is characterized by the fact that there is *one* member of the class in question, namely the *first*, which stands in a relation R to every other whole number, R being the transitive and totally non-symmetrical relation of "predecessor," while no positive whole number stands in the relation R to this first one; and by the further fact that whatever number (say 2, or n) one chooses, there is *one* number (say 3, or $n + 1$) and *only one*, such that, while (n R n + 1) is true, *no* whole number m exists such that (n R m) while (m R (n + 1)). In this case (n + 1) is called the *next successor of n*. And thus the relation "next successor" is defined in terms of R, and of the absence of intermediates. A further characteristic of the whole numbers is this, that if any property Q belongs to the *first* whole number, and if Q is such that, in case Q belongs to any whole number, n, Q belongs to the "next successor" of n (say to $n + 1$), then Q belongs to *all* of the whole numbers. This characteristic of the whole number series is defined and applied by combining the

[2] The use of the foregoing definition, and the classifications of possible serial types which the definition permits, have now become common property. The significance of the definition, and the wealth of ordinal properties that could be stated in terms of it, were gradually brought to light in the latter half of the nineteenth century through the researches of C. S. Peirce, of Dedekind, of Cantor, and of various other logical and mathematical writers. The results have been summed up, and placed in various new lights, in Russell's *Principles of Mathematics*.

other relational properties of the series with the logical properties of classes, and *is of the most fundamental importance for deduction throughout mathematical theory*. Thus still another norm of deductive reasoning is established for a certain class of cases.

Such simple considerations concerning classes and relations define then, the series of the whole numbers, and predetermine the inexhaustible wealth of the Theory of Whole Numbers. An extension of such an ordinal series "backwards" gives us the *negative whole numbers*. The series of the *"rational numbers"* can be characterized as to its ordinal type by defining the relation R, for that series, and also by choosing the elements of the series, *so* that whatever pair (i, k) of distinct rational numbers exists, such that $(i\ R\ k)$ is true, there also exists j different from i and from k such that $(i\ R\ j)$ and $(j\ R\ k)$. A series of this type is now called *"dense."* Upon the basis of the *dense* series of the rational numbers we can define another series, that of the "cuts" or *Schnitte* of the rational numbers. This new series is (in Dedekind's sense) "continuous." It is defined in terms of still another union of a certain sort of classification with the relational properties already in question. This series of the "cuts" of the rational numbers is the series of the "real numbers." And Cantor has worked out a more precise characterization of the properties of the continuous series of "real numbers" (the so-called "arithmetical continuum") by a still further synthesis of the properties of certain sub-classes which such a series contains, with the general properties of the relation R, whereby the series as a whole is determined.

In consequence, mathematical science is now in possession of a complete definition of the "arithmetical continuum" in purely ordinal terms.

But the numbers are not merely subject to *dyadic* ordinal relations. As usually employed in arithmetic and algebra, they are also subject to *triadic* relations, in terms of which the *operations* of ordinary addition (a + b = c), and of multiplication (pq = r) are defined. The momentous problem arises as to *how these triadic relations are themselves related to the dyadic ordinal relations of the number-series*. This problem has been attacked with complete success by the modern students of the foundations of mathematics. It has been shown, first, that the simple series of the *whole numbers*, defined as above, is such as to enable us to define *for that series* the operations of the addition and multiplication of its own terms upon the basis of considerations that involve solely the dyadic relational properties of this whole-number series as it stands. That is, in case of a series such as the whole numbers, positive and negative, the triadic relations involved in addition and in multiplication, can be defined in terms of the dyadic relations whereby the series is ordered. But in case of the dense series of the rational numbers, and still more in case of the "arithmetical continuum" of the "real numbers," and again yet more in case of the "complex numbers" of algebra, *such a reduction of the triadic relations of these numbers to the dyadic relations of the whole numbers can be accomplished only indirectly*, by means of special definitions, which enable us to regard these other series and in fact the whole system of the "complex numbers," as derived, through a sort of "logical genesis," from the original whole number series, by a *series of combinations* of the terms, classes, and relations, of the latter series, and by further combinations of the results of these first combinations. All this "genesis" we have not here room to follow. It is enough to say that the result of this research is to show that all the properties which make the numbers of ordinary algebra subject to the endlessly varied operations of *calculation*, can be reduced to properties which depend: (1) Upon the dyadic relations of order which hold in the whole-number system itself, and (2) Upon the properties and ordinal relations of certain derived logical entities (*pairs* of whole numbers, *classes* of these pairs, *pairs* of real numbers, etc.). And in brief, we can say: All the properties of the numbers which are used in ordinary algebra, are properties of their order-system, while this order-system is *indirectly definable* on the basis of the properties of the whole-number system, and of the properties of certain classes and relations of objects which the whole-number system enables us to define.

The number-system of ordinary algebra being once defined, it is possible to deal, in a systematic way, with the problems which are presented by the physical and ideal *Quantities* with which mathematical theories so frequently deal. *Quantities* are objects, either physical or ideal, that fall into series by virtue of relations of the nature of *greater* and *less*. They have therefore their serial order-systems. They also, in general, are subject to relations of *equality*. In case they are *Intensive* Quantities, their order-systems are definable *only* by means of such dyadic relations, that is, by means of relations of *greater-less*, and by means of the symmetrical relation of *equality*. Extensive Quantities are such as, *over and above* these dyadic relations, of *greater, less, equal*, are subject to *triadic* relations in terms of which the *sum* of any two extensive quantities that belong to the same system of quantities can be defined. In the realm of the quantities, however, there is no *general* mode of "logical genesis" which makes it possible for us to define triadic relations of the type (a + b = c) upon the sole basis of the dyadic relations *greater, less*, and *equal*. Herein the quantities differ, as logical objects, from the number-series viewed as pure algebra views the latter. The "logical genesis" of the rational and of the "real" numbers,—a genesis of which we have just made mention, has no precise and general correspondent process in the world of quantities. Therefore, those triadic relations of most sets of extensive quantities upon which their addition depends, are defined, either (1) upon the basis of empirical inductions (as is the case with physical weights, with quantities of energy, etc.), or (2) upon the basis of voluntarily assumed postulates (as is the case with many systems of ideal quantities, such as for instance the extensive quantities of Pure Metrical Geometry as they are usually treated), or (3) upon some union of postulate and of physical experience (as is frequently the case in the applications of geometry, and in such a science as Mechanics).[3]

Given, however, some workable and sufficiently general definition of a triadic relation upon which an addition-operation can be founded, then the number-system can be at once introduced into the theory of any system of quantities. The exactness of a physical theory of such a *set* of quantities depends upon such an introduction. The order-system of such a realm of extensive quantities becomes correspondent to the order-system either of a *part* of the numbers, or of the *entire* system of the real or of the complex numbers. Thus, what makes deductive inference in the realm of quantity possible depends solely upon the ordinal properties of this realm.

The application of the foregoing principles regarding serial order-types to the theory and description of more complicated

[3] In the very notable case of geometrical theory, a special form of reduction of the "metrical" to the "ordinal" properties of space-forms also exists, whereby the bases of metrical geometry can be indirectly reduced to principles that are stateable wholly in projective, that is, in ordinal terms. This case is of vast importance for the logic of geometry, but cannot further be studied here.

order-systems, involves a set of processes to which we have now made frequent reference namely: The *Correlation of Series. Upon such correlations the whole theory of Mathematical Functions depends,*—a theory which admits of infinitely numerous variations and applications, and which plays its part in every extended and exact theoretical science. The norms of deductive inference which are definable here are numerous and complex, but vastly important.

The *simplest type of correlation* is that which takes place when a relation of "one-one correspondence" can be established between the members of two series, or between the members of definable parts of such series. In other cases, a "one-many" relation can be established, whereby to every member (say p) of a given series S, there corresponds some determinate number, a pair (q, r) or a triad (q, r, s) of elements, chosen from some series S', or else so that q belongs to S', r to S", etc.; while, given $(q, r,$ etc.$)$, p is uniquely determined. The possibilities thus suggested may be still further varied without any necessary sacrifice of exactness of definition. In very numerous instances, especially where the operations possible in case of numbers and quantities are in question, we may have a correspondence and correlation of series so established that, to each set of pairs (p, q), or of triads (p, q, r) etc. (whereof p shall be chosen from one series, q from another or from the same series, and so on), there corresponds some determinate element x, or some set of elements $(x, y, z,$ etc.$)$, while the element x (or the set $x, y,$ etc.$)$ can be defined as elements of some series or order-system that thus *results from* or *that is definable in terms of the* "*functional relation*," whose laws lie at the basis of the correlation in question. In general, let $a, \beta,$ and γ be, not now single individuals viewed merely as such, but *pairs, triads,* or other sets of objects. Let the elements whereof each of the sets $a, \beta,$ and γ, consists, be all chosen in a determinate way from certain series of objects already defined (number-series, points on lines, series of lines or of other geometrical figures, physical quantities, etc.). Suppose that some general law exists which one can state in the form: "If R' (a) and R'' (β) are both of them true, R''' (γ) is true." Then such a law establishes a *functional* relation, or a *system of functional relations,* amongst the various series from which the elements of a, of β, and of γ, respectively, are chosen.

For instance, R' (a) may stand for some combination of quantities of different forms of physical energy (coal burned, water-power supplied, etc.). These forms of energy may be combined in the production of certain industrial products. Each of these quantities, in a special case, will then be a member of its own series (weight of coal, amount of water used at a certain "head," etc.). R″ (β) may be a combination of the costs of these various forms of energy, when the energy is obtained under certain conditions. And then, again, each of these elements of cost will have its place in its own series, determined by a price-list (price of coal per ton, of water per cubic metre, etc.). Hereupon, in ways determined by the mode of production, by the waste or the use of energy, etc., there may correspond to a given combination R′ (α) and a combination R″ (β), a given set of costs of a set of industrial products, expressed by R‴ (γ). In such a case the costs of the products will appear as in *"functional relations"* to the sources of energy used, and to the costs of each of these sources. Wherever such a correlation of series, or of sets or systems of series appears, the result is an Order determined by the correlations.

As Klein long since pointed out, the various types of Geometrical Science, the different geometries (metrical, projective, etc.), may be classified in terms of the "invariants" (that is, of the unchanging laws of the results of correlation) to which the different geometrical "transformations" are subject. And the geometrical "transformations" (projections, systematic deformations, dualities, inversions, etc.) involve correlations of sets of series such that (with the foregoing definition of the symbols used), R′ (α), and R″ (β), etc., imply, as their combined result R‴ (γ), in ways which the relational properties of the geometrical world enable the geometer to define. In general a mathematical "transformation" means a definition of one system of relations by means of a correspondence with other systems of relations and of related terms. Its "invariant" is a law or a relational property or construction which is exemplified by each and by all of the correlated systems.

A very highly important condition of the orderly character of the systems within which such "functional relations," and such "transformations" are possible, is the existence of relational properties that admit of *eliminations*, of the type discussed in our general account of relations (§ 18, near the close). *What transitivity is in the definition of a single series, the more general relational properties which permit elimination are, in the definition of the complex geometrical and physical order-systems which admit of definite and lawfully repeated correlations and transformations.*

It remains to say a word as to the significance of the Symmetrical Relations in the constitution of all such order-types. If a = b = c = d, etc., the set of objects between any two of which such a dyadic symmetrical transitive relation as = obtains, may be called a *Level*. On a topographical map, the lines that indicate levels, the "contour-lines," run through points any two of which stand for physical points, on the surface mapped, such that they are at *equal* heights above some "base-level" (usually above sea-level). Isothermal lines, isobars, parallels of latitude, and countless other symbols for levels, are conspicious features of the diagrams that are used to depict the orderly structure of real or ideal objects. Yet the members of such a level are not ordered by means of their symmetrical transitive *levelling* relations. They are ordered, if at all, in terms of serial relations, or in terms of the foregoing correlations of systems of series. Yet levelling processes and relations are constantly used in the definition of order-systems. The topographical map, or the "weather map" illustrates this fact. And the vast range of usefulness which the Equation has in mathematics is one of the best known features of that science. Why are relations which by themselves do *not* order, so useful in the definition of types of order?

The answer to this question is three-fold: —

1. The symmetrical relations, and especially the symmetrical transitive relations, enable us to classify, and so *form the basis for all the most exactly definable classifications of the Science of Order*.

2. For this very reason, many of the most important series in the theoretical sciences are *Series of Levels*. Such, for instance, are the series of contour-lines, isobars, etc., on a map.

3. And again, for the same reason, many of the most important *laws* of an ordered world are defined in terms of levels. The "invariants" of a system of "transformations" establish, in general, such levels. That is, when two or more systems are correlated through a "transformation," the results of such correlation leave certain relations that belong to each system unchanged by the passage from one system to the other. Thus a level is established. For instance, the law of the Conservation of Energy is a law expressed by asserting that, between any two states *A* and *B* of a given "closed system" in the physical world there obtains a certain

symmetrical transitive relation, namely the relation expressed by saying that: "The total energy present in the system in the state A is equal in quantity to the total energy present in the system in the state B." In other words, the total energy remains invariant through the transformation. Thus the statement of the "invariant" law of any system of correlations or of transformations always includes some elements that can be expressed by symmetrical transitive relations. All this is the result of the same *inseparable union of the concepts of Class and of Relation,*—a union which we have illustrated from the beginning of our sketch of Order.

It will be noted, as we now look back, that the various norms of deductive inference, in all the various cases here in question, depend upon the relational properties of the order-systems which are under consideration, and so, in the last analysis, upon the properties of single relations. Thus Formal Logic, as a "Normative science," is incidental to the application of the Theory of Order to this or that process of deductive inference.

The Logical Genesis of the Types of Order

§ 21. In our first section, the study of methodology showed us the relation of all scientific procedure to the Theory of Order. In our second section we have portrayed, in a largely empirical fashion, the Types of Order which characterize the exact sciences. Two of the concepts absolutely essential to the Theory of Order, we have already treated, indeed, so as to show *why they are necessary.* These are the concepts of Relation and of Class. For not only are these concepts actually used in the definition of every type of order, but as we have seen, *their necessity depends upon the fact that without them no rational activity of any kind is possible.* We have consequently insisted that these concepts unite in a very characteristic way—"creation" and "discovery," an element of contingency and an element of absoluteness. That a particular physical or psychical *relation,* such as that of father and child, should be present in the world, is as empirical a fact as the existence of colors or tones. That there should be physical objects to *classify,* this again is a matter of experience. And furthermore, every classification of real or of ideal objects is determined in any special instance, by a norm or principle of classification which we voluntarily choose. And in so far classifications are arbitrary, and may

812 LOGIC AND METHODOLOGY

be said to be "creations" or "constructions." Yet, whatever else the world contains, if it only contains a reasonable being who knows and intends his own acts, then this being is aware of a certain relation, the relation between performing and not performing any act which he considers in advance of action. And thus relations amongst acts are in such wise necessary facts, that whoever acts at all, or whoever, even in ideal, contemplates *possible courses of action*, must regard at least some of these relations as present in the realm of his conceived *modes of action*. In a similar fashion, as we have seen, every sort of action determines a kind of classification of some world, physical or ideal. In so far, therefore, as the nature of relations and of classes in general determines the existence and the meaning of types of orderly activity, these types of orderly activity, and the order-systems which express their nature, are both empirical objects, "found" (since we experience their presence in our world); and are also *necessary* objects, because if we try to conceive that they are *not* there, our very conception involves modes of action, and hence restores these necessary relations and classes to the world from which we had tried to banish them. We "construct" relational systems and classes in our ideal world. But we also "find" that at least *some* of these constructions are necessary.

A frequently asserted modern view, to which we have made some reference in the foregoing, namely the view called **Pragmatism**, asserts that all truth, including logical truth, has its basis in the fact that our hypotheses, or other assertions, prove to be *successful*, or show by their empirical workings that they meet the needs which they were intended to meet. From this point of view the logical hypothesis: "That there are classes, relations, and order systems," would be true merely in so far as the acts of conceiving such objects, and of treating them as real, have, under the empirical conditions under which we do our thinking, a successful result. And thus logical truth, and the logical existence and validity of classes, of relations, and of the various types of order, would stand in the same position in which all the "working hypotheses" of an empirical science stand. These order-systems would exist, and their laws would be valid, precisely in so far as such ways of actively conceiving of the world have successful workings.

But, in the foregoing, we have already indicated that, so far as the existence of classes and of relations in general is in question, and in so far as the validity of certain logical laws is concerned, we are obliged to maintain a position which we may characterize by the term Absolute Pragmatism. This position differs from that of the pragmatists now most in vogue. There are *some* truths that are known to us *not* by virtue of the special successes which this or that hypothesis obtains in particular instances, but by virtue of the fact that *there are certain modes of activity, certain laws of the rational will, which we reinstate and verify, through the very act of attempting to presuppose that these modes of activity do not exist, or that these laws are not valid.* Thus, whoever says that there are no classes whatever in his world, inevitably classifies. Whoever asserts that for him there are no real relations, and that, in particular the logical relation between affirmation and denial does not exist, so that for him *yes* means the same as *no,*—on the one hand himself asserts and denies, and so makes a difference between *yes* and *no;* and, on the other hand, asserts the existence of a relational *sameness* even in denying the difference between *yes* and *no.*

In brief, whatever actions are such, whatever types of action are such, whatever results of activity, whatever conceptual constructions are such, that the very act of getting rid of them, or of thinking them away, logically implies their presence, are known to us indeed both empirically and pragmatically (since we note their presence and learn of them through action); but they are also absolute. And any account which succeeds in telling what they are has absolute truth. Such truth is a "construction" or "creation," for activity determines its nature. It is "found," for we observe it when we act.

It consequently follows that whoever attempts to justify the existence of any of the more complicated systems of order that we have been describing in the foregoing section, has a right to seek for some absolute criterion, whereby he may distinguish what systems of order are necessary facts in the world,—that is, in the world that the logician has a right to regard as necessary,— and what, if any, amongst these forms are either capricious, and unnecessary, or else are suggested by the particular facts of experience in such wise as to remain merely contigent.

The logician's world is the world of hypotheses, and of theories, and of the ideal constructions that are used in these theories and hypotheses. Now theories and hypotheses may be merely suggested to us by physical phenomena, so that, if we had different sensations from our present ones, or if our perceptions followed some other routine than the observed one, we should have no need for these hypotheses and resulting theories. In so far, the hypotheses are contingent, and the theories have only conditional value. Furthermore, some of our activities are indeed arbitrary, so that we may, as the common expression is, "do as we like." And when such modes of activity play their part in the choice or in the definition of our hypotheses, the logician cannot regard them as necessary. But such logical facts as the difference between *yes* and *no*, are not dependent on the contingent aspect of our sensations, but on our rational consciousness of what we intend to do or not to do. Such facts have not the contingency of the empirical particulars of sense. And some modes of action, such as affirmation and denial, are absolute modes.

We can indeed suspend the process of affirmation and denial, but only by suppressing every rational consciousness about what we ourselves purpose to do. The particular deed may be arbitrary. But the absolute modes of activity just suggested are not arbitrary. We cannot choose to do without them, without seeking to choose, since choice is action, and involves, for instance, the aforesaid difference between affirming and denying that we mean to do thus and thus.

§ 22. Considerations of this sort show us that the Theory of Order must undertake a task which the foregoing sketch has only suggested. It now appears that the logician's world has in it *some* necessary elements and laws upon which order-systems may be founded. But this fact does not of itself suffice to tell us *what ones* amongst the enormously complicated order-systems of mathematics include contingent and arbitrary elements, and what ones are indeed in such wise necessary that whoever knows what his own orderly activity is, must recognize that these order-systems belong to his logical world. Let us illustrate the issue thus brought to our attention.

In the physical world, we meet with the difference between *greater* weights and *less* weights. We meet with this difference empirically, and test it by experiment. The result is that we get tests, such as the balance, whereby we can arrange physical weights in a series of Levels, each level consisting of observed weights any two of which are equal, while the series of these levels is determined by the transitive and totally non-symmetrical relation of greater and less. The familiar operations of putting two weights in one scale-pan of a balance and finding a single weight that, put into the other scale-pan, will balance them, enables us to define for the weights an operation of *summation*,—a *triadic relation* of weights. This operation empirically conforms to the laws of the addition of quantities. Hereupon, by processes not further to be followed in this discussion, we establish an ideal and hypothetical correlation between physical weights and the number-system of arithmetic; and so the physical world, so far as weights are concerned, is conceived in orderly terms, in a way that makes many physical theories logically possible.

Now it is obvious that the existence of physical weights, and that all of the aforegoing relations, so far as they are physical relations, are, from our human point of view, both empirical and contingent. We can easily conceive of a physical world without any such phenomena. For if all our knowledge of nature came to us through sight and smell alone, in the form of colours, odours, etc., and if we never saw anything that suggested to us the comparing of weights, we should of course know of no physical facts that would define for us this order-system.

On the other hand, in defining the system of the weights as in the case of any other extensive quantities, we use our empirical facts for the sake of establishing some kind of correlation between the quantities of our physical world and the facts and laws of the number-system. *But what shall we say about the number-system itself?* It is a system, whose first principles can be stated as hypotheses of a very general nature concerning objects that can be distinguished, numbered, etc. Is our experience of the existence of such objects althogether as contingent as our experience of the existence of weights in the physical world? One obvious answer is suggested by the fact that we can apply the system of the whole numbers to characterize our own acts. Any orderly succession of deeds in which we pass from one to the next has certain of the characters of the series of ordinal whole numbers. In any orderly activity that we begin, we have a first act followed by a second, followed by a third, and so on. It therefore may occur to our minds that our knowledge of at least the whole numbers, like our knowledge of the difference between *yes* and *no*, may be founded upon the consciousness of our own activity and some of its necessary characters. But this view, when first stated, meets with the very obvious difficulty that, during our actual human lives, we perform only at best a very limited number of distinct acts, while the whole number-series, as the mathematician conceives it is an *infinite* sequence. Furthermore, nothing about the empirical nature of our activity as human beings seems to determine the number of deeds that we shall do in our short lives. But the whole numbers of the mathematician present themselves as an order-system such that every member of the series *must* have its next successor. No mere observation of the contingent sequence of our own empirical deeds can therefore by itself warrant the necessity that the infinite sequence of the whole numbers should have a place in the logician's world at all.

Yet this consideration is, once more, only a suggestion of a difficulty, but not a decisive proof that the whole-number series is devoid of absolute necessity. For perhaps there is indeed something about the nature of our activity, in so far as it is rational,—something which necessitates a *possible* next deed after any deed that has been actually accomplished. And this possibility may prove to have something absolute about it. Such considerations deserve at least a further study.

To sum up:—The order-systems of mathematics are suggested in *some* cases by contingent empirical phenomena. In *other* aspects these order-systems may prove upon analysis to be absolutely necessary facts, in the same sense in which the existence of classes and relations of some sort are necessary facts in our world. And thus may be stated *the central problem of the Theory of Order.* This problem is:—*What are the necessary "logical entities," and what are their necessary laws? What objects must the logician's world contain? What order-systems must he conceive, not as contingent and arbitrary, but as so implied in the nature of our rational activity that the effort to remove them from our world would inevitably imply their reinstatement,* just as the effort to remove relations and classes from the world would involve recognizing both classes and relations as, in some new way, present.

It is precisely in this form that the problem of the theory of order appears to be, at the present time, undergoing a most progressive series of changes, enlargements, and enrichments. The "Deduction of the Categories" is taking on decidedly new forms in recent discussion. The principles that will enable us in the future to make an indubitable endless progress in this field at least possible, remain very briefly to be considered as our sketch closes.

§ 23. Common to all the recent logicians who have dealt seriously with the problem thus defined is the tendency to reduce all the order-systems of mathematics to a form defined, so far as possible, in terms of a *few* simple and necessary "logical entities," and "fundamental hypotheses" about relational properties and about the objects whose relations are in question.

In all the older attempts to characterize the mathematical systems of an orderly type; great stress was laid upon the assumption of so-called "self-evident" *Axioms*. The example of Euclid in his Geometry, and the Aristotelian logical theory regarding the necessity of founding all proof upon "immediate" certainties,—these were the paramount influences in determining this tendency. But the more the logician considers the so-called "self-evident" principles of the older mathematical statements, the more reason does he see to condemn self-evidence as in itself a fitting logical guide. *When we call an assertion self-evident we generally do so because we have not yet sufficiently considered the complexity of the relations involved.* And many propositions have been supposed to be self-evident truths that upon closer acquaintance have turned out to be decidedly inexact in their meaning, or altogether incorrect.

In two cases, in the foregoing discussion, we have had occasion to indicate for logical purposes how inadequate the older assumptions regarding the axioms of mathematics and other sciences have been. The first case was presented to us by the presupposition of induction, to the effect that the realm of the objects of possible experience has in any of its definable collections of fact *a determinate constitution*. In mentioning this presupposition in § 10, we stated that it is not self-evident. In § 19 this presupposition appeared in the form of the postulate: *That there are Individuals.* The substantial identity of the two postulates appears upon due reflection. But, as we remarked (in § 19), the postulate: That there are individuals, is too complex to be self-evident, although, upon the other hand, a study of the conception of an individual led us to the assertion, not very fully discussed in this sketch, that this postulate is indeed *at once pragmatic and absolute.* As we said, in our former passage, the principle in question has metaphysical aspects that cannot here be discussed.

At all events, however, we gain, and we do *not* lose, by regarding the postulate of individuality not as "self-evident" but as the expression of an extremely complex, but at the same time fundamental demand of the rational will,—a demand without which our activity becomes rationally meaningless.

The other case of a so-called "axiom" was mentioned in § 18, where we spoke of the principle: That things equal to the same thing are equal to each other. We gain instead of losing when this principle no longer seems self-evident, because we have come to observe that it involves a *synthesis* of the logically independent characters, transitivity and symmetry,—a synthesis which always needs to be justified, either by experience or by definition, or by demonstration, or finally, if that is possible, by the method which we have already applied in dealing with the concepts of class and of relation.

As a fact, therefore, most modern investigators of the Theory of Order have abandoned the view that the fundamental types of order can be defined in terms of merely "self-evident" axioms. These investigators have therefore come to be divided, largely, into two classes: (1) those who, in company with the Pragmatists, are disposed to admit a maximum of the empirical and the contingent into the theory of order; and (2) those who are disposed, like the present writer, to regard the fundamental principles of logic as sufficient to require the existence of a realm of ideal, *i.e.* of possible objects, which is infinitely rich, which contains systems such as the order-system of the numbers, and which conforms to laws that are in foundation the same as the laws to which one conforms when he distinguishes between *yes* and *no,* and when he defines the logical properties of classes and relations.

The writers of the first class would maintain, for instance, that whether or no such distinctions as that between *yes* and *no* have a necessary validity over and above that which belongs to physical objects, such systems as the *ordinal whole numbers* are simply hypothetical generalizations from experience, are empirically known to be valid so far as our process of counting extends, and are regarded in mathematics as absolute, so to speak, *by courtesy.* The field within which such logical empiricists very naturally find their most persuasive instances, is the field presented by geometrical theories. Geometry is a field in which purely logical considerations, and very highly contingent physical facts and relations, have been, in the past, brought into a most extraordinary union, which only recent research has begun to disentangle. Is Geometry at bottom a physical science? Or is it rather a branch of pure logic, the discussion of an order-system or order-systems that possess a logically ideal necessity? The modern discussion of the Principles of Geometry has indeed greatly emphasized the enormous part that a purely logical Theory of Order plays in the development of geometry. But such a theory depends after all upon assumptions. Some of these assumptions, such as the famous Euclidian postulate regarding parallels, appear to some of the writers in question to have an obviously empirical foundation, as contingent as is the physical law of gravitation, and as much subject to verifications which are only approximate as that law is.

Over against these logical empiricists there are those who, however they analyze such special cases as that of geometry, agree with Mr. Bertrand Russell (in his *Principles of Mathematics*) in viewing the pure Theory of Order as dependent upon certain "logical constants." Such "logical constants" Mr. Russell assumes to be fundamental and inevitable facts of a realistically conceived world of purely logical entities, whose relation to our will or activity Mr. Russell would indeed declare to be factitious and irrelevant. Given the "logical constants," Mr. Russell regards the order-systems as creatures of definition: although, from his point of view, definition also appears to be a process by which one reports the existence, in the logician's realm, of certain *beings*, namely, classes, relation, series, orders, of the degrees of complexity described in our foregoing sketch. The Theory of Order for Mr. Russell is the systematic characterization of these creatures of definition. It asserts that the properties of these systems follow from their definitions. And pure mathematics consists of propositions of the type "p implies q," propositions p and q being defined, in terms of the "logical constants," and *so*, that, whatever entities there be (Mr. Russell's "variables") which are defined in terms of proposition p, are also such that proposition q holds of them. In the main Mr. Russell's procedure carries out with great finish ideas already developed by the school of Peano. Mr. Russell's doctrines serve, then, as examples of logical opinions which are not, in the ordinary sense, empiristic.

But the "burning questions" already mentioned as prominent in recent logical theory have shown how difficult it is to make articulate the theory of Mr. Russell, the somewhat similar position of Frege in Germany, and the methods of the school of Peano, without making more "pressing" than ever the question as to *what* classes, series, order types, and systems are to be regarded as unquestionably existing in the world which the theory of order studies, when it abstracts from physical experience and confines itself to the entities and systems of entities which can be defined solely in terms of the "logical constants." There is no doubt of the great advance made in recent times by the writers of this school in actually working out the deductive consequences of certain postulates, when these are once used for the purpose of defining a system. And every such working out is indeed a discovery of permanent importance for the theory of order. To define, for instance, what are called ideal "space-forms," upon the basis of principles more or less similar to, or more or less general than, the postulates of Euclid, is to reach actual and positive results valid for all future Theory of Order. But as the present state of the Theory of Assemblages shows, serious doubts may rise in any one case as to whether such definitions and postulates do not involve latent contradictions, which render the theories in question inadequate to tell us what order-systems are indeed the necessary ones, and what the range of those entities is whose existence can be validated by considerations as fundamental as those which we have already used in speaking of classes and relations in general.

§ 24. One method of escape from the difficulties thus suggested is a way that, in principle, was pointed out a good many years since by an English logician, Mr. A. B. Kempe. In the year 1886, in the *Philosophical Transactions of the Royal Society*, Mr. A. B. Kempe published a memoir on the "Theory of Mathematical Form," in which, amongst other matters, he discussed the fundamental conceptions both of Symbolic logic and of Geometry. The ideas there indicated were further developed, by Mr. Kempe, in an extended paper "On the Relation between the Logical Theory of Classes and the Geometrical Theory of Points," in the *Proceedings of the London Mathematical Society* for 1890. Despite the close attention that has since then been devoted to the study of the foundations of geometry, Mr. Kempe's views have remained almost unnoticed. They concern, however, certain matters which recent research enables us to regard with increasing interest.

In 1905 the present writer published, in the *Transactions of the*

American Mathematical Society, a paper entitled "The Relation of the Principles of Logic to the Foundations of Geometry." This paper attempts (1) to show that the principles which Mr. Kempe developed can be stated in a different, and as the author believes, in a somewhat more precise way; and (2) that the principles in question, namely the principles which are involved in any account of the nature of logical classes and their relations, are capable of a restatement in terms of which we can define an extremely general order-system. This order-system is the one which Mr. Kempe had partially defined, but which the present author's paper attempted to characterize and develop in a somewhat novel way. The thesis of that paper, taken in conjunction with Mr. Kempe's results may be restated thus:—

Both classes and propositions are objects without which the logician cannot stir a step. Their relations and laws have therefore, in the foregoing sense, an absolute validity. But, if we state these relations as laws in a definite way, and if we thereupon define a further principle regarding the existence of certain logical entities which in many respects are similar to classes and propositions,—a principle not heretofore expressly considered by logicians,—we hereupon find ourselves forced to conceive the existence of a system called, in the paper of 1905, "The System Σ." *This system has an order which is determined entirely by the fundamental laws of logic, and by the one additional principle thus mentioned.* The new principle in question is precisely analogous to a principle which is fundamental in geometrical theory. This is the principle that, between any two points on a line, there is an intermediate point, so that the points on a line constitute, for geometrical theory, *at least a dense series.* In its application to the entities of pure logic this principle appears indeed at first sight to be extraneous and arbitrary. For the principle corresponding to the geometrical principle which defines dense series of points, does not apply at all to the logical world of propositions. And, again, it does not apply with *absolute* generality to the objects known as classes. But it *does* apply to a set of objects, to which in the foregoing repeated reference has been made. This set of objects may be defined as, "certain possible modes of action that are open to any rational being who can act at all, and who can also reflect upon his own modes of possible action." Such objects as "the modes of action" have never been regarded heretofore as logical entities in the sense in which classes and propositions have been so regarded. But in fact our modes of action are subject to the same general laws to which propositions and classes are subject. That is:—

(1) To any "mode of action," such as "to sing" or "singing" (expressed in English either by the infinitive or by the present participle of the verb) there corresponds a mode of action, which is the *contradictory* of the first, for example "not to sing" or "not singing." Thus, in this realm, to every x there corresponds *one*, and essentially *only* one, $\bar{x}$.

(2) Any pair of modes of action, such for instance as "singing" and "dancing," have their "logical product," precisely as classes have a product, and their "logical sum," again, precisely as the classes possess a sum. Thus the "mode of action" expressed by the phrase: "To sing and to dance" is the logical product of the "modes of action" "to sing" and "to dance." The mode of action expressed by the phrase, "Either to sing or to dance," is the logical sum of "to sing" and "to dance." These logical operations of addition and multiplication depend upon triadic relations of modes of action, precisely analogous to the triadic relation of classes. So then, to any x and y, in this realm, there correspond $x\,y$ and $x + y$.

(3) Between any two modes of action a certain dyadic, transitive and not totally non-symmetrical relation may either obtain or not obtain. This relation may be expressed by the verb "implies." It has precisely the same relational properties as the relation $-\!\!\!<$ of one class or proposition to another. Thus the mode of action expressed by the phrase, "To sing *and* to dance," *implies* the mode of action expressed by the phrase "to sing." In other words "Singing *and* dancing," implies "singing."

(4) There is a mode of action which may be symbolized by a o. This mode of action may be expressed in language by the phrase, "to do nothing," or "doing nothing." There is another mode of action which may be symbolized by 1. This is the mode of action expressed in language by the phrase "to do something," that is, to act positively in any way whatever which involves "*not doing nothing*." The modes of action o and 1 are contradictories each of the other.

In consequence of these considerations, *the modes of action are a set of entities that in any case conform to the same logical laws to which classes and propositions conform.* The so-called "Algebra of Logic" may be applied to them. A set of modes of action may therefore be viewed as a system within which the principles of logical order must be regarded as applicable.

Now it would indeed be impossible to attempt to define with any exactness "the *totality* of all possible modes of action." Such an attempt would meet with all the difficulties which the Theory of Assemblages has recently met with in its efforts to define certain extremely inclusive classes. Thus, just as "the class of all classes" has been shown by Mr. Russell to involve fairly obvious and elementary contradictions, and just as "the greatest possible cardinal number" in the Cantorian theory of cardinal numbers, and equally "the greatest possible ordinal number" have been shown to involve logical contradictions, so (and unquestionably) the concept of the "totality of all possible modes of action" involves a contradiction. There is in fact no such totality.

On the other hand, it is perfectly possible to define a certain set, or "logical universe" of modes of action such that all the members of this set are "possible modes of action," *in case* there is some rational being who is capable of performing some one single possible act, and is also capable of noting, observing, recording, in some determinate way every mode of action of which he is actually capable, and which is a mode of action whose possibility is *required* (that is, is made logically a necessary entity) by the *single* mode of action in terms of which this system of modes of action is defined. Such a special system of possible modes of action may be determined, in a precise way, by naming *some one* mode of action, which the rational being in question is supposed to be capable of conceiving, and of noting or recording in some reflective way any mode of action once viewed as possible. The result will be that any such system will possess its own logical order-type. And some such system must be recognized as belonging to the realm of genuinely valid possibilities by any one who is himself a rational being. The order-type of this system will therefore possess a genuine validity, a "logical reality," which cannot be questioned without abandoning the very conception of rational activity itself. For the question is not whether there exists any being who actually exemplifies these modes of activity in the same way in which "singing and dancing" are exemplified in our human world. The logical question is whether the special sets of modes of action whose logical existence as a set of possible modes of action is required (in case there is any one rational being who can conceive of any one mode of action), is a genuinely valid system, which as such has logical existence.

Now the logical system of such modes of action illustrates a principle, which, as just admitted, *does not apply to the Calculus of Propositions.* Nor does this principle apply, with complete generality, to the Calculus of Classes. But what we may here call the Calculus of Modes of Action, while it makes use of all the laws of the Algebra of Logic, also permits us to make use of the principle here in question, and in fact, in case a system of modes of action, such as has just been indicated, is to be defined at all, *requires* us to make use of this principle. The principle in question may be dogmatically stated thus: "If there exist two distinct modes of action p and r, such that p —< r, then there always exists a mode of action q such that p —< q —< r, while p and q are distinct modes of action and q and r are equally distinct." This principle could be otherwise stated thus "for any rational being who is able to reflect upon and to record his own modes of action, if there be given any two modes of action such that one of them implies the other, there always exists at least one determinate mode of action which is implied by the first of these modes of action and which implies the second, and which is yet distinct from both of them." That this principle holds true of the modes of action which are open to any rational being to whom any one mode of action is open, can be shown by considerations for which there is here no space, but which are of the nature heretofore repeatedly defined in this paper. For the question is not whether there actually lives any body who actually does all these things. *That,* from the nature of the case, is impossible. The question is as to the definition of a precisely definable set of modes of action. And this principle holds for the Calculus of possible modes of action, because, as can be shown, the denial of such a principle for a rational being of the type in question, would involve self-contradiction.

Now the consideration developed by Kempe, and further elaborated in the paper of 1905, before cited, may be applied, and in fact must be applied to the order-system of such a determinate realm of modes of action. Such a realm is in fact of the form of the foregoing system Σ. A comparison of Kempe's results with the newer results developed in the author's later paper would hereupon show.—

(1) That the members, elements, or "modes of action" which

constitute this logically necessary system Σ exist in sets both finite and infinite in number, and both in "dense" series, in "continuous" series, and in fact in all possible serial types.

(2) That such systems as the whole number series, the series of the rational numbers, the real numbers, etc., consequently enter into the constitution of this system. The arithmetical continuum, for instance, is a part of the system Σ.

(3) That this system also includes in its complexities all the types of order which appear to be required by the at present recognized geometrical theories, projective and metrical.

(4) That the relations amongst the logical entities in question, namely the *modes of action*, of which this system Σ is composed, are not only dyadic, but in many cases polyadic in the most various way. Kempe, in fact, shows with great definiteness that the triadic relations of ordinary logic, which are used in defining "sums" and "products," are really dependent upon tetradic relations into which 0 or 1, one or both may enter. In addition to these tetradic relations the logical order-system also depends for some of its most remarkable properties upon a totally symmetrical tetradic relation that, in the sense described in § 18, is transitive by pairs. These special features of the system of logical entities are here mentioned for the sake of merely hinting how enormously complex this order-system is. The matter here cannot be further discussed in its technical details. The result of these considerations is *that it at present appears to be possible to define, upon the basis of purely logical relations, and upon the basis of the aforegoing principles concerning rational activity, an order-system of entities inclusive not only of objects having the relation of the number system, but also of objects illustrating the geometrical types of order, and thus apparently including all the order-systems upon which, at least at present, the theoretical natural sciences depend for the success of their deductions.*

And so much must here serve as a bare indication of the problems of the Theory of Order, problems which, at the present day, are rapidly undergoing reconsideration and which form an inexhaustible topic for future research. Of the fundamental philosophical importance of such problems no student of the Categories, no one who understands the significance of Kant's great undertaking, no one who takes Truth seriously, ought to be in doubt. The Theory of Order will be a fundamental science in the philosophy of the future.

Moral and
Religious Experience

Part VII

Moral and Religious Experience

With regard to the problem of evil, Royce was assuredly no polly-anna. In his essay on "The Problem of Job."* he separates himself from that brand of "false idealism," which regards evil as "merely an illusion." (*SGE*, p. 17; below, 2:845.) Over against such an abstract and insensitive view, Royce makes his own position quite clear. "I regard evil as a distinctly real fact, a fact just as real as the most helpless and hopeless sufferer finds it to be when he is in pain." (*SGE*, p. 16; below, 2:845.)

Royce, of course, was no stranger to pain, having undergone a series of personal misfortunes.[1] His colleague of many years, George Herbert Palmer, once said of Royce that "to his happy home came many sorrows, 'afflictions sorted, anguish of all sizes.' "[2] In the presence of such experience, the task of man is to work it through, to idealize his situation and become a creative factor in the life of the universe. This is the "religious mission of sorrow."

Royce does not have, however, an orthodox approach to the problem of evil.

Here is our problem. And it is a hard one. In brief, as you may say, religion must take its choice. Either the evil in the world is of no great importance, and then religion is useless; or the need of salvation is great, and the way is straight and narrow; and then evil is deeply rooted in the very nature of reality, and religion seems a failure. (*SRI*, p. 227; below, 2:1047.)

[1] Royce's personal life is still considerably shrouded but it is known that his trip to Australia in 1888 was precipitated by a severe emotional depression, for his head "had broken down with too much work." See Ralph Barton Perry, *The Thought and Character of William James* (Boston: Little, Brown and Co., 1935) 1:800.

[2] George Herbert Palmer, "Josiah Royce," in *Contemporary Idealism in America* (New York: Macmillan Co., 1932), p. 9.

Royce's attempt to avoid this dilemma reveals still another way in which he articulates the relationship between the "Absolute and the Individual." In order to deal with the moral and religious dimensions of this problem, Royce forged a powerful perspective from which to proceed, the philosophy of loyalty. *"In loyalty, when loyalty is properly defined, is the fulfillment of the whole moral law."* (PL, p. 15; below, 2:860.) His preliminary definition of loyalty is quite simple and obvious: *"The willing and practical and thoroughgoing devotion of a person to a cause."* (PL, pp. 16–17; below, 2:861.) Royce's concluding definition, however, is more formidable: *"Loyalty is the will to manifest, so far as is possible, the Eternal, that is, the conscious and superhuman unity of life, in the form of the acts of an individual Self."* (PL, p. 357; below, 2:996.)

Given such a context, the struggle—the commitment—is all important, whereas the nature of the cause less so. Royce, of course, was severely criticized for this view, in that it seemed to preach indifference as to the quality of the task undertaken. His response to this and other objections seems weak and not to the point (e.g., PL, pp. 59–70; below, 2:877–82). In several instances Royce merely shows that loyalty is assumed by the nature of the objections. Royce's approach here is reminiscent of James's effort to rebuke the critics of his *Pragmatism*, who accused him of a crass acceptance of expediency in place of a theory of truth. James attempted to answer his critics on their own terms, as if his *Pragmatism* could be separated from a life-long endeavor to rework in radical terms a metaphysical statement of human behavior. So too with Royce. How can one take seriously the objection that Royce doesn't distinguish between good and evil causes? In order to respond adequately to this objection, Royce would have to make visible the central contentions of his metaphysics. In this way, Royce would maintain that all human *activity*, however fragmentary or, within limits of our perspective, disposed to evil, can conceivably be shown to participate in the fullness of being. On logical as well as metaphysical grounds, Royce would disagree with James that "separateness" is to be experienced to the very end. Although Royce would admit that our awareness is blocked by "human narrowness and the vicissitudes of the world of time," he would also hold that *"all the loyal, whether they individually know the fact or not, are, and in all times have been, one genuine and religious brotherhood."* (SRI, pp. 279, 280).

The dilemma posed earlier, relative to the role of religion, is therefore restated, rather than solved. Religion should not be asked to fulfill an explanatory purpose, particularly with regard to the problem of evil. "The world is infinite. With our present view we could not expect to grasp directly the unity of its meaning." (*SRI*, p. 237; below, 2:1053.) In addition to those inexplicable evils which we wish to destroy, as physical anguish, pestilence and oppression, Royce points also to those "ills" which upon confrontation involve us in growth. "Such ills we remove only in so far as we assimilate them, idealise them, take them up into the plan of our lives, give them meaning, set them in their place in the whole." (*SRI*, p. 235; below, 2:1052.) This process provides sources of religious insight and engenders a sense of salvation, for out of evil we are able to bring good. Royce, however, insists that such insight and personal growth does *not* enable us to understand the "countless and terrible ills" which afflict us at every turn for no apparent redeeming reason. Through "loyal endeavor" and "religious insight," we gather but a hint of "larger spiritual processes," which may, if known, account for all of our suffering. Royce has no illusions about the ultimate explanatory character of our religious insight. A close reading of "The Religious Meaning of Sorrow,"* will reveal Royce as extremely sensitive to the opaque quality of much of our suffering, as undergone from our point of view. In the midst of Royce's complex argumentation, we should not forget that at the heart of his moral and religious thought is a request for a change in attitude, nothing less than a "conversion." Invoking William James, Royce tells us that in its metaphysical form *"Loyalty is the Will to Believe in something eternal, and to express that belief in the practical life of a human being."* (*PL*, p. 357; below, 2:997.)

28

The Problem of Job

In speaking of the problem of Job, the present writer comes to the subject as a layman in theology, and as one ignorant of Hebrew scholarship. In referring to the original core of the Book of Job he follows, in a general way, the advice of Professor C. H. Toy; and concerning the text of the poem he is guided by the translation of Dr. Gilbert. What this paper has to attempt is neither criticism of the book, nor philological exposition of its obscurities, but a brief study of the central problem of the poem from the point of view of a student of philosophy.

The problem of our book is the personal problem of its hero, Job himself. Discarding, for the first, as of possibly separate authorship, the Prologue, the Epilogue and the addresses of Elihu and of the Lord, one may as well come at once to the point of view of Job, as expressed in his speeches to his friends. Here is stated the problem of which none of the later additions in our poem offer any intelligible solution. In the exposition of this problem the original author develops all his poetical skill, and records thoughts that can never grow old. This is the portion of our book which is most frequently quoted and which best expresses the genuine experience of suffering humanity. Here, then, the philosophical as well as the human interest of our poem centres.

[Reprinted from *SGE*, pp. 1–28.]

I

Job's world, as he sees it, is organized in a fashion extremely familiar to us all. The main ideas of this cosmology are easy to be reviewed. The very simplicity of the scheme of the universe here involved serves to bring into clearer view the mystery and horror of the problem that besets Job himself. The world, for Job, is the work of a being who, in the very nature of the case, ought to be intelligible (since he is wise), and friendly to the righteous, since, according to tradition, and by virtue of his divine wisdom itself, this God must know the value of a righteous man. But—here is the mystery—this God, as his works get known through our human experiences of evil, appears to us not friendly, but hopelessly foreign and hostile in his plans and his doings. The more, too, we study his ways with man, the less intelligible seems his nature. Tradition has dwelt upon his righteousness, has called him merciful, has magnified his love towards his servants, has described his justice in bringing to naught the wicked. One has learned to trust all these things, to conceive God in these terms, and to expect all this righteous government from him. Moreover, tradition joins with the pious observation of nature in assuring us of the omnipotence of God. Job himself pathetically insists that he never doubts, for an instant, God's power to do whatever in heaven or earth he may please to do. Nothing hinders God. No blind faith thwarts him. Sheol is naked before him. The abyss has no covering. The earth hangs over chaos because he orders it to do so. His power shatters the monsters and pierces the dragons. He can, then, do with evil precisely what he does with Rahab or with the shades, with the clouds or with the light or with the sea, namely, exactly what he chooses. Moreover, since he knows everything, and since the actual value of a righteous man is, for Job, an unquestionable and objective fact, God cannot fail to know this real worth of righteousness in his servants, as well as the real hatefulness and mischief of the wicked. God knows worth, and cannot be blind to it, since it is as real a fact as heaven and earth themselves.

Yet despite all these unquestioned facts, this God, who can do just what he chooses, "deprives of right" the righteous man, in Job's own case, and "vexes his soul," becomes towards him as a "tyrant," "persecutes" him "with strong hand," "dissolves" him "into storm," makes him a "byword" for outcasts, "casts" him "into the mire," renders him "a brother to jackals," deprives him of the poor joy

of his "one day as a hireling," of the little delight that might come
to him as a man before he descends hopelessly to the dark world of
the shades, "watches over" him by day to oppress, by night to
"terrify" him "with dreams and with visions"—in brief, acts as his
enemy, "tears" him "in anger," "gnashes upon" him "with his teeth."
All these are the expressions of Job himself. On the other hand, as,
with equal wonder and horror the righteous Job reports, God on
occasion does just the reverse of all this to the notoriously and deliberately wicked, who "grow old," "wax mighty in power," "see
their offspring established," and their homes "secure from fear."
If one turns from this view of God's especially unjust dealings with
righteous and with wicked individuals to a general survey of his
providential government of the world, one sees vast processes going
on, as ingenious as they are merciless, as full of hints of a majestic
wisdom as they are of indifference to every individual right.

> A mountain that falleth is shattered,
> And a rock is removed from its place;
> The waters do wear away stones,
> Its floods sweep the earth's dust away;
> And the hope of frail man thou destroyest.
> Thou subdu'st him for aye, and he goes;
> Marring his face thou rejectest him.

Here is a mere outline of the divine government as Job sees it. To
express himself thus is for Job no momentary outburst of passion.
Long days and nights he has brooded over these bitter facts of
experience, before he has spoken at all. Unweariedly, in presence of
his friends' objections, he reiterates his charges. He has the right
of the sufferer to speak, and he uses it. He reports the facts that he
sees. Of the paradox involved in all this he can make nothing. What
is clear to him, however, is that this paradox is a matter for reasoning,
not for blind authority. God ought to meet him face to face, and
have the matter out in plain words. Job fears not to face his judge,
or to demand his answer from God. God knows that Job has done
nothing to deserve this fury. The question at issue between maker
and creature is therefore one that demands a direct statement and a
clear decision. "Why, since you can do precisely as you choose,
and since you know, as all-knower, the value of a righteous servant,
do you choose, as enemy, to persecute the righteous with this fury
and persistence of hate?" Here is the problem.

The human interest of the issue thus so clearly stated by Job lies, of course, in the universality of just such experiences of undeserved ill here upon earth. What Job saw of evil we can see ourselves to-day whenever we choose. Witness Armenia. Witness the tornadoes and the earthquakes. Less interesting to us is the thesis mentioned by Job's friends, in the antiquated form in which they state it, although to be sure, a similar thesis, in altered forms, is prevalent among us still. And of dramatic significance only is the earnestness with which Job defends his own personal righteousness. So naïve a self-assurance as is his is not in accordance with our modern conscience, and it is seldom indeed that our day would see any man sincerely using this phraseology of Job regarding his own consciousness of rectitude. But what is to-day as fresh and real to us as it was to our poet is the fact that all about us, say in every child born with an unearned heredity of misery, or in every pang of the oppressed, or in every arbitrary coming of ill fortune, some form of innocence is beset with an evil that the sufferer has not deserved. Job wins dramatic sympathy as an extreme, but for the purpose all the more typical, case of this universal experience of unearned ill fortune. In every such case we therefore still have the interest that Job had in demanding the solution of this central problem of evil. Herein, I need not say, lies the permanent significance of the problem of Job,—a problem that wholly outlasts any ancient Jewish controversy as to the question whether the divine justice always does or does not act as Job's friends, in their devotion to tradition, declare that it acts. Here, then, is the point where our poem touches a question, not merely of an older religion, but of philosophy, and of all time.

II

The general problem of evil has received, as is well known, a great deal of attention from the philosophers. Few of them, at least in European thought, have been as fearless in stating the issue as was the original author of Job. The solutions offered have, however, been very numerous. For our purposes they may be reduced to a few.

First, then, one may escape Job's paradox by declining altogether to view the world in teleological terms. Evils, such as death, disease, tempests, enemies, fires, are not, so one may declare, the works of

God or of Satan, but are natural phenomena. Natural, too, are the phenomena of our desires, of our pains, sorrows and failures. No divine purpose rules or overrules any of these things. That happens to us, at any time, which must happen, in view of our natural limitations and of our ignorance. The way to better things is to understand nature better than we now do. For this view—a view often maintained in our day—there is no problem of evil, in Job's sense, at all. Evil there indeed is, but the only rational problems are those of natural laws. I need not here further consider this method, not of solving but of abolishing the problem before us, since my intent is, in this paper, to suggest the possibility of some genuinely teleological answer to Job's question. I mention this first view only to recognize, historically, its existence.

In the second place, one may deal with our problem by attempting any one, or a number, of those familiar and popular compromises between the belief in a world of natural law and the belief in teleological order, which are all, as compromises, reducible to the assertion that the presence of evil in the creation is a relatively insignificant, and an inevitable, incident of a plan that produces sentient creatures subject to law. Writers who expound such compromises have to point out that, since a burnt child dreads the fire, pain is, on the whole, useful as a warning. Evil is a transient discipline, whereby finite creatures learn their place in the system of things. Again, a sentient world cannot get on without some experience of suffering, since sentience means tenderness. Take away pain (so one still again often insists), take away pain, and we should not learn our share of natural truth. Pain is the pedagogue to teach us natural science. The contagious diseases, for instance, are useful in so far as they lead us in the end to study Bacteriology, and thus to get an insight into the life of certain beautiful creatures of God whose presence in the world we should otherwise blindly overlook! Moreover (to pass to still another variation of this sort of explanation), created beings obviously grow from less to more. First the lower, then the higher. Otherwise there could be no Evolution. And were there no evolution, how much of edifying natural science we should miss! But if one is evolved, if one grows from less to more, there must be something to mark the stages of growth. Now evil is useful to mark the lower stages of evolution. If you are to be, first an infant, then a man, or first a savage, then a civilized being, there must be evils attendant upon the earlier stages of your life—evils that make growth welcome and conscious. Thus, were there no colic and croup, were there no tumbles and crying-spells in infancy, there would be no sufficient incentives to loving parents to hasten the growing robustness of their children, and no motives to impel the children to long to grow big! Just so, cannibalism is valuable as a mark of a lower grade of evolution. Had there been no cannibalism we should realize less joyously than we do what a respectable thing it is to have become civilized! In brief, evil is, as it were, the dirt of the natural order, whose value is that, when you wash it off, you thereby learn the charm of the bath of evolution.

The foregoing are mere hints of familiar methods of playing about the edges of our problem, as children play barefoot in the shallowest reaches of the foam of the sea. In our poem, as Professor Toy expounds it, the speeches ascribed to Elihu contain the most hints of some such way of defining evil, as a merely transient incident of the discipline of the individual. With many writers explanations of this sort fill much space. They are even not without their proper place in popular discussion. But they have no interest for whoever has once come into the presence of Job's problem as it is in itself. A moment's thought reminds us of their superficiality. Pain is useful as a warning of danger. If we did not suffer, we should burn our hands off. Yes, but this explanation of one evil presupposes another, and a still unexplained and greater evil, namely, the existence of the danger of which we need to be thus warned. No doubt it is well that the past sufferings of the Armenians should teach the survivors, say the defenseless women and children, to have a wholesome fear in future of Turks. Does that explain, however, the need for the existence, or for the murderous doings of the Turks? If I can only reach a given goal by passing over a given road, say of evolution, it may be well for me to consent to the toilsome journey. Does that explain why I was created so far from my goal? Discipline, toil, penalty, surgery, are all explicable as means to ends, if only it be presupposed that there exists, and that there is quite otherwise explicable, the necessity for the situations which involve such fear-ful expenses. One justifies the surgery, but not the disease; the toil, but not the existence of the need for the toil; the penalty, but not the situation which has made the penalty necessary, when one points out that evil is in so many cases medicinal or disciplinary or prophy-lactic—an incident of imperfect stages of evolution, or the price of a distant good attained through misery. All such explanations, I insist, trade upon borrowed capital. But God, by hypothesis, is no borrower. He produces his own capital of ends and means. Every evil is explained on the foregoing plan only by presupposing at least an equal, and often a greater and a preëxistent evil, namely, the very state of things which renders the first evil the only physically possible way of reaching a given goal. But what Job wants his judge to explain is not that evil A is a physical means of warding off some other greater evil B, in this cruel world where the waters wear away even the stones, and where hopes of man are so much frailer than the stones; but why a God who can do whatever he wishes chooses situations where such a heaped-up mass of evil means become what we should call physical necessities to the ends now physically possible.

No real explanation of the presence of evil can succeed which declares evil to be a merely physical necessity for one who desires, in this present world, to reach a given goal. Job's business is not with physical accidents, but with the God who chose to make this present nature; and an answer to Job must show that evil is not a physical but a logical necessity—something whose non-existence would simply contradict the very essence, the very perfection of God's own nature and power. This talk of medicinal and disciplinary evil, perfectly fair when applied to our poor fate-bound human surgeons, judges, jailors, or teachers, becomes cruelly, even cynically trivial when applied to explain the ways of a God who is to choose, not only the physical means to an end, but the very *Physis* itself in which path and goal are to exist together. I confess, as a layman, that whenever, at a funeral, in the company of mourners who are immediately facing Job's own personal problem, and who are sometimes, to say the least, wide enough awake to desire not to be stayed with relative comforts, but to ask that terrible and uttermost question of God himself, and to require the direct answer—that whenever, I say, in such company I have to listen to these half-way answers, to these superficial plashes in the wavelets at the water's edge of sorrow, while the black, unfathomed ocean of finite evil spreads out before our wide-opened eyes—well, at such times this trivial speech about useful burns and salutary medicines makes me, and I fancy others, simply and wearily heartsick. Some words are due to children at school, to peevish patients in the sickroom who need a little temporary quieting. But quite other speech is due to men and women when they are wakened to the higher reason of

Job by the fierce anguish of our mortal life's ultimate facts. They deserve either our simple silence, or, if we are ready to speak, the speech of people who ourselves inquire as Job inquired.

III

A third method of dealing with our problem is in essence identical with the course which, in a very antiquated form, the friends of Job adopt. This method takes its best known expression in the doctrine that the presence of evil in the world is explained by the fact that the value of free will in moral agents logically involves, and so explains and justifies, the divine permission of the evil deeds of those finite beings who freely choose to sin, as well as the inevitable fruits of the sins. God creates agents with free will. He does so because the existence of such agents has of itself an infinite worth. Were there no free agents, the highest good could not be. But such agents, because they are free, can offend. The divine justice of necessity pursues such offenses with attendant evils. These evils, the result of sin, must, logically speaking, be permitted to exist, if God once creates the agents who have free will, and himself remains, as he must logically do, a just God. How much ill thus results depends upon the choice of the free agents, not upon God, who wills to have only good chosen, but of necessity must leave his free creatures to their own devices, so far as concerns their power to sin.

This view has the advantage of undertaking to regard evil as a logically necessary part of a perfect moral order, and not as a mere incident of an imperfectly adjusted physical mechanism. So dignified a doctrine, by virtue of its long history and its high theological reputation, needs here no extended exposition. I assume it as familiar, and pass at once to its difficulties. It has its share of truth. There is, I doubt not, moral free will in the universe. But the presence of evil in the world simply cannot be explained by free will alone. This is easy to show. One who maintains this view asserts, in substance, "All real evils are the results of the acts of free and finite moral agents." These agents may be angels or men. If there is evil in the city, the Lord has *not* done it, except in so far as his justice has acted in readjusting wrongs already done. Such ill is due to the deeds of his creatures. But hereupon one asks at once, in presence of any ill, "Who did this?" Job's friends answer: "The sufferer himself; his deed wrought his own undoing. God punishes only the sinner. Every one suffers for his own wrongdoing. Your ill is the result of your crime."

But Job, and all his defenders of innocence, must at once reply: "Empirically speaking, this is obviously, in our visible world, simply not true. The sufferer may suffer innocently. The ill is often undeserved. The fathers sin; the child, diseased from birth, degraded, or a born wretch, may pay the penalty. The Turk or the active rebel sins. Armenia's helpless women and babes cry in vain unto God for help."

Hereupon the reply comes, although not indeed from Job's friends: "Alas! it is so. Sin means suffering; but the innocent may suffer *for* the guilty. This, to be sure, is God's way. One cannot help it. It is so." But therewith the whole effort to explain evil as a logically necessary result of free will and of divine justice alone is simply abandoned. The unearned ills are not justly due to the free will that indeed partly caused them, but to God who declines to protect the innocent. God owes the Turk and the rebel their due. He also owes to his innocent creatures, the babes and the women, his shelter. He owes to the sinning father his penalty, but to the son, born in our visible world a lost soul from the womb, God owes the shelter of his almighty wing, and no penalty. Thus Job's cry is once more in place. The ways of God are not thus justified.

But the partisan of free will as the true explanation of ill may reiterate his view in a new form. He may insist that we see but a fragment. Perhaps the soul born here as if lost, or the wretch doomed to pangs now unearned, sinned of old, in some previous state of existence. Perhaps Karma is to blame. You expiate to-day the sins of your own former existences. Thus the Hindoos varied the theme of our familiar doctrine. This is what Hindoo friends might have said to Job. Well, admit even that, if you like; and what then follows? Admit that here or in former ages the free deed of every present sufferer earned as its penalty every ill, physical or moral, that appears as besetting just this sufferer to-day. Admit that, and what logically follows? It follows, so I must insist, that the moral world itself, which this free-will theory of the source of evil, thus abstractly stated, was to save, is destroyed in its very heart and centre.

For consider. A suffers ill. B sees A suffering. Can B, the onlooker, help his suffering neighbor, A? Can he comfort him in any true way? No, a miserable comforter must B prove, like Job's friends, so long as B, believing in our present hypothesis, clings strictly to the logic of this abstract free-will explanation of the origin of evil. To A he says: "Well, you suffer for your own ill-doing. I therefore simply cannot relieve you. This is God's world of justice. If I tried to hinder God's justice from working in your case, I should at best only postpone your evil day. It would come, for God is just. You are hungry, thirsty, naked, sick, in prison. What can I do about it? All this is your own deed come back to you. God himself, although justly punishing, is not the author of evil. You are the sole originator of the ill." "Ah!" so A may cry out, "but can you not give me light, insight, instruction, sympathy? Can you not at least teach me to become good?" "No," B must reply, if he is a logical believer in the sole efficacy of the private free will of each finite agent as the one source, under the divine justice, of that agent's ill: "No, if you deserved light or any other comfort, God, being just, would enlighten you himself, even if I absolutely refused. But if you do not deserve light, I should preach to you in vain, for God's justice would harden your heart against any such good fortune as I could offer you from without, even if I spoke with the tongues of men and of angels. Your free will is yours. No deed of mine could give you a good free will, for what I gave you from without would not be *your* free will at all. Nor can any one but you cause your free will to be this or that. A great gulf is fixed between us. You and I, as sovereign free agents, live in God's holy world in sin-tight compartments and in evil-tight compartments too. I cannot hurt you, nor you me. You are damned for your own sins, while all that I can do is to look out for my own salvation." This, I say, is the logically inevitable result of asserting that every ill, physical or moral, that can happen to any agent, is solely the result of that agent's own free will acting under the government of the divine justice. The only possible consequence would indeed be that we live, every soul of us, in separate, as it were absolutely fire-proof, free-will compartments, so that real coöperation as to good and ill is excluded. What more cynical denial of the reality of any sort of moral world could be imagined than is involved in this horrible thesis, which no sane partisan of the abstract and traditional free-will explanation of the source of evil will to-day maintain, precisely because no such partisan really knows or can know what his doctrine logically means, while still continuing to maintain it. Yet whenever one asserts with pious obscurity, that "No harm can come to the righteous," one in fact implies, with logical necessity, just this cynical consequence.

IV

There remains a fourth doctrine as to our problem. This doctrine is in essence the thesis of philosophical idealism, a thesis which I myself feel bound to maintain, and, so far as space here permits, to explain. The theoretical basis of this view, the philosophical reasons for the notion of the divine nature which it implies, I cannot here explain. That is another argument. But I desire to indicate how the view in question deals with Job's problem.

This view first frankly admits that Job's problem is, upon Job's presuppositions, simply and absolutely insoluble. Grant Job's own presupposition that God is a being other than this world, that he is its external creator and ruler, and then all solutions fail. God is then either cruel or helpless, as regards all real finite ill of the sort that Job endures. Job, moreover, is right in demanding a reasonable answer to his question. The only possible answer is, however, one that undertakes to develop what I hold to be the immortal soul of the doctrine of the divine atonement. The answer to Job is: God is not in ultimate essence another being than yourself. He is the Absolute Being. You truly are one with God, part of his life. He is the very soul of your soul. And so, here is the first truth: When you suffer, *your sufferings are God's sufferings*, not his external work, not his external penalty, not the fruit of his neglect, but identically his own personal woe. In you God himself suffers, precisely as you do, and has all your concern in overcoming this grief.

The true question then is: Why does God thus suffer? The sole possible, necessary, and sufficient answer is, Because without suffering, without ill, without woe, evil, tragedy, God's life could not be perfected. This grief is not a physical means to an external end. It is a logically necessary and eternal constituent of the divine life. It is logically necessary that the Captain of your salvation should be perfect through suffering. No outer nature compels him. He chooses this because he chooses his own perfect selfhood. He is perfect. His world is the best possible world. Yet all its finite regions know not only of joy but of defeat and sorrow, for thus alone, in the completeness of his eternity, can God in his wholeness be triumphantly perfect.

This, I say, is my thesis. In the absolute oneness of God with the sufferer, in the concept of the suffering and therefore triumphant God, lies the logical solution of the problem of evil. The doctrine of philosophical idealism is, as regards its purely theoretical aspects, a fairly familiar metaphysical theory at the present time. One may, then, presuppose here as known the fact that, for reasons which I have not now to expound, the idealist maintains that there is in the universe but one perfectly real being, namely, the Absolute, that the Absolute is self-conscious, and that his world is essentially in its wholeness the fulfillment *in actu* of an all-perfect ideal. We ourselves exist as fragments of the absolute life, or better, as partial functions in the unity of the absolute and conscious process of the world. On the other hand, our existence and our individuality are not illusory, but are what they are in an organic unity with the whole life of the Absolute Being. This doctrine once presupposed, our present task is to inquire what case idealism can make for the thesis just indicated as its answer to Job's problem.

In endeavoring to grapple with the theoretical problem of the place of evil in a world that, on the whole, is to be conceived, not only as good, but as perfect, there is happily one essentially decisive consideration concerning good and evil which falls directly within the scope of our own human experience, and which concerns matters at once familiar and momentous as well as too much neglected in philosophy. When we use such words as good, evil, perfect, we easily deceive ourselves by the merely abstract meanings which we associate with each of the terms taken apart from the other. We forget the experiences from which the words have been abstracted. To these experiences we must return whenever we want really to comprehend the words. If we take the mere words, in their abstraction, it is easy to say, for instance, that if life has any evil in it at all, it must needs not be so perfect as life would be were there no evil in it whatever. Just so, speaking abstractly, it is easy to say that, in estimating life, one has to set the good over against the evil, and to compare their respective sums. It is easy to declare that, since we hate evil, wherever and just so far as we recognize it, our sole human interest in the world must be furthered by the removal of evil from the world. And thus viewing the case, one readily comes to say that if God views as not only good but perfect a world in which we find so much evil, the divine point of view must be very foreign to ours, so that Job's rebellious pessimism seems well in order, and Prometheus appears to defy the world-ruler in a genuinely humane spirit. Shocked, however, by the apparent impiety of this result, some teachers, considering divine matters, still misled by the same one-sided use of words, have opposed one falsely abstract view by another, and have strangely asserted that the solution must be in proclaiming that since God's world, the real world, in order to be perfect, must be without evil, what we men call evil must be a mere illusion—a mirage of the human point of view—a dark vision which God, who sees all truth, sees not at all. To God, so this view asserts, the eternal world in its wholeness is not only perfect, but has merely the perfection of an utterly transparent crystal, unstained by any color of ill. Only mortal error imagines that there is any evil. There is no evil but only good in the real world, and that is why God finds the world perfect, whatever mortals dream.

Now neither of these abstract views is my view. I consider them both the result of a thoughtless trust in abstract words. I regard evil as a distinctly real fact, a fact just as real as the most helpless and hopeless sufferer finds it to be when he is in pain. Furthermore, I hold that God's point of view is not foreign to ours. I hold that God willingly, freely, and consciously suffers in us when we suffer, and that our grief is his. And despite all this I maintain that the world from God's point of view fulfills the divine ideal and is perfect. And I hold that when we abandon the one-sided abstract ideas which the words good, evil, and perfect suggest, and when we go back to the concrete experiences upon which these very words are founded, we can see, even within the limits of our own experience, facts which make these very paradoxes perfectly intelligible, and even commonplace.

As for that essentially pernicious view, nowadays somewhat current amongst a certain class of gentle but inconsequent people— the view that all evil is *merely* an illusion and that there is no such thing in God's world—I can say of it only in passing that it is often advanced as an idealistic view, but that, in my opinion, it is false idealism. Good idealism it is to regard all finite experience as an appearance, a hint, often a very poor hint, of deeper truth. Good idealism it is to admit that man can err about truth that lies beyond his finite range of experience. And very good idealism it is to assert that all truth, and so all finite experience, exists in and for the mind of God, and nowhere outside of or apart from God. But it is not good idealism to assert that any facts which fall within the range of finite experience are, even while they are experienced, mere illusions. God's truth is inclusive, not exclusive. What you experience God experiences. The difference lies only in this, that God sees in unity what you see in fragments. For the rest, if one said, "The source and seat of evil is only the error of mortal mind," one would but have changed the name of one's problem. If the evil were but the error, the error would still be the evil, and altering the name would not have diminished the horror of the evil of this finite world.

V

But I hasten from the false idealism to the true; from the abstractions to the enlightening insights of our life. As a fact, idealism does not say: The finite world is, as such, a mere illusion. A sound idealism says, whatever we experience is a fragment, and, as far as it goes, a genuine fragment of the truth of the divine mind. With this principle before us, let us consider directly our own experiences of good and of evil, to see whether they are abstractly opposed to each other as the mere words often suggest. We must begin with the elementary and even trivial facts. We shall soon come to something deeper.

By good, as we mortals experience it, we mean something that, when it comes or is expected, we actively welcome, try to attain or keep, and regard with content. By evil in general, as it is in our experience, we mean whatever we find in any sense repugnant and intolerable. I use the words repugnant and intolerable because I wish to indicate that words for evil frequently, like the words for good, directly refer to our actions as such. Commonly and rightly, when we speak of evil, we make reference to acts of resistance, of struggle, of shrinking, of flight, of removal of ourselves from a source of mischief—acts which not only follow upon the experience of evil, but which serve to define in a useful fashion what we mean by evil. The opposing acts of pursuit and of welcome define what we mean by good. By the evil which we experience we mean precisely whatever we regard as something to be gotten rid of, shrunken from, put out of sight, of hearing, or of memory, eschewed, expelled, assailed, or otherwise directly or indirectly resisted. By good we mean whatever we regard as something to be welcomed, pursued, won, grasped, held, persisted in, preserved. And we show all this in our acts in presence of any grade of good or evil, sensuous, æsthetic, ideal, moral. To shun, to flee, to resist, to destroy, these are our primary attitudes towards ill; the opposing acts are our primary attitudes towards the good; and whether you regard us as animals or as moralists, whether it is a sweet taste, a poem, a virtue, or God that we look to as good, and whether it is a burn or a temptation, an outward physical foe, or a stealthy, inward, ideal enemy, that we regard as evil. In all our organs of voluntary movement, in all our deeds, in a turn of the eye, in a sigh, a groan, in a hostile gesture, in an act of silent contempt, we can show in endlessly varied ways the same general attitude of repugnance.

But man is a very complex creature. He has many organs. He performs many acts at once, and he experiences his performance of these acts in one highly complex life of consciousness. As the next feature of his life we all observe that he can at the same time shun one object and grasp at another. In this way he can have at once present to him a consciousness of good and a consciousness of ill. But so far in our account these sorts of experience appear merely as facts side by side. Man loves, and he *also* hates, loves this, and hates that, assumes an attitude of repugnance towards one object, while he welcomes another. So far the usual theory follows man's life, and calls it an experience of good and ill as mingled but exclusively and abstractly opposed facts. For such a view the final question as to the worth of a man's life is merely the question whether there are more intense acts of satisfaction and of welcome than of repugnance and disdain in his conscious life.

But this is by no means an adequate notion of the complexity of man's life, even as an animal. If every conscious act of hindrance, of thwarting, of repugnance, means just in so far an awareness of some evil, it is noteworthy that men can have and can show just such tendencies, not only towards external experiences, but towards their own acts. That is, men can be seen trying to thwart and to hinder even their own acts themselves, at the very moment when they note the occurrence of these acts. One can consciously have an impulse to do something, and at that very moment a conscious disposition to hinder or to thwart as an evil that very impulse. If, on the other hand, every conscious act of attainment, of pursuit, of reinforcement, involves the awareness of some good, it is equally obvious that one can show by one's acts a disposition to reinforce or to emphasize or to increase, not only the externally present gifts of fortune, but also one's own deeds, in so far as one observes them. And in our complex lives it is common enough to find ourselves actually trying to reinforce and to insist upon a situation which involves for us, even at the moment of its occurrence, a great deal of repugnance. In such cases we often act as if we felt the very thwarting of our own primary impulses to be so much of a conscious good that we persist in pursuing and reinforcing the very situation in which this thwarting and hindering of our own impulses is sure to arise.

In brief, as phenomena of this kind show, man is a being who can to a very great extent find a sort of secondary satisfaction in the very act of thwarting his own desires, and thus of assuring for the time his own dissatisfactions. On the other hand, man can to an indefinite degree find himself dissatisfied with his satisfactions and disposed to thwart, not merely his external enemies, but his own inmost impulses themselves. But I now affirm that in all such cases you cannot simply say that man is preferring the less of two evils, or the greater of two goods, as if the good and the evil stood merely side by side in his experience. On the contrary, in such cases, man is not merely setting his acts or his estimates of good and evil side by side and taking the sum of each; but he is making his own relatively primary acts, impulses, desires, the objects of all sorts of secondary impulses, desires, and reflective observations. His whole inner state is one of tension; and he is either making a secondary experience of evil out of his estimate of a primary experience of good, as is the case when he at once finds himself disposed to pursue a given good and to thwart this pursuit as being an evil pursuit; or else he is making a secondary experience of good out of his primary experience of evil, as when he is primarily dissatisfied with his situation, but yet secondarily regards this very dissatisfaction as itself a desirable state. In this way man comes not only to love some things and also to hate other things, he comes to love his own hates and to hate his own loves in an endlessly complex hierarchy of superposed interests in his own interests.

Now it is easy to say that such states of inner tension, where our conscious lives are full of a warfare of the self with itself, are contradictory or absurd states. But it is easy to say this only when you dwell on the words and fail to observe the facts of experience. As a fact, not only our lowest but our highest states of activity are the ones which are fullest of this crossing, conflict, and complex interrelation of loves and hates, of attractions and repugnances. As a merely physiological fact, we begin no muscular act without at the same time initiating acts which involve the innervation of opposing sets of muscles, and these opposing sets of muscles hinder each other's freedom. Every sort of control of movement means the conflicting play of opposed muscular impulses. We do nothing simple, and we will no complex act without willing what involves a certain measure of opposition between the impulses or partial acts which go to make up the whole act. If one passes from single acts to long series of acts, one finds only the more obviously this interweaving of repugnance and of acceptance, of pursuit and of flight, upon which every complex type of conduct depends.

One could easily at this point spend time by dwelling upon numerous and relatively trivial instances of this interweaving of conflicting motives as it appears in all our life. I prefer to pass such instances over with a mere mention. There is, for instance, the whole marvelous consciousness of play, in its benign and in its evil forms. In any game that fascinates, one loves victory and shuns defeat, and yet as a loyal supporter of the game scorns anything that makes victory certain in advance; thus as a lover of fair play preferring to risk the defeat that he all the while shuns, and partly thwarting the very love of victory that from moment to moment fires his hopes. There are, again, the numerous cases in which we prefer to go to places where we are sure to be in a considerable measure dissatisfied; to engage, for instance, in social functions that absorbingly fascinate us despite or even in view of the very fact that, as long as they continue, they keep us in a state of tension which makes us, amongst other things, long to have the whole occasion over. Taking a wider view, one may observe that the greater part of the freest products of the activity of civilization, in ceremonies, in formalities, in the long social drama of flight, of pursuit, of repartee, of contest and of courtesy, involve an elaborate and systematic delaying and hindering of elemental human desires, which we continually outwit, postpone and thwart, even while we nourish them. When students of human nature assert that hunger and love rule the social world, they recognize that the elemental in human nature is trained by civilization into the service of the highest demands of the Spirit. But such students have to recognize that the elemental rules the higher world only in so far as the elemental is not only cultivated, but endlessly thwarted, delayed, outwitted, like a constitutional monarch, who is said to be a sovereign, but who, while he rules, must not govern.

But I pass from such instances, which in all their universality are still, I admit, philosophically speaking, trivial, because they depend upon the accidents of human nature. I pass from these instances to point out what must be the law, not only of human nature, but of every broader form of life as well. I maintain that this organization of life by virtue of the tension of manifold impulses and interests is not a mere accident of our imperfect human nature, but must be a type of the organization of every rational life. There are good and bad states of tension, there are conflicts that can only be justified when resolved into some higher form of harmony. But I insist that, in general, the only harmony that can exist in the realm of the spirit is the harmony that we possess when we thwart the present but more elemental impulse for the sake of the higher unity of experience; as when we rejoice in the endurance of the tragedies of life, because they show us the depth of life, or when we know that it is better to have loved and lost than never to have loved at all, or when we possess a virtue in the moment of victory over the tempter. And the reason why this is true lies in the fact that the more one's experience fulfills ideals, the more that experience presents to one, not of ignorance, but of triumphantly wealthy acquaintance with the facts of manifold, varied and tragic life, full of tension and thereby of unity. Now this is an universal and not merely human law. It is not those innocent of evil who are fullest of the life of God, but those who in their own case have experienced the triumph over evil. It is not those naturally ignorant of fear, or those who, like Siegfried, have never shivered, who possess the genuine experience of courage; but the brave are those who have fears, but control their fears. Such know the genuine virtues of the hero. Were it otherwise, only the stupid could be perfect heroes.

To be sure it is quite false to say, as the foolish do, that the object of life is merely that we may "know life" as an irrational chaos of experiences of good and of evil. But knowing the good in life is a matter which concerns the form, rather than the mere content of life. One who knows life wisely knows indeed much of the content of life; but he knows the good of life in so far as, in the unity of his experience, he finds the evil of his experience not abolished, but subordinated, and in so far relatively thwarted by a control which annuls its triumph even while experiencing its existence.

VI

Generalizing the lesson of experience we may then say: It is logically impossible that a complete knower of truth should fail to
know, to experience, to have present to his insight, the fact of actually existing evil. On the other hand, it is equally impossible for one
to know a higher good than comes from the subordination of evil
to good in a total experience. When one first loving, in an elemental
way, whatever you please, himself hinders, delays, thwarts his elemental interest in the interest of some larger whole of experience,
he not only knows more fact, but he possesses a higher good than
would or could be present to one who was aware neither of the
elemental impulse, nor of the thwarting of it in the tension of a
richer life. The knowing of the good, in the higher sense, depends
upon contemplating the overcoming and subordination of a less
significant impulse, which survives even in order that it should be
subordinated. Now this law, this form of the knowledge of the
good, applies as well to the existence of moral as to that of sensuous
ill. If moral evil were simply destroyed and wiped away from the
external world, the knowledge of moral goodness would also be
destroyed. For the love of moral good is the thwarting of lower
loves for the sake of the higher organization. What is needed, then,
for the definition of the divine knowledge of a world that in its
wholeness is perfect, is not a divine knowledge that shall ignore,
wipe out and utterly make naught the existence of any ill, whether
physical or moral, but a divine knowledge to which shall be present
that love of the world as a whole which is fulfilled in the endurance
of physical ill, in the subordination of moral ill, in the thwarting of
impulses which survive even when subordinated, in the acceptance
of repugnances which are still eternal, in the triumph over an enemy
that endures even through its eternal defeat, and in the discovery
that the endless tension of the finite world is included in the contemplative consciousness of the repose and harmony of eternity.
To view God's nature thus is to view his nature as the whole idealistic theory views him, not as the Infinite One beyond the finite
imperfections, but as the being whose unity determines the very
constitution, the lack, the tension, and relative disharmony of the
finite world.

 The existence of evil, then, is not only consistent with the perfection of the universe, but is necessary for the very existence of that

perfection. This is what we see when we no longer permit ourselves to be deceived by the abstract meanings of the words good and evil into thinking that these two opponents exist merely as mutually exclusive facts side by side in experience, but when we go back to the facts of life and perceive that all relatively higher good, in the trivial as in the more truly spiritual realm, is known only in so far as, from some higher reflective point of view, we accept as good the thwarting of an existent interest that is even thereby declared to be a relative ill, and love a tension of various impulses which even thereby involves, as the object of our love, the existence of what gives us aversion or grief. Now if the love of God is more inclusive than the love of man, even as the divine world of experience is richer than the human world, we can simply set no human limit to the intensity of conflict, to the tragedies of existence, to the pangs of finitude, to the degree of moral ill, which in the end is included in the life that God not only loves, but finds the fulfillment of the perfect ideal. If peace means satisfaction, acceptance of the whole of an experience as good, and if even we, in our weakness, can frequently find rest in the very presence of conflict and of tension, in the very endurance of ill in a good cause, in the hero's triumph over temptation, or in the mourner's tearless refusal to accept the lower comforts of forgetfulness, or to wish that the lost one's preciousness had been less painfully revealed by death—well, if even we know our little share of this harmony in the midst of the wrecks and disorders of life, what limit shall we set to the divine power to face this world of his own sorrows, and to find peace in the victory over all its ills.

But in this last expression I have pronounced the word that serves to link this theory as to the place of evil in a good world with the practical problem of every sufferer. Job's rebellion came from the thought that God, as a sovereign, is far off, and that, for his pleasure, his creature suffers. Our own theory comes to the mourner with the assurance: "Your suffering, just as it is in you, is God's suffering. No chasm divides you from God. He is not remote from you even in his eternity. He is here. His eternity means merely the completeness of his experience. But that completeness is inclusive. Your sorrow is one of the included facts." I do not say: "God sympathizes with you from without, would spare you if he could, pities you with helpless external pity merely as a father pities his children." I say: "God here sorrows, not *with* but *in* your sorrow. Your grief is identically his grief, and what you know as your loss, God knows as his loss, just in and through the very moment when you grieve."

But hereupon the sufferer perchance responds: "If this is God's loss, could he not have prevented it? To him are present in unity all the worlds; and yet he must lack just this for which I grieve." I respond: "He suffers here that he may triumph. For the triumph of the wise is no easy thing. Their lives are not light, but sorrowful. Yet they rejoice in their sorrow, not, to be sure, because it is mere experience, but because, for them, it becomes part of a strenuous whole of life. They wander and find their home even in wandering. They long, and attain through their very love of longing. Peace they find in triumphant warfare. Contentment they have most of all in endurance. Sovereignty they win in endless service. The eternal world contains Gethsemane."

Yet the mourner may still insist: "If my sorrow is God's, his triumph is not mine. Mine is the woe. His is the peace." But my theory is a philosophy. It proposes to be coherent. I must persist: "It is your fault that you are thus sundered from God's triumph. His experience in its wholeness cannot now be yours, for you just as you—this individual—are now but a fragment, and see his truth as through a glass darkly. But if you see his truth at all, through even the dimmest light of a glimmering reason, remember, that truth is in fact your own truth, your own fulfillment, the whole from which your life cannot be divorced, the reality that you mean even when you most doubt, the desire of your heart even when you are most blind, the perfection that you unconsciously strove for even when you were an infant, the complete Self apart from whom you mean nothing, the very life that gives your life the only value which it can have. In thought, if not in the fulfillment of thought, in aim if not in attainment of aim, in aspiration if not in the presence of the revealed fact, you can view God's triumph and peace as your triumph and peace. Your defeat will be no less real than it is, nor will you falsely call your evil a mere illusion. But you will see not only the grief but the truth, your rescue, your triumph."

Well, to what ill-fortune does not just such reasoning apply? I insist: our conclusion is essentially universal. It discounts any evil that experience may contain. All the horrors of the natural order, all the concealments of the divine plan by our natural ignorance, find their general relation to the unity of the divine experience indicated in advance by this account of the problem of evil.

"Yes," one may continue, "ill-fortune you have discovered, but how about moral evil? What if the sinner now triumphantly retorts: 'Aha! So my will is God's will. All then is well with me.' " I reply: What I have said disposes of moral ill precisely as definitely as of physical ill. What the evil will is to the good man, whose goodness depends upon its existence, but also upon the thwarting and the condemnation of its aim, just such is the sinner's will to the divine plan. God's will, we say to the sinner, is your will. Yes, but it is your will thwarted, scorned, overcome, defeated. In the eternal world you are seen, possessed, present, but your damnation is also seen including and thwarting you. Your apparent victory in this world stands simply for the vigor of your impulses. God wills you not to triumph. And that is the use of you in the world—the use of evil generally—to be hated but endured, to be triumphed over through the very fact of your presence, to be willed down even in the very life of which you are a part.

But to the serious moral agent we say: What you mean when you say that evil in this temporal world ought not to exist, and ought to be suppressed, is simply what God means by seeing that evil ought to be and is endlessly thwarted, endured, but subordinated. In the natural world you are the minister of God's triumph. Your deed is his. You can never clean the world of evil; but you can subordinate evil. The justification of the presence in the world of the morally evil becomes apparent to us mortals only in so far as this evil is overcome and condemned. It exists only that it may be cast down. Courage, then, for God works in you. In the order of time you embody in outer acts what is for him the truth of his eternity.

29

The Philosophy of Loyalty

I. The Nature and the
Need of Loyalty

One of the most familiar traits of our time is the tendency to revise
tradition, to reconsider the foundations of old beliefs, and sometimes mercilessly to destroy what once seemed indispensable. This
disposition, as we all know, is especially prominent in the realms
of social theory and of religious belief. But even the exact sciences
do not escape from the influence of those who are fond of the
reëxamination of dogmas. And the modern tendency in question
has, of late years, been very notable in the field of Ethics. Conventional morality has been required, in company with religion, and
also in company with exact science, to endure the fire of criticism.
And although, in all ages, the moral law has indeed been exposed
to the assaults of the wayward, the peculiar moral situation of our
time is this, that it is no longer either the flippant or the vicious who
are the most pronounced or the most dangerous opponents of our
moral traditions. Devoted reformers, earnest public servants, ardent
prophets of a coming spiritual order,—all these types of lovers of
humanity are represented amongst those who to-day demand great
and deep changes in the moral standards by which our lives are

[The complete text of *The Philosophy of Loyalty* is reprinted here from
PL.]

to be governed. We have become accustomed, during the past few generations,—during the period of Socialism and of Individualism, of Karl Marx, of Henry George, of Ibsen, of Nietzsche, of Tolstoi, —to hear unquestionably sincere lovers of humanity sometimes declaring our traditions regarding the rights of property to be immoral, and sometimes assailing, in the name of virtue, our present family ties as essentially unworthy of the highest ideals. Individualism itself, in many rebellious forms, we often find asserting that it speaks in the name of the true morality of the future. And the movement begun in Germany by Nietzsche—the tendency towards what that philosophical rhapsodist called the "transmutation of all moral values"—has in recent years made popular the thesis that all the conventional morality of the past, whatever may have been its inevitableness, or its temporary usefulness, was in principle false, was a mere transition stage of evolution, and must be altered to the core. "Time makes ancient good uncouth": in this well-known word one might sum up the spirit of this modern revolt against moral traditions.

Now when we review the recent moral controversies that express this sort of questioning, some of us find ourselves especially troubled and bewildered. We all feel that if the foundations of the exact sciences are to be criticised by the restless spirit of our reforming age, the exact sciences are indeed well able to take care of themselves. And as for religion,—if its fortunes have indeed, of late, deeply troubled and perplexed many gentle hearts, still both believers and doubters have now generally come to view with a certain resignation this aspect of the fate of our time, whether they regard religious doubt as the result of God's way of dealing with a wayward world, or as a sign of man's transition to a higher stage of enlightenment.

But restlessness regarding the very foundations of morality—that seems to many of us especially discouraging. For that concerns both the seen and the unseen world, both the truths that justify the toil spent upon exact science, and the hopes for the love of which the religions of men have seemed dear. For what is science worth, and what is religion worth, if human life itself, for whose ennoblement science and religion have both labored, has no genuine moral standards by which one may measure its value? If, then, our moral standards themselves are questioned, the iron of doubt—so some of us feel—seems to enter our very hearts.

I

In view, then, of the fact that the modern tendency to revise traditions has inevitably extended itself, in new ways, to the region of morals, I suppose that a study of some of the foundations of the moral life is a timely undertaking. It is such an undertaking that I propose as the task of the present course of lectures. My purpose, in these discussions, is both a philsophical and a practical purpose. I should indeed be glad, if there were time, to attempt, in your company, a systematic review of all the main problems of philosophical ethics. That is, I should like, were that possible, to discuss with you at length the nature, the foundation, and the truth of the moral law, approaching that problem from all those various sides which interest philosophers. And, as a fact, I shall indeed venture to say something, in the course of these lectures, regarding each of these topics. But I well know that there is no space, in eight lectures, for any adequate treatment of that branch of philosophy which is called Ethics. Nor do you come here merely or mainly for the sake of hearing what a student of philosophy chances to think about the problems of his own calling. Accordingly, I shall not try, in this place, to state to you any system of moral philosophy. Rather is it the other aspect of my purpose in appealing to you—the practical aspect, which I must especially try to bear in mind throughout these lectures.

Our age, as I have said, is a good deal perplexed regarding its moral ideals and its standards of duty. It has doubts about what is really the best plan of human life. This perplexity is not wholly due to any peculiar waywardness of our time, or to any general lack of moral seriousness. It is just our moral leaders, our reformers, our prophets, who most perplex us. Whether these revolutionary moral teachers are right or wrong, they beset us, they give us no rest, they call in doubt our moral judgments, they undertake to "transmute values." And the result, for many of us, is a practical result. It tends to deprive us of that confidence which we all need in order to be ready to do good works. It threatens to paralyze the effectiveness of many conscientious people. Hence any effort to reason calmly and constructively about the foundations of the moral life may serve, not merely to clarify our minds, but to give vigor to our deeds. In these lectures, then, I shall ask you to think indeed about moral problems, but to think for the sake of action. I shall try to give you some fragments of a moral philosophy; but I shall try to justify the philosophy through its application to life. I do not much care whether you agree with the letter of any of my philosophical formulas; but I do want to bring to your consciousness, by means of these formulas, a certain spirit in terms of which you may henceforth be helped to interpret the life that we all in common need to live. Meanwhile, I do not want merely to refute those reformers and prophets of whose perplexing assaults upon our moral traditions I have just spoken, nor yet do I want to join myself with them in perplexing you still further. I want, as far as I can, to indicate some ways whereby we may clarify and simplify our moral situation.

I indeed agree with the view that, in many ways, our traditional moral standards ought to be revised. We need a new heaven and a new earth. We do well to set out to seek for both, however hard or doubtful may be the quest. In so far as our restlessness about moral matters—our unsettlement—implies a sense of this need, it is a good thing. To use a comparison suggested by modern Biblical criticism—our conventional morality is indeed a sort of Pentateuch, made up of many ancient documents. It has often been edited afresh. It needs critical reëxamination. I am a student of philosophy. My principal business has always been criticism. I shall propose nothing in this course which I have not tried to submit to critical standards, and to revise repeatedly.

But, on the other hand, I do not believe that unsettlement is finality. Nor to my mind is the last word of human wisdom this: that the truth is inaccessible. Nor yet is the last word of wisdom this: that the truth is merely fluent and transient. I believe in the eternal. I am in quest of the eternal. As to moral standards, in particular, I do not like that mere homesickness and spiritual estrangement, and that confusion of mind about moral ideals, which is nowadays too common. I want to know the way that leads our human practical life homewards, even if that way prove to be infinitely long. I am discontented with mere discontent. I want, as well as I can, not merely to help you to revise some of your moral standards, but to help you to give to this revision some definitive form and tendency, some image and hint of finality.

Moreover, since moral standards, as Antigone said, are not of to-day or yesterday, I believe that revision does not mean, in this field, a mere break with the past. I myself have spent my life in revising my opinions. And yet, whenever I have most carefully revised my moral standards, I am always able to see, upon reviewing my course of thought, that at best I have been finding out, in some new light, the true meaning that was latent in old traditions. Those traditions were often better in spirit than the fathers knew. We who revise may sometimes be able to see this better meaning that was latent in forms such as are now antiquated, and perhaps, in their old literal interpretation, even mischievous. Revision does not mean mere destruction. We can often say to tradition: That which thou sowest is not quickened except it die. But we can sometimes see in the world of opinion a sort of resurrection of the dead,—a resurrection wherein what was indeed justly sown in dishonor is raised in honor,—glorified,—and perhaps incorruptible. Let us bury the natural body of tradition. What we want is its glorified body and its immortal soul.

II

I have entitled these lectures, "The Philosophy of Loyalty." I may as well confess at once that my title was suggested to me, early last summer, by a book that I read—a recent work by a distinguished ethnologist, Dr. Rudolf Steinmetz of The Hague, entitled "The Philosophy of War." War and loyalty have been, in the past, two very closely associated ideas. It will be part of the task of these lectures to break up, so far as I can, in your own minds, that ancient and disastrous association, and to show how much the true conception of loyalty has been obscured by viewing the warrior as the most typical representative of rational loyalty. Steinmetz, however, accepts, in this respect, the traditional view. According to him, war gives an opportunity for loyal devotion so notable and important that, if war were altogether abolished, one of the greatest goods of civilization would thereby be hopelessly lost. I am keenly conscious of the sharp contrast between Steinmetz's theory of loyalty and my own. I agree with Steinmetz, as you will later see, regarding the significance of loyalty as a central principle of the moral life. I disagree with him very profoundly as to the relation of war both to true loyalty and to civilization in general. The very contrast has suggested to me the adoption of the form of title which Steinmetz has used.

The phrase, "Philosophy of Loyalty," is intended to indicate first, that we are here to consider loyalty as an ethical principle. For philosophy deals with first principles. And secondly, my title means to suggest that we are to view the matter critically and discriminatingly, as well as practically. For philosophy is essentially a criticism of life. Not everything, then, that calls itself loyalty, and not every form of loyalty, shall be put in our discussion on the same level with every other moral quality that uses or that deserves the ancient name in question. Moreover, the term "loyalty" comes to us as a good old popular word, without any exact definition. We are hereafter to define our term as precisely as possible, yet so as to preserve the spirit of the former usage. In estimating the place of loyalty in the moral life, we are, moreover, to follow neither traditional authority nor the voice of private prejudice. We are to use our reason as best we can; for philosophy is an effort to think out the reasons for our opinions. We are not to praise blindly, nor to condemn according to our moods. Where loyalty seems to be a good, we are to see why; when what men call loyalty leads them astray, we are to find wherein the fault lies. Since loyalty is a relative term, and always implies that there is some object, some cause, to which any given loyalty is to be shown, we must consider what are the fitting objects of loyalty. In attempting an answer to these various questions, our philosophy of loyalty must try to delve down to the roots of human conduct, the grounds for our moral standards, as far as our time permits.

But when all these efforts have been made towards a philosophical treatment of our topic, when certain discriminations between true and mistaken loyalty have been defined, when we have insisted upon the fitting objects of loyalty, and have throughout indicated our reasons for our theses, there will then stand out one great practical lesson, which I shall try to illustrate from the start, and to bring to its fruition as our lectures close. And the lesson will be this: *In loyalty, when loyalty is properly defined, is the fulfilment of the whole moral law.* You can truthfully centre your entire moral world about a rational conception of loyalty. Justice, charity, industry, wisdom, spirituality, are all definable in terms of enlightened loyalty. And, as I shall maintain, this very way of viewing the moral world—this deliberate centralization of all the duties and of all the virtues about the one conception of rational loyalty—is of great service as a means of clarifying and simplifying the tangled moral problems of our lives and of our age.

Thus, then, I state the task which our title is intended to set before us. The rest of this opening lecture must be devoted to clearing our way—and to a merely preliminary and tentative view of our topic. I must first attempt a partial and provisional definition of the term "loyalty" as I shall use that term. I wish that I could begin with a final and adequate definition; but I cannot. Why I cannot, you will see in later lectures. At the moment I shall try to direct your minds, as well as I can, merely to some of the features that are essential to my conception of loyalty.

III

Loyalty shall mean, according to this preliminary definition: *The willing and practical and thoroughgoing devotion of a person to a cause.* A man is loyal when, first, he has some *cause* to which he is loyal; when, secondly, he *willingly* and *thoroughly* devotes himself to this cause; and when, thirdly, he expresses his devotion in some *sustained and practical way*, by acting steadily in the service of his cause. Instances of loyalty are: The devotion of a patriot to his country, when this devotion leads him actually to live and perhaps die for his country; the devotion of a martyr to his religion; the devotion of a ship's captain to the requirements of his office when, after a disaster, he works steadily for his ship and for the saving of his ship's company until the last possible service is accomplished, so that he is the last man to leave the ship, and is ready if need be to go down with his ship.

Such cases of loyalty are typical. They involve, I have said, the willingness of the loyal man to do his service. The loyal man's cause is his cause by virtue of the assent of his own will. His devotion is his own. He chooses it, or, at all events, approves it. Moreover, his devotion is a practical one. He does something. This something serves his cause. Loyalty is never mere emotion. Adoration and affection may go with loyalty, but can never alone constitute loyalty. Furthermore, the devotion of the loyal man involves a sort of restraint or submission of his natural desires to his cause. Loyalty without self-control is impossible. The loyal man serves. That is, he does not merely follow his own impulses. He looks to his cause for guidance. This cause tells him what to do, and he does it. His devotion, furthermore, is entire. He is ready to live or to die as the cause directs.

And now for a further word about the hardest part of this

preliminary definition of loyalty: A loyal man, I have said, has a cause. I do not yet say that he has a good cause. He might have a bad one. I do not say, as yet, what makes a cause a good one, and worthy of loyalty. All that is to be considered hereafter. But this I now premise: If one is loyal, he has a cause which he indeed personally values. Otherwise, how could he be devoted to it? He therefore takes interest in the cause, loves it, is well pleased with it. On the other hand, loyalty never means the mere emotion of love for your cause, and never means merely following your own pleasure, viewed *as* your private pleasure and interest. For if you are loyal, your cause is viewed by you as something outside of you. Or if, like your country, your cause includes yourself, it is still much larger than your private self. It has its own value, so you as a loyal person believe. This essential value it would keep (so you believe) even if your private interest were left out of account. Your cause you take, then, to be something objective—something that is not your private self. It does not get its value merely from your being pleased with it. You believe, on the contrary, that you love it just because of its own value, which it has by itself, even if you die. That is just why one may be ready to die for his cause. In any case, when the loyal man serves his cause, he is not seeking his own private advantage.

Moreover, the cause to which a loyal man is devoted is never something *wholly* impersonal. It concerns other men. Loyalty is social. If one is a loyal servant of a cause, one has at least possible fellow-servants. On the other hand, since a cause, in general, tends to unite the many fellow-servants in one service, it consequently seems to the loyal man to have a sort of impersonal or superpersonal quality about it. You can love an individual. But you can be loyal only to a tie that binds you and others into some sort of unity, and loyal to individuals only through the tie. The cause to which loyalty devotes itself has always this union of the personal and the seemingly superindividual about it. It binds many individuals into one service. Loyal lovers, for instance, are loyal not merely to one another as separate individuals, but to their love, to their union, which is something more than either of them, or even than both of them viewed as distinct individuals.

So much for a preliminary view of what loyalty is. Our definition is not complete. It raises rather than solves problems about the nature of loyalty. But thus indeed we get a first notion of the general nature of loyalty.

IV

But now for a next step. Many people find that they have a need of loyalty. Loyalty is a good thing for them. If you ask, however, why loyalty may be needed by a given man, the answer may be very complex. A patriot may, in your opinion, need loyalty, first because his country needs his service, and, as you add, he actually owes this service, and so needs to do his duty, viz. to be loyal. This first way of stating a given man's need of a given loyalty, turns upon asserting that a specific cause rightly requires of a certain man a certain service. The cause, as one holds, is good and worthy. This man actually ought to serve just that cause. Hence he stands in need of loyalty, and of just this loyalty.

But in order thus to define this man's need of loyalty, you have to determine what causes are worthy of loyalty, and why this man ought to serve his own cause. To answer such questions would apparently presuppose a whole system of morals,—a system which at this stage of our argument we have not yet in sight.

But there is another,—a simpler, and, at the outset, a lower way of estimating the value of loyalty. One may, for the time, abstract from all questions as to the value of causes. Whether a man is loyal to a good cause or to a bad cause, his own personal attitude, when he is loyal, has a certain general quality. Whoever is loyal, whatever be his cause, is devoted, is active, surrenders his private self-will, controls himself, is in love with his cause, and believes in it. The loyal man is thus in a certain state of mind which has its own value for himself. To live a loyal life, whatever be one's cause, is to live in a way which is certainly free from many well-known sources of inner dissatisfaction. Thus hesitancy is often corrected by loyalty; for the cause plainly tells the loyal man what to do. Loyalty, again, tends to unify life, to give it centre, fixity, stability.

Well, these aspects of loyalty are, so far as they go, good for the loyal man. We may therefore define our need of loyalty in a certain preliminary way. We may take what is indeed a lower view of loyalty, regarding it, for the moment, in deliberate abstraction from the cause to which one is loyal. We may thus regard loyalty, for the moment, just as a personal attitude, which is good for the loyal man himself.

Now this lower view of our need of loyalty is the one to which in the rest of this lecture I want you to attend. All that I now say is preliminary. Results belong later. Let us simply abstract from the question whether a man's cause is objectively worthy of his loyalty or not. Let us ask: What does a man gain by being loyal? Suppose that some cause, outside of and also inclusive of his private self, so appeals to a man that he believes it to be worthy, and becomes heartily loyal to it. What good does he get personally out of his loyalty? In order to answer this question, even in this preliminary way, I must indeed go rather far afield, and define for you, still very tentatively, one of the best-known and hardest of the problems of our personal life.

V

What do we live for? What is our duty? What is the true ideal of life? What is the true difference between right and wrong? What is the true good which we all need? Whoever begins seriously to consider such questions as these soon observes certain great truths about the moral life which he must take into account if his enterprise is to succeed, that is, if he is ever to answer these questions.

The first truth is this: We all of us first learned about what we ought to do, about what our ideal should be, and in general about the moral law, through some authority external to our own wills. Our teachers, our parents, our playmates, society, custom, or perhaps some church,—these taught us about one or another aspect of right and wrong. The moral law came to us from without. It often seemed to us, in so far, something other than our will, something threatening or socially compelling, or externally restraining. In so far as our moral training is still incomplete, the moral law may at any moment have to assume afresh this air of an external authority merely in order to win our due attention. But if we have learned the moral law, or any part of it, and if we do not ask any longer how we first learned, or how we may still have to learn afresh our duty, but if, on the contrary, we rather ask: "What reason can I now give to myself why a given act is truly right? What reason can I give why my duty is my duty?"—then, indeed, we find that no external authority, viewed merely as external, can give one any reason why an act is truly right or wrong. Only a calm and reasonable view of what it is that I myself really will,—only this can decide such a question. My duty is simply my own will brought to my clear self-consciousness. That which I can rightly view as good for me is simply the object of my own deepest desire set plainly before my insight. For your own will and your own desire, once fully brought to self-consciousness, furnish the only valid reason for you to know what is right and good.

This comment which I now make upon the nature of the moral law is familiar to every serious student of ethics. In one form or another this fact, that the ultimate moral authority for each of us is determined by our own rational will, is admitted even by apparently extreme partisans of authority. Socrates long ago announced the principle in question when he taught that no man is willingly base. Plato and Aristotle employed it in developing their ethical doctrines. When St. Augustine, in a familiar passage in his Confessions, regards God's will as that in which, and in which alone, our wills can find rest and peace, he indeed makes God's will the rule of life; but he also shows that the reason why each of us, if enlightened, recognizes the divine will as right, is that, in Augustine's opinion, God has so made us for himself that our own wills are by nature inwardly restless until they rest in harmony with God's will. Our restlessness, then, so long as we are out of this harmony, gives us the reason why we find it right, if we are enlightened, to surrender our self-will.

If you want to find out, then, what is right and what is good for you, bring your own will to self-consciousness. Your duty is what you yourself will to do in so far as you clearly discover who you are, and what your place in the world is. This is, indeed, a first principle of all ethical inquiry. Kant called it the Principle of the Autonomy or self-direction of the rational will of each moral being.

But now there stands beside this first principle a second principle, equally inevitable and equally important. This principle is, that I can never find out what my own will is by merely brooding over my natural desires, or by following my momentary caprices. For by nature I am a sort of meeting place of countless streams of ancestral tendency. From moment to moment, if you consider me apart from my training, I am a collection of impulses. There is no one desire that is always present to me. Left to myself alone, I can never find out what my will is.

You may interpose here the familiar thesis that there is one desire which I always have, namely, the desire to escape from pain and to get pleasure. But as soon as you try to adjust this thesis to the facts of life, it is a thesis which simplifies nothing, and which at best simply gives me back again, under new names, that chaos of conflicting passions and interests which constitutes, apart from training, my natural life. What we naturally desire is determined for us by our countless instincts and by whatever training they have received. We want to breathe, to eat, to walk, to run, to speak, to see, to hear, to love, to fight, and, amongst other things, we want to be more or less reasonable. Now, if one of these instinctive wants of ours drives us at any moment to action, we normally take pleasure in such action, in so far as it succeeds. For action in accordance with desire means relief from tension; and that is usually accompanied with pleasure. On the other hand, a thwarted activity gives us pain. But only under special circumstances does this resulting pleasure or pain of the successful or of the hindered activity come to constitute a principal object of our desire. We all do like pleasure, and we all do shun pain. But a great deal of what we desire is desired by instinct, apart from the memory or the expectation of pleasure and pain, and often counter to the warnings that pleasure and pain have given to us. It is normal to desire food because one is hungry, rather than because one loves the pleasures of the table. It is water that the thirsty man in the desert longs for, rather than pleasure, and rather than even mere relief from pain as such. For much of the pain appears to his consciousness as largely due to his longing for water. Pain, then, is indeed an evil, but it is in part secondary to thwarted desire; while, when pain appears as a brute fact of our feelings, which we indeed hate, such pain is even then only one amongst the many ills of life, only one of the many undesirable objects. The burnt child, indeed, dreads the fire; but the climbing child, instinctively loving the ways of his remote arboreal ancestors, is little deterred by the pain of an occasional fall.

Furthermore, if I even admitted that I always desire pleasure and relief from pain, and nothing else, I should not learn from such a principle what it is that, on the whole, I am to will to do, in order to express my desire for pleasure, and in order to escape from pain. For no art is harder than the art of pleasure seeking. I can never learn that art alone by myself. And so I cannot define my own will, and hence cannot define my duty, merely in terms of pleasure and pain.

VI

So far, then, we have a rather paradoxical situation before us. Yet it is the moral situation of every one of us. If I am to know my duty, I must consult my own reasonable will. I alone can show myself why I view this or this as my duty. But on the other hand, if I merely look within myself to find what it is that I will, my own private individual nature, apart from due training, never gives me any answer to the question: What do I will? By nature I am a victim of my ancestry, a mass of world-old passions and impulses, desiring and suffering in constantly new ways as my circumstances change, and as one or another of my natural impulses comes to the front. By nature, then, apart from a specific training, I have no personal will of my own. One of the principal tasks of my life is to learn to have a will of my own. To learn your own will,—yes, to create your own will, is one of the largest of your human undertakings.

Here, then, is the paradox. I, and only I, whenever I come to my own, can morally justify to myself my own plan of life. No outer authority can ever give me the true reason for my duty. Yet I, left to myself, can never find a plan of life. I have no inborn ideal naturally present within myself. By nature I simply go on crying out in a sort of chaotic self-will, according as the momentary play of desire determines.

Whence, then, can I learn any plan of life? The moral education of any civilized person easily reminds you how this question is, in one respect, very partially, but, so far as ordinary training goes, constantly answered. One gets one's various plans of life suggested through the models that are set before each one of us by his fellows. Plans of life first come to us in connection with our endless imitative activities. These imitative processes begin in our infancy, and run on through our whole life. We learn to play, to speak, to enter into our social realm, to take part in the ways and so in the life of mankind. This imitative social activity is itself due to our instincts as social beings. But in turn the social activities are the ones that first tend to organize all of our instincts, to give unity to our passions and impulses, to transform our natural chaos of desires into some sort of order—usually, indeed, a very imperfect order. It is our social existence, then, as imitative beings,—it is this that suggests to us the sorts of plans of life which we get when we learn a calling, when we find a business in life, when we discover our place in the social world. And so our actual plans of life, namely, our callings, our more or less settled daily activities, come to us from without. We in so far learn what our own will is by first imitating the wills of others.

Yet no,—this, once more, is never the whole truth about our social situation, and is still less the whole truth about our moral situation. By ourselves alone, we have said, we can never discover in our own inner life any one plan of life that expresses our genuine will. So then, we have said, all of our plans get suggested to us by the social order in which we grow up. But on the other hand, our social training gives us a mass of varying plans of life,—plans that are not utterly chaotic, indeed, but imperfectly ordered,—mere routine, not ideal life. Moreover, social training tends not only to teach us the way of other people, but to heighten by contrast our vague natural sense of the importance of having our own way. Social training stimulates the will of the individual self, and also teaches this self customs and devices for self-expression. We never merely imitate. Conformity attracts, but also wearies us. Meanwhile, even by imitation, we often learn how to possess, and then to carry out, our own self-will. For instance, we learn speech first by imitation; but henceforth we love to hear ourselves talk; and our whole plan of life gets affected accordingly. Speech has, indeed, its origin in social conformity. Yet the tongue is an unruly member, and wags rebelliously. Teach men customs, and you equip them with weapons for expressing their own personalities. As you train the social being, you make use of his natural submissiveness. But as a result of your training he forms plans; he interprets these plans with reference to his own personal interests; he becomes aware who he is; and he may end by becoming, if not original, then at least obstreperous. And thus society is constantly engaged in training up children who may, and often do, rebel against their mother. Social conformity gives us social power. Such power brings to us a consciousness of who and what we are. Now, for the first time, we begin to have a real will of our own. And hereupon we may discover this will to be in sharp conflict with the will of society. This is what normally happens to most of us, for a time at least, in youth.

You see, so far, how the whole process upon which man's moral life depends involves this seemingly endless play of inner and outer. How shall my duty be defined? Only by my own will, whenever that will is brought to rational self-consciousness. But what is my will? By nature I know not; for by birth I am a mere eddy in the turbulent stream of inherited human passion. How, then, shall I get a will of my own? Only through social training. That indeed gives me plans, for it teaches me the settled ways of my world. Yet no,—for such training really teaches me rather the arts whereby I may express myself. It makes me clever, ambitious, often rebellious, and in so far it teaches me how to plan opposition to the social order. The circular process thus briefly indicated goes on throughout the lives of many of us. It appears in new forms at various stages of our growth. At any moment we may meet new problems of right and wrong, relating to our plans of life. We hereupon look within, at what we call our own conscience, to find out what our duty is. But, as we do so, we discover, too often, what wayward and blind guides our own hearts so far are. So we look without, in order to understand better the ways of the social world. We cannot see the inner light. Let us try the outer one. These ways of the world appeal to our imitativeness, and so we learn from the other people how we ourselves are in this case to live. Yet no,—this very learning often makes us aware of our personal contrast with other people, and so makes us self-conscious, individualistic, critical, rebellious; and again we are thrown back on ourselves for guidance. Seeing the world's way afresh, I see that it is not my way. I revive. I assert myself. My duty, I say, is my own. And so, perhaps, I go back again to my own wayward heart.

It is this sort of process which goes on, sometimes in a hopelessly circular way, when, in some complicated situation, you are morally perplexed, and after much inner brooding give up deciding by yourself and appeal to friends for advice. The advice at first pleases you, but soon may arouse your self-will more than before. You may become, as a result, more wayward and sometimes more perplexed, the longer you continue this sort of inquiry. We all know what it is to seek advice, just with the result of finding out what it is that we do not want to do.

Neither within nor without, then, do I find what seems to me a settled authority,—a settled and harmonious plan of life,—unless, indeed, one happy sort of union takes place between the inner and the outer, between my social world and myself, between my natural waywardness and the ways of my fellows. This happy union is the one that takes place whenever my mere social conformity, my docility as an imitative creature, turns into exactly that which, in these lectures, I shall call loyalty. Let us consider what happens in such cases.

VII

Suppose a being whose social conformity has been sufficient to enable him to learn many skilful social arts,—arts of speech, of prowess in contest, of influence over other men. Suppose that these arts have at the same time awakened this man's pride, his self-confidence, his disposition to assert himself. Such a man will have in him a good deal of what you can well call social will. He will be no mere anarchist. He will have been trained into much obedience. He will be no natural enemy of society, unless, indeed, fortune has given him extraordinary opportunities to win his way without scruples. On the other hand, this man must acquire a good deal of self-will. He becomes fond of success, of mastery, of his own demands. To be sure, he can find within himself no one naturally sovereign will. He can so far find only a general determination to define some way of his own, and to have his own way. Hence the conflicts of social will and self-will are inevitable, circular, endless, so long as this is the whole story of the man's life. By merely consulting convention, on the one hand, and his disposition to be somebody, on the other hand, this man can never find any one final and consistent plan of life, nor reach any one definition of his duty.

But now suppose that there appears in this man's life some one of the greater social passions, such as patriotism well exemplifies. Let his country be in danger. Let his elemental passion for conflict hereupon fuse with his brotherly love for his own countrymen into that fascinating and blood-thirsty form of humane but furious ecstacy, which is called the war-spirit. The mood in question may or may not be justified by the passing circumstances. For that I now care not. At its best the war-spirit is no very clear or rational state of anybody's mind. But one reason why men may love this spirit is that when it comes, it seems at once to define a plan of life, —a plan which solves the conflicts of self-will and conformity. This plan has two features: (1) it is through and through a social plan, obedient to the general will of one's country, submissive; (2) it is through and through an exaltation of the self, of the inner man, who now feels glorified through his sacrifice, dignified in his self-surrender, glad to be his country's servant and martyr,—yet sure that through this very readiness for self-destruction he wins the rank of hero.

Well, if the man whose case we are supposing gets possessed by some such passion as this, he wins for the moment the consciousness of what I call loyalty. This loyalty no longer knows anything about the old circular conflicts of self-will and of conformity. The self, at such moments, looks indeed *outwards* for its plan of life. "The country needs me," it says. It looks, meanwhile, *inwards* for the inspiring justification of this plan. "Honor, the hero's crown, the soldier's death, the patriot's devotion—these," it says, "are my will. I am not giving up this will of mine. It is my pride, my glory, my self-assertion, to be ready at my country's call." And now there is no conflict of outer and inner.

How wise or how enduring or how practical such a passion may prove, I do not yet consider. What I point out is that this war-spirit, for the time at least, makes self-sacrifice seem to be self-expression, makes obedience to the country's call seem to be the proudest sort of display of one's own powers. Honor now means submission, and to obey means to have one's way. Power and service are at one. Conformity is no longer opposed to having one's own will. One has no will but that of the country.

As a mere fact of human nature, then, there are social passions which actually tend to do at once two things: (1) to intensify our self-consciousness, to make us more than ever determined to express our own will and more than ever sure of our own rights, of our own strength, of our dignity, of our power, of our value; (2) to make obvious to us that this our will has no purpose but to do the will of some fascinating social power. This social power is the cause to which we are loyal.

Loyalty, then, fixes our attention upon some one cause, bids us look without ourselves to see what this unified cause is, shows us thus some one plan of action, and then says to us, "In this cause is your life, your will, your opportunity, your fulfilment."

Thus loyalty, viewed merely as a personal attitude, solves the paradox of our ordinary existence, by showing us outside of ourselves the cause which is to be served, and inside of ourselves the will which delights to do this service, and which is not thwarted but enriched and expressed in such service.

I have used patriotism and the war-spirit merely as a first and familiar illustration of loyalty. But now, as we shall later see, there is no necessary connection between loyalty and war; and there are many other forms of loyalty besides the patriotic forms. Loyalty has its domestic, its religious, its commercial, its professional forms, and many other forms as well. The essence of it, whatever forms it may take, is, as I conceive the matter, this: Since no man can find a plan of life by merely looking within his own chaotic nature, he has to look without, to the world of social conventions, deeds, and causes. Now, a loyal man is one who has found, and who sees, neither mere individual fellow-men to be loved or hated, nor mere conventions, nor customs, nor laws to be obeyed, but some social cause, or some system of causes, so rich, so well knit, and, to him, so fascinating, and withal so kindly in its appeal to his natural self-will, that he says to his cause: "Thy will is mine and mine is thine. In thee I do not lose but find myself, living intensely in proportion as I live for thee." If one could find such a cause, and hold it for his lifetime before his mind, clearly observing it, passionately loving it, and yet calmly understanding it, and steadily and practically serving it, he would have one plan of life, and this plan of life would be his own plan, his own will set before him, expressing all that his self-will has ever sought. Yet this plan would also be a plan of obedience, because it would mean living for the cause.

Now, in all ages of civilized life there have been people who have won in some form a consciousness of loyalty, and who have held to such a consciousness through life. Such people may or may not have been right in their choice of a cause. But at least they have exemplified through their loyalty one feature of a rational moral life. They have known what it was to have unity of purpose.

And again, the loyal have known what it was to be free from moral doubts and scruples. Their cause has been their conscience. It has told them what to do. They have listened and obeyed, not because of what they took to be blind convention, not because of a fear of external authority, not even because of what seemed to themselves any purely private and personal intuition, but because, when they have looked first outwards at their cause, and then inwards at themselves, they have found themselves worthless in their own eyes, except when viewed as active, as confidently devoted, as willing instruments of their cause. Their cause has forbidden them to doubt; it has said: "You are mine, you cannot do otherwise." And they have said to the cause: "I am, even of my own will, thine. I have no will except thy will. Take me, use me, control me, and even thereby fulfil me and exalt me." That is again the speech of the devoted patriots, soldiers, mothers, and martyrs of our race. They have had the grace of this willing, this active loyalty.

Now, people loyal in this sense have surely existed in the world, and, as you all know, the loyal still exist amongst us. And I beg you not to object to me, at this point, that such devoted people have often been loyal to very bad causes; or that different people have been loyal to causes which were in deadly war with one another, so that loyal people must often have been falsely guided. I beg you, above all, not to interpose here the objection that our modern doubters concerning moral problems simply cannot at present see to what one cause they ought to be loyal, so that just herein, just in our inability to see a fitting and central object of loyalty, lies the root of our modern moral confusion and distraction. All those possible objections are indeed perfectly fair considerations. I shall deal with them in due time; and I am just as earnestly aware of them as you can be. But just now we are getting our first glimpse of our future philosophy of loyalty. All that you can say of the defects of loyalty leaves still untouched the one great fact that, if you want to find a way of living which surmounts doubts, and centralizes your powers, it must be some such a way as all the loyal in common have trodden, since first loyalty was known amongst men. What form of loyalty is the right one, we are hereafter to see. But unless you can find some sort of loyalty, you cannot find unity and peace in your active living. You must find, then, a cause that is really worthy of the sort of devotion that the soldiers, rushing cheerfully to certain death, have felt for their clan or for their country, and that the martyrs have shown on behalf of their faith. This cause must be indeed rational, worthy, and no object of a false devotion. But once found, it must become your conscience, must tell you the truth about your duty, and must unify, as from without and from above, your motives, your special ideals, and your plans. You ought, I say, to find such a cause, if indeed there be any ought at all. And this is my first hint of our moral code.

But you repeat, perhaps in bewilderment, your question: "Where, in our distracted modern world, in this time when cause wars with cause, and when all old moral standards are remorselessly criticised and doubted, are we to find such a cause—a cause, all-embracing, definite, rationally compelling, supreme, certain, and fit to centralize life? What cause is there that for us would rationally justify a martyr's devotion?" I reply: "A perfectly simple consideration, derived from a study of the very spirit of loyalty itself, as this spirit is manifested by all the loyal, will soon furnish to us the unmistakable answer to this question." For the moment we have won our first distant glimpse of what I mean by the general nature of loyalty, and by our common need of loyalty.

II. Individualism

In my opening lecture I undertook to define the personal attitude which I called loyalty, and to show that, for our own individual good, we all need loyalty, and need to find causes to which we can be loyal. This was but the beginning of our philosophy of loyalty. Before I take my next step, I must ask you briefly to review the results that we have already reached.

I

By loyalty, as you remember, I mean in this preliminary view of loyalty, the willing and practical and thoroughgoing devotion of a person to a cause. By a cause that is adapted to call forth loyalty I mean, for the first, something which seems to the loyal person to be larger than his private self, and so to be, in some respect, external to his purely individual will. This cause must, in the second place, unite him with other persons by some social tie, such as a personal friendship, or his family, or the state may, in a given case, represent. The cause, therefore, to which the loyal man is devoted, is something that appears to him to be at once personal (since it concerns both himself and other people), and impersonal, or rather, if regarded from a purely human point of view, superpersonal, because it links several human selves, perhaps a vast number of selves, into some higher social unity. You cannot be loyal to a merely impersonal abstraction; and you also cannot be loyal simply to a collection of various separate persons, viewed merely as a collection. Where there is an object of loyalty, there is, then, an union of various selves into one life. This union constitutes a cause to which one may indeed be loyal, if such is his disposition. And such an union of many in one, if known to anybody for whom a person means merely a human person, appears to be something impersonal or superpersonal, just because it is more than all those separate and private personalities whom it joins. Yet it is also intensely personal, because the union is indeed an union of selves, and so not a merely artificial abstraction.

That such causes and that a thoroughgoing, willing, practical devotion to them, such as our definition of loyalty demands—that, I say, such things exist in the world, I tried at the last time to illustrate to you. My illustrations were inadequate; for it is simply impossible to show you briefly how Protean the forms of human loyalty are, and yet how similar, amidst all this endless variety of forms, the spirit of loyalty remains, whatever the causes in question may be, and whoever the loyal people are. We began, of course, with marked, traditional, and familiar illustrations. The loyal captain, steadfastly standing by his sinking ship until his last possible duty for the service to which he belongs has been accomplished; the loyal patriot, eager to devote every power to living, and, if need be, to dying for his endangered country; the loyal religious martyr, faithful unto death, —these are indeed impressive and typical instances of loyalty; but they are not the only possible instances. Anybody who, for a time, is in charge of the lives of others (for instance, any one who takes a party of children on a pleasure trip) may have the opportunity to possess and to show as genuine a loyalty as does the true-hearted captain of the sinking ship. For danger is everywhere, and to be in charge of life is always an occasion for loyalty. Anybody who has friends may devote his life to some cause which his friendship defines for him and makes, in his eyes, sacred. Anybody who has given his word in a serious matter may come to think himself called upon to sacrifice every private advantage in order to keep his word. Thus, then, anything which can link various people by fixed social ties may suggest to somebody the opportunity for a lifelong loyalty. The loyal are, therefore, to be found in all orders of society. They may be of very various degrees of intelligence, of power, of effectiveness. Wherever there are mothers and brethren, and kindred of any degree, and social organizations of any type; wherever men accept offices, or pledge their word, or, as in the pursuit of science or of art, coöperate in the search for truth and for beauty,—there are to be found causes which may appeal to the loyal interest of somebody. Loyalty may thus exist amongst the lowliest and amongst the loftiest of mankind. The king and the peasant, the saint and the worldling, all have their various opportunities for loyalty. The practical man of the world and the seemingly lonely student of science may be equally loyal.

But whatever the cause to which one is loyal, and whoever it be that is loyal, the spirit of loyalty is always the one which our preliminary definition set forth, and which our former discussion attempted more precisely to describe. Whenever a cause, beyond your private self, greater than you are,—a cause social in its nature and capable of linking into one the wills of various individuals, a cause thus at once personal and, from the purely human point of view, superpersonal,—whenever, I say, such a cause so arouses your interest that it appears to you worthy to be served with all your might, with all your soul, with all your strength, then this cause awakens in you the spirit of loyalty. If you act out this spirit, you become, in fact, loyal. And upon the unity of this spirit, amidst all its countless varieties, our future argument will depend. It is essential to that argument to insist that the humblest as well as the wisest and mightiest of men, may share in this one spirit.

Now, loyalty, thus defined, is, as we have maintained, something which we all, as human beings, need. That is, we all need to find causes which shall awaken our loyalty. I tried to indicate to you at the last time the grounds for this our common need for loyalty. In order to do so, I began with a confessedly lower view of loyalty. I have asked you, for the time, in this opening study, to abstract altogether from the cause to which any man is loyal, to leave out of account whether that cause is or is not in your opinion worthy, and to begin by considering what good the loyal man gets out of the personal attitude of loyalty, whatever be his cause. Only by thus beginning can we prepare the way for a higher view of loyalty.

Loyalty, I have said, be the cause worthy or unworthy, is for the loyal man a good, just as, even if his beloved be unworthy, love may in its place still be a good thing for a lover. And loyalty is for the loyal man not only a good, but for him chief amongst all the moral goods of his life, because it furnishes to him a personal solution of the hardest of human practical problems, the problem: "For what do I live? Why am I here? For what am I good? Why am I needed?"

The natural man, more or less vaguely and unconsciously, asks such questions as these. But if he looks merely within his natural self, he cannot answer them. Within himself he finds vague cravings for happiness, a chaos of desires, a medley of conflicting instincts. He has come—

> Into this universe, the why not knowing,
> Nor whence, like water, willy-nilly flowing.

He must, then, in any case consult society in order to define the purpose of his life. The social order, however, taken as it comes, gives him customs, employment, conventions, laws, and advice, but no one overmastering ideal. It controls him, but often by the very show of authority it also inflames his self-will. It rebukes and amuses; it threatens and praises him by turns; but it leaves him to find out and to justify the sense of his own life as he can. It solves for him no ultimate problems of life, so long as his loyalty is unawakened.

Only a cause, then, an absorbing and fascinating social cause, which by his own will and consent comes to take possession of his life, as the spirits that a magician summons might by the magician's own will and consent take control of the fortunes of the one who has called for their aid,—only a cause, dignified by the social unity that it gives to many human lives, but rendered also vital for the loyal man by the personal affection which it awakens in his heart, only such a cause can unify his outer and inner world. When such unity comes, it takes in him the form of an active loyalty. Whatever cause thus appeals to a man meets therefore one of his deepest personal needs, and in fact the very deepest of his moral needs; namely, the need of a life task that is at once voluntary and to his mind worthy.

II

So far the former discussion led us. But already, at this point, an objection arises,—or rather, there arise a whole host of objections,—whereof I must take account before you will be ready to comprehend the philosophy of loyalty which I am to propose in later lectures. These objections, familiar in the present day, come from the partisans of certain forms of Individualism which in our modern world are so prevalent. I shall devote this lecture to a study of the relations of the spirit of loyalty to the spirit of individualism. Individualism is as Protean as loyalty. Hence my task involves meeting various very different objections.

Somewhat more than a year since, I was attempting to state in the presence of a company of young people my arguments for loyalty. I was trying to tell that company, as I am trying to tell you, how much we all need some form of loyalty as a centralizing motive in our personal lives. I was also deploring the fact that, in our modern American life, there are so many social motives that seem to take away from people the true spirit of loyalty, and to leave them distracted, unsettled as to their moral standards, uncertain why or for what they live. After I had said my word, my hearers were invited to discuss the question. Amongst those who responded was a very earnest youth, the son of a Russian immigrant. My words had awakened my young friend's righteous indignation. "Loyalty," so he in effect said, "has been in the past one of humanity's most disastrous failings and weaknesses. Tyrants have used the spirit of loyalty as their principal tool. I am glad," he went on, "that we are outgrowing loyalty, whatever its forms or whatever the causes that it serves. What we want in the future is the training of individual judgment. We want enlightenment and independence. Let us have done with loyalty."

I need hardly remark that my opponent's earnestness, his passion for the universal triumph of individual freedom, his plainness of speech, his hatred of oppression, were themselves symptoms of a very loyal spirit. For he had his cause. That was plain. It was a social cause,—the one need of the many for release from the oppressor. He spoke like a man who was devoted to that cause. I honored his loyalty to humanity, in so far as he understood the needs of his fellows. His spirit, then, as he spoke, simply illustrated my own thesis. He was awake, resolute, eager. He had his ideal. And his loyalty to the cause of the oppressed had given to him this fine self-possession. He was a living instance of my view of the value of loyalty to the loyal man.

So, in fact, he was not my opponent. But he thought that he was. And his view of loyalty, his conception that loyalty is by its nature, as a spirit of devotion and of self-sacrifice for a cause, necessarily a spirit of subservience, of slavish submission,—this view, I say, although it was clearly refuted by the very existence of his own loyalty to the cause of the relief of the people from the oppressor, was still a misunderstanding of himself and of life,—a misunderstanding such as is nowadays only too common. Here, then, is one form which current objections to the spirit of loyalty often take.

Another and a decidedly different objection to my own views about loyalty was expressed to me, also within the past year, by a friend high in official position in a distant community,—a teacher who has charge of many youth, and who is profoundly concerned for their moral welfare. "I wish," he said, "that, if you address the youth who are under my charge, you would tell them that loyalty to their various organizations, to their clubs, to their secret societies, to their own student body generally, is no excuse for mischief-makers, and gives to loyal students no right to encourage one another to do mischief, and then to stand together to shield offenders for the sake of loyalty. Loyalty hereabouts," he in substance went on, speaking of his own community, "is a cloak to cover a multitude of sins. What these youth need is the sense that each individual has his own personal duty, and should develop his own conscience, and should not look to loyalty to excuse him from individual responsibility."

The objection which was thus in substance contained in my friend's words, was of course partly an objection to the special causes to which these students were loyal; that is, it was an objection to their clubs, and to their views about the special rights of the student body. In so far, of course, this objection does not yet concern us; for I am not now estimating the worth of men's causes, but am considering only the inner value of the loyal spirit to the man who has that spirit, whatever be the cause to which this man is loyal. In part, however, this objection was founded upon a well-known form of ethical individualism, and is an objection that does here concern us. For his own good, so my critic seemed to hold, each man needs to develop his own individual sense of personal duty and of responsibility. Loyalty, as my critic further held, tends to take the life out of a young man's conscience, because it makes him simply look outside of himself to see what his cause requires him to do. In other words, loyalty seems to be opposed to the development of that individual autonomy of the moral will which, as I told you in the last lecture, Kant insists upon, and which all moralists must indeed emphasize as one of our highest goods. If I look to my cause to tell me what to do, am I not resigning my moral birthright? Must I not always judge my own duty? Now, does not loyalty tend to make me ask my club or my other social cause simply to tell me what to do?

And yet, as you see, even the objector who pointed out this difficulty about loyalty cannot have been as much my opponent as he seemed to believe that he was. For he himself, by virtue of his own autonomous choice of his career, is a very loyal teacher, devoted to his office, and loyal to the true welfare of his students as he sees that welfare. I am sure that his spirit must be the very loyalty which I have been describing to you. He is an independent sort of man, who has chosen his cause and is now profoundly loyal. Otherwise, how could he love, as he does, the hard tasks of his office and live, as he does, in his devotion to that office, accepting its demands as his own? He works like a slave at his own task,—and of course he works lovingly. Yet he seemed to condemn the loyalty of his students to their clubs as essentially slavish. Is there not some misunderstanding here?

But yet another, and once more a very different form of individualism I find, at times, opposed by my objectors to the loyalty whose importance I am maintaining. The objection here in question is familiar. It may be stated thus: The modern man—yes, the modern woman also, as we sometimes are told—can be content only with the completest possible self-development and the fullest self-expression which the conditions of our social life permit. We all of us have individual rights, so such an objector vigorously insists. Duties, perhaps, as he adds, we also occasionally have, under rather exceptional, perhaps abnormal and annoying, conditions. But whether or no the duties get in our way and hinder our growth, the rights at least are ours. Now, there is no good equal to winning what is your right; namely, this free self-expression, this untrammelled play of the spirit. You have opinions; utter them. They are opposed to current moral traditions; then so much the better; for when you utter them you know, because of their unconventional sound, that they must be your own. Even so, your social ties prove irksome. Break them. Form new ones. Is not the free spirit eternally young? From this point of view loyalty does indeed appear to be slavish. Why sacrifice the one thing you have,—your chance to be yourself, and nobody else?

I need not further pursue, at the moment, the statement of the case for this special type of modern individualism. In this form individualism does not stand, like the enthusiasm of my young Russian, for sympathy with the oppressed, but rather for the exuberance of the vitality of certain people who, as I shall hereafter try to show, have not yet found out what to do with themselves. In any case, individualism of this sort, as I have said, is familiar enough. You know it well in recent literature. Plays, romances, essays, embody its teachings. You know this form of individualism also in real life. You read of its doings in the current newspapers. As you go about your own daily business, it sometimes, to show its moral dignity, jostles you more than even our modern congestion of population makes necessary; or it passes you by all too swiftly and perilously, in its triumphant and intrepid—self-assertion. In brief, the people who have more rights than duties have gained a notable and distinguished ethical position in our modern world. The selfish we had always with us. But the divine right to be selfish was never more ingeniously defended, in the name of the loftiest spiritual dignity, than it is sometimes defended and illustrated to-day.

But even now I have not done with stating the case of my objectors. Still another form of modern individualism exists, and this form is again very different from any of the foregoing forms. Yet once more I must let a friend of mine state the case for this sort of individualism. This is no longer the enthusiastic revolt against the oppressor which my young Russian expressed; nor is it the interest in moral independence of judgment which the teacher of youth emphasized; nor is it the type of self-assertion which prefers rights to duties; it is, on the contrary, the individualism of those who seek, and who believe that they find, an interior spiritual light which guides them and which relieves them of the need of any loyalty to externally visible causes. Such people might themselves sometimes speak of their fidelity to their inner vision as a sort of loyalty. But they would not define their loyalty in the terms which I have used in defining the loyal spirit. The friend of whom I have spoken stated the case for such people by saying: "Loyalty, such as you define, is not a man's chief good. Spirituality, contemplative self-possession, rest in the light of the truth, interior peace—these constitute, if one can attain to them, man's chief good. Good works for other men, and what externally appears as loyal conduct—such things may and will result from the attainment of inner perfection, but will so result merely because the good soul overflows, just as, to adapt the famous metaphor of Plotinus, just as the sun shines. The true good is to be at one with yourself within. Then you are at the centre of your world, and whatever good deeds you ought to do will result from the mere fact that you are thus self-possessed, and are therefore also in possession of light and peace. It is, then, spirituality rather than loyalty which we principally need." Thus, then, my friend's objection was stated.

I have thus let four different kinds of individualism state their case, as against my own thesis that loyalty is man's chief moral good. Perhaps the foregoing objections are the principal ones which my thesis in the present day has to meet; although, as I said, a host of special objections can be made merely by varying the form of these. The objections, as you will have observed, are founded upon very various and mutually conflicting principles. Yet each one of them seems somewhat formidable, especially at this stage of my argument, where I am maintaining, not that loyalty is good because or in so far as its cause is objectively and socially a good cause, but that loyalty is a centrally significant good for the loyal man himself, apart from the cause to which he is loyal, and so apart from the usefulness to other people which his loyalty may possess.

III

The scholastic philosopher, Thomas Aquinas, in his famous theological treatise, the Summa, always, in each one of the articles into which his work is divided, gives his opponents the word before he states his own case. And after thus setting forth in order the supposed reasons for the very views which he intends to combat, and immediately before beginning his detailed argument for the theses that he proposes to defend, he confronts his various opponents with some single counter-consideration,—a Scriptural passage, a word from the Fathers, or whatever brief assertion will serve his purpose, —as a sort of indication to all of his opponents together that they somehow must be in the wrong. This brief opening of his confutation is always formally introduced by the set phrase: *Sed contra est,* "But on the contrary stands the fact that," etc.

And so now, having sketched various objections, due to equally various forms of individualism, I may venture my own *Sed contra est* before I go on to a better statement of my case. Against all my four opponents stands the following fact:—

A little while since the Japanese won much admiration from all of us by the absolute loyalty to their own national cause which they displayed during their late war. Hereupon we turned for information to our various authorities upon things Japanese, and came to know something of that old moral code Bushido which Nitobe in his little book has called the Soul of Japan. Well, whatever our other views regarding Japanese life and policy, I think that we have now come to see that the ideal of Bushido, the ancient Japanese type of loyalty, despite the barbarous life of feuds and of bloodshed in which it first was born, had very many elements of wonderful spiritual power about it. Now, Bushido did indeed involve many anti-individualistic features. But it never meant to those who believed in it any sort of mere slavishness. The loyal Japanese Samurai, as he is described to us by those who know, never lacked his own sort of self-assertion. He never accepted what he took to be tyranny. He had his chiefs; but as an individual, he was proud to serve them. He often used his own highly trained judgment regarding the applications of the complex code of honor under which he was reared. He was fond of what he took to be his rights as a man of honor. He made much, even childlike, display of his dignity. His costume, his sword, his bearing, displayed this sense of his importance. Yet his ideal at least, and in large part his practice, as his admirers depict him, involved a great deal of elaborate cultivation of a genuine spiritual serenity. His whole early training involved a repression of private emotions, a control over his moods, a deliberate cheer and peace of mind, all of which he conceived to be a necessary part of his knightly equipment. Chinese sages, as well as Buddhistic traditions, influenced his views of the cultivation of this interior self-possession and serenity of soul. And yet he was also a man of the world, a warrior, an avenger of insults to his honor; and above all, he was loyal. His loyalty, in fact, consisted of all these personal and social virtues together.

This Japanese loyalty of the Samurai was trained by the ancient customs of Bushido to such freedom and plasticity of conception and expression that, when the modern reform came, the feudal loyalties were readily transformed, almost at a stroke, into that active devotion of the individual to the whole nation and to its modern needs and demands,—that devotion, I say, which made the rapid and wonderful transformation of Japan possible. The ideal of Bushido, meanwhile, spread from the old military class to a great part of the nation at large. It is plainly not the only Japanese ideal. And I am not disposed to exaggerate what I hear of the part that the old Japanese loyalty actually plays in determining the present morality of the plain people of that country. But there can be no doubt that Bushido has been an enviable spiritual possession of vast numbers of Japanese. It is indeed universally agreed that this ideal of loyalty has been conceived in Japan as requiring a certain impersonalism, a certain disregard of the central importance of the ehtical individual. And I myself do not believe, in fact, that the Japanese have rightly conceived the true worth of the individual. And yet, after all, is not this Japanese ideal of loyalty a sort of counter-instance which all the various opponents of loyalty, whose cases have heretofore been stated, ought to consider?

For Japanese loyalty has not been a mere tool for the oppressors to use. Herein it has indeed strongly differed from that blind and pathetic loyalty of the ignorant Russian peasant, which my young friend had in mind when he condemned loyalty. Japanese loyalty has led, on the contrary, to a wonderful and cordial solidarity of national spirit. If it has discouraged strident self-assertion, it has not suppressed individual judgment. For the modern transformation of Japan has surely depended upon a vast development of personal ingenuity and plasticity, not only intellectual but moral. This loyalty has not made machines out of men. It has given rise to a wonderful development of individual talent. Japanese loyalty, furthermore, if indeed strongly opposed to the individualism which knows its rights rather than its duties, has expressed itself in an heroic vigor of life which the most energetic amongst those who love to assert themselves might well envy. And meanwhile this loyalty, in some at least of its representatives, has included, has used, has elaborately trained an inner serenity of individual self-control, a spiritual peace and inner perfection which I find enviable, and which many of our own nervous wanderers upon the higher plane might find indeed restful if they could attain to it. There is, then, not so much opposition between the good which the loyal may win, and the various personal goods which our partisans of individualism emphasized. I do not believe that the Japanese ought to be our models. Our civilization has its own moral problems, and must meet them in its own way. But I am sure that our various partisans of ethical individualism, when they conceive that they are opponents of the spirit of loyalty, ought to consider those aspects of Japanese loyalty which most of us do indeed find enviable. This counter-instance serves to show that, at least in some measure, the various personal goods which the different ethical individualists seek, have been won, and so can be won, by means of the spirit of loyalty.

IV

With this counter-instance once before you, I may now go on to a closer analysis of the rational claims of ethical individualism.

Whether he takes account of the physical or of the natural world, every man inevitably finds himself as apparently occupying the centre of his own universe. The starry heavens form to his eyes a sphere, and he himself, so far as he can ever see, is at the centre of that sphere. Yes, the entire and infinite visible world, to be even more exact, seems to each of you to have its centre about where the bridge of your own nose chances to be. What is very remote from us we all of us find it difficult to regard as real in the same warm and vital sense in which the world near to us is real. It is for us all a little hard to see how the people who live far from our own dwelling-place, say, the Australians or the Siberians, can really fail to observe how distant they are from the place where, after all, it is from our point of view most natural to have one's abiding-place. And the people of alien races must surely feel, if they share our so natural insight regarding them, that they are indeed a strange sort of folk.

This inevitable illusion of perspective is, of course, responsible for what is called our natural selfishness. But on the other hand, this illusion is no mere illusion. It suggests, even while it distorts, the true nature of things. The real world has a genuine relation to the various personalities that live in it. The truth is diversified by its relation to these personalities. Values do indeed alter with the point of view. The world as interpreted by me is a fact different from the world as interpreted by you; and these different interpretations have all of them their basis in the truth of things. So far as moral values are concerned, it is therefore indeed certain that no ethical doctrine can be right which neglects individuals, and which disregards, I will not say their right, but their duty to centralize their lives, and so their moral universe, about their own purposes. As we seem to be at the centre of the starry heavens, so each of us is indeed at the centre of his own realm of duty. No impersonal moral theory can be successful. Individualism in ethics has therefore its permanent and, as I believe, its absolute justification in the nature of things.

And the first principle of a true individualism in ethics is indeed that moral autonomy of any rational person which I mentioned at the last time, and which Kant so beautifully defended. Only your own will, brought to a true knowledge of itself, can ever determine for you what your duty is. And so far, then, I myself, in defending loyalty as a good thing for the loyal, am speaking as an ethical individualist. My whole case depends upon this fact. And so, in following my argument, you need not fear that I want to set some impersonal sort of life as an ideal over against the individualism of the opponents of loyalty whose various cases I have just been stating. I contend only that their opposition to loyalty, their view that one's individual purposes can be won otherwise than by and through loyalty, is due merely to their failure to comprehend what it is that the ethical individual needs, and what it is that in all, even of his blindest strivings, he is still seeking. What I hold is, that he inevitably seeks his own form of loyalty, his own cause, and his opportunity to serve that cause, and that he can actually and rationally find spiritual rest and peace in nothing else. Let me indicate to you my reasons for this view; and then, as I hope, you will see that my opponents do not at heart mean to oppose me. As the matter stands, they merely oppose themselves, and this through a mere misapprehension.

To my opponent, wherever he is, I therefore say: Be an individual; seek your own individual good; seek that good thoroughly, unswervingly, unsparingly, with all your heart and soul. But I persist in asking: Where, in heaven above and in earth beneath, have you to look for this your highest good? Where can you find it?

V

The first answer to this question might very naturally take the form of saying: "I seek, as my highest individual good, my own happiness." But, as I pointed out to you in my opening discussion, this answer only gives you your problem back again, unsolved. Happiness involves the satisfaction of desires. Your natural desires are countless and conflicting. What satisfies one desire defeats another. Until your desires are harmonized by means of some definite plan of life, happiness is therefore a mere accident. Now it comes and now it flies, you know not why. And the mere plan to be happy if you can is by itself no plan. You therefore cannot adopt the pursuit of happiness as your profession. The calling that you adopt will in any case be something that the social order in which you live teaches you; and all plans will in your mind be practically secondary to your general plan to live in some sort of tolerable relation to your social order. For you are indeed a social being.

If, next, you simply say: "Well, then, I will live as my social order requires me to live,"—again, as we have seen, you find yourself without any determinate way of expressing your own individuality. For if the social order is indeed not as chaotic in its activities as by nature you yourself are, it is quite unable of itself to do more than to make of you, in one way or another, a link in its mechanism, or a member of one of its numerous herds, in any case a mere vehicle for carrying its various influences. Against this fate, as an ethical individual, you justly revolt. If this chance social existence furnishes to you your only plan of life, you therefore live in a sad but altogether too common wavering between blind submission and incoherent rebellion. As Kant says of the natural human being, your state so far remains this, that you can neither endure your fellow-man nor do without him. You do your daily work perhaps, but you complain of your employer. You earn your bread, but you are bitter because of hard times, and because of the social oppressions that beset you. You are insufferably dreary when alone, but are bored when in company. Your neighbors determine your customs; but in return for the art of life thus acquired, you persistently criticise your neighbors for their offences against custom. Imitation and jealousy, slavish conventionality, on the one hand, secret or open disorder, on the other, bickerings that inflame, and gayeties that do not cheer—these, along with many joys and sorrows that come by accident, constitute upon this level the chronicle of your life. It is such a chronicle that the daily newspapers, in the most of their less violently criminal reports, constantly rehearse to us, so far as they are not taken up with reporting the really greater social activities of mankind. Thus the merely social animal escapes from the chaos of his natural desires, only to sink to the pettiness of a hewer of wood and drawer of water for his lord, the social order. He may become fairly happy for a longer or shorter time; but that is so far mere chance. He may even think himself fairly contented, but that is, upon this level, mere callousness.

But if, indeed, you are a genuine individualist, you cannot accept this fate. If you are an effective individualist, you do not remain a prey to that fate. You demand your liberation. You require your birthright of the social order which has brought your individuality into being. You seek the salvation of yourself from this intolerable bondage. Now, I have already counselled you to seek such liberty in the form of loyalty; that is, of a willing and whole-souled devotion to a fascinating social cause. But perhaps this does not yet seem to you the solution. And therefore you may next turn to a very familiar form of individualism. You may say, "Well, then, my ideal shall be Power. I seek to be master of my fate."

That the highest good for the individual is to be defined in terms of Power,—this, I say, is a well-known doctrine. It is very old. It is in each generation renewed, for the young men define it ever afresh. In our time it has been emphasized by Nietzsche's view that the central principle of ethical individuality is *Der Wille zur Macht*—the will to be mighty.

If this is now your doctrine, the power that you seek will, of course, not be mere brute force. Those have ill interpreted Nietzsche,—that heavily burdened invalid, doomed to solitude by his sensitiveness, and yet longing amidst his sufferings for an influence over his fellow-men of which he never became conscious before the end came to him,—those have ill interpreted him who have found in his passionate aphorisms only a glorification of elemental selfishness. No,—power for Nietzsche, as for all ethical individualists of serious significance, is power idealized through its social efficacy, and conceived in terms of some more or less vague dream of a completely perfected and ideal, but certainly social, individual man. And Nietzsche's particular dream of power has all the pathos of the hopeless invalid's longing for escape from his disease. The tragedy of his personal life was one only of the countless tragedies to which the seekers after power have fallen victims.

Well, if it is power that you seek, your ideal may not be expressed as Nietzsche expressed his, but in any case you will be seeking some socially idealized type of power. Warriors, statesmen, artists, will be before your mind as examples of what power, if attained, would be. In your sphere you will be seeking to control social conditions, and to centre them about your individual interests. Our present question is: Can you hope to attain the highest individual good by such a quest for power as this?

When we remember that the principal theme of heroic tragedy in all ages has been the fate of the seekers after individual power, and that one of the favorite topics of comedy, from the beginning of comedy until to-day, has been the absurdity of the quest of these very lovers of power, our question begins to suggest its own answer. Regarding few topics have the sages, the poets, and the cynical critics of mankind more agreed than regarding the significance of the search for power, whenever power is sought otherwise than as a mere means to some more ideal goal. Let us then merely recall the well-known verdict that tragedy and comedy, and the wisdom of the ages, have passed upon the lust of power.

The objections to defining your individual good in terms merely of power are threefold. First, the attainment of power is a matter of fortune. Set your heart upon power, make it your central good in life, and you have staked the worth of your moral individuality upon a mere venture. In the end old age and death will at best make a mockery of whatever purely individual powers your life as a human being can possess for yourself alone. While life lasts, the attainment of power is at best but a little less uncertain than the attainment of a purely private individual happiness. This is the first objection to power as the highest individual good. It is an objection as sound as it is old; and in this objection the poets and the sages are at one; and the cynics join in the verdict.

Secondly, the lust for power is insatiable. To say, I seek merely power, not as a means to an end, but as my chief good, is to say that, for my own sake alone, I condemn myself to a laborious quest that is certain, from my own point of view and however fortune favors me, to give me a constantly increasing sense that I have not found what I need. Thus, then, I condemn myself to an endless disappointment. This objection is also well known; and it is easily illustrated. After fortune had long seemed to be actually unable to thwart Napoleon, he went on to destroy himself, merely because his lust for power grew with what it fed upon, until the fatal Russian campaign became inevitable.

Thirdly, in the often quoted words of Spinoza, "The power of man is infinitely surpassed by the power of external things;" and hence the seeker after merely individual power has undertaken a battle with the essentially irresistible forces of the whole universe. Therefore, to adapt other words of Spinoza, when such a seeker after power "ceases to suffer, he ceases also to be." The larger one's powers, the more are the places in which he comes in contact with the world that he would conquer, and the more are the ways in which he feels its force. It is with the seeker after individual power as it has lately been with some of our greater corporations. The vaster the capital of these corporations, and the more widely spread the interests that they control, the more numerous are their enemies, the harder the legislative enactments that they have to fear, the greater their fines if they are convicted of misdoing. Power means increasing opportunities for conflict. Hence the mere seeker for power not only, by the accidents of fortune, may meet his downfall, but also, himself, actively pursues his own destruction.

Whoever pursues power, and only power, wars therefore with unconquerable fate. But you may retort: "Are the loyal also not subject to fortune, like others?" And, in reply, I call at once attention to the fact that precisely such fate is what the loyal also unhesitatingly face; but they meet it in a totally different spirit. They, too, are indeed subject to fortune; their loyalty, also, is an insatiable passion to serve their cause; they also know what it is to meet with tasks that are too vast for mortals to accomplish. Only their very loyalty, since it is a willing surrender of the self to the cause, is no hopeless warfare with this fate, but is a joyous acceptance in advance of the inevitable destiny of every individual human being. In such matters, as you well know, "the readiness is all." Loyalty discounts death, for it is from the start a readiness to die for the cause. It defies fortune; for it says: "Lo, have I not surrendered my all? Did I ever assert that just I must be fortunate?" Since it views life as service of the cause, it is content with an endless quest. Since nothing is too vast to undertake for the cause, loyalty regards the greatness of its tasks as mere opportunity. But the lust of power, on the contrary, has staked its value not upon the giving up of self-will, but upon the attainment of private possessions, upon the winning of the hopeless fight of the individual with his private fate. Hence, in a world of wandering and of private disasters and unsettlement, the loyal indeed are always at home. For however they may wander or lose, they view their cause as fixed and as worthy. To serve the cause is an honor; and this honor they have in their own possession. But in this same world the seekers for power are never at home. If they have conquered Western Europe, power lies still hidden in the Far East, and they wander into the snows of a Russian winter in pursuit of that ghost of real life which always beckons to them from the dark world beyond. Napoleon's loyal soldiers won, indeed, their goal when they died in his service. But he lost. They were more fortunate than was their leader. They had their will, and then slept. He lived on for a while, and failed.

Such considerations may suffice to show wherein consists the blindness of those who in our day seem to themselves to have more rights than duties. This homily of mine about the vanity of the lust for power is, of course, a very old story. You may think these remarks but wearisome moral platitudes. But we all have to learn this sort of lesson sometime afresh, and for ourselves. And if the story of the fate of the lust for power is old, it is none the less true. And it is a story that we in America seem to need to have told to us anew to-day. Any financial crisis with its tragedies can serve by way of illustration.

But perhaps this is not the form of individualism which is asserted by the ethical individualist whom I am now addressing. Perhaps you say: "It is not mere power that I want. I demand moral autonomy, personal independence of judgment. I want to call my soul my own. The highest good is an active self-possession." Well, in this case I wholly agree with your demand, precisely in so far as you make that demand positive. I only undertake to supplement your own statement of your demand, and to oppose your denial of the supreme value of loyalty. For what end, I insist, is your moral independence good? Do you find anything finally important in the mere fact that you are unlike anybody else, or that you think good what another man condemns? What worth could you find in an independence that should merely isolate you, that should leave you but a queer creature, whose views are shared by nobody? No,—you are still a social being. What you really mean is, that you want to be heard and respected as regards your choice of your own cause. What you actually intend is, that nobody else shall determine, apart from this your own choice, the special loyalty that shall be yours.

Now, I, who have defined loyalty as the willing devotion of a self to a cause, am far from demanding from you any unwilling devotion to any cause. You are autonomous, of course. You can even cut loose from all loyalty if you will. I only plead that, if you do so, if you wholly decline to devote yourself to any cause whatever, your assertion of moral independence will remain but an empty proclaiming of a moral sovereignty over your life, without any definite life over which to be sovereign. For the only definite life that you can live will be a social life. This social life may indeed be one of enmity to society. But in that case your social order will crush you, and then your moral independence will die without any of the comfort of the loyal man's last glimpse of the banner for which he sheds his blood. For the loyal man's cause survives him. Your independence will die with you, and while it lives, nobody else will find its life worth insuring. Your last word will then be simply the empty phrase: "Lo, I asserted myself." But in the supposed case of your enmity to society, you will never know what it was that you thus asserted when you asserted yourself. For a man's self has no contents, no plans, no purposes, except those which are, in one way or another, defined for him by his social relations. Or, again, your life may indeed be one of social conformity, of merely conventional morality. But such a life you, as individualist, have learned to despise,—I think justly. Your only recourse, then, is to assert your autonomy by choosing a cause, and by loyally living, and, when need be, dying for that cause. Then you will not only assert yourself by your choice of a cause, but express yourself articulately by your service. The only way to be practically autonomous is to be freely loyal.

Such considerations serve to indicate my answer to those individualists who insist upon moral independence. My young Russian and my friend, the teacher, were individualists of this type. My answer to them both, as you see, is that the only coherent moral independence which you can define is one that has to find its expression in a loyal life. There is endless room, as we shall hereafter see, for a rational autonomy in your choice of your cause.

But you may still insist that one other form of individualism remains open to you. You may say: "I seek spirituality, serenity, an inward peace, which the world cannot give or take away. Therefore my highest good lies not in loyalty, but in this interior perfection." But once more I answer you with the whole verdict of human experience regarding the true nature of spiritual self-possession. You seek serenity. Yes, but you do not want your serenity to mean mere apathy. You seek peace, but you do not want dreamless sleep, nor yet the repose of a swoon. The stones seem to remain serene when you by chance stumble over them; some tropical islanders slumber peacefully in their huts when there is no work pressing. But the types of serenity that are for you in question are not of such sort. You are an ethical individualist. Your repose must therefore be the only repose possible to a being with a conscious and a vital will of his own. It must be the repose of activity; the assurance of one who lives energetically, even because he lives in the spirit. But in what spirit shall you live? Are you not a man? Can you live with an active will of your own without living amongst your brethren? Seek, then, serenity, but let it be the serenity of the devotedly and socially active being. Otherwise your spiritual peace is a mere feeling of repose, and, as such, contents at its best but one side of your nature, namely, the merely sensuous side. The massive sensation that all things are somehow well is not the highest good of an active being. Even one of the most typical of mystics, Meister Eckhart, once stated his case, regarding a true spiritual life, thus: "That a man should have a life of rest and peace in God is good; that he should bear a painful life with patience is better; but that he should find his rest even in his painful life, that is best of all." Now, this last state, the finding of one's rest and spiritual fulfilment even in one's very life of toil itself,—this state is precisely the state of the loyal, in so far as their loyalty gets full control of their emotional nature. I grant you that not all the loyal are possessed of this serenity; but that is because of their defects of nature or of training. Their loyalty would be more effective, indeed, if it were colored throughout by the serenity that you pursue. But your own peace of spirit will be meaningless unless it is the peace of one who is willingly devoted to his cause. "The loving," says Bayard Taylor, in his lyric of Sebastopol, "the loving are the daring." And I say: The truly serene of spirit are to be found at their best amongst the loyal.

In view of such considerations, when I listen to our modern ethical individualists,—to our poets, dramatists, essayists who glorify personal initiative—to our Walt Whitman, to Ibsen, and, above all, when I listen to Nietzsche,—I confess that these men move me for a time, but that erelong I begin to listen with impatience. Of course, I then say, be indeed autonomous. Be an individual. But for Heaven's sake, set about the task. Do not forever whet the sword of your resolve. Begin the battle of real individuality. Why these endless preliminary gesticulations? "Leave off thy—grimaces," and begin. There is only one way to be an ethical individual. That is to choose your cause, and then to serve it, as the Samurai his feudal chief, as the ideal knight of romantic story his lady,—in the spirit of all the loyal.

III. Loyalty to Loyalty

The two foregoing lectures have been devoted to defending the thesis that loyalty is, for the loyal individual himself, a supreme good, whatever be, for the world in general, the worth of his cause. We are next to consider what are the causes which are worthy of loyalty.

I

But before I go on to this new stage of our discussion, I want, by way of summary of all that has preceded, to get before your minds as clear an image as I can of some representative instance of loyalty. The personal dignity and worth of a loyal character can best be appreciated by means of illustrations. And I confess that those illustrations of loyalty which my earlier lectures used must have aroused some associations which I do not want, as I go on to my further argument, to leave too prominent in your minds. I chose those instances because they were familiar. Perhaps they are too familiar. I have mentioned the patriot aflame with the war-spirit, the knight of romance, and the Japanese Samurai. But these examples may have too much emphasized the common but false impression that loyalty necessarily has to do with the martial virtues and with the martial vices. I have also used the instance of the loyal captain standing by his sinking ship. But this case suggests that the loyal have their duties assigned to them by some established and customary routine of the service to which they belong. And that, again, is an association that I do not want you to make too prominent. Loyalty is perfectly consistent with originality. The loyal man may often have to show his loyalty by some act which no mere routine predetermines. He may have to be as inventive of his duties as he is faithful to them.

Now, I myself have for years used in my own classes, as an illustration of the personal worth and beauty of loyalty, an incident of English history, which has often been cited as a precedent in discussions of the constitutional privileges of the House of

Commons, but which, as I think, has not been sufficiently noticed by moralists. Let me set that incident now before your imagination. Thus, I say, do the loyal bear themselves: In January, 1642, just before the outbreak of hostilities between King Charles I and the Commons, the King resolved to arrest certain leaders of the opposition party in Parliament. He accordingly sent his herald to the House to demand the surrender of these members into his custody. The Speaker of the House in reply solemnly appealed to the ancient privileges of the House, which gave to that body jurisdiction over its own members, and which forbade their arrest without its consent. The conflict between the privileges of the House and the royal prerogative was herewith definitely initiated. The King resolved by a show of force to assert at once his authority; and, on the day following that upon which the demand sent through his herald had been refused, he went in person, accompanied by soldiers, to the House. Then, having placed his guards at the doors, he entered, went up to the Speaker, and, naming the members whom he desired to arrest, demanded, "Mr. Speaker, do you espy these persons in the House?"

You will observe that the moment was an unique one in English history. Custom, precedent, convention, obviously were inadequate to define the Speaker's duty in this most critical instance. How, then, could he most admirably express himself? How best preserve his genuine personal dignity? What response would secure to the Speaker his own highest good? Think of the matter merely as one of the Speaker's individual worth and reputation. By what act could he do himself most honor?

In fact, as the well-known report, entered in the Journal of the House, states, the Speaker at once fell on his knee before the King and said: "Your Majesty, I am the Speaker of this House, and, being such, I have neither eyes to see nor tongue to speak save as this House shall command; and I humbly beg your Majesty's pardon if this is the only answer that I can give to your Majesty."

Now, I ask you not, at this point, to consider the Speaker's reply to the King as a deed having historical importance, or in fact as having value for anybody but himself. I want you to view the act merely as an instance of a supremely worthy personal attitude. The beautiful union of formal humility (when the Speaker fell on his knee before the King) with unconquerable self-assertion (when the reply rang with so clear a note of lawful defiance); the willing and complete identification of his whole self with his cause (when the Speaker declared that he had no eye or tongue except as his office gave them to him),—these are characteristics typical of a loyal attitude. The Speaker's words were at once ingenious and obvious. They were in line with the ancient custom of the realm. They were also creative of a new precedent. He had to be inventive to utter them; but once uttered, they seem almost commonplace in their plain truth. The King might be offended at the refusal; but he could not fail to note that, for the moment, he had met with a personal dignity greater than kingship,—the dignity that any loyal man, great or humble, possesses whenever he speaks and acts in the service of his cause.

Well—here is an image of loyalty. Thus, I say, whatever their cause, the loyal express themselves. When any one asks me what the worthiest personal bearing, the most dignified and internally complete expression of an individual is, I can therefore only reply: Such a bearing, such an expression of yourself as the Speaker adopted. Have, then, your cause, chosen by you just as the Speaker had chosen to accept his office from the House. Let this cause so possess you that, even in the most thrilling crisis of your practical service of that cause, you can say with the Speaker: "I am the servant of this cause, its reasonable, its willing, its devoted instrument, and, being such, I have neither eyes to see nor tongue to speak save as this cause shall command." Let this be your bearing, and this your deed. Then, indeed, you know what you live for. And you have won the attitude which constitutes genuine personal dignity. What an individual in his practical bearing can be, you now are. And herein, as I have said, lies for you a supreme personal good.

II

With this image of the loyal self before us, let us now return to the main thread of our discourse. We have deliberately declined, so far, to consider what the causes are to which men ought to be loyal. To turn to this task is the next step in our philosophy of loyalty.

Your first impression may well be that the task in question is endlessly complex. In our opening lecture we defined indeed some general characteristics which a cause must possess in order to be a fitting object of loyalty. A cause, we said, is a possible object of loyalty only in case it is such as to join many persons into the unity of a single life. Such a cause, we said, must therefore be at once personal, and, for one who defines personality from a purely human point of view, superpersonal. Our initial illustrations of possible causes were, first, a friendship which unites several friends into some unity of friendly life; secondly, a family, whose unity binds its members' lives together; and, thirdly, the state, in so far as it is no mere collection of separate citizens, but such an unity as that to which the devoted patriot is loyal. As we saw, such illustrations could be vastly extended. All stable social relations may give rise to causes that may call forth loyalty.

Now, it is obvious that nobody can be equally and directly loyal to all of the countless actual social causes that exist. It is obvious also that many causes which conform to our general definition of a possible cause may appear to any given person to be hateful and evil causes, to which he is justly opposed. A robber band, a family engaged in a murderous feud, a pirate crew, a savage tribe, a Highland robber clan of the old days—these might constitute causes to which somebody has been, or is, profoundly loyal. Men have loved such causes devotedly, have served them for a lifetime. Yet most of us would easily agree in thinking such causes unworthy of anybody's loyalty. Moreover, different loyalties may obviously stand in mutual conflict, whenever their causes are opposed. Family feuds are embittered by the very strength of the loyalty of both sides. My country, if I am the patriot inflamed by the war-spirit, seems an absolutely worthy cause; but my enemy's country usually seems hateful to me just because of my own loyalty; and therefore even my individual enemy may be hated because of the supposed baseness of his cause. War-songs call the individual enemy evil names just because he possesses the very personal qualities that, in our own loyal fellow-countrymen, we most admire. "No refuge could save the hireling and slave." Our enemy, as you see, is a slave, because he serves his cause so obediently. Yet just such service we call, in our own country's heroes, the worthiest devotion.

Meanwhile, in the foregoing account of loyalty as a spiritual good to the loyal man, we have insisted that true loyalty, being a willing devotion of the self to its cause, involves some element of autonomous choice. Tradition has usually held that a man ought to be loyal to just that cause which his social station determines for him. Common sense generally says, that if you were born in your country, and still live there, you ought to be loyal to that country, and to that country only, hating the enemies across the border whenever a declaration of war requires you to hate them. But we have declared that true loyalty includes some element of free choice. Hence our own account seems still further to have complicated the theory of loyalty. For in answering in our last lecture the ethical individualists who objected to loyalty, we have ourselves deliberately given to loyalty an individualistic coloring. And if our view be right, and if tradition be wrong, so much the more difficult appears to be the task of defining wherein consists that which makes a cause worthy of loyalty for a given man, since tradition alone is for us an insufficient guide.

To sum up, then, our apparent difficulties, they are these: Loyalty is a good for the loyal man; but it may be mischievous for those whom his cause assails. Conflicting loyalties may mean general social disturbances; and the fact that loyalty is good for the loyal does not of itself decide whose cause is right when various causes stand opposed to one another. And if, in accordance with our own argument in the foregoing lecture, we declare that the best form of loyalty, for the loyal individual, is the one that he freely chooses for himself, so much the greater seems to be the complication of the moral world, and so much the more numerous become the chances that the loyalties of various people will conflict with one another.

III

In order to overcome such difficulties, now that they have arisen in our way, and in order to discover a principle whereby one may be guided in choosing a right object for his loyalty, we must steadfastly bear in mind that, when we declared loyalty to be a supreme good for the loyal man himself, we were not speaking of a good that can come to a few men only—to heroes or to saints of an especially exalted mental type. As we expressly said, the mightiest and the humblest members of any social order can be morally equal in the exemplification of loyalty. Whenever I myself begin to look about my own community to single out those people whom I know to be, in the sense of our definition, especially loyal to their various causes, I always find, amongst the most exemplary cases of loyalty, a few indeed of the most prominent members of the community, whom your minds and mine must at once single out because their public services and their willing sacrifices have made their loyalty to their chosen causes a matter of common report and of easy observation. But my own mind also chooses some of the plainest and obscurest of the people whom I chance to know, the most straightforward and simple-minded of folk, whose loyalty is even all the more sure to me because I can certainly affirm that they, at least, cannot be making any mere display of loyalty in order that they should be seen of men. Nobody knows of their loyalty except those who are in more or less direct touch with them; and these usually appreciate this loyalty too little. You all of you similarly know plain and wholly obscure men and women, of whom the world has never heard, and is not worthy, but who have possessed and who have proved in the presence of you who have chanced to observe them, a loyalty to their chosen causes which was not indeed expressed in martial deeds, but which was quite as genuine a loyalty as that of a Samurai, or as that of Arnold von Winkelried when he rushed upon the Austrian spears. As for the ordinary expressions of loyalty, not at critical moments and in the heroic instants that come to the plainest lives, but in daily business, we are all aware how the letter carrier and the housemaid may live, and often do live, when they choose, as complete a daily life of steadfast loyalty as could any knight or king. Some of us certainly know precisely such truly great personal embodiments of loyalty in those who are, in the world's ill-judging eyes, the little ones of the community.

Now these facts, I insist, show that loyalty is in any case no aristocratic gift of the few. It is, indeed, too rare a possession to-day in our own American social order; but that defect is due to the state of our present moral education. We as a nation, I fear, have been forgetting loyalty. We have been neglecting to cultivate it in our social order. We have been making light of it. We have not been training ourselves for it. Hence we, indeed, often sadly miss it in our social environment. But all sound human beings are made for it and can learn to possess it and to profit by it. And it is an essentially accessible and practical virtue for everybody.

This being true, let us next note that all the complications which we just reported are obviously due, in the main, to the fact that, as loyal men at present are, their various causes, and so their various loyalties, are viewed by them as standing in mutual, sometimes in deadly conflict. In general, as is plain if somebody's loyalty to a given cause, as for instance to a family, or to a state, so expresses itself as to involve a feud with a neighbor's family, or a warlike assault upon a foreign state, the result is obviously an evil; and at least part of the reason why it is an evil is that, by reason of the feud or the war, a certain good, namely, the enemy's loyalty, together with the enemy's opportunity to be loyal, is assailed, is thwarted, is endangered, is, perhaps, altogether destroyed. If the loyalty of A is a good for him, and if the loyalty of B is a good for him, then a feud between A and B, founded upon a mutual conflict between the causes that they serve, obviously involves this evil, namely, that each of the combatants assails, and perhaps may altogether destroy, precisely what we have seen to be the best spiritual possession of the other, namely, his chance to have a cause and to be loyal to a cause. The militant loyalty, indeed, also assails, in such a case, the enemy's physical comfort and well-being, his property, his life; and herein, of course, militant loyalty does evil to the enemy. But if each man's having and serving a cause is his best good, the worst of the evils of a feud is the resulting attack, not upon the enemy's comfort or his health or his property or his life, but upon the most precious of his possessions, his loyalty itself.

If loyalty is a supreme good, the mutually destructive conflict of loyalties is in general a supreme evil. If loyalty is a good for all sorts and conditions of men, the war of man against man has been especially mischievous, not so much because it has hurt, maimed, impoverished, or slain men, as because it has so often robbed the defeated of their causes, of their opportunities to be loyal, and sometimes of their very spirit of loyalty.

If, then, we look over the field of human life to see where good and evil have most clustered, we see that the best in human life is its loyalty; while the worst is whatever has tended to make loyalty impossible, or to destroy it when present, or to rob it of its own while it still survives. And of all things that thus have warred with loyalty, the bitterest woe of humanity has been that so often it is the loyal themselves who have thus blindly and eagerly gone about to wound and to slay the loyalty of their brethren. The spirit of loyalty has been misused to make men commit sin against this very spirit, holy as it is. For such a sin is precisely what any wanton conflict of loyalties means. Where such a conflict occurs, the best, namely, loyalty, is used as an instrument in order to compass the worst, namely, the destruction of loyalty.

It is true, then, that some causes are good, while some are evil. But the test of good and evil in the causes to which men are loyal is now definable in terms which we can greatly simplify in view of the foregoing considerations.

If, namely, I find a cause, and this cause fascinates me, and I give myself over to its service, I in so far attain what, for me, if my loyalty is complete, is a supreme good. But my cause, by our own definition, is a social cause, which binds many into the unity of one service. My cause, therefore, gives me, of necessity, fellow-servants, who with me share this loyalty, and to whom this loyalty, if complete, is also a supreme good. So far, then, being loyal myself, I not only get but give good; for I help to sustain, in each of my fellow-servants, his own loyalty, and so I help him to secure his own supreme good. In so far, then, my loyalty to my cause is also a loyalty to my fellows' loyalty. But now suppose that my cause, like the family in a feud, or like the pirate ship, or like the aggressively warlike nation, lives by the destruction of the loyalty of other families, or of its own community, or of other communities. Then, indeed, I get a good for myself and for my fellow-servants by our common loyalty; but I war against this very spirit of loyalty as it appears in our opponent's loyalty to his own cause.

And so, a cause is good, not only for me, but for mankind, in so far as it is essentially a *loyalty to loyalty*, that is, is an aid and a furtherance of loyalty in my fellows. It is an evil cause in so far as, despite the loyalty that it arouses in me, it is destructive of loyalty in the world of my fellows. My cause is, indeed, always such as to involve some loyalty to loyalty, because, if I am loyal to any cause at all, I have fellow-servants whose loyalty mine supports. But in so far as my cause is a predatory cause, which lives by overthrowing the loyalties of others, it is an evil cause, because it involves disloyalty to the very cause of loyalty itself.

IV

In view of these considerations, we are now able still further to simplify our problem by laying stress upon one more of those very features which seemed, but a moment since, to complicate the matter so hopelessly. Loyalty, as we have defined it, is the willing devotion of a self to a cause. In answering the ethical individualists, we have insisted that all of the higher types of loyalty involve autonomous choice. The cause that is to appeal to me at all must indeed have some elemental fascination for me. It must stir me, arouse me, please me, and in the end possess me. Moreover, it must, indeed, be set before me by my social order as a possible, a practically significant, a living cause, which binds many selves in the unity of one life. But, nevertheless, if I am really awake to the significance of my own moral choices, I must be in the position of accepting this cause, as the Speaker of the House, in the incident that I have narrated, had freely accepted his Speakership. My cause cannot be merely forced upon me. It is I who make it my own. It is I who willingly say: "I have no eyes to see nor tongue to speak save as this cause shall command." However much the cause may seem to be assigned to me by my social station, I must coöperate in the choice of the cause, before the act of loyalty is complete.

Since this is the case, since my loyalty never is my mere fate, but is always also my choice, I can of course determine my loyalty, at least to some extent, by the consideration of the actual good and ill which my proposed cause does to mankind. And since I now have the main criterion of the good and ill of causes before me, I can define a principle of choice which may so guide me that my loyalty shall become a good, not merely to myself, but to mankind.

This principle is now obvious. I may state it thus: In so far as it lies in your power, so choose your cause and so serve it, that, by reason of your choice and of your service, there shall be more loyalty in the world rather than less. And, in fact, so choose and so serve your individual cause as to secure thereby the greatest possible increase of loyalty amongst men. More briefly: *In choosing and in serving the cause to which you are to be loyal, be, in any case, loyal to loyalty.*

This precept, I say, will express how one should guide his choice of a cause, in so far as he considers not merely his own supreme good, but that of mankind. That such autonomous choice is possible, tends, as we now see, not to complicate, but to simplify our moral situation. For if you regard men's loyalty as their fate, if you think that a man must be loyal simply to the cause which tradition sets before him, without any power to direct his own moral attention, then indeed the conflict of loyalties seems an insoluble problem; so that, if men find themselves loyally involved in feuds, there is no way out. But if, indeed, choice plays a part,—a genuine even if limited part, in directing the individual's choice of the cause to which he is to be loyal, then indeed this choice may be so directed that loyalty to the universal loyalty of all mankind shall be furthered by the actual choices which each enlightened loyal person makes when he selects his cause.

V

At the close of our first discussion we supposed the question to be asked, Where, in all our complex and distracted modern world, in which at present cause wars with cause, shall we find a cause that is certainly worthy of our loyalty? This question, at this very moment, has received in our discussion an answer which you may feel to be so far provisional,—perhaps unpractical,—but which you ought to regard as, at least in principle, somewhat simple and true to human nature. Loyalty is a good, a supreme good. If I myself could but find a worthy cause, and serve it as the Speaker served the House, having neither eyes to see nor tongue to speak save as that cause should command, then my highest human good, in so far as I am indeed an active being, would be mine. But this very good of loyalty is no peculiar privilege of mine; nor is it good only for me. It is an universally human good. For it is simply the finding of a harmony of the self and the world,—such a harmony as alone can content any human being.

In these lectures I do not found my argument upon some remote ideal. I found my case upon taking our poor passionate human nature just as we find it. This "eager anxious being" of ours, as Gray calls it, is a being that we can find only in social ties, and that we, nevertheless, can never fulfil without a vigorous self-assertion. We are by nature proud, untamed, restless, insatiable in our private self-will. We are also imitative, plastic, and in bitter need of ties. We profoundly want both to rule and to be ruled. We must be each of us at the centre of his own active world, and yet each of us longs to be in harmony with the very outermost heavens that encompass, with the lofty orderliness of their movements, all our restless doings. The stars fascinate us, and yet we also want to keep our own feet upon our solid human earth. Our fellows, meanwhile, overwhelm us with the might of their customs, and we in turn are inflamed with the naturally unquenchable longing that they should somehow listen to the cries of our every individual desire.

Now this divided being of ours demands reconciliation with itself; it is one long struggle for unity. Its inner and outer realms are naturally at war. Yet it wills both realms. It wants them to become one. Such unity, however, only loyalty furnishes to us,— loyalty, which finds the inner self intensified and exalted even by the very act of outward looking and of upward looking, of service and obedience,—loyalty, which knows its eyes and its tongue to be never so much and so proudly its own as when it earnestly insists that it can neither see nor speak except as the cause demands, —loyalty, which is most full of life at the instant when it is most ready to become weary, or even to perish in the act of devotion to its own. Such loyalty unites private passion and outward conformity in one life. This is the very essence of loyalty. Now loyalty has these characters in any man who is loyal. Its emotions vary, indeed, endlessly with the temperaments of its adherents; but to them all it brings the active peace of that rest in a painful life,— that rest such as we found the mystic, Meister Eckhart, fully ready to prize.

Loyalty, then, is a good for all men. And it is in any man just as much a true good as my loyalty could be in me. And so, then, if indeed I seek a cause, a worthy cause, what cause could be more worthy than the cause of loyalty to loyalty; that is, the cause of making loyalty prosper amongst men? If I could serve that cause in a sustained and effective life, if some practical work for the furtherance of uiversal human loyalty could become to me what the House was to the Speaker, then indeed my own life-task would be found; and I could then be assured at every instant of the worth of my cause by virtue of the very good that I personally found in its service.

Here would be for me not only an unity of inner and outer, but an unity with the unity of all human life. What I sought for myself I should then be explicitly seeking for my whole world. All men would be my fellow-servants of my cause. In principle I should be opposed to no man's loyalty. I should be opposed only to men's blindness in their loyalty, I should contend only against that tragic disloyalty to loyalty which the feuds of humanity now exemplify. I should preach to all others, I should strive to practise myself, that active mutual furtherance of universal loyalty which is what humanity obviously most needs, if indeed loyalty, just as the willing devotion of a self to a cause, is a supreme good.

And since all who are human are as capable of loyalty as they are of reason, since the plainest and the humblest can be as true-hearted as the great, I should nowhere miss the human material for my task. I should know, meanwhile, that if indeed loyalty, unlike the "mercy" of Portia's speech, is not always mightiest in the mightiest, it certainly, like mercy, becomes the throned monarch better than his crown. So that I should be sure of this good of loyalty as something worthy to be carried, so far as I could carry it, to everybody, lofty or humble.

Thus surely it would be humane and reasonable for me to define my cause to myself,—if only I could be assured that there is indeed some practical way of making loyalty to loyalty the actual cause of my life. Our question therefore becomes this: Is there a practical way of serving the universal human cause of loyalty to loyalty? And if there is such a way, what is it? Can we see how personally so to act that we bring loyalty on earth to a fuller fruition, to a wider range of efficacy, to a more effective sovereignty over the lives of men? If so, then indeed we can see how to work for the cause of the genuine kingdom of heaven.

VI

Yet I fear that as you have listened to this sketch of a possible and reasonable cause, such as could be a proper object of our loyalty, you will all the while have objected: This may be a definition of a possible cause, but it is an unpractical definition. For what is there that one can do to further the loyalty of mankind in general? Humanitarian efforts are an old story. They constantly are limited in their effectiveness both by the narrowness of our powers, and by the complexity of the human nature which we try to improve. And if any lesson of philanthropy is well known, it is this, that whoever tries simply to help mankind as a whole, loses his labor, so long as he does not first undertake to help those nearest to him. Loyalty to the cause of universal loyalty—how, then, shall it constitute any practical working scheme of life?

I answer at once that the individual man, with his limited powers, can indeed serve the cause of universal loyalty only by limiting his undertakings to some decidedly definite personal range. He must have his own special and personal cause. But this cause of his can indeed be chosen and determined so as to constitute a deliberate effort to further universal loyalty. When I begin to show you how this may be, I shall at once pass from what may have seemed to you a very unpractical scheme of life, to a realm of familiar and commonplace virtuous activities. The only worth of my general scheme will then lie in the fact that, in the light of this scheme, we can, as it were, see the commonplace virtues transfigured and glorified by their relation to the one highest cause of all. My thesis is *that all the commonplace virtues, in so far as they are indeed defensible and effective, are special forms of loyalty to loyalty,* and are to be justified, centralized, inspired, by the one supreme effort to do good, namely, the effort to make loyalty triumphant in the lives of all men.

The first consideration which I shall here insist upon is this: Loyalty, as we have all along seen, depends upon a very characteristic and subtle union of natural interest, and of free choice. Nobody who merely follows his natural impulses as they come is loyal. Yet nobody can be loyal without depending upon and using his natural impulses. If I am to be loyal, my cause must from moment to moment fascinate me, awaken my muscular vigor, stir me with some eagerness for work, even if this be painful work. I cannot be loyal to barren abstractions. I can only be loyal to what my life can interpret in bodily deeds. Loyalty has its elemental appeal to my whole organism. My cause must become one with my human life. Yet all this must occur not without my willing choice. I must control my devotion. It will possess me, but not without my voluntary complicity; for I shall accept the possession. It is, then, with the cause to which you personally are loyal, as it was with divine grace in an older theology. The cause must control you, as divine grace took saving control of the sinner; but only your own will can accept this control, and a grace that merely compels can never save.

Now that such an union of choice with natural interest is possible, is a fact of human nature, which every act of your own, in your daily calling, may be used to exemplify. You cannot do steady work without natural interest; but whoever is the mere prey of this passing interest does no steady work. Loyalty is a perfect synthesis of certain natural desires, of some range of social conformity, and of your own deliberate choice.

In order to be loyal, then, to loyalty, I must indeed first choose forms of loyal conduct which appeal to my own nature. This means that, upon one side of my life, I shall have to behave much as the most unenlightened of the loyal do. I shall serve causes such as my natural temperament and my social opportunities suggest to me. I shall choose friends whom I like. My family, my community, my country, will be served partly because I find it interesting to be loyal to them.

Nevertheless, upon another side, all these my more natural and, so to speak, accidental loyalties, will be controlled and unified by a deliberate use of the principle that, whatever my cause, it ought to be such as to further, so far as in me lies, the cause of universal loyalty. Hence I shall not permit my choice of my special causes to remain a mere chance. My causes must form a system. They must constitute in their entirety a single cause, my life of loyalty. When apparent conflicts arise amongst the causes in which I am interested, I shall deliberately undertake, by devices which we shall hereafter study in these lectures, to reduce the conflict to the greatest possible harmony. Thus, for instance, I may say, to one of the causes in which I am naturally bound up:—

> I could not love thee, dear, so much,
> Loved I not honour more.

And in this familiar spirit my loyalty will aim to be, even within the limits of my own personal life, an united, harmonious devotion, not to various conflicting causes, but to one system of causes, and so to one cause.

Since this one cause is my choice, the cause of my life, my social station will indeed suggest it to me. My natural powers and preferences will make it fascinating to me, and yet I will never let mere social routine, or mere social tradition, or mere private caprice, impose it upon me. I will be individualistic in my loyalty, carefully insisting, however, that whatever else I am, I shall be in all my practical activity a loyal individual, and, so far as in me lies, one who chooses his personal causes for the sake of the spread of universal loyalty. Moreover, my loyalty will be a growing loyalty.

Without giving up old loyalties I shall annex new ones. There will be evolution in my loyalty.

The choice of my cause will in consequence be such as to avoid unnecessary conflict with the causes of others. So far I shall indeed negatively show loyalty to loyalty. It shall not be my cause to destroy other men's loyalty. Yet since my cause, thus chosen and thus organized, still confines me to my narrow personal range, and since I can do so little directly for mankind, you may still ask whether, by such a control of my natural interests, I am indeed able to do much to serve the cause of universal loyalty.

Well, it is no part of the plan of this discourse to encourage illusions about the range of influence that any one poor mortal can exert. But that by the mere force of my practical and personal loyalty, if I am indeed loyal, I am doing something for the cause of universal loyalty, however narrow my range of deeds, this a very little experience of the lives of other people tends to teach me. For who, after all, most encourages and incites me to loyalty? I answer, any loyal human being, whatever his cause, so long as his cause does not arouse my hatred, and does not directly injure my chance to be loyal. My fellow's special and personal cause need not be directly mine. Indirectly he inspires me by the very contagion of his loyalty. He sets me the example. By his loyalty he shows me the worth of loyalty. Those humble and obscure folk of whom I have before spoken, how precious they are to us all as inspiring examples, because of their loyalty to their own.

From what men, then, have I gained the best aid in discovering how to be myself loyal? From the men whose personal cause is directly and consciously one with my own? That is indeed sometimes the case. But others, whose personal causes were apparently remote in very many ways from mine, have helped me to some of my truest glimpses of loyalty.

For instance: There was a friend of my own youth whom I have not seen for years, who once faced the choice between a scholarly career that he loved, on the one hand, and a call of honor, upon the other,—who could have lived out that career with worldly success if he had only been willing to conspire with his chief to deceive the public about a matter of fact, but who unhesitatingly was loyal to loyalty, who spoke the truth, who refused to conspire, and who, because his chief was a plausible and powerful man, thus deliberately wrecked his own worldly chances once for all, and retired into a misunderstood obscurity in order that his fellow-men might henceforth be helped to respect the truth better. Now, the worldly career which that friend thus sacrificed for the sake of his loyalty is far from mine; the causes that he has since loyally served have not of late brought him near to me in worldly doings. I am not sure that he should ever have kept our interests in close touch with one another even if we had lived side by side. For he was and is a highly specialized type of man, austere, and a little disposed, like many scholars, to a life apart. For the rest, I have never myself been put in such a place as his was when he chose to make his sacrifice, and have never had his great choice set before me. Nor has the world rewarded him at all fairly for his fidelity. He is, then, as this world goes, not now near to me and not a widely influential man. Yet I owe him a great debt. He showed me, by the example of his free sacrifice, a good in loyalty which I might otherwise have been too blind to see. He is a man who does not love flattery. It would be useless for me now to offer to him either words of praise or words of comfort. He made his choice with a single heart and a clear head, and he has always declined to be praised. But it will take a long time, in some other world, should I meet him in such a realm, to tell him how much I owe to his example, how much he inspired me, or how many of his fellows he had indirectly helped to their own loyalty. For I believe that a good many others besides myself indirectly owe far more to him than he knows, or than they know. I believe that certain standards of loyalty and of scientific truthfulness in this country are to-day higher than they were because of the self-surrendering act of that one devoted scholar.

Loyalty, then, is contagious. It infects not only the fellow-servant of your own special cause, but also all who know of this act. Loyalty is a good that spreads. Live it and you thereby cultivate it in other men. Be faithful, then, so one may say, to the loyal man; be faithful over your few things, for the spirit of loyalty, secretly passing from you to many to whom you are a stranger, may even thereby make you unconsciously ruler over many things. Loyalty to loyalty is then no unpractical cause. And you serve it not by becoming a mere citizen of the world, but by serving your own personal cause. We set before you, then, no unpractical rule when we repeat our moral formula in this form: Find your own cause, your interesting, fascinating, personally engrossing cause; serve it with all your might and soul and strength; but so choose your cause, and so serve it, that thereby you show forth your loyalty to loyalty, so that because of your choice and service of your cause, there is a maximum of increase of loyalty amongst your fellow-men.

VII

Yet herewith we have only begun to indicate how the cause of loyalty to loyalty may be made a cause that one can practically, efficaciously, and constantly serve. Loyalty, namely, is not a matter merely of to-day or of yesterday. The loyal have existed since civilization began. And, even so, loyalty to loyalty is not a novel undertaking. It began to be effective from the time when first people could make and keep a temporary truce during a war, and when first strangers were regarded as protected by the gods, and when first the duties of hospitality were recognized. The way to be loyal to loyalty is therefore laid down in precisely the rational portion of the conventional morality which human experience has worked out.

Herewith we approach a thesis which is central in my whole philosophy of loyalty. I announced that thesis in other words in the opening lecture. My thesis is that *all those duties which we have learned to recognize as the fundamental duties of the civilized man, the duties that every man owes to every man, are to be rightly interpreted as special instances of loyalty to loyalty.* In other words, all the recognized virtues can be defined in terms of our concept of loyalty. And this is why I assert that, when rightly interpreted, loyalty is the whole duty of man.

For consider the best-known facts as to the indirect influence of certain forms of loyal conduct. When I speak the truth, my act is directly an act of loyalty to the personal tie which then and there binds me to the man to whom I consent to speak. My special cause is, in such a case, constituted by this tie. My fellow and I are linked in a certain unity,—the unity of some transaction which involves our speech one to another. To be ready to speak the truth to my fellow is to have, just then, no eye to see and no tongue to speak save as this willingly accepted tie demands. In so far, then, speaking the truth is a special instance of loyalty. But whoever speaks the truth, thereby does what he then can do to help everybody to speak the truth. For he acts so as to further the general confidence of man in man. How far such indirect influence may extend, no man can predict.

Precisely so, in the commercial world, honesty in business is a service, not merely and not mainly to the others who are parties to the single transaction in which at any one time this faithfulness is shown. The single act of business fidelity is an act of loyalty to that general confidence of man in man upon which the whole fabric of business rests. On the contrary, the unfaithful financier whose disloyalty is the final deed that lets loose the avalanche of a panic, has done far more harm to general public confidence than he could possibly do to those whom his act directly assails. Honesty, then, is owed not merely and not even mainly to those with whom we directly deal when we do honest acts; it is owed to mankind at large, and it benefits the community and the general cause of commercial loyalty.

Such a remark is in itself a commonplace; but it serves to make concrete my general thesis that every form of dutiful action is a case of loyalty to loyalty. For what holds thus of truthfulness and of commercial honesty holds, I assert, of every form of dutiful action. Each such form is a special means for being, by a concrete deed, loyal to loyalty.

We have sought for the worthy cause; and we have found it. This simplest possible of considerations serves to turn the chaotic mass of separate precepts of which our ordinary conventional moral code consists into a system unified by the one spirit of universal loyalty. By your individual deed you indeed cannot save the world, but you can at any moment do what in you lies to further the cause which both for you and for the human world constitutes the supreme good, namely, the cause of universal loyalty. Herein consists your entire duty.

Review in the light of this simple consideration, the usually recognized range of human duties. How easily they group themselves about the one principle: *Be loyal to loyalty.*

Have I, for instance, duties to myself? Yes, precisely in so far as I have the duty to be actively loyal at all. For loyalty needs not only a willing, but also an effective servant. My duty to myself is, then, the duty to provide my cause with one who is strong enough and skilful enough to be effective according to my own natural powers. The care of health, self-cultivation, self-control, spiritual power—these are all to be morally estimated with reference to the one principle that, since I have no eyes to see or tongue to speak save as the cause commands, I will be as worthy an instrument of the cause as can be made, by my own efforts, out of the poor material which my scrap of human nature provides. The highest personal cultivation for which I have time is thus required by our principle. But self-cultivation which is not related to loyalty is worthless.

Have I private and personal rights, which I ought to assert? Yes, precisely in so far as my private powers and possessions are held in trust for the cause, and are, upon occasion, to be defended for the sake of the cause. My rights are morally the outcome of my loyalty. It is my right to protect my service, to maintain my office, and to keep my own merely in order that I may use my own as the cause commands. But rights which are not determined by my loyalty are vain pretence.

As to my duties to my neighbors, these are defined by a well-known tradition in terms of two principles, justice and benevolence. These two principles are mere aspects of our one principle. Justice means, in general, fidelity to human ties in so far as they are ties. Justice thus concerns itself with what may be called the mere forms in which loyalty expresses itself. Justice, therefore, is simply one aspect of loyalty—the more formal and abstract side of loyal life. If you are just, you are decisive in your choice of your personal cause, you are faithful to the loyal decision once made, you keep your promise, you speak the truth, you respect the loyal ties of all other men, and you contend with other men only in so far as the defence of your own cause, in the interest of loyalty to the universal cause of loyalty, makes such contest against aggression unavoidable. All these types of activity, within the limits that loyalty determines, are demanded if you are to be loyal to loyalty. Our principle thus at once requires them, and enables us to define their range of application. But justice, without loyalty, is a vicious formalism.

Benevolence, on the other hand, is that aspect of loyalty which directly concerns itself with your influence upon the inner life of human beings who enjoy, who suffer, and whose private good is to be affected by your deeds. Since no personal good that your fellow can possess is superior to his own loyalty, your own loyalty to loyalty is itself a supremely benevolent type of activity. And since your fellow-man is an instrument for the futherance of the cause of universal loyalty, his welfare also concerns you, in so far as, if you help him to a more efficient life, you make him better able to be loyal. Thus benevolence is an inevitable attendant of loyalty. And the spirit of loyalty to loyalty enables us to define wherein consists a wise benevoence. Benevolence without loyalty is a dangerous sentimentalism. Thus viewed, then, loyalty to universal loyalty is indeed the fulfilment of the whole law.

IV. Conscience

One of the main purposes of these lectures is to simplify our conceptions of duty and of the good. When I am in a practical perplexity, such as often arises in daily life, that friend can best advise me who helps me to ignore useless complications, to see simply and directly, to look at the central facts of my situation. And even so, when a moralist attempts a rational theory of duty, he ought, like the practical adviser of a friend in perplexity, to do what he can to rid our moral situation of its confusing complications. In these lectures I am trying to accomplish this end by centralizing our duties about the one conception of loyalty.

I

Conventional morality, as it is usually taught to us, consists of a maze of precepts. Some of these precepts we have acquired through the influence of Christianity. Some of them are distinctly unchristian, or even antichristian. Whatever their origin, whether Christian or Greek or barbarian, they lie side by side in our minds; and sometimes they tend to come into conflict with one another. Be just; but also be kind. Be generous; but also be strict in demanding what is your due. Live for others; but be careful of your own dignity, and assert your rights. Love all mankind; but resent insults, and be ready to slay the enemies of your country. Take no thought for the morrow; but be careful to save and to insure. Cultivate yourself; but always sacrifice yourself. Forget yourself; but never be so thoughtless in conduct that others shall justly say, "You have forgotten yourself." Be moderate in all things; but know no moderation in your devotion to righteousness. Such are a few of the well-known paradoxes of our popular morality. And these paradoxes are, for the most part, no mere accidents. Nearly all of these apparently conflicting moral maxims express some significant truth. What we want is a method of finding our way through the maze, a principle that shall unify our moral life, and that shall enable us to solve its paradoxes.

Such a centralizing and unifying principle we tried to propose at the last lecture. Our topic in the foregoing discussion was the question: By what criterion may we know that a proposed cause is one which is worthy of our loyalty? We answered the question by asserting that there is in any case *one* cause which is worthy of every man's loyalty. And that is the cause of loyalty itself. Do what you can to make men loyal, and to keep them in a loyal attitude; this was the sense of the general precept that we derived from our study of the value of loyalty to those who are loyal. Whoever follows this precept inevitably defines for himself a cause, and becomes loyal to that cause. His sovereign and central moral maxim may otherwise be stated thus: *Be loyal to loyalty.*

Our reasons for asserting that this maxim is a sound guide to dutiful action were these: First, the primal fact that loyalty, in any man who possesses it, is his supreme good. Secondly, the further fact that such loyalty is not a good which only a few are able to get,—an aristocratic possession of a small company of saints; but it is, on the contrary, a good which is accessible to all sorts and conditions of men, so far as they have normal human interests and normal self-control. We saw that there is no sort of wholesome human life which does not furnish opportunities for loyalty. And whoever is loyal wins, whatever his social station, and precisely in so far as he is loyal, the same general form of spiritual fulfilment, namely, self-possession through self-surrender. The keeper of a lonely lighthouse and the leader of a busy social order, the housemaid and the king, have almost equal opportunities to devote the self to its own chosen cause, and to win the good of such devotion. In consequence of these two considerations, whoever undertakes to further the general cause of loyalty, is certainly aiming at the supreme good of mankind at large. His cause, therefore, is certainly a worthy cause.

Nor is the undertaking to further the general cause of loyalty itself an unpractical undertaking,—a vague philanthropy. On the contrary, of all the efforts that you can make on behalf of your fellow-men, the effort to make them loyal to causes of their own is probably the most generally and widely practicable. It is notoriously hard, by any direct philanthropic effort, to give good fortune to any man, except to some few of those with whose fortunes you are most closely linked. Certain forms of suffering can be relieved by the hospitals, or by private skill and kindness. But when the sufferer is relieved, he stands once more merely on the threshold of life, and the question, What can you do to give him life itself? is not yet answered. If, hereupon, you try to make your fellow-man prosperous, by offering to him unearned good fortune, you may in fact merely teach him to be wasteful and indolent. If you seek to deal out happiness to him by devices of your own, you find that he generally prefers to look for happiness in his own way. If you attempt to give him contentment, you come into conflict with his insatiable natural desires.

But if you undertake to make him loyal, there is indeed much that you can do. For, as I pointed out at the close of the last lecture, all of what common sense rightly regards as your ordinary duties to mankind may be viewed, and ought to be viewed, as practically effective ways of helping on the cause of general loyalty. Thus, you can speak the truth to your fellow, and can thereby help him to a better confidence in mankind. This confidence in mankind will aid him in turn to speak the truth himself. And in truth-speaking there will be for him much real peace, for truth-speaking is a form of loyalty and will aid him to be otherwise loyal to his own. Precisely so, there are as many other ways of helping him to be loyal as there are other such obvious and commonly recognized duties to be done in your ordinary and peaceful dealings with him.

Let me mention one further instance that was not used amongst our illustrations at the last meeting: The true value of courtesy in ordinary human intercourse lies in the fact that courtesy is one expression of loyalty to loyalty, and helps every one who either receives or witnesses courtesy to assume himself a loyal attitude towards all the causes that are represented by the peaceful and reasonable dealings of man with man. The forms of courtesy, in fact, are largely derived from what once were, or still are, more or less ceremonious expressions of loyal devotion. Courtesy, then, may be defined as an explicit assumption of a loyal bearing. To adopt such a bearing with a real sincerity of heart is to express, in your passing actions, loyalty to universal loyalty. To act thus towards your individual fellow-man is then and there to help all who know of your act to be loyal. Courtesy, then, is a duty owed not so much to the individual to whom you are courteous, as to humanity at large.

There are, then, many ways of aiding your fellow-man to be loyal. Now, as we also set forth at the last lecture, one of the most effective of these ways lies in being loyal yourself to some personally chosen and determinate social cause which constitutes your business. This special cause need not be one in which the particular fellow-man whom you are just now to help is, at the moment, directly interested. Your very loyalty to your own cause will tend to prove infectious. Whoever is loyal to his own therefore helps on the cause of universal loyalty by his every act of devotion, precisely in so far as he refrains from any hostile attack upon the loyalty of other people, and simply lets his example of loyalty work. Whoever makes the furtherance of universal loyalty his cause, lacks, therefore, neither practical means nor present opportunity for serving his cause.

To each man our principle therefore says: *Live in your own way a loyal life and one subject to the general principle of loyalty to loyalty.* Serving your own cause, but so choose it and so serve it that in consequence of your life loyalty amongst men shall prosper. Fortunes may indeed make the range of your choice of your calling very narrow. Necessity may bind you to an irksome round of tasks. But sweeten these with whatever loyalty you can consistently get into your life. Let loyalty be your pearl of great price. Sell all the happiness that you possess or can get in disloyal or in non-loyal activities, and buy that pearl. When you once have found, or begun to find, your personal cause, be as steadily faithful to it as loyalty to loyalty henceforth permits. That is, if you find that a cause once chosen does indeed involve disloyalty to loyalty, as one might find who, having sworn fidelity to a leader, afterwards discovered his leader to be a traitor to the cause of mankind, you may have altogether to abandon the cause first chosen. But never abandon a cause except for the sake of some higher or deeper loyalty such as actually requires the change.

Meanwhile, the principle of loyalty to loyalty obviously requires you *to respect loyalty in all men, wherever you find it*. If your fellow's cause has, in a given case, assailed your own, and if, in the world as it is, conflict is inevitable, you may then have to war with your fellow's cause, in order to be loyal to your own. But even then, you may never assail whatever is sincere and genuine about his spirit of loyalty. Even if your fellow's cause involves disloyalty to mankind at large, you many not condemn the loyalty of your fellow in so far as it is loyalty. You may condemn only his blindly chosen cause. All the loyal are brethren. They are children of one spirit. Loyalty to loyalty involves the active furtherance of this spirit wherever it appears. Fair play in sport, chivalrous respect for the adversary in war, tolerance of the sincere beliefs of other men,—all these virtues are thus to be viewed as mere variations of loyalty to loyalty. Prevent the conflict of loyalties when you can, minimize such conflict where it exists, and, by means of fair play and of the chivalrous attitude towards the opponent, utilize even conflict, where it is inevitable, so as to further the cause of loyalty to loyalty. Such maxims are obvious consequences of our principle. Do we not gain, then, a great deal from our principle in the way of unifying our moral code?

II

But next, as to those just-mentioned paradoxes of popular morality, do we not gain from our principle a guide to help us through the maze? "Be just; but also be kind." These two precepts, so far as they are sound, merely emphasize, as we pointed out at the close of our last lecture, two distinct but inseparable aspects of loyalty. My cause links my fellow and myself by social ties which, in the light of our usual human interpretation of life, appear to stand for super-personal interests,—for interests in property rights, in formal obligations, in promises, in various abstractly definable re-relations. If I am loyal, I respect these relations. And I do so since, from the very definition of a cause to which one can be loyal, this cause will become nothing unless these ties are preserved intact. But to respect relations as such is to be what men call just. Meanwhile, our common cause also personally interests both my fellow and myself. So far as we both know the cause, we love it, and delight in it. Hence in being loyal to our cause, I am also being kind to my fellow. For hereby I further his delight in just so far as I help him to insight. But kindness which is not bound up with loyalty is as a sounding brass and as a tinkling cymbal, a mere sentimentalism. And abstract justice, apart from loyalty, is a cruel formalism. My fellow wants to be loyal. This is his deepest need. If I am loyal to that need, I therefore truly delight him. But kindness that is not bound up with loyalty may indeed amuse my fellow for a moment. Yet like "fancy," such kindness "dies in the cradle where it lies." Even so, if I am loyal, I am also just. But justice that is no aspect of loyalty has no reason for existence. The true relations of benevolence and justice can therefore be best defined in terms of our conception of loyalty. If any one says, "I will show thee my justice or my kindness without my loyalty," the loyal man may rightly respond, "I will show thee my kindness and my justice by my loyalty."

In a similar fashion, the moral problems regarding the right relations of strictness to generosity, of prudent foresight to present confidence, of self-surrender to self-assertion, of love to the righteous resistance of enemies,—all these moral problems, I say, are best to be solved in terms of the principle of loyalty to loyalty. As to the problem of the true concern and regard for the self, the loyal man cultivates himself, and is careful of his property rights, just in order to furnish to his cause an effective instrument; but he aims to forget precisely so much of himself as is, at any time, an obstruction to his loyalty; and he also aims to be careless of whatever about his private fortunes may be of no importance to his service of the cause. When he asserts himself, he does so because he has neither eyes to see nor tongue to speak save as his cause commands; and it is of precisely such self-sacrificing self-assertion that the foes of his cause would do well to beware. All the paradoxes about the care of self and the abandonment of self are thus soluble in terms of loyalty. Whoever knows and possesses the loyal attitude, *ipso facto* solves these paradoxes in each special case as it arises. And whoever comprehends the nature of loyalty to loyalty, as it is expressed in the form of fair play in sport, of chivalry in war, of tolerance in belief, and of the spirit that seeks to prevent the conflict of loyalties where such prevention is possible,—whoever, I say, thus comprehends what loyalty to loyalty means, holds the key to all the familiar mysteries about the right relation of the love of man to the strenuous virtues, and to the ethics of conflict.

III

As you see, it is my deliberate intention to maintain that the principle of loyalty to loyalty is a sufficient expression of what common sense calls "the dictates of conscience." When I state this thesis, it leads me, however, to a somewhat new question, which the title of this lecture is intended to emphasize.

Stated practically, this our next question takes the form of asking: Is the principle of loyalty to loyalty not only a means of solving certain perplexities, but an actually general, safe, and sufficient test of what is right and wrong in the doubtful moral situations which may arise in daily life? We have shown that the well-recognized duties and virtues, such as those which have to do with truth-speaking, with courtesy, with fair play in sport, and with chivalrous regard for enemies, can indeed be regarded, if we choose, as special forms of loyalty to loyalty. But it is indeed one thing (as you may now interpose) to interpret in terms of our principle certain virtues or duties that we already recognize. It is another thing to use the concept of loyalty to loyalty as an universal means of finding out what it is right to do when one is otherwise in doubt. Is our principle always a serviceable practical guide? Or, to use the well-known term, does our principle adequately express what people usually mean by the "dictates of conscience"?

The word "conscience," which here becomes important for our philosophy of loyalty, is a term of many uses. The problem as to the true nature of the human conscience is a complicated and difficult one. I shall here deal with the matter only in so far as is necessary for our own distinctly practical purpose. In expounding my precept, *Be loyal to loyalty*, I have set forth what does indeed pretend to be a general guiding maxim for conduct. But most of us, when we say, "My conscience dictates this or this sort of conduct," are not disposed to think of conscience as definable in terms of any one maxim. Our conscience seems to us to represent, in our ordinary lives, a good many related but nevertheless distinct motives, such as prudence, charity, reasonableness, piety, and so on. Conscience also seems to us somewhat mysterious in many of its demands, so that we often say, "I do not precisely know why this or this is right; but I feel sure that it is right, for my conscience tells me so." Since, then, conscience seems so complex and sometimes so mysterious a power, you may naturally hesitate to accept the views of a moralist who attempts, as you may think, to simplify too much the requirements of conscience. You may still insist that the moral doctrine which I have so far set forth is in one respect like all other philosophies of conduct that fill the history of ethical thought; because, as you may insist, this theory is powerless to tell any one what to do when a really perplexing case of conscience arises.

The reproach that moral philosophers have fine-sounding principles to report, but can never tell us how these principles practically apply, except when the cases are such as common sense has already decided,—this is an old objection to philosophical ethics. I want to show you how I myself meet that objection, and in what way, and to what extent, as I think, the principle of loyalty to loyalty does express the true dictates of conscience, and does tell us what to do in doubtful cases.

What is conscience? You will all agree that the word names a mental possession of ours which enables us to pass some sort of judgment, correct or mistaken, upon moral questions as they arise. My conscience, then, belongs to my mental equipment, and tells me about right and wrong conduct. Moreover, my conscience approves or disapproves my conduct, excuses me or accuses me. About the general nature and office of the conscience we all of us, as I suppose, so far agree. Our differences regarding our conscience begin when questions arise of the following sort: Is our conscience inborn? Is it acquired by training? Are its dictates the same in all men? Is it God-given? Is it infallible? Is it a separate power of the mind? Or is it simply a name for a collection of habits of moral judgment which we have acquired through social training, through reasoning, and through personal experience of the consequences of conduct?

IV

In trying to meet these questions so far as they here concern us, it is important next to note a few fundamental features which characterize the personal life of all of us. The first of these features appears if one, instead of stopping with the question, "What is my conscience?" goes deeper still and asks the question, "Who and what am I?" This latter question also has indeed countless aspects, and a complete answer to it would constitute an entire system of metaphysics. But for our present purpose it is enough to note that I cannot answer the question, "Who am I?" except in terms of some sort of statement of the plans and purposes of my life. In responding to the question, "Who are you?" a man may first mention his name. But his name is a mere tag. He then often goes on to tell where he lives, and where he comes from. His home and his birthplace, however, are already what one may call purposeful aspects of his personality. For dwelling-place, country, birthplace, and similar incidental facts about a man tend to throw light upon his personality mainly because they are of importance for a further knowledge of his social relations, and so of his social uses and activities.

But the answer to the question, "Who are you?" really begins in earnest when a man mentions his calling, and so actually sets out upon the definition of his purposes and of the way in which these purposes get expressed in his life. And when a man goes on to say, "I am the doer of these and these deeds, the friend of these friends, the enemy of these opposing purposes, the member of this family, the one whose ideals are such and such, and are so and so expressed in my life," the man expresses to you at length whatever is most expressible and worth knowing in answer to the question, "Who are you?"

To sum up, then, I should say that a person, an individual self, may be defined as a human life lived according to a plan. If a man could live with no plan at all, purposelessly and quite passively, he would in so far be an organism, and also, if you choose, he would be a psychological specimen, but he would be no personality. Wherever there is personality, there are purposes worked out in life. If, as often happens, there are many purposes connected with the life of this human creature, many plans in this life, but no discoverable unity and coherence of these plans, then in so far there are many glimpses of selfhood, many fragmentary selves present in connection with the life of some human organism. But there is so far no one self, no one person discoverable. You are one self just in so far as the life that goes on in connection with your organism has some one purpose running through it. By the terms "this person" and "this self," then, we mean this human life in so far as it expresses some one purpose. Yet, of course, this one purpose which is expressed in the life of a single self need not be one which is defined by this self in abstract terms. On the contrary, most of us are aware that our lives are unified, after a fashion, by the very effort that we more or less vaguely make to assert ourselves somehow as individuals in our world. Many of us have not yet found out how it would be best to assert ourselves. But we are trying to find out. This very effort to find out gives already a certain unity of purpose to our lives.

But in so far as we have indeed found out some cause, far larger than our individual selves, to which we are fully ready to be loyal, this very cause serves to give the required unity to our lives, and so to determine what manner of self each of us is, even though we chance to be unable to define in abstract terms what is the precise nature of this very cause. Loyalty may be sometimes almost dumb; it is so in many of those obscure and humble models of loyalty of whom I have already spoken. They express their loyalty clearly enough in deeds. They often could not very well formulate it in words. They could not give an abstract account of their business. Yet their loyalty gives them a business. It unifies their activities. It makes of each of these loyal beings an individual self,—a life unified by a purpose. This purpose may in such cases come to consciousness merely as a willing hunger to serve the cause, a proud obedience to the ideal call. But in any case, wherever loyalty is, there is selfhood, personality, individual purpose embodied in a life.

And now, further, if the argument of our first and second lectures is right, wherever a human selfhood gets practically and consciously unified, there is some form of loyalty. For, except in terms of some sort of loyal purpose, as we saw, this mass of instincts, of passions, of social interests, and of private rebelliousness, whereof the nature of any one of us is orginally compounded, can never get any effective unity whatever.

To sum up so far,—a self is a life in so far as it is unified by a single purpose. Our loyalties furnish such purposes, and hence make of us conscious and unified moral persons. Where loyalty has not yet come to any sort of definiteness, there is so far present only a kind of inarticulate striving to be an individual self. This very search for one's true self is already a sort of life-purpose, which, as far as it goes, individuates the life of the person in question, and gives him a task. But loyalty brings the individual to full moral self-consciousness. It is devoting the self to a cause that, after all, first makes it a rational and unified self, instead of what the life of too many a man remains,—namely, a cauldron of seething and bubbling efforts to be somebody, a cauldron which boils dry when life ends.

V

But what, you may now ask, has all this view of the self to do with conscience? I answer that the nature of conscience can be understood solely in terms of such a theory of the self as the one just sketched.

Suppose that I am, in the foregoing sense, a more or less completely unified and loyal self. Then there are two aspects of this selfhood which is mine. I live a life; and I have, as a loyal being, an ideal. The life itself is not the ideal. They are and always remain in some sense distinct. For no one act of my life, and no limited set of acts of mine, can ever completely embody my ideal. My ideal comes to me from my cause, as the ideal of the Speaker of the House of Commons, in the story that we have already used to illustrate loyalty, came to him from the House. My cause, however, is greater than my individual life. Hence it always sets before me an ideal which demands more of me than I have yet done,— more, too, than I can ever at any one instant accomplish. Even because of this vastness of my ideal, even because that to which I am loyal is so much greater than I ever become, even because of all this can my ideal unify my life, and make a rational self of me.

Hence, if I am indeed one self, my one ideal is always something that stands over against my actual life; and each act of this life has to be judged, estimated, determined, as to its moral value, in terms of the ideal. My cause, therefore, as it expresses itself to my own consciousness through my personal ideal,—my cause and my ideal taken together, and viewed as one, perform the precise function which tradition has attributed to conscience. My cause, then, for our philosophy of loyalty, *is* my conscience,—my cause as interpreted through my ideal of my personal life. When I look to my cause, it furnishes me with a conscience; for it sets before me a plan or ideal of life, and then constantly bids me contrast this plan, this ideal, with my transient and momentary impulses.

To illustrate: Were I a loyal judge on the bench, whose cause was my official function, then my judicial conscience would be simply my whole ideal as a judge, when this ideal was contrasted with any of my present and narrower views of the situation directly before me. If, at a given moment, I tended to lay unfair stress upon one side of a controversy that had been brought into my court, my ideal would say: But a judge is impartial. If I were disposed to decide with inadvised haste, the ideal would say: But a judge takes account of the whole law bearing on the case. If I were offered bribes, my judicial conscience would reject them as being once for all ideally intolerable. In order to have such a judicial conscience, I should, of course, have to be able to view my profession as the carrying out of some one purpose, and so as one cause. This purpose I should have learned, of course, from the traditions of the office. But I should have had willingly to adopt these traditions as my own, and to conceive my own life in terms of them, in order to have a judicial conscience of my own. Analogous comments could be made upon the conscience of an artist, of a statesman, of a friend, or of a devoted member of a family, of any one who has a conscience. To have a conscience, then, is to have a cause, to unify your life by means of an ideal determined by this cause, and to compare the ideal and the life.

If this analysis is right, your conscience is simply that ideal of life which constitutes your moral personality. In having your conscience you become aware of your plan of being yourself and nobody else. Your conscience presents to you this plan, however, in so far as the plan or ideal in question is distinct from the life in which you are trying to embody your plan. Your life as it is lived, your experiences, feelings, deeds,—these are the embodiment of your ideal plan, in so far as your ideal plan for your own individual life as this self, gets embodied at all.

But no one act of yours ever expresses your plan of life perfectly. Since you thus always have your cause beyond you, there is always more to do. So the plan or ideal of life comes to stand over against your actual life as a general authority by which each deed is to be tested, just as the judicial conscience of the judge on the bench tests each of his official acts by comparing it with his personal ideal of what a judge should be. My conscience, therefore, is the very ideal that makes me this rational self, the very cause that inspires and that unifies me. Viewed as something within myself, my conscience is the spirit of the self, first moving on the face of the waters of natural desire, and then gradually creating the heavens and the earth of this life of the individual man. This spirit informs all of my true self, yet is nowhere fully expressed in any deed. So that, in so far as we contrast the ideal with the single deed, we judge ourselves, condemn ourselves, or approve ourselves.

Our philosophy of loyalty thus furnishes us with a theory of a certain kind of consciousness which, in any case, precisely fulfils the functions of the traditional conscience. I need hardly say that the conscience which I have now described is not in its entirety at all innate. On the contrary, it is the flower rather than the root of the moral life. But unquestionably we should never get it unless we possessed an innate power to become reasonable, unless we were socially disposed beings, unless we were able so to develop our reason and our social powers as to see that the good of mankind is indeed also our own good, and, in brief, unless we inherited a genuine moral nature.

With this view of the nature of conscience, what can we say as to the infallability of such a conscience? I answer: My conscience is precisely as fallible or as infallible as my choice of a cause is subject to error, or is of such nature as to lead me aright. Since loyalty, in so far as it is loyalty, is always a good, the conscience of any loyal self is never wholly a false guide. Since loyalty may be in many respects blind, one's conscience also may be in many respects misleading. On the other hand, your conscience, at any stage of its development, is unquestionably the best moral guide that you then have, simply because, so far as it is viewed as an authority outside of you, it is your ideal, your cause, set before you; while, in so far as it is within you, it is the spirit of your own self, the very ideal that makes you any rational moral person whatever. Apart from it you are a mere pretence of moral personality, a manifold fermentation of desires. And as you have only your own life to live, your conscience alone can teach you how to live that life. But your conscience will doubtless grow with you, just as your loyalty and your cause will grow. The best way to make both of them grow is to render up your life to their service and to their expression.

Conscience, as thus defined, is for each of us a personal affair. In so far as many of us are fellow-servants of the same cause, and, above all, in so far as all of us, if we are enlightened, are fellow-servants of the one cause of universal loyalty, we do indeed share in the same conscience. But in so far as no two of us can live the same life, or be the same individual human self, it follows that no two of us can possess identical consciences, and that no two of us should wish to do so. Your conscience is not mine; yet I share with you the same infinite realm of moral truth, and we are subject to the same requirement of loyalty to loyalty. This requirement must interpret itself to us all in endlessly varied ways. The loyal are not all monotonously doing the same thing. Yet they individually partake of the one endlessly varied and manifold spirit of loyalty.

As to whether conscience is in any sense divine, we shall learn something in our closing lecture upon the relations of Loyalty and Religion.

VI

So far as is needful for our present practical purpose, the theory of the conscience which our philosophy of loyalty requires is now before you. We needed this theory in order to prepare the way for answering the question: In how far does the law, *Be loyal to loyalty*, enable us to decide cases of moral doubt? In how far does this principle furnish a means of discovering these special precepts about single cases which common sense calls the "dictates of conscience"?

How do moral doubts arise in the mind of a loyal person? I answer: Moral doubts arise in the loyal mind when there is an apparent conflict between loyalties. As a fact, that cause, which in any sense unifies a life as complex as my human life is, must of course be no perfectly simple cause. By virtue of my nature and of my social training, I belong to a family, to a community, to a calling, to a state, to humanity. In order to be loyal to loyalty, and in order to be a person at all, I must indeed unify my loyalty. In the meantime, however, I must also choose special causes to serve; and if these causes are to interest me, if they are to engross and to possess me, they must be such as together appeal to many diverse sides of my nature; they must involve me in numerous and often conflicting social tasks; they can form one cause only in so far as they constitute an entire system of causes. My loyalty will be subject, therefore, to the ancient difficulty regarding the one and the many. Unless it is one in its ultimate aim, it will be no loyalty to universal loyalty; unless it is just to the varied instincts and to the manifold social interests of a being such as I am, it cannot engross me.

Despite this great difficulty, however, the loyal all about us show us that this union of one and many in life is, at least in great portions of long human careers, a possible thing. We never completely win the union; we never realize to the full the one loyal life; but in so far as we are loyal, we win enough of this unity of life to be able to understand the ideal, and to make it our own guide. Our question still remains, however, this: Since the only loyal life that we can undertake to live is so complex, since the one cause of universal loyalty can only be served, by each of us, in a personal life wherein we have to try to unify various special loyalties, and since, in many cases, these special loyalties seem to us to conflict with one another,—how shall we decide, as between two apparently conflicting loyalties, which one to follow? Does our principle tell us what to do when loyalties thus seem to us to be in conflict with one another?

It is, of course, not sufficient to answer here that loyalty to loyalty requires us to do whatever can be done to harmonize apparently conflicting loyalties, and to remove the conflict of loyalties from the world, and to utilize even conflict, where it is inevitable, so as to further general loyalty. That answer we have already considered in an earlier passage of this discussion. It is a sound answer; but it does not meet those cases where conflict is forced upon us, and where we ourselves must take sides, and must annul or destroy one or two conflicting loyalties. One or two illustrations of such a type will serve to show what sorts of moral doubts our own philosophy of loyalty has especially to consider.

At the outset of our Civil War, many men of the border states, and many who had already been in the service of the Union, but who were conscious of special personal duties to single states of the Union, found themselves in presence of a well-known conflict of loyalties. Consider the personal problem that the future General Lee had to solve. Could the precept, *Be loyal to loyalty, and to that end, choose your own personal cause and be loyal thereto,*—could this principle, you may say, have been of any service in deciding for Lee his personal problem at the critical moment?

Or again, to take a problem such as some of my own students have more than once urged, in various instances, as a test case for my theory of loyalty to decide: A young woman, after a thorough modern professional training, begins a career which promises not only worldly success, but general good to the community in which she works. She is heartily loyal to her profession. It is a beneficent profession. She will probably make her mark in that field if she chooses to go on. Meanwhile she is loyal to her own family. And into the home, which she has left for her work, disease, perhaps death, enters. Her younger brothers and sisters are now unexpectedly in need of such care as hers; or the young family of her elder brother or sister, through the death of their father or mother, has come to be without due parental care. As elder sister or as maiden aunt this young woman could henceforth devote herself to family tasks that would mean very much for the little ones in question. But this devotion would also mean years of complete absorption in these family tasks, and would also mean an entire abandonment of the profession so hopefully begun, and of all the good that she can now be fairly sure of doing if she continues in that field.

What are the dictates of conscience? How shall this young woman solve her problem? How shall she decide between these conflicting loyalties? To be loyal to the family, to the needs of brothers, sisters, nephews, nieces,—surely this is indeed devotion of a self to a cause. But to be loyal to her chosen profession, which, in this case, is no mere hope, but which is already an actual and successful task,—is not that also loyalty to a cause? And does the principle, *Be loyal to loyalty*, decide which of these two causes is the one for this young woman to serve?

These two cases of conscience may serve as examples of the vast range of instances of a conflict of loyalties. And now you may ask: What will our principle do to decide such cases?

VII

I reply at once by emphasizing the fact that the precept, *Be loyal to loyalty*, implies two characteristics of loyal conduct which are, to my mind, inseparable. The first characteristic is Decisiveness on the part of the loyal moral agent. The second characteristic is Fidelity to loyal decisions once made, in so far as later insight does not clearly forbid the continuance of such fidelity. Let me indicate what I mean by these two characteristics.

Loyalty to loyalty is never a merely pious wish. It is personal devotion. This devotion shows itself by action, not by mere sentiments. Loyalty to loyalty hence requires the choice of some definite mode of action. And this mode of action involves, in critical cases, some new choice of a personal cause, through which the loyal agent undertakes to serve henceforth, as best he can, the general cause of the loyalty of mankind. Now, my special choice of my personal cause is always fallible. For I can never know with certainty but that, if I were wiser, I should better see my way to serving universal loyalty than I now see it. Thus, if I choose to be loyal to loyalty by becoming a loyal clerk or a watchman or a lighthouse keeper, I can never know but that, in some other calling, I might have done better. Now, it is no part of the precept, *Be loyal to loyalty*, to tell me, or to pretend to tell me, what my most effective vocation is. Doubts about that topic are in so far not moral doubts. They are mere expressions of my general ignorance of the world and of my own powers. If I indeed happen to know that I have no power to make a good clerk or a good watchman, the precept about loyalty then tells me that it would be disloyal to waste my powers in an undertaking for which I am so unfit. If, of various possible ways of undertaking to be loyal to loyalty, my present insight already tells me that one will, in my case, certainly succeed best of all, then, indeed, the general principle of loyalty requires me to have neither eyes to see nor tongue to speak save as this best mode of service commands. But if, at the critical moment, I cannot predict which of two modes of serving the cause of loyalty to loyalty will lead to the more complete success in such service, the general principle certainly cannot tell me which of these two modes of service to choose.

And, nevertheless, the principle does not desert me, even at the moment of my greatest ignorance. It is still my guide. For it now becomes the principle, *Have a cause; choose your cause; be decisive*. In this form the principle is just as practical as it would be if my knowledge of the world and of my own powers were infallible. For it forbids cowardice; it forbids hesitancy beyond the point where further consideration can be reasonably expected, for the present, to throw new light on the situation. It forbids me to play Hamlet's part. It requires me, in a loyal spirit and in the light of all that I now know, to choose and to proceed to action, not as one who believes himself omniscient, but as one who knows that the only way to be loyal is to act loyally, however ignorantly one has to act.

Otherwise started, the case is this. I hesitate at the critical moment between conflicting causes. For the sake of loyalty to loyalty, which one of two conflicting special causes shall I henceforth undertake to serve? This is my question. If I knew what is to be the outcome, I could at once easily choose. I am ignorant of the outcome. In so far I indeed cannot tell which to choose. But in one respect I am, nevertheless, already committed. I have already undertaken to be loyal to loyalty. In so far, then, I already have my cause. If so, however, I have neither eyes to see nor tongue to speak save as this my highest cause commands. Now, what does this my highest cause, loyalty to loyalty, command? It commands simply but imperatively that, since I must serve, and since, at this critical moment, my only service must take the form of a choice between loyalties, I shall choose, even in my ignorance, what form my service is henceforth to take. The point where I am to make this choice is determined by the obvious fact that, after a certain waiting to find out whatever I can find out, I always reach the moment when further indecision would of itself constitute a sort of decision,—a decision, namely, to do nothing, and so not to serve at all. Such a decision to do nothing, my loyalty to loyalty forbids; and therefore my principle clearly says to me after a fair considera- tion of the case: *Decide, knowingly if you can, ignorantly if you must, but in any case decide, and have no fear.*

The duty of decisiveness as to one's loyalty is thus founded upon considerations analogous to those which Professor James has em- phasized, in speaking of certain problems about belief in his justly famous essay on the Will to Believe. *As soon as further indecision would itself practically amount to a decision to do nothing,*—and so would mean a failure to be loyal to loyalty,—*then at once decide.* This is the only right act. If you cannot decide knowingly, put your own personal will into the matter, and thereupon decide ignorantly. For ignorant service, which still knows itself as a will- ing attempt to serve the cause of universal loyalty, is better than a knowing refusal to undertake any service whatever. The duty to decide is, in such cases, just that upon which our principle insists.

Decision, however, is meaningless unless it is to be followed up by persistently active loyalty. Having surrendered the self to the chosen special cause, loyalty, precisely as loyalty to loyalty, for- bids you to destroy the unity of your own purposes, and to set the model of disloyalty before your fellows, by turning back from the cause once chosen, unless indeed later growth in knowledge makes manifest that further service of that special cause would henceforth involve unquestionable disloyalty to universal loyalty. Fidelity to the cause once chosen is as obvious an aspect of a thorough devotion of the self to the cause of universal loyalty, as is decisiveness.

Only a growth in knowledge which makes it evident that the special cause once chosen is an unworthy cause, disloyal to universal loyalty,—only such a growth in knowledge can absolve from fidelity to the cause once chosen. In brief, the choice of a special personal cause is a sort of ethical marriage to this cause, with the exception that the duty to choose some personal cause is a duty for everybody, while marriage is not everybody's duty. The marriage to your cause is not to be dissolved unless it becomes unquestionably evident that the continuance of this marriage involves positive unfaithfulness to the cause of universal loyalty. But like any other marriage, the marriage of each self to its chosen personal cause is made in ignorance of the consequences. Decide, then, in the critical case, and, "forsaking all others, cleave to your own cause." Thus only can you be loyal to loyalty.

If you once view the matter in this way, you will not suppose that our principle would leave either the future General Lee or our supposed young professional woman without guidance. It would say: Look first at the whole situation. Consider it carefully. See, if possible, whether you can predict the consequences to the general loyalty which your act will involve. If, after such consideration, you still remain ignorant of decisive facts, then look to your highest loyalty; look steadfastly at the cause of universal loyalty itself. Remember how the loyal have always borne themselves. Then, with your eyes and your voice put as completely as may be at the service of that cause, arouse all the loyal interests of your own self, just as they now are, to their fullest vigor; and hereupon firmly and freely decide. Henceforth, with all your mind and soul and strength belong, fearlessly and faithfully, to the chosen personal cause until the issue is decided, or until you positively know that this cause can no longer be served without disloyalty. So act, and you are morally right.

Now, that is how Lee acted. And that, too, is how all the loyal of our own Northern armies acted. And to-day we know how there was indeed loyalty to loyalty upon both sides, and how all those loyal actually served the one cause of the now united nation.

They loyally shed their blood, North and South, that we might be free from their burden of hatred and of horror. Precisely so should the young woman of our ideal instance choose. It is utterly vain for another to tell her which she ought to choose,—her profession or her family. But it would be equally vain, and an insult to loyalty, lightly to say to her: Do as you please. One can say to her: Either of these lives,—the life of the successful servant of a profession, or the life of the devoted sister or aunt,—either, if loyally lived, is indeed a whole life. Nobody ought to ask for a more blessed lot than is either of these lives,—however obscure the household drudgery of the one may be, however hard beset by cares the worldly success of the other may prove, or however toilsome either of them in prospect is, so long as either is faithfully lived out in full devotion. For nobody has anything better than loyalty, or can get anything better. But one of them alone can you live. No mortal knows which is the better for your world. With all your heart, in the name of universal loyalty, choose. And then be faithful to the choice. So shall it be morally well with you.

Now, if this view of the application of our precept is right, you see how our principle is just to that mysterious and personal aspect of conscience upon which common sense insists. Such a loyal choice as I have described demands, of course, one's will,—one's conscious decisiveness. It also calls out all of one's personal and more or less unconsciously present instincts, interests, affections, one's socially formed habits, and whatever else is woven into the unity of each individual self. Loyalty, as we have all along seen, is a willing devotion. Since it is willing, it involves conscious choice. Since it is devotion, it involves all the mystery of finding out that some cause awakens us, fascinates us, reverberates through our whole being, possesses us. It is a fact that critical decisions as to the direction of our loyalty can be determined by our own choice. It is also a fact that loyalty involves more than mere conscious choice. It involves that response of our entire nature, conscious and unconscious, which makes loyalty so precious. Now, this response of the whole nature of the self, when the result is a moral decision, is what common sense has in mind when it views our moral decisions as due to our conscience, but our conscience as a mysterious higher or deeper self.

As a fact, the conscience is the ideal of the self, coming to consciousness as a present command. It says, *Be loyal.* If one asks,

Loyal to what? the conscience, awakened by our whole personal response to the need of mankind replies, *Be loyal to loyalty.* If, hereupon, various loyalties seem to conflict, the conscience says: *Decide.* If one asks, *How decide?* conscience further urges, *Decide as I, your conscience, the ideal expression of your whole personal nature, conscious and unconscious, find best.* If one persists, *But you and I may be wrong,* the last word of conscience is, *We are fallible, but we can be decisive and faithful; and this is loyalty.*

V. Some American Problems in Their Relation to Loyalty

In the philosophy of loyalty, whose general statement has been contained in the foregoing lectures, I have made an effort to reconcile the conception of loyalty with that of a rational and moral individualism. To every ethical individualist I have said: In loyalty alone is the fulfilment of the reasonable purposes of your individualism. If you want true freedom, seek it in loyalty. If you want self-expression, spirituality, moral autonomy, loyalty alone can give you these goods. But equally I have insisted upon interpreting loyalty in terms that emphasize the significance of the individual choice of that personal cause to which one is to be loyal. This evening, as I approach the application of our philosophy of loyalty to some well-known American problems, it is important for us to bear in mind from the outset this synthesis of individualism and loyalty which constitutes our whole ethical doctrine.

I

The traditional view of loyalty has associated the term, in the minds of most of you, with moral situations in which some external social power predetermines for the individual, without his consent, all the causes to which he ought to be loyal. Loyalty so conceived appears to be opposed to individual liberty. But in our philosophy of loyalty there is only one cause which is rationally and absolutely determined for the individual as the right cause for him as for everybody,—this is the general cause defined by the phrase *loyalty to loyalty*. The way in which any one man is to show his loyalty to loyalty is, however, in our philosophy of loyalty, something which varies endlessly with the individual, and which can never be precisely defined except by and through his personal consent. I can be loyal to loyalty only in my own fashion, and by serving my own special system of causes. How wide a range of moral freedom of conscience this fact gives me, we began at the last time to see. In order to make that fact still clearer, let me sum up our moral code afresh, and in another order than the one used at the last time.

As our philosophy of loyalty states the case, the moral law is: (1) be loyal; (2) to that end have a special cause or a system of causes which shall constitute your personal object of loyalty, your business in life; (3) choose this cause, in the first place, for yourself, but decisively, and so far as the general principle of loyalty permits, remain faithful to this chosen cause, until the work that you can do for it is done; and (4) the general principle of loyalty to which all special choices of one's cause are subject, is the principle: Be loyal to loyalty, that is, do what you can to produce a maximum of the devoted service of causes, a maximum of fidelity, and of selves that choose and serve fitting objects of loyalty.

From the point of view of this statement of the moral law, we are all in the wrong in case we have no cause whatever to which we are loyal. If you are an individualist in the sense that you are loyal to nothing, you are certainly false to your duty. Furthermore, in order that you should be loyal at all, the cause to which you are loyal must involve the union of various persons by means of some social tie, which has in some respects an impersonal or superindividual character, as well as a distinct personal interest for each of the persons concerned.

On the other hand, my statement of the moral principle gives to us all an extremely limited right to judge what the causes are to which any one of our neighbors ought to devote himself. Having defined loyalty as I have done as a devotion to a cause, outside the private self, and yet chosen by this individual self as his cause; having pointed out the general nature which such a cause must possess in order to be worthy,—namely, having shown that it must involve the mentioned union of personal and impersonal interests;

having, furthermore, asserted that all rightly chosen loyalty is guided by the intent not to enter into any unnecessary destruction of the loyalty of others, but is inspired by loyalty to loyalty, and so seeks, as best the loyal individual can, to further loyalty as a common good for all mankind,—having said so much, I must, from my point of view, leave to the individual the decision as to the choice of the cause or causes to which he is loyal, subject only to these mentioned conditions. I have very little right to judge, except by the most unmistakable expression of my fellow's purpose, whether he is actually loyal, in the sense of my definition, or not.

I may say of a given person that I do not understand to what cause he is loyal. But I can assert that he is disloyal only when I know what cause it is to which he has committed himself, and what it is that he has done to be false to his chosen fidelity. Or again, I can judge that he lacks loyalty if he makes it perfectly evident by his acts or by his own confessions that he has chosen no cause at all. If he is unquestionably loyal to something, to his country or to his profession or to his family, I may criticise his expression of loyalty, in so far as I clearly see that it involves him in unnecessary assault upon the loyalty of others, or upon their means to be loyal. Thus, all unnecessary personal aggression upon what we commonly call the rights of other individuals are excluded by my formula, simply because in case I deprive my fellow of his property, his life, or his physical integrity, I take away from him the only means whereby he can express in a practical way whatever loyalty he has. Hence such aggression, unless necessary, involves disloyalty to the general loyalty of mankind, is a crime against humanity at large, and is inconsistent with any form of loyalty. Such is the range of judgment that we have a right to use in our moral estimates of other people. The range thus indicated is, as I have insisted, large enough to enable us to define all rationally defensible special principles regarding right and wrong acts. Murder, lying, evil speaking, unkindness, are from this point of view simply forms of disloyalty.

But my right to judge the choices of my fellow is thus very sharply limited. I cannot say that he is disloyal because his personal cause is not my cause, or because I have no sympathy with the objects to which he devotes himself. I have no right to call him disloyal because I should find that if I were to do what he does, I should indeed be disloyal to causes that I accept. I may not judge a man to be without an object of loyalty merely because I do not understand what the object is with which he busies himself. I may regard his cause as too narrow, if I clearly see that he could do better service than he does to the cause of universal loyalty. But when I observe how much even the plainest and humblest of the loyal sometimes unconsciously do to help others to profit by the contagion of their own loyalty, by the example of their faithfulness, I must be cautious about judging another man's cause to be too narrow. You cannot easily set limits to the occupations that the sincere choice of somebody will make expressions of genuine loyalty. The loyal individual may live largely alone; or mainly in company. His life may be spent in the office or in the study or in the workshop or in the field; in arctic exploration, in philanthropy, in a laboratory. And yet the true form and spirit of loyalty, and of loyalty to loyalty, when once you get an actual understanding of the purposes of the self that is in question, is universal and unmistakable.

I hesitate, therefore, to decide for another person even such a question as the way in which his most natural and obvious opportunities for loyalty shall be used. It is true that nature furnishes to us all opportunities for loyalty which it seems absurd to neglect. Charity, as they say, begins at home. Still more obviously does loyalty naturally begin at home. People who wholly neglect their natural family ties often thereby make probable that they are disloyal people. Yet the well-known word about hating father and mother in the service of a universal cause paradoxically states a possibility to which the history of the early Christian martyrs more than once gave an actual embodiment. If the martyr might break loose from all family ties in his loyal service of his faith, one cannot attempt to determine for another person at just what point the neglect of a naturally present opportunity for loyalty becomes an inevitable incident of the choice of loyalty that one has made. Nature, after all, furnishes us merely our opportunities to be loyal. Some of these must be used. None of them may be so ignored that thereby we deliberately increase the disloyalty of mankind. But the individual retains the inalienable duty, which nobody, not even his most pious critical neighbor, can either perform or wholly judge for him,—the duty to decide wherein his own loyalty lies. Yet the duty to be loyal to loyalty is absolutely universal and rigid.

As we also saw at the last time, since fidelity and loyalty are indeed inseparable, the breaking of the once plighted faith is always a disloyal act, unless the discovery that the original undertaking involves one in disloyalty to the general cause of loyalty requires the change. Thus, indeed, the once awakened and so far loyal member of the robber band would be bound by his newly discovered loyalty to humanity in general, to break his oath to the band. But even in such a case, he would still owe to his comrades of the former service a kind of fidelity which he would not have owed had he never been a member of the band. His duty to his former comrades would change through his new insight. But he could never ignore his former loyalty, and would never be absolved from the peculiar obligation to his former comrades,— the obligation to help them all to a higher service of humanity than they had so far attained.

You see, from this point of view, how the requirements of the spirit of loyalty are in one sense perfectly stern and unyielding, while in another sense they are and must be capable of great freedom of interpretation. In judging myself, in deciding how I can best be loyal to loyalty, in deciding what special causes they are through which I am to express my loyalty, in judging whether my act is justified by my loyalty,—in all these respects I must be with myself, at least in principle, entirely rigid. As I grow in knowledge, I shall better learn how to be loyal. I shall learn to serve new causes, to recover from vain attempts at a service of which I was incapable, and in general to become a better servant of the cause. But at each point of my choice my obligation to be loyal, to have a cause, to have for the purposes of voluntary conduct no eyes and ears and voice save as this cause directs,—this obligation is absolute. I cannot excuse myself from it without being false to my own purpose. I may sleep or be slothful, but precisely in so far as such relaxation fits me for work. I may amuse myself, but because amusement is again a necessary preliminary to or accompaniment of loyal service. I may seek my private advantage, but only in so far as, since I am an instrument of my cause, it is indeed my duty, and is consistent with my loyalty, to furnish to the cause an effective instrument. But the general principle remains: Working or idle, asleep or awake, joyous or sorrowful, thoughtful or apparently careless, at critical moments, or when engaged in the most mechanical routine, in so far as my will can determine what I am,

I must be whatever my loyalty requires me to be. And in so far my voluntary life is from my point of view a topic for judgments which are in principle perfectly determinate.

Profoundly different must be my judgment in case of my estimate of the loyalty of my fellow. The tasks of mankind are not only common but also individual. So long as you are sure of your own loyalty, and do not break your trust, I cannot judge that you are actually disloyal. I can only judge in some respects whether your loyalty is or is not enlightened, is or is not successful, is or is not in unnecessary conflict with the loyalty of others. I have to be extremely wary of deciding what the loyalty of others demands of them. But this I certainly know, that if a man has made no choice for himself of the cause that he serves, he is not yet come to his rational self, he has not yet found his business as a moral agent.

II

Such are our general results regarding the nature of loyalty as an ethical principle. This complete synthesis of loyalty with a rational individualism must be borne in mind as we attempt a certain practical application of these principles to the problem of our present American life. If there is any truth in the foregoing, then our concept especially helps us in trying to define what it is that we most need in the social life of a democracy, and what means we have of doing something to satisfy the moral needs of our American community, while leaving the liberties of the people intact.

Liberty without loyalty—of what worth, if the foregoing principles are sound, could such liberty be to any people? And yet, if you recall the protest of my young friend, the Russian immigrant's son, as cited to you in a former lecture, you will be reminded of the great task that now lies before our American people,—the task of teaching millions of foreign birth and descent to understand and to bear constantly in mind the value of loyalty, the task also of keeping our own loyalty intact in the presence of those enormous complications of social life which the vastness of our country, and the numbers of our foreign immigrants are constantly increasing. The problem here in question is not merely the problem of giving instruction in the duties of citizenship to those to whom our country is new, nor yet of awakening and preserving patriotism. It is the problem of keeping alive what we now know to be the central principle of the moral life in a population which is constantly being altered by new arrivals, and unsettled by great social changes.

If you recall what was said in our former lecture regarding modern individualism in general, you will also see that our American immigration problem is only one aspect of a world-wide need of moral enlightenment,—a need characteristic of our time. One is tempted to adapt Lincoln's great words, and to say that in all nations, but particularly in America, we need in this day to work together to the end that loyalty of the people, by the people, and for the people shall not perish from the earth.

It is not, indeed, that loyal people no longer are frequent amongst us. The faithful who live and die in loyalty so far as they know loyalty are indeed not yet uncommon. The loyalty of the common people is precisely the most precious moral treasure of our world. But the moral dangers of our American civilization are twofold. First, loyalty is not sufficiently prominent amongst our explicit social ideals in America. It is too much left to the true-hearted obscure people. It is not sufficiently emphasized. Our popular literature too often ignores it or misrepresents it. This is one danger, since it means that loyalty is too often discouraged and confused, instead of glorified and honored. In the long run, if not checked, this tendency must lead to a great decrease of loyalty. The second danger lies in the fact that when loyalty is indeed emphasized and glorified, it is then far too seldom conceived as rationally involving loyalty to universal loyalty. Hence we all think too often of loyalty as a warlike and intolerant virtue, and not as the spirit of universal peace. Enlightened loyalty, as we have now learned, means harm to no man's loyalty. It is at war only with disloyalty, and its warfare, unless necessity constrains, is only a spiritual warfare. It does not foster class hatreds; it knows of nothing reasonable about race prejudices, and it regards all races of men as one in their need of loyalty. It ignores mutual misunderstandings. It loves its own wherever upon earth its own, namely, loyalty itself, is to be found. Enlightened loyalty takes no delight in great armies or in great navies for their own sake. If it consents to them, it views them merely as transiently necessary calamities. It has no joy in national prowess, except in so far as that prowess means a furtherance of universal loyalty. And it regards the war-spirit, which in our first lecture we used as an example of loyalty,—it regards this spirit, I say, as at its best an outcome of necessity or else of unenlightened loyalty, and as at its worst one of the basest of disloyalties to universal loyalty.

Now, it is precisely this enlightened form of loyalty, this conception of loyalty to loyalty, which we most need to have taught to our American people,—taught openly, explicitly,—yet not taught, for the most part, by the now too familiar method of fascinating denunciations of the wicked, nor by the mere display of force, social or political, nor by the setting of class against class, nor yet by any glorification of mere power, nor by appeals merely to patriotic but confused fervor. We want loyalty to loyalty taught by helping many people to be loyal to their own special causes, and by showing them that loyalty is a precious common human good, and that it can never be a good to harm any man's loyalty except solely in necessary defence of our own loyalty.

III

From the point of view of the foregoing discussion, if you want to do the best you can to teach loyalty, not now to single individuals, but to great masses of people,—masses such as our whole nation,—you should do three things: (1) You should aid them to possess and to keep those physical and mental powers and possessions which are the necessary conditions for the exercise of loyalty. (2) You should provide them with manifold opportunities to be loyal, that is, with a maximum of significant, rational enterprises, such as can be loyally carried out; you should, if possible, secure for them a minimum of the conditions that lead to the conflicts of various forms of loyalty; and you should furnish them a variety of opportunities to get social experience of the value of loyalty. (3) You should explicitly show them that loyalty is the best of human goods, and that loyalty to loyalty is the crown and the real meaning of all loyalty.

Helping the people to the attainment and preservation of their powers obviously involves the sort of care of public health, the sort of general training of intelligence, the sort of protection and assistance, which our philanthropists and teachers and public-spirited people generally regard as important. There is no doubt that in our modern American life our social order does give to great numbers of people care and assistance and protection, such as earlier stages of civilization lacked. But the other side of the task of providing our people with the means of ethical advancement, the side that has to do with letting them know what loyalty is, and with giving them opportunities to be loyal, this side, I say, of what we ought to do to further the moral progress of our people, is at present very imperfectly accomplished.

With prosperity, as we may well admit, sympathy, benevolence, public spirit, even the more rational philanthropy which seeks not merely to relieve suffering, but to improve the effective powers of those whom we try to help,—all these things have become, in recent decades, more and more prominent on the better side of our civilization. And yet I insist, just as prosperity is not virtue, and just as power is not morality, so too even public charity, and even the disposition to train people, to make them more intelligent, to give them new power, all such dispositions are insufficient to insure the right moral training of our people, or the effective furtherance of ideal life amongst them.

What men need involves opportunity for loyalty. And such opportunity they get, especially through the suggestion of objects to which they can be loyal. If you want to train a man to a good life, you must indeed do what you can to give him health and power. And you do something for him when, by example and by precept, you encourage him to be sympathetic, public-spirited, amiable, or industrious. But benevolence, sympathy, what some people love to call altruism,—these are all mere fragments of goodness, mere aspects of the dutiful life. What is needed is loyalty. Meanwhile, since loyalty is so plastic a virtue, since the choice of the objects of loyalty must vary so widely from individual to individual, and since, above all, you can never force anybody to be loyal, but can only show him opportunities for loyalty, and teach him by example and precept what loyalty is, the great need of any higher civilization is a vast variety of opportunities for individual loyalty, and of suggestion regarding what forms of loyalty are possible.

Now, I need not for a moment ignore the fact that every higher civilization, and of course our own, presents to any intelligent person numerous opportunities to be loyal. But what I must point out in our present American life is, that our opportunities for loyalty are not rightly brought to our consciousness by the conditions of our civilization, so that a great mass of our people are far too little reminded of what chances for loyalty they themselves have, or of what loyalty is. Meanwhile our national prosperity and our national greatness involve us all in many new temptations to disloyalty, and distract our minds too much from dwelling upon the loyal side of life; so that at the very moment when our philanthropy is growing, when our sympathies are constantly aroused through the press, the drama, and our sensitive social life generally, our training in loyalty is falling away. Our young people grow up with a great deal of their attention fixed upon personal success, and also with a great deal of training in sympathetic sentiments; but they get far too little knowledge, either practical or theoretical, of what loyalty means.

IV

The first natural opportunity for loyalty is furnished by family ties. We all know how some of the conditions of our civilization tend with great masses of our population to a new interpretation of family ties in which family loyalty often plays a much less part than it formerly did in family life. Since our modern family is less patriarchal than it used to be, our children, trained in an individualistic spirit, frequently make little of certain duties to their parents which the ancient family regarded as imperative and exalted as ideal. Many of us deliberately prefer the loss of certain results of the patriarchal family tie, and are glad that in the modern American family the parental decisions regarding the marriage choices of children are so much less decisive than they used to be. Many insist that other weakenings of the family tie, such as divorce legislation and the practice of divorce have involved, are in the direction of a reasonable recognition of individual interests.

I will not try to discuss these matters at length. But this I can say without hesitation: The family ties, so far as they are natural, are opportunities for loyalty; so far as they are deliberately chosen or recognized, are instances of the choice of a loyalty. From our point of view, therefore, they must be judged as all other opportunities and forms of loyalty are judged. That such opportunities and forms alter their character as civilization changes is inevitable, and need be no matter for superstitious cares regarding whatever was arbitrary in traditional views of family authority. But, after all, fidelity and family devotion are amongst the most precious opportunities and instances of loyalty. Faithlessness can never become a virtue, however your traditions about the forms of faithfulness may vary in their external details. Whoever deliberately breaks the tie to which he is devoted loses the opportunity and the position of the loyal self, and in so far loses the best sort of thing that there is in the moral world. No fondness for individualism will ever do away with this fact. We want more individuals and more rational individualism; but the only possible ethical use of an individual is to be loyal. He has no other destiny.

When a man feels his present ties to be arbitrary or to be a mechanical bondage, he sometimes says that it is irrational to be a mere spoke in a wheel. Now, a loyal self is always more than a spoke in a wheel. But still, at the worst, it is better to be a spoke in the wheel than a spoke out of the wheel. And you never make ethical individuals, or enlarge their opportunities, merely by breaking ties. Hence, so far as a change in family tradition actually involves a loss of opportunities and forms of loyalty, which tradition used to emphasize, our new social order has lost a good thing. Do we see at present just what is taking its place? If the patriarchal family must pass away or be profoundly altered, surely we should not gain thereby unless there were to result a new family type, as rich in appeal to our human affections and our domestic instincts as the old forms ever were.

But in our present American life the family tie has been weakened, and yet no substitute has been found. We have so far lost certain opportunities for loyalty.

Now, how shall we hope to win back these opportunities? I answer: We can win back something of what we have lost if only we in this country can get before ourselves and our public a new, a transformed conception of what loyalty is. The loyalties of the past have lost their meaning for many people, simply because people have confounded loyalty with mere bondage to tradition, or with mere surrender of individual rights and preferences. Such people have forgotten that what has made loyalty a good has never been the convention which undertook to enforce it, but has always been the spiritual dignity which lies in being loyal.

As to individual rights and preferences, nobody can ever attain either the one or the other, in full measure, apart from loyalty to the closest and the most lasting ties which the life of the individual in question is capable of accepting with hearty willingness. Ties once loyally accepted may be broken in case, but only in case, the further keeping of those ties intact involves disloyalty to the universal cause of loyalty. When such reason for breaking ties exists, to break them becomes a duty; and then, indeed, a merely conventional persistence in what has become a false position, is itself a disloyal deed. But ties may never be broken except for the sake of other and still stronger ties. No one may rationally say: "Loyalty can no longer bind me, because, from my deepest soul, I feel that I want my individual freedom." For any such outcry comes from an ignorance of what one's deepest soul really wants.

Disloyalty is moral suicide. Many a poor human creature outlives all that, in the present life, can constitute his true self,—outlives as a mere psychological specimen any human expression of his moral personality, and does so because he has failed to observe that his loyalty, so far and so long as it has been his own, has been the very heart of this moral personality. When loyalty has once been fully aroused, and has then not merely blundered but died, there may, indeed, remain much fluttering eagerness of life; as if a stranded ship's torn canvas were still flapping in the wind. But there cannot remain freedom of personal existence. For the moral personality that once was loyal, and then blindly sought freedom, is, to human vision, dead. What is, in such a case, left of the so-called life is merely an obituary. Curious people of prominence have sometimes expressed a wish to read their own obituaries. But it is hardly worth while to live them.

People sometimes fail to observe this fact, partly because they conceive loyalty as something which convention forces upon the individual, and partly because they also conceive loyalty, where it exists, as merely a relation of one individual to other individuals. Both views, as we now know, are wrong. No convention can predetermine my personal loyalty without my free consent. But then, if I loyally consent, I mean to be faithful; I give myself; I am henceforth the self thus given over to the cause; and therefore essential unfaithfulness is, for me, moral suicide. Meanwhile, however, no mere individual can ever be my whole object of loyalty; for to another individual human being I can only say, "So far as in me lies I will be loyal to *our* tie, to *our* cause, to *our union*."

For this reason the loyal are never the mere slaves of convention; and, on the other hand, they can never say one to another, "Since we have now grown more or less tired of one another, our loyalty ceases." To tire of the cause to which my whole self is once for all committed, is indeed to tire of being my moral self. I cannot win my freedom in that way. And no individual, as individual, ever has been, or ever can be, my whole cause. My cause has always been a tie, an union of various individuals in one.

Now, can our American people learn this lesson in so far as this lesson is illustrated by family ties? Can they come to see that loyalty does not mean the bondage of one individual to another, but does mean the exaltation of individuals to the rank of true personalities by virtue of their free acceptance of enduring causes, and by virtue of their lifelong service of their common personal ties? If this lesson can be learned by those serious-minded people who have been misled, in recent times, by a false form of individualism, then we shall indeed not get rid of our moral problems, but we shall vastly simplify our moral situation. And a rational individualism will still remain our possession. How to treat the disloyal remains indeed a serious practical problem. But we shall never learn to deal with that problem if we suppose that the one cure for disloyalty, or the one revenge which we can take upon the disloyal, lies in a new act of disloyalty, that is, in the mere assertion of our individual freedom. Train our people to know the essential preciousness of loyalty. In that way only can you hope to restore to the family, not, indeed, all of its older conventional forms, but its true dignity. The problem, then, of the salvation of the family life of our nation resolves itself into the general problem of how to train our people at large into loyalty to loyalty.

V

The second great opportunity for loyalty is furnished, to the great mass of our people, by their relations to our various political powers and institutions, and to our larger social organizations generally. And here we meet, in the America of to-day, with many signs that our political and social life form at present a poor school in the arts of loyalty to loyalty.

Loyalty, indeed, as I have repeatedly said, we still have present all about us. The precious plain and obscure people, who are loyal to whatever they understand to be worthy causes, and, on the other hand, those prominent and voluntary public servants, who in so many cases are our leaders in good works,—these we have so far still with us. And new forms of loyalty constantly appear in our social life. Reform movements, trades-unions, religious sects, partisan organizations, both good and evil, arouse in various ways the loyalty of great numbers of people. Yet these special loyalties do not get rightly organized in such form as to further loyalty to loyalty. Narrow loyalties, side by side with irrational forms of individualism and with a cynical contempt for all loyalty,—these are what we too often see in the life of our country. For where the special loyalties are, amongst our people, most developed, they far too often take the form of a loyalty to mutually hostile partisan organizations, or to sects, or to social classes, at the expense of loyalty to the community or to the whole country. The labor-unions demand and cultivate the loyalty of their members; but they do so with a far too frequent emphasis upon the thesis that in order to be loyal to his own social class, or, in particular, to his union, the laborer must disregard certain duties to the community at large, and to the nation,—duties which loyalty to loyalty seems obviously to require. And party loyalty comes to be misused by corrupt politicians to the harm of the state. Therefore loyalty to special organizations such as labor-unions comes to be misdirected by such leaders as are disloyal, until the welfare of the whole social order is endangered.

The result is that the very spirit of loyalty itself has come to be regarded with suspicion by many of our social critics, and by many such partisans of ethical individualism as those whose various views we studied in our second lecture. Yet surely if such ethical individualists, objecting to the mischiefs wrought by the corrupt politicians, or by the more unwise leaders of organized labor, imagine that loyalty is responsible for these evils, such critics have only to turn to the recent history of corporate misdeeds and of the unwise management of corporations in this country, in order to be reminded that what we want, at present, from some of the managers of great corporate interests is more loyalty, and less of individualism of those who seek power. And I myself should say that precisely the same sort of loyalty is what we want both from the leaders and from the followers of organized labor. There is here one law for all.

Meanwhile, in case of the ill-advised labor agitations, and of the corrupt party management, the cure, if it ever comes, surely will include cultivating amongst our people the spirit of loyalty to loyalty. Loyalty in itself is never an evil. The arbitrary interference with other men's loyalties, the disloyalty to the universal cause of loyalty, is what does the mischief here in question. The more the laborer is loyal to his union, if only he learns to conceive this loyalty as an instance of loyalty to loyalty, the more likely is his union to become, in the end, an instrument for social harmony, and not, as is now too often the case, an influence for oppression and for social disorganization. The loyalty which the trades-unions demand of their members is at present too often viewed as a mere class loyalty, and also as opposed to the individual freedom of choice on the part of those laborers who do not belong to a given union, or even to those who are in the union, but whose right choice and interests are sometimes hindered by their own union itself. But our people must learn that loyalty does not mean hostility to another man's loyalty. Loyalty is for all men, kings and laborers alike; and whenever we learn to recognize that fact, loyalty will no longer mean fraternal strife, and will no longer excuse treason to the country for the sake of fidelity to corrupt leaders or to mischievous agitations.

VI

But you may hereupon ask how the masses of our people are to learn such a lesson of loyalty to loyalty. I admit that the problem of teaching our people what the larger loyalty means is at present peculiarly difficult. And it is rendered all the more difficult by the fact that, for us Americans, loyalty to our nation, as a whole, is a sentiment that we find to be at present by no means as prominent in the minds of our people as such sentiments have been in the past in other nations. Let me explain what I mean by this assertion.

The history of our sentiment towards our national government is somewhat different from the history of the sentiment of patriotism in other countries. We have never had a king as the symbol of our national dignity and unity. We have, on the other hand, never had a war against a privileged class. Our constitutional problem which led to the Civil War was a different problem from that which the French Revolution, or the English political wars of the seventeenth century, have exemplified. At one time loyalty to the nation stood, in the minds of many of our people, in strong contrast to their loyalty to their state, or to their section of the country. This contrast led in many cases to a bitter conflict between the two sorts of loyal interests. At last such conflicts had to be decided by war. The result of the war was such that, from one point of view, the national government and the authority of the nation, as a whole, have won a position that is at present politically unquestionable. The supremacy of the national government in its own sphere is well recognized. Within its legal limits, its power is popularly regarded as irresistible. The appearance of its soldiers at any moment of popular tumult is well known to be the most effective expression of public authority which we have at our disposal, even although the body of soldiers which may be accessible for such a show of force happens to be a very small body. Viewed, then, as a legal authority and as a physical force, our national government occupies at present a peculiarly secure position. And so, the President of the United States is, at any moment, more powerful than almost any living monarch. All this, viewed as the outcome of our long constitutional struggle, would seem of itself to suggest that the American people have become essentially loyal to our national government.

But, nevertheless, is this quite true? I think that almost any thoughtful American has to admit that in time of peace we do not regard our national government with any such intense sentiments of loyalty as would seem from report to be the living, the vital, the constant possession of Japanese patriots when they consider their traditional devotion to the nation and to their emperor. For them their country is part of a religion. In their consciousness it is said especially to be the land sacred to the memory of their dead. The living, as they say, are but of to-day. The dead they have always with them in memory, even if not in the determinate form of any fixed belief with regard to the precise nature of the life beyond the grave. It is said that the Japanese are very free as to the formulation of all their religious opinions. But in any case their religion includes a reverence for the historic past, a devotion to the dead whose memory makes their country sacred, and a present loyalty which is consciously determined by these religious motives.

Now, the most patriotic American can hardly pretend that he consciously views his country, taken as a whole, in any such religious way. The country is to us an unquestionable political authority. Were it in danger, we should rally to its defence. We have a good many formal phrases of reverence for its history and for its dignity,—phrases which had a much more concrete meaning for our predecessors, when the country was smaller, or when the country was in greater danger from its foes. But, at present, is not our national loyalty somewhat in the background of our practical consciousness? Are we really at present a highly patriotic people? Certainly, the observer of a presidential canvass can hardly think of that canvass as a religious function, or believe that a profound reverence for the sacred memory of the fathers is at present a very prominent factor in determining our choice of the party for which we shall vote at the polls.

And if you say that political dissensions are always of such a nature as to hide for the moment patriotism behind a mist of present perplexities, you may well be asked in reply whether anywhere else, outside of political dissensions, we have in our national life functions, ceremonies, expressions of practical devotion to our nation as an ideal, which serve to keep our loyalty to our country sufficiently alive, and sufficiently a factor in our lives. When can the ordinary American citizen say in time of peace that he performs notable acts of devotion to his country, such that he could describe those acts in the terms that the Speaker of the House of Commons used, in the story that I reported to you in my former lecture? In other words, how often, in your own present life, or in the lives of your fellow-citizens, as now you know them, is it the case that you do something critical, significant, involving personal risk or sacrifice to yourself, and something which is meanwhile so inspired by your love of your nation as a whole that you can say that just then you have neither eyes to see nor tongue to speak save as the country itself, in your opinion, requires you to see and to speak?

Now, all this state of things is opposed to our easily forming a conception of what loyalty to loyalty demands of us in our social and political relations. But the faults in question are not peculiar to our American people. They seem to my mind to be merely symptomatic of something which naturally belongs to the general type of civilization upon which, in our national history, we are entering. The philosopher Hegel, in one of his works on the philosophy of history, depicts a type of civilization, which, in his mind, was especially associated with the decline and fall of the Roman Empire, as well as with the political absolutism of the seventeenth and of the early eighteenth centuries in modern Europe. This type itself was conceived by him as a general one, such that it might be realized in very various ages and civilizations. Hegel called this type of social consciousness the type of the social mind, or of the "Spirit," that had become, as he said, "estranged from itself." Let me explain what Hegel meant by this phrase.

A social consciousness can be of the provincial type; that is, of the type which belongs to small commonwealths or to provinces, such as our own thirteen colonies once were. Or, on the other hand, the social life can be that of the great nation, which is so vast that the individuals concerned no longer recognize their social unity in ways which seem to them homelike. In the province the social mind is naturally aware of itself as at home with its own. In the Roman Empire, or in the state of Louis XIV, nobody is at home. The government in such vast social orders represents the law, a dictation that the individual finds relatively strange to himself. Or, again, the power of the state, even when it is attractive to the individual, still seems to him like a great nature force, rather than like his own loyal self, writ large. The world of the "self-estranged social mind" of Hegel's definition we might, to use a current phraseology, characterize as the world of the imperialistic sort of national consciousness, or simply as the world of imperialism. In such a world, as Hegel skilfully points out, the individual comes to regard himself as in relation to the social powers, which, in the first place, he cannot understand. The fact that, as in our present civilization, he is formally a free citizen, does not remove his character of self-estrangement from the social world in which he moves. Furthermore, since such a society is so vast as to be no longer easily intelligible, not only its political, but also its other social powers, appear to the individual in a similarly estranged and arbitrary fashion. In Hegel's account stress is laid upon the inevitable conflicts between wealth and governmental authority, between corporate and political dignities,—conflicts which characterize the imperial stage of civilization in question. In the world of the "self-estranged social mind," loyalty passes into the background, or tends to disappear altogether. The individual seeks his own. He submits to major force. Perhaps he finds such submission welcome, if it secures him safety in the acquisition of private gain, or of stately social position. But welcome or unwelcome, the authority to which he submits, be it the authority of the government or the authority which wealth and the great aggregations of capital imply, is for him just the fact, not a matter for loyalty.

Such a formula as the one which Hegel suggests is always inadequate to the wealth of life. But we are able to understand our national position better when we see that our nation has entered in these days into the realm of the "self-estranged spirit," into the social realm where the distant and irresistible national government, however welcome its authority may be, is at best rather a guarantee of safety, an object for political contest, and a force with which everybody must reckon, than the opportunity for such loyalty, as our distinctly provincial fathers used to feel and express in their early utterances of the national spirit. In the same way in this world of the self-estranged spirit, the other forces of society arouse our curiosity, interest us intensely, must be reckoned with, and may be used more or less wisely to our advantage. But they are the great industrial forces, the aggregations of capital, the combinations of enormous physical power, employed for various social ends. These vast social forces are like the forces of nature. They excite our loyalty as little as do the trade-winds or the blizzard. They leave our patriotic sentiments cold. The smoke of our civilization hides the very heavens that used to be so near, and the stars to which we were once loyal. The consequences of such social conditions are in part inevitable. I am not planning any social reform which would wholly do away with these conditions of the world of the self-estranged spirit. But these conditions of our national social order do not make loyalty to loyalty a less significant need. They only deprive us of certain formerly accessible opportunities for such loyalty. They lead us to take refuge in our unpatriotic sects, partisan organizations, and unions. But they make it necessary that we should try to see how, under conditions as they are, we can best foster loyalty in its higher forms, not by destroying the sects or the unions, but by inspiring them with a new loyalty to loyalty.

As the nation has in so many respects become estranged from our more intimate consciousness, we have lost a portion of what, in the days before the war, used to absorb the loyalty of a large proportion of our countrymen. I speak here of loyalty to the separate states and to the various provinces of our country. Such provincial loyalty still exists, but it has no longer the power that it possessed when it was able to bring on civil war, and very nearly to destroy the national unity. Instead of dangerous sectionalism, we now have the other dangerous tendency towards a war of classes, which the labor-unions and many other symptoms of social discontent emphasize. We have that corrupt political life which partisan mismanagement exemplifies. And we have that total indifference to all forms of loyalty which our seekers after individual power sometimes exhibit, and which occasionally appears as so serious an evil in the conduct of the businesss of certain great corporations.

All these, I insist, are in our present American life symptoms of the state of the self-estranged spirit. The decline of family loyalty, of which I spoke a while since, may be regarded as another symptom of the same general tendency. Loyalty itself, under such conditions, remains too often unconscious of its true office. Instead of developing into the true loyalty to loyalty, it fails to recognize its own in the vast world of national affairs. It is dazzled by the show of power. It limits its devotion to the service of the political party, or of the labor-union, or of some other sectarian social organization. In private life, as we have seen, it too often loses control of the family. In public life it appears either as the service of a faction, or as a vague fondness for the remote ideals.

VII

And nevertheless, as I insist, loyalty to loyalty is not a vague ideal. The spirit of loyalty is practical, is simple, is teachable, and is for all normal men. And in order to train loyalty to loyalty in a great mass of people, what is most of all needed is *to help them to be less estranged than they are from their own social order.*

To sum up, then, this too lengthy review, the problem of the training of our American people as a whole to a larger and richer social loyalty is *the problem of educating the self-estranged spirit of our nation to know itself better.* And now that we have the problem before us, what solution can we offer?

The question of what methods a training for loyalty should follow, is the special problem of our next lecture. But there is indeed one proposal, looking towards a better training of our nation to loyalty, which I have here to make as I close this statement of our national needs. The proposal is this. We need and we are beginning to get, in this country, a new and wiser provincialism. I mean by such provincialism no mere renewal of the old sectionalism. I mean the sort of provincialism which makes people want to idealize, to adorn, to ennoble, to educate, their own province; to hold sacred its traditions, to honor its worthy dead, to support and to multiply its public possessions. I mean the spirit which shows itself in the multiplying of public libraries, in the laying out of public parks, in the work of local historical associations, in the enterprises of village improvement societies,—yes, even in the genealogical societies, and in the provincial clubs. I mean also the present form of that spirit which has originated, endowed, and fostered the colleges and universities of our Western towns, cities, and states, and which is so well shown throughout our country in our American pride in local institutions of learning. Of course, we have always had something of this provincialism. It is assuming new forms amongst us. I want to emphasize how much good it can do in training us to higher forms of loyalty.

That such provincialism is a good national trait to possess, the examples of Germany and of Great Britain, in their decidedly contrasting but equally important ways, can show us. The English village, the English country life, the Scotsman's love for his own native province,—these are central features in determining the sort of loyalty upon which the British Empire as a whole has depended. Germany, like ourselves, has suffered much from sectionalism. But even to-day the German national consciousness presupposes and depends upon a highly developed provincial life and loyalty. One of the historical weaknesses of France has been such a centralization of power and of social influence about Paris as has held in check the full development of the dignity of provincial consciousness in that country. Now, in our country we do not want any mutual hatred of sections. But we do want a hearty growth of provincial ideals. And we want this growth just for the sake of the growth of a more general and effective patriotism. We want to train national loyalty through provincial loyalty. We want the ideals of the various provinces of our country to be enriched and made definite, and then to be strongly represented in the government of the nation. For, I insist, it is not the sect, it is not the labor-union, it is not the political partisan organization, but it is the widely developed provincial loyalty which is the best mediator between the narrower interests of the individual and the larger patriotism of our nation. Further centralization of power in the national government, without a constantly enriched and diversified provincial consciousness, can only increase the estrangement of our national spirit from its own life. On the other hand, history shows that if you want a great people to be strong, you must depend upon provincial loyalties to mediate between the people and their nation.

The present tendency to the centralization of power in our national government seems to me, then, a distinct danger. It is a substitution of power for loyalty. *To the increase of a wise provincialism in our country, I myself look for the best general social means of training our people in loyalty to loyalty.* But of course such training in loyalty to loyalty must largely be a matter of the training of individuals, and to the problem of individual training for loyalty our next lecture will be devoted.

VI. Training for Loyalty

Two objections which have been expressed to me by hearers of the foregoing lectures of this course deserve a word of mention here, as I begin the present discussion of the work of training individuals for a loyal life.

I

The first of these objections concerns my use of the term "loyalty." "Why," so the objection runs, why can you not avoid the endless repetition of your one chosen term, 'loyalty'? Why would not other words, such as fidelity, devotion, absorption, trustworthiness, faithfulness, express just as well the moral quality to which you give the one name that you have employed?"

The second objection concerns my definition of the term "loyalty," and is closely connected with the first objection. It runs as follows: "Why do you insist that the cause which the loyal man serves must be a *social* cause? Why might one not show the same essential moral quality that you define, when the cause that he serves is something quite unearthly, or something earthly but quite unsocial? Saint Simeon on his pillar, Buddha seeking enlightenment under his lonely tree, the Greek geometer attempting to square the circle,—were they not as faithful as your loyal man is? And were their causes social causes?"

I reply to these objections together. I have defined my present usage of the popular term "loyalty" in my own distinctly technical way. Loyalty so far means for us, in these lectures, the willing, the thoroughgoing, and the practical devotion of a self to a cause. And a cause means, in these lectures, something that is conceived by its loyal servant as unifying the lives of various human beings into one life. Now, I know of no other word whose popular usage comes closer than does that of the good old word "loyalty" to embodying the meaning that I have given to the term. I think, then, that I have a right to my technical definition. It is based upon popular usage, and goes beyond that usage only in a very natural way. I intend soon to show you that we are now ready to substitute for this first technical definition another and a still more significant definition which will reveal to us, for the first time, the true spirit of the enterprise in which all the loyal are actually engaged. But I can reach this higher definition only through the simpler definition. To that, inadequate as it is, my discussion must cling until we are ready for something better.

Granting, however, my own definition of my term, I cannot easily use any other popular or philosophical term in the same way. I cannot substitute the word "devotion" for the term "loyalty," since loyalty is to my mind a very special kind of devotion. A man might be devoted to the pursuit of pleasure; but that would not make him loyal. Fidelity, again, is, in my own account, but one aspect of loyalty. Loyalty includes fidelity, but means more, since, besides fidelity, decisiveness and the acceptance of a cause also belong to loyalty; and the fidelity of a dog to his master is only a pathetic hint of loyalty, or a fragment of the disposition that, in human beings, expresses itself in the full reasonableness of loyal life. The same comment holds in case of the word "faithfulness." As for *absorption*, the loyal are absorbed in their cause, but the angry man is absorbed in his passion. Yet such absorption is not what I have in mind. The loyal, again, possess *trustworthiness*, but a watch may also be trustworthy; and that word ill expresses the voluntary nature of the spirit of loyalty.

I cannot find, then, another term to meet my purpose. My usage of this term is justified mainly by that simplification of our conceptions of the moral life which our theory has made possible.

As for my insistence upon the social aspect of the loyal life, that insistence implies two assertions about such cases as those of the lonely saint on the pillar, or Buddha seeking enlightenment, or the geometer trying to solve his problem. The first assertion is that all such lonely enterprises have moral value only when they are indeed a part of one's service of the cause of humanity. The saint on the pillar was presumably trying to add to the store of merits which the universal church was supposed to possess. If so, he had a social cause which he served; namely, the church,—the mystic union of all the faithful. His cause may have been wrongly conceived by him, but it was, in our sense, a cause, and a social one. The Buddha of the legend was seeking to save not only himself but mankind. He was loyal, therefore, in our sense. As for the geometer, his search for the solution of his problem concerned one of the deepest common interests of the human mind; namely, an interest in the discovery and possession of rational truth. Truth is for everybody; and it unifies the lives of all men. Whoever seeks for a truth, as important as geometrical truth is, and seeks it with a serious devotion, has a social cause. And no utterly lonely devotion to anything is morally worthy of a human being.

My second assertion as to the social aspect of causes is this. Sometimes men have indeed sought to serve God in an actually unsocial way, and have been devoted to a world of unseen and superhuman beings. But such beings, if they are real and are worthy of a moral devotion at all, are worthy of the devotion of all mankind; and in such devotion, if it is indeed justified, all men may be blessed. The worship of the gods, even when a lonely worshipper has expressly tried not to think of his fellows, has therefore always implied a loyalty to the cause of one's own people, or else of mankind at large. The Christian's devotion to God is inseparably bound up with his loyalty to the mystic union of the faithful in the church. The non-social aspect of genuine worship is therefore but apparent. Religion seeks a certain fulfilment of the purposes of the moral life,—a fulfilment which we are hereafter to study. On the other hand, loyalty itself, as a devotion to a cause which unifies many human lives, is, as we shall see, profoundly religious in its spirit. For men, viewed merely as natural phenomena, are many, and mutually conflicting creatures. Loyalty aims at their unity, and such unity, as we shall see, is always something that has its supernatural meaning. In brief, then, to worship divine powers in a genuinely ethical spirit, is always to serve a cause which is also, in the human sense, social,—the cause of the state, or of the church, or of humanity; while, on the other hand, loyally to serve causes is to aim to give human life a supernatural,— an essentially divine meaning.

And these are the reasons why I have insisted upon the social aspect of loyalty.

Bear, then, I pray you, with my too often repeated term; accept its apparently too narrow definition. We are on the way towards a view of the spiritual unity of all human life,—a view which may serve to justify this technical usage of a term, this long dwelling upon the details of the moral life, these seemingly commonplace comments upon social problems.

II

How shall individuals be trained for a loyal life? That is the question of the present lecture. In trying to answer this question I shall first dwell, briefly, and very inadequately, upon the place that a training for loyalty should occupy in the education of the young. Then I shall speak of the way in which mature people are trained for such forms of loyalty as belong to the actual business of the social world.

Whether you like my use of terms or not, you will agree that training the young for a willing and thoroughgoing devotion of the self to a social cause, must be a long and manifold task. Before true loyalty can appear in any but rather crude and fragmentary forms in the life of a growing human being, a long discipline of the whole mind must have preceded. One must have become capable of conceiving what a social cause is. One must have learned decisiveness and fidelity through an elaborate general preparation of the will. Therefore, while the beginnings of loyalty extend far back into the life of childhood, its full development must belong to mature years. Affection, obedience, a gradually increasing persistence in wholesome activities, a growing patience and self-control, all these, in the natural growth of a human being, are preliminaries to the more elaborate forms of loyalty. By themselves

they are not loyalty. In accordance with the general trend of
modern educational theory, we therefore naturally point out that,
in training children for future loyalty, teachers must avoid trying
to awaken any particular sort of loyalty before its fitting basis is
laid, and before a sufficient age has been reached. The basis in
question involves a rich development of social habits. The age for
true and systematic loyalty can hardly precede adolescence. One
must obtain the material for a moral personality before a true conscience can be won. Conscience, as we have seen, is the flower and
and not the root of the moral life.

But there is one contribution which childhood early makes to a
possible future loyalty,—a contribution which we sometimes fail
to take sufficiently into account. That contribution is the well-
known disposition to idealize heroes and adventures, to live an
imaginary life, to have ideal comrades, and to dream of possible
great enterprises. I have for years insisted, along with many others
who have studied our educational problems, that these arts of
idealization which childhood so often and so spontaneously prac-
tises, are not only in themselves fascinating and joyous, but are
also a very important preliminary to that power to conceive the
true nature of social causes upon which later loyalty depends. If
I have never been fascinated in childhood by my heroes and by
the wonders of life, it is harder to fascinate me later with the call
of duty. Loyalty, as we have already seen, and as we have yet
further to see, is an idealizing of human life, a communion with
invisible aspects of our social existence. Too great literalness in the
interpretation of human relations is, therefore, a foe to the development of loyalty. If my neighbor is to me merely a creature of a
day, who walks and eats and talks and buys and sells, I shall never
learn to be loyal to his cause and to mine. But the child who plays
with ideal comrades, or who idealizes with an unconscious wisdom
our literal doings and his own, is, in his own way, getting glimpses
of that real spiritual world whose truth and whose unity we have
hereafter more fully to consider. It is in his fantasies, then, that a
child begins to enter into the kingdom of heaven. Such fantasies
may need to be carefully guarded. They may take a dangerous or
even a disastrous turn in the life of one or another child. But in
their better phases they are not mere illusions and are great bless-
ings. They are prophecies of the coming of conscience, and of a
possible union with the world of an actually divine truth.

Yet since loyalty involves conduct, such fantasies of childhood are indeed but a preparation for loyalty. And higher loyalty belongs later. But in normal childhood there do indeed appear, in a fragmentary way, forms of conduct which already include a simple, but, so far as it goes, an actual loyalty to the causes the child already understands. You all know some of these forms. The members of a gang of boys, sometimes of bad boys, show a certain loyalty to the cause represented by the gang. School children develop the code of honor that forbids the telling of tales to the teacher. Truthfulness becomes a conscious virtue early in normal childhood, and has its own childish casuistry,—often an amusing one.

The rule, of course, regarding all such childhood beginnings of loyalty is that we should always respect whatever is in the least socially tolerable about the expressions of even the crudest loyalty. The parent or teacher who trifles with the code of honor of children by encouraging the talebearer, or by even requiring that a child should become an informer, is simply encouraging disloyalty. He outrages the embryonic conscience of his young charges.

For the rest, children appreciate the loyalty or disloyalty of our conduct towards them sooner than they can define their own duty. And the one who would train for loyalty must therefore be, in his dealings with children, peculiarly scrupulous about his own loyalty.

III

But after all, whatever be the best training of childhood for a coming moral life, the rapid development of loyalty itself belongs to adolescence, just as the outcome of that development is reached only in mature life. Upon the importance of youth as the natural period for training in more elaborate forms of loyal conduct, our recent authority regarding adolescence, President Stanley Hall, has insisted. In normal youth various forms of loyalty, of a highly complex character, appear with a great deal of spontaneity. Two of these forms have become important in the life of the youth of many nations, and certainly in the life of our own American youth to-day. The one form is loyalty to the fraternal organization,— very generally to a secret fraternity. The other form is loyalty to one's own side in an athletic contest, or to one's college or other institution, viewed as an athletic entity.

Both of these forms of loyalty have their excesses, and lead to well-known abuses. The secret fraternities may become organizations for general mischief and disorder; the athletic contests may involve overmuch passion, and may even do harm to the general loyalty by fostering the spirit of unfair play. Now, it is notable that both of these sorts of abuses increase when the fraternities and the athletic organizations are imitated in the lower schools by the children. The resulting dangers show that loyalty ought not to be a prematurely forced plant. It should grow, in its various forms, in its due time. Hence those in charge of our secondary schools should not be misled by their knowledge of the preciousness of loyalty into encouraging an overhasty development of secret fraternities and of fully formed athletic organizations amongst those who are not old enough to reap the fruits of such forms of loyalty. The coming of true loyalty may be seriously hindered by the too early organization of the perfectly natural gang of boys into some too elaborate social structure. Harm has been done of late years by too much aping of athletic and fraternity life in connection with the lower grades of schools.

But when youth is fairly reached, and the secret fraternity and the athletic organization become spontaneously prominent, it is plain that our efforts to train our youth to a higher life must recognize these natural types of loyalty, but must do so without over-emphasizing their cruder features. We must always build upon what we have; and therefore any unnecessary hostility to the fraternities and to the athletic life is profoundly objectionable. But the most unhappy features of the athletic, and in some measure of the fraternity, life in our colleges and universities are due to the false social prominence which the public opinion of those who have nothing to do with college life often forces upon our youth. The athletic evils, such as they are, of our academic world, are not due to the college students themselves nearly so much as to the absurd social prominence which the newspapers and the vast modern crowds give to contests which ought to be cheerful youthful sports, wherein a natural loyalty is to be trained, but wherein a national prominence of the games and the contestants is utterly out of place. It is as absurd to overemphasize such matters as it is wicked to interfere unnecessarily with any other aspect of youthful moral development. It is the extravagant publicity of our inter-collegiate sports which is responsible for their principal evils. Leave wholesome youth to their natural life, not irritated and not aroused to unwise emotions by the exaggerated comments of the press, and our athletic organizations would serve their proper function of training the muscles as well as the souls of our youth to loyalty. As for the fraternities,—the false social prominence which their graduate members sometimes force upon them is a distinct hindrance to the work that they can do in training youth for a loyal life.

Fair play in sport is a peculiarly good instance of loyalty. And in insisting upon the spirit of fair play, the elders who lead and who organize our youthful sports can do a great work for the nation. The coach, or the other leader in college sports, to whom fair play is not a first concern, is simply a traitor to our youth and to our nation. If the doctrine of these lectures is right, we can see with what stupendous human interests he is trifling.

As to other ways in which the loyalty of our youth can be trained, we still too much lack, in this country, dignified modes of celebrating great occasions. Once the Fourth of July was a day for training patriotic loyalty; it has now degenerated, and is probably irretrievably lost to the cause of true loyalty. Memorial Day and our national Thanksgiving Day are our best holidays for expressing loyalty to the community and to the nation. Let us cherish them, and preserve them from desecration. But with us both holidays and public ceremonials have a certain democratic tendency to degeneration. We need more means for symbolizing loyalty, both in public monuments and in ceremonials, as well as in forms of common public service to our community. European nations glorify the army as a practical teacher of loyalty to the youth. The loyalty thus won is mingled with the war-spirit, and is therefore dear bought. But we unquestionably need substitutes for military service as a means of training for a loyal life. It belongs to the task of our social leaders to invent and to popularize such substitutes. Herein lies one of the great undertakings of the future.

IV

The true sphere of a complete loyalty is mature life. We constantly need, all of us, individual training in the art of loyalty.

How is this work accomplished in the social order? In answering this question, let history and our daily social experience be our guides. The main lessons that these guides teach us, as I think, are three: First, our loyalty is trained and kept alive by the influence of personal leaders. Secondly, the higher forms of training for loyalty involve a momentous process which I shall call the Idealizing of the Cause. Thirdly, loyalty is especially perfected through great strains, labors, and sacrifices in the service of the cause.

Of the three factors here mentioned, the first and second are inseparable and universal. If we are to be made loyal, we want personal leaders, and highly idealized causes. In exceptional cases a man may seem to be his own sole leader in loyalty. But this is rare. Always, to be sure, a loyal man uses his own leadership, since, as we saw in our fourth lecture, his conscience is his leader. But usually he needs the aid of other personal leaders besides himself. As for the idealizing of the cause,—I have called it a momentous process. How momentous we shall soon see. For it is by this process that we are introduced into the true spiritual world.

Let me illustrate my theses. We are all familiar with the history of clubs and of sectarian social organizations generally. Now how are these social enterprises, good or evil, made to succeed?

You all know that if a club or a sect is to be begun, or if a political or social movement is to be rendered effective, two things are necessary: first, a leader, or a group of leaders, eager, enthusiastic, convinced, or, at the worst, capable of speaking as if they were convinced,—leaders persistent, obstinate, and in their own fitting way aggressive; and, secondly, a cause that can be idealized so that, when the leaders talk of it in their glowing exhortations, it seems to be a sort of supernatural being, in one sense impersonal, but in another sense capable of being personified, an exalted but still personally interesting spiritual power. The two aspects of loyalty, the personal and the seemingly superpersonal, must thus be emphasized together.

Consider, in particular, the process of making almost any new club succeed. Some group of persons, sometimes a single leader, must be found, willing to devote time and energy to directing the new organization. The leader or leaders must believe the enterprise worth while, must proclaim its importance in vigorous terms, and must patiently stand by the club through all the doubtful first period of its existence. But the personal influence of these leaders cannot be enough to arouse any genuine loyalty in the members of the club, unless the organization itself can be made to appear as a sort of ideal personality, of a higher than merely human type. If the leaders impress their companions as being people who are concerned merely with their own private importance, they in vain persist in their propaganda. In that case the club is nicknamed as their particular pet or as their fad; one makes light of their energy, one maligns their motives, and the club crumbles into nothing. In order to succeed, the leaders must give to the club the character of a sort of ideal entity, often of an improvised mythological goddess, who is to be conceived as favoring her devotees, as bestowing upon them extraordinary social or spiritual benefits. Even the convivial festivals of the club, if such festivals there be, must have some sort of ceremonial dignity about them,—a dignity such as suggests the impersonal or superpersonal rank of the club as an ideal. The club must become a cause, in whose service the members are one. If it is a reform club, or other body engaged in a propaganda, then social interests that lie outside of the boundaries of the club's separate being serve to define this cause; the club is then merely an instrument to further a loyalty that is intelligible apart from the existence of this very instrument; and in such a case the leaders of the club have mainly to insist effectively upon the importance of this already existing loyalty. But if the club is to be an end in itself,—an organization that exists for its own sake and for the sake of its own members,—the process of learning to ascribe to the new club the ideal dignity of a common cause is sometimes a difficult process. The devices used by the leaders are, upon occasion, very direct. One simply calls the club an ideal; one personifies it in various poetical ways; and one praises it as a sort of superhuman being. Or, more practically still, one incorporates the club, endows it with a legal personality, and makes it a property owner. But other devices are more indirect. Club ceremonials and festivals, some more or less rudimentary club ritual, perhaps also the various familiar devices of the secret societies, the air of mystery, club emblems and symbols,—all serve to give to the club the appearances, at least, of a fitting cause for the exercise of loyalty. Another indirect device consists in naming the club after famous or beloved people, now dead, whose honor and whose memory idealize the new organization. Or, again, one arbitrarily calls the club ancient and dignifies it by a more or less conscious myth about its past. All such devices serve to call out loyalty in ways that may be comparatively trivial, but that may also be of a very profound significance, if the new organization is actually a fitting object of loyalty.

With proper changes the foregoing account applies to the plans that are useful in establishing a new religious sect. Always you find the same union of personal enthusiasm on the part of leaders with a disposition to define the ideal of the new organization in terms that transcend the limits of individual human life. Man, even when he is a member of a purely convivial social body, is prone to try to conceive both his own life, and also that of this social body, in superhuman terms. Experience thus shows that a procedure of the sort just described does succeed, in many cases, in training people—sometimes small groups, sometimes great bodies of men— to new forms of loyalty.

The plans whereby an actually ancient institution is kept in possession of the loyalty of its own natural servants do not in their essence differ from the ones just characterized. The loyalty of a body of alumni to their university is a classic instance of a loyalty kept alive by the union of an institution with the personality of its living leaders. Even so, the loyalty of the sons of a subjugated nationality, such as the Irish or the Poles, to their country, is kept alive through precisely such an union of the influence of individual leaders with the more impersonal reverence for the idealized, although no longer politically existent nationality.

You see, so far, how the personal leaders and the superhuman cause are inseparable in the training of loyalty. The cause comes to be idealized partly because the leaders so vigorously insist that it is indeed ideal. On the other hand, the leaders become and remain personally efficacious by reason of the dignity that the cause confers upon them. Were they considered apart from their cause, they would seem to be merely ambitious propagandists, seeking gain or notoriety. To those without the range of their personal influence, they often seem such. Yet if they did not speak for the cause, and so give to it the life of their personal enthusiasm, nobody would be taught to regard their cause as ideal. The cause thus needs to become incarnate, as it were, in the persons of the leaders; but the leaders get their personal influence through the fact that they seem to be incarnations of the cause.

Facts of this sort are familiar. You can observe them whenever you attend an anniversary meeting, or other such ceremonial, of your own club, and whenever you listen to those who represent any successful propaganda. But how vastly significant such facts may be in determining the lives of whole generations and nations and races of men, you can only judge if you read the general history of humanity in the light of the principles now pointed out. If our philosophy of loyalty has any truth, the history of human loyalty concerns whatever is most important in the annals of mankind. And the whole history of loyalty is the history of the inseparable union of the personal influence of leaders with the tendency to idealize causes.

V

But the idealization of the cause, although never possible without the aid of living persons, may also depend upon still other factors than the direct personal influence of leaders. When we consider the general history of loyalty amongst men, our attention is soon attracted to a deeply instructive process whereby, in certain cases, —some of them very great and wonderful cases,—causes have been idealized not only by the personal influence of the leaders, but also by certain deeply pathetic motives to which the leaders could constantly appeal. I refer to the process illustrated by the history of lost causes.

I referred a moment ago to the loyalty of the Irish and of the Poles to their own lost nationalities. Now such loyalty to a lost cause may long survive, not merely in the more or less unreal form of memories and sentiments, but in a genuinely practical way. And such loyalty to a lost cause may be something that far transcends the power of any mere habit. New plans, endless conspiracies, fruitful social enterprises, great political organizations,—yes, in the extreme case,—new religions, may grow up upon the basis of such a loyalty to a cause whose worldly fortunes seem lost, but whose vitality may outlast centuries, and may involve much novel growth of opinion, of custom, and of ideals.

The most notable religious development which the world has ever seen, the religion of Israel, together with its successor, Christianity,—this whole religious evolution,—is, as we must here point out, the historical result of a national loyalty to a lost cause. The political unity of all the tribes of Israel, attained but for a moment, so to speak, under David and Solomon, and then lost from the visible world of history, survived as an ideal. Only as such a lost ideal could this conception of what Israel once was and ought again to be inspire the Old Testament prophets to speak the word of the Lord regarding the way of righteousness whereby, as the prophets held, the prosperity of Israel was to be restored. Only this same lost political ideal, and this resulting discovery of the prophetic theory of the divine government of human affairs, could lead over to that later religious interpretation and to that rewriting of the whole ancient history of Israel, which we now read in our Old Testament. Only upon the same basis could the Messianic idea come to be defined; and only thus could the prophetic doctrine of the universal future triumph of righteousness come to be formulated. And so through an historical process, every step of which depended upon a pathetic and yet glorious loyalty to a lost national cause, the ideals in question were at once universalized and intensified until, through Israel, all the nations of Christendom have been blessed. In consequence, to-day, in speaking of its own hopes of the salvation of mankind, and in describing its coming kingdom of heaven, Christianity still uses the familiar terms: Zion, the throne of David, Jerusalem,—terms whose original application was to places and to persons first made notable in their own time merely by reason of the petty tribal feuds of an obscure province. Thus loyalty, steadfast and yet developing through centuries, gradually transformed what were once seemingly insignificant matters of local politics into the most sacred concerns of a world religion.

Loyalty to lost causes is, then, not only a possible thing, but one of the most potent influences of human history. In such cases, the cause comes to be idealized through its very failure to win temporary and visible success. The result for loyalty may be vast. I need not remind you that the early Christian church itself was at first founded directly upon a loyalty to its own lost cause,—a cause which it viewed as heavenly just because here on earth the enemies seemed to have triumphed, and because the Master had departed from human vision. The whole history of Christianity is therefore one long lesson as to how a cause may be idealized through apparent defeat, and how even thereby loyalty may be taught to generation after generation of men, and may develop into endlessly new forms, and so may appeal to peoples to whom the cause in question was originally wholly strange. This history shows us how such a teaching and such an evolution of an idea may be furthered by what seems at first most likely to discourage loyalty, that is, by loss, by sorrow, by worldly defeat.

Loyalty to a lost cause, whatever the grade of dignity of the cause, depends in part, of course, upon the same motives which the simpler and more direct forms of loyalty employ.

But when a cause is lost in the visible world, and when, nevertheless, it survives in the hearts of its faithful followers, one sees more clearly than ever that its appeal is no longer to be fully met by any possible present deed. Whatever one can just now do for the cause is thus indeed seen to be inadequate. All the more, in consequence, does this cause demand that its followers should plan and work for the far-off future, for whole ages and æons of time; should prepare the way for their Lord, the cause, and make his paths straight. Activity becomes thus all the more strenuous, just because its consequences are viewed as so far-reaching and stupendous. Man's extremity is loyalty's opportunity. The present may seem dark. All the greater the work yet to be done. The distant future must be conquered. How vast the undertaking,—how vast, but therefore how inspiring!

All this larger and broader devotion of those loyal to a lost cause is colored and illuminated by strong emotion. Sorrow over what has been lost pierces deep into the hearts of the faithful. So much the more are these hearts stirred to pour out their devotion. Meanwhile, the glamour of memory is over the past. Whatever was commonplace about the former visible fortunes of the lost cause is now forgotten. For the memory of those who sorrow over loss is, as we all know, fond of precious myths, and views these myths as a form in which truth appears. In the great days that have passed away—in the days before the cause suffered defeat—there was indeed tragedy; but there was glory. Legend, often truer,—yes, as Aristotle said of poetry, more philosophical than history,—thus reads into that past not what the lost cause literally was, but what it meant to be. Its body is dead. But it has risen again. The imagination, chastened by all this grief, stirred by all this deep need, not only reforms the story of the past, but builds wonderful visions of what is yet to be.

Loyalty for the lost cause is thus attended by two comrades, grief and imagination. Yet loyalty, always strenuous and active, is not enervated by these deep emotions, nor yet confused by the wealth of these visions; but rather devotes itself to resolving upon what shall be. Grief it therefore transforms into a stimulating sense of need. If we have lost, then let us find. Loyalty also directs its deeds by the visions that imagination furnishes; and meanwhile it demands in turn that the imagination shall supply it with visions that can be translated into deeds. When it hears from the imagination the story of the coming triumph, it does not become passive. Rather does it say: Watch, for ye know not the day or the hour when the triumph of the cause is to come.

> Hora novissima
> Tempora pessima
> Sunt, vigilemus.

This wonderful awakening from the prostration of grief to the stern but fascinating resolve to live and to be active for the lost cause, this freeing of the imagination through the very agony of missing the dear presence in the visible world, and this complete control both of such passion and of such imagination through the will to make all things work together for the good of the cause,— all this is the peculiar privilege of those who are loyal to a cause which the world regards as lost, and which the faithful view as ascended into a higher realm, certain to come again in renewed might and beauty. Thus may grief minister to loyalty.

And I may add, as an obvious truth of human nature, that loyalty is never raised to its highest levels without such grief. For what one learns from experience of grief over loss is precisely the true link between loyalty as a moral attitude, and whatever is eternally valuable in religion. One begins, when one serves the lost causes, to discover that, in some sense, one ought to devote one's highest loyalty precisely to the causes that are too good to be visibly realized at any one moment of this poor wretched fleeting time world in which we see and touch and find mere things, mere sensations, mere feelings of the moment. Loyalty wants the cause in its unity; it seeks, therefore, something essentially superhuman. And therefore, as you see, loyalty is linked with religion. In its highest reaches it always is, therefore, the service of a cause that is just now lost—and lost because the mere now is too poor a vehicle for the presentation of that ideal unity of life of which every form of loyalty is in quest. Loyalty to loyalty, that cause of causes upon which I have so much insisted in the foregoing, is indeed just now in far too many ways a lost cause amongst men. But that is the fault of the men, not of the cause. Let us rejoice that we can serve a cause of which the world, as it is, is not yet worthy.

The history of the lost causes is instructive, however, not only as showing us a new aspect of the value of loyalty, namely, what I have just called the link between loyalty and religion, but also as showing us something of the way in which grief, and imagination, and the stirring of our whole human nature to its very depths, through loss and through defeat, have served in the past as means of training in loyalty. This school of adversity has often been a hard one. But the loyalty that has been trained in this school has produced for us some of humanity's most precious spiritual treasures. Thus, then, through personal leaders and through suffering, loyalty learns to idealize its cause.

VI

What is the lesson of all the foregoing when we ask: How shall we ourselves seek training in loyalty?

The first answer is obvious: Whatever our cause, we need personal leaders. And how shall we be surest of finding such personal leaders? Shall we look exclusively to those who are fellow-servants of our own chosen special causes? We all do this. Yet this is often not enough. Familiarity and personal misunderstandings often interfere with the guidance that our fellow-servants give us. We need the wider outlook. Close friendships are amongst the most powerful supports of loyalty. Yet when people confine themselves to regarding their close friends as their leaders in loyalty, they often become narrow and forget the cause of universal loyalty. Much of the art of loyalty, consequently, depends upon training yourself to observe the loyal who are all about you, however remote their cause is from yours, however humble their lives. It is well also, whenever you have to fight, to learn the art of honoring your opponent's loyalty, even if you learn of it mainly through feeling the weight and the sharpness of his sword. "It is a deep cut; but a loyal enemy was he who could give it to me"—to think in such terms is to lighten the gloom of conflict with what may sometimes be more precious than a transient victory; for at such moments of honoring the loyally dangerous enemy, we begin to learn that all the loyal are in spirit serving, however unwittingly, the same universal cause. To be sure, when men have once sufficiently learned that lesson, they cease to fight. But while fighting lasts, if you cannot love your enemy, it is a beautiful thing to be able to enjoy the sight of his loyalty.

But men have not to fight one another in order to display loyalty. Open your eyes, then, to observe better the loyalty of the peaceful, as well as of the warriors. Consider especially the loyalty of the obscure, of the humble, of your near neighbors, of the strangers who by chance come under your notice. For such exemplars of loyalty you always have. Make them your leaders. Regard every loyal man as your leader in the service of the cause of universal loyalty.

VII

But our review of the history of loyalty taught us another lesson. We need not only leaders. We need to idealize our causes; that is, to see in them whatever most serves to link them to the cause of universal loyalty. And the procedure whereby our causes are to be idealized is one involving a range of possible experiences and activities far too vast to be adequately surveyed in our present discussion. Here belong all those practically valuable relations between loyalty and art, and between loyalty and religion, which the history of mankind illustrates and which we can use in our own training for loyalty. Art supports loyalty whenever it associates our cause with beautiful objects, whenever it sets before us the symbols of our cause in any worthy expression, and whenever, again, by showing us any form of the beautiful, it portrays to us that very sort of learning and unity that loyalty ceaselessly endeavors to bring into human life. Thus viewed, art may be a teacher of loyalty. To say this is in no wise to prejudge the famous question regarding the main purpose of art, and the relation of this purpose of art to the moral life. I am attempting here no theory of art. But it belongs to our present province merely to insist that part of our education in loyalty is to be won through whatever love of beauty and whatever knowledge of the beautiful we possess. The monuments of any cause that possesses monuments should associate our love of this cause with our love for beauty. Our personal causes, if they are worthy at all, need beautiful symbols to express to us their preciousness. Whatever is beautiful appears to us to embody harmonious relations. And the practical search for harmony of life constitutes loyalty. And thus training for loyalty includes the knowledge of the beautiful.

Still more universal in its efficacy as an idealizer of private and personal causes is religion. In how far a genuinely religious experience results from loyalty, and in how far loyalty bears witness to any religiously significant truth, we have hereafter to see. Our closing lectures will deal with the bearing of loyalty upon religion. But we have here to mention, in passing, the converse relation; namely, the influence of religion upon loyalty. We have to point out how large a part of the function of religion in human affairs consists in the idealizing of our loyalties, by linking our causes, whatever they are, to a world which seems to us to be super-human.

VIII

Art and religion, however, are not our only means for teaching ourselves to view our personal causes as linked with universal human interests, and with an unseen superhuman world. Sorrow, defeat, disappointment, failure, whenever these result from our efforts to serve a cause, may all be used to teach us the same lesson. How such lessons have been taught to humanity at large, the history of those lost causes which have been, even because of the loss, transformed into causes of permanent and world-wide importance, has now shown us. This lesson of the history of the lost causes is, however, one that has deep importance for our individual training. We do not always read this lesson aright. To keep our loyalty steadfast through defeat is something that we often view as a sort of extra strain upon loyalty,—the overcoming of a painful hindrance to loyalty. We ought not so to view the matter. Defeat and sorrow, when they are incurred in the service of a cause, ought rather to be a positive aid to loyalty. If we rightly view them, they will prove to be such an aid. For they enable us to see whether we have really given ourselves to the cause, or whether what we took for loyalty was a mere flare of sanguine emotion. When sorrow over a defeat in the service of our cause reverberates all through us, it can be made to reveal whatever loyalty we have. Let us turn our attention to this revelation, even while we suffer. We shall then know for what we have been living. And whoever, once deliberately dwelling upon his cause at a moment of defeat, does not find the cause dearer to him because of his grief, has indeed yet to learn what loyalty is. The cause, furthermore, when viewed in the light of our sorrow over our loss of its present fortunes, at once tends to become idealized,—as the lost throne of David was idealized by Israel, and as the departed Master's cause was idealized by the early church.

The disciples, in the well-known story, say concerning their lost Master to the stranger whom they meet on the lonely road to Emmaus: "We had trusted that it was he who should have redeemed Israel." But soon after "their eyes were opened, and they knew him, and he vanished out of their sight." Amongst all the legends of the risen Lord, this one most completely expresses the spirit of that loyalty which, triumphing even through defeat, winning the spirit even through the loss of a visible presence, was thereafter to conquer its world.

Now, the lesson of such experiences, as history records them, relates not merely to great movements and to mankind at large. It is a personal lesson. It concerns each one of us. I repeat: View your sorrow by itself, and it is a blind and hopeless fact; view your cause in the light of your sorrow, and the cause becomes transfigured. For you learn hereby that it was not this or that fortune, nor even this or that human life which constituted your cause. There was from the beginning, about your cause, something that to human vision seems superpersonal, unearthly as well as earthly. Now the memory of whatever is lost about your cause is peculiarly adapted to bring to your consciousness what this superpersonal element has been. I have already mentioned the merely psychological aspects of the process that, in such cases, goes on. The glamour which memory throws about the past, the awakening of the imagination when some visible presence is removed, the stimulating reaction from the first stroke of sorrow whenever we are able once more to think of our cause itself, the transformation of our own ideas about the cause, by virtue of the very fact that, since our loss has so changed life, the cause can no longer be served in the old way, and must be the object of new efforts, and so of some new form of devotion,—all these are the idealizing motives which are present when defeat comes. I insist,—human loyalty can never be perfected without such sorrow. Regard defeat and bereavement, therefore, as loyalty's opportunity. Use them deliberately as means for idealizing the cause, and so far bringing your personal cause into closer touch with the cause of universal loyalty.

The most familiar of all those blows of fortune which seem to us, for the moment, to make our personal cause a lost cause, is death, when it comes to those with whom our personal cause has so far been bound up. And yet what motive in human life has done more to idealize the causes of individuals than death has done? Death, viewed as a mere fact of human experience, and as a merely psychological influence, has been one of the greatest idealizers of human life. The memory of the dead idealizes whatever interest the living have in former days shared with the departed. Reverence for the dead dignifies the effort to carry on the work that they began, or that, if they died in childhood, our fond desire would have had them live to do. From the beginning a great portion of the religious imagination of mankind has centered about the fact of death. And the same motive works to-day in the minds of all the loyal, whatever their faith.

Idealize your cause. This has been our maxim for the present aspect of our personal training in loyalty. I have offered merely some hints as to how this maxim may be carried into effect. How science can join with art and with religion, how joyous friendly intercourse can in its own place coöperate with our experiences of sorrow to teach us the lessons of idealizing our common causes,— all this I can only indicate.

And thus we have before us two of the methods whereby individual loyalty is trained. The deliberate fixing of our attention upon the doings of loyal people, the deliberate use of those methods of human nature which tend to idealize our cause,—these are means for training in loyalty.

Yet one method remains,—it is the most commonplace, yet often the hardest of all. Loyalty means giving the Self to the Cause. And the art of giving is learned by giving. Strain, endurance, sacrifice, toil,—the dear pangs of labor at the moments when perhaps defeat and grief most seem ready to crush our powers, and when only the very vehemence of labor itself saves us from utter despair,— these are the things that most teach us what loyalty really is. I need not enlarge here upon an ancient and constantly repeated lesson of life,—a lesson which is known to all of you. The partisans of war often glorify war as a moralizer of humanity, because, as they say, only the greatest strains and dangers can teach men true loyalty. I do not think that war is needed for such lessons. The loyalty of the most peaceful enables us all to experience, sooner or later, what it means to give, whatever it was in our power to give, for the cause, and then to see our cause take its place, to human vision, amongst the lost causes. When such experiences come, let us face them without hesitation. For all these things together,—our personal friends who inspire us to the service of our own causes, the hosts of the loyal whom we know so little, but who constitute the invisible church of those who live in the spirit, the griefs that teach us the glory of what our human vision has lost from its field, the imagination that throws over all the range of human life its idealizing light, the labors that leave us breathless, the crushing defeats that test our devotion,—well, these, these are all only the means and the ministers whereby we are taught to enter the realm of spiritual truth.

VII. Loyalty, Truth, and Reality

In closing my last lecture I said that whatever trains us in the arts of loyalty enables us to enter into a world of spiritual truth. These words were intended to indicate that the loyal life has another aspect than the one hitherto most emphasized in these lectures. Our foregoing account has been deliberately one-sided. We have been discussing the moral life as if one could define a plan of conduct without implying more about man's place in the real universe than we have yet made explicit in these lectures. Hence our discussion, so far, is open to obvious objections.

For, in talking about the good of loyalty, we have indeed appealed to human experience to show us wherein that good consists. But our very appeal also showed us that loyalty is good for a man precisely because he believes that his cause itself, even apart from his service, is good, and that both his cause and its goodness are realities, founded in facts which far transcend his individual life and his personal experience. Now, one may well doubt whether this belief of a loyal man is, in any individual case, a well-founded belief. And if it is not well founded, one may well question whether the loyal man's good is not, after all, an illusory good, which will vanish from his experience as soon as he becomes enlightened. Since any instance of loyalty is subject to this sceptical inquiry, one may doubt whether even what we have called the supreme cause, that of loyalty to loyalty, is a good cause. For any or all loyalties may be founded in illusion, and then it would be an illusion that the fostering of loyalty amongst men is a finally worthy undertaking.

I

Objections of this sort are best stated by those to whom they actually occur as serious difficulties regarding the discussions contained in the foregoing lectures. A dear friend of mine, without receiving any instigation from me to help me by such an act, has so aptly summed up the objections here in question, that I can best show you precisely where we now stand by reading to you a portion of a letter which he has written to me, after hearing the first portion of my account of the good of loyalty.

" 'Loyalty to loyalty,' " writes my friend, "doesn't seem ultimate. Is it not loyalty to all *objects* of true loyalty that is our ultimate duty? The object, not the relation,—the universe and the devotion to it, not the devotion alone, is the object of our ultimate devotion. . . . Is it not the glory of this goal that lends dignity to all loyal search,—our own or that of others? It is because of this goal that we cheer on all to pursue it. . . . It is because of what we believe about the end of the various loyalties that we are so glad of all the loyalties which make it possible to attain that end. The port gives value to the courses steering for it. . . . Except for our knowledge of the value of their destination, and of all life lived in quest of that destination, should we be anxious to urge all seekers along their courses? . . . Loyalty is a relation. . . . Can we be loyal to anything, ultimately, except the universe which is the object of all love and all knowledge?"

So far my friend's statement of his difficulty. As you will see, from these two closing lectures of my course which still remain, I cordially share my friend's objection to the definition of loyalty so far insisted upon in these lectures. Our definition of loyalty, and of its relation to the ultimate good which the loyal are seeking, has so far been inadequate. But, as I told you in the opening lecture, we deliberately began with an inadequate definition of the nature of loyalty. We were obliged to do so. I expressly said this in my opening statement. Why we were obliged to do so, and why, thus far in these lectures, we have confined ourselves to developing and to illustrating the consequences of this imperfect definition of loyalty, our closing lectures will of themselves, I hope, make clear. A similar difficulty can be urged against any mere moralism, that is, against any purely ethical theory of the moral life. One wants a doctrine of the real world, or a religion, to help out one's ethics. For, as I have replied to my friend, morality, viewed by itself, has a character that can well be suggested by the parable of the talents. The moral life, regarded simply as the moral life, is the service of a master who seems, to those who serve him, to have gone away into a far country. His servants have faith in him, but the service of his cause always has, for the moral, a certain mystery about it. They can indeed become sure, apart from any solution of this mystery, that their own supreme personal good lies in serving their lord. For not otherwise can they find even the relative peace that lies in a service of duty. But those who serve are not thus altogether secured against a pessimism regarding the whole outcome of human endeavor. For if loyalty is indeed our best, may not even this best itself be a failure?

Or, to use further the similitude of the parable of the talents: It may be indeed our supreme good to serve the master who has gone into the far country. Yet we do not merely want to serve him; we want, like Job, to meet him face to face. Suppose that we should discover the master to be indeed unworthy or a phantom or a deceiver, would even this, our best good, the service of his cause, seem permanently valuable? Should we not say, some day: To serve him was our best chance of life; but after all even that service was vanity.

In any case, our loyalty implies a faith in the master,—an assurance that life, at its best, is indeed worth while. Our philosophy of loyalty must therefore include an attempt to see the master of life himself, and to find out whether in truth he is, what our loyalty implies that he is, a master worth serving.

To sum up: So far we have defined the moral life as loyalty, and have shown why the moral life is for us men the best life. But now we want to know what truth is behind and beneath the moral life. With my friendly correspondent, we want to see the relation of loyalty to the real universe.

II

What must be true about the universe if even loyalty itself is a genuine good, and not a merely inevitable human illusion?

Well, loyalty is a service of causes. A cause, if it really is what our definition requires, links various human lives into the unity of one life. Therefore, if loyalty has any basis in truth, human lives can be linked in some genuine spiritual unity. Is such unity a fact, or is our belief in our causes a mere point of view, a pathetic fallacy? Surely, if any man, however loyal, discovers that his cause is a dream, and that men remain as a fact sundered beings, not really linked by genuine spiritual ties, how can that man remain loyal? Perhaps his supreme good indeed lies in believing that such unities are real. But if this belief turns out to be an illusion, and if a man detects the illusion, can he any longer get the good out of loyalty?

And as for even this personal good that is to be got out of loyalty, we have all along seen that such good comes to a loyal man's mind in a very paradoxical way. A loyal man gets good, but since he gets it by believing that his cause has a real existence outside of his private self, and is of itself a good thing, he gets the fascination of loyalty not as a private delight of his own, but as a fulfilment of himself through self-surrender to an externally existing good,—through a willing abandonment of the seeking of his own delight. And so the loyal man's good is essentially an anticipation of a good that he regards as not his own, but as existent in the cause. The cause, however, is itself no one fellow-man, and no mere collection of fellow-men. It is a family, a country, a church, or is such a rational union of many human minds and wills as we have in mind when we speak of a science or an art. Now, can such causes contain any good which is not simply a collection of separate human experiences of pleasure or of satisfaction? Thus, then, both the reality and the good of a loyal man's cause must be objects of the loyal man's belief in order that he should be able to get the experience of loyalty. And if his loyalty is indeed well founded, there must be unities of spiritual life in the universe such that no one man ever, by himself, experiences these unities as facts of his own consciousness. And these higher unities of life must possess a degree and a type of goodness,—a genuine value, such that no one man, and no mere collection of men, can ever exhaustively experience this goodness, or become personally possessed of this value.

How paradoxical a world, then, must the real world be, if the faith of the loyal is indeed well founded! A spiritual unity of life, which transcends the individual experience of any man, must be real. For loyalty, as we have seen, is a service of causes that, from the human point of view, appear superpersonal. Loyalty holds these unities to be good. If loyalty is right, the real goodness of these causes is never completely manifested to any one man, or to any mere collection of men. Such goodness, then, if completely experienced at all, must be experienced upon some higher level of consciousness than any one human being ever reaches. If loyalty is right, social causes, social organizations, friendships, families, countries, yes, humanity, as you see, must have the sort of unity of consciousness which individual human persons fragmentarily get, but must have this unity upon a higher level than that of our ordinary human individuality.

Some such view, I say, must be held if we are to regard loyalty as in the end anything more than a convenient illusion. Loyalty has its metaphysical aspect. It is an effort to conceive human life in an essentially superhuman way, to view our social organizations as actual personal unities of consciousness, unities wherein there exists an actual experience of that good which, in our loyalty, we only partially apprehend. If the loyalty of the lovers is indeed well founded in fact, then they, as separate individuals, do not constitute the whole truth. Their spiritual union also has a personal, a conscious existence, upon a higher than human level. An analogous unity of consciousness, an unity superhuman in grade, but intimately bound up with, and inclusive of, our apparently separate personalities, must exist, if loyalty is well founded, wherever a real cause wins the true devotion of ourselves. Grant such an hypothesis, and then loyalty becomes no pathetic serving of a myth. The good which our causes possess, then, also becomes a concrete fact for an experience of a higher than human level. That union of self-sacrifice with self-assertion which loyalty expresses becomes a consciousness of our genuine relations to a higher social unity of consciousness in which we all have our being. For from this point of view we are, and we have our worth, by virtue of our relation to a consciousness of a type superior to the human type. And meanwhile the good of our loyalty is itself a perfectly concrete good, a good which is present to that higher experience, wherein our cause is viewed in its truth, as a genuine unity of life. And because of this fact we can straightforwardly say: We are loyal not for the sake of the good that we privately get out of loyalty, but for the sake of the good that the cause—this higher unity of experience—gets out of this loyalty. Yet our loyalty gives us what is, after all, our supreme good, for it defines our true position in the world of that social will wherein we live and move and have our being.

I doubt not that such a view of human life,—such an assertion that the social will is a concrete entity, just as real as we are, and of still a higher grade of reality than ourselves,—will seem to many of you mythical enough. Yet thus to view the unity of human life is, after all, a common tendency of the loyal. That fact I have illustrated in every lecture of this course. That such a view need not be mythical, that truth and reality can be conceived only in such terms as these, that our philosophy of loyalty is a rational part of a philosophy which must view the whole world as one unity of consciousness, wherein countless lesser unities are synthesized,— this is a general philosophical thesis which I must next briefly expound to you.

III

My exposition, as you see, must be, in any case, an attempt to show that the inevitable faith of the loyal—their faith in their causes, and in the real goodness of their causes—has truth, and since I must thus, in any case, discourse of truth, I propose briefly to show you that whoever talks of any sort of truth whatever, be that truth moral or scientific, the truth of common sense or the truth of a philosophy, inevitably implies, in all his assertions about truth, that the world of truth of which he speaks is a world possessing a rational and spiritual unity, is a conscious world of experience, whose type of consciousness is higher in its level than is the type of our human minds, but whose life is such that our life belongs as part to this living whole. This world of truth is the one that you must define, so I insist, if your are to regard any proposition whatever as true, and are then to tell, in a reasonable way, what you mean by the truth of that proposition.

The world of truth is therefore essentially a world such as that in whose reality the loyal believe when they believe their cause to be real. Moreover, this truth world has a goodness about it, essentially like that which the loyal attribute to their causes. Truth seeking and loyalty are therefore essentially the same process of life merely viewed in two different aspects. Whoever is loyal serves what he takes to be a truth, namely, his cause. On the other hand, whoever seeks truth for its own sake fails of his business if he seeks it merely as a barren abstraction, that has no life in it. If a truth seeker knows his business, he is, then, in the sense of our definition, serving a cause which unifies our human life upon some higher level of spiritual being than the present human level. He is therefore essentially loyal. Truth seeking is a moral activity; and on the other hand, morality is wholly inadequate unless the light of eternal truth shines upon it.

This, I say, will be my thesis. Some of you will call it very mystical, or at least a very fantastic thesis. It is not so. It ought to be viewed as a matter of plain sense. It is, I admit, a thesis which many of the most distinguished amongst my colleagues, who are philosophers, nowadays view sometimes with amusement, and sometimes with a notable impatience. This way of regarding the world of truth, which I have just defined as mine, is especially and most vivaciously attacked by my good friends, the pragmatists,—a group of philosophers who have of late been disposed to take truth under their especial protection, as if she were in danger from the tendency of some people who take her too seriously.

When I mention pragmatism, I inevitably bring to your minds the name of one whom we all honor,—the philosopher who last year so persuasively stated, before the audience of this Institute, the pragmatist theory of philosophical method, and of the nature of truth. It is impossible for me to do any justice, within my limits, to the exposition which Professor James gave of his own theory of truth. Yet since the antithesis between his views and those which I have now to indicate to you may be in itself an aid to my own exposition, I beg you to allow me to use, for the moment, some of his assertions about the nature of truth as a means of showing, by contrast, how I find myself obliged to interpret the same problem. The contrast is accompanied, after all, by so much of deeper agreement that I can well hope that my sketch of the current situation in the philosophical controversies about truth may not seem to you merely a dreary report of differences of opinion.

Professor James, in discussing the nature of truth, in his recent book on pragmatism, begins, as some of you will remember, by accepting the classic definition of truth as the agreement of our ideas with reality. Whoever knows or possesses a truth has, then, in his mind, an idea, an opinion, a judgment, or some complex of such states of mind. If his views are true, then these his ideas or opinions are in agreement with something called reality. Thus, for instance, if a loyal man believes his cause, say, his friendship or his club or his nation, to be a reality, and if his belief is true, his loyal opinion is in agreement with the real world. So far, of course, all of you will accept the definition of truth here in question.

Professor James now goes on to point out that, in some cases, our ideas agree with what we call real things by copying those things. So, if, with shut eyes, you think of the clock on the wall, your image of the clock is a copy of its dial. But, as my colleague continues, our power to copy real objects by ideas of our own is obviously a very limited power. You believe that you have at least some true ideas about many objects which are far too complex or too mysterious for you to copy them. Your power to become sure that your ideas do copy the constitution of anything whatever which exists outside of you is also very limited, because, after all, you never get outside of your own experience to see what the real things would be if taken wholly in themselves. Hence, on the whole, one cannot say that the agreement of our ideas with reality which constitutes their truth is essentially such as to demand that our ideas should be copies. For we believe that we have true ideas even when we do not believe them to be copies.

Moreover (and herewith we approach a consideration which is, for my colleague's theory of truth, very essential), not only does truth not consist merely in copying facts; but also truth cannot be defined in terms of any other static or fixed relation between ideas and facts. The only way to conceive that agreement between ideas and facts which constitutes truth is to think of the "practical consequences" which follow from possessing true ideas. "True ideas," in Professor James's words, "lead us, namely, through the acts and other ideas which they instigate, into or up to or towards other parts of experience with which we feel all the while that the original ideas remain in agreement. The connections and transitions come to us, from point to point, as being progressive, harmonious, satisfactory. This function of agreeable leading is what we mean by an idea's verification." So far my colleague's words. He goes on, in his account, to mention many illustrations of the way in which the truth of ideas is tested, both in the world of common sense, and in the world of science, by the usefulness, by the success, which attaches to the following out of true ideas to their actual empirical consequences. The wanderer lost in the woods gets true ideas about his whereabouts whenever he hits upon experiences and ideas which set him following the path which actually leads him home. In science, hypotheses are tested as to their truth, by considering what experiences they lead us to anticipate, and by then seeing whether these anticipations can be fulfilled in a satisfactory way. "True," says Professor James, "is the name for whatever idea starts the verification process." For instance, then, the verifiable scientific hypothesis, if once tested by the success of its results in experience, is in so far declared true. And similarly, the idea of following a given path in the woods in order to get home is declared true, if you follow the path and get home.

In consequence, every true idea is such in so far as it is useful in enabling you to anticipate the sort of experience that you want; and every idea that is useful as a guide of life is in so far true. The personal tests of usefulness, as of truth, are for every one of us personal and empirical. My own direct tests of truth are of course thus limited to my own experience. I find my own ideas true just in so far as I find them guiding me to the experience that I want to get. But of course, as my colleague constantly insists, we give credit, as social beings, to one another's verifications. Hence I regard as true many ideas that I personally have not followed out to any adequately experienced consequences. The "overwhelmingly large" number of the ideas by which we live, "we let pass for true without attempting to verify." We do this, says Professor James, "because it *works* to do so, everything we know conspiring with the belief, and nothing interfering." That is, we regard as true those ideas which we personally find it convenient, successful, expedient to treat as verifiable, even though we never verify them. The warrant of these unverifiable truths is, however, once more, the empirical usefulness of living as if they were verfiable. "Truth lives," says Professor James, "for the most part on a credit system.

. . . But this all points to direct face-to-face verification some-where, without which the fabric of truth collapses like a financial system with no cash basis whatever. You accept my verification of one thing, I yours of another. We trade on each other's truth. But beliefs verified concretely by *somebody* are the posts of the whole superstructure." The indirectly verifiable ideas, that is, the ideas which somebody else verifies, or even those which nobody yet verifies, but which agree sufficiently with verified ideas, we accept because it is advantageous to accept them. It is the same thing, then, to say that an idea is true because it is useful and to say that it is useful because it is true.

Agreement with reality thus turns out, as my colleague insists, "to be an affair of leading,—leading that is useful because it is into quarters that contain objects that are important." And my col-league's account of truth culminates in these notable expressions: " 'The true,' to put it very briefly, is only the expedient in the way of our thinking, just as 'the right' is only the expedient in the way of our behaving." "Pragmatism faces forward towards the future." That is, an idea is true by virtue of its expedient outcome. "It pays for our ideas to be validated, verified. Our obligation to seek truth is part of our general obligation to do what pays. The payment true ideas bring are the sole why of our duty to follow them."

The sum and substance of this theory of truth, as you see, is that the truth of an idea is determined by its "success" in yielding what my colleague frequently calls "the cash values in terms of experience," which appear as consequences of holding this idea. These values may either take the form of direct verifications in terms of sensible facts, as when one finds one's way out of the woods and sees one's home; or else the form of practically satisfy-ing and expedient beliefs, which clash with no sensible experience, and which are personally acceptable to those who hold them. It is "expedient" to connect the latter beliefs with sensible cash values when you can. If you cannot turn them into such cash, you are at liberty to hold them, but with the conviction that, after all, the personally expedient is the true.

In any case, as you see, whatever else truth is, it is nothing static. It changes with the expediencies of your experience. And there-fore those who conceive the realm of truth as essentially eternal are the objects of my colleague's most charming philosophical fury.

IV

We have, then, an authoritative exposition of pragmatism before us. You must see that this doctrine, whether it be true doctrine, or whether it be indeed simply for some people an expedient doctrine, is certainly one that concerns our philosophy of loyalty, now that indeed we have reached the place where the relation between loyalty and truth has become, for us, a critically important relation. May we venture to ask ourselves, then: Is this pragmatism a fair expression of what we mean by truth?

In reply let me at once point out the extent to which I personally agree with my colleague, and accept his theory of truth. I fully agree with him that whenever a man asserts a truth, his assertion is a deed,—a practical attitude, an active acknowledgment of some fact. I fully agree that the effort to verify this acknowledgment by one's own personal experience, and the attempt to find truth in the form of a practical congruity between our assertions and our attained empirical results, is an effort which in our individual lives inevitably accompanies and sustains our every undertaking in the cause of truth seeking. Modern pragmatism is not indeed as orginal as it seems to suppose itself to be in emphasizing such views. The whole history of modern idealism is full of such assertions. I myself, as a teacher of philosophy, have for years insisted upon viewing truth in this practical way. I must joyously confess to you that I was first taught to view the nature of truth in this way when I was a young student of philosophy; and I was taught this by several great masters of modern thought. These masters were Kant, Fichte, Hegel, and Professor James himself, whose lectures, as I heard them in my youth at the Johns Hopkins University, and whose beautiful conversations and letters in later years, inspired me with an insight that helped me, rather against his own advice, to read my German idealists aright, and to see what is, after all, the eternal truth beneath all this pragmatism. For Professor James's pragmatism, despite its entertaining expressions of horror of the eternal, actually does state one aspect of eternal truth. It is, namely, eternally true that all search for truth is a practical activity, with an ethical purpose, and that a purely theoretical truth, such as should guide no significant active process, is a barren absurdity. This, however, is so far precisely what Fichte spent his life in teaching. Professor James taught me, as a student, much the same lesson; and I equally prize and honor all of my masters for that lesson; and I have been trying to live up to it ever since I first began to study the nature of truth.

So far, then, I am a pragmatist. And I also fully agree that, if we ever get truth, the attainment of truth means a living and practical success in those active undertakings in terms of which we have been trying to assert and to verify our truth. I doubt not that to say, "This is true," is the same as to say: "The ideas by means of which I define this truth are the practically and genuinely successful ideas, the ideas such that, when I follow them, I really fulfil my deepest needs." All this I not only admit; but I earnestly insist that truth is an ethical concept; and I thank from my heart the great pragmatist who so fascinated his audience last year in this place; I thank him that he taught them what, in my youth, he helped to teach me, namely, that winning the truth means winning the success which we need, and for which the whole practical nature of our common humanity continually groans and travails together in pain until now.

And yet, and yet all this still leaves open one great question. When we seek truth, we indeed seek successful ideas. But what, in Heaven's name, constitutes success? Truth-seeking is indeed a practical endeavor. But what, in the name of all the loyal, is the goal of human endeavor? Truth is a living thing. We want leading and guidance. "Lead, kindly light,"—thus we address the truth. We are lost in the woods of time. We want the way, the truth, and the life. For nothing else does all our science and our common sense strive. But what is it to have genuine abundance of life? For what do we live?

V

Here our entire philosophy of loyalty, so far as it has yet been developed, comes to our aid. The loyal, as we have said, are the only human beings who can have any reasonable hope of genuine success. If they do not succeed, then nobody succeeds. And of course the loyal do indeed live with a constant, although not with an exclusive, reference to their own personal experience and to that of other individual men. They feel their present fascination for their cause. It thrills through them. Their loyalty has, even for them, in their individual capacity what Professor James calls a cash value.

And of course they like to have their friends share such cash values. Yet I ask you: Are the loyal seeking *only* the mere collection of their private experiences of their personal thrills of fascination? If you hear loyal men say: "We are in this business just for what we as individuals—we and our individual fellows—can get out of it," do you regard that way of speech as an adequate expression of their really loyal spirit? When Arnold von Winkelried rushed on the Austrian spears, did he naturally say: "Look you, my friends, I seek, in experiential terms, the cash value of my devotion; see me draw the cash." My colleague would of course retort that the hero in question, according to the legend, said, as he died: "Make way for liberty." He therefore wanted liberty, as one may insist, to get these cash values. Yes, but liberty was no individual man, and no mere heap of individual men. Liberty was a cause, a certain superhuman unity of the ideal life of a free community. It was indeed expedient that one man should die for the people. But the people also was an *unio mystica* of many in one. For that cause the hero died. And no man has ever yet experienced, in his private and individual life, the whole true cash value of that higher unity. Nor will all the individual Swiss patriots, past, present, or future, viewed as a mere collection of creatures of a day, ever draw the cash in question. If the cause exists, the treasure exists, and is indeed a cash value upon a level higher than that of our passing human life. But loyalty does not live by selling its goods for present cash in the temple of its cause. Such pragmatism it drives out of the temple. It serves, and worships, and says to the cause: "Be thine the glory."

Loyalty, then, seeks success and from moment to moment indeed thrills with a purely fragmentary and temporary joy in its love of its service. But the joy depends on a belief in a distinctly superhuman type of unity of life. And so you indeed cannot express the value of your loyalty by pointing at the mere heap of the joyous thrills of the various loyal individuals. The loyal serve a real whole of life, an experiential value too rich for any expression in merely momentary terms.

Now, is it not very much so with our love of any kind of truth? Of course, we mortals seek for whatever verification of our truths we can get in the form of present success. But can you express our human definition of truth in terms of any collection of our human experiences of personal expediency?

Well, as to our concept of truth, let us consider a test case by way of helping ourselves to answer this question. Let us suppose that a witness appears, upon some witness-stand, and objects to taking the ordinary oath, because he has conscientious scruples, due to the fact that he is a recent pragmatist, who has a fine new definition of truth, in terms of which alone he can be sworn. Let us suppose him, hereupon, to be granted entire liberty to express his oath in his own way. Let him accordingly say, using, with technical scrupulosity, my colleague's definition of truth: "I promise to tell whatever is expedient and nothing but what is expedient, so help me future experience." I ask you: Do you think that this witness has expressed, with adequacy, that view of the nature of truth that you really wish a witness to have in mind? Of course, if he were a typical pragmatist, you would indeed be delighted to hear his testimony on the witness-stand or anywhere else. But would you accept his formula?

But let me be more precise as to the topic of this witness's possible testimony. I will use for the purpose Kant's famous case. Somebody, now dead, let us suppose, has actually left with the witness a sum of money as a wholly secret deposit to be some time returned. No written record was made of the transaction. No evidence exists that can in future be used to refute the witness if he denies the transaction and keeps the money. The questions to be asked of the witness relate, amongst other things, to whatever it may be that he believes himself to know about the estate of the deceased. I now ask, not what his duty is, but simply what it is that he rationally means to do in case he really intends to tell the truth about that deposit. Does he take merely the "forward-looking" attitude of my colleague's pragmatism? Does he mean merely to predict, as expedient, certain consequences which he expects to result either to himself or to the heirs of the estate? Of course his testimony will have consequences. But is it these which he is trying to predict? Are they his true object? Or does the truth of his statement mean the same as the expediency, either to himself or to the heirs, of any consequences whatever which may follow from his statement? Does the truth of his statement about the deposit even mean the merely present empirical fact that he now feels a belief in this statement or that he finds it just now congruent with the empirical sequences of his present memories? No, for the witness is not trying merely to tell how he feels. He is trying to tell the truth about the deposit. And the witness's belief is not the truth of his belief. Even his memory is not the truth to which he means to be a witness. And the future consequences of his making a true statement are for the witness irrelevant, since they are for the law and the heirs to determine. Yet one means something perfectly definite by the truth of the testimony of that witness. And that truth is simply inexpressible in such terms as those which my colleague employs. Yet the truth here in question is a simple truth about the witness's own personal past experience.

Now, such a case is only one of countless cases where we are trying to tell the truth about something which we all regard as being, in itself, a matter of genuine and concrete experience, while nevertheless we do not mean, "It is expedient just now for me to think this," nor yet, "I predict such and such consequences for my own personal experience, or for the future experience of some other individual man; and these predicted consequences constitute the truth of my present assertion." I say there are countless such cases where the truth that we mean is empirical indeed, but transcends all such expediencies and personal consequences. The very assertion, "Human experience, taken as a totality of facts, exists," is a momentous example of just such an assertion. We all believe that assertion. If that assertion is not actually true, then our whole frame of natural science, founded as it is on the common experience of many observers, crumbles into dust, our common sense world is nothing, business and society are alike illusions, loyalty to causes is meaningless. Now that assertion, "Human experience, that is, the totality of the experiences of many men, really exists," is an assertion which you and I regard as perfectly true. Yet no individual man ever has verified, or ever will verify, that assertion. For no man, taken as this individual man, experiences the experience of anybody but himself. Yet we all regard that assertion as true.

My colleague, of course, would say, as in fact he has often said, that his assertion is one of the numerous instances of that process of trading on credit which he so freely illustrates. We do not verify this assertion. But we accept it on credit as verifiable. However, the credit simile is a dangerous one here, so long as one conceives that the verification which would pay the cash would be a payment in the form of such human experience as you and I possess. For the assertion, "The experience of many men exists," is an assertion that is essentially unverifiable by any one man. If the "cash value" of the assertion means, then, its verifiability by any man, then the credit in question is one that simply cannot be turned into such cash by any conceivable process, occurring in our individual lives, since the very idea of the real existence of the experience of many men excludes, by its definition, the direct presence of this experience of various men within the experience of any one of these men. The credit value in question would thus be a *mere* fiat value, so long as the only cash values are those of the experiences of individual men, and the truth of our assertion would mean simply that we find it expedient to treat as verifiable what we know cannot be verified. Hereupon, of course, we should simply be trading upon currency that has no cash value. Whoever does verify the fact that the experience of many men exists, if such a verifier there be, is a superhuman being, an union of the empirical lives of many men in the complex of a single experience. And if our credit of the assertion that many men exist is convertible into cash at all, that cash is not laid up where the moth and rust of our private human experience doth from moment to moment corrupt the very data that we see; but is laid up in a realm where our experiences, past, present, future, are the object of a conspectus that is not merely temporal and transient. Now all the natural sciences make use of the persuasion that the experiences of various men exist, and that there is a unity of such experiences. This thesis, then, is no invention of philosophers.

My colleague, in answer, would of course insist that as a fact you and I are now believing that many men exist, and that human experience in its entirety exists, *merely* because, in the long run, we find that this belief is indeed congruous with our current and purely personal experience, and is therefore an expedient idea of ours. But I, in answer, insist that common sense well feels this belief to be indeed from moment to moment expedient, and yet clearly distinguishes between that expediency and the truth which common sense all the while attributes to the belief. The distinction is precisely the one which my fancied illustration of the pragmatist on the witness-stand has suggested. It is a perfectly universal distinction and a commonplace one. Tell me, "This opinion is true," and whatever you are talking about I may agree or disagree or doubt; yet in any case you have stated a momentous issue. But tell me, "I just now find this belief expedient, it feels to me congruous" and you have explicitly given me just a scrap of your personal biography, and have told me no other truth whatever than a truth about the present state of your feelings.

If, however, you emphasize my colleague's wording to the effect that a truth is such because it proves to be an idea that is expedient "in the long run," I once more ask you: *When* does a man experience the whole of the real facts about the "long run"? At the beginning of the long run, when the end is not yet, or at the end, when, perhaps, he forgets, like many older men, what were once the expediencies of his youth? What decides the truth about the long run? My exalted moments, when anything that I like seems true, or my disappointed moments, when I declare that I have always had bad luck? To appeal to the genuinely real "long run" is only to appeal in still another form to a certain ideally fair conspectus of my own whole life,—a conspectus which I, in my private human experience, never get. Whoever gets the conspectus of my whole life, to see what, in the long run, is indeed for me expedient,—whoever, I say, gets that conspectus, if such a being there indeed is,— is essentially superhuman in his type of consciousness. For he sees what I only get in the form of an idea; namely, the true sense and meaning of my life.

In vain, then, does one try adequately to define the whole of what we mean by truth either in terms of our human feelings of expediency or in terms of our instantaneous thrills of joy in success, or in terms of any other verifications that crumble as the instant flies. All such verifications we use, just as we use whatever perishes. Any such object is a fragment, but we want the whole. Truth is itself a cause, and is largely as one must admit, for us mortals, just now, what we called, in our last lecture, a lost cause—else how should these pragmatists be able thus to imagine a vain thing, and call that truth which is but the crumbling expediency of the moment? Our search for truth is indeed a practical process. The attainment of truth means success. Our verifications, so far as we ever get them, are momentary fragments of that success. But the genuine success that we demand is an ethical success, of precisely the type which all the loyal seek, when they rejoice in giving all for their cause.

VI

But you will now all the more eagerly demand in what sense we can ever get any warrant for saying that we know any truth whatever. In seeking truth we do not seek the mere crumbling successes of the passing instants of human life. We seek a city out of sight. What we get of success within our passing experience is rationally as precious to us as it is, just because we believe that attainment to be a fragment of an essentially superhuman success, which is won in the form of a higher experience than ours,—a conspectus wherein our human experiences are unified. But what warrant have we for this belief?

I will tell you how I view the case. We need unity of life. In recognizing that need my own pragmatism consists. Now, we never find unity present to our human experience in more than a fragmentary shape. We get hints of higher unity. But only the fragmentary unity is won at any moment of our lives. We therefore form ideas—very fallible ideas—of some unity of experience, an unity such as our idea of any science or any art or any united people or of any community or of any other cause, any other union of many human experiences in one, defines. Now, if our ideas are in any case indeed true, then such an unity is as a fact successfully experienced upon some higher level than ours, and is experienced in some conspectus of life which wins what we need, which approves our loyalty, which fulfils our rational will, and which has in its wholeness what we seek. And then we ourselves with all our ideas and strivings are in and of this higher unity of life. Our loyalty to truth is a hint of this unity. Our transient successes are fragments of the true success. But suppose our ideas about the structure of this higher unity to be false in any of their details. Suppose, namely, any of our causes to be wrongly viewed by us. Then there is still real that state of facts, whatever it is, which, if just now known to us, would show us this falsity of our various special ideas. Now, only an experience, a consciousness of some system of contents, could show the falsity of any idea. Hence this real state of facts, this constitution of the genuine universe, whatever it is, must again be a reality precisely in so far as it is also a conspectus of facts of experience.

We therefore already possess at least one true idea, precisely in so far as we say: "The facts of the world are what they are; the real universe exposes our errors and makes them errors." And when we say this, we once more appeal to a conspectus of experience in which ours is included. For I am in error only in case my present ideas about the true facts of the whole world of experience are out of concord with the very meaning that I myself actively try to assign to these ideas. My ideas are in any detail false, only if the very experience to which I mean to appeal, contains in its conspectus contents which I just now imperfectly conceive. In any case, then, the truth is possessed by precisely that whole of experience which I never get, but to which my colleague also inevitably appeals when he talks of the "long run," or of the experiences of humanity in general.

Whatever the truth, then, or the falsity of any of my special convictions about this or that fact may be, the real world, which refutes my false present ideas in so far as they clash with its wholeness, and which confirms them just in so far as they succeed in having significant relations to its unity,—this real world, I say, is a conspectus of the whole of experience. And this whole of experience is in the closest real relation to my practical life, precisely in so far as, for me, the purpose of my life is to get into unity with the whole universe, and precisely in so far as the universe itself is just that conspectus of experience that we all mean to define and to serve whatever we do, or whatever we say.

But the real whole conspectus of experience, the real view of the totality of life, the real expression of that will to live in and for the whole, which every assertion of truth and every loyal deed expresses—well, it must be a conspectus that includes whatever facts are indeed facts, be they past, present, or future. I call this whole of experience an eternal truth. I do not thereby mean, as my colleague seems to imagine, that the eternal first exists, and that then our life in time comes and copies that eternal order. I mean simply that the whole of experience includes all temporal happenings, contains within itself all changes, and, since it is the one whole that we all want and need, succeeds in so far as it supplements all failures, accepts all, even the blindest of services, and wins what we seek. Thus winning it is practically good and worthy.

But if one insists, How do you know all this? I reply: I know simply that to try to deny the reality of this whole of truth is simply to reaffirm it. Any special idea of mine may be wrong, even as any loyal deed may fail, or as any cause may become, to human vision, a lost cause. But to deny that there is truth, or that there is a real world, is simply to say that the whole truth is that there is no whole truth, and that the real fact is that there is no fact real at all. Such assertions are plain self-contradictions. And on the other hand, by the term "real world," defined as it is for us by our ideal needs, we mean simply that whole of experience in which we live, and in unity with which we alone succeed.

Loyalty, then, has its own metaphysic. This metaphysic is expressed in a view of things which conceives our experience as bound up in a real unity with all experience,—an unity which is essentially good, and in which all our ideas possess their real fulfilment and success. Such a view is true, simply because if you deny its truth you reaffirm that very truth under a new form.

Truth, meanwhile, means, as pragmatism asserts, the fulfilment of a need. But we all need the superhuman, the city out of sight, the union with all life,—the essentially eternal. This need is no invention of the philosophers. It is the need which all the loyal feel, whether they know it or not, and whether they call themselves pragmatists or not. To define this need as pragmatism in its recent forms has done, to reduce truth to expediency, is to go about crying *cash, cash,* in a realm where there is no cash of the sort that loyalty demands, that every scientific inquiry presupposes, and that only the unity of the experiences of many in one furnishes.

If we must, then, conceive recent pragmatism under the figure of a business enterprise,—a metaphor which my colleague's phraseology so insistently invites,—I am constrained therefore to sum up its position thus: First, with a winning clearness, and with a most honorable frankness it confesses bankruptcy, so far as the actually needed cash payments of significant truth are concerned. Secondly, it nevertheless declines to go into the hands of any real receiver, for it is not fond of anything that appears too absolute. And thirdly, it proposes simply and openly to go on doing business under the old style and title of the truth. "After all," it says, "are we not, every one of us, fond of credit values?"

But I cannot conceive the position of the loyal to be, in fact, so hopelessly embarrassed as this. The recent pragmatists themselves are, in fact, practically considered very loyal lovers of genuine truth. They simply have mistaken the true state of their accounts. We all know, indeed, little enough. But the loyal man, I think, whether he imagines himself to be a recent pragmatist or not, has a rational right to say this: My cause partakes of the nature of the only truth and reality that there is. My life is an effort to manifest such eternal truth, as well as I can, in a series of temporal deeds. I may serve my cause ill. I may conceive it erroneously. I may lose it in the thicket of this world of transient experience. My every human deed may involve a blunder. My mortal life may seem one long series of failures. But I know that my cause liveth. My true life is hid with the cause and belongs to the eternal.

VIII. Loyalty and Religion

We began these lectures with a confessedly inadequate definition of loyalty. At the last time we laid a basis for a new definition of loyalty. In this concluding lecture, we are to develop that definition, and to draw conclusions regarding the relation of loyalty to religion. Both enterprises will require a further development of our theory of truth.

I

Loyalty, so we said at the outset, is the willing and thoroughgoing devotion of a person to a cause. We defined a cause as something that unifies many human lives in one. Our intent in making these definitions was mainly practical. Our philosophy of loyalty was and is intended to be a practical philosophy. We used our definition first to help us to find out the purpose of life, and the supreme good which human beings can seek for themselves. We found this good to be, indeed, of a paradoxical seeming. It was a good found only by an act of sacrifice. We then developed the conception of loyalty to loyalty, and learned that, with this means of defining the one cause which is worthy of all men's devotion, we could unify and simplify the chaotic code of our conventional morality, could do full justice to the demands of a rational ethical individualism, and could leave to every man his right and his duty to choose some special personal cause of his own, while we could yet state the ideal of a harmony of all human causes in one all-embracing cause. Upon this basis we also could form a theory of conscience,— a theory which views conscience at once as rational and universal in its authority, and yet as individual in its expression in the life of each man, so that every man's conscience remains his own, and is, to himself, in many ways, mysterious; while the whole business of any man's conscience is, nevertheless, to direct that man to find his individual place in the one, universal, rational, moral order.

Hereupon we illustrated our theory of loyalty by applying it to a study of some of our own national problems. And next, our account of the practice of loyalty culminated in a doctrine of the nature of training for loyalty. Here we found the great paradox of loyalty afresh illustrated. Loyalty wins not only by sacrifice, but also by painful labor, and by the very agony of defeat. In this our human world the lost causes have proved themselves, in history, to be the most fruitful causes. In sum, loyalty is trained both through the presence of personal leaders, and through that idealization of our causes which adversity nourishes, which death illumines, and which the defeats of present time may render all the clearer and more ideally fascinating.

All these results showed us that loyalty has about it a character such as forbids us, after all, to interpret the true good of loyalty in terms of our merely individual human experiences. Man discovers, indeed, even within the limits of his own personal experience, that loyalty is his ethical destiny, and that without it he can win no peace; while, with loyalty once in possession of his active powers, he seems to himself to have solved the personal problem of the purpose of his life. But loyalty thus appears, after all, in the individual life, in a deeply mysterious form. It says to a man: "Your true good can never be won and verified by you in terms to which the present form and scope of our human experience is adequate. The best that you can get lies in self-surrender, and in your personal assurance that the cause to which you surrender yourself is indeed good. But your cause, if it is indeed a reality, has a good about it which no one man, and no mere collection of men, can ever verify. This good of the cause is essentially superhuman in its type, even while it is human in its embodiment. For it belongs to an union of men, to a whole of human life which transcends the individuality of any man, and which is not to be found as something belonging to any mere collection of men. Let your supreme good, then, be this, that you regard the cause as real, as good, and that, if the cause be lost to any merely human sight, you hold it to be nevertheless living in its own realm,—not apart, indeed, from human life, but in the form of the fulfilment of many human lives in one."

Now, this mysterious speech of loyalty implies something which is not only moral, but also metaphysical. Purely practical considerations, then, a study of our human needs, an ideal of the business of life,—these inevitably lead us into a region which is more than merely a realm of moral activities. This region is either one of delusions or else one of spiritual realities of a level higher than is that of our present individual human experience.

In the last lecture we undertook to consider this larger realm of spiritual unities which must be real in case our loyalty is not based upon illusion. And we attempted to sketch a general theory of truth which might show us that such spiritual unities are indeed realities, and are presupposed by our every effort to define truth. Thus our ethical theory has transformed itself into a general philosophical doctrine; and loyalty now appears to us not only as a guide of life but as a revelation of our relation to a realm which we have been obliged to define as one of an eternal and all-embracing unity of spiritual life.

We have called this realm of true life, and of genuine and united experience,—this realm which, if our argument at the last time was sound, includes our lives in that very whole which constitutes the real universe,—we have called this realm, I say, an eternal world,— eternal, simply because, according to our theory, it includes all temporal happenings and strivings in the conspectus of a single consciousness, and fulfils all our rational purposes together, and is all that we seek to be. For, as we argued, this realm of reality is conscious, is united, is self-possessed, and is perfected through the very wealth of the ideal sacrifices and of the loyal devotion which are united so as to constitute its fulness of being. In view of the philosophy that was thus sketched, I now propose a new definition of loyalty; and I say that this definition results from all of our previous study: *Loyalty is the will to manifest, so far as is possible, the Eternal, that is, the conscious and superhuman unity of life, in the form of the acts of an individual Self.* Or, if you prefer to take the point of view of an individual human self, if you persist in looking at the world just as we find it in our ordinary experience, and if you regard the metaphysical doctrine just sketched merely as an ideal theory of life, and *not* as a demonstrable philosophy, I can still hold to my definition of loyalty by borrowing a famous phrase from the dear friend and colleague some of whose views I at the last time opposed. I can, then, simply state my new definition of loyalty in plainer and more directly obvious terms thus: *Loyalty is the Will to Believe in something eternal, and to express that belief in the practical life of a human being.*

This, I say, is my new definition of loyalty, and in its metaphysical form, it is my final definition. Let me expound it further, and let me show a little more in detail how it results from the whole course of our inquiry.

II

However kindly you may have followed the discussion of my last lecture, some of you will feel doubts as to the theory of truth and of reality which I opposed to the doctrines of recent pragmatism, and which I now lay at the basis of my final definition of loyalty. I approached my own theory by the way of a polemic against my colleague's recently stated views regarding the nature of truth. But polemic often hinders our appreciation of some aspects of the questions at issue, even while it may help us to emphasize others. So let me now point out, apart from a polemic against other theories of truth, what is my main motive for viewing the real world as I do, and why I suppose that viewing the world as I do helps us to understand better the business of loyalty.

People who have faith in this or in that form of superhuman and significant reality often ask what they can do to turn their faith into something that more resembles clear insight. Shall they look into the evidences that are adduced in favor of this or of that miraculous story? Shall they themselves seek for the miraculous in their own personal experience? Will psychical research throw any light on the mysteries of being? Or, perhaps, will some sort of special mystical training reveal the higher truth? What is the way that leads towards the spiritual world? And thus those who doubt whether there are such higher realities to be found still sometimes try to get rid of these doubts by various appeals either to more or less magical arts, or to extraordinary personal experiences, or to mystical transformations of their personal life.

Now, whatever may be said of wonders, or of mystical revelations, our philosophy of loyalty is naturally interested in pointing out a road to the spiritual world, if, indeed, there be such a world, —a road, I say, which has a plain relation to our everyday moral life. And it seems to me, both that there is a genuinely spiritual world, and that there is a path of inquiry which can lead from such a practical faith in the higher world as loyalty embodies in its deeds, to a rational insight into the general constitution of this higher realm. I do not offer my opinions upon this subject as having any authority. I can see no farther through stone walls than can my fellow, and I enjoy no special revelations from any super-human realm. But I ask you, as thoughtful people, to consider what your ordinary life, as rational beings, implies as its basis and as its truth.

What I was expounding at the close of my last lecture was a view of things which seems to me to be implied in any attempt to express, in a reasonable way, where we stand in our universe.

We all of us have to admit, I think, that our daily life depends upon believing in realities which are, in any case, just as truly beyond the scope of our ordinary individual experience as any spiritual realm could possibly be. We live by believing in one another's minds as realities. We give credit to countless reports, documents, and other evidences of present and past facts; and we do all this, knowing that such credit cannot be adequately verified by any experience such as an individual man can obtain. Now, the usual traditional account of all these beliefs of ours is that they are forced upon us, by some reality which is, as people say, wholly independent of our knowledge, which exists by itself apart from our experience, and which may be, therefore, entirely alien in its nature to any of our human interests and ideals.

But modern philosophy,—a philosophy in whose historical course of development our recent pragmatism is only a passing incident,—that philosophy which turns upon analyzing the bases of our knowledge, and upon reflectively considering what our human beliefs and ideas are intended to mean and to accomplish, has taught us to see that we can never deal with any wholly independent reality. The recent pragmatists, as I understand them, are here in full and conscious agreement with my own opinion. We can deal with no world which is out of relation to our experience. On the contrary, the real world is known to us in terms of *our* experience, is defined for us by *our* ideas, and is the object of *our* practical endeavors. Meanwhile, to declare anything real is to assert that it has its place in some realm of experience, be this experience human or superhuman. To declare that anything whatever is a fact, is simply to assert that some proposition, which you or I or some other thinking being can express in the form of intelligible ideas, is a true proposition. And the truth of propositions itself is nothing dead, is nothing independent of ideas and of experience, but is simply the successful fulfilment of some demand,—a demand which you can express in the form of an assertion, and which is fulfilled in so far, and only in so far, as some region of live experience contains what meets that demand. Meanwhile, every proposition, every assertion that anybody can make, is a deed; and every rational deed involves, in effect, an assertion of a fact. If the prodigal son says, "I will arise and go to my father," he even thereby asserts something to be true about himself, his father, and his father's house. If an astronomer or a chemist or a statistician or a man of business reports "this or this is a fact," he even thereby performs a deed,— an act having an ideal meaning, and embodying a live purpose; and he further declares that the constitution of experience is such as to make this deed essentially reasonable, successful, and worthy to be accepted by every man.

The real world is therefore *not* something independent of us. It is a world whose stuff, so to speak,—whose content,—is of the nature of experience, whose structure meets, validates, and gives warrant to our active deeds, and whose whole nature is such that it can be interpreted in terms of ideas, propositions, and conscious meanings, while in turn it gives to our fragmentary ideas and to our conscious life whatever connected meaning they possess. Whenever I have purposes and fail, so far, to carry them out, that is because I have not yet found the true way of expressing my own relation to reality. On the other hand, precisely in so far as I have understood some whole of reality, I have carried out successfully some purpose of mine.

There is, then, no merely theoretical truth, and there is no reality foreign, in its nature, to experience. Whoever actually lives the whole conscious life such as *can* be lived out with a definitely reasonable meaning,—such a being, obviously superhuman in his grade of consciousness, not only knows the real world, but *is* the real world. Whoever is conscious of the whole content of experience possesses all reality. And our search for reality is simply an effort to discover what the whole fabric of experience is into which our human experience is woven, what the system of truth is in which our partial truths have their place, what the ideally significant life is for the sake of which every deed of ours is undertaken. When we try to find out what the real world is, we are simply trying to discover the sense of our own individual lives. And we can define that sense of our lives only in terms of a conscious life in which ours is included, in which our ideas get their full meaning expressed, and in which what we fail to carry out to the full is carried out to the full.

III

Otherwise stated, when I think of the whole world of facts,—the "real world,"—I inevitably think of something that is *my own* world, precisely in so far as that world is any object of any reasonable idea of mine. It is true, of course, that, in forming an idea of my world of facts, I do not thereby give myself, at this instant, the least right to spin out of my inner consciousness any adequate present ideas of the detail of the contents of my real world. In thinking of the real world, I am indeed thinking of the whole of that very system of experience in which my experience is bound up, and in which I, as an individual, have my very limited and narrow place. But just now I am not in possession of that whole. I have to work for it and wait for it, and faithfully to be true to it. As a creature living along, from moment to moment, in time, I therefore indeed have to wait ignorantly enough for coming experience. I have to use as I can my fallible memory in trying to find out about my own past experience. I have no way of verifying what your experience is, except by using tests—and again the extremely fallible tests—which we all employ in our social life. I need the methods of the sciences of experience to guide me in the study of whatever facts fall within their scope. I use those practical and momentary successes upon which recent pragmatism insists, whenever I try to get a concrete verification of my opinions. And so far I stand, and must rightly stand, exactly where any man of common sense, any student of a science, any plain man, or any learned man stands. I am a fallible mortal, simply trying to find my way as I can in the thickets of experience.

And yet all this my daily life, my poor efforts to remember and to predict, my fragmentary inquiries into this or that matter of science or of business, my practical acknowledgment of your presence as real facts in the real world of experience, my personal definition of the causes to which I devote myself,—these are all undertakings that are overruled, and that are rendered significant, simply in so far as they are reasonable parts of one all-embracing enterprise. This enterprise is my active attempt to find out my true place in the real world. But now I can only define my real world by conceiving it in terms of experience. I can find my place in the world only by discovering where I stand in the whole system of experience. For what I mean by a fact is something that somebody finds. Even a merely possible fact is something only in so far as somebody actually *could* find it. And the sense in which it *is* an actual fact that somebody *could* find in his experience a determinate fact, is a sense which again can only be defined in terms of concrete, living, and not merely possible experience, and in terms of some will or purpose expressed in a conscious life. Even possible facts, then, are *really* possible only in so far as something is actually experienced, or is found by somebody. Whatever is real, then, be it distant or near, past or future, present to your mind or to mine, a physical fact or a moral fact, a fact of our possible human experience, or a fact of a superhuman type of experience, a purpose, a desire, a natural object or an ideal object, a mechanical system or a value,—whatever, I say, is real, *is real as a content present to some conscious being*. Therefore, when I inquire about the real world, I am simply asking what contents of experience, human or superhuman, are actually and consciously found by somebody. My inquiries regarding facts, of whatever grade the facts may be, are therefore inevitably an effort to find out *what the world's experience is*. In all my common sense, then, in all my science, in all my social life, I am trying to discover what the universal conscious life which constitutes the world contains as its contents, and views as its own.

But even this is not the entire story of my place in the real world. For I cannot inquire about facts without forming my own ideas of these facts. In so far as my ideas are true, my own personal ideas are therefore active processes that go on within the conscious life of the world. If my ideas are true, they succeed in agreeing with the very world consciousness that they define. But this agreement, this success, if itself it is a fact at all, is once more a fact of experience,—yet not merely of my private experience, since I myself never personally find, within the limits of my own individual experience, the success that every act of truth seeking demands. If I get the truth, then, at any point of my life, my success is real only in so far as some conscious life, which includes my ideas and my efforts, and which also includes the very facts of the world whereof I am thinking, actually observes my success, in the form of a conspectus of the world's facts, and of my own efforts to find and to define them.

In so far, then, as I get the truth about the world, I myself am a fragmentary conscious life that is included within the conscious conspectus of the world's experience, and that is in one self-conscious unity with that world consciousness. And it is in this unity with the world consciousness that I get my success, and am in concord with the truth.

But of course any particular idea of mine, regarding the world, or regarding any fact in the world, may be false. However, this possibility of my error is itself a real situation of mine, and involves essentially the same relation between the world and myself which obtains in case I have true ideas. For I can be in error about an object only in case I really mean to agree with that object, and to agree with it in a way which only my own purposes, in seeking this agreement, can possibly define. It is only by virtue of my own undertakings that I can fail in my undertakings. It is only because, after all, I am loyal to the world's whole truth that I can so express myself in fallible ideas, and in fragmentary opinions that, as a fact, I may, at any moment, undertake too much for my own momentary success to be assured, so that I can indeed in any one of my assertions fail justly to accord with that world consciousness which I am all the while trying to interpret in my own transient way. But when I thus fail, I momentarily fail *to interpret my place in the very world consciousness whose life I am trying to define.* But my failure, when and in so far as it occurs, is once more a fact,—and therefore a fact for the world's consciousness. If I blunder, but am sincere, if I think myself right, but am not right, then my error is a fact for a consciousness which includes my fallible attempts to be loyal to the truth, but which sees how they just now lose present touch with their true cause. Seeing this my momentary defeat, the world consciousness sees, however, my loyalty, and in its conspectus assigns, even to my fragmentary attempts at truth, their genuine place in the single unity of the world's consciousness. My very failure, then, like every loyal failure, is still a sort of success. It is an effort to define my place in the unity of the world's conspectus of all conscious life. I cannot fall out of that unity. I cannot flee from its presence. And I err only as the loyal may give up their life for their cause. Whether I get truth, then, or whether I err in detail, *my loyal search for truth insures the fact that I am in a significant unity with the world's conscious life.*

The thesis that the world is one whole and a significant whole of conscious life is, for these reasons, a thesis which can only be viewed as an error, by reinstating this very assertion under a new form. For any error of mine concerning the world is possible only in so far as I really mean to assert the truth about the world; and this real meaning of mine can exist only as a fact within the conspectus of consciousness for which the real whole world exists, and within which I myself live.

This, then, in brief, is my own theory of truth. This is why I hold this theory to be no fantastic guess about what may be true, but a logically inevitable conclusion about how every one of us, wise or ignorant, is actually defining his own relation to truth, whether he knows the fact or not. I expressed my theory at the last time in terms of a polemic against the recent pragmatists; but as a fact their view, in its genuine and deeper meaning, is no more opposed to mine than my young Russian's vehement protest against loyalty, quoted in my second lecture, was, in its true spirit, opposed to my own view. My young Russian, you may remember, hated what he took to be loyalty, just because he was so loyal. And even so my friends, the recent pragmatists, reassert my theory of truth even in their every attempt to deny it. For, amongst other things, they assert that their own theory of truth is actually true. And that assertion implies just such a conspectus of all truth in one view,—just such a conspectus as I too assert.

IV

We first came in sight of this theory of truth, in these discussions, for a purely practical reason. Abstract and coldly intellectual as the doctrine, when stated as I have just stated it, may appear, we had our need to ask what truth is, because we wanted to know whether the loyal are right in supposing, as they inevitably do suppose, that their personal causes, and that their cause of causes, namely, universal loyalty, that any such causes, I say, possess genuine foundation in truth. Loyalty, as we found, is a practical service of superhuman objects. For our causes transcend expression in terms of our single lives. If the cause lives, then all conscious moral life—even our poor human life—is in unity with a superhuman conscious life, in which we ourselves dwell; and in this unity we win, in so far as we are loyal servants of our cause, a success which no transient human experience of ours, no joyous thrill of the flying moment, no bitterness of private defeat and loss, can do more or less than to illustrate, to illumine, or to idealize.

We asked: Is this faith of the loyal in their causes a pathetic fallacy? Our theory of truth has given us a general answer to this intensely practical question. The loyal try to live in the spirit. But, if thereupon they merely open their eyes to the nature of the reasonable truth, they see that it is in the spirit only that they do or can live. They would be living in this truth, as mere passing fragments of conscious life, as mere blind series of mental processes, even if they were not loyal. For all life, however dark and fragmentary, is either a blind striving for conscious unity with the universal life of which it is a fragment, or else, like the life of the loyal, is a deliberate effort to express such a striving in the form of a service of a superhuman cause. *And all lesser loyalties, and all serving of imperfect or of evil causes, are but fragmentary forms of the service of the cause of universal loyalty.* To serve universal loyalty is, however, to view the interests of all conscious life as one; and to do this is to regard all conscious life as constituting just such an unity as our theory of truth requires. Meanwhile, since truth seeking is indeed itself a practical activity, what we have stated in our theory of truth is itself but an aspect of the very life that the loyal are leading. Whoever seeks any truth is loyal, for he is determining his life by reference to a life which transcends his own. And he is loyal to loyalty; for whatever truth you try to discover is, if true, valid for everybody, and is therefore worthy of everybody's loyal recognition. The loyal, then, are truth seekers; and the truth seekers are loyal. And all of them live for the sake of the unity of all life. And this unity includes us all, but is superhuman.

Our view of truth, therefore, meets at once an ethical and a logical need. The real world is precisely that world in which the loyal are at home. Their loyalty is no pathetic fallacy. Their causes are real facts in the universe. The universe as a whole possesses that unity which loyalty to loyalty seeks to express in its service of the whole of life.

Herewith, however, it occurs to us to ask one final question. Is not this real world, whose true unity the loyal acknowledge by their every deed, and whose conscious unity every process of truth seeking presupposes,—is not this also the world which religion recognizes? If so, what is the relation of loyalty to religion?

The materials for answering this question are now in our hands. We have been so deliberate in preparing them for our present purpose, just for the sake of making our answer the simpler when it comes.

V

We have now defined loyalty as the will to manifest the eternal in and through the deeds of individual selves. As for religion,—in its highest historical forms (which here alone concern us),— religion, as I think, may be defined as follows. Religion (in these its highest forms) *is the interpretation both of the eternal and of the spirit of loyalty through emotion, and through a fitting activity of the imagination.*

Religion, in any form, has always been an effort to interpret and to make use of some superhuman world. The history, the genesis, the earlier and simpler forms of religion, the relations of religion and morality in the primitive life of manknd, do not here concern us. It is enough to say that, in history, there has often been a serious tension between the interests of religion and those of morality. For the higher powers have very generally seemed to man to be either nonmoral or immoral. This very tension, only too frequently, still exists for many people to-day. One of the greatest and hardest discoveries of the human mind has been the discovery of how to reconcile, not religion and science, but religion and morality. Whoever knows even a small portion of the history of the cults of mankind is aware of the difficulties to which I refer. The superhuman has been conceived by men in terms that were often far enough from those which loyalty requires. Whoever will read over the recorded words of a writer nowadays too much neglected, the rugged and magnificently loyal Old Testament prophet Amos, can see for himself how bravely the difficulty of conceiving the superhuman as the righteous, was faced by one of the first who ever viewed the relation of religion and morality as our best teachers have since taught us to view them. And yet such a reader can also see how hard this very task of the prophet was. When we remember also that so great a mind as that of the originator of Buddhism, after all the long previous toil of Hindoo thought upon this great problem, could see no way to reconcile religion and morality, except by bringing them both to the shores of the mysterious and soundless ocean of Nirvana, and sinking them together in its depths (an undertaking which Buddha regarded as the salvation of the world), we get a further view of the nature of the problem. When we remember that St. Paul, after many years of lonely spiritual struggle, attempted in his teaching to reconcile morality and religion by an interpretation of Christianity which has ever since kept the Christian world in a most inspiring ferment of theological controversy and of practical conflict, we are again instructed as to the seriousness of the issue. But as a fact, the experience of the civilized man has gradually led him to see how to reconcile the moral life and the religious spirit. Since this reconciliation is one which our theory of truth, and of the constitution of the real world, substantially justifies, we are now ready for a brief review of the entire situation.

People often say that mere morality is something very remote from true religion. Sometimes people say this in the interests of religion, meaning to point out that mere morality can at best make you only a more or less tolerable citizen, while only religion can reconcile you, as such people say, to that superhuman world whose existence and whose support alone make human life worth living. But sometimes almost the same assertion is made in the interest of pure morality, viewed as something independent of religion. Some people tell you, namely, that since, as they say, religion is a collection of doubtful beliefs, of superstitions, and of more or less exalted emotions, morality is all the better for keeping aloof from religion. Suffering man needs your help; your friends need as much happiness as you can give them; conventional morality is, on the whole, a good thing. Learn righteousness, therefore, say they, and leave religion to the fantastic-minded who love to believe. The human is what we need. Let the superhuman alone.

Now, our philosophy of loyalty, aiming at something much larger and richer than the mere sum of human happiness in individual men, has taught us that there is no such sharp dividing line between the human and the superhuman as these attempts to sunder the provinces of religion and morality would imply. The loyal serve something more than individual lives. Even Nietzsche, individualist and ethical naturalist though he was, illustrates our present thesis. He began the later period of his teaching by asserting that "God is dead"; and (lest one might regard this as a mere attack upon monotheism, and might suppose Nietzsche to be an old-fashioned heathen polytheist) he added the famous remark that, in case any gods whatever existed, he could not possibly endure being himself no god. "*Therefore,*" so he reasoned, "*there are no gods.*" All this seems to leave man very much to his own devices. Yet Nietzsche at once set up the cult of the ideal future being called the *Uebermensch* or Superman. And the *Uebermensch* is just as much of a god as anybody who ever throned upon Olympus or dwelt in the sky. And if the doctrine of the "Eternal Recurrence," as Nietzsche defined it, is true, the *Uebermensch* belongs not only to the ideal future, but has existed an endless number of times already.

If our philosophy of loyalty is right, Nietzsche was not wrong in this appeal to the superhuman. The superhuman we indeed have always with us. Life has no sense without it. But the superhuman need not be the magical. It need not be the object of superstition. And if we are desirous of unifying the interests of morality and religion, it is well indeed to begin, as rugged old Amos began, by first appreciating what righteousness is, and then by interpreting righteousness, in a perfectly reasonable and non-superstitious way, in superhuman terms. Then we shall be ready to appreciate what religion, whose roots are indeed by no means wholly in our moral nature, nevertheless has to offer us as a supplement to our morality.

VI

Loyalty is a service of causes. But, as we saw, we do not, we cannot, wait until somebody clearly shows us how good the causes are in themselves, before we set about serving them. We first practically learn of the goodness of our causes through the very act of serving them. Loyalty begins, then, in all of us, in elemental forms. A cause fascinates us—we at first know not clearly why. We give ourselves willingly to that cause. Herewith our true life begins. The cause may indeed be a bad one. But at worst it is our way of interpreting the true cause. If we let our loyalty develop, it tends to turn into the service of the universal cause.

Hence I deliberately declined, in this discussion, to *base* my theory of loyalty upon that metaphysical doctrine which I postponed to my latest lectures. It is a very imperfect view of the real world which most youth get before them before they begin to be loyal. Hosts of the loyal actually manifest the eternal in their deeds, and know not that they do so. They only know that they are given over to their cause. The first good of loyalty lies, then, in the fact which we emphasized in our earlier lectures. Reverberating all through you, stirring you to your depths, loyalty first unifies your plan of life, and thereby gives you what nothing else can give, —your self as a life lived in accordance with a plan, your conscience as your plan interpreted for you through your ideal, your cause expressed as your personal purpose in living.

In so far, then, one can indeed be loyal without being consciously and explicitly religious. One's cause, in its first intention, appears to him human, concrete, practical. It is *also* an ideal. It is *also* a superhuman entity. It also really *means* the service of the eternal. But this fact may be, to the hard-working, and especially to the unimaginative, and, in a worldly sense, fairly successful man, a latent fact. He then, to be sure, gradually idealizes his cause as he goes; but this idealizing in so far becomes no very explicitly emphasized process in his life, although, as we have seen, some tendency to deify the cause is inevitable.

Meanwhile, such an imperfectly developed but loyal man may also accept, upon traditional grounds, a religion. This religion will then tell him about a superhuman world. But in so far the religion need not be, to his mind, an essential factor in his practical loyalty. He may be superstitious; or he may be a religious formalist; or he may accept his creed and his church simply because of their social respectability and usefulness; or, finally, he may even have a rich and genuine religious experience, which still may remain rather a mysticism than a morality, or an æsthetic comfort rather than a love of his cause.

In such cases, loyalty and religion may long keep apart. But the fact remains that loyalty, if sincere, involves at least a latent belief in the superhuman reality of the cause, and means at least an unconscious devotion to the one and eternal cause. But such a belief is also a latent union of morality and religion. Such a service is an unconscious piety. The time may come, then, when the morality will consciously need this union with the religious creed of the individual whose growth we are portraying.

This union must begin to become an explicit union whenever that process which, in our sixth lecture, we called the idealizing of the cause, reaches its higher levels. We saw that those higher levels are reached in the presence of what seems to be, to human vision, a lost cause. If we believe in the lost cause, we become directly aware that we are indeed seeking a city out of sight. If such a cause is real, it belongs to a superhuman world. Now, every cause worthy, as we said, of lifelong service, and capable of unifying our life plans, shows sooner or later that it is a cause *which we cannot successfully express in any set of human experiences of transient joys and of crumbling successes.* Human life taken merely as it flows, viewed merely as it passes by in time and is gone, is indeed a lost river of experience that plunges down the mountains of youth and sinks in the deserts of age. Its significance comes solely through its relations to the air and the ocean and the great deeps of universal experience. For by such poor figures I may, in passing, symbolize that really rational relation of our personal experience to universal conscious experience,—that relation to which I have devoted these last two lectures.

Everybody ought to serve the universal cause in his own individual way. For this, as we have seen, is what loyalty, when it comes to know its own mind, really means. But whoever thus serves inevitably *loses* his cause in our poor world of human sense-experience, because his cause is too good for this present temporal world to express it. And that is, after all, what the old theology meant when it called you and me, as we now naturally are, lost beings. Our deepest loyalty lies in devoting ourselves to causes that are just now lost to our poor human nature. One can express this, of course, by saying that the true cause is indeed real enough, in the higher world, while it is our poor human nature which is lost. Both ways of viewing the case have their truth. Loyalty means a transformation of our nature.

Lost causes, then, we must serve. But as we have seen, in our sixth lecture, loyalty to a lost cause has two companions, grief and imagination. Now, these two are the parents of all the higher forms of genuinely ethical religion. If you doubt the fact, read the scriptures of any of the great ethical faiths. Consult the psalter, the hymns, the devotional books, or the prayers of the church. Such religion interprets the superhuman in forms that our longing, our grief, and our imagination invent, but also in terms that are intended to meet the demands of our highest loyalty. For we are loyal to that unity of life which, as our truer moral consciousness learns to believe, owns the whole real world, and constitutes the cause of causes. In being loyal to universal loyalty, we are serving the unity of life.

This true unity of the world-life, however, is at once very near to us and very far from us. Very near it is; for we have our being in it, and depend upon it for whatever worth we have. Apart from it we are but the gurgling stream soon to be lost in the desert. In union with it we have individual significance in and for the whole. But we are very far from it also, because our human experience throws such fragmentary light upon the details of our relation to its activities. Hence in order to feel our relations to it as vital relations, we have to bring it near to our feelings and to our imaginations. And we long and suffer the loneliness of this life as we do so. But because we know of the details of the world only through our empirical sciences, while these give us rather materials for a rational life than a view of the unity of life, we are indeed left to our imagination to assuage grief and to help in the training of loyalty. For here, that is, precisely as to the *details* of the system of facts whereby our life is linked to the eternal, our science forsakes us. We can know *that* we are thus linked. *How* we are linked, our sciences do not make manifest to us.

Hence the actual content of the higher ethical religions is endlessly rich in legend and in other symbolic portrayal. This portrayal is rich in emotional meaning and in vivid detail. What this portrayal attempts to characterize is, in its general outline, an absolute truth. This truth consists in the following facts: *First, the rational unity and goodness of the world-life; next, its true but invisible nearness to us, despite our ignorance; further, its fulness of meaning despite our barrenness of present experience; and yet more, its interest in our personal destiny as moral beings; and finally, the certainty that, through our actual human loyalty, we come, like Moses, face to face with the true will of the world, as a man speaks to his friend.* In recognizing these facts, we have before us what may be called the creed of the Absolute Religion.

You may well ask, of course, whether our theory of truth, as heretofore expounded, gives any warrant to such religious convictions. I hold that it does give warrant to them. The symbols in which these truths are expressed by one or another religion are indeed due to all sorts of historical accidents, and to the most varied play of the imaginations both of the peoples and of the religious geniuses of our race. But that our relations to the world-life are relations wherein we are consciously met, from the other side, by a superhuman and yet strictly personal conscious life, in which our own personalities are themselves bound up, but which also is not only richer but is more concrete and definitely conscious and real than we are,—this seems to me to be an inevitable corollary of my theory of truth.

VII

And now, finally, to sum up our whole doctrine of loyalty and religion. Two things belonging to the world-life we know—two at least, if my theory is true: *it is defined in terms of our own needs; and it includes and completes our experience.* Hence, in any case, it is precisely as live and elemental and concrete as we are; and there is not a need of ours which is not its own. If you ask why I call it good—well, the very arguments which recent pragmatism has used are, as you remember, here my warrant. A truth cannot be a merely theoretical truth. True is that which successfully fulfils an idea. Whoever, again, is not succeeding, or is facing an evil, or is dissatisfied, is inevitably demanding and defining facts that are far beyond him, and that are not yet consciously his own. A knower of the totality of truth is therefore, of necessity, in possession of the fulfilment of all rational purposes. If, however, you ask why this world-life permits any evil whatever, or any finitude, or any imperfections, I must indeed reply that here is no place for a general discussion of the whole problem of evil, which I have repeatedly and wearisomely considered in other discussions of mine. But this observation does belong here. Our theory of evil is indeed no "shallow optimism," but is founded upon the deepest, the bitterest, and the dearest moral experience of the human race. The *loyal*, and they alone, know the one great good of suffering, of ignorance, of finitude, of loss, of defeat—*and that is just the good of loyalty*, so long as the cause itself can only be viewed as indeed a living whole. Spiritual peace is surely no easy thing. We win that peace only through stress and suffering and loss and labor. But when we find the preciousness of the idealized cause emphasized through grief, we see that, whatever evil is, it at least *may* have its place in an ideal order. What would be the universe without loyalty; and what would loyalty be without trial? And when we remember that, from this point of view, our own griefs are the griefs of the very world consciousness itself, in so far as this world-life is expressed in our lives, it may well occur to us that the life of loyalty with all its griefs and burdens and cares may be the very foundation of the attainment of that spiritual triumph which we must conceive as realized by the world spirit.

Perhaps, however, one weakly says: "If the world will attains in its wholeness what we seek, why need we seek that good at all?" I answer at once that our whole philosophy of loyalty instantly shows the vanity of such speech. Of course, the world-life does *not* obtain the individual good that is involved in my willing loyalty unless indeed *I am loyal*. The cause may in some way triumph without me, but not as *my* cause. We have never defined our theory as meaning that the world-life is *first* eternally complete, but *then* asks us, in an indifferent way, to copy its perfections. Our view is that each of us who is loyal is doing his unique deed in that whole of life which we have called the eternal simply because it is the conspectus of the totality of life, past, present, and future. If my deed were not done, the world-life would miss my deed. Each of us can say that. The very basis of our theory of truth, which we found upon the deeds, the ideas, the practical needs, of each of us, gives every individual his unique place in the world order—his deed that nobody else can do, his will which is his own. "Our wills are ours to make them thine." The unity of the world is *not* an ocean in which we are lost, but a life which is and which needs all our lives in one. Our loyalty defines that unity for us as a living, active unity. We have come to the unity through the understanding of our loyalty. It is an eternal unity only in so far as it includes all time and change and life and deeds. And therefore, when we reach this view, since the view simply fulfils what loyalty demands, our loyalty remains as precious to us, and as practical, and as genuinely a service of a cause, as it was before. It is no sort of "moral holiday" that this whole world-life suggests to us. It is precisely as a whole life of ideal strivings in which we have our places as individual selves and are such selves only in so far as we strive to do our part in the whole,—it is thus, and thus only, that our philosophy of loyalty regards the universe.

Religion, therefore, precisely in so far as it attempts to conceive the universe as a conscious and personal life of superhuman meaning, and as a life that is in close touch with our own meaning, is eternally true. But now it is just this *general* view of the universe as a rational order that is indeed open to our rational knowledge. No part of such a doctrine gives us, however, the present right as human beings to determine with any certainty the details of the world-life, except in so far as they come within the scope of our scientific and of our social inquiries. Hence, when religion, in the service of loyalty, interprets the world-life to us with symbolic detail, it gives us indeed merely symbols of the eternal truth. That this truth is indeed eternal, that our loyalty brings us into personal relations with a personal world-life, which values our every loyal deed, and needs that deed, all this is true and rational. And just this is what religion rightly illustrates. But the parables, the symbols, the historical incidents that the religious imagination uses in its portrayals,—these are the more or less sacred and transient *accidents* in which the "real presence" of the divine at once shows itself to us, and hides the detail of its inner life from us. These accidents of the religious imagination endure through many ages; but they also vary from place to place and from one nation or race of men to another, and they ought to do so. Whoever sees the living truth of the personal and conscious and ethical unity of the world *through* these symbols is possessed of the absolute religion, whatever be his nominal creed or church. Whoever overemphasizes the empirical details of these symbols, and then asks us to accept these details as literally true, commits an error which seems to me simply to invert that error whereof, at the last time, I ventured to accuse my pragmatist friends. Such a literalist, who reads his symbols as revelations of the detailed structure of the divine life, seems to me, namely, to look for the eternal *within* the realm of the mere data of human sense and imagination. To do this, I think, is indeed to seek the risen Lord in the open sepulchre.

Concerning the living truth of the whole conscious universe, one can well say, as one observes the special facts of human sense and imagination: "He is not here; he is arisen." Yet equally from the whole circle of the heaven of that entire self-conscious life which *is* the truth, there comes always, and to all the loyal, the word: "Lo, I am with you always, even unto the end of the world."

30

Individual Experience
and Social Experience
as Sources of Religious Insight

I

As we have defined religion, the main concern of any religion that
we are to recognise is with the salvation of man, and with whatever
objects or truths it is important to know if we are to find the way of
salvation. Now the experiences which teach us that we need what I
have ventured to call by the traditional name salvation, are, from my
point of view, experiences common to a very large portion of mankind. They are great and, in certain respects at least, simple experiences. You can have them and estimate them without being
committed to any one form of religious faith, without accepting
any special creed about supernatural things, and even without
hoping to find out any way of salvation whatever. The essential
conditions for discovering that man needs salvation are these: You
must find that human life has some highest end; and you must also
find that man, as he naturally is, is in great danger of failing to attain
this supreme goal. If you discover these two facts (and I personally
hold them to be facts whose reality you can experience), then the
quest for the salvation of man interests you, and is defined for you in

[Reprinted from *SRI*, pp. 37–75.]

genuinely empirical terms. Given the problem, you may or you may not see how to solve it. You may or you may not appeal to what you suppose to be a revelation to guide you on the way. But in any case, granted these conditions, granted that your experience has shown you your need of salvation—then the problem of religion is upon your hands. Soluble or insoluble, the topic of a revelation from above, or of a scientific inquiry, or of a philosophy, or of a haphazard series of efforts to better your condition, this problem, if it once comes to hold your attention, will make of you a religious inquirer. And so long as this is the case, no degree of cynicism or of despair regarding the finding of the way to salvation, will deprive you of genuinely religious interest. The issue will be one regarding facts of live experience. The concerns that for you will seem to be at stake will be perfectly human, and will be in close touch with every interest of daily life.

To conceive the business of religion in this way simplifies our undertaking, in so far as it connects religion not merely with doubtful dogmas and recondite speculations, but rather with personal and practical interests and with the spirit of all serious endeavour.

Upon the other hand, this way of defining religion does, indeed, also complicate certain aspects of our present task. For if, from our point of view, religion thus becomes, in one way or another, the concern of everybody who has once seen that life has a highest goal, and that we are all naturally in great danger of missing this goal—still any effort to study the nature of religious insight seems to require us to be somehow just to all the endless varieties of human opinion regarding what the highest goal of human life is, and regarding the way to attain that goal after we have once defined it. In some sense, in our further inquiry, nothing human can be alien to us, in case it involves any deep experience of man's purpose in living, or of man's peril as a seeker after the attainment of his purpose; or any assurance regarding the presence or the power which, entering into some sort of union with any man's own spiritual life, seems to that man an apt Deliverer from his evil plight, a genuinely saving principle in his life.

How great the resulting complications that threaten our investigation seem to be the conclusion of our former lecture showed us. Countless souls, trusting to their individual experience, have learned, as we at the last time indicated, to define their ideal, and their need, and, upon occasion, to discover the power that they took to be their saving principle—their deliverer. Who amongst all these were right, either in their judgment as to their need or in their consciousness that they had found the way that leads to peace, to triumph, to union with the goal of human life? Were all of them more or less right? Were any of them wholly deluded? Are there as many supreme aims of life as there are individuals? Are there as many ways of salvation as there are religions that men follow? And by what means shall we decide such questions? Grave and infinitely complicated seem the issues which these queries arouse.

Upon one side, then, our problem is pathetically simple, human, practical, even commonplace. Daily experience, in serious-minded people, illustrates it. The plainest facts of our life exemplify it. It concerns nothing more recondite than that tragedy of natural human failure which you may constantly witness all about you, if not within you. Upon the other side, no questions more bring you into contact with the chaotic variety of human opinion, and with the complexities of the whole universe, than do the religious questions, when thus defined in terms of men's deepest needs and of men's hopes and faiths regarding the possible escape from their most pressing peril of failure.

Our first lecture gave us a glimpse of this simplicity of the main definition of our problem and of this complication with regard to the conflicting proposals that are made toward its special formulation and toward its solution. We have now to study further the sources of insight upon which every solution of our problem must depend.

II

Our present lecture will be devoted to three tasks. First, we shall try to show that the religious consciousness of mankind, when it is concerned with the need and with the way of salvation, must needs appear in many various and apparently conflicting forms, but that, nevertheless, these conflicts need not discourage us. For, as we shall attempt still further to explain, the underlying motives of the higher religions are, after all, much more in agreement than the diversities of creeds and the apparent chaos of religious experiences would lead us to imagine. In order to make this deeper unity of the higher religious life of mankind plain, we shall try to show, more fully than we did in the last lecture, how the consciousness of the ideal of life, and of the need of salvation, naturally arises in the experience of the individual man. The religious paradox, as, in our former lecture, we defined that paradox, depends upon the fact that the principal religious motives are indeed perfectly natural and human motives, which need no mysterious movings from another world to explain their presence in our lives; while, on the other hand, these very motives, when once they appear, force us to seek for relief from spiritual sources that cannot satisfy unless they are far above our natural human level of life—that is, unless they are in some definable sense superhuman. But about superhuman matters it is not surprising that ignorant mortals should widely differ, despite the deeper unity that underlies all our nobler religious needs.

Thus the unity of the religious concerns of mankind is perfectly compatible with the fact that men differ so widely in faith. The mysteries of religion belong to our natural failure to conceive readily and to grasp adequately the religious objects. But our religious need is not a mystery; and our religious interests are as natural as is our ignorance. The higher forms of the religious consciousness are due to perfectly human motives but lead to a stubborn quest for the superhuman. To understand whence the higher religions get their moving principle, you have only to survey our natural life as it is, in all its pathetic and needy fallibility. But if the higher religions are to find what they seek, they call for sources of insight which you cannot define, unless we are able to know a reality that transcends human nature as it is—unless we can come into genuine intercourse with a spiritual realm that is above man. This naturalness of the religious motives, this supernatural and naturally baffling character of the religious objects, I am, then, first to illustrate still further than I at the last time was able to do.

I shall thus be led, in the second place, to the mention of that source of religious insight to which, at the close of the former lecture, I directed your attention, namely, to our social experience. Society, in a certain sense, both includes and transcends the individual man. Perhaps, then, something can be done toward solving the problem of the religious paradox, and toward harmonising the varieties of religious opinion, by considering the religious meaning of our social consciousness. The religious paradox is that the needy and ignorant natural man must somehow obtain the spiritual power to get into a genuine touch with a real life that is above his own level. If he is to be saved, something that is divine must come to be born in the humble manger of his poor natural life. How is this apparition of the divine in the human, of the supernatural in the natural, conceivable? It is that question which most of all divides men into various religious sects. Perhaps a study of our social experience, which, indeed, often tends to mould our naturally narrow selfishness into nobler spiritual forms, may throw light upon this problem. And so I shall, in this second part of the present discourse, state the case for our social experience as a source of religious insight.

We shall, however, no sooner state this case than we shall begin to see how inadequate our ordinary social experience is to give us full religious insight. Therefore, in the third place, I shall try to estimate more critically both the merits and the imperfections of this second source of religious light, and thus I shall be led, as I close, to the mention of a third source, from which, as I hold, we can learn what neither our unaided private experience nor our ordinary social experience ever adequately shows.

III

Let me proceed at once to the first of these three undertakings. I am further to illustrate, on the one hand, the unity and the naturalness of the religious motives; on the other hand, I am to emphasise the mysterious seeming of the religious objects. And I am thus to show the reason why the faiths of men are so diverse but their religious needs so nearly common.

At the last time I tried to define for you, in my own terms, what the supreme purpose of human life is, or, in other words, what that highest good is which we are all in such peril of missing that we need salvation from this peril. My definition was this: We are naturally creatures of wavering and conflicting motives, passions, desires. The supreme aim of life is to triumph over this natural chaos, to set some one plan of life above all the others, to give unity to our desires, to organise our activities, to win, not, indeed, the passionless peace of Nirvana, but the strength of spirit which is above the narrowness of each one of our separate passions. We need to conceive of such a triumphant and unified life, and successfully to live it. That is our goal: Self-possession, unity, peace, and spiritual power through and yet beyond all the turmoil of life—the victory that overcometh in the world.

Now this definition of the ideal life will have seemed to some of you too much a merely philosophical formula. You will say that this is not what plain men have in mind when they ask God's help, or lament their sins, or look to religion for consolation.

I grant you that, since I am here concerned with philosophy and not with preaching, I, of course, prefer, for my present purpose, a formulation of the ideal of life in reflective, in thoughtful terms. But I cannot admit that plain men, in their religious moods, are not concerned with the ideal of life which I thus reflectively formulate. I am trying to formulate the ideal of life that seems to me to underlie all the higher religions. It is one thing, however, to feel an interest and another thing to become conscious of the meaning of the interest. No matter how inarticulate may be a man's sense of his need, that sense, if deep and genuine, may imply a view of life which a whole system of ethics and of metaphysics may be needed to expound. Philosophy ought to be considerate, and to use more or less technical speech, but it need not be on that account inhuman. Its concern is with what common-sense means but does not express in clearly conscious terms. It does not want to substitute its formulas for life. It does desire to add its thoughtfulness to the intensity of life's great concerns and to enlighten us regarding what aims life has always really intended to pursue.

My own effort to formulate the supreme end of life does not seem to me to be foreign to common-sense. I think that this way of stating the purpose of life may help us to see through many of the apparently hopeless diversities of human opinion regarding what the highest good is.

It is customary to describe that longing for salvation which is, from the point of view of these lectures, the foundation of religion, by saying that the man who begins to get religious interest discovers that when left to himself he is out of harmony with what James calls "the higher powers," that is, with what a Christian calls God. In other words, as a customary formula states the case, the religiously disposed man begins by learning that the chief end of his existence is to come into harmony with God's will. And this discovery, as such a view supposes, teaches him, for the first time, what his ideal of life ought to be. And therefore, as many say, something that is of the nature of a mysterious revelation from without is needed to initiate the religious process and to show us our goal. On the other hand, writers like James, who insist upon interpreting religion, so far as that is possible, in terms of personal experience rather than in terms of external revelation, have nevertheless been led to agree with many of the partisans of revelation in regarding this sense of our disharmony with the "higher powers" as something that must have an essentially superhuman source. For James, our sense of religious need is an experience which mysteriously wells up from the subliminal self, from the soundless depths of our own subconsciousness. James, therefore, conceives it probable that, through the subliminal or subconscious self, we are actually aroused to religious interest by spiritual beings whose level is higher than our own, and whose will, expressed to us through the vague but often intense sense of need which the religiously minded feel, does set for us an ideal task which is of greater worth than our natural desires, and which, when we can get into harmony with these powers through the aid of their subliminal influences, does give a new sense to life.

Now in contrast with such views regarding the origin of that deeper sense of need which is indeed the beginning of religion, I have to insist that the basis of the religious interest is something much less mysterious than James's supposed workings of the "higher powers" through our subliminal selves, and is also something much more universally human than is the opportunity to come under the influence of any one revelation. Men who never heard of Christianity, and men who have never felt conscious of any external revelation from above, as well as men who have had no such sudden uprushes from their own subconscious natures as James's "religious geniuses" have reported, are able to win a genuine religious interest, to be aware of an intense need for salvation, and to set before themselves, in however inarticulate a fashion, the very ideal of life which I have been trying in my own way to formulate. The need and the ideal can come into sight in a manner that indeed does not in the least either exclude or require a belief in one or in another reported revelation, but that links both the need and the ideal to our ordinary personal experience by ties which are not at all mysterious. Let me show you, then, better than my time permitted in the former lecture, how an individual may naturally experience what I have called his need of salvation.

Nothing is more obvious about the natural course of our lives than is the *narrowness* of view to which we are usually subject. We are not only the victims of conflicting movies, but we are often too narrow to know that this is true. For we see our various life interests, so to speak, one at a time. We forget one while we are living out another. And so we are prone to live many lives, seldom noting how ill harmonised they are. Home life, for instance, may be one thing; business life in principle another; sport or social ambition another. And these various lives may be lived upon mutually inconsistent plans. We forget one part of ourselves in our temporary absorption in some other part. And if, as our naturally complex and often conflicting motives determine, these our various lives are out of harmony with one another, we constantly do irrevocable deeds that emphasise and perpetuate the results of this disharmony. And as we grow older our motives alter; yet because of our natural narrowness of interest, we often do not recognise the change. Our youth consequently lays a poor foundation for our age; or perhaps our mature life makes naught of the aspirations of our youth. We thus come to spend a great part of our days thwarting ourselves through the results of our fickleness, yet without knowing who it is that thwarts us. We love, and, like Siegfried, forget our former beloved, and perhaps live to feel the fatal spear-thrust that avenges our treason to our own past. The deeper tragedies of life largely result from this our narrowness of view.

But over against this narrowness of our ordinary activities there, indeed, stand certain moments when we get a wider vision of ourselves, when we review life, or foresee it with a broad outlook. These are, indeed, moments of insight. We all know how tragic they often are, because they show us at a glance how with the left hand we have undone the right hand's work, how we have loved and forgotten, how we have sworn fealty to many masters, and have cheated one while we served another, how absorption in business has made us unworthy of home, or how we have wantonly sacrificed a friend in order to win a game, or gained our bit of the world through what, upon review, we have to call the loss of our souls. Such moments of insight come to us sometimes when our friends die, and when memory reminds us of our neglected debts of love or of gratitude to them, or when worldly defeat reawakens the long-forgotten unworldly aspirations that we abandoned in order to do what has ended in earning the defeat. These are, I repeat, often tragic moments. But they enlighten. And they show us our need. And they arise as naturally as does any other incident of a reasonable life.

What need do they show? I answer, the need to possess what by mere nature we never come to possess, namely, the power to "see life steadily and see it whole," and then to live triumphantly in the light of this vision. Can a plain man who is no philosopher feel this need? I answer, Yes, whenever he has his moments of vision; whenever he feels the longing for the clean, straight, unswerving will, for the hearty whole life; whenever he sees and regrets his fickleness, just because it means self-defeat; whenever he seeks to be true to himself. At such moment his highest aim is the aim that there should be a highest aim in life, and that this aim should win what it seeks. He has the longing, however inarticulate, for integrity of spirit and for success in winning the fruits of integrity.

When the plain man feels what I venture thus to formulate, how will he express his longing? He will, of course, not use my present formulas. He will seize upon whatever expressions the creed or the language of his tribe may suggest to him. He may say, and perhaps truthfully: "This is the ideal that God sets before me. This is the divine will regarding my life." For at such times he conceives of God as the being who has widest vision and who knows him best. Therefore he conceives of God's plan as the fulfilment of his own rational plan. But the interior source of the plain man's view regarding the divine will is simply his better vision of the meaning of his life, the vision that comes at moments when he is not forgetful of the whole; when he does not want to swear fidelity to one beloved, and then, like Siegfried, pursue and win another; when he wants to be true to the whole of himself. No wonder that he, indeed, conceives this supreme goal of life as the goal set for him by some will higher than his own private will. He is right. For, as we shall see, throughout our later study, we are, indeed, helpless either to hold before us this our personal vision of the triumphant life and of the unity of the spirit, or to turn the vision into a practical reality, unless we come into touch and keep in touch with an order of spiritual existence which is in a perfectly genuine sense superhuman, and in the same sense supernatural, and which certainly is not our natural selves.

But in any case the plain man must needs interpret his vision of the ideal in terms of whatever conception of God, or of the triumphant life, or of spiritual power, his traditions and his stage of personal development may suggest to him. Hence the endless varieties in the formulation of the religious ideal. Whatever is suggested to a man, at his moments of wider vision, as a law or as a motive which, *if* it were the ruling motive or the supreme law would make life a consistent whole—this he takes to be God's will, or the truth that is to save him if, indeed, salvation is possible.

If this account of the sources of the religious motive is right, we need not view the religious interest as the result of an arbitrary intrusion from above—as if the gods loved to disturb us and to trouble our peace. Nor need we, with James, speak of a marvellous and capricious uprush from below the level of our natural consciousness. Yet just as little need we think of religion as having no concern with what is, indeed, superhuman. Religion is, indeed, our own affair; for it grows out of our personal vision of the transformation that a divinely enlarged power to comprehend, to survey, to harmonise, to triumph over our natural life would give. This vision comes to us at moments, in glimpses—and is seen through a glass darkly. Our need is to see face to face and to live in the light thus to be discovered. And so to live would be salvation. The word salvation is fitting, because the need is so great and because the transformation would be so profound. The endlessly various interpretations of this one ideal and of the nature of the saving process are due to the wealth of life and to the imposing multitude of motives and of experiences that the religious consciousness has to consider. But beneath and above all the varieties of religious experience lies the effort to win in reality what the vision of the harmonious and triumphant life suggests to us in our moments of clearness. Since our own natures leave us hopelessly remote from this goal, while our glimpses of spiritual harmony and power reveal to us its preciousness, our religious need is supreme, and is accompanied with the perfectly well-warranted assurance that we cannot attain the goal unless we can get into some sort of communion with a real life infinitely richer than our own—a life that is guided by a perfect and unwavering vision, and that somehow conquers and annuls all fickleness, conflict, and estrangement. Such a life rightly seems to us to be superhuman in its breadth of view and in its spiritual power, if indeed there be such a life at all. If there is no such life, none the less we need it, and so need salvation. If salvation is possible, then there is in the universe some being that knows us, and that is the master of life. And we seek ourselves to know even as we are known and to live as the wise one would have us live.

Thus simple and, for all to whom even the occasional moments of wider vision come, universal are the religious motives. James was wrong when he sought them in any capricious interference of the subliminal self, or of its superhuman controls, with our natural selves. It is we who in our natural lives are capricious and narrowly interfere with our own freedom. It is we who are the disturbers of our own peace. The religious ideal grows out of the vision of a spiritual freedom and peace which are not naturally ours. No two of us get that vision in quite the same way. But all its forms show us the same far-off shining light. The problem of religious insight is the problem whether that light is a mirage.

No wonder, then, that men differ as to their special efforts to solve such a problem. But it is now our task to seek for further sources of insight.

IV

The foregoing discussion may seem to have led us far from the study of our social experience as a source of religious insight. But in fact it is a necessary preliminary to that study and leads us very near to it.

If one principal source of our need of salvation is the natural narrowness of our view of the meaning of our own purposes and motives, and the consequent fickleness and the forgetful inconsistency with which we usually live out our days, it seems right, in searching for a way that may lead toward salvation, to get such help as we can by looking to our normal social experience for whatever guidance it can give. The social world is wide, even if it is still full of conflict. It broadens our outlook at every turn. A man corrects his own narrowness by trying to share his fellow's point of view. Our social responsibilities tend to set limits to our fickleness. Social discipline removes some of our inner conflicts, by teaching us not to indulge caprices. Human companionship may calm, may steady our vision, may bring us into intercourse with what is in general much better than a man's subliminal self, namely, his public, his humane, his greater social self, wherein he finds his soul and its interests writ large. Perhaps, then, whatever the ultimate goal, the way out of the distractions of the natural self, the way toward the divine insight and power that we need, lies through our social experience.

No wonder, then, that in the religious discussions of to-day our social experience is that source of insight upon which a great number of our teachers, whether they are professional religious teachers or not, most frequently insist. Our present time is an age of great concern with social problems and reforms. No wonder, then, that we have all learned to widen our vision, and to control our wayward-ness, by remembering that man is a being who can be neither under-stood nor directed in case you try to view him in isolation. As for salvation, many of our most influential leaders now teach us that the problem of our day is the problem of saving, not the individual as an individual, but the social order as a whole. The two tendencies which seem to be most potent in the political realm are the general tendencies known by the admittedly vague names of democracy and socialism. Solidarity, collectivism, the common life—these are the watchwords of some of the most widely influential movements of our time.

And these watchwords have, for many of us, not only a political, but a religious meaning. I need not remind you of the popular influence of such dramas as "The Servant in the House," or of the numbers of clergymen to whom the preaching of religion has come to mean, in the main, the preaching of beneficent social reforms. If teachers who thus view religion as, on the whole, a movement to-ward the increase of social welfare are asked what their counsel is to the individual regarding the salvation of his soul, they will reply: "If you want to be saved, come out of yourself." Some of them would add: "Forget yourself." But whether they use this latter ex-tremely ambiguous and doubtful form of advice, they very gen-erally agree that to seek to save your own soul by any merely or mainly inward and non-social process is to secure perdition. "It is love that saves," they are fond of telling us. And in this doctrine, as interpreted in the light of our modern social movements, many see the entire essence of Christianity adapted to our present situation.

Nor is the tendency here in question limited to the practical counsels of which I have just reminded you. There are those students of the psychology and the philosophy of religion who are disposed to conceive that the whole essence of the religion of all times, the entire meaning of religious beliefs and practices, can be exhaustively and accurately described in the purely human and social terms which these practical counsels attempt to embody. A recent writer on the psychology of religion defines religion as man's consciousness of his highest social values, and maintains that all religious beliefs are attempts to express this consciousness in whatever terms a given stage of civilisation makes natural and possible.

One can easily suggest to any student of general history some of the facts which such a writer has in mind. Have not the gods often been conceived as tribal deities, and so simply as representatives of the welfare and of the will of the community over against the waywardness and the capriciousness of the individual? Was not the transition from polytheism to the various forms of pantheism and of monotheism determined by the social processes that formed kingdoms or empires, and that finally led over to the modern appreciation of the value of the common interest of an ideally united humanity? Were not the prophets of Israel social reformers? Was not the work of Jesus an anticipation and a prophecy of the coming consciousness of the brotherhood of man, as the lovers of mankind now conceive that brotherhood? What has religion had to teach us, some will insistently ask, more saving, unifying, sustaining, than this love of man for man?

From such a point of view, as you see, our social experience is our principal source of religious insight. And the salvation that this insight brings to our knowledge is salvation through the fostering of human brotherhood. Such salvation accrues to the individual so far as he gives himself over to the service of man, and to mankind in so far as men can only be saved together and not separately.

I am just now depicting, not judging, a view concerning the solution of religious problems which you know to be, in our day, as potent as it is varied and problematic in its teaching. Can this view satisfy? Does this way of stating the case really indicate to us any adequate source of religious insight, any way in which we can define the true salvation of man?

V

We cannot answer this question without taking account of the views of those of our recent teachers to whom this purely social theory of the religious objects and values is indeed profoundly unsatisfactory. That such opponents of the adequacy of the interpretation of religion just suggested are to be found amongst the believers in familiar religious traditions, we need not at any length set forth. The traditions of the great religions of the world do not interpret the old faiths in this way, just because these religious traditions all agree in regarding the human social order as something which exists for the sake of an essentially superhuman order. As these various faiths assert, man can never be saved by purely human means, whether you call these means preventive medicine, or socialism, or universal brotherhood, or even love, so long as love means simply human love. As for Christianity, in all its older forms, it has emphasised the love of man, but always in a certain union with the love of God which tradition could never conceive as adequately expressible in terms of our recent social movements. The "Servant in the House" is supposed to be a modern apparition of the Christ; but he is explicitly a heretic regarding the old faith of the church.

But with tradition as tradition, these lectures have to do only by way of occasional illustration. What interests us more, for our present purpose, is the fact that, despite the predominance of the social interpretations of religion of which I have just reminded you, there are still some of our recent teachers who stoutly insist that our social experience does not adequately show us any way of salvation whatever.

And here first I must call attention to certain of the most modern and least theologically disposed of our leaders, namely, to those who emphasise the most characteristic recent forms of individualism. I have mentioned Nietzsche in my former lecture. Surely he stands for opposition to tradition and he expresses tendencies that are potent to-day. But while he lived and wrote, he aspired to be a sort of Antichrist, and preached the doctrine that a religion of love can never save, because, as he insists, what the self needs is power, and power is not to be won by attempting to please a world of slaves. Nietzsche may seem to you, as he has seemed to so many, a hopeless abnormity; but his Titanism is in fact a wayward modern expression of a motive that has always played its notable part in the search for salvation, ever since heroism and the resolute will were first discovered by man. Nietzsche's insight too, such as it is, is a social insight. It comes through noting that, even if the individual needs his social world as a means of grace and a gateway to salvation, the social order, in its turn, needs individuals that are worth saving, and can never be saved unless it expresses itself through the deeds and the inner life of souls deeply conscious of the dignity of selfhood, of the infinite worth of unique and intensely conscious personal life.

As a fact, individualism is as potent an ethical motive in the life of to-day as is the collectivism just characterized. Each of these tendencies, in our present social order, feeds upon and intensifies the other. Socialism opposes, and yet inevitably encourages, the purposes of the very individual who feels his social ties as a galling restraint. It preaches solidarity and brotherhood and love; but wins a ready hearing from those who view all these tendencies mainly as means whereby they may hope to have their own way, and to become, as Nietzsche's Superman, "beyond good and evil"— masters in the coming world of triumphant democracy. The social experience of our time is full of ambiguous lessons. Its way toward salvation leads not only over the Hill of Difficulty, but both ways around the hill; and it shows us no one straight and narrow road to peace. Whoever would traverse its wilderness and reach salvation needs to supplement his social insight by a use of other and deeper sources.

And as to what these deeper sources of insight are, the teacher whom I have already repeatedly cited—William James—asserts a doctrine that, as you already know, I do not regard as adequate, but that I must again here emphasise, because its contrast with that social theory of religion which I just characterised is so instructive.

James, in his "Varieties of Religious Experience," shows the utmost liberality toward differences of faith, and insists in the opening chapters of his book that religious experience is a field where one must beware of defining sharp boundary lines or of showing a false exclusiveness. Yet *one* boundary line he himself defines with the greatest sharpness; and in respect of *one* matter he is rigidly exclusive. Religious experience, he insists, is, as you will remember from our first lecture, the experience of an individual who feels himself to be "alone with the divine." And the social types of religious experience James rigidly excludes from the "varieties" whereof he takes account. And James's reason for this procedure is explicit. In its social aspects religion, so he insists, always becomes, or has already become, conventional. James no longer finds in the religious life of communities the novelty and independence of vision which he prizes. The essence of true religious experience lies, for him, in its originality, in its spontaneity, and so in the very solitude which is a condition, to James's mind, for the discovery of that which saves.

The words "originality" and "spontaneity" emphasise the features which, as I think, James most meant to emphasise. The problem of salvation, for James, must be an essentially individual problem; for nobody else ever faced *your* need of salvation, or had your personal issues to meet. If you win religious insight, you will have to win it very much as you will have to die—alone. Of course James does not hesitate to test the value of religious experience, in his pragmatic fashion, by its social as well as by its individual consequences. The fruits of the spirit accrue to the general advantage; and the saint, in James's opinion, must indeed undertake to edify, not only himself, but also his brethren. But the effects of religious insight must not be confused with the sources. James insists that the sources are mainly from within the individual and are only incidentally social. A religious discovery has in common with a poetic creation the fact that the religious genius, like the artist, sees his vision, and produces his spiritual miracle, in solitude.

If you ask whether this position which James assumes is anything more than his own private opinion, and if you want to know his grounds for it, a closer examination of his book will show you why he thus deliberately turns his back upon the favourite recent interpretation of religion as an essentially social phenomenon. James, in common with the traditional faiths, although not in conformity with their formulas, always conceived religious experience as an intercourse with objects and with powers that, whatever their deeper bases in our "subliminal" nature, do not adequately express themselves in our everyday, worldly, overt human nature. And in our social life, where the conventional reigns, where man imitates man or contends with man, where crowds bustle and the small-talk or the passionate struggle of the day fill the mind, where lovers pursue their beloved and are jealous of their rivals, and laborers toil and sweat, and worldly authorities display their pomp, you meet not the solution, but the problem of life. James, as man, was full of social interests, and, as psychologist, was fond of studying social processes. But when a man wants peace and spiritual triumph, James observes that, as an empirical fact, he does not readily find them in the market-place, or on the battle-field, or in the law courts, unless, indeed, he comes to these places already full of the light that the saintly souls have often found in the wilderness or in their meditations. In brief, James always emphasises the mystical element in religious experience and is full of the assurance that religion cannot find its food in the commonplace; while our social life is a realm where the commonplace holds sway. Or again, James holds that when the faithful have thought of their religious experience as an intercourse with beings of a level wholly superhuman, they may, indeed, have been wrong in their creeds, but were right in holding that man as he lives in his social world can never save man. Our social consciousness is too barefaced and open in its union of triviality and pathos. What we want as the saving power is, for a teacher such as James, something more mysterious, deep, subconscious or superconscious, and in this sense, indeed, superhuman.

Still I am only depicting, not yet judging. I have now briefly stated opinions that favour and opinions that oppose an interpretation of religious insight in terms of our social experience. But what are the merits of the case? In what sense can there be a religion of the social consciousness?

VI

The answer to this question involves, I think, two considerations, both of them exemplified by the various views here in question, both of them familiar, both of them easily misinterpreted. The first is the very consideration upon which our popular teachers of salvation through love most insist. We ourselves came upon that consideration at the close of our first lecture. Man is, indeed, a being who cannot be saved alone, however much solitude may help him, at times, toward insight. For he is bound to his brethren by spiritual links that cannot be broken. The second consideration is this: So long as man views his fellow-man *merely* as fellow-man, he only complicates his problem, for both he and his fellow equally need salvation. Their plight is common; their very need of salvation chains them together in the prison of human sorrow. If, to adapt the symbolism of ancient stories to our case, the angel of love is to appear in their prison, is to loosen their chains, is to open the doors, it must be, in some wise, as an angel, not as a merely human presence, that love must appear.

Perhaps the best way to indicate wherein lies the strength and the weakness, the irresistible authority and the pathetic limitation of our social experience as a religious guide, and the best way also to indicate its true relations to the religious experience of the human individual, is to remind ourselves of a very few familiar cases in which an individual finds that his own way toward salvation, if any such way is to exist for him at all, lies through his social world, so that he cannot be saved without the help of his fellows.

Our first instance shall be an extreme one, in which the sense of need is intense and the longing for salvation acute, but where there is little or no hope of finding the way, although one knows that if the way could be found it would bring one into touch with a new type of human companionship. We all know how the sense of guilt may take the form of a feeling of overwhelming loneliness. Now the sense of guilt, if deep and pervasive and passionate, involves at least a dim recognition that there is some central aim of life and that one has come hopelessly short of that aim. I may regret a blunder, and yet have no hint that there is any unified and supreme ideal of life. For a blunder is a special affair involving the missing of some particular aim. I may even bitterly repent a fault, and still think of that fault as a refusal to pursue some one separate moral purpose— a violation of this or of that maxim of conduct. But the true sense of guilt in its greater manifestation involves a confession that the whole self is somehow tainted, the whole life, for the time being, wrecked. But the bankruptcy of the self implies that there is one highest purpose which gives the self its value; the sense of total failure is itself a revelation of the value of what was lost. Hence the highly idealising tendency of the great experiences of moral suffering. They lead us to think not of this or of that special good, but of salvation and perdition in their general bearing upon life. The depth of the despair shows the grandeur of what has been missed; and it is therefore not surprising that experiences of this sort have been, for so many, the beginnings of religious insight. To believe that one is cut off from salvation may be the very crisis that in the end saves.

Now some of those who feel this overmastering might of their guilt lay most stress upon their assurance that God has condemned them. And religious tradition has of course emphasised this way of stating the case. But it is perfectly natural, and is surely a humane experience, to feel the sense of guilt primarily in the form of a belief that one is an outcast from human sympathy and is hopelessly alone. The more abnormal types of the sense of guilt, in nervous patients, frequently exemplify this terror of the lonely soul, this inner grief over the homelessness of the remorseful outcast. But actual guilt may be present with or without the more abnormal nervous conditions just mentioned, and, when present, may bring home to the rueful mind the despair of the awakened but forsaken sinner, and may bring it in the form of the feeling of guilty solitude.

A well-known expression of such a mood you find in Kipling's lyric of the "Poor little sheep that have gone astray." In these verses the outcast sons of good families, the "gentlemen-rankers," dwell together in an agonised companionship of common loneliness. Their guilt and their lost homes are for them inseparably associated.

Or again: Beneath all the fantastic imagery of Coleridge's "Ancient Mariner," the poet uses a perfectly recognisable type of the sense of guilt as the means to make his tale of wonders seem, despite all its impossibilities, human and even plausible. The incidents are the miracles of a magic dream; but the human nature depicted is as real as is the torment of any guilty conscience. Somehow—no matter how, or under how arbitrary conditions—the hero has committed a crime without precisely intending it to be a crime. His tale is one of a young man's adventurous insolence. His deed has all the too familiar characters of the typical sins of wayward youth. And that is why the gay young wedding guest must hear his tale. He— the mariner—in his own youth, had consciously meant to be only a little wanton and cruel. He awakened, as many a light-minded youth later awakes, to find that, as a fact, he had somehow struck at the very centre of life, at the heart of love, at the laws that bind the world together, at the spirit of the universe. When one thus awakes, he sees that nature and God are against him. But, worst of all, he has become a curse to his fellows; and in turn they curse him; and then they leave him alone with the nightmare life in death of utter solitude. To his mind there are no living men. He sees about him only "the curse in a dead man's eye." What life he can still see is no longer, to his morbid eyes, really human:

> The many men, so beautiful!
>   And they all dead did lie;
> And a thousand, thousand slimy things
>   Lived on; and so did I.

The Ancient Mariner's escape from the horrors of this despair, the beginnings of his salvation, date from the first movings of love in his heart toward all living beings. His salvation is won when, at the end, he finds God along with the goodly company at the kirk. In brief, the curse of his guilt is to be "alone on a wide, wide sea."

His salvation comes in preaching love and companionship, and in uniting himself hereby to the God who loves all things both great and small.

Now one does not often think of the "Ancient Mariner" as a poem of religious experience; but apart from its brilliant play with natural magic, its human charm actually depends upon this well-founded picture of the loneliness of guilt and of the escape through loving union with one's kind. And the poet deliberately gives to this picture the form and the sense of a religious process of salvation.

If you turn from the dreamy product of Coleridge's youthful fancy to the opposite pole of modern literature, you find an instance of almost the same motives at the basis of that most impressive romance of the Russian Dostoieffsky: "Crime and Punishment." Dostoieffsky had himself lived long in what he called "The House of the Dead," in Siberia, before he learned how to write this masterpiece. He had been forced to sojourn amongst the guilty of the most various grades. He had come to universalise their experiences and to struggle himself with one form of the problem of salvation. Those who, like Dante, have looked upon hell, sometimes have, indeed, wonders to tell us. Dostoieffsky condenses the whole problem of salvation from guilt in this picture of an individual. Raskolnikow, the hero, after his thoughtfully conceived crime, and after his laborious effort at self-justification, finds himself the prey of a simply overwhelming sense that he walks alone amongst men, and that, in the crowded streets of the city, he is as one dead amongst spectres. There is nowhere, I think, a more persuasive picture of the loneliness of great guilt. Raskolnikow could not be more the victim of supernatural forces if he were Coleridge's Ancient Mariner. Like the Ancient Mariner, Raskolnikow in the end finds the way to salvation through love—the love which the martyred Sonia teaches him—herself, as our Russian most persuasively pictures her, at once outcast and saint. The author uses religious conceptions which are both ancient and, in his use of them, unconventional. But the central one of these is the familiar conception that salvation involves a reconciliation both with the social and with the divine order, a reconciliation through love and suffering—an escape from the wilderness of lonely guilt to the realm where men can understand one another.

In such elemental ways the process of salvation can be made to appear as essentially a social process, just because its opposite, perdition, seems to mean banishment from amongst men.

Another group of cases presents to us the same need for human companionship as a means to salvation, but presents it in the winning guise of salvation beginning through love, without the main stress being laid upon the previous despair. In such cases the despair may be mentioned but at once relieved. The religion of friendship and of love is a familiar human experience. James, in his fear of debasing religion by romantic or by grosser associations, unjustly neglects it in his study of "varieties." In fact, to seem to find the divine in the person of your idealised friend or beloved is a perfectly normal way of beginning your acquaintance with the means of grace. You meet, you love, and—you seem to be finding God. Or, to use our present interpretation of what reveals the divine, love seems to furnish you with a vision of a perfect life, to give you a total survey of the sense of your own life, and to begin to show you how to triumph. If there be any divine life, you say, this is my vision of its beauty and its harmony. So the divine appears in one of Browning's later lyrics.

> Such a starved bank of moss,
>   Till, that May morn,
> Blue ran the flash across;
>   Violets were born!
>
> Sky—what a scowl of cloud
>   Till, near and far,
> Ray on ray split the shroud
>   Splendid! a star!
>
> World—how it walled about
>   Life with disgrace,
> Till God's own smile came out;
>   That was thy face!

In the sonnets of Shakespeare this religion of friendship has found some of its most perfect expressions.

> Haply I think of thee, and then my state,
>   Like to the lark's, at break of day arising
> From sullen earth, sings hymns at heaven's gate.

And again, in Mrs. Browning's "Sonnets from the Portuguese," the religion of love not only uses speech intensely personal, fond, intimate, but also, and deliberately, accompanies all this with words derived from reflective metaphysics, or from theology, and intended to express the miracle that the nearest movings of affection are also a revelation of the highest powers of the spiritual world.

> How do I love thee? Let me count the ways.
>   I love thee to the depth and breadth and height
>   My soul can reach, when feeling out of sight
> For the ends of Being, and Ideal Grace.
> I love thee to the level of everyday's
>   Most quiet need, by sun and candle light.
>   I love thee freely, as men strive for Right;
>   I love thee purely, as they turn from Praise;
>   I love thee with the passion put to use
> In my old griefs, and with my childhood's faith;
>   I love thee with a love I seemed to lose
> With my lost saints,—I love thee with the breath,
>   Smiles, tears, of all my life!—and, if God choose,
> I shall but love thee better after death.

Surely one could not better express, than this sonnet does, the naturalness of the religious motive—the mystery of the religious object.

And finally, turning from these cases to those which are social in the larger sense, every patriotic song which deifies one's country, every other form of the religion of patriotism, exemplifies the experience of the devoted lover of his country by teaching that it is "man's perdition to be safe" in case his social world calls for the sacrifice of his life, and that salvation comes through service.

James is indeed wrong then to neglect the social roads that lead toward the experience of what one takes to be divine. There is no love so simple-minded that, if it be true love, the way of salvation may not seem to be opened through it to the lover.

But observe that, as we review these instances, they show us how the social world wherein they bid us seek our salvation is a world whose very essence is transformed by love and by its vision into something that seems to the lover mystical, superhuman, and more than our literal and commonplace social life directly exemplifies. Those who have failed to find in their actual social life such inspirations may, indeed, have to look, as the typical mystics have generally done, elsewhere, for their vision of the divine, than in so much of the social world as they know. And such will, indeed, seek their vision of salvation in solitude. When they tell us of their experience, they may well remind the social enthusiast, as well as the lover, that the religion of love is no religion at all, unless it conceives its human object not only as this creature, or as this collection of needy men and women, but as a hint, or revelation, or incarnation of a divine process—of a process which is not only human but superhuman, and which can never be comprehended in the "mart and the crowded street" unless by the soul that is either mystical enough to meet God also "in the bush," or rationally enlightened enough to know that human life is indeed a revelation of something that is also superhuman.

I conclude, then, for the moment, thus: Social experience seems to lie on the way to salvation. Normally the way to salvation, if there be any such way, must lead through social experience. But when our social experience shows us any such way upward it does so, if it truly does so, because human social life is the hint, the likeness, or the incarnation of a life that lies beyond and above our present human existence. For human society as it now is, in this world of care, is a chaos of needs; and the whole social order groans and travails together in pain until now, longing for salvation. It can be saved, as the individual can be saved, only in case there is some way that leads upward, through all our turmoil and our social bickerings, to a realm where that vision of unity and self-possession which our clearest moments bring to us becomes not merely vision, but fulfilment, where love finds its own, and where the power of the spirit triumphs. Of such a realm the lovers dream and the religions tell. Let us appeal to a further source of insight. Concerning the realities that we need, let us next consult our Reason.

31

The Religious Mission of Sorrow

It very often happens to us that to reach any notable result, either in life or in insight, is even thereby to introduce ourselves to a new problem. In the present state of the undertaking of these lectures such is our experience. The religious insight whose source is the loyal spirit was our topic in the foregoing lecture. If my own view is correct, this source is by far the most important that we have yet considered. It unites the spirit and the meaning of all the foregoing sources. Rightly interpreted, it points the way to a true salvation.

Yet the very last words of our sketch of the fruits of loyalty were of necessity grave words. Intending to show through what spirit man escapes from total failure, we were brought face to face with the tragedies which still beset the higher life. "Adversity"— poor Griselda faced it in the tale. We left the loyal spirit appearing to us—as it does appear in its strongest representatives, able, some-how, in the power that is due to its insight, to triumph over fortune. But side by side with this suggestion of the nature of that which overcomes the world stood the inevitable reminder of the word: "In this world ye shall have tribulation."

How is tribulation related to religious insight? That is our present problem. It has been forced upon our attention by the study of the place and the meaning of loyalty. Some understanding of this prob-

[Reprinted from *SRI*, pp. 213–54.]

lem is necessary to any further comprehension of the lessons of all the foregoing sources of insight, and is of peculiar significance for any definition of the office of religion.

To nearly all of us, at some time in our lives, and to many of us at all times, the tragic aspect of human life seems to be a profound hindrance to religious insight of any stable sort. I must here first bring more fully to your minds why this is so—why the existence of tragedy in human existence appears to many moods, and to many people, destructive of faith in any religious truth and a barrier against rational assurance regarding the ultimate triumph of anything good. Then I want to devote the rest of this lecture to showing how sorrow, how the whole burden of human tribulation, has been, and reasonably may be, not merely a barrier in the way of insight, but also a source of religious insight. And this is the explanation of the title of the present lecture.

I

We approach our problem fully mindful of the limitations to which the purpose of these lectures confines us. The problem of evil has many metaphysical, theological, moral, and common-sense aspects upon which I can say nothing whatever in the present context. Human sorrow appears in our pathway in these lectures as a topic for us to consider, first, because whatever source of religious insight we have thus far consulted has shown us man struggling with some sort of ill, and, secondly, because there are aspects of this very struggle which will provide us with a new source of religious insight, and which will thus tend to throw new light upon the meaning of all the other sources. A thorough-going study of the problem of evil would require of us a complete philosophy not only of religion but of reality. But we are limiting ourselves, in these discussions, to a survey of certain sources.

The reasons why the existence and the prominence of evil in human life seem to all of us at some times, and to many of us at all times, a hindrance to the acceptance of any religious solution of the problems of life are familiar. I need then only to remind you what they are.

Without going into any subtleties regarding the definition of evil, it is obvious that our first characteristic reaction when we meet with what we take to be an evil is an effort to get rid of it, to shun its presence, or to remove it from existence. Pain, cold, burning heat, disease, starvation, death, our enemies, our dangers, these are facts that, precisely so far as we find them evil, we face with the determination to annul altogether their evil aspect.

A characteristic result of this tendency appears in the fact that man, who of all animals is most clearly aware of the presence of evil in his world, is for that very reason not only an ingenious deviser of new inventions for getting good things and for supplying his needs, but is also the most destructive of animals. He wars with his natural surroundings, and still more with his fellow-men, in ways that show how the instinctive aversions upon which his estimates of evil are founded are reinforced by the habits which he forms in his contests with ill fortune. Man the destroyer of evil thus appears, in much of his life, as a destroyer who is also largely moved by a love of destruction for its own sake. This love plays a great part in the formation of even very high levels of our social and moral con- sciousness. The heroes of song and story, and often of history as well, are fascinating partly, or chiefly, because they could kill and did so. We love victory over ill. Killing seems to involve such a victory. So we love killing, at least in the hero tales. The result is often a certain inconsistency. The gods offered Achilles the choice between a short life full of the glorious slaying of enemies and a long life of harmless obscurity. He chose the short life; and there- fore he is to be remembered forever. For even when he would not fight, his "destructive wrath sent the souls of many valiant heroes to Hades, and left themselves a prey to the dogs and birds of the air." And when he returned to battle, what became of Hector? The song of the Nibelungs opens by assuring us that the old stories tell of many wonders, and of heroes worthy of praise (*von Helden lobebaeren*), and of great labours (*von grosser Arebeit*). These "great labours" consisted mainly in the slaying of other men. And this slaying was obviously "worthy of praise"; for it gave us a model for all our own struggle with evil. As for the heroes of history, of course, we love to dwell upon their constructive labours. But, after all, what sort of comparison is there in what the plain man, apart from a higher enlightenment, usually calls glory, between Washington and Napoleon? No doubt there will always be admir- ers of Napoleon who will think of him as a misunderstood reformer labouring for the building up of an ideal Europe. But even such admirers will join with the plain man in dwelling, with especial fascination, upon the Napoleon of Austerlitz. And they will not forget even Borodino. No doubt the lovers of Washington find him glorious. But where, in his career, belongs the glory of having put an end to the Holy Roman Empire, or of having destroyed the polity of the Europe of the old maps?

Man the destroyer thus glories in his prowess, and adores the heroes who were the ministers of death. And since, of course, his warfare is always directed against something that he takes to be an evil, the principle which directs his glorious conflicts seems to be one easy of general statement, inconsistent as some of the reasonings founded upon it seem to be. This principle is: "All evil ought to be destroyed. There ought to be none. It should be swept out of existence."

Of course, when the principle of the warfare with evil is thus abstractly stated, it does not tell us what we are to regard as an evil. It leaves the wise estimate of good and evil to be learned through a closer study of the facts of life. No doubt, then, Achilles, and the other heroes of song and story, may have become as glorious as they are by reason of our excessive love of destruction due to some imperfect estimate of the true values of life. And therefore the mere statement of the principle leaves open a very wide range for difference of opinion and for inconsistency of view as to what it is that ought to be destroyed. The natural estimate of the plain man, when he loves the heroes of old, seems to imply that one of the chief ills that man ought to destroy usually takes the form of some other man. And this way of estimating men in terms of their success in killing other men has its obvious inconsistencies. But, after all, as one may insist, much is gained when we have made up our minds as to what ought to be done with evil, whether evil is incorporated in our enemies, in our pains, or in our sins. We may leave to advancing civilization, or perhaps to some triumph of religion, the correction of our excessive fondness for the destruction of human life. What is essentially important is that it is part of man's mission to destroy evil. And about this general teaching the saints and the warriors, so it seems, may well agree.

Religion, it may be said, can have nothing to urge against this fundamental axiom. So far all appears clear. Evil ought to be driven out of the world. Common-sense says this. Every struggle with climate or with disease or with our foes is carried on in this spirit. The search for salvation is itself—so one may insist—simply another instance of this destructive conflict with impending ills. All that is most elemental in our hatreds thus agrees with whatever is loftiest in our souls, in facing evils with our "everlasting No." All the differences of moral opinion are mere differences as to what to destroy. Man is always the destroyer of ill.

II

But if you grant the general principle thus stated, the presence of evil in this world, in the forms that we all recognise, and in the degree of importance that it attains in all our lives, seems, indeed, a very serious hindrance in the way of religious insight. And the reason is plain. Religion, as we have said, in seeking salvation, seeks some form of communion with the master of life. That is, it seeks to come into touch with a power, a principle, or a mind, or a heart, that, on the one hand, possesses, or, with approval, surveys or controls the real nature of things, and that, on the other hand, welcomes us in our conflicts with evil, supports our efforts, and secures our success. I have made no effort, in these lectures, to define a theological creed. Such a creed forms a topic in which I take great interest but which lies beyond the limitations of this discourse. Yet our study of the historical relations between religion and morality, our earlier analysis of the religious need, have shown us that unless you are able to make some sort of effective appeal to principles that link you with the whole nature of things, your religious need must remain unsatisfied, and your last word will have to take, at best, the form of a moral, not a religious doctrine. Religion does not require us to solve all mysteries; but it does require for its stability some assurance that, so far as concerns our need of salvation, and despite the dangers that imperil our salvation, those that are with us, when we are rightly enlightened, are more than those that are against us.

In order to make this fact yet clearer, let us suppose that all such assurance is taken away from us. Review the result. Let it be supposed that we need salvation. Let it be granted that, as we naturally are, in our blindness and narrowness, and in the caprices of our passions, we cannot find the way out unless we can get into touch with some spiritual unity and reasonable life such as the loyal man's cause seems to reveal to him. Let it be further supposed, however, that all human causes are, in their way and time, as much subject

to chance and to the capricious blows of fortune as we ourselves
individually are. Let it be imagined that the cause of causes, the unity
of the whole spiritual world, is, in fact, a mere dream. Let the insight of the reason and of the will, which, when taken in their unity,
have been said by me to reveal to us that the universe is in its
essence Spirit, and that the cause of the loyal is not only a reality, but
the reality—let this insight, I say, be regarded as an illusion. Let no
other spiritual view of reality prove probable. Then, indeed, we shall
be left merely with ideals of life in our hands, but with no assurance
that real life, in its wholeness, approves or furthers these ideals. Our
need of salvation will then, to be sure, still remain. Our definition of
what salvation would be if it should become ours will be unchanged.
But, having thus abandoned as illusory or as uncertain all the sources
of insight which I have so far been defending, we shall have upon
our hands only the moral struggle for the good as our best re-
source. We shall then hope for no assurance of salvation. We shall
abandon religion to the realm of mythical consolations, and shall face
a grim world with only such moral courage as we can muster for
the uncertain conflict. Our loyalty itself will lose its religious aspect.
For the objective goodness of our cause—the divine grace which its
presence seems to offer to our life—will no longer mean anything
but a faint and uncertain hope, which we shall keep or not according to the caprices of our personal resolutions. Such, I say, would
be the outcome of rejecting all sources of religious insight into the
real nature of things.

The result, in the case now supposed, will be one which any honest man will indeed accept if he must, but which no one can regard
as including any satisfactory religious insight whatever. I certainly
do not here present these considerations as in themselves any arguments for religion, or as in themselves furnishing support for our
previous arguments regarding the nature and the merits of the
sources of insight which we have been reviewing. The case for
which I have argued in the foregoing lectures must indeed stand or
fall solely upon its own merits. And if the reason and the will, as
the spirit of loyalty interprets and unifies their teachings, do *not*
really show us any truth about the whole nature of things, I would
not for a moment ask to have their teachings tolerated merely because, without such teachings, we should lose our grounds for holding to a religious interpretation of life. If we *must* fall back upon
mere moral resoluteness, and abandon any assurance as to the re-

ligious objects, and as to the way and the attainment of salvation, I, for one, am quite ready to accept the call of life, and to fight on for a good end so long as I can, without seeking for religious consolations that have once been shown to be mythical. But I have indicated to you, in general, my grounds for holding that our previous sources actually *do* give us an insight which is not only moral but religious, and *do* throw light upon our relations to a reason which moves in all things, to a divine will which expresses itself in all the universe, and to a genuine revelation of its purposes which this makes of itself when it inspires our loyalty. My present purpose is, not to reinforce these grounds by the mere threat that their rejection would involve an abandonment of any well-grounded religious assurance, but to present to you the fact that religion is, indeed, a search for a really divine foundation for the saving process.

Religion differs from morality in looking beyond our own active resoluteness for something—not ourselves—that gives a warrant, founded in the whole nature of things—a warrant for holding that this resoluteness will succeed and will bring us into union with that which saves.

Hence it is, indeed, true that if there is *no* master of life with whom we can come into touch, *no* triumph of the good in the universe, *no* real source of salvation—religion must result in disappointment. And then our only recourse must, indeed, be the moral will. This recourse is one that, as we have seen, many in our time are quite ready to accept. And such, in my own opinion, are for reasons that they do not themselves admit actually well on their way toward real salvation. Only it is useless to attribute to them, in their present stage of conviction, any conscious and assured possession of religious insight. To sum up, then, religion demands the presence of the master of life as a real being, and depends upon holding that the good triumphs.

But if we attempt to combine the two assertions, "All evil ought to be destroyed" and "In the universe as a whole the good triumphs," and hereupon to face the facts of human life as religion finds them, we are at once involved in familiar perplexities. With many of these perplexities the limitations of the present discussion, as already explained, forbid us to deal. I am merely trying to show, for the moment, why the presence of evil in our lives seems to be a hindrance in the way of religious insight. And it is enough if I emphasize at this point what must readily come to the consciousness of all of you when you consider the situation in which our whole argument seems now to have placed us.

The very existence of the religious need itself presupposes not only the presence, but the usual prevalence of very great evils in human life. For unless man is in great danger of missing the pearl of great price, he stands in no need of a saving process. A religious man may come to possess an acquired optimism—the hard-won result of the religious process which seems to him to have pointed out the way of salvation. But a man who begins with the assurance that all is ordinarily well with human nature is precluded from religion, in our sense of the word religion, by his very type of optimism. Such an optimist of the "first intention," such a believer that in the main it is well with human nature, can be, as we have seen, a moralist, although he is usually a very simple-minded moralist, as unaware of the graver moral problems as he is cheerfully indifferent to the hard case in which most of his brethren live. But whoever sees the deep need of human salvation, as the various cynics and rebels and sages and prophets whom we cited in our first lecture have seen it, has begun by recognising the bitterness of human loss and defeat— the gravity of the evil case of the natural man. Were not the world as it now is very evil, what, then, were the call for religion? Religion takes its origin in our sense of deep need—in other words, in our recognition that evil has a very real place in life. "*Tempora pessima*"—"The times are very evil"—is thus no phrase of a merely mediæval type of world-hatred. The woes of man are the presupposed basis of fact upon which the search for salvation rests.

And the further one goes in the pursuit of the sources of religious insight, the more, as we have ourselves found, does one's original recognition of the ill of the human world become both deepened and varied. From the solitude of one's individual sorrows one goes out to seek for religious relief in the social world, only to find how much more manifold the chaos of ordinary social life is than is the conflict of one's private passions. If one asks guidance from reason, reason appears at first as a sort of spirit brooding upon the face of the depths of unreason. When loyalty itself is created, it finds itself beset by adversities. If evil drives us to seek relief in religion, religion thus teaches us to know, better and better, the tragedy of life. Its first word is, thus, about evil and about the escape from evil. But its later words appear to have been a persistent discourse upon our tribulations.

But how can religion, thus presupposing the presence of evil in our life, and illustrating this presence anew at every step, undertake to lead us to any assurance of the triumph of a good principle in the real world, in case, as seems so far obvious, such a triumph of a good principle would mean that all evil is to be simply destroyed and wiped out of existence?

Briefly restating the situation, it is this: If the evils of human life are indeed but transient and superficial incidents, or if—to use a well-known extreme form of statement—evil is an "unreality" altogether—then religion is superfluous. For there is no need of salvation unless man's ordinary case is, indeed, very really a hard case, that is, unless evil is a reality, and a deep-rooted one. But, on the other hand, if evil is thus deep-rooted in the very conditions of human life as they are, and if it persists upon higher levels even of the religious life, religion seems in danger of total failure. For unless goodness is somehow at the real heart of things—is, so to speak, the core of reality— the hope of salvation is a dream, and religion deceives us. But goodness, by the hypothesis that we are just now considering, requires that evil should be wholly abolished. How can that which should not exist at all, namely, evil, be in such wise the expression of the real nature of things that on the one hand religion is needed to save us from evil, and yet is able to do so only by bringing us to know that the real nature of things is good? Here is our problem. And it is a hard one.

In brief, as you may say, religion must take its choice. Either the evil in the world is of no great importance, and then religion is useless; or the need of salvation is great, and the way is straight and narrow; and then evil is deeply rooted in the very nature of reality, and religion seems a failure.

III

I believe that there is some advantage in stating in this somewhat crabbed and dialectical fashion, a problem which most of us usually but means to an end. Their end is to help us to a clear and rational sometimes tends to clear away the clouds with which emotion from approach through much more direct and pathetic experience. One advantage in crabbedness and in fondness for dialectic is that it moment to moment surrounds certain great problems of life. As I said earlier, in speaking of the office of the reason, abstract ideas are survey of the connections of things. When you are to examine the landscape from a height, in order to obtain a wide prospect, you may have to use a glass, or a compass, or some other instrument of abstraction, in order to define what the distance tends to render obscure, or what the manifoldness of the scenery surveyed makes it hard rightly to view in its true relations. And, in such cases, the glass or the compass is but an auxiliary, intended to help in the end your whole outlook. Now the world of good and evil is a world of wide prospects, of vast distances, of manifold features. A bit of dialectics, using abstract and one-sided considerations in succession, may prepare the way for seeing the whole better.

The plain man well knows the problem that I have just been characterising. He knows how it may enter his religious life. Only he does not usually think of it abstractly. It pierces his heart. Stunned by a grief, he may say: "I have trusted God, and now he forsakes me. How can a good God permit this horror in my life?" Yet the plain man, if religiously minded, also knows what is meant by saying, "Out of the depths have I cried." And he knows, too, that part of the preciousness of his very idea of God depends upon the fact that there *are* depths, and that out of them one *can* cry, and that God is precisely a being who somehow hears the cry from the depths. God, "pragmatically viewed," as some of our recent teachers express the matter, is thus often defined for the plain man's religious experience as a helper in trouble. Were there no trouble, there would be, then, it would seem, no cry of the soul for such a being, and very possibly no such being conceived by the soul that now cries. Yet this very God—one cries to him because he is supposed to be all-powerful, and to do all things well, and therefore to be a very present help in time of trouble. All this seems clear enough at the time when one is on the way up, out of the depths, or when one begins to praise God in the Psalmist's words, because, as one now says: "He hath planted my feet upon a rock, and hath established my goings." But how does all this seem at the moment when one suddenly falls into the pit of sorrow, and when one's eyes are turned downward; when he who doeth all things well permits the utmost treachery of fortune, and when the one who can hear every cry seems deaf to one's most heart-rending pleadings? The familiar explanation that all this is a penalty for one's sins may awaken an echo of Job's protest in the mind of the man who knows not how he has deserved this woe, or may arouse the deeper and now consciously dialectical comments on the mystery involved in the fact that God permits sin. "Why was I made thus blind and sinful?" one may cry. And hereupon religious insight becomes, indeed, confused enough, and may turn for relief to that well-known type of defiance which, if not religious, is at least moral; for it is a protest against evil. If at such moments God is, indeed, to our darkened vision, and, for us, who wait for his blessing, as if he were sleeping or on a journey, one can at least, as moral agent, utter this protest against ill, and wonder why his omnipotence does not make it effective. One thus begins, as it were, to try heroically to do the absent God's work for him.

All these are familiar experiences. They find us, too often, unprepared. They find us when emotion tends to cloud every insight. They illustrate a certain dialectical process which belongs to all human life and which plays its part in the whole history of religion. Perhaps it is well to state an aspect of this dialectical process abstractly, crabbedly, and unemotionally, as we have just done, in order that we may make ourselves the more ready to face the issue when life exemplifies it with crushing suddenness, and when

> The painful ploughshare of passion
> Grinds down to our uttermost rock.

The problem, as just abstractly stated, is this. Religion seems to face this dilemma: Either there are no great and essential ills about human life; and then there is no great danger of perdition, and no great need of salvation, and religion has no notable office; or there are great and essential ills, and man's life is in bitter need of salvation; but in that case evil is deeply rooted in the very nature of the reality from which we have sprung; and therefore religion has no right to assure us of communion with a real master of life who is able to do with evil what not only ought to be done with it, but ought always to have been done with it by any being able to offer man any genuine salvation. For (as we are assuming) what ought to be done, yes, what ought to have been done with evil from the beginning, is and was this: To banish it altogether from existence.

This, I say, is, when abstractly stated, the dilemma in which religion seems to be placed. Of this dilemma the countless struggles of the human soul when, in the spirit of some practical religion, it seeks for salvation and faces its woes are examples. These struggles are infinitely pathetic and in life are often confusing to insight. Is there any value in considering this abstract statement of the principles upon which this dilemma seems to be founded? Possibly there is, if we can hereby be led also to consider—not indeed, in this place, the problems of theology, or the metaphysics of evil, but a new source of insight.

IV

This new source of insight begins to come to us when we observe, as we can often observe if we listen with closer attention to the voices of our own hearts, that the general principle, "Evil ought simply to be put out of existence," does *not* express our whole attitude toward all evils, and gives only an imperfect account either of our more commonplace and elemental or of our more elevated, heroic, and reasonable estimates of life.

The principle: "Evil ought to be simply abolished," is, indeed, one that we unquestionably apply, in our ordinary life, to a vast range of natural ills. But it is not universal. Let us first indicate its apparent range. Physical pain, when sufficiently violent, is an example of an ill that appears to us, in all its greater manifestations, plainly intolerable. So it seems to us to illustrate the principle that "Evil ought to be put out of existence." We desire, with regard to it, simply its abolition. The same is true of what one may call *unassimilated* griefs of all levels—the shocks of calamity at the moment when they first strike, the anguish of loss or of disappointment precisely when these things are new to us and appear to have no place in our life-plan. These are typical ills. And they all illustrate ills that seem to us to be worthy only of destruction. The magnitude of such ills as factors in the individual and in the social world often appears to us immeasurable. Pestilence, famine, the cruelties of oppressors, the wrecks of innocent human lives by cruel fortunes— all these seem, for our ordinary estimates, facts that we can in no wise assimilate, justify, or reasonably comprehend. That is, we can see, in the single case, no reason why such events should form part of human life—except that so it indeed is. They seem, to our natural understanding, simply opaque data of experience, to be annulled or removed if we can. And to such ills, from our human point of view, the principle: "They ought to be simply driven out of existence," is naturally applied without limitation. The apparent range of this principle is therefore, indeed, very wide.

Now it forms no part of our present discourse to consider in detail the possible theological or metaphysical basis for a possible explanation of such ills. I have elsewhere written too much and too often about the problem of evil to be subject to the accusation of neglecting the pathos and the tragedy of these massive ills. This, however, I can at once say. *In so far as* ills appear to us thus, they are, indeed, *no* sources of religious insight. On the other hand, even when thus viewed, in all their blackness, they can be, and are, sources of moral enthusiasm and earnestness. Man the destroyer, when, awaking to the presence of such ills in his world, he contends with them, gets a perfectly definite moral content into his life. And he has his right to do so. Whatever his religion, he is morally authorised to labour against these unmediated evils with the heartiest intolerance. When such labour takes on social forms, it helps toward the loftiest humanity. The war with pain and disease and oppression, the effort to bind up wounds and to snatch souls from destruction—all these things constitute some of man's greatest opportunities for loyalty. Nevertheless, when man loyally wars with the ills such as physical anguish and pestilence and famine and oppression, he does *not* thereby tend to discover, through his own loyal act, why such individual ills are permitted in the world. In so far as these evils give him opportunity for service, they appeal to his loyalty as a warrior against them. If his cause includes, for him, activities that enter into this warfare with ills that are to be destroyed, these ills have thus indirectly conduced to his religious life. But it is his loyalty that in such cases is his source of religious insight. The ills themselves that he thus destructively fights remain to him as opaque as before. Why they find their place in the world he does not see. Now that they are found there, he knows what to do with them—namely, to annul them, to put them out of existence, as a part of his loyal service. But if he is religiously minded, he does not for a moment conceive that the ills with which he wars are there simply to give him the opportunity for his service. So far then it is, indeed, true that the ills which we have simply to destroy offer us no source of religious insight.

But now, as I must insist, *not all* the ills that we know are of this nature. Wide and deep and terrible as are those conflicts with the incomprehensible ills of fortune whose presence in the world we do not understand, there are other ills. And toward these other ills we take an attitude which is not wholly destructive. We find them, upon a closer view, inseparably bound up with good—so closely bound up therewith that we could not conceive a life wherein this sort of good which is here bound up with this sort of ill could be separated therefrom. In these cases the principle: "Evil should be simply put out of existence," proves to be a palpable falsity. As our knowledge of such ills grows clearer, we commonly find that there is, indeed, something about them, as they at any one moment appear to us, which ought, indeed, to be annulled, set aside, destroyed. But this annulling of one momentary or at least transient aspect of the ill is but part, in such cases, of a constructive process, which involves growth rather than destruction—a passage to a new life rather than a casting wholly out of life. Such ills we remove only in so far as we assimilate them, idealise them, take them up into the plan of our lives, give them meaning, set them in their place in the whole.

Now such ills, as I must insist, play a very great part in life and especially in the higher life. Our attitude toward them constitutes, above all, on the very highest levels of our reasonableness, a very great part of our attitude toward the whole problem of life. In the presence of these idealised evils, man the destroyer becomes transformed into man the creator. And he does so without in the least abandoning his justified moral distinctions, without indulging in any sort of "moral holiday," and without becoming unwilling to destroy when he cannot otherwise rationally face the facts before him than by destroying. He is not less strenuous in his dealing with his moral situation because he has discovered how to substitute growth for destruction and creative assimilation for barren hostility. He is all the more effectively loyal in the presence of such ills, because he sees how they can become, for his consciousness, parts of a good whole.

Ills of this sort may become, and in the better cases do become, sources of religious insight. Their presence in our world enables us the better to comprehend its spiritual unity. And because they are often very deep and tragic ills, which we face only with very deep and dear travail of spirit, they hint to us how, from the point of view of a world-embracing insight, the countless and terrible ills of the other sort, which we *cannot* now understand, and which, at present, appear to us merely as worthy of utter destruction, may still also have their places, as stages and phases of expression, in the larger life to which we belong. In our own power to assimilate and spiritualise our own ills, we can get at times a hint of such larger spiritual processes. In these very processes we also, through our loyal endeavour, can act our own real part; although *what* the larger processes are we cannot expect at present to comprehend better than a sympathising dog, whose master is devoting his life to furthering the highest spiritual welfare of a nation or of all mankind, can know why his master's face is now grief-stricken and now joyous.

In other words, the ills that we *can* spiritualise and idealise without merely destroying them hint to us that, despite the uncomprehended chaos of seemingly hopeless tragedy with which for our present view human life seems to be beset, the vision of the spiritual triumph of the good which reason and loyalty present to us need not be an illusion, but is perfectly consistent with the facts. The world is infinite. With our present view we could not expect to grasp directly the unity of its meaning. We have sources of insight which tend to our salvation by showing us, in general, although certainly not in detail, the nature of the spiritual process which, as these sources of insight persistently point out, constitutes the essence of reality. Whether these sources are themselves valid and trustworthy is a question to be considered upon its own merits. I have stated my case so far as our brief review requires it to be stated. I must leave to your own considerateness the further estimate of what these sources teach, both as to the reality of the master of life and as to the nature of the process of salvation. My present concern is simply with the cloud that the presence of evil seems to cause to pass over the face of all these sources. I cannot undertake wholly to dispel this cloud by showing you in detail why pestilences or why broken hearts are permitted to exist in this world. But I can show you that there are, indeed, ills, and very dark ills in life, which not only are there, but are essential to the highest life. I do not exaggerate our power to solve mysteries when I insist that *these* ills constitute not an opaque hindrance to insight, not a cloud over the sun of reason and of loyalty, but rather a source of insight. And, as I insist, they constitute such a source without being in the least an excuse for any indolence in our moral struggle with precisely those aspects of such ills as we ought to destroy. They show us how the triumph of the moral will over such adversities is perfectly consistent with the recognition that the most rational type of life demands the existence of just such adversities. Their presence in our world does not excuse sloth, does not justify a "moral holiday," does not permit us to enjoy any mere luxury of mystical contemplation of the triumph of the divine in the world, without ourselves taking our rational and strenuous part in the actual attainment of such triumph. But what these forms of ill show us is that there are accessible cases in which if—but only if—one does the divine will—one can know of the doctrine that teaches how the divine will can and does become perfect, not through the mere abolition of evil, but through suffering. Such cases of ill are true sources of insight. They reveal to us some of the deepest truths about what loyalty, and spiritual triumph, and the good really are. They make for salvation. They drive away clouds and bring us face to face with the will of the world.

I have so far spoken of evil in general. For the present purpose I need a name for the ills that one rationally faces only when one, through some essentially active, constructive, moral process, creatively assimilates and idealises them, and thus wins them over to be a part of good—not when one merely drives them out of existence. One name for such ills is Griselda's name: "Adversities." But I have chosen, in the title of this lecture, to use the vaguer untechnical name: Sorrow. A great physical pain, you in general cannot, at least at the moment, idealise. You then and there face it only as something intolerable, and can see no good except through its mere abolition. The same is true of any crushing blow of fortune, precisely in so far as it crushes. All such things you then and there view narrowly. Their mystery lies in the very fact that they are thus, for the moment, seen only narrowly. Hence, they are *ipso facto* hindrances to insight. But a sorrow—when you use the word you have already begun to assimilate and idealise the fact that you call a sorrow. That you have begun to idealise it, the very luxury of deep grief often vaguely hints, sometimes clearly shows. For sorrows may have already become tragically precious to you. Would you forget your lost love, or your dead, or your "days that are no more," even if you could? Is mere destruction, then, your *only* tendency in the presence of such sorrows. A closer view of your attitude toward such sorrows shows that they are not only clouding but revealing. They begin, they may endlessly continue, to show you the way into the spiritual realm and the nature of this realm.

By sorrow, then, I here mean an experience of ill which is not wholly an experience of that which as you then and there believe ought to be simply driven out of existence. The insight of which sorrow is the source, is an insight that tends to awaken within you a new view of what the spiritual realm is. This view is not in the least what some recent writers have blindly proclaimed it to be—

a philosopher's artificial abstraction—a cruel effort to substitute a "soft" doctrine of the study for a moral and humane facing of the "hard" facts of human life. No, this view is the soul of the teaching of all the world's noblest and most practical guides to the most concrete living. This view faces hardness, it endures and overcomes. Poets, prophets, martyrs, sages, artists, the heroes of spirituality of every land and clime, have found in it comfort, resolution, and triumph. The philosopher, at best, can report what these have seen. And "soft," indeed, is the type of thoughtful effort which declines to follow with its ideas what all these have learned to express in their lives and in their religion.

V

Because I am here not stating for you a merely speculative doctrine concerning the place of evil in a good and rational spiritual world, I once more need, at this point, to appeal as directly as I can to life. Let me present to you, from recent literature, a noteworthy instance of the use of our present source of insight. The instance is confessedly one where no complete and determinate religious creed is defended as the result of the use of the insight in question. And an actually eternal truth about the spiritual world—a very old truth in the lore of the wise, but a deeply needed truth for our own day —is illustrated by the instance which the tale portrays.

I refer to a recent short story, published in the *Atlantic Monthly* for November, 1910, and written by Cornelia A. P. Comer. It is entitled "The Preliminaries." It is, to my mind, an impressive union of a genuinely effective realism and a deep symbolism. The characters are very real human beings. Their problem is one of the most familiar problems of daily life—the problem as to the advisability of the proposed marriage of two young lovers. The conditions of the problem are hard facts, of a general type that is unfortunately frequent enough under our confusing modern conditions. These facts are viewed in the tale as such people might well view them. And yet the issues involved are, like all the problems of young lovers, issues that are bound up with all the interests of religion and with the whole problem of the reality of a spiritual world. These issues are treated as they truly are, with a result that is fairly supernatural in its ancient but always new appeal to a source of insight that we can reach only through sorrow.

Since the question inevitably concerns the prospects of the proposed marriage, the first statement of the problem is fully in harmony with the spirit of recent pragmatism. The truth of the assertion: "We ought to marry," is surely a truth that, as the pragmatists would say, the young lovers who make the assertion should regard as quite inseparable from the probable results to which this marriage will lead in concrete life. Such a truth then is, one would say, wholly empirical. A marriage proposal, to use the favourite phrase of pragmatism, is a "working hypothesis." Such hypotheses must be submitted to the test of experience. No such test, it would seem, would be absolute. What does poor humanity know as to the real values of our destiny? Meanwhile the whole problem of good and evil is in question. Marriage, especially under certain conditions, will lead to one or another sorrow. Can one face sorrow with any really deeper trust in life? Is life really a good at all, since there is so much sorrow in it? Must not any prudent person be afraid of life? Ought the lovers to defy fortune and to ignore obvious worldly prudence?

Such is the first statement of the problem. Its treatment in this admirable sketch shows an insight into the nature of good and evil which I had myself come to regard as very little present to the minds of the story-tellers of to-day, who are so often dominated by the recent love of power, by the tedious blindness of modern individualism, by false doctrines as to the merely temporal expediency of truth, and by the merely glittering show of unspiritual worldly efficiency. I rejoice to find that, in a literature which has been, of late, so devastated by a popularly trivial interpretation of pragmatism, and by an equally trivial disregard for the "rule of reason," there is still place for so straightforward and practical a recognition of eternal truth as the wise woman who has written this short story exemplifies.

The issue regarding this particular marriage proposal is stated at once in the opening words of the tale:

"Young Oliver Pickersgill was in love with Peter Lannithorne's daughter. Peter Lannithorne was serving a six-year term in the penitentiary for embezzlement."

The young hero is depicted as a high-minded youth of unquestionable and prosperous social position in his community. His beloved is a loyal daughter who is convinced that her father's crime was due solely to a momentary and benevolent weakness, and to a mind confused by care for the needs and too importunate requirements of his own family. Not unjustly attributing the father's final downfall to the impatience, to the agonising discontent, and to the worldly ambition of her own mother, the daughter with spirit replies to the lover's proposal by saying plainly: "I will never marry any one who doesn't respect my father as I do." The lovers somewhat easily come to terms, at least apparently, as to this sole present ground for disagreement. The youth, not without inward difficulty, is ready to accept the daughter's version of her father's misadventure. In any case, love makes him indifferent to merely worldly scruples, and he has no fear of his own power to face his community as the loving husband of a convict's daughter; though there is, indeed, no doubt as to the father's actual guilt, and although Lannithorne is known to have admitted the justice of his sentence.

But to love, and to be magnanimously hopeful—this is not the same as to convince other people that such a marriage is prudent, or is likely, as the pragmatists would say, to have "expedient work-ings." Young Oliver has to persuade Ruth's mother on the one hand, his own father on the other, that such a marriage is reasonable. Both prove to be hard to convince. To the ordinary scruples of worldly prudence which young lovers generally have to answer, they easily add seemingly unanswerable objections. The mother—the convict's wife—now a brilliantly clear-witted but hopelessly narrow-minded invalid—a broken woman of the world—prag-matically enlightened, in a way, by the bitter experience of sorrow, but not in the least brought thereby to any deeper insight, faces the lover as an intruder upon her daughter's peace and her own desolation. She has known, she says, what the bitterness of an un-happy marriage can be and is. If she herself has had her share of blame for her husband's downfall, that only the more shows her such truth as, in this dark world, she still can grasp. "I do not want my daughters to marry"—this is, to her, the conclusion of the whole matter. The bitterness of her own marriage has taught her this les-son, which she expounds to the lover with all the passion of wounded pride and the dear-bought lore of life as she has learned it. But of course, as she admits, she may be wrong. Let the lover consult her husband at the jail. He—the convict—is a well-meaning man, after all. He fell; but he is not at heart a criminal. Let him say whether he wants his daughter to take up the burden of this new tragedy. So the mother concludes her parable.

The lover, baffled, but still hopeful, next turns to his own father for consent and encouragement. But now he has to listen to the teachings of a loftier yet to him profoundly discouraging prudence. Oliver's father is a truly high-minded man of the world, with a genuinely religious feeling in the background of his mind, and is intensely devoted to his son. But from this proposed match he recoils with a natural horror. The world is full of good girls. Why not choose one who brings no such sorrow with her? Peter Lannithorne was in his crime no worse, indeed, than many other men who are not in jail. He even meant on the whole well, and blundered, until at last from blunder he drifted into crime. He then took his penalty like a man, and owned that it was just. But, after all, he was found out. Such a taint lasts. It cannot be removed by repentance. The proposed marriage can only lead to misery. Peter Lannithorne himself, who, after all, "knows what's what," would be the first to admit this fact, if one asked his advice. If the son must persist in making light of a loving father's wisdom—well, let him then consult Peter Lannithorne himself. Ask the convict in his prison what a man needs and expects in the family of the woman whom he is to marry. This is the father's firm but kindly ultimatum.

Terrified by the gravity of repeated warnings, and dispirited by having to leave his dearest problem to the decision of the convict himself, Oliver determines to face the inevitable. He arranges for the interview at the jail, and is left by the warden alone with the prisoner in the prison library. Suddenly, as he faces his man, the youth finds himself in the presence of one who has somehow been transformed as if by a supernatural power. As for the convict's person—

His features were irregular and unnoticeable; but the sum-total of them gave the impression of force. It was a strong face, yet you could see that it had once been a weak one. It was a tremendously human face, a face like a battleground, scarred and seamed and lined with the stress of invisible conflicts. . . . Not a triumphant face at all, and yet there was peace in it. Somehow, the man had achieved something, arrived somewhere, and the record of the journey was piteous and terrible. Yet it drew the eyes in awe as much as in wonder, and in pity not at all.

Oliver, reassured by the new presence, and glad to find himself at last facing a man who has nothing left to fear in life, states as well as possible his main problem. The father of his beloved listens, first with surprise at the news, then with seriousness. Oliver finds himself forced to cut deep when he repeats his own father's appeal to know the convict's opinion about what a man expects to meet in his

future wife's family, and then pauses with a keen sense of the cruelty
of his own position. But Lannithorne, who has long since become
accustomed to feeling the ploughshare of passion grind down to
his uttermost rock, is perfectly ready with his response. As the
youth pauses and then begins a new appeal—

The man looked up and held up an arresting hand. "Let me clear the
way for you a little," he said. "It was a hard thing for you to come and
seek me out in this place. I like your coming. Most young men would
have refused, or come in a different spirit. I want you to understand
that if in Ruth's eyes, and my wife's, and your father's, my counsel
has value, it is because they think I see things as they are. And that
means, first of all, that I know myself for a man who committed a
crime and is paying the penalty. I am satisfied to be paying it. As I
see justice, it is just. So, if I seem to wince at your necessary allusions
to it, that is part of the price. I don't want you to feel that you are
blundering or hurting me more than is necessary. You have got to lay
the thing before me as it is."

Something in the words, in the dry, patient manner, in the endurance
of the man's face, touched Oliver to the quick and made him feel all
manner of new things: such as a sense of the moral poise of the universe, acquiescence in its retributions, and a curious pride, akin to
Ruth's own, in a man who could meet him after this fashion, in this
place.

Hereupon, fully aroused, the youth tells with freedom why the
problem seems so hard for the young people, and how their elders
all insist upon such frightful discouragements, and how much he
longs to know the truth about life, and whether all such doubts and
scruples as those of his own father and of Ruth's mother are well
founded. At last the prisoner begins his reply:

"They haven't the point of view," he said. "It is life that is the great
adventure. Not love, not marriage, not business. They are just chapters
in the book. The main thing is to take the road fearlessly—to have
courage to live one's life."

"Courage?"

Lannithorne nodded.

"That is the great word. Don't you see what ails your father's point
of view, and my wife's? One wants absolute security in one way for
Ruth; the other wants absolute security in another way for you. And
security—why, it's just the one thing a human being can't have, the
thing that's the damnation of him if he gets it! The reason it is so hard
for a rich man to enter the Kingdom of Heaven is that he has that
false sense of security. To demand it just disintegrates a man. I don't
know why. It does."

Oliver shook his head uncertainly.

"I don't quite follow you, sir. Oughtn't one to try to be safe?"

"One ought to try, yes. That is common prudence. But the point is that, whatever you do or get, you aren't after all secure. There is no such condition, and the harder you demand it, the more risk you run. So it is up to a man to take all reasonable precautions about his money, or his happiness, or his life, and trust the rest. What every man in the world is looking for is the sense of having the mastery over life. But I tell you, boy, there is only one thing that really gives it!"

"And that is——?"

Lannithorne hesitated perceptibly. For the thing he was about to tell this undisciplined lad was his most precious possession; it was the price of wisdom for which he had paid with the years of his life. No man parts lightly with such knowledge.

"It comes," he said, with an effort, "with the knowledge of our power to endure. That's it. *You are safe only when you can stand everything that can happen to you.* Then, and then only! Endurance is the measure of a man! . . . Sometimes I think it is harder to endure what we deserve, like me," said Lannithorne, "than what we don't. I was afraid, you see, afraid for my wife and all of them. Anyhow, take my word for it. Courage is security. There is no other kind."

Then—Ruth and I——"

"Ruth is the core of my heart!" said Lannithorne thickly. "I would rather die than have her suffer more than she must. But she must take her chances like the rest. It is the law of things. If you know yourself fit for her, and feel reasonably sure you can take care of her, you have a right to trust the future. Myself, I believe there is some One to trust it to."

The speaker of this hard-won wisdom, after this appeal to the eternal, utters his last tremulous word as from a father's loving heart, and then the interview must end. The author concludes:

Finding his way out of the prison yard a few minutes later, Oliver looked, unseeing, at the high walls that soared against the blue spring sky. He could not realise them, there was such a sense of light, air, space, in his spirit.

Apparently, he was just where he had been an hour before, with all his battles still to fight, but really he knew they were already won, for his weapon had been forged and put in his hand. He left his boyhood behind him as he passed that stern threshold, for the last hour had made a man of him, and a prisoner had given him the master-key that opens every door.

VI

Now this, I insist, is insight. It is no "soft" doctrine. It is far beyond the sort of pragmatism that accepts the test of momentary results.

As far as it goes, it is religious insight. It is insight, moreover, into the nature of certain ills which cannot, yes, which in principle, and even by omnipotence, could not, be simply removed from existence without abolishing the conditions which are logically necessary to the very highest good that we know. Life in the spirit simply presupposes the conditions that these ills exemplify.

What sorrow is deeper than the full recognition of one's own now irrevocable deed, if one has, hereupon, fully to confess that this deed is, from one's own present point of view, a crime? Yet how could such ills be simply removed from existence if any range of individual expression, of freedom, of power to choose is to be left open at all? How can one possess spiritual effectiveness—the privilege that youth most ardently demands—without assuming the risk involved in taking personal responsibility for some aspects of the lives of our fellows? As for our blunders, what more precious privilege do we all claim than the privilege of making our own blunders, or at least a due proportion of them? When we act, every act is done for eternity, since it is irrevocable. When we love, we ask the privilege to bind up other destinies with our own. The tragedies of such a world as ours are, therefore, not such as could be simply wiped out of existence, unless one were ready to deprive every individual personality both of its range of free choice and of its effectiveness of action. When we suffer, then, in such a world, we know indeed that there need have been no such suffering had there been no world at all. But precisely when our ills are most bound up with our own personal wills, we know that no mere removal of such ills could have occurred without the abolition of all the conditions which our spiritual freedom, our longing for effectiveness, and our love for union with other personalities make us regard as the conditions of the highest good. No God could conceivably give you the good of self-expression without granting you the privilege, not only of choosing wrongly, but of involving your brethren in the results of your misdeed. For when you love your kind, you aim to be a factor in their lives; and to deprive you of this privilege would be to insure your total failure. But if you possess this privilege, you share in a life that, in proportion to its importance and depth and range and richness of spiritual relations, is full of the possibilities of tragedy.

Face such tragedy, however, and what does it show you? The possibility, not of annulling an evil, or of ceasing to regret it, but of showing spiritual power, first, through idealising your grief, by seeing even through this grief the depth of the significance of our relations as individuals to one another, to our social order, and to the whole of life; secondly, through enduring your fortune; and thirdly, through conquering, by the might of the spirit, those goods which can only be won through such sorrow. What those goods are, the convict has just, if only in small part, told us. Griselda told us something about them which is much deeper still. For adversity and loyalty are, indeed, simply inseparable companions. There could not be loyalty in a world where the loyal being himself met no adversities that personally belonged to and entered his own inner life. That this is true, let every loyal experience bear witness.

Now such sorrows, such idealised evils, which are so interwoven with good that if the precious grief were wholly removed from existence, the courage, the fidelity, the spiritual self-possession, the peace through and in and beyond tribulation which such trials alone make possible, would also be removed—they surely show us that the abstract principle: "Evil ought to be abolished," is false. They show us that the divine will also must be made perfect through suffering. Since we can comprehend the meaning of such experiences only through resolute action, through courage, through loyalty, through the power of the spirit, they in no wise justify sloth, or mere passivity, or mystical idleness. The active dealing with such sorrow gives, as James himself once well asserts, a new dimension to life. No experiences go further than do these to show us how, in our loyalty and in our courage, we are becoming one with the master of life, who through sorrow overcomes.

Let man, the destroyer, then remember that there is one ill which he could not destroy, even if he were God, without also destroying all the spiritual prowess in which all those rejoice who, inspired by an ambition infinitely above that of Achilles, long to be one with God through bearing and overcoming the sorrows of a world.

We have thus indicated a source of insight. To tell more about what it reveals would at once lead me, as you see, close to the most vital of all Christian teachings, the doctrine of the Atonement. But such a study belongs elsewhere.

Community as Lived

Part VIII

Community as Lived

Royce was an idealist in the vernacular sense of that word as well as in its technical and philosophical reference. He was sensitive to the charge that philosophical idealism was essentially an unpractical doctrine. For Royce, such a criticism failed to comprehend that "loyalty is the practical aspect and expression of an idealistic philosophy." (*RQP*, p. vii.)[1]

The essays contained in this section, although simply written, evoke many of the major themes of Royce's thought, especially those dealing with the nature of the community. Of particular fascination is Royce's development of the meaning of provincialism. Royce defined the meaning of one's province as primarily a domain, sufficiently unified, geographically and socially to generate a sense of pride and identity for its inhabitants. (*RQP*, p. 61; below, 2:1069). In *The Philosophy of Loyalty*, he called for a "new and wiser provincialism," as distinguished from a "mere renewal of the old sectionalism." (*PL*, p. 245; above, 2:953.) In Royce's view, the idealization of the "provincial" experience would aid in the resolution of a serious "American problem," namely, "*the problem of educating the self-estranged spirit of our nation to know itself better.*" (*PL*, p. 245; above, 2:952.)

Royce sees no contradiction in the deepening of "provincial" experience as a way of fostering an enhanced sense of national life. Actually, he holds that "they cannot prosper apart." (*RQP*, p. 66;

[1] Cf. also Royce's comment that "Professor James' pragmatism despite its entertaining expressions of horror of the eternal, actually does state one aspect of eternal truth. It is, namely, that all search for truth is a practical activity, with an ethical purpose, and that a purely theoretical truth, such as should guide no significant active process, is a barren absurdity." (*PL*, p. 326; above, 2:984.)

below, 2:1071.) And the possibility of an international, "great community," depends likewise on the participating presence of nations,
thoroughly self-conscious in their own right. It is not loyalty to a
cause which Royce fears as the source of tension and unrest. To the
contrary, it is the individual without roots, without commitment,
and without care, who dilutes the energies necessary to build a
community. Further, when under duress, the "detached individual
or nation" often abandons restraint and out of disrespect for the
variety of life-styles, moves to suppress them.

In one of his last writings, Royce warns us that we must avoid
the plight of the "detached individual," who belongs "to no community which he loves and to which he can devote himself. . . .
For mere detachment, mere self-will, can never be satisfied with
itself, can never win its goal. What saves us on any level of human
social life is union." (*HGC*, pp. 51–52; below, 2:1156).

32

Provincialism

I propose, in this address, to define certain issues which, as I think, the present state of the world's civilization, and of our own national life, make both promiment and critical.

I

The word "provincialism," which I have used as my title, has been chosen because it is the best single word that I have been able to find to suggest the group of social tendencies to which I want to call your especial attention. I intend to use this word in a somewhat elastic sense, which I may at once indicate. When we employ the word "provincialism" as a concrete term, speaking of "a provincialism," we mean, I suppose, any social disposition, or custom, or form of speech or of civilization, which is especially characteristic of a province. In this sense one speaks of the provincialisms of the local dialect of any English shire, or of any German country district. This use of the term in relation to the dialects of any language is very common. But one may also apply the term to name, not only the peculiarities of a local dialect, but the fashions, the manners, and customs of a given restricted region of any country. One also often employs the word "provincialism" as an abstract term, to name not only the customs or social tendencies themselves, but that fondness for them, that pride in them, which may make the inhabitants of a

[Reprinted from *RQP*, pp. 57–108.]

province indisposed to conform to the ways of those who come from without, and anxious to follow persistently their own local traditions. Thus the word "provincialism" applies both to the social habits of a given region, and to the mental interest which inspires and maintains these habits. But both uses of the term imply, of course, that one first knows what is to be meant by the word "province." This word, however, is one of an especially elastic usage. Sometimes, by a province, we mean a region as restricted as a single English county, or as the smallest of the old German principalities. Sometimes, however, one speaks of the whole of New England, or even of the Southern states of our Union, as constituting one province; and I know of no easy way of defining how large a province may be. For the term, in this looser sense, stands for no determinate political or legal division of a country. Meanwhile we all, in our minds, oppose the term "province" to the term "nation," as the part is opposed to the whole. Yet we also often oppose the terms "provincial" and "metropolitan," conceiving that the country districts and the smaller towns and cities belong even to the province, while the very great cities belong rather to the whole country, or even to the world in general. Yet here the distinction that we make is not the same as the former distinction between the part of a country and the whole country. Nevertheless, the ground for such an identification of the provincial with that which pertains to country districts and to smaller cities can only lie in the supposed tendency of the great city to represent better the interests of the larger whole than do the lesser communities. This supposition, however, is certainly not altogether well founded. In the sense of possessing local interests and customs, and of being limited to ideas of their own, many great cities are almost as distinctly provincial as are certain less populous regions. The plain people of London or of Berlin have their local dialect; and it seems fair to speak of the peculiarities of such dialects as provincialisms. And almost the same holds true of the other social traditions peculiar to individual great cities. It is possible to find, even amongst the highly cultivated classes of ancient cities, ideas and fashions of behavior as characteristically local, as exclusive in their indifference to the ways of outsiders, as are the similarly characteristic ways and opinions of the country districts of the same nationality. And so the opposition of the provincial to the metropolitan, in manners and in beliefs, seems to me much less important than the other opposition of the province, as the more or less restricted part of the nation as the whole. It is this latter opposition that I shall therefore emphasize in the present discussion. But I shall not attempt to define how large or how well organized, politically, a province must be. For my present purpose a county, a state, or even a large section of the country, such as New England, might constitute a province. For me, then, a province shall mean any one part of a national domain, which is, geographically and socially, sufficiently unified to have a true consciousness of its own unity, to feel a pride in its own ideals and customs, and to possess a sense of its distinction from other parts of the country. And by the term "provincialism" I shall mean, first, the tendency of such a province to possess its own customs and ideals; secondly, the totality of these customs and ideals themselves; and thirdly, the love and pride which leads the inhabitants of a province to cherish as their own these traditions, beliefs, and aspirations.

II

I have defined the term used as my title. But now, in what sense do I propose to make provincialism our topic? You will foresee that I intend to discuss the worth of provincialism, *i.e.* to consider, to some extent, whether it constitutes a good or an evil element in civilization. You will properly expect me, therefore, to compare provincialism with other social tendencies; such tendencies as patriotism, the larger love of humanity, and the ideals of higher cultivation. Precisely these will constitute, in fact, the special topics of my address. But all that I have to say will group itself about a single thesis, which I shall forthwith announce. My thesis is that, in the present state of the world's civilization, and of the life of our own country, the time has come to emphasize, with a new meaning and intensity, the positive value, the absolute necessity for our welfare, of a wholesome provincialism, as a saving power to which the world in the near future will need more and more to appeal.

The time was (and not very long since), when, in our own country, we had to contend against very grave evils due to false forms of provincialism. What has been called sectionalism long threatened our national unity. Our Civil War was fought to overcome the ills due to such influences. There was, therefore, a time when the virtue of true patriotism had to be founded upon a vigorous condemnation of certain powerful forms of provincialism. And our national education at that time depended both upon our learning common federal ideals, and upon our looking to foreign lands for the spiritual guidance of older civilizations. Furthermore, not only have these things been so in the past, but similar needs will, of course, be felt in the future. We shall always be required to take counsel of the other nations in company with whom we are at work upon the tasks of civilization. Nor have we outgrown our spiritual dependence upon older forms of civilization. In fact we shall never outgrow a certain inevitable degree of such dependence. Our national unity, moreover, will always require of us a devotion that will transcend in some directions the limits of all our provincial ideas. A common sympathy between the different sections of our country will, in future, need a constantly fresh cultivation. Against the evil forms of sectionalism we shall always have to contend. All this I well know, and these things I need not in your presence emphasize. But what I am to emphasize is this: The present state of civilization, both in the world at large, and with us, in America, is such as to define a new social mission which the province alone, but not the nation, is able to fulfil. False sectionalism, which disunites, will indeed always remain as great an evil as ever it was. But the modern world has reached a point where it needs, more than ever before, the vigorous development of a highly organized provincial life. Such a life, if wisely guided, will not mean disloyalty to the nation; and it need not mean narrowness of spirit, nor yet the further development of jealousies between various communities. What it will mean, or at least may mean,—this, so far as I have time, I wish to set forth in the following discussion. My main intention is to define the right form and the true office of provincialism,—to portray what, if you please, we may well call the Higher Provincialism,—to portray it, and then to defend it, to extol it, and to counsel you to further just such provincialism.

Since this is my purpose, let me at once say that I address myself, in the most explicit terms, to men and women who, as I hope and presuppose, are and wish to be, in the wholesome sense, provincial. Every one, as I maintain, ought, ideally speaking, to be provincial,— and that no matter how cultivated, or humanitarian, or universal in purpose or in experience he may be or may become. If in our own country, where often so many people are still comparative strangers to the communities in which they have come to live, there are some of us who, like myself, have changed our provinces during our adult

years, and who have so been unable to become and to remain in the
sense of European countries provincial; and if, moreover, the life of
our American provinces everywhere has still too brief a tradition,—
all that is our misfortune, and not our advantage. As our country
grows in social organization, there will be, in absolute measure, more
and not less provincialism amongst our people. To be sure, as I hope,
there will also be, in absolute measure, more and not less patriotism,
closer and not looser national ties, less and not more mutual sectional
misunderstanding. But the two tendencies, the tendency toward
national unity and that toward local independence of spirit, must
henceforth grow together. They cannot prosper apart. The national
unity must not kill out, nor yet hinder, the provincial self-consciousness. The loyalty to the Republic must not lessen the love and the
local pride of the individual community. The man of the future
must love his province more than he does to-day. His provincial
customs and ideals must be more and not less highly developed, more
and not less self-conscious, well-established, and earnest. And therefore, I say, I appeal to you as to a company of people who are, and
who mean to be, provincial as well as patriotic,—servants and lovers
of your own community and of its ways, as well as citizens of the
world. I hope and believe that you all intend to have your community live its own life, and not the life of any other community, nor yet
the life of a mere abstraction called humanity in general. I hope that
you are fully aware how provincialism, like monogamy, is an essential basis of true civilization. And it is with this presupposition that I
undertake to suggest something toward a definition and defence of
the higher provincialism and of its office in civilization.

III

With this programme in mind, let me first tell you what seem to me
to be in our modern world, and, in particular, in our American
world, the principal evils which are to be corrected by a further
development of a true provincial spirit, and which cannot be corrected without such a development.

The first of these evils I have already mentioned. It is a defect
incidental, partly to the newness of our own country, but partly
also to those world-wide conditions of modern life which make
travel, and even a change of home, both attractive and easy to
dwellers in the most various parts of the globe. In nearly every one

of our American communities, at least in the northern and in the western regions of our country, there is a rather large proportion of people who either have not grown up where they were born, or who have changed their dwelling-place in adult years. I can speak all the more freely regarding this class of our communities, because, in my own community, I myself, as a native of California, now resident in New England, belong to such a class. Such classes, even in modern New England, are too large. The stranger, the sojourner, the newcomer, is an inevitable factor in the life of most American communities. To make him welcome is one of the most gracious of the tasks in which our people have become expert. To give him his fair chance is the rule of our national life. But it is not on the whole well when the affairs of a community remain too largely under the influence of those who mainly feel either the wanderer's or the new resident's interest in the region where they are now dwelling. To offset the social tendencies due to such frequent changes of dwelling-place we need the further development and the intensification of the community spirit. The sooner the new resident learns to share this spirit, the better for him and for his community. A sound instinct, therefore, guides even our newer communities, in the more fortunate cases, to a rapid development of such a local sentiment as makes the stranger feel that he must in due measure conform if he would be permanently welcome, and must accept the local spirit if he is to enjoy the advantages of his community. As a Californian I have been interested to see both the evidences and the nature of this rapid evolution of the genuine provincial spirit in my own state. How swiftly, in that country, the Californians of the early days seized upon every suggestion that could give a sense of the unique importance of their new provincial life. The associations that soon clustered about the tales of the life of Spanish missionaries and Mexican colonists in the years before 1846,—these our American Californians cherished from the outset. This, to us often half-legendary past, gave us a history of our own. The wondrous events of the early mining life,—how earnestly the pioneers later loved to rehearse that story; and how proud every young Californian soon became of the fact that his father had had his part therein. Even the Californian's well-known and largely justified glorification of his climate was, in his own mind, part of the same expression of his tendency to idealize whatever tended to make his community, and all its affairs, seem unique, beloved, and deeply founded upon some significant natural basis. Such a foundation was, indeed, actually there; nature had, indeed, richly blessed his land; but the real interest that made one emphasize and idealize all these things, often so boastfully, was the interest of the loyal citizen in finding his community an object of pride. Now you, who know well your own local history, will be able to observe the growth amongst you of this tendency to idealize your past, to glorify the bounties that nature has showered upon you, all in such wise as to give the present life of your community more dignity, more honor, more value in the eyes of yourselves and of strangers. In fact, that we all do thus glorify our various provinces, we well know; and with what feelings we accompany the process, we can all observe for ourselves. But it is well to remember that the special office, the principal use, the social justification, of such mental tendencies in ourselves lies in the aid that they give us in becoming loyal to our community, and in assimilating to our own social order the strangers that are within our gates. It is the especial art of the colonizing peoples, such as we are, and such as the English are, to be able by devices of this sort rapidly to build up in their own minds a provincial loyalty in a new environment. The French, who are not a colonizing people, seem to possess much less of this tendency. The Chinese seem to lack it almost altogether. Our own success as possessors of new lands depends upon this one skill in making the new lands where we came to dwell soon seem to us glorious and unique. I was much impressed, some years ago, during a visit to Australia and New Zealand, with the parallel developments in the Australasian colonies. They too have already their glorious past history, their unique fortunes, their romances of the heroic days,— and, in consequence, their provincial loyalty and their power to assimilate their newcomers. So learn to view your new community that every stranger who enters it shall at once feel the dignity of its past, and the unique privilege that is offered to him when he is permitted to belong to its company of citizens,—this is the first rule of the people of every colonizing nation when they found a new province.

Thus, then, I have pointed out the first evil with which our provincialism has to deal—the evil due to the presence of a considerable number of not yet assimilated newcomers in most of our communities. The newcomers themselves are often a boon and welcome indeed. But their failure to be assimilated constitutes, so long as it endures, a source of social danger, because the community needs well-knit organization. We meet this danger by the development of a strong provincial spirit amongst those who already constitute the centralized portion of the community. For thus a dignity is given to the social order which makes the newcomer long to share in its honors by deserving its confidence. But this aspect of provincialism, this usefulness of local pride, is indeed the best known aspect of my topic. I pass at once to the less frequently recognized uses of the provincial spirit, by mentioning the second of the evils with which a wise provincialism is destined to contend.

IV

This second modern evil arises from, and constitutes, one aspect of the levelling tendency of recent civilization. That such a levelling tendency exists, most of us recognize. That it is the office of the province to contend against some of the attendant evils of this tendency, we less often observe. By the levelling tendency in question I mean that aspect of modern civilization which is most obviously suggested by the fact that, because of the ease of communication amongst distant places, because of the spread of popular education, and because of the consolidation and of the centralization of industries and of social authorities, we tend all over the nation, and, in some degree, even throughout the civilized world, to read the same daily news, to share the same general ideas, to submit to the same overmastering social forces, to live in the same external fashions, to discourage individuality, and to approach a dead level of harassed mediocrity. One of the most marked of all social tendencies is in any age that toward the mutual assimilation of men in so far as they are in social relations with one another. One of the strongest human predispositions is that toward imitation. But our modern conditions have greatly favored the increase of the numbers of people who read the same books and newspapers, who repeat the same phrases, who follow the same social fashions, and who thus, in general, imitate one another in constantly more and more ways. The result is a tendency to crush the individual. Furthermore there are modern economic and industrial developments, too well known to all of you to need any detailed mention here, which lead toward similar results. The independence of the small trader or manufacturer becomes lost in the great commercial or industrial combination. The vast corporation succeeds and displaces the individual. Ingenuity and initiative become subordinated to the discipline of an impersonal social order. And each man, becoming, like his fellow, the servant of masters too powerful for him to resist, and too complex in their undertakings for him to understand, is, in so far, disposed unobtrusively to conform to the ways of his innumerable fellow-servants, and to lose all sense of his unique moral destiny as an individual.

I speak here merely of tendencies. As you know, they are nowhere unopposed tendencies. Nor do I for an instant pretend to call even these levelling tendencies wholly, or principally, evil. But for the moment I call attention to what are obviously questionable, and in some degree are plainly evil, aspects of these modern tendencies. Imitation is a good thing. All civilization depends upon it. But there may be a limit to the number of people who ought to imitate precisely the same body of ideas and customs. For imitation is not man's whole business. There ought to be some room left for variety. Modern conditions have often increased too much what one might call the purely mechanical carrying-power of certain ruling social influences. There are certain metropolitan newspapers, for instance, which have far too many readers for the good of the social order in which they circulate. These newspapers need not always be very mischievous ones. But when read by too vast multitudes, they tend to produce a certain monotonously uniform triviality of mind in a large proportion of our city and suburban population. It would be better if the same readers were divided into smaller sections, which read different newspapers, even if these papers were of no higher level. For then there would at least be a greater variety in the sorts of triviality which from day to day occupied their minds. And variety is the beginning of individual independence of insght and of conviction. As for the masses of people who are under the domination of the great corporations that employ them, I am here not in the least dwelling upon their economic difficulties. I am pointing out that the lack of initiative in their lives tends to make their spiritual range narrower. They are too little disposed to create their own world. Now every man who gets into a vital relation to God's truth becomes, in his own way, a creator. And if you deprive a man of all incentive to create, you in so far tend to cut him off from God's truth. Or, in more common language, independence of spirit flourishes only when a man at least believes that he has a chance to change his fortunes if he persistently wills to do so. But the servant of some modern forms of impersonal social organization tends to lose this belief that he has a chance. Hence he tends to lose independence of spirit.

Well, this is the second of the evils of the modern world which, as I have said, provincialism may tend to counteract. Local spirit, local pride, provincial independence, influence the individual man precisely because they appeal to his imitative tendencies. But thereby they act so as to render him more or less immune in presence of the more trivial of the influences that, coming from without his community, would otherwise be likely to reduce him to the dead level of the customs of the whole nation. A country district may seem to a stranger unduly crude in its ways; but it does not become wiser in case, under the influence of city newspapers and of summer boarders, it begins to follow city fashions merely for the sake of imitating. Other things being equal, it is better in proportion as it remains self-possessed,—proud of its own traditions, not unwilling indeed to learn, but also quite ready to teach the stranger its own wisdom. And in similar fashion provincial pride helps the individual man to keep his self-respect even when the vast forces that work toward industrial consolidation, and toward the effacement of in-dividual initiative, are besetting his life at every turn. For a man is in large measure what his social consciousness makes him. Give him the local community that he loves and cherishes, that he is proud to honor and to serve,—make his ideal of that community lofty,—give him faith in the dignity of his province,—and you have given him a power to counteract the levelling tendencies of modern civiliza-tion.

V

The third of the evils with which a wise provincialism must contend is closely connected with the second. I have spoken of the constant tendency of modern life to the mutual assimilation of various parts of the social order. Now this assimilation may occur slowly and stead-ily, as in great measure it normally does; or, on the other hand, it may take more sudden and striking forms, at moments when the popular mind is excited, when great emotions affect the social or-der. At such times of emotional disturbance, society is subject to tendencies which have recently received a good deal of psycho-logical study. They are the tendencies to constitute what has often been called the spirit of the crowd or of the mob. Modern readers of the well-known book of Le Bon's on "The Crowd" well know what the tendencies to which I refer may accomplish. It is true that the results of Le Bon are by no means wholly acceptable. It is true that the psychology of large social masses is still insufficiently understood, and that a great many hasty statements have been made about the fatal tendency of great companies of people to go wrong. Yet in the complex world of social processes there can be no doubt that there exist such processes as the ones which Le Bon characterizes. The mob-spirit is a genuine psychological fact which occasionally becomes important in the life of all numerous communities. Moreover, the mob-spirit is no new thing. It has existed in some measure from the very beginning of social life. But there are certain modern conditions which tend to give the mob-spirit new form and power, and to lead to new social dangers that are consequent upon the presence of this spirit.

I use the term "mob-spirit" as an abbreviation for a very large range of phenomena, phenomena which may indeed be classed with all the rest of the imitative phenomena as belonging to one genus. But the mob-phenomena are distinguished from the other imitative phenomena by certain characteristic emotional tendencies which belong to excited crowds of people, and which do not belong to the more strictly normal social activities. Man, as an imitative animal, naturally tends, as we have seen, to do whatever his companions do, so long as he is not somehow aroused to independence and to individuality. Accordingly, he easily shares the beliefs and temperaments of those who are near enough to him to influence him. But now suppose a condition of things such as may readily occur in any large group of people who have somehow come to feel strong sympathy with one another, and who are for any reason in a relatively passive and impressible state of mind. In such a company of people let any idea which has a strong emotional coloring come to be suggested, by the words of the leader, by the singing of a song, by the beginning of any social activity that does not involve clear thinking, that does not call upon a man to assert his own independence. Such an idea forthwith tends to take possession in an extraordinarily strong degree of every member of the social group in question. As a consequence, the individual may come to be, as it were, hypnotized by his social group. He may reach a stage where he not merely lacks a disposition to individual initiative, but becomes for the time simply unable to assert himself, to think his own thoughts, or even to remember his ordinary habits and principles of conduct. His judgment for the time becomes one with that of the mass. He may not himself observe this fact. Like the hypnotized subject, the member of the excited mob may feel as if he were very independently expressing himself. He may say: "This idea is my own idea," when as a fact the ruling idea is suggested by the leaders of the mob, or even by the accident of the momentary situation. The individual may be led to acts of which he says: "These things are my duty, my sacred privilege, my right," when as a fact the acts in question are forced upon him by the suggestions of the social mass of which at the instant he is merely a helpless member. As the hypnotized subject, again, thinks his will free when an observer can see that he is obliged to follow the suggestions of the hypnotizer, so the member of the mob may feel all the sense of pure initiative, although as a fact he is in bondage to the will of another, to the motives of the moment.

All such phenomena are due to very deep-seated and common human tendencies. It is no individual reproach to any one of us that, under certain conditions, he would lose his individuality and become the temporary prey of the mob-spirit. Moreover, by the word "mob" itself, or by the equivalent word "crowd," I here mean no term that reflects upon the personal characters or upon the private intelligence of the individuals who chance to compose any given mob. In former ages when the defenders of aristocratic or of monarchical institutions used to speak with contempt of the mob, and oppose to the mob the enlightened portion of the community, the wise who ought to rule, or the people whom birth and social position secured against the defects of the mob, the term was used without a true understanding of the reason why crowds of people are upon occasion disposed to do things that are less intelligent than the acts of normal and thoughtful people would be. For the modern student of the psychology of crowds, a crowd or a mob means not in any wise a company of wicked, of debased, or even of ignorant persons. The term means merely a company of people who, by reason of their sympathies, have for the time being resigned their individual judgment. A mob might be a mob of saints or of cutthroats, of peasants or of men of science. If it were a mob it would lack due social wisdom whatever its membership might be. For the members of the mob are sympathizing rather than criticising. Their ruling ideas then, therefore, are what Le Bon calls atavistic ideas; ideas such as belong to earlier and cruder periods of civilization. Opposed to the mob in which the good sense of individuals is lost in a blur of emotion, and in a helpless suggestibility,—opposed to the mob, I say, is the small company of thoughtful individuals who are taking counsel together. Now our modern life, with its vast unions of people, with its high development of popular sentiments, with its passive and sympathetic love for knowing and feeling whatever other men know and feel, is subject to the disorders of larger crowds, of more dangerous mobs, than have ever before been brought into sympathetic union. One great problem of our time, then, is how to carry on popular government without being at the mercy of the mob-spirit. It is easy to give this mob-spirit noble names. Often you hear of it as "grand popular enthusiasm." Often it is highly praised as a loyal party spirit or as patriotism. But psychologically it is the mob-spirit whenever it is the spirit of a large company of people who are no longer either taking calm counsel together in small groups, or obeying an already established law or custom, but who are merely sympathizing with one another, listening to the words of leaders, and believing the large print headings of their newspapers. Every such company of people is, in so far, a mob. Though they spoke with the tongues of men and of angels, you could not then trust them. Wisdom is not in them nor in their mood. However highly trained they may be as individuals, their mental processes, as a mob, are degraded. Their suffrages, as a mob, ought not to count. Their deeds come of evil. The next mob may undo their work. Accident may render their enthusiasm relatively harmless. But, as a mere crowd, they cannot be wise. They cannot be safe rulers. Who, then, are the men who wisely think and rightly guide? They are, I repeat, the men who take counsel together in small groups, who respect one another's individuality, who meanwhile criticise one another constantly, and earnestly, and who suspect whatever the crowd teaches. In such men there need be no lack of wise sympathy, but there is much besides sympathy. There is individuality, and there is a willingness to doubt both one another and themselves. To such men, and such groups, popular government ought to be intrusted.

Now these principles are responsible for the explanation of the well-known contrast between those social phenomena which illustrate the wisdom of the enlightened social order, and the phenomena which, on the contrary, often seem such as to make us despair for the moment of the permanent success of popular government. In the rightly constituted social group where every member feels his own responsibility for his part of the social enterprise which is in hand, the result of the interaction of individuals is that the social group may show itself wiser than any of its individuals. In the mere crowd, on the other hand, the social group may be, and generally is, more stupid than any of its individual members. Compare a really successful town meeting in a comparatively small community with the accidental and sometimes dangerous social phenomena of a street mob or of a great political convention. In the one case every individual may gain wisdom from his contact with the social group. In the other case every man concerned, if ever he comes again to himself, may feel ashamed of the absurdity of which the whole company was guilty. Social phenomena of the type that may result from the higher social group, the group in which individuality is respected, even while social loyalty is demanded,—these phenomena may lead to permanent social results which as tradition gives them a fixed character may gradually lead to the formation of permanent institutions, in which a wisdom much higher than that of any individual man may get embodied. A classic instance of social phenomena of this type, and of the results of such social activities as constantly make use of individual skill, we find in language. However human language originated, it is certain that it was never the product of the mob-spirit. Language has been formed through the efforts of individuals to communicate with other individuals. Human speech is, therefore, in its structure, in its devices, in its thoughtfulness, essentially the product of the social activities of comparatively small groups of persons whose ingenuity was constantly aroused by the desire of making some form of social coöperation definite, and some form of communication amongst individuals effective. The consequence is that the language of an uncultivated people, who have as yet no grammarians to guide them and no literature to transmit the express wisdom of individual guides from generation to generation, may, nevertheless, be on the whole much more intelligent than is any individual that speaks the language.

Other classic instances of social processes wherein the group appears wiser than the individual are furnished to us by the processes that resulted through centuries of development in the production of the system of Roman law or of the British constitution. Such institutions embody more wisdom than any individual who has taken part in the production of these institutions has ever possessed. Now the common characteristic of all such social products seems to me to be due to the fact that the social groups in which they originated were always such as encouraged and as in fact necessitated an emphasis upon the contrasts between various individuals. In such groups what Tarde has called "the universal opposition" has always been an effective motive. The group has depended upon the variety and not the uniformity of its members. On the other hand, the other sort of social group, the mob, has depended upon the emotional agreement, the sympathy, of its members. It has been powerful only in so far as they forgot who they individually were, and gave themselves up to the suggestions of the moment.

It follows that if we are to look for the source of the greatest dangers of popular government, we must expect to find them in the influence of the mob spirit. Le Bon is right when he says that the problem of the future will become more and more the problem how to escape from the domination of the crowd. Now I do not share Le Bon's pessimism when he holds, as he seems to do, that all popular government necessarily involves the tendency to the prevalence of the mob-spirit. So far as I can see Le Bon and most of the other writers who in recent times have laid so much stress upon the dangers of the mob, have ignored, or at least have greatly neglected, that other social tendency, that tendency to the formation of smaller social groups, which makes use of the contrasts of individuals, and which leads to a collective wisdom greater than any individual wisdom. But why I do insist upon this is that the problem of the future for popular government must involve the higher development, the better organization, the more potent influence, of the social groups of the wiser type, and the neutralization through their influence of the power of the mob-spirit. Now the modern forms of the mob-spirit have become so portentous because of a tendency that is in itself very good, even as may be the results to which it often leads. This tendency is that toward a very wide and inclusive human sympathy, a sympathy which may be as undiscriminating as it often is kindly. Sympathy, however, as one must recollect, is not necessarily even a kindly tendency. For one may sympathize with any emotion,—for instance, with the emotions of a cruelly ferocious mob. Sympathy itself is a sort of neutral basis for more rational mental development. The noblest structures may be reared upon its soil. The basest absurdities may, upon occasion, seem to be justified, because an undiscriminating sympathy makes them plausible. Now modern conditions have certainly tended, as

I have said, to the spread of sympathy. Consider modern literature with its disposition to portray any form of human life, however ignoble or worthless, or on the other hand, however lofty or inspiring, —to portray it not because of its intrinsic worth but because of the mere fact that it exists. All sorts and conditions of men,—yes, all sorts and conditions of emotion, however irrational, have their hearing in the world of art to-day, win their expression, charm their audience, get, as we say, their recognition. Never were men so busy as now with the mere eagerness to sympathize with, to feel whatever is the lot of any portion of humanity. Now, as I have said, this spread of human sympathy, furthered as it is by all the means at the disposal of modern science, so far as that science deals with humanity, is a good thing just in so far as it is a basis upon which a rational philanthropy and a more intelligent social organization can be founded. But this habit of sympathy disposes us more and more to the influence of the mob. When the time of popular excitement comes, it finds us expert in sharing the emotions of the crowd, but often enervated by too frequent indulgence in just such emotion. The result is that modern mobs are much vaster, and in some respects more excitable than ever they were before. The psychological conditions of the mob no longer need include the physical presence of a crowd of people in a given place. It is enough if the newspapers, if the theatre, if the other means of social communication, serve to transmit the waves of emotional enthusiasm. A nation composed of many millions of people may fall rapidly under the hypnotic influence of a few leaders, of a few fatal phrases. And thus, as our third evil, we have not only the general levelling tendency of modern social life, but the particular tendency to emotional excitability which tends to make the social order, under certain conditions, not only monotonous and unideal, but actively dangerous.

Yet, as we have seen, this evil is not, as Le Bon and the pessimists would have it, inherent in the very fact of the existence of a social order. There are social groups that are not subject to the mob-spirit. And now if you ask how such social groups are nowadays to be fostered, to be trained, to be kept alive for the service of the nation, I answer that the place for fostering such groups is the province, for such groups flourish under conditions that arouse local pride, the loyalty to one's own community, the willingness to remember one's own ways and ideals, even at the moment when the nation is carried away by some levelling emotion. The lesson would then be: Keep the province awake, that the nation may be saved from the disastrous hypnotic slumber so characteristic of excited masses of mankind.

VI

I have now reviewed three types of evils against which I think it is the office of provincialism to contend. As I review these evils, I am reminded somewhat of the famous words of Schiller in his "Greeting to the New Century," which he composed at the outset of the nineteenth century. In his age, which in some respects was so analogous to our own, despite certain vast differences, Schiller found himself overwhelmed as he contemplated the social problem of the moment by the vast national conflict, and the overwhelming forces which seemed to him to be crushing the more ideal life of his nation, and of humanity. With a poetic despair that we need indeed no longer share, Schiller counsels his reader, in certain famous lines, to flee from the stress of life into the still recesses of the heart, for, as he says, beauty lives only in song, and freedom has departed into the realm of dreams. Now Schiller spoke in the romantic period. We no longer intend to flee from our social ills to any realm of dreams. And as to the recesses of the heart, we now remember that out of the heart are the issues of life. But so much my own thesis and my own counsel would share in common with Schiller's words. I should say to-day that our national unities have grown so vast, our forces of social consolidation have become so paramount, the resulting problems, conflicts, evils, have been so intensified, that we, too, must flee in the pursuit of the ideal to a new realm. Only this realm is, to my mind, so long as we are speaking of social problems, a realm of real life. It is the realm of the province. There must we flee from the stress of the now too vast and problematic life of the nation as a whole. There we must flee, I mean, not in the sense of a cowardly and permanent retirement, but in the sense of a search for renewed strength, for a social inspiration, for the salvation of the individual from the overwhelming forces of consolidation. Freedom, I should say, dwells now in the small social group, and has its securest home in the provincial life. The nation by itself, apart from the influence of the province, is in danger of becoming an incomprehensible monster, in whose presence the individual loses his right, his self-consciousness, and his dignity. The province must save the individual.

But, you may ask, in what way do I conceive that the wise provincialism of which I speak ought to undertake and carry on its task? How is it to meet the evils of which I have been speaking? In what way is its influence to be exerted against them? And how can the province cultivate its self-consciousness without tending to fall back again into the ancient narrowness from which small communities were so long struggling to escape? How can we keep broad humanity and yet cultivate provincialism? How can we be loyally patriotic, and yet preserve our consciousness of the peculiar and unique dignity of our own community? In what form are our wholesome provincial activities to be carried on?

I answer, of course, in general terms, that the problem of the wholesome provincial consciousness is closely allied to the problem of any individual form of activity. An individual tends to become narrow when he is what we call self-centred. But, on the other hand, philanthropy that is not founded upon a personal loyalty of the individual to his own family and to his own personal duties is notoriously a worthless abstraction. We love the world better when we cherish our own friends the more faithfully. We do not grow in grace by forgetting individual duties in behalf of remote social enterprises. Precisely so, the province will not serve the nation best by forgetting itself, but by loyally emphasizing its own duty to the nation and therefore its right to attain and to cultivate its own unique wisdom. Now all this is indeed obvious enough, but this is precisely what in our days of vast social consolidation we are some of us tending to forget.

Now as to the more concrete means whereby the wholesome provincialism is to be cultivated and encouraged, let me appeal directly to the loyal member of any provincial community, be it the community of a small town, or of a great city, or of a country district. Let me point out what kind of work is needed in order to cultivate that wise provincialism which, as you see, I wish to have grow not in opposition to the interests of the nation, but for the very sake of saving the nation from the modern evil tendencies of which I have spoken.

First, then, I should say a wholesome provincialism is founded upon the thought that while local pride is indeed a praiseworthy accompaniment of every form of social activity, our province, like our own individuality, ought to be to all of us rather an ideal than a mere boast. And here, as I think, is a matter which is too often forgotten. Everything valuable is, in our present human life, known to us as an ideal before it becomes an attainment, and in view of our human imperfections, remains to the end of our short lives much more a hope and an inspiration than it becomes a present achievement. Just because the true issues of human life are brought to a finish not in time but in eternity, it is necessary that in our temporal existence what is most worthy should appear to us as an ideal, as an Ought, rather than as something that is already in our hands. The old saying about the bird in the hand being worth two in the bush does not rightly apply to the ideal goods of a moral agent working under human limitations. For him the very value of life includes the fact that its goal as something infinite can never at any one instant be attained. In this fact the moral agent glories, for it means that he has something to do. Hence the ideal in the bush, so to speak, is always worth infinitely more to him than the food or the plaything of time that happens to be just now in his hands. The difference between vanity and self-respect depends largely upon this emphasizing of ideals in the case of the higher forms of self-consciousness, as opposed to the emphasis upon transient temporal attainments in the case of the lower forms. Now what holds true of individual self-consciousness ought to hold true of the self-consciousness of the community. Boasting is often indeed harmless and may prove a stimulus to good work. It is therefore to be indulged as a tribute to our human weakness. But the better aspect of our provincial consciousness is always its longing for the improvement of the community.

And now, in the second place, a wise provincialism remembers that it is one thing to seek to make ideal values in some unique sense our own, and it is quite another thing to believe that if they are our own, other people cannot possess such ideal values in their own equally unique fashion. A realm of genuinely spiritual individuality is one where each individual has his own unique significance, so that none could take another's place. But for just that very reason all the unique individuals of the truly spiritual order stand in relation to the same universal light, to the same divine whole in relation to which they win their individuality. Hence all the individuals of the true spiritual order have ideal goods in common, as the very means whereby they can win each his individual place with reference to the possession and the employment of these common goods. Well, it is with provinces as with individuals. The way to win independence is by learning freely from abroad, but by then insisting upon our own intepretation of the common good. A generation ago the Japanese seemed to most European observers to be entering upon a career of total self-surrender. They seemed to be adopting without stint European customs and ideals. They seemed to be abandoning their own national independence of spirit. They appeared to be purely imitative in their main purposes. They asked other nations where the skill of modern sciences lay, and how the new powers were to be gained by them. They seemed to accept with the utmost docility every lesson, and to abandon with unexampled submissiveness, their purpose to remain themselves. Yet those of us who have watched them since, or who have become acquainted with representative Japanese students, know how utterly superficial and illusory that old impression of ours was regarding the dependence, or the extreme imitativeness, or the helpless docility, of the modern Japanese. He has now taught us quite another lesson. With a curious and on the whole not unjust spiritual wiliness, he has learned indeed our lesson, but he has given it his own interpretation. You always feel in intercourse with a Japanese how unconquerable the spirit of his nation is, how inaccessible the recesses of his spirit have remained after all these years of free intercourse with Europeans. In your presence the Japanese always remains the courteous and respectful learner so long as he has reason to think that you have anything to teach him. But he remains as absolutely his own master with regard to the interpretation, the use, the possession of all spiritual gifts, as if he were the master and you the learner. He accepts the gifts, but their place in his national and individual life is his own. And we now begin to see that the feature of the Japanese nationality as a member of the civilized company of nations is to be something quite unique and independent. Well, let the Japanese give us a lesson in the spirit of true provincialism. Provincialism does not mean a lack of plasticity, an unteachable spirit; it means a determination to use the spiritual gifts that come to us from abroad in our own way and with reference to the ideals of our own social order.

And therefore, thirdly, I say in developing your provincial spirit, be quite willing to encourage your young men to have relations with other communities. But on the other hand, encourage them also to make use of what they thus acquire for the furtherance of the life of their own community. Let them win aid from abroad, but let them also have, so far as possible, an opportunity to use this which they acquire in the service of their home. Of course economic conditions rather than deliberate choice commonly determine how far the youth of a province are able to remain for their lifetime in a place where they grow up. But so far as a provincial spirit is concerned, it is well to avoid each of two extremes in the treatment of the young men of the community,—extremes that I have too often seen exemplified. The one extreme consists in maintaining that if young men mean to be loyal to their own province, to their own state, to their own home, they ought to show their loyalty by an unwillingness to seek guidance from foreign literature, from foreign lands, in the patronizing of foreign or distant institutions, or in the acceptance of the customs and ideas of other communities than their own. Against this extreme let the Japanese be our typical instance. They have wandered far. They have studied abroad. They have assimilated the lore of other communities. And they have only gained in local consciousness, in independence of spirit, by the ordeal. The other extreme is the one expressed in that tendency to wander and to encourage wandering, which has led so many of our communities to drive away the best and most active young men. We want more of the determination to find, if possible, a place for our youth in their own communities.

Finally, let the province more and more seek its own adornment. Here I speak of a matter that in all our American communities has been until recently far too much neglected. Local pride ought above all to centre, so far as its material objects are concerned, about the determination to give the surroundings of the community nobility, dignity, beauty. We Americans spend far too much of our early strength and time in our newer communities upon injuring our landscapes, and far too little upon endeavoring to beautify our towns and cities. We have begun to change all that, and while I have no right to speak as an æsthetic judge concerning the growth of the love of the beautiful in our country, I can strongly insist that no community can think any creation of genuine beauty and dignity in its public buildings or in the surroundings of its towns and cities too good a thing for its own deserts. For we deserve what in such realms we can learn how to create or to enjoy, or to make sacrifices for. And no provincialism will become dangerously narrow so long as it is constantly accompanied by a willingness to sacrifice much in order to put in the form of great institutions, of noble architecture, and of beautiful surroundings an expression of the worth that the community attaches to its own ideals.

33

Race Questions and Prejudices

The numerous questions and prejudices which are aroused by the
contact of the various races of men have always been important
factors in human history. They promise, however, to become, in
the near future, still more important than they have ever been before. Such increased importance of race questions and prejudices, if it
comes to pass, will be due not to any change in human nature, and
especially not to any increase in the diversity or in the contrasting
traits of the races of men themselves, but simply to the greater
extent and complexity of the work of civilization. Physically speaking, great masses of men are to-day brought into more frequent
and closer contact than was formerly possible, because of the ease
with which at present the numerous means of communication can
be used, because of the increase of peaceful migrations, and because
of the imperial ambitions of several of the world's great peoples.
Hence whatever contact, conflict, or mutual influence the races of
men have had in the past, we find to-day more ways and places
in which men find themselves in the presence of alien races, with
whom they have to learn to live in the same social order. When we
think of East Indian coolies now present as laborers, side by side
with the native negroes, and with white men, in the British West
Indies; when we remember the problem of South Africa, as it was
impressed upon our minds a few years since, at a moment when
Dutchmen and Englishmen fought for the land, while Kaffirs and

[Reprinted from *RQP*, pp. 3–53.]

Zulus watched the conflict; when we recall what the recent war between Japan and Russia has already meant for the future of the races of men in the far East; and when, with a few only of such typical instances in mind, we turn back to our own country, and think how many different race-problems confront us,—we then see that the earliest social problem of humanity is also the most recent problem. This is the problem of dealing with the men who seem to us somehow very widely different from ourselves, in physical constitution, in temperament, in all their deeper nature, so that we are tempted to think of them as natural strangers to our souls, while nevertheless we find that they are stubbornly there in our world, and that they are men as much determined to live as we are, and are men who, in turn, find us as incomprehensible as we find them. Of these diverse races, what ones are the superior and what ones are the inferior races? What race or races ought to rule? What ones ought to yield to their natural masters? To which one of these races has God, or nature, or destiny, ordained the rightful and final sovereignty of the earth? Which of these types of men is really the human type? Are they by their presence and their rivalry essentially perilous to one another's interests? And if so, what one amongst them is there whose spread, or whose increase in power or in number, is most perilous to the true cause of civilization? Is it a "yellow peril," or a "black peril," or perhaps, after all, is it not rather some form of "white peril," which most threatens the future of humanity in this day of great struggles and of complex issues? Are all men equal, as the Eighteenth Century theorists insisted? Or if the actual inequality of men in power, in value, in progressiveness, is an obvious fact, then how is this fact related to racial distinctions?

Such are a few of the questions that crowd upon us when we think about the races of men, and about their various relations to civilization. I do not mean, in this brief discussion, to exhaust any of these questions, but I want to call attention to a few principles which seem to me to be serviceable to any one who wants to look at race questions fairly and humanely.

I

It will be natural for some of my readers to interpose, at this point, the suggestion that the principal guidance in any attempt to answer such questions as the foregoing must come from an appeal to the results of the modern scientific study of the races of men. Why speculate and moralize, one may say? Have not the races of men been studied in recent times with elaborate care? What can tell us how to deal with the race-problems, in case we neglect the results of anthropology and of ethnology? And if we consult those sciences, do they not already give us a basis for decision regarding all such matters—a basis which is far more valuable than any chance observations of an amateur can be?

As a fact, if I supposed that, in their present stage of progress, the sciences which deal with man had already attained to exact results regarding the mental and moral differences, prospects, and destinies, of the different stocks of the *genus homo,* nobody would be humbler than I should be in accepting, and in trying to use the verdict that would then have been obtained. But I confess that, as a student of ethics and of certain other aspects of our common human nature, I have been a good deal baffled in trying to discover just what the results of science are regarding the true psychological and moral meaning of race-differences. I shall later speak further of some of the difficulties of this scientific aspect of our topic. It is enough to say here that when I consult any of the known *Rassentheoretiker* for light, I do indeed learn that the concept of race is the key to the comprehension of all history, and that, if you only form a clear idea of the important types of men (types such, for instance, as the marvellous *Germanen* of Chamberlain's *Grundzüge des Neunzehnten Jahrhunderts*), you can then determine with exactness precisely who ought to rule and who ought to yield, and can predict the forms of civilization, the *Weltanschauungen,* and the other possessions, which will be characteristic of each type of men, so long as that type shall endure. When I observe, however, that the *Rassentheoretiker* frequently uses his science to support most of his personal prejudices, and is praised by his sympathizers almost equally for his exact knowledge and for his vigorous display of temperament, I begin to wonder whether a science which mainly devotes itself to proving that we ourselves are the salt of the earth, is after all so exact as it aims to be. It is with some modern race-theories, as it is with some forms of international yacht racing. I know nothing about yachting; but whenever any form of the exalted sport of international yachting proves to be definable as a sort of contest in which the foreigner is invariably beaten, I for my part take no interest in learning more about the rules of that particular game. And precisely so, when men marshal all the resources of their science to prove that their own race-prejudices are infallible, I can feel no confidence in what they imagine to be the result of science. Much of our modern race-theory reminds me, in its spirit, altogether too much of some of the conversations in the "Jungle Book,"—or of the type of international courtesy expressed in "The Truce of the Bear,"—too much, I say to seem like exact science. Mowgli's remarks addressed to Red Dog may have been good natural history; but scientific Zoölogy does not proceed in that way.

While I deeply respect, then, the actual work of the sciences which deal with man, and while I fully recognize their modern progress, I greatly doubt that these sciences as yet furnish us with the exact results which representative race-theorists sometimes insist upon. Hence I am unable to begin this little study by a mere report of what science has established regarding the mental and moral varieties of men. I must rather make my beginning with a mention of two instances which have recently been much in my mind, and which bear upon the meaning of race prejudices. One of these instances is to-day in everybody's mind.

II

I refer then, first, to the wonderful lesson that Japan has been teaching us regarding what human energy and devotion have done and can do, and can do also in case of a race that is indeed remote enough from our own. I remember well the Japan of the geography text-books of my childhood, text-books which were even then antiquated enough; but I believed them. Japan was a weird land, according to the old text-books,—a land from which foreigners were excluded, a land where all things were as perverse as possible, where criminals were boiled in oil, where Catholic missionaries had long ago been martyred. Whatever the Japanese were, they were plainly men of the wrong race. Later, however, I learned something of the contemporary history of Japan as it then was. The scene was now, indeed, vastly changed. The Japanese had opened their land; and hereupon, lo! in a magic way, they were imitating, so we heard, *all* of our European customs. So we next had to alter our own opinion as to their essential nature.

They became in our eyes a plastic race of wonderful little children, small of stature, quick of wit, light-minded—a folk who took up any suggestion precisely as the playful children often do. They, too, were playing, it seemed, with our whole Western civilization. Plainly, then, they were a race who had no serious life of their own at all. Those of us who disliked them noted that they thus showed an ape-like unsteadiness of conduct. This, then, was their racial characteristic. Those who admired them thought of them as a new sort of pets, to be humored and instructed with all our superior condescension. Well, as time went on, and I grew to manhood, I myself came to know some of these Japanese as students. Hereupon, however, I gradually learned to see such men in a wholly new light. I found them, with all their steadfast courtesy, pleasantly, but impenetrably reserved—keepers of their own counsel, men whose life had, as I soon found, a vast background of opinions and customs that I could not fathom. When, I said, shall I ever see what is behind that Japanese smile? What is in their hearts? With an immovable self-consciousness they resisted every effort to alter, from without, any of their essential ideals. Politely, whenever you pressed them, they declined to admit that any of our Western arts or opinions were equal in value to their own most cherished national ideal treasures. And this they did even at the moment when they were present, most respectfully, as learners. They learned well; but plainly they meant to use this learning for their own purposes. An enthusiastic lady in an American University town was once seeking to draw from a Japanese visitor some admission of the importance of Christianity for the higher civilization of his country. "Confess," she insisted, "confess what a boon our missionaries have brought you in introducing Christianity into your land." "You are right," answered the Japanese, with his usual courteous smile, "you are right; the missionaries in introducing Christianity, have indeed brought us a great good. They have completed the variety of religions in Japan."

This impenetrable Japanese self-consciousness, this unconquerable polite and obstinate reserve, what did it mean? Well, Mr. Hearn and his kin have now let us know in a literary way something of the true heart of Japan. And the recent war has shown us what Japan meant by imitating our Western ways, and also what ancestral ideals have led her sons to death in battle, and still hold the nation so closely knit to their Emperor. Already I have heard some tender souls amongst us say: "It is *they* who are racially *our* superiors." Some of us may live to see Japanese customs pervading our land, and all of our professional imitators trying to be Japanese.

Well, I myself am no worshipper of any new fancy or distant civilization, merely because of its temporary prominence. But the true lesson which Japan teaches us to-day is, that it is somewhat hard to find out by looking at the features of a man's face, or at the color of his skin, or even at the reports of travellers who visit his land, what it is of which his race is really capable. Perhaps the Japanese are not of the right race; but we now admit that so long as we judged them merely by their race, and by mere appearances, we were judging them ignorantly, and falsely. This, I say, has been to me a most interesting lesson in the fallibility of some of our race judgments.

III

So much, then, for one lesson of experience. I have recently been much impressed by another lesson, but by one of a very different character, occurring, so to speak, at the other extremity of the world of modern race-problems. The negro has so far shown none of the great powers of the Japanese. Let us, then, provisionally admit at this stage of our discussion that the negro is in his present backward state as a race, for reasons which are not due merely to circumstances, but which are quite innate in his mental constitution. I shall indeed return to that topic later on. But, for the moment, let that view pass as if it were finally accepted. View the negro, then, for the instant merely as a backward race. But let the race-question here be our own pressing Southern question: How can the white man and the negro, once forced, as they are in our South, to live side by side, best learn to live with a minimum of friction, with a maximum of coöperation? I have long learned from my Southern friends that this end can only be attained by a firm and by a very constant and explicit insistence upon keeping the negro in his proper place, as a social inferior—who, then, as an inferior, should, of course, be treated humanely, but who must first be clearly and unmistakably taught where he belongs. I have observed that the pedagogical methods which my Southern friends of late years have found it their duty to use, to this end, are methods such as still keep awake a good deal of very lively and intense irritation in the minds not only of the pupils but also of the teachers. Now irritation, viewed merely in itself, is not an enlightening state of mind. It is, therefore, according to our modern views, not a very pedagogical state of mind. I am myself, for instance, a fairly irritable person, and I am also a teacher. But at the moments when I am irritated I am certainly not just then a good teacher. Is, however, the irritation which seems to be the accompaniment of some of the recent Southern methods of teaching the negro his place an inevitable evil, a wholly necessary accompaniment of the present transition period in the South? *Must* such increase of race-hatred first come, in order that later, whenever the negro has fully learned his lesson, and aspires no more beyond his station, peace may come? Well, concerning just this matter I lately learned what was to me, in my inexperience, a new lesson. I have had occasion three times, in recent summers, to visit British West Indies, Jamaica, and Trinidad, at a time when few tourists were there. Upon visiting Jamaica I first went round the coast of the island, visiting its various ports. I then went inland, and walked for miles over its admirable country roads. I discussed its condition with men of various occupations. I read some of its official literature. I then consulted with a new interest its history. I watched its negroes in various places, and talked with some of them, too. I have since collected such further information as I had time to collect regarding its life, as various authorities have discussed the topic, and this is the result:—

Jamaica has a population of surely not more than 14,000 or 15,000 whites, mostly English. Its black population considerably exceeds 600,000. Its mulatto population, of various shades, numbers, at the very least, some 40,000 or 50,000. Its plantation life, in the days before emancipation, was much sadder and severer, by common account, than ours in the South ever was. Both the period of emancipation and the immediately following period were of a very discouraging type. In the sixties of the last century there was one very unfortunate insurrection. The economic history of the island has also been in many ways unlucky even to the present day. Here, then, are certainly conditions which in some respects are decidedly such as would seem to tend toward a lasting state of general irritation, such as you might suppose would make race-questions acute. Moreover, the population, being a tropical one, has serious moral burdens to contend with of the sort that result from the known influences of such climates upon human character in the men of all races.

And yet, despite all these disadvantages, to-day, whatever the problems of Jamaica, whatever its defects, our own present Southern race-problem in the forms which we know best, simply does not exist. There is no public controversy about social race equality or superiority. Neither a white man nor a white woman feels insecure in moving about freely amongst the black population anywhere on the island. The colony has a Legislative Assembly, although one of extremely limited legislative powers. For the choice to this assembly a suffrage determined only by a decidedly low rate-qualification is free to all who have sufficient property, but is used by only a very small portion of the negro population. The negro is, on the whole, neither painfully obstrusive in his public manners, nor in need of being sharply kept in his place. Within the circles of the black population itself there is meanwhile a decidedly rich social differentiation. There are negroes in government service, negroes in the professions, negroes who are fairly prosperous peasant proprietors, and there are also the poor peasants; there are the thriftless, the poor in the towns,—yes, as in any tropical country, the beggars. In Kingston and in some other towns there is a small class of negroes who are distinctly criminal. On the whole, however, the negroes and colored population, taken in the mass, are orderly, law-abiding, contented, still backward in their education, but apparently advancing. They are generally loyal to the government. The best of them are aspiring, in their own way, and wholesomely self-conscious. Yet there is no doubt whatever that English white men are the essential controllers of the destiny of the country. But these English whites, few as they are, control the country at present, with extraordinarily little friction, and wholly without those painful emotions, those insistent complaints and anxieties, which at present are so prominent in the minds of many of our own Southern brethern. Life in Jamaica is not ideal. The economical aspect of the island is in many ways unsatisfactory. But the negro race-question, in our present American sense of that term, seems to be substantially solved.

How? By race-mixture?

The considerable extent to which race-mixture went in the

earlier history of Jamaica is generally known. Here, as elsewhere, however, it has been rather the social inequality of the races, than any approach to equality, which has been responsible for the mixture, in so far as such has occurred. It was the social inequality of the plantation days that began the process of mixture. If the often-mentioned desire to raise the "color" of their children, has later led the colored population to seek a further amalgamation of the two stocks, certainly that tendency, so far as it is effective, has been due to the social advantages of the lighter color—and not due to any motive which has decreased the ancient disadvantages under which the darker race has had to suffer. If race-amalgamation is indeed to be viewed as always an evil, the best way to counteract the growth of that evil must everywhere be the cultivation of racial self-respect and not of racial degradation. As a fact, it is not the amalgamation of the stocks, so far as that has occurred, which has tended to reduce the friction between the races in Jamaica. As to the English newcomers to the island, they probably do not tend to become amalgamated with the colored stocks in Jamaica, more than in any other region where the English live. The English stock tends, here as elsewhere, to be proud of itself, and to keep to itself. How then has the solution of what was once indeed a grave race-question been brought about in Jamaica?

I answer, by the simplest means in the world—the simplest, that is, for Englishmen—viz.: by English administration, and by English reticence. When once the sad period of emanicipation and of subsequent occasional disorder was passed, the Englishman did in Jamaica what he has so often and so well done elsewhere. He organized his colony; he established good local courts, which gained by square treatment the confidence of the blacks. The judges of such courts were Englishmen. The English ruler also provided a good country constabulary, in which native blacks also found service, and in which they could exercise authority over other blacks. Black men, in other words, were trained, under English management, of course, to police black men. A sound civil service was also organized; and in that educated negroes found in due time their place, while the chiefs of each branch of the service were and are, in the main, Englishmen. The excise and the health services, both of which are very highly developed, have brought the law near to the life of the humblest negro, in ways which he sometimes finds, of course, restraining, but which he also frequently finds beneficent. Hence he is accustomed to the law; he sees its ministers often, and often, too, as men of his own race; and in the main, he is fond of order, and learns to be respectful toward the established ways of society. The Jamaica negro is described by those who know him as especially fond of bringing his petty quarrels and personal grievances into court. He is litigious just as he is vivacious. But this confidence in the law is just what the courts have encouraged. That is one way, in fact, to deal with the too forward and strident negro. Encourage him to air his grievances in court, listen to him patiently, and fine him when he deserves fines. That is a truly English type of social pedagogy. It works in the direction of making the negro a conscious helper toward good social order.

Administration, I say, has done the larger half of the work of solving Jamaica's race-problem. Administration has filled the island with good roads, has reduced to a minimum the tropical diseases by means of an excellent health-service, has taught the population loyalty and order, has led them some steps already on the long road "up from slavery," has given them, in many cases, the true self-respect of those who themselves officially coöperate in the work of the law, and it has done this without any such result as our Southern friends nowadays conceive when they think of what is called "negro domination." Administration has allayed ancient irritations. It has gone far to offset the serious economic and tropical troubles from which Jamaica meanwhile suffers.

Yes, the work has been done by administration,—and by reticence. For the Englishman, in his official and governmental dealings with backward peoples, has a great way of being superior without very often publicly saying that he is superior. You well know that in dealing, as an individual, with other individuals, trouble is seldom made by the fact that you are actually the superior of another man in any respect. The trouble comes when you tell the other man, too stridently, that you are his superior. Be my superior, quietly, simply showing your superiority in your deeds, and very likely I shall love you for the very fact of your superiority. For we all love our leaders. But tell me that I am your inferior, and then perhaps I may grow boyish, and may throw stones. Well, it is so with races. Grant then that yours is the superior race. Then you can afford to say little about that subject

in your public dealings with the backward race. Superiority is
best shown by good deeds and by few boasts.

IV

So much for the lesson that Jamaica has suggested to me. The
widely different conditions of Trinidad suggest, despite the differences, a somewhat similar lesson. Here also there are great defects
in the social order; but again, our Southern race-problem does not
exist. When, with such lessons in mind, I recall our problem, as I
hear it from my brethren of certain regions of our Union, I see
how easily we can all mistake for a permanent race-problem a
difficulty that is essentially a problem of quite another sort. Mr.
Thomas Nelson Page in his recent book on the "Southerners'
Problem" speaks, in one notable passage, of the possibility which
he calls Utopian, that perhaps some day the negro in the South
may be made to coöperate in the keeping of order by the organization under State control of a police of his own race, who shall
deal with blacks. He even mentions that the English in the East
Indies use native constabulary. But this possibility is not Utopian.
When I hear the complaint of the Southerner, that the race-problem is such as constantly to endanger the safety of his home, I
now feel disposed to say: "The problem that endangers the
sanctity of your homes and that is said sometimes to make lynching
a necessity, is not a race-problem. It is an administrative problem.
You have never organized a country constabulary. Hence, when
various social conditions, amongst which the habit of irritating
public speech about race-questions is indeed one, though only
one, condition, have tended to the producing and to the arousing
of extremely dangerous criminals in your communities, you have
no adequate means of guarding against the danger. When you
complain that such criminals, when they flee from justice, get
sympathy from some portion of their ignorant fellows and so are
aided to get away, you forget that you have not first made your
negro countryman familiar with, and fond of, the law, by means
of a vigorous and well-organized and generally beneficent administration constantly before his eyes, not only in the pursuit of
criminals, but in the whole care of public order and health. If you
insist that in some districts the white population is too sparse or too
poor, or both, to furnish an efficient country constabulary con-

stantly on duty, why, then, have you not long since trained black men to police black men? Sympathy with the law grows with responsibility for its administration. If it is revolting to you to see black men possessed of the authority of a country constabulary, still, if you will, you can limit their authority to a control over their own race. If you say all this speech of mine is professorial, unpractical, Utopian, and if you still cry out bitterly for the effective protection of your womankind, I reply merely, look at Jamaica. Look at other English colonies.

In any case, the Southern race-problem will never be relieved by speech or by practices such as increase irritation. It will be relieved when administration grows sufficiently effective, and when the negroes themselves get an increasingly responsible part in this administration in so far as it relates to their own race. That may seem a wild scheme. But I insist: It is the English way. Look at Jamaica, and learn how to protect your own homes.

I have reviewed two very different lessons which I have recently had brought home to me regarding race-problms. What is there which is common to these two lessons? Is it not this: In estimating, in dealing with races, in defining what their supposedly unchangeable characteristics are, in planning what to do with them, we are all prone to confuse the accidental with the essential. We are likely to take for an essential race-characteristic what is a transient incident, or a product of special social conditions. We are disposed to view as a fatal and overwhelming race-problem what is a perfectly curable accident of our present form of administration. If we are indeed of a superior race ourselves, we shall, however, best prove the fact by learning to distinguish the accidental from the essential in our relations with other races. I speak with no lack of sympathy for the genuine and bitter trials of our Southern brethren when I say that I suppose the mistake which I now point out, the mistake of confusing the essential and the accidental, is the mistake that they are now making in many of their sincerest expressions of concern over their race-problem.

So much for the two lessons that have led me to the present discussion. But now let me pass to a somewhat wider view of race-problems. Let me ask a little more generally, What, if anything, can be known to be essential about the characteristics of a race of men and consequently an essentially important consideration in our dealings with alien races? Speaking so far as we can, apart from prejudice, what can we say about what it is which distinguishes the various races of men from one another?

V

The term "race" is popularly used in a very vague way. The newspapers not long ago said, during trouble in Poland, that the Russian soldiers then in Warsaw showed "race-antipathy" in their conflicts with the people. We all know, however, that the mutual hatred of Russians and Poles is due mainly to political and to religious causes. Frenchmen of the northern provinces, who are anthropologically wholly indistinguishable, as Professor Ripley tells us, from the inhabitants of many western German districts, still have what they call a "race-antipathy" for the men across the border. Thus almost any national or political or religious barrier, if it is old enough, may lead to a consciousness of difference of race. On the other hand, there are, of course, unquestionable physical varieties of mankind, distinguished by well-known physical contrasts. But the anthropologists still almost hopelessly disagree as to what the accurate classification of these true races may be. Such a classification, however, does not concern us here. We are now interested in the minds of men. We want to know what the races of men are socially good for. And not in the study of skulls or of hair, or of skin color, and not in the survey of all these bewildering complications with which physical anthropology deals, shall we easily find an answer to our more practical questions, viz., to our questions regarding the way in which these various races of men are related to the interests of civilization, and regarding the spirit in which we ought to estimate and practically to deal with these racial traits of mankind.

For after all, it is a man's mind, rather than his skull, or his hair, or his skin, that we most need to estimate. And if hereupon we ask ourselves just how these physical varieties of the human stock, just how these shades of color, these types of hair, these forms of skull, or these contours of body, are related to the mental powers and to the moral characteristics of the men in question, then, if only we set prejudice wholly aside, and appeal to science to help us, we find ourselves in the present state of knowledge almost hopelessly at sea. We know too little as yet about the natural history of the human mind, our psychology is far too infantile a science, to give us any precise information as to the way in which the inherited, the native, the constitutional aspects of the minds of men really vary with their complexions or with their hair. Yet that, of course, is just what we most want to know. It is easy to show that an Australian is just now far below our mental level. But how far is his degradation due to the inherited and unchangeable characters of his race, and how far to his long struggle with the dreary desert? How far is he, as we now find him, a degenerate, whose ancestors were on some far higher level? In other words, is his type of mind a true variety of the human mind, inbred and unchangeable? How far is it, so to speak, a mere incident? Upon what level were the minds of our own ancestors in the early stone age of Europe? How did their minds then compare with the minds of those ancestors of the Australian who were then their contemporaries? Who shall answer such questions? Yet just such questions we should have to answer before we could decide upon the true relations of race and of mind.

To be sure, anthropology has made a beginning, and a very important beginning, in the study of the mental types of primitive man. By various comparative and archæological methods we can already learn a good deal about the minds of our own ancestors. We can also study various races as they are to-day. We know, about the early stages of human culture, far more than we knew a little while since. But one result may forthwith be stated regarding what we have so far learned concerning the early history of the human mind, whether it is the mind of our ancestors, or of other races. Of course, we cannot doubt that, just as now we widely differ in mental life, so always there must have been great contrasts between the minds of the various stocks of men. No doubt, if the science of man were exact, it would indeed include a race-psychology. But my present scepticism concerns the present state of science, and the result of such study as we have yet made of the racial psychology of man is distinctly disappointing to those who want to make their task easy by insisting that the physical varieties of mankind are in our present state of knowledge sufficient guides to an interpretation of the whole inner contrast of the characters and of the mental processes of men. For what anthropology thus far shows us is, that, so soon as you go back beyond those stages of cultivation where history is possible, and so soon a you view men as they are apart from the higher culture—well, then, all men, so far as we can yet study them, appear to us not, of course, the same in mind, but yet surprisingly alike in their minds, in their morals, and in their arts. Widely as the primitive men differ, in certain broad features they remain, for our present knowledge, notably similar. And these common features are such as are by no means altogether flattering to our racial pride, when we think that our own ancestors, too, were, not very long since, comparatively, primitive men like the rest.

All the more primitive men, namely, are largely alike in the grossness and in the unpromising stupidity of their superstitions, and in their moral defects and virtues. Very many of them, belonging to the most various races, resemble one another in possessing customs which we now, for the most part, profoundly abhor, and which we are at present prone to view as characteristic of essentially debased minds. Such customs as cannibalism, or as human sacrifice, or as the systematic torturing of prisoners of war, such horrors as those of the witchcraft from whose bondage Europeans escaped only since the seventeenth century—such things, I say, are characteristic of no one race of men. To surround one's life with a confused mass of spiritual horrors, to believe in ghosts, or in vampires, in demons, in magic, in witchcraft, and in hostile gods of all sorts, to tangle up one's daily activities in a net of superstitious customs, to waste time in elaborate incantations, to live in fantastic terrors of an unseen world, to be terrified by tabus of all kinds, so that numerous sorts of useful deeds are superstitiously forbidden, to narrate impossible stories and believe in them, to live in filth, to persecute, to resist light, to fight against progress, to be mentally slothful, dull, sensuous, cruel, to be the prey of endless foolishness, to be treacherous, to be destructive— well, these are the mental traits of no one or two races of men. These are simply the common evil, traits of primitive humanity, traits to which our own ancestors were very long ago a prey, traits against which civilized man has still constantly to fight. Any frenzied mob of civilized men may relapse in an hour to the level of a very base savagery. All the religions of men, without exception, and however lofty the heights that they have since climbed, appear to have begun with much the same chaos of weird customs and of unreasonable delusions. Man's mental burdens have thus been, in all races, of very much the same sort, except, to be sure, that civilization, side by side with the good that it has created, has invented some new mental burdens, such as our increasing percentage of insanity in recent times illustrates.

The souls of men, then, if viewed apart from the influences of culture, if viewed as they were in primitive times, are by no means as easy to classify as the woolly-haired and the straight-haired races at first appear to be. If you study the thoughts of the various peoples, as the anthropologist Bastian has loved to mass them together in his chaotic and learned monographs, or as Fraser has surveyed some of them in his "Golden Bough," well, these primitive thoughts appear, in all their own chaos, and in all their vast varieties of detail, to be the outcome not of racial differences so much as of a few essentially human, although by no means always very lofty, motives. These fundamental motives appear, with almost monotonous regularity, in the superstitions, the customs, the legends, of all races. Esquimaux and Australians, negroes and Scotch Highlanders of former days, ancient Japanese and Hindoos, Polynesians and early Greeks,—all these appear side by side, in such comparative studies of the primitive mind of man, side by side as brothers in error and in ignorance, so soon as you proceed to study by the comparative method their early magic, their old beliefs, their early customs. Yet only by such a study could you hope to distinguish what really belongs to the mind of a race of men, as distinct from what belongs to culture.

If, then, it is the mind and the heart of man that you really want to know, you will find it hard, so soon as you leave civilization out of account, to tell what the precise meaning of the term "race of men" is, when that term is conceived as characterizing a distinct hereditary variety of human mental constitution. A race-psychology is still a science for the future to discover.

Perhaps, however, as you may say, I have not been just, in this very summary statement, to what, after all, may prove to be the best test of the true racial differences amongst the various types of the human mind. Some races, namely, have proved themselves to be *capable of civilization.* Other races have stubbornly refused civilization, or have remained helplessly degraded even when surrounded by civilization. Others still have perished at the first contact with civilization. The Germanic ancestors of the present western Europeans were barbarians, although of a high type. But when they met civilization, they first adopted, and then improved it. Not so was it with the Indians, with the Polynesians. Here, then, is the test of a true mental difference amongst races. Watch them when they meet civilization. Do they show themselves first teachable and then originative? Then they are mentally higher races. Do they stagnate or die out in the presence of civilization? Then they are of the lower types. Such differences, you will say, are deep and ineradicable, like the differences between the higher and the lower sorts of individual men. And such differences will enable us to define racial types of mind.

I fully agree that this test is an important one. Unfortunately, the test has never been so fairly applied by the civilized nations of men that it can give us any exact results. Again, the facts are too complex to be estimated with accuracy. Our Germanic ancestors accepted civilization when they met with it. Yes, but they met civilization under conditions peculiarly favorable to their own education. They had been more or less remotely influenced by its existence, centuries before they entered the field of history. When they entered this field, they met civilization first as formidable foes; they were long in contact with it without being themselves enslaved; and then later, in numerous cases, they met civilization as conquerors, who, in the course of their very efforts to conquer, found thus the opportunity and later something of the leisure to learn, and who had time to discover by centuries of hard experience, how great were the advantages the cultivation of the Roman empire had to offer them. But suppose that Cæsar in the first century B.C. had already had the opportunity to undertake the civilization of Germany by means of our own modern devices. Suppose that he had then possessed unlimited supplies of rum, of rifles, and of machine guns. Suppose in brief that, by the aid of such gentle arts as we now often use, he had very greatly abbreviated the period of probation and of schooling that was open to the German barbarians to learn the lessons that the cultivated peoples had to teach. Suppose that Roman syndicates had been ready to take possession, at once, of the partly depopulated lands of the north, and to keep the few surviving natives thenceforth in their place, by showing them how cultivated races can look down upon savage folk. Well, in that case, the further history of civilization might have gone on without the aid of the Germanic peoples. The latter would then have quickly proved their natural inferiority once for all. They would have furnished one instance more for the race-partisans to cite in order to show how incapable the lower races are of ascending from barbarism to civilization. Dead men not only tell no tales; they also, strange to say, attend no schools, and learn no lessons. And hereby they prove themselves in the eyes of certain students of race-questions to have been always of a much lower mental type than the cultivated men who killed them. Their surviving descendants, if sufficiently provided with the means of corruption, and if sufficiently down-trodden, may remain henceforth models of degradation. For man, whatever his race, is an animal that you unquestionably can debase to whatever level you please, if you only have power, and if you then begin early enough, and devote yourself persistently enough to the noble and civilized task of proving him to be debased.

I do not doubt, then, that some races are more teachable than others. But I do very much doubt our power to estimate how teachable a race is, or what can be made of them, or what hereditary mental powers they have until we have given them centuries of opportunity to be taught. Fortune and the defects of the Roman Empire gave to the Germanic peoples an extraordinary opportunity to learn. So the world found out how teachable they were. Let their descendants not boast unduly until they, too, have given to other races, not indeed the opportunities of conquerors, but some equal opportunity to show of what sort of manhood they are capable.

Yet, you may insist, civilization itself had an origin. Were not the races that first won civilized rank superior in mental type to those that never showed themselves capable of such originality? Well, I reply, we do not know as yet precisely where, and still less how, civilization originated. But this seems clear, viz.: first, that physical environment and the forms of social aggregation which this environment determined, had a very great share in making the beginnings of civilization possible; while, secondly, whatever part race-qualities played in early civilization, certainly no one race has the honor of beginning the process. Neither Chinese nor Egyptian, neither Caucasian nor Mongol, was the sole originator of civilization, The African of the tropical swamps and forests, the Australian of the desert, the Indian of our prairies, was sufficiently prevented by his physical envirnoment from being the originator of a great civilization. What each of these races would have done in another environment, we cannot tell. But the Indian of Central America, of Mexico, and of Peru, shows us that race alone did not predetermine how remote from the origination of a higher civilization a stock must needs remain. Chinese civilization, and, in recent times, Japanese civilization, have shown us that one need not be a Caucasian in order to originate a higher type of wisdom.

In brief, then there is hardly any one thing that our actual knowledge of the human mind enables us to assert, with any scientific exactness, regarding the permanent, the hereditary, the unchangeable mental characteristics which distinguish even the most widely sundered physical varieties of mankind. There is, to be sure, one exception to this rule, which is itself instructive. It is the case where we are dealing with physical and social degeneracy, the result of circumstances and of environment, and where such degeneracy has already gone so far that we have before us highly diseased human types, such as can no longer be reclaimed. But such types are not racial types. They are results of alcohol, of infection, or in some instances, of the long-continued pressure of physical environment. In such cases we can sometimes say, Here is a hopelessly degraded stock of men. But, then, civilization can create such stocks, out of any race of men, by means of a sufficient amount of oppression and of other causes of degradation, if continued through generations.

No race of men, then, can lay claim to a fixed and hereditary type of mental life such as we can now know with exactness to be unchangeable. We do not scientifically know what the true racial varieties of mental type really are. No doubt there are such varieties. The judgment day, or the science of the future, may demonstrate what they are. We are at present very ignorant regarding the whole matter.

VI

What, then, in the light of these considerations, is there which can be called fundamentally significant about our numerous modern race-problems? I answer, scientifically viewed, these problems of ours turn out to be not so much problems caused by anything which is essential to the existence or to the nature of the races of men themselves. Our so-called race-problems are merely the problems caused by our antipathies.

Now, the mental antipathies of men, like the fears of men, are very elemental, wide-spread, and momentous mental phenomena.

But they are also in their fundamental nature extremely capricious, and extremely suggestible mental phenomena. Let an individual man alone, and he will feel antipathies for certain other human beings very much as any young child does—namely, quite capriciously—just as he will also feel all sorts of capricious likings for people. But train a man first to give names to his antipathies, and then to regard the antipathies thus named as sacred merely because they have a name, and then you get the phenomena of racial hatred, of religious hatred, of class hatred, and so on indefinitely. Such trained hatreds are peculiarly pathetic and peculiarly deceitful, because they combine in such a subtle way the elemental vehemence of the hatred that a child may feel for a stranger, or a cat for a dog, with the appearance of dignity and solemnity and even of duty which a name gives. Such antipathies will always play their part in human history. But what we can do about them is to try not to be fooled by them, not to take them too seriously because of their mere name. We can remember that they are childish phenomena in our lives, phenomena on a level with a dread of snakes, or of mice; phenomena that we share with the cats and with the dogs, not noble phenomena, but caprices of our complex nature.

Upon the theoretical aspects of the problem which such antipathies present, psychology can already throw some light. Man, as a social being, needs and possesses a vast range of simply elemental tendencies to be socially sensitive when in the presence of other men. These elemental tendencies appear, more or less untrained, in the bashfulness of childhood, in the stage fright of the unskilled, in the emotional disturbances of young people who are finding their way in the world, in the surprises of early love, in the various sorts of anthropophobia which beset nervous patients, in the antipathies of country folk toward strangers, in the excitements of mobs, in countless other cases of social stress or of social novelty. Such sensitiveness may arise in advance of or apart from any individual experience which gives a conscious reason why one should feel thus. A common feature of all such experiences is the fact that one human being finds other human beings to be *portentous*, even when the socially sensitive being does not in the least know why they should be so. That such reactions have an instinctive basis is unquestionable. Their general use is that they prepare one, through interest in men, to be ready for social training, and to be submissively plastic. In milder forms, or upon the basis of agreeable social relations, such instinctive emotions easily come to be moulded into the most fascinating of human interests; and the social life is impossible without this basis of the elemental concerns which man feels merely because of the fact that other men are there in his world. If decidedly intense, however, such instinctively determined experiences are apt, like other intense disturbances, to be prevailingly painful. And since novelty, oddity, and lack of social training on the part of the subject concerned are motives which tend to make such social reflexes intense, a very great number of the cruder and more childish social reactions involve antipathies; for a social antipathy is merely a painful, and so, in general, an overintense, reflex disturbance in the presence of another human being. No light need be thrown, by the mere occurrence of such an antipathy, upon any permanently important social character of the hated object. The chance intensity of the passing experience may be alone significant. And any chance association may serve to secure, in a given case, the intensity of disturbance which makes the object hated. Oddities of feature or of complexion, slight physical variations from the customary, a strange dress, a scar, a too steady look, a limp, a loud or deep voice, any of these peculiarities, in a stranger, may be, to one child, or nervous subject, or other sensitive observer, an object of fascinated curiosity; to another, slightly less stable observer, an intense irritation, an object of terror, or of violent antipathy. The significant fact is that we are all instinctively more or less sensitive to such features, simply because we are by heredity doomed to be interested in all facts which may prove to be socially important. Whether we are fascinated, or horror-stricken, or angry, is, apart from training, largely a matter of the momentary subjective intensity of the disturbance.

But all such elemental social experiences are *ipso facto*, highly suggestible. Our social training largely consists in the elimination or in the intensification or in the systematizing of these original reactions through the influence of suggestion and of habit. Hence the antipathy, once by chance aroused, but then named, imitated, insisted upon, becomes to its victims a sort of sacred revelation of truth, sacred merely because it is felt, a revelation merely because it has won a name and a social standing.

What such sacred revelations, however, really mean, is proved by the fact that the hungry traveller, if deprived of his breakfast long enough, by means of an accidental delay of his train, or the tired camper in the forest, may readily come to feel whatever racial antipathy you please toward his own brother, if the latter then wounds social susceptibilities which the abnormal situation has made momentarily hyperæsthetic.

I have said little or nothing, in this paper, of human justice. I have spoken mainly of human illusions. We all have illusions, and hug them. Let us not sanctify them by the name of science.

For my part, then, I am a member of the human race, and this is a race which is, as a whole, considerably lower than the angels, so that the whole of it very badly needs race-elevation. In this need of my race I personally and very deeply share. And it is in this spirit only that I am able to approach our problem.

34

On Certain Limitations
of the Thoughtful Public
in America

No one who is engaged in any part of the work of the higher education in this country can doubt that, at the present time, our thoughtful public,—the great company of those who read, reflect, and aspire,—is a larger factor in our national life than ever before. When foreigners accuse us of extraordinary love for gain, and of practical materialism, they fail to see how largely we are a nation of idealists. Yet that we are such a nation is something constantly brought to the attention of those whose calling requires them to observe any of the tendencies prevalent in our recent intellectual life in America.

I

When I speak, in this way, of contemporary American idealists, I do not now specially refer to the holders of any philosophical opinions, or even to the representatives of any one type of religious faith. I here use the term in no technical sense. In this discussion, I mean by the word "idealist," a man or woman who is

An address first delivered at Vassar College. [Reprinted from *RQP*, pp. 111–65.]

consciously and predominantly guided, in the purposes and in the great choices of life, by large ideals, such as admit of no merely material embodiment, and such as contemplate no merely private and personal satisfaction as their goal. In this untechnical sense the Puritans were idealists. The signers of our Declaration of Independence were idealists. Idealism inspired us during our Civil War. Idealism has expressed itself in the rich differentiation of our national religious life. Idealism has founded our colleges and universities.

Well, using the term "idealism" in this confessedly untechnical sense, I say that many of our foreign judges have failed to see how largely we Americans are to-day a nation of idealists. To be sure, we are by no means alone amongst modern men in our idealism. But elsewhere sometimes the consequences of long-continued and oppressive militarism, sometimes the stress of certain social problems, and sometimes the burdens of ancient imperial responsibility, have tended more to discourage, or even quite to subdue, many forms of that fidelity to ideals upon which surely all higher civilization in any country depends. But, with us, ever since the close of the Civil War, numerous forces have been at work to render us as a nation more thoughtful, more aspiring, and more in love with the immaterial things of the spirit, and that too even at the very moment when our material prosperity, with all of its well-known corrupting temptations, has given us much opportunity, had we chosen to take it, to be what the mistaken foreign critics often suppose us to be,—a people really sunk in practical materialism.

Moreover, in saying all this, as to our general growth in spiritual interests, I am not at all unmindful of that other side,—that grosser material side of our national life, upon which our foreign critics so often insist. The growth of unwise luxury, the brute power of ill-used wealth, the unideal aspects of our political life, the evils of our great cities,—what enlightened American is there who does not recognize the magnitude of such ills in our midst? But you cannot prove the absence of light merely by exploring the darker chasms and caverns of our national existence. Vast as are those recesses of night, the light of large and inspiring ideas shines upon still vaster regions of our American life. Side by side with the excesses of mere luxury you find, amongst our people, a true and increasing, a self-sacrificing and intelligent love of the beautiful for its own sake. Side by side with the misuse of money, you observe the encouraging frequency of the great and humane deeds that wealth can do. Nor is this all. An ardent and often successful struggle for social reform, and a civic pride that aims, sometimes even from the very depths of municipal degradation, at the accomplishment of great and honorable public services,—these are tendencies that are growing amongst us, and that are never wholly or permanently checked even by the closest contact with the very worst of our national defects.

Yet, of course, the real proof of the prevalence of what I have called idealism, in the great masses of our people, is above all to be sought not in any particular good deeds of wealthy men, nor yet in the public life of the great cities, but in the intellectual and religious life of the community at large. And here it is, as I say, that the college teacher, or any other worker professionally concerned with the higher mental interests of our people, has a chance to estimate the strength and magnitude of these interests in the unseen.

In our country it is extraordinarily easy, and as one may at once admit it is too easy, to get a hearing for any seemingly new and large-minded doctrine relating either to social reform or to inspiring changes of creed. Whoever desires the reputation of the founder of a new sect has merely to insist upon his plan for reforming society and saving souls,—has merely to announce repeatedly to the public the high valuation that he sets upon his own ideas concerning nobler topics in order to win a respectful hearing from many, and, if his ideas have any measure of coherence and of humanitarian interest, an often all too kindly acquiescence from at least a few. And the faithfulness of these few may soon assume the pathetic intensity that so often marks the devotion of the followers of small sects. Need I mention many instances in order to remind you of the nature of these now so familiar processes in our American life? The late Mr. Henry George was, up to the time of the appearance of his "Progress and Poverty," a man quite unknown to the nation at large,—a California newspaper man, with no obvious authority to teach concerning economic problems. His book received, at the time of its appearance, little or no support from the professional economists, and excited at first, I believe, little very close attention from their side. George himself was no party manager. He used hardly any showy devices for attracting popular attention. He was simply in earnest. Yet we all know how the sect of his followers grew. And any busy man who has sometimes received letters from propagandists of that particular sect will also know, I suppose, how humane, how faithful, how strenuous, how unworldly, and one may add, how unweariedly obstinate they may be in their efforts to convert the doubter and to lead people to see, and if possible to love, their new way of social salvation. A similar, and even more swiftly contagious kindliness made possible the dramatic, if temporary, success of Mr. Bellamy's book, "Looking Backward." And again, a case in point is the movement in connection with which Bryan gained his first national prominence in 1896, a movement which came near proving successful, and which was then for a time so dangerous. That movement had its origin quite as much in practical idealism as in material distress. Its fundamental motives were in considerable measure philanthropic, humane, and, in an abstract way, vaguely large-minded. That was precisely what made this movement most dangerous. Unwise philanthropy, uninstructed large-mindedness, can often prove injurious to the very interests they seek to further. Our greatest national danger now lies in an extravagant love of ideally fascinating enterprises, whose practical results are as hard to foresee and to estimate as was the end that lay before the noble-hearted Childe Rolande of Browning's well-known poem, when he searched for the goal of his journey in the midst of the shifting landscapes, and the treacherous pathways of his romantic wilderness.

Well, these, I say, are instances of our American idealism in social matters. In religion, a similar tendency has been strong in our life from the very first. It has not only multiplied sects among us, but it has also wrought great good by giving lasting strength to their missionary and to their other philanthropic enterprises. Moreover it has endowed them with an importance for the daily life of the people that no established State church could ever have won by a merely external show of authority. The same interest in ideals has kept the sects themselves from stagnation, has insisted upon an adjustment of whatever in their fashions of teaching was non-essential to the vital needs of each generation of people. On the other hand, this idealism often shows itself less worthily in the form of a hasty desire for whatever seems new, or remote, or fantastic in faith. At the present day there is hardly a conceivable creed about ultimate matters, be it never so quaint or so unreasonable that, if its apparent intents are only humane, and its catch words impressive, this creed once earnestly taught cannot very quickly find a body of adherents, not only in our country at large, but in some of the most thoughtful and sophisticated communities which our country contains. It is not the ignorant amongst us who are the prey of strange new doctrines, so much as a portion of the most considerate classes of our public. And we are indeed not obliged to be bigoted in order to feel that, at present, this spiritual plasticity of our American public has gone too far. We ought to be docile; but the disposition to prove all things can easily outrun the power to hold fast that which is good.

As a consequence, if new sects thus easily find followers, and often faithful and permanent followers, there is also the other side of the picture. There are those of our people who waste life in merely floating from doctrine to doctrine. In such minds the art of holding fast has wholly been lost, in favor of the easier art of at least playing with all the things that belong in the realms of the spirit. For such souls, new doctrines are like new pictures, or new plays, or like the passing events of a social season. The more ardent amongst such people grow temporarily enthusiastic upon every new occasion where they listen to what they cannot comprehend. The more disillusioned find the novelties in doctrine more or less of a bore, just as some folk always find the plays and the parties tedious. But both the ardent and the disillusioned, in such social groups as I now have in mind, do indeed treat the new doctrines and the various rival plans of salvation altogether too much as they treat the social occasions, the plays, or the pictures. They expect something new to take the place of the old at each moment of their experience. And whether ardent or bored they continue their life-long quest for spiritual sensations.

Such excesses of the higher life in our country are only too easy to observe and, upon occasion, to ridicule. I have not mentioned them however for the sake of ridicule. Spinoza said that human affairs are neither to be wept over nor to be laughed at, but to be understood; and Spinoza's word, despite its seeming fatalism, had from any point of view its large measure of truth. I am speaking at present of symptoms. These symptoms, like other incidents of so complex a life as ours, have both their good and their evil aspects. Devotion to ideals has its dangers as it has its glories. I have to point out the one as an aid toward a comprehension of the other.

I turn to still other and better aspects of the tendency here in question. If one asks what the devotion to ideals has of late accomplished with purest success in the intellectual life of our country, I myself should be disposed to name, as one of the noblest, most positive, and most unsullied products of American idealism in recent years, the whole modern educational movement. The reform of academic methods and interests, both in the younger and in the older universities and colleges has been such, within the past twenty-five years, as to constitute one of the most substantial and significant events in our national history. The general public still understands all too little of the vast work that has been accomplished. By the fault of too large a portion of the newspaper press of the country the more trivial aspects of our academic life,—the public athletic contests, and the idle gossip of the hour,—are continually exaggerated, while the serious and the most progressive tendencies of this same life are as persistently slighted and are often misrepresented. Yet despite the false perspective in which our colleges are thus often made to appear, the general public has nevertheless somehow learned to support nobly the interests of academic reform. The vast sums that have been dedicated to the cause of learning, the cordial approval that our more enlightened people have given to the attempts at bettering higher education,— these have been most encouraging features of our educational movement. Nor has this movement confined itself to the Universities and Colleges. In its connection with the lower schools it is still in the period of storm and stress and hope. But it is indeed, in all its forms, a movement in the interest of ideals. It has needed at every step great sacrifices, strenuous devotion, wide sympathies, and far-reaching foresight. And these have been forthcoming. When an intelligent American wants to vindicate the honor of his country to foreigners, I know in our recent history of no purer instance of single-hearted patriotism, devoted to humane and unsullied ideals, and successful against all sorts of foes, not only without but within,—I know, I say, of no purer instance of such true patriotism than is furnished by just the great educational reform movement, and especially the academic movement of the last quarter of a century. For this has indeed been no mere effort of dreamers. It has been a practical movement. It has been guided by administrators who were often of the highest executive talent,—men quite capable, in many instances, of winning worldly success in wholly different and more showy regions of public life. It has been supported by benefactors who were often tempted by all sorts of more selfish interests to use their wealth otherwise. It has given to great numbers of youth a light and guidance that have meant for them escape from spiritual bondage, and an opportunity to become in their turn benefactors. It has furnished to our country a constantly increasing class of cultivated workers, ready to enter practical life with the ardor of a genuine idealism in their hearts and minds. And great as this academic movement has been, its influence is only beginning. Its real fruits are still to be gathered.

So far, then, I have surveyed a number of forms of recent American idealism. I have meant to be fair to both sides of the shield. Not all golden is our devotion to ideals. Yet this devotion is too marked a feature of our national spirit to justify the neglect of those among our foreign critics who regard us as mainly workers for wealth, or as lovers of mere material power. It may not be unfitting, upon this occasion, for us to ask ourselves what can yet be done to make our national idealism more intelligent, better organized, and, above all, more effective.

II

For, after all that we have thus far said, when we try to sum up the amount of influence exerted by these various forms of idealism upon the actual life of our country, we are obliged to confess that our thoughtful public is not yet as efficacious as it ought to be. Too frequently we find the lovers of the ideal engaged in unprofitable conflicts with their spiritual kindred. Plan wars with plan; reform stands in hostile array over against reform. Meanwhile the children of this world are wiser in their generation than the children of light. The people who dwell in the realms of thought and of higher faith consequently find themselves unable to organize effectively their reforms. They indeed associate, discourse, and take counsel together. But their enemies remain too often the better managers. While, as I just said, the academic movement is the great instance amongst us, in recent times, of the possible practical success of ideal interests, this educational progress stands too much alone. Our tree of life flourishes, and puts forth countless leaves; but it does not yet bear sufficient fruit for the healing of the nation. Our national idealism is more characteristic of our intellectual and religious life than it is productive of permanent, organized, and substantial results. Whenever the servants of ill perfect their devices for corrupting anywhere the state, and misusing its resources, the lovers of good things find themselves too frequently helpless to thwart such mischief. Yet amongst us the conscious servants of ill are really in a very decided minority. Our youth are exceptionally high-minded and aspiring. Our social life is full of admirable purposes. Our people are very generally interested in the things of the spirit. Yet the enemy seems to have possession of far too many of the effective weapons of social and of political warfare. When we try to meet him in the field, we are too scattered, too fantastic, or too uncertain in mind, to be ready for an effective fight. Our thoughtfulness involves too much idle curiosity, too much vaguely restless ardor, too much unwillingness to accept the necessary material limitations under which human work is to be done. And therefore we are indeed often, in practical undertakings, "beaten down" like Tennyson's Lancelot in his quest for the Grail, "beaten down by little men, mean knights." The enemy, the power of evil at work, in whatever form in our land,—the enemy at least always knows his own purpose. But we, we lovers of the ideal, spend far too much of our time vaguely wandering from one club-meeting or lecture or recent book to another, trying to discover just what it is that we are thinking about. While we, with eager minds, inquire into the shifting thing sometimes called the New Thought, the enemy is steadily engaged in serving the purposes of the Old Adam. And those purposes need no course of lectures to define them, no laborious clambering toward any "higher plane" to survey them. The devil within is always ready to explain them directly and personally to all comers. The consequence is precisely that appearance of grosser materialism which our foreign critics falsely take to be characteristic of our country. But much more characteristic of us is the intensity, the manifoldness, the restlessness, and in all but a few regions, the relative ineffectiveness of our national idealism.

Look where you will, even in the regions where ideas best and most beneficently express themselves in our social life, and you find the same limitations of our thoughtful public exemplified, setting bounds to our spiritual progress even in the best regions of our activity, and resulting in too many cases, in a more or less complete inability to do wholesome reforming work where work is most needed. In speaking thus, I have in mind no one section of our country, no one type of activity, no one special class of our thoughtful public. As myself a Californian, and as one often called upon to visit, in connection with professional duties, very various parts of our land, I have felt the limitations of which I speak in the West as well as in the East, amongst good men and women, in the life of the professional classes as well as in the life of the people of the world.

Wherever you go, you find the typical American sensitive to ideas, curious about doctrines, concerned for his soul's salvation, still more concerned for the higher welfare of his children, willing to hear about great topics, dissatisfied with merely material objects, seeking even wealth rather with a view to its more ideal uses than with a mere desire for its sensuous gratifications, disposed to plan great things for his country and for his community, proud of both, jealous of their honor, and discontented with the life that now is. His piety has its ideal fervor none the less when it is the piety of the free thinker than when it is that of the faithful. He forms and supports great associations for public-spirited ends. He encourages science and learning. He pauses in the midst of the rush of business to discuss religion, or education, or psychical research, or mental healing, or socialism. His well-known and characteristic devotion to his children keeps fresh in his heart a childlike love of plans and hopes and beliefs that belong not so much to the marketplace, as to the far-off future, and to the home land of the Platonic ideas.

Yet this same American is unable to give his idealism any adequate expression in his social life. His country towns and his manufacturing cities are too often full of hideous ugliness. Even the best of his great cities are in appearance whatever they happen to be. In founding new cities and in occupying new lands he first devotes himself to burning the forests, to levelling with ruthless eagerness the hill-slopes, to inflicting upon the land, whatever its topography, the unvarying plan of his system of straight streets and of rectangular street crossings. In brief, he begins his new settlements by a feverish endeavor to ruin the landscape. Now all this he does not at all because he is a mere materialist but (as a colleague of mine, Professor George Palmer, has pointed out), he does this because mere nature is, as such, vaguely unsatisfactory to his soul, because what is merely found must never content us, and because our present life itself is felt to be not yet ideal. Hence, the first desire is to change, to disturb, to bring the new with us.

In the regions thus so quickly altered by man's hand, a community spirit, a strong local pride, quickly springs up. The church, the school, the university, appear within a very few years, and seem at first as if they were quite at home. One is firmly determined, in each young community, that they shall all be the best of their kind anywhere to be found. The social order thus established has also its representative literature,—its poets, its artists, its public heroes, even its swiftly acquired local traditions, as well as its self-conscious social independence, somewhat too ardently and tremulously asserted, of the mere wornout ideals and authority of the older regions of the country.

Nor are the interests in ideal things confined to such expressions. Confident faith in the future and in the might of the new life asserts itself in such newer regions of our land in the overhasty construction of great railways, that pierce the mountains or invade the deserts, long before a less restlessly ideal people would have seen sufficient prospect of any adequate return for the material outlay. Our pioneer makers of railways have often seemed as if they were themselves amongst the prophets, the poets, or even the fanatics of our newer communities. But the result of this eagerness is too often a swift bankruptcy. The young community flies too near the sun, and then lies prostrate and wingless in the despair of hard times.

Hereupon begins the grosser period. The community soon really possesses through mere accumulation more wealth and power; yet merciless money-getters have profited by the failures of the first period, and these now take possession of the creations of the pioneers, crush out weaker opponents, obtain too much influence in local politics, and give to the life of the community just that outward seeming of mere materialism of which we have spoken. And now the better men learn more thoughtfully to look about them, only to observe, at this stage, what vast opportunities have been lost, what noble natural beauties have been hopelessly defaced, what ideal kingdoms have been carelessly created only to be conquered by the enemy.

The real struggle with evil herewith begins. The social order, so hastily and easily organized at the outset, through the finely ideal political instincts of our people, now becomes infected by various political diseases. Corruption grows too prominent in politics. The Philistines seem to have captured and blinded the Sampson whose deeds made the pioneer days so wonderful. Satan seems to have triumphed.

Yet this triumph is never so real as it seems. The good are still in the majority. The heart of society is still healthy. The church, the school, the university, the public library, the literary circles, the intellectual clubs,—these not only remain, but multiply, and in these one finds centres for the propagation of ideal interests. Would-be reformers become numerous. But alas, they war among themselves. They are too often crude, strident, prejudiced. Greed too often wins possession of the strongest material forces of the community. The reformers lift their too familiar voices in vain. The prophets true and false speak their many words. Many listen and applaud. Yet at the elections the prophets do not win. The thoughtful public remains the most characteristic, but too often the least effective, portion of the community.

Such is the tale of too many of our newer communities. Shall I speak still of the older communities? There indeed the processes are more complex; but the lesson, like the outcome, is too often the same. The great limitation of our thoughtful public in America remains its inability to take sufficient control of affairs. And in pointing out this limitation, I have already indicated, in a measure, both its causes and the directions in which we ought to look for a cure, if a cure is possible, for this ineffectiveness of our American idealism. Let me pass then to a closer study of this latter aspect of the case. I have not undertaken this discussion for the sake of merely criticising my brethren; but for the sake of suggesting some few ways of improving our state, in so far as any poor suggestions of mine can hope to possess value.

III

Yet, as I go on to this side of our topic, I must indeed admit quite freely that I have no panacea, no quack remedy to suggest, as any infallible cure for the ineffectiveness of our national idealism, or as any one saving device for overcoming the limitations of our thoughtful public. Such ills as the one here in question always lie deep in the very constitution of our temperaments. We cannot, by merely taking thought, add a cubit to our stature. One of the very limitations of our thoughtful public which are here under discussion lies in the fact that many of us suppose great reforms to be possible merely through good resolutions. Yet good resolutions have their place in accomplishing reforms. Our mere human consciousness never by itself transforms our temperaments; but it may do something toward lessening their ill effects, and toward intensifying or enlarging the range of their good qualities. Where limitations have to be overcome, a due measure of consciousness as to where the fault lies does not come amiss. Accordingly, with a full sense of the little that I can do by such mere practical advice as lies within my scope, I still wish not merely to point out the ailment, but to show how it may be attacked. That it is no hopeless ailment, such successes of our idealism as the modern educational movement have already shown us. May we not hope to escape in time and at last, in a measure from the ineffectiveness that now besets the efforts of the thoughtful people of our country?

Reform, in such matters, must come, if at all, from within. The kingdom of heaven is within you; and that truth is precisely what all ideally minded people know. It is this knowledge which makes them lovers of the unseen. I cannot then offer any pedagogical device for raising the thoughtful public of our country to a higher level of effectiveness, unless my device appeals directly to the individual. The public as a whole is whatever the processes that occur, for good or evil, in individual minds, may determine. No one of us is individually called upon for any very large share in determining other peoples' lives. The work of any one man, in this life, has a narrow range. Yet, on the other hand, the forest is made of the trees; and great reforms are due to the combined action of numerous individuals.

I appeal then to the individual lover of ideals. I say, upon such as you are, and upon such as you aspire to be, the future of our country depends. If you fail, in union with your spiritual kind, to win, and to win for good, the controlling voice in the nation's affairs, corruption, grossness, despotism, social ruin, will sooner or later make naught of our liberties, of all the dear memory of our country's fathers, and of the great work that we in America ought to do for mankind. And if such as you are find not the way to overcome, in time, these present limitations of the effectiveness of our thoughtful public, you will fail to win and to retain control of the constantly increasing complications of our national life. Our ideals will grow vaguer and more restless, even while our material activities become more steadily enchained by the powers of evil. We shall end where others have ended, in national disaster, in social dissolution, in humiliation, in the clutches of some domestic or foreign conqueror.

But in case you win effective control over your personal ideals and over your own processes of giving them expression, you yourself as an individual will indeed accomplish but an infinitesimal portion of the nation's vast task. Yet still it will be the nation's task in which, in your measure, you will be engaged. For no man liveth unto himself, and no man dieth unto himself. I appeal then to you, and to the public, only through such as you are. If you, together with the others who love the coming of the kingdom of heaven, succeed in solving your personal problems, the good cause will win in public as in private. And what you need to find is some little task that you can effectually do. That task you need to perform.

To the individual, then, I address myself. Nor do I forget that I am speaking to students who already know what one means by high ideals, and by hearty aspirations, and who stand at the beginning of life's great tasks. There comes a sad time in many lives, when people who have long struggled in vain with foes without and foes within, grow weary of the cultivation of ideal interests. Those to whom I am especially privileged to speak, upon this occasion, have not reached this stage. I hope that when any of you reach it, you will pass it successfully, for nothing better have we in this life than our ideals and our hopes, and our power to do a little work. Just now you are privileged to have a faith, still unsullied, in such ideals, and a hope to do good work. I want to indicate some of the ways in which one may wisely nourish this faith, and undertake this work.

IV

My first word of advice, addressed thus especially to the thoughtful amongst us, relates to a certain moderation, to a certain temperance, that, as I believe, we must all cultivate in dealing with our own consciousness of what our ideals are. Devotion to what we believe to be a high cause demands of us, indeed, a certain thoroughness of surrender, a certain persistence in service, which, in its own due time and place, ought to know indeed no bounds. On the other hand, when thoughtful people cultivate ideals, they do so, in part, by thinking over these ideals, by reasoning about them, by becoming conscious of what they are, by trying to convert others to these ideals, and, in general, by giving these ideals articulate expression. The faithfulness of the unlearned may be dumb, half-conscious, incapable of giving any reason for itself. The fidelity of the thoughtful seeks definite formulation in a creed, propagates its cause by spoken and by written words, voices itself in a doctrine that can be defended or assailed by argument,—in brief, seeks to add knowledge to faith, insight to service, and teaching to example. You often hear how important it is to be not only devoted, but wise, clear of head as well as persistent in service. Now such tendencies are an important factor in the lives of all thoughtful people. Their highest expression is a reasoned philosophy, which undertakes to investigate, to compare, to harmonize, and then, finally, to formulate and to teach systems of ideals. Now I am myself by calling a teacher of philosophy. I believe in persistent thoughtfulness as a most important factor in the higher life of humanity. I try to become as conscious as I properly can become of what my ideals are, and of why I hold them, and of how they go together to make one whole, and of why other lovers of reason ought, if I am right, to accept my ideals. Over against the inconsiderate partisans of this or of that form of unreasoning faith, I often have, as teacher of philosophy, to maintain the importance, for certain great purposes, of giving a reason for the faith that is in us. And so, as you see, I am in every way disposed to favor, in its place, not only the thoughtful spirit of inquiry, but the disposition to formulate ideals in a definite and conscious way, to maintain them through argument, and to propagate them by the spoken and by the written word. I believe in the human reason, as a vastly important factor in the development of all our ideals.

And yet,—I can here speak all the more frankly just because my profession is that of the reasoner,—I constantly see mischief done by an unwise exaggeration of the tendency to reason, to argue, to trust to mere formulas, to seek for the all-solving word; in brief, to bring to consciousness what for a given individual ought to remain unconscious. Thoughtfulness is, for us in this life, like any other human power and privilege. It must be exercised with a proper moderation. Thought must indeed be free. But freedom means responsibility. Thought in any individual, must freely set limits to its own finite task. And when the thoughtful lovers of ideals forget this fact, they may become mere wranglers, or doctrinaires, or pedants, or, on the other hand, in the end, through failure in thinking, they may become cynics. Now some may wonder that, as a teacher of philosophy, I should at once lay the first stress upon this defect of the lovers of ideals, as a defect so often attendant upon the processes of unhappy thinkers. Some may wonder that I first confess the errors of my own calling. Yet why should I not do so? What defects has one more occasion to observe than those which occur in the erring human effort to pursue his own calling? If one loves his calling and believes in it, does he therefore ignore these defects? Shall one make a business of the art of seeing clearly, and yet entirely ignore the imperfections that may naturally beset his own organ of vision?

Very well then, I first observe that many thoughtful lovers of ideals, many students, many reformers, many teachers, are too much disposed to trust to constant argument, reasoning, or reflection, to keep them faithful to their own ideals, and to win others to these ideals. Or again, some lovers of the ideal, even when they profess not to argue, but to be followers of intuition, still in many cases are too fond of abstract formulas, of catch words or phrases. Such mistake fads for eternal truths. Now all such have not observed the inevitable limitations of the human thinking process in each individual mind. They do not observe that any one of us can think clearly and reflectively and can formulate exactly and successfully only in case we think with due moderation, and think during the time properly set apart for thought, trying to formulate only what we have more or less expert right to understand, and then devoting the rest of life to naïveté and to relatively unreflective action. As a professional reasoner, I have a profound contempt for deliberate excesses in the work of reasoning; I personally try to avoid such excesses. As one busy with formulating theories, I have a great hatred for the excessive use of formulas.

I remember well, from my student days, a pathetic incident that may illustrate the spirit in which I make this confession. While

I was studying philosophy, one winter at Leipzig, I enjoyed many happy hours in company with a musical friend of mine, an advanced student at the Conservatory, who had devoted himself since childhood to the violin, and who has since won an important place in his profession. He often took me to attend the musical evenings at the Conservatory, and so helped me, as a mere listener, to enter the wondrous world of tones where he was making his home. But alas! for the moment, my friend, although so faithful and advanced a student of music, was himself no public performer at the Conservatory evenings, although in previous years he had been a prominent and favorite student player. Overwork had given him, for the time, one of those well-known functional nervous troubles of coördination, or "occupation disorders"; namely, in his case, a "violinist's arm." Neuralgic pains whenever he played had forced him to suspend his efforts. Prolonged rest for his arm was needed. My friend was perforce spending this year in the study of musical theory, and in other more general intellectual tasks relating to his art. Naturally this forced restraint was hard, and wounded ambition would often express itself; but still my friend was a man of general mental skill, who had therefore not a few resources in his distress. One evening we were together at the Conservatory. Many students played. Among them my friend's principal contemporary and rival, a young violinist of no small skill, won abounding applause by a very brilliant performance. And my friend, sitting beside me with wounded wing, must merely listen! It would have been more than human not to rebel a little. But my friend could at least remember that he himself had his own variety of mental occupations. He did remember this fact, yet he grieved inwardly and deeply. As we were walking home he was silent for a time, and then his wrath at the chains that bound him burst forth. We spoke of the rival. We could not avoid the topic. "Confound that fellow!" said my friend. "Confound that fellow; he can't do anything *but* fiddle!"

Well, I speak somewhat in my friend's general spirit, although I hope without any bitterness toward any particular rival student when I now say: "I am indeed not nearly as much of a reasoner as I desire to be. My skill in this art is far below my ambition. But, poor as I am, reasoning is indeed my own art. I love it. I prize it. I cultivate it. It is a great part of my life. And yet,—and yet I still insist,—let that reasoner, that thoughtful lover of ideals, that philosopher, if such there be, let him be confounded who cannot do anything *but* reason." And in the same way I say to you of the thoughtful public: Woe unto the man or woman who can do nothing but be thoughtful.

Yet why do I thus warn you? Pedantry, it will be said, is a disease of professors and of bookish men. The young, the ardent, and the general company of the faithful to ideals in our land, whatever their faults, are surely not pedants. An overcultivation of the merely abstract reason is not a besetting sin of most people. I reply that there are many forms of pedantry; there are many grounds for being on one's guard against it. The misuse of the reasoning process enters the life of the thoughtful in more ways than one. The love of abstract formulas, of mere phrases, or of falsely simplified thoughtful processes is not confined to the professors.

I remember once discussing with a young lady who was a college student of psychology, some points in the text-book of my honored colleague Professor William James. We spoke in particular of his wonderful chapter on Habit, so full, as some of you may know, not only of theoretical wisdom, but of wholesome practical advice about the formation and control of habits. I asked my young friend what she thought of this chapter. She replied, with adorable naïveté, that she had found this chapter full of advice which must be very valuable indeed "for the young men for whom it was intended." Well, my young friend had certainly observed part of the significance of Professor James's chapter; but she did not admit having observed that his comments upon Habit apply to us all, whether young men or not. And now, just so, I should be sorry to have my word about the misuse of reason and the false love of abstract formulas supposed to apply only to those philosophers, if such there be, for whom it was indeed also intended. The lesson is general, and human. Especially does it apply to all the thoughtful public of America.

For this fault of a too abstract thoughtfulness is committed, in substance, whenever people try to reform all the world, or even any great region of our complex lives, by insisting upon any one set of phrases, of human conceptions and words, which the individual himself has found somehow dear to his own consciousness. Not merely the partisans of technical reasoning, but the apostles of intuition, too, can commit our fault, whenever they trust in any mere abstraction. The people of one idea, the people to whom this or that single device for saving souls is alone important, the followers of fads,—these fall prey to this form of error. They mistake the power to define for the power to accomplish, the abstraction for the life, the single thought for all the wealth of truth that our human world contains, the exercise of an individual reason for the whole task of reforming our nature. And does not our modern America, both in the East and in the West, really suffer too much, nowadays, from mere fads? What shall I do to be saved? says the inquirer,—and the answer is,—"Practice this or that system of mind cure, whose teaching can be made clear in just so many lessons. Follow Delsarte, study your attitudes, or oratory, or some other formal accomplishment. Accept this or that doctrine of the New Thought." Now the people who cultivate ideals in this spirit often suppose themselves to be free from the philosopher's overwrought love of the reason. "We follow," they say, "spiritual intuitions. We thus avoid abstractions and wrangling." "Yes," one may reply, "but you none the less are anxious for some all-embracing formula, some one saving principle that shall do all manner of work." Now the human mind, in its present form of consciousness, is simply incapable of formulating all its practical devices under any one simple rule. We have to learn both to work and to wait. We have to learn to obey as well as to formulate. What saves the world can never be any one man's formulated scheme. Restless search for the immediate presence of the ideal is often vain, like the pioneer idealism that burns the forests merely to see what they hide. Let the forests grow. They are better than the empty hillsides. Much of the best in human nature simply escapes our present definitions, is known only by its fruits, and prospers best in the forest shade of unconsciousness. But a thoughtful lover of ideals, whether a philosopher or not, is of course thinking of something that he *can* formulate,—is trying to make his ideas conscious, explicit, teachable, and so abstract. Hence so much of his life's business as he best formulates is likely for that very reason to be narrow when compared with his whole human task and with his own best and deepest aims. We are primarily creatures of instinct; and instinct is not merely the part of us that allies us with the lower animals. The highest in us is also based upon instinct. And only a portion of your instincts can ever be formulated. You will be able in this life to tell what they mean in only a few instances. But your life's best work will depend upon all of your good instincts together. Hence a great part of your life's work will never become a matter of your own personal and private consciousness at all. It is one of the duties then of the thoughtful lover of ideals to know that he cannot turn into conscious thinking processes all of his ideal activities. Accordingly, he must indeed cultivate a wise naïveté, and that alongside of his reflective processes. That is why the companionship of children becomes the more useful to us the more thoughtful we are. They show us the beauty of unconsciousness, and help us to compensate for our tendency to abstraction by reminding us of what it is to live straightforwardly.

And now, I say, this rule of mine applies to the very lover of ideals whom I now chance to be addressing. We who teach philosophy are constantly receiving inquires from people who seem not to know how little in human life can as yet be reduced to any abstractly stateable formulas at all. Teachers inquire as to the final and correct theory of the development of the human mind, as to the precise number of powers that the mind possesses, or as to the one secret of method in education. Newspapers or magazines call for popular discussions of the most serious and complex issues, as if these could finally be dealt with in any brief shape. A newspaper once asked me to contribute to a so-called symposium whose problem was to be this: What characteristics will the ideal man of the future possess? As I only knew about the ideal future man this, that when he comes, he will, as in him lies, adequately attend to his own business, I felt unable to contribute anything original to the proposed discussion. The first condition of knowing how to think about ideal subjects consists in being aware not only what can be profitably formulated at all, but when and for what purpose a given formulation is profitable. When I visit a convalescent friend who is beginning to feel joyous after a long illness, I do not in general discuss the problem of evil. When I too am to enjoy the company of my friend, I do not first undertake to inquire into the metaphysical problem as to whether my friend exists at all. And yet just such problems have their place in philosophy. Now just so, when I vote, since, as it chances, I am no expert in sociology or in economic problems, I generally have no really very good reason that I can formulate, in a conscious and philosophical way, why I vote just as I do. I vote largely on grounds of sympathy and of instinct. I know better than to try to do otherwise. If I tried to formulate a political theory, it would be a very poor one; for I have no scientific comprehension of politics, no philosophy adequate to directing my choice of parties. For my business is largely with other branches of philosophy. I am a member of one or two deliberative bodies, where I often hear lengthy debates upon complex practical questions. The debates for a time instruct me; but later they often weary me, if they continue, without instructing me. When people ask me my reason for my own vote in such complex practical cases, or wonder why I am anxious for a vote to be reached, I often say that just because my profession is reasoning, I have learned to know some of the limits of the art, and to recognize that about some complex practical issues, after a certain point, it is vain to reason further, since only personal reactions, incapable of adequate reflective formulation, will decide. Hence I grow weary of the much speaking. I know that at such times I seem unreasonable; but I merely want to vote; and more formulations will in such cases make me no wiser.

People often say that men act upon conscious reasoning processes, and women upon intuitions which they refuse to formulate. The assertion is, like most proverbial assertions, inadequate to the wealth of life's facts. Certainly women often enough act with a mysterious swiftness of unconscious wisdom. But so do many of the most effective men. I have, however, often observed that some educated women, some women who enter public life as reformers, and perhaps too many college-bred women, are nowadays troubled with an overfondness both for mere formulas and for abstract arguments about complex practical issues that only a happy instinctive choice and wholesome sentiment can ever successfully decide so long as we remain what we are; namely, frail and ignorant human beings, who see through a glass darkly. The fault of being overfond of abstractions, or of trying to formulate bad reasons for one's instinctive actions, does not characterize the man of business or the successful executive. One does not meet this fault in the market-place. But just this fault does characterize some of our most cultivated and thoughtful people in this country. And among these people I find a good many intellectual women.

What then is the happy medium? Shall I cease to think? No, not so. Be thoughtful, reason out some of your ideals for yourself. Know something, and know that something well. Have the region where you have a right to mistrust your instincts, to be keenly and mercilessly critical, to question, to doubt, and to formulate, and then devotedly to maintain and to teach. But let that region be the little clearing in your life's forest,—the place where you see, and comprehend, and are at home. Let there be such a place. You need it. It may be art, or theology, or Greek, or administrative work, or politics, or philosophy, or domestic economy, or general business, wherein you find this your chosen intellectual dwelling. In that region be indeed the creature of hard-won insight, of clear consciousness, of definite thinking about what it is yours to know. There the formula is in order. There the ideal is won by your investigations, and defended by your arguments. I say, have such a region. We need those who know. In that region, believe only when you know why you believe. But remember, life is vast, and your little clearing is very small. In the rest of life, cultivate näiveté, accept authority, dread fads, follow as faithfully as your instinct permits other lovers of the ideal who are here wiser than you, and be sure that though your head splits you will never think out all your problems, or formulate all your ideals so long as you are in this life. If this precept were followed in this country there would be more experts, and fewer popular crazes, more effective work done, and less time wasted in hopeless efforts at general reforms. *De te fabula*, I say to every studious soul who is disposed to be too thoughtful rather than wisely effective. Be in your devotion to effective leaders relatively uncritical in many things, in order to be thoughtfully knowing in some. Be childlike in much of life in order to become maturely wise in some things.

V

If you are once aware of the vanity of trying to formulate everything, and to argue about all sorts of problems, you will not be tempted to pursue unwisely mere novelties of formulation for their own sake. I have spoken more than once of the feverish desire for new ideas in which our thoughtful public wastes much time. An entirely false interpretation of the doctrine of evolution has led some people to imagine that in any department of our lives, novelty as such must mean true progress toward the goal. Hence you constantly hear of the New Education, the New Psychology, the New Thought, the New Humanity, and whatever else can be adorned by the mere prefixing of this adjective. And yet people do not speak adoringly of the New Blizzard, or of the New Weather in general. We all of us have a fondness, not altogether wise, for the so-called news of the day, quite apart from its meaning; and the newspapers daily verify for us the ancient fact that bad men lie and steal and murder. Such news, which alas is no news, but the ancient sorrow of our race, we do indeed greet with a certain keenness of interest which is neither altogether rational nor highly ideal. But still the lovers of the ideal do not in such cases suppose that some new form of burglary must, because of the fatal law of evolution, be higher in nature, or nobler, or more worthy of study than the older arts of the thieves. So nobody preaches in praise of the New Burglary. Nor do we suppose that evolution implies, as any universal law, that the New Blizzard, when it comes, is an object worthy of admiration above all former caprices of our climate. We know that if news, in this sense, is indeed interesting, still the weather is the weather, and the thieves break through and steal, and that no news makes more ideal these ancient aspects of the visible world. Now much that is proposed as new in thought, or in the less exact sciences, or in complex arts such as education, has indeed its importance as embodying real progress. When we know that to be the case, we welcome the new, not because it is merely new, but because it is a substantial addition to what is already known to be a good. But, on the other hand, much that is novel in opinion is novel only as the latest change of the weather is new. And I warn you, not indeed blindly to condemn, but cautiously to suspect doctrines that are obliged to advertise, very ostentatiously, the supposed fact that they are new, in order to get a public hearing. In really progressive sciences, as for instance in psychology itself, the most important advances need not be thus loudly heralded. They make their own way, not because they are merely new, but because they are maturely conceived and carefully worked out. As for the world of faith, it is as vain to be a mere seeker of novelties as it is to be a mere conservative. In our deeper faiths the newest and the oldest of humanity's deeds, interests, and experiences lie side by side. What is new for one soul is not new for another. Love and death and our duty, these are the oldest and the newest things in human destiny. The new love is not on that account the true one. The new coming of death teaches still the ancient lessons of the burial psalm.

The new duty is no duty unless it is an example of the most venerable of truths. "These things" says Antigone, "are not of to-day or of yesterday, and no man knows whence they came." As a fact, what you and I really most need and desire is not the new, nor yet the old. It is the eternal. The genuine lover of truth is neither a conservative nor a radical. He is beyond that essentially trivial opposition. He cares nothing for the time in which these things came to pass. For him their interest lies in their truth. Time is but an image, an imitation of the eternal. Evolution itself is only a fashion in which the everlasting appears. For God there is nothing new. Before the mountains were brought forth, or ever thou hadst founded the earth, from everlasting thou art God.

Be docile then; be ready to learn what is new to you. But avoid this disease of merely running after every thought that loudly proclaims, or every plan that stridently asserts, "Behold, I am new." Say to every such claimant for your reverence: "Are you such that you can grow old and still remain as good as ever? Then indeed I will trust you."

But is there nothing, then, in the idea of progress? Are there not certainly progressive moments, whose new stages will therefore be good? Yes. The actual discoveries of empirical science, once submitted to careful test, do indeed form a progressive series. Here the new, once assured by critical verification, is good. But the existence in any particular field of inquiry or of action of a progress that you and I can regard as certain, is never something to be merely presumed. The presumption is valid only after due examination. Only the expert can decide then, with clearness, whether the new is good. This holds in finance and in business as genuinely as in politics or in religion. Therefore it is only, once more, within the relatively narrow range of your expertness, that you can judge whether the new really is, as such, likely to be the good. Outside of that range, favor no novelties unless they appeal to your personal sentiments, to your most humane sympathies, to your best cultivated, but still in general partly unconscious, tastes and instincts. In brief, then, I say to our thoughtful public, overcome your limitations, first by minute and faithful study of a few things and by clearness of ideas about them; then by child-like simplicity in the rest of life, by faithfulness to enlightened leaders, by resignation as opposed to restlessness, and above all by work rather than by idle curiosity. Organize through a willingness to recognize that we must often differ in insight, but that what we need is to *do* something together. Avoid this restless longing for mere novelty. Learn to wait, to believe in more than you see, and to love not what is old or new, but what is eternal.

35

The Possibility of
International Insurance

Near the beginning of the present war I wrote a little book entitled "War and Insurance," in which I stated and defended the thesis that the cause of the world's peace would be aided if in future the principle of insurance were gradually and progressively introduced into international business.

Insurance has already proved to be, in the modern life of individual nations, a cause of no little growth in social organization, in human solidarity, in reasonableness, and in peace. The best workings of the insurance principle have been, on the whole, its indirect workings. It has not only taught men, in manifold ways, both the best means and the wisdom of "bearing one another's burdens"; but it has also established many indirect, and for that very reason all the more potent, types of social linkage, which the individual policy-holder or underwriter very seldom clearly and consciously estimates at their true value.

These indirect and less frequently noticed types of linkage have already transformed our civilization, so that ours is already an age and a civilization of insurance. Thus the greatest service of insurance has been done, so to speak, beneath the surface of our social life; and the most significant changes of our modern world through the indirect influence of insurance have grown up as if in the dark,

[Reprinted from *HGC*, pp. 71-92.]

becoming manifest only after they have been long developing their effectiveness. This fact furnishes a reason for looking forward most hopefully to great and good indirect results when once insurance assumes a definite international form.

Thus, for instance, one of the most significant indirect results of the development of fire insurance in the social life of our own nation has been the fact that fire insurance has made possible, and has systematized, a method of business whereby great numbers of people who would otherwise have no way of acquiring homes of their own, are now able, through thrift and patience, to become in time the owners of dwelling houses.

The method of business in question consists simply in this, that the home-seeker at the outset induces some one to advance the money whereby the house can be built, while the man for whom the new house is built makes the one who has advanced this money not only his mortgagee, but also the holder of an insurance policy whereby the advance made on the new house is rendered secure. Without fire insurance this security, in great numbers of cases, could not be furnished.

In analogous ways, fidelity insurance, working in more or less indirect fashion, enables countless young men to begin life in positions of trust, and thus to find their places as people worthy of confidence in a world where they might otherwise be doomed to live only as temporary employees.

Life insurance may be used by the otherwise needy man to capitalize his own future, and thus to win his way through a period of struggle. And in all such cases social linkages are formed which depend upon the use of insurance and which tend to bind men in far-reaching unions such as without insurance would be impossible. Such social linkages are peace breeding, and are profoundly civilizing.

It is therefore not merely the "mutual" aspect of insurance wherein its most beneficent influence is manifested. Its greatest social power depends upon the fact that a man does not in general purchase an insurance policy merely for the transient creature of to-day called "himself." A man purchases insurance for his "beneficiary." His beneficiaries may include people or corporations of whose very existence he, the individual, is little aware. But his linkages with such beneficiaries may join him to the whole social order.

It is because the men of to-day are thus united through insurance in groups of greater complexity, stability, and value than any other sort of business or institution makes possible that we owe as much as we do to the indirect influences which the relations of insurers, adventurers, and beneficiaries make possible and effective.

Were any group of nations to begin in a businesslike and practicable way to do what the individual fellow members of a social order have now the means of doing, namely to insure against risks of some insurable sort, we should have a good reason to expect that analogous and beneficent indirect workings would ere long follow from even a modest beginning in the art of international insurance.

The vast and unexpected transformations which, as the experience of the nineteenth century showed, insurance has introduced into the social order of individual peoples are of a type so much needed in the mutual relations of various nations that no opportunity should be neglected to make such a beginning in this new art of international insurance.

And since the present war seemed to me, and still seems, to furnish a great, although so tragic an opportunity to make such a beginning, I could not forego the chance which the moment offered to indicate, as I tried to do in my book, the general nature of this opportunity as I then saw it. First sketches of novel plans are very generally crude. The details of my own first statement of a mode of beginning international insurance were, as I myself said, wholly tentative, and were meant to be subject to a thorough revision. For such revision there has still been no sufficient time. But I already see aspects of the subject which need, as I believe, some recognition.

And I still believe that if insurance "of the nations, for the nations, and by the nations" once appeared in a practicable form, it would thenceforward not "vanish from the earth," but would tend, more than any international influence has yet tended, to "make the community of mankind visible," and so to further, gradually, perhaps slowly, but powerfully, the cause of peace.

Among the critics of my book there are, (despite all the objections to my plan which have been urged, and despite all the difficulties that lie in the way of introducing into international relations the principle of insurance,) some friendly counselors, who have said: "If we could but see, or devise, some definite procedure whereby a beginning could be made in the insurance of any risks that are common to several nations, then, were this procedure such as, if proposed and undertaken, would involve a feasible and practicable business of international insurance, however modest this beginning, we should be even now quite willing to look with favor upon the discussion of the enterprise."

In fact, for such critics, it is precisely the way of beginning international insurance, on however limited a scale, that they most want to have explained. It is for such readers and critics of my plan that the present article is written.

Since the present war began, I have met with a good many expressions which have come from authoritative sources, and which have related to the ways in which so destructive and widespread a conflict, especially if it continues long, is likely to affect the future conduct of the various forms of insurance which already exist. Said, in effect, in a letter to me, a man prominent in his own part of the insurance world: "By its very nature war tends to impair, and in the long run to destroy, all sorts of interests which, apart from war, have constituted or have determined insurable risks."

Such comments seem to be obvious enough. They are just now, as I believe, frequent. But they so far leave unanswered the question: "What shall be done, or can be done, to protect, after the close of this war, those vast common interests which the insurance organizations now have in charge, but which wars, and, above all, great wars, tend plainly and dangerously to assail?" It is precisely this question to which my present discussion offers at least a partial answer.

The experts in each special branch of insurance must discover for themselves and must define in their own way the relations which war in general, and this war in particular, may be expected to have to the interests which they represent. But there is one type of problems, common to a number of distinct forms of insurance, to which I may next direct attention.

The problems to which I refer are those presented by the sort of insurance business which is called reinsurance. These problems are certain to be very considerably affected by the results of the present war. Some of them are already much affected. This, as I learn, upon inquiry from experts, is especially the case in some regions of the fire insurance field. But problems of reinsurance also play their part in life insurance and in marine insurance.

And at or after the close of the present war, large alterations and readjustments will be needed to adapt the future conduct of reinsurance to the new conditions that will result from the vast and widespread destruction which the war has already produced, and will continue to produce until it ends, and perhaps long after it has ended.

Without trespassing upon the special field of any expert in insurance, it seems reasonable for a layman to venture a mere hint regarding some of the ways in which this effect of the war upon the future conduct of reinsurance may be expected to show itself.

At any time, whether in peace or in war, an underwriter who has already undertaken to carry a given risk, and who regards this risk as altered in its probable value by events that have happened since he made his contract, may, like anyone else who has to face a problem which involves his own risks and fortunes, seek to make a new contract with a second insurer, who, for a consideration, based upon a new estimate of the risk as it appears in the light of the new facts, shall undertake to carry and to fulfil an agreed portion of the obligations which the first underwriter insured.

Such reinsurance may take place in exceptional ways, and may be confined to some one case or to some few individual cases. Reinsurance contracts of this sort are comparatively familiar in marine insurance, and often come to be mentioned in the newspapers of the day when some vessel is long overdue, and when those underwriters who first insured her now go into the market to reinsure their risks. Such reinsurance contracts, when thus confined to individual cases and made subject to no general prior agreements among the various underwriters concerned, may more or less closely approach the character of mere wagers.

Reinsurance contracts possess, however, the character and the social and financial value of typical insurance transactions when they are made systematically, not merely because an underwriter desires not to carry longer a risk previously assumed, but in accordance with general agreements whereby various underwriters combine to carry in union some class that includes several, sometimes many, different insurance undertakings.

This is the case if underwriters A and B agree in advance that A may at pleasure, or subject to certain rules, reinsure with B such and such of the risks that A undertakes to carry; or, again, if A and B agree that of some class of risks which A assumes B shall be bound in advance to carry, for a suitable consideration, such and such a proportion. There are companies—some of them especially prominent in the fire-insurance field—which devote themselves mainly to various types of reinsurance.

It will be noticed, on the basis of such facts, that reinsurance has already become, in a perfectly natural way, and quite apart from any philosopher's speculations, a business which has a wide international extent and importance; although, as yet, no group of nations has taken part in the conduct of reinsurance.

But as soon as we give a little attention to this side of our problem, we stand face to face with the fact that a perfectly definite form of genuinely international insurance has already come, through the course of evolution, very near, not only to general practicability, but to actual existence. The nations therefore already have at hand an opportunity whose preciousness, as I believe, can hardly be overrated. Let us briefly consider what this opportunity is and implies.

That the State may, under certain conditions, undertake to insure its subjects or some class of its subjects, against various sorts of risks, is already a principle well recognized; although, of course, the expediency of state insurance in this or in that special form is a topic that involves many matters of controversy. Most of the forms of modern social insurance involve a greater or less approach to using the State as an insurer of its own subjects. At the beginning of this war our national Government undertook to carry for our shippers some of the special risks to which the war has subjected our commerce. To speak of state insurance, then, is not to mention a wholly strange idea.

If, however, there exist, as has been for years the case, forms and plans of reinsurance which involve interests that are already international in their scope and extent, and in the variety of the problems and interests concerned; and if, at the conclusion of the present war, the whole business of reinsurance, in adjusting itself to the needs and demands of the future, will have to solve problems that will deeply concern the underwriters of many nations; why should not these international problems of the future of reinsurance, involving, as they necessarily will do, the future conduct and agreements of insurance corporations belonging to many peoples, be put at once under the care of a suitable international organ?

That is, why should not we make, and promptly make, a beginning at the international conduct of the business of reinsurance? I refer especially to so much of this business of reinsurance as will in fact, at the end of the present war, demand, of and for the underwriters of different nations, readjustments, new contracts, new agreements among existing corporations belonging to various peoples; while these new problems and contracts will be too complex and too difficult to be readily and adequately and advantageously met by individual agreements among the many widely distributed private corporations that have to deal with the now rapidly changing situation of the whole insurance world, and that will have to deal with this situation in the future.

What sort of international organ would be suited to deal with these problems of reinsurance? The answer is furnished, I believe, by the International Board of Trustees, which in my book I have defined and proposed as the general organ for conducting this sort of insurance.

The choice and formation of this Board of Trustees would involve no new and strife-breeding treaties among the various nations. The board, when once constituted, would have no political powers or functions whatever. Its conduct of the trust funds committed to its care would need no supervision from any arbitration tribunal. No diplomatists would have any voice in its doings. Its funds themselves could be protected, and the longer it existed the more varied and effective this perfectly peaceful self-protection would become, if the board were at the outset constituted as, with reasonable probability, it could be constituted.

Its business would consist, in general, in selling various sorts of policies to the nations which, for any reason, chose to have dealings with the International Insurance Trustees. Nations that made trust agreements with the board could withdraw from them at pleasure, in a perfectly peaceful way, by the expedient of surrendering, upon terms determined by previous agreements, the policies that they had come to possess. The Board of Trustees would have a strong interest in so planning its policies and in so administering its international business as to retain and increase its reputation as an insurance corporation deserving of patronage, and able to offer policies which the insuring nations would find advantageous to themselves.

In my book I have in general defined the nature, constitution, and possible functions of this International Board of Insurance Trustees. My critics have doubted whether I could name a set of insurable risks, common to various nations, and sufficiently attractive to induce a group of nations to do a practicable business with the board when once it had been formed.

My present article points out that, from the end of the present war, there will be a constant increase and variety of reinsurance plans and contracts needed by the private insurance companies of various nations. If the conduct of this new reinsurance business is not put under the care of an Internationl Board of Trustees, the business, of course, will in one way or another come in time to be done.

But, apart from international co-operation, directed to this end, such business will depend upon special agreements made amongst individual corporations belonging to different nations, and will be subject to complications and to competitive hindrances such as must rapidly increase under the new conditions. New and large investments of private capital will be called for, and, for some time, will be harder to obtain, to organize, and to adjust to current requirements than was the case in the conduct of these larger undertakings of the insurance world before the war.

At this point, if only these new problems of reinsurance receive the attention due to the international scope, and to the vast importance of the commercial interests involved, it becomes possible to bring into existence a corporation whose functions, at the very beginning of its life, would be those of a "treaty company" undertaking reinsurance.

Its first contracts might be made, on the one hand, with those already existing private corporations which in any nation desired to reinsure some of their existing or future risks, or which needed to find a systematic way of readjusting their business to the new conditions.

On the other hand, the contracts of this new treaty company from the very outset might in part be made with those nations which, for the sake of aiding their own underwriters in dealing with the manifold and complex problems of the new era, decided to undertake, in whatever way they found suited to the new conditions, the reinsurance of risks which their own insurance corporations had already undertaken to carry, or which these insurance corporations desired in future to undertake and to reinsure.

Such a business, or part thereof, may actually come to constitute the task of some new private corporation which will be formed in the near future, after the present war. There will no doubt be new "treaty companies." Some of them will do an international business.

They will be needed. They will also need large new investments of capital in order to carry on their reinsurance business.

What I propose is that this possible new reinsurance corporation should actually begin its life as the international board of insurance trustees which, in my book, I have in outline described, and have proposed. At the outset, although not for any very long period, I propose that the functions of the Board of Trustees be provisionally limited to this perfectly practicable activity of reinsurance.

The reasons why such a reinsurance board of trustees would have ample reinsurance business with which to begin its task have now been indicated. The motives which would at first tend to make such international reinsurance attractive to the individual nations have also been sketched.

The individual nation would at first be induced to take out policies with the international board by the desire, or by the actual need, of aiding its own underwriters to adjust their business to the complications of the new life after this war, or at any rate in some near future time. The board itself would be an entirely new sort of international organ. It would have as its most important task that of finding and of making practicable still other forms of international insurance. Its indirect influence would from the very beginning far outrank in importance its direct accomplishment. Its mode of development would be guided by experience.

At no point in the growth of its work would any fundamental transformation of human nature be needed as a condition prior to its possessing a genuine, a peace-making, and a potent influence. Once having been constituted, with international reinsurance for its first enterprise, it would gradually discover new enterprises, and would increase both its direct workings and its indirect furthering of the cause of humanity by each of its new enterprises.

It would stand in opposition to none of the other peace-making influences which may come to take part in international affairs. It might well tend, in the long run, to transform international relations as, in our recent history, insurance has transformed the social life of individual nations. I submit that the time is ripe for the beginning, in this form, of international insurance; and that the prospect is impressive.

36

The Hope of
the Great Community

These words are written at a moment when the issues of the great war are still undecided. They are founded upon no foresight of the course which the world's political and military fortunes are to follow. They therefore refer wholly to ideals, to duties, to hopes, and to the interests of humanity.

There are moments when the lover of mankind, in these days, seems to catch a glimpse of a wonderful dawn light. If this dawn soon gives place to the coming day, an era of inspiring promise for the best hopes of all human ages will begin. If the clouds persistently gather again, as at some moments they do; if the night returns, as, for all that the present writer can know, it may return,—then the world must wait again for centuries, and must wait in sorrow, for that which the wise and the faithful of many generations have longingly expected.

"More than they that watch for the morning," the true lovers of mankind now watch to see whether the seeming promise of the dawn is to be, in any genuine sense, fulfilled. More than the spoilers of mankind ever before scoffed at the hope of humanity, powerful enemies of the good now confidently look for the triumph of Satan. The outcome of the present struggle between good and ill remains still a mystery.

[Reprinted from *HGC*, pp. 25–70.]

All that one can hope to do at such a moment, is to try to clarify his ideas about what ought to be—wholly powerless as the lover of the ideal is to determine, through any skilfully devised engines of destruction, or through any efficiency of the general staff of any national army, what shall be. All that one can now utter must be called at best "A Song before Sunrise." We do not know whether the sun for which the genuine lovers of mankind and of the ideal long, will ever rise in any future which we human beings can foresee for our own race.

Every idealist believes himself to have rational grounds for the faith that somewhere, and in some world, and at some time, the ideal will triumph, so that a survey, a divine synopsis of all time, somehow reveals the lesson of all sorrow, the meaning of all tragedy, the triumph of the spirit. But it is not ours to say, in the world in which we at present have to live from one day to another, and to follow the fortunes of man from one newspaper to another,—when and how the true revelation of the world's meaning is faced and found. We often do our best when we fix our mind on the thought which Kant expressed in the words: "If justice meets utter wreck, then there is no worth whatever in the continued existence of human life in this world." That word, at least, relieves us from the requirement of trying to prove that justice in mortal affairs will escape total wreck.

Perhaps the time will come when, indeed, there will be no further worth in the continued existence of men on this planet. If the purposes and deeds which some of the powerful enemies of mankind now boastfully attempt to make successful ever become permanently triumphant, then in truth there will be no further worth in the continued existence of human beings. As a matter of fact, this planet has seen its "Age of Reptiles." The sabre-toothed tiger has also had its day. Perhaps the ideals of those who defend and praise the destruction of mothers and of their babes on the "Lusitania" represent the sort of humanity that is henceforth, for an indefinite time, to win possession of the powers which are to control the fortunes of human civilization. About such matters a genuine idealist has no philosophical right, just as he has no scientific right, to make any particular prediction. His business is with the justice whose nature is such that if here on earth it is permanently wrecked, then the life of man becomes utterly worthless. There are to-day boastful powers, as hopeful of their own success as Milton's fallen angels were when

> Satan exalted sat,
> By merit raised to that bad eminence,

on his throne before them, and made preparations for a sort of sub-marine campaign against the salvation of man. The lover of ideals has no more right to make predictions about the hopes of these boastful powers, than Milton's good angels would have had to make predictions about the results of Satan's subsequent search for this little earth, and about what his visits to the Garden of Eden would accomplish.

In Milton's tale these visits accomplished the Fall of Man. The good and the bad angels have been struggling for the final pos-session of man ever since. The struggle continues to-day. And there can be no doubt that the evil powers are prodigiously efficient, and that the servants of ill are devotedly loyal to their diabolical cause. As for humanity, man, like the sabre-toothed tiger, may ere long have had his day and may have ceased to be. The lover of ideals can make no predictions as to such results. He can only "watch for the morning" until, for him and for some of his human fellows, the darkness has indeed settled down. It remains, however, still worth while to tell what hopes one's "Song before Sunrise" would express if one were permitted not merely to watch and some-times to hope for the morning, but to tell what the sun would show us if it had already risen for humanity, or will show us whenever for humanity it does rise, if indeed on this planet it ever is to rise.

I

In order rightly to estimate the ideal issues which are at stake in the present crisis of humanity, it is first necessary to make clear a matter concerning which there is a good deal of confusion in recent discussion. Some of this confusion is benevolent and well-meaning; some of it is due to wilful disregard of certain ethical issues which ought to be as obvious as they are deep. The matter to which I refer can best be brought nearer to clearness by contrasting two views of the world's present moral situation which frequently ap-pear in recent expressions concerning the morals of the war. Ac-cording to one of these views, the present war is essentially a conflict between nations and between national ideals. The essence of this doctrine is, that just as the conflicting powers are nations, so the main moral concern ought to be expressed in hopes that this or that nation will obtain a deserved success.

Opposed to this view is a second and very different view of the moral situation of the world and of the meaning of the war. According to this view, the present war is a conflict more conscious, more explicit, and for that very reason more dangerous than any we have ever had before, a conflict between the community of mankind and the particular interests of individual nations. Consequently, no nation engaged in this war is, or can be, right in its cause, except in so far as it is explicitly aiming towards the triumph of the community of mankind. As a fact, the various warring nations are at present acting with a decidedly various degree of clearness about their relation to the unified interests of humanity; that is, to what I call the cause of the community of mankind. Hence the various nations differ in the degree to which, at any stage of the conflict, their cause is just. In certain respects and with regard to certain of their enterprises, they may be, and are, explicitly aware that they intend to serve the community of mankind; while in other respects, or in regard to other matters, they may act with a more or less explicitly deliberate hostility to the cause of the community of mankind. Their moral position may, therefore, vary accordingly. But owing to the vastness and to the definiteness of many of the special international passions and issues concerned in the present conflict, the outcome of the war promises to be either a victory or a defeat, not for any one of the warring nations nearly so much as for humanity in its wholeness, and hence for what I shall venture also to call the church universal. It is important, therefore, to indicate as clearly as possible what in this discussion I mean by the community of mankind, and what by the church universal.

Ancient Israel somewhat early reached a religious ideal which it expressed in the doctrine of some of its Prophets, that the redeemed and transformed Jerusalem of the future was to be the centre of a redeemed humanity, the spiritual ruler of a kingdom which should have no end. In reaching this ideal, the religion of the Prophets did not look forward merely to a political conquest of the rest of the world by the future people of Israel. The ideal of the transformed humanity of the future had, indeed, in case of the religion of the Prophets, its political metaphors and inevitably its political coloring. The subsequent results when the ideal religion of the Prophets degenerated into the formalities of later Judaism, were in many ways disastrous both for the morals and for the religion of Judaism. But the ideal city of Zion, the centre of a new heaven and earth, passed over as an ideal into the possession of the early Christian church. The Apostle Paul gave to its inner life the character which he called "charity," and which he expounded to the Corinthians in one of the greatest documents of Christian literature.

The often misunderstood heart and essence of the Pauline vision of charity is that it is a virtue belonging to a community, a community which Paul conceives as finding its future home in a heaven where the Divine Spirit both informs it and fulfils its life and its desire. Charity does not mean mere love of individuals for individuals; since if, according to Paul, I gave all my goods to feed the poor, and my body to be burned, I might still be without charity, and then be as a sounding brass or as a tinkling cymbal. Charity, for Paul, is not a merely mystical power to prophesy, nor does it consist in any other form of merely individual efficiency or proficiency. It is a virtue which Paul recommends to his Corinthians as to an united community who, in the bonds of the spirit, are one body despite the multitude of the members. Charity never faileth, and outlasts all earthly vicissitudes in its own heavenly world, because there we know even as we are known, and our mutual relations are those of a perfected spiritual community.

Paul viewed the salvation of humanity as consisting in the triumph of the Christian church. This triumph was for him something miraculous, catastrophic, and future; and his expectations regarding the triumph and end of humanity were obviously quite mythical. But this triumph of humanity, this hope of all the faithful, this salvation of a community through an universally significant human transformation, without which no salvation of an individual man would be possible, this idea, in terms of which the Apostle Paul universalized the ideal Jerusalem of the early Prophets, this became the most essential and characteristic idea of the Christian church.

The historical church has never been true to it and has seldom understood it. Most Christians suppose that the salvation of men is an affair involving the distinct, and in many ways the isolated, spiritual fortunes of individual men. Such Christians, however, have not understood what the vision of the New Jerusalem was in which the seer of the Apocalypse gloried. What the tree of life bears for the healing of the nations, such Christians have never rightly comprehended. What the farewell address of the Logos of the Fourth Gospel meant, when the departing Lord prayed to the Father, "That those whom Thou has given me may be One as We are One," such individualistic Christianity (which has been only too popular in the various Protestant sects) has neglected, if not forgotten. But however ill-comprehended, the "sign" in which and by which Christianity conquered the world was the sign of an ideal community of all the faithful, which was to become the community of all mankind, and which was to become some day the possessor of all the earth, the exponent of true charity, at once the spirit and the ruler of the humanity of the future.

Such is a bare suggestion of that ideal of the community of mankind which it was the historical mission of Christianity to introduce into the world, to keep alive through centuries of human crimes, oppressions, rebellions, and hatreds, and to hold before the world for the healing of the nations. The present situation of humanity depends upon the fact that for good reasons, which have to do not merely with the sentimental and romantic aspirations of humanity, but also with the most serious business in which men are engaged, the idea of the community of mankind has become more concrete, more closely related to the affairs of daily life, has become more practicable than ever before. At this very moment the material aspect of civilization favors, as never before, the natural conditions upon which the community of mankind, if it were reasonably successful, would depend for its prosperity. The growth of the natural sciences as well as of the technical industries of mankind also makes possible and comprehensive forms and grades of coöperation which men have never before known. Some motives which tend to render the genuine Pauline charity, the genuine love of the unity of the great community to which all civilized men may, when enlightened, consciously belong,—such motives, I say, have been furthered by the arts, the industries, the sciences, and the social developments of the nineteenth and twentieth centuries, as thousands of years of previous human activity have never furthered them. The brilliant coloring, the luxuriant images with which the fancy of the seer of the Apocalypse adorned his New Jerusalem, readily suggest themselves to the imagination of the lover of human kind, who dwells on some of the more benign aspects of our recent civilization, and who considers how far-reaching the abundant powers of human life are tending to become under the influence of those humane arts and sciences which of late have so successfully combated disease, and have brought together nations and races of men who once could not in the least feel their brotherhood, or mutually understand the tongues which they spoke.

These benevolent and benign influences do not, indeed, of themselves constitute the true Pauline charity; but within the last two centuries we have for the first time seen glimpses of how, under perfectly human conditions, they could become a basis for a charity which might transform our society in many of its most significant features into a social order worthy both of a new heaven and of a new earth. In brief, the last two centuries have given us a right to hope for the unity of mankind, a right of which we had only mythical glimpses and mystical visions before. This right we gained through the recent development both of our natural sciences and of our modern humanities. The idea of the human community has tended of late to win a certain clearness which it never could possess until now.

Paul could believe in his vision of the redeemed humanity of the future, because he had his own perfectly concrete and human, if to him unsatisfactory, experiences of the apparently miraculous life which was present in his enthusiastic little churches. When he talked of the redeemed humanity in heaven, and had his vision of the charity that never faileth, he could say to his brethren: "Thus the Spirit manifests itself amongst you." When, in an unquestionably more fantastic manner and language, the author of the Fourth Gospel made the speaker of the farewell addresses characterize the present life and the future life of his little company of disciples, whom "having loved them, he loved them to the end," the writer of this Gospel could use his concrete, although historically idealized, portrait of the last meeting between the Lord and his disciples as the basis and background of this vision of the salvation of mankind.

In our day this vision of the salvation of mankind, while indeed far enough away from us to cause constant and grave concern, and to demand endless labor, has been for a long time becoming clearer than ever, while both science and industry have tended to bring men together in new fashions of coöperation, in new opportunities and exercises that involve an expressed charity in its true form, as a devotion not merely to individuals but to the united life of the community. The belief that mankind can be and in the end shall be one, has thus for a long time had an increased concreteness, definiteness, practical applicability, and despite all the vast evils of our modern social order, a genuine hopefulness. What has to be borne in mind is, that in former centuries, and above all in ancient times, the community of mankind was hindered from becoming an object either of experience or of reasonable hope by the confusions of men's tongues, by the mutual hostilities of nations, of religions, and of sects, and by the absence of means whereby men might learn to work together. Since the beginning of the modern world, not only have the sciences and the arts helped us to work together in a material way and to understand one another regarding our various ideas, but very many of our modern intellectual and practical modes of progress have possessed a significance not only material, but deeply spiritual and, what is more to the point in our present discussion, wisely international. The modern world has become in many ways more and more an international world. And this, I insist, has been true not merely as to its technical and material ties, but as to its spiritual union.

It has been this vision upon which a recent international crime has so violently intruded. The hope of the community lies in trying to keep before us a vision of what the community of mankind may yet become despite this tragic calamity.

II

In speaking at such a moment of the community of mankind viewed simply as an ideal of the future, there are two matters which, as I believe, we ought to bear in mind. First, its members will not be merely individual human beings, nor yet mere collections or masses of human beings, however vast, but communities of some sort, communities such as, at any stage of civilization in which the great community is to be raised to some higher level of organization, already exist. Ethical individualism has been, in the past, one great foe of the great community. Ethical individualism, whether it takes the form of democracy or of the irresponsible search on the part of individuals for private happiness or for any other merely individual good, will never save mankind. Equally useless, however, for the attainment of humanity's great end would be any form of mere ethical collectivism, that is, any view which regarded the good of mankind as something which masses or crowds or disorganized collections of men should win.

For this reason Bentham's utilitarianism, in the form which he gave to it, and which the English political Liberals of the middle of the nineteenth century emphasized, does not express what the community of mankind needs for its existence and for its general welfare. That is why mere philanthropy, merely seeking for the greatest happiness for the greatest number, merely endeavoring to alleviate the pains of individual men or of collections of men, will never bring about the end for which mankind has always been seeking, and for the sake of which our individual life is worth living. That, too, is the reason why at the present time many humane people, despite their former horror of war, in view of its sorrows and of the misery which it causes, find to their surprise that, as Mr. Robert Herrick has said in a recent number of "The New Republic," war seems to them now no longer as great an evil as it used to seem; for in each of the warring peoples the war has brought about new consciousness of unity, a new willingness to surrender private good to the welfare of the community, a new sense of the sacredness of duty, a new readiness to sacrifice.

Such converts to the doctrine that war is good ascribe their sudden conversion to the wonder and reverence which have been aroused in them by the sight of France regenerated through the very dangers which the invader has brought with him, awakened to a new sense that the value of life lies not in what individuals get out of it, but in what the exertions and the perils of war call out and illustrate, namely, the supreme and super-individual value of loyalty. Loyalty, the devotion of the self to the interests of the community, is indeed the form which the highest life of humanity must take, whether in a political unity, such as in a nation, or in the church universal, such as Paul foresaw. Without loyalty, there is no salvation. Therefore loyalty can never completely express itself in the search for individual happiness, whether the happiness that is in question be that of the individual who teaches, or that of the mere collections of masses of individuals for whom some philanthropist seeks happiness.

Therefore it is indeed true that, if the only alternative for mankind were either to continue the arts of war or to lose its vision of high attainment in the form of a mere search for happiness, then it would be better that war should rage, with all its horrors, so long as humanity lasts, rather than that what Emerson called "hearts in sloth and ease" should live in an endlessly dissatisfied search for pleasures which deceive and which fade in the enjoyment, and for a happiness which no human individual can possibly attain, unless indeed he is viewed as a member of the community.

The detached individual is an essentially lost being. That ethical truth lies at the basis of the Pauline doctrine of original sin. It lies also at the basis of the pessimism with which the ancient southern Buddhism of the original founder of that faith, Gotama Buddha, viewed the life of man. The essence of the life of the detached individual is, as Gotama Buddha said, an unquenchable desire for bliss, a desire which "hastens to enjoyment, and in enjoyment pines to feel desire." Train such a detached individual by some form of highly civilized cultivation, and you merely show him what Paul called "the law." The law thus shown he hereupon finds to be in opposition to his self-will. Sin, as the Pauline phrase has it, "revives."

The individual, brought by his very cultivation to a clearer consciousness of the conflict between his self-will and the social laws which tradition inflicts upon him, finds a war going on in his own members. His life hereupon becomes only a sort of destruction of what is dearest to him. For as a social being, he has to recognize both the might of his social order and the dignity of its demands. But as a detached individual, he naturally hates restraint; that is, as Paul says, he hates the law. However correct his outward conduct may be, he inwardly says: "Oh, wretched man that I am, who shall deliver me from the body of this death?"

Such is the picture of the essentially disastrous life of the detached individual which you find in the much misunderstood, and in our day comparatively unpopular seventh chapter of the Epistle to the Romans. In the following chapter, Paul characterizes the only mode of salvation which can be offered with any hope to such a detached individual. Gotama Buddha sought the salvation of the detached individual through an act of resignation whereby all desires are finally abandoned. Paul describes what is essentially salvation through loyalty, salvation through the willing service of a community, the salvation of those whom he characterizes by the words: "They are in Christ Jesus, and walk not after the flesh, but after the spirit." But for Paul the being whom he called Christ Jesus was in essence the spirit of the universal community.

The lesson with regard to which both Buddhism and Christianity agree, is the lesson that for the detached individual there is no salvation. Since, therefore, you can never make the detached individual securely and steadily happy, it is useless to try to save him, or any mere crowd or collection of detached individuals, by mere philanthropy. Since the detached individual is essentially a lost being, you cannot save masses of lost individuals through the triumph of mere democracy. Masses of lost individuals do not become genuine freemen merely because they all have votes. The suffrage can show the way of salvation only to those who are already loyal, who already, according to their lights, live in the spirit, and are directed not by a mere disposition to give good things to everybody, or to give all their goods to feed the poor, or to give their body to be burned, but by a genuinely Pauline charity.

Since then, it is only the consciously united community—that which is in essence a Pauline church—which can offer salvation to distracted humanity and can calm the otherwise insatiable greed and longing of the natural individual man, the salvation of the world will be found, if at all, through uniting the already existing communities of mankind into higher communities, and not through merely freeing the peoples from their oppressors, or through giving them a more popular government, unless popular government always takes the form of government by the united community, through the united community, and for the united community.

Therefore, while the great community of the future will unquestionably be international by virtue of the ties which will bind its various nationalities together, it will find no place for that sort of internationalism which despises the individual variety of nations, and which tries to substitute for the vices of those who at present seek merely to conquer mankind, the equally worthless desire of those who hope to see us in future as "men without a country." Whatever that form of loyalty which is now patriotism expresses, must be in spirit preserved by the great community of the future. That unity within the national growth which the observers of the war watch with such fascination, when they see how each people is better knit and more serious, more conscious of the sacredness of its national life than it was before the great peril, that unity will not, and must not, be lost when the new international life comes into existence. There can be no true international life unless the nations remain to possess it. There can never be a spiritual body unless that body, like the ideal Pauline church, has its many members. The citizens of the world of the future will not lose their distinct countries. What will pass away will be that insistent mutual hostility which gives to the nations of to-day, even in times of peace, so many of the hateful and distracting characters of a detached individual man. In case of human individuals, the sort of individualism which is opposed to the spirit of loyalty, is what I have already called the individualism of the detached individual, the individualism of the man who belongs to no community which he loves and to which he can devote himself with all his heart, and his soul, and his mind, and his strength. In so far as liberty and democracy, and independence of soul, mean that sort of individualism, they never have saved men and never can save men. For mere detachment, mere self-will, can never be satisfied with itself, can never win its goal. What saves us on any level of human social life is union. And when Webster said, in his familiar reply to Hayne, that what alone could save this country must be described as "Liberty and Union, now and forever, one and inseparable!"—Webster expressed in fine phrase, and with special reference to this country, the true doctrine of the church universal.

Liberty alone never saves us. Democracy alone never saves us. Our political freedom is but vanity unless it is a means through which we come to realize and practise charity, in the Pauline sense of that word. Hence the community of mankind will be international in the sense that it will ignore no rational and genuinely self-conscious nation. It will find the way to respect the liberty of the individual nations without destroying their genuine spiritual freedom. Its liberty and union, when attained, will be "now and forever, one and inseparable."

III

I have now mentioned one character which, as I believe, must belong to the international community of the future. Hereupon I must turn to a second character, which seems to me of equal importance with the first, although reformers and the creators of Utopias have almost uniformly neglected, or misunderstood this second character.

The distinct national unities must remain intact, each with its own internal motives for loyalty and with its modes of expression whereby the loyalty of its individual citizens will be won and sustained in the community of mankind, which the ideal future must contain if humanity is to be really saved. In the far-off future, as in the past, humanity will include amongst its number nations whose citizens belong not merely to various national types but to distinct races. No dream of universal conquest, if it were carried out, could ever lead to anything but to a more or less universal community of hate, to a social world essentially distracted, much as the world of the Gentiles, depicted by Paul at the outset of the Epistle to the Romans, was distracted. In and for such a community, no man, still less a nation, could deeply feel or long retain any genuine loyalty. Neither the pan-Germanists nor the pan-Slavists, neither the partisans of the white race nor those who hope for the supremacy of the yellow race, have any true conception of what the community of mankind is intended to be or of what the spirit of loyalty demands that it shall be. Both the nations and the races are needed for the future of mankind. The problem of humanity is to see that their liberty and their union shall remain "forever one and inseparable."

But what the lovers of national rivalries, who look forward to an endless strife of peoples, as well as the makers of the Utopias of universal peace, have equally failed to see is that amongst the many social functions of a nation or, for that matter, of any human community, the political functions of such a community, at any rate, as they have been conceived and carried out up to the present time, are ethically amongst the least important.

Greece never attained political unity. To-day it rules the world, as Germany will never rule it, though its inventions and its efficiency should continue and grow for a thousand years. Greece rules a spiritual world, and rules it spiritually. No modern nation that has won political power has ever expressed its best contribution to humanity through this political power, or has ever made a contribution to the community of mankind which is nearly equal to the contribution made by Greece, and made by a nation which proved wholly incapable of political unity. The greatest rival which Greece has ever possessed as a contributor to the cause of the community of mankind is the nation Israel—by which I mean, not the Israel whose history was rewritten from the point of view of later Judaism and was so misrepresented in what we call the Old Testament. The Israel of which I speak is the Irsael of the great formative period of the prophetic religion, the Israel whose religious beginnings are sketched for us in that brief and impressive fragment of poetry called the Song of Deborah—the Israel whose maturer consciousness found its voice in Amos and Isaiah, and in the records of the prophetic literature. Even after its formative period was past, and after Judaism had nearly quenched the spiritual fire which had burned in the religion of the Prophets, Israel still gave us the Psalms, still expressed, in the great speeches which an unknown master put into the mouth of Job, ideas and problems which are with us to-day, and which will record some of the great problems of human destiny for all coming ages of mankind, just as the great Greek tragedians of the formative period of the Hellenic mind have spoken for all time. But Israel, like Greece, never won, and from the nature of the case could not win, a lasting political unity.

When we remember how all the highest products of the German mind have so far been the products of times when the national unity in a political sense was not yet attained, while the mightiest accomplishment of Prussian domination has thus far been that, like the base Indian of Othello's last words, this Prussian domination, in dealing with the magnificent ideal legacy of the Germanic mind, has simply "thrown a pearl away, richer than all his tribe"; and when we remember how an analogous rule holds in case of several other European nations, we are reminded that, on the whole, there seems to be some opposition between the political power of a nation and its power to contribute to the ideal goods of the community of mankind.

The political contributions of nations either to the unity or to the life of the great community are by no means their only or, on the whole, their principal contributions. For that very reason it is not wise to hope that when the Holy City of the community of mankind descends from heaven to earth, it will come in political form. According to a well-known tradition, the Master said: "My kingdom is not of this world, else would my servants fight." I do not think that this reported word of the Master represents what the ideal course of human progress ought to be. The ideal community of mankind, whenever it really descends from heaven to earth, will indeed appear in a definitely worldly fashion. If the ideal is approximately realized, the kingdom will be in this world, yet its servants will not fight, simply because they will be loyally engrossed in much better business than fighting. That upon which I here insist is, that in learning such business they will not principally be guided by political arts and motives.

IV

But if the great community is not to win its loyal consciousness through inventing new political forms and through depending upon political institutions for its principal advances, must it then be confined to "the empire of the air"? Must it always be dependent upon its poets and its prophets? or upon their brethren, the great scientific discoverers, the genuinely inventive leaders of thought? Must its kingdom be a wholly ideal kingdom? Must its fortunes be those which, in a somewhat disheartening sequence of faiths and of practices, have so far constituted the history of religion?

I do not believe this. I believe that the future will invent, and will in due time begin very actively and productively to practise, forms of international activity which will be at once ideal in their significance and business-like in their methods, so that we shall no longer be dependent upon the extremely rare and precious beings called prophets or poets, to show us the way towards the united life of the great community. I have recently ventured to point out certain ways in which international business is already approaching a stage wherein, if the spoilers do not indeed too seriously wreck or too deeply impair our progress, we may actively begin to further international unity, without in the least interfering with the free internal development of the social orders of individual nations. It is not at all necessary to look towards the triumph of Socialism or of any other equally revolutionary social tendency, whether political or non-political, in order to foresee possible modes of international unification, which, if they were once tried, if a fair beginning of some such international activity were made, would almost certainly prove to be self-sustaining as well as conducive to a mutual understanding amongst the nations.

There is, for instance, a type of business which has been invented only within a little more than a century. In origin it is due to no poet and to no prophet. It has already transformed the civilization of the principal nations of Europe. The transformation in question is nowhere, except by accident, very closely bound up with political changes. The social transformations which it has already wrought within the communities of single nations, are not due to the spread of socialistic doctrines or to any notable political tensions or strifes within the communities which have thus been influenced.

The form of business which I have in mind is the form known as insurance. Within the life of a single civilized people, it is capable of accomplishing an immense variety of types of social service. The internal organization of Germany itself has been prodigiously furthered, the social unity and the impressive efficiency of the German people have been in recent decades very vastly furthered by the use which Bismarck and those who followed him were led to make of various forms of "state insurance" and of "social insurance," largely as means of meeting the demands which the socialistic movement was already making upon the state in general. What has been proved is that the type of business called insurance is so plastic and has such vast direct as well as indirect effects, that, within a single nation, if the purpose is to give a community such unity and such organization as naturally hold the attention and win the practical loyalty of the members of the community, the insurance type of organization is the best type invented for the purpose in question. This is no place to speak of the details of recent social insurance which Germany has so largely and so successfully used. It is enough to say that the business of insurance depends upon devices which are, so to speak, essentially unifying, essentially reconciling, essentially such as to exemplify a type of social community to which in a recent book of my own I have ventured to give a name, not, as I hope, too technical.

An insuring financial organization, whether it be an ordinary corporation or, as in Germany's case, a state or a government, has what I may call a mediating, a reconciling, a unifying function. If you regard the insurer as an individual man—and such in special cases he may be,—he mediates between the interests of two persons whose concerns, apart from the work of the insurer, are subject to an often painful conflict. These two persons may be called "the adventurer" and "the beneficiary." The adventurer is somebody who takes a risk, a practically significant risk. Like all risks, this one does not affect the fortunes of the adventurer alone. For the adventurer has, or at some time in the future will have, heirs or successors, or a family or other co-adventurers, who may, or who under certain conditions will benefit by the adventurer's undertakings if they succeed, but who will otherwise get quite the reverse of benefit out of the adventurer's failure. Thus the interests of the adventurer and of his possible beneficiaries, who may or will win if he wins, or who may or will lose if he loses, stand in a relation involving a certain rivalry, a tension, a source of possible conflict of the most varied kind. In other words, the adventurer and the possible beneficiary constitute what, in my "War and Insurance," I have called "a dangerous pair" of human beings. That is, their conflicting interests may lead to misunderstandings, to mutual wrongs, and to personal and social unrest of the most varied sorts.

Into this "dangerous pair" the insurer, in case his insurance enterprise is well founded and successful, introduces a reconciling element. It is the nature of his business to guarantee the beneficiary against the losses with which in the course of his fortunes the adventurer may meet. In consequence the dangerous pair becomes a genuine community, whose type is triadic and whose form is that of all the communities which I call "communities of interpretation." These are groups whose members comprise within themselves either individuals or communities. But in each of these communities, one of the members has the essentially spiritual function or task of representing or interpreting the plans, or purposes, or ideas, of one of his two fellows to the other of these two in such wise that the member of the community whom I call the "interpreter" works to the end that these three shall coöperate as if they were one, shall be so linked that they shall become members one of another, and that the community of the whole shall prosper and be preserved.

In "War and Insurance" I have defended the thesis that, if the principle of insurance were introduced into international affairs, even in a very small degree, it would involve, first the creation of an entirely new sort of international body—namely, an "international board of trustees." The functions of this board would not be those of a court of arbitration. They would not be diplomatic functions. The board would have no political powers or duties whatever. Hence its functions would constitute an entire novelty in human history. How such a board would be possible, how its funds might be protected from predatory assaults and kept free from the danger of being risked in international quarrels, my book has in a general way explained.

Since any reader of this book who may have time in the distractions of the present conflict to give it even the least careful attention, very naturally asks at once what common interests of the nations there are to insure, it is possibly worth while to say that in an article in *The New York Times* for July 25, 1915, I have pointed out certain international interests which, in fact, are greatly intensified by some of the conditions of the present conflict, and which are so definitely related to existing forms of the insurance business, that were a few nations at the close of the present war to appoint an international board of trustees to take practical charge of just these perfectly definable interests, and to treat them so as to meet the conditions which the nations concerned could readily agree upon without departing from fields of insurance that already exist and that have already acquired international importance, then a beginning in international insurance could actually be made at once upon the conclusion of the present war.

Were such an international board of trustees once appointed, were some such essentially simple and familiar type of insurance enterprise once undertaken, under perfectly reasonable and business-like conditions, a beginning would be made in a process that would, from the very first, tend to make the unity of the various nations of mankind something practical and obvious, as well as certain to possess, as time went on, more and more significance for all concerned in such a process. For, as a fact, there are certain forms of insurance which, as I have just said, are already international in their scope. At the close of the present war, some of these forms of insurance will be in need of new international devices to render them useful and prosperous under the new financial conditions that will inevitably succeed the conflict.

Nobody has as yet attempted to devise an international board of trustees fitted to take charge of such international social interests. But in the article to which I have referred, I have endeavored not merely to show how the still very distant ideal of an international insurance against risks directly connected with war would be valuable if we could secure such a form of international insurance, but also to show that a special type of international insurance would be perfectly practicable and business-like at the close of the present war, if a few nations were to agree upon a plan for appointing an international board of trustees and for intrusting to it the new enterprise. This new enterprise would involve no essentially new type of insurance. It would be based upon international needs which are already recognized, which have already created certain very successful corporations, which actually do an international business. To make these already existing types of insurance international in my present sense, only the explicit recognition of a suitable international organ is necessary.

This new international organ would not be political in its nature, would not attempt to do the work of "a league of peace," while of course it would have no sort of opposition to the formation of any league of peace which proves in the future to be practicable. The new type of international organ would be founded upon no international treaty such as would need or invite arbitration. The nations that entered into the new enterprise would merely intrust certain funds to the new international board of trustees, and would remain perfectly free to retire from all relations to the enterprise at any moment, by the device which any ordinary holder of an insurance policy can use at present, namely, by surrendering the policy to the board of trustees.

The effects of the new enterprise would be in the main indirect. That is, the new enterprise would meet an actual need, and if it were reasonably devised, would meet that need at once, and would in so far do good. But if successful, it would lead to new enterprises of the type. The principle of insurance would, however, be definitely introduced into international affairs. Once introduced, and once made in the least effective, that principle might, I believe, safely be left to vindicate itself and its power to bring to consciousness the great community of the future. The realm of peace may, indeed, be far enough away from our distracted human nature. But the way towards peace, the way towards the winning of self-consciousness for the great community, the way towards a genuine and practically effective coöperation of the nations, at once in the spirit of sound and business-like devotion, and in its primitive true Pauline charity,—that way already lies open.

Part IX

Annotated Bibliography
of the Published Works of
Josiah Royce

Ignas K. Skrupskelis

Annotated Bibliography
of the Published Works of
Josiah Royce

The present bibliography is primarily a listing of what Royce himself published. Although I have tried to provide a complete list, it is probable that much has escaped unnoticed, particularly newspaper pieces, which could have been published with hardly a trace, and which would be recoverable only by a stroke of luck. Secondarily, the bibliography lists items, including letters, published or reprinted after Royce's death. No systematic effort to locate these has been made, however, and only those that I chanced to come upon are included. Reprintings in textbooks and anthologies have been completely ignored.

Where the same item appears in several places, observed differences have been noted, but the several texts have not been compared systematically. Some of the information provided about the writings is, most likely, trivial. The inclusion of trivia, however, seems unavoidable, because it is difficult to anticipate what will prove useful in the future.

A compilation of this sort is especially dependent upon the help of others. Librarians and archivists, too numerous to mention, have answered inquiries and provided access to their materials. Several student assistants and my wife have spent dull hours turning the pages of crumbling magazines. Father Frank M. Oppenheim and Professor John Clendenning, both Roycean scholars, have been especially helpful. Professor James Willard Oliver of the University of South Carolina often provided encouragement, while the committee on research of the University of South Carolina provided financial assistance. I hope that this common effort has advanced the study of Royce and that it will serve as a basis for further work.

Throughout, cross-references to items in the bibliography will be made in italics as follows:
1. Student writings, *S* followed by the entry number (*S–3, S–5*);
2. Writings in the main body, date of publication followed by the entry number (*1885–1, 1916–5*);
3. Posthumous publications, *P* and the entry number (*P–4, P–8*);
4. Published letters, *L* and the entry number (*L–6, L–14*).

A list of unpublished letters referred to, with their locations, is appended at the end of the bibliography.

List of Abbreviations

FE	*Fugitive Essays, P–1.*
Haskell	Daniel C. Haskell. *The Nation 1865–1917.* 2 vols. New York: New York Public Library, 1951–53.
HGC	*The Hope of the Great Community, 1916–5.*
IJE	*International Journal of Ethics.*
Poole's	*Poole's Index to Periodical Literature.*
RAP	*The Religious Aspect of Philosophy, 1885–1.*
RLE	*Royce's Logical Essays, P–5.*
Royce Papers	Collection of Royce manuscripts and other materials in the Harvard University Archives.
RPJR	*The Religious Philosophy of Josiah Royce, P–4.*
SGE	*Studies of Good and Evil, 1898–8.*
SPJR	*The Social Philosophy of Josiah Royce, P–8.*

Royce Bibliographies

Rand, Benjamin. "A Bibliography of the Writings of Josiah Royce." In *Philosophical Review*, 25 (1916): 515–22 (*Papers in Honor of Josiah Royce*, pp. 287–94; this offprint is the same text as that in the *Philosophical Review*, but with different page numbers and separately bound).

Smith, John Edwin. "Bibliography." In *Royce's Social Infinite*, pp. 171–73. New York: Liberal Arts Press, 1950. Intended as an addendum to the Rand bibliography.

Cotton, James Harry. "Selected Bibliography." In *Royce on the Human Self*, pp. 305–11. Cambridge: Harvard University Press, 1954.

Humbach, Karl-Theo. "Bibliographie des Schriften von und über Royce." In *Das Verhältnis von Einzelperson und Gemeinschaft nach Josiah Royce*, pp. 181–206. Heidelberg: Carl Winter, 1962.

Oppenheim, Frank M. "A Critical Annotated Bibliography of the Published Works of Josiah Royce." *The Modern Schoolman*, 41 (1964): 339–65. Reprinted without the annotations and with additional entries in *Revue Internationale de Philosophie*, 21, nos. 79–80, (1967): 138–58.

Devaux, André-A. "Bibliographie des traductions d'ouvrages de Royce et des etudes sur l'œuvre de Royce." *Revue Internationale de Philosophie*, 21, nos. 79–80 (1967): 159–82.

The bibliographies by Humach and Devaux are especially useful for writings about Royce. Humbach provides the most extensive list available of reviews of Royce's books.

Cotton includes a partial list of the unpublished Royce manuscripts in the Harvard University Archives. A much earlier list is that of Jacob Loewenberg, "A Bibliography of the Unpublished Writings of Josiah Royce," *Philosophical Review*, 26 (1917): 578–82. Both of these, however, are incomplete and often unreliable. The Harvard University Archives has a manuscript "Index to the Josiah Royce Papers," completed in 1958 by Victoria Hernandez, Boyd Cruise, and Frank M. Oppenheim, S. J.

Student Publications

Included here are those items which Royce wrote before his graduation from the University of California and which appeared in student publications. Many of these items were published unsigned. Most of these are attributed to Royce on the basis of his own claims. Probably in the summer of 1875, Royce compiled a notebook called "General Index of Notes, MSS., &c.." In this notebook, he claims authorship for many unsigned pieces. In compiling it, he had on hand copies of the *Berkeleyan*. Items appearing in them were numbered to correspond to their numbering in the notebook. The notebook and some of the numbered copies can be found among the Royce Papers in a box labelled "Miscellaneous." Items listed in this notebook will be identified by the word "Index" following the entry.

1. "Is the Assassination of Tyrants ever Justifiable?" *Lincoln Observer*, vol. 2, no. 4, 1869.

This is the student paper of the Lincoln Grammar School in San Francisco, from which Royce graduated in June of 1869. The piece is signed with the initials "J.R." It is attributed to Royce on the grounds that a copy of this paper was given to the Harvard University Archives by the Royce family. Presumably, Royce himself preserved it as a souvenir of his school days. Most similar souvenirs contain items by Royce. The attribution is made somewhat uncertain by the fact that his "General Index" does not mention it, although it does mention earlier writings, and that a James F. Ryan was attending the school at the same time. If it is by him, it would be the earliest known published writing by Royce, although still earlier efforts survive in manuscript. The essay reaches the conclusion that, except where commanded by God, assassination is always harmful.

2. "Sound and Silence." *Neolæan Review,* 1 (April, 1873): 1. Index.
   The *Neolæan Review* was published by the Neolæan Literary Society, a student society of the University of California. The item is signed "X. Z." The essay claims that nature is most powerful when it works silently, and that the same is true of human undertakings. It further asserts that we should learn from this in evaluating our own efforts and those of others.

3. "Personification in Early Tongues." *Neolæan Review,* 1 (October, 1873): 1, 3. Index.
   Initialed "J.R., '75." Attempts to explain why some languages have a masculine and a feminine gender for inanimate objects. This is attributed to the tendency of primitive man to personify inanimate objects.

All of the items which follow appeared in the *Berkeleyan,* the student newspaper of the University of California. Royce is listed as one of the editors on five issues, from February 1875 through June 1875. The listing is chronological.

4. "Recent Discussions on Class Feeling." 1 (January, 1874): 7. Index.
   Initialed "J.R., '75." A polemical essay on the removal of the jealousies and conflicts which arise between members of different societies and classes.

5. "The Problem of Class Feeling." 1 (February, 1874): 5. Index.
   Initialed "J.R., '75." Continues the discussion of the previous item.

6. "The Modern Novel as a Mode of Conveying Instruction and Accomplishing Reform." 1 (April, 1874): 10–11. Index.
   Prize oration delivered on March 23, 1874. The topic is one of a number of stock topics available for orations to college students of the day.

7. "Literary Education." 1 (May, 1874): 4–5. Index.
   Initialed "J.R., '75." Written in response to an essay published in the *Berkeleyan.* Emphasises the value of a literary education for the scientist.

8. "Comments Suggested by a Principle in the Science of History." 1 (August, 1874): 4. Index.
Initialed "J.R., '75." The General Index refers to this item as "Ideas as Social Forces." Claims that ideas do influence events, although they need not be consciously pursued.

9. "The Prince of Denmark, the Moor of Venice, and their Creator." 1 (December, 1874): 3–5. Index.
Signed.

10. "The Literary Artist and the Work of Literary Art." 2 (January, 1875): 3–5. Index.
Signed.

11. "McCollough's Hamlet." 2 (February, 1875): 5. Index.
Unsigned. Comments on the performance of the actor McCollough presented in San Francisco.

12. "Editorial Responsibility." 2 (February, 1875): 8. Index.
Unsigned. Explains how the new editors of the *Berkeleyan*, Royce among them, have divided up their responsibilities.

13. "The Death of President Durant." 2 (February, 1875): 8. Index.
Unsigned editorial. Durant had served as president of the university.

14. "Draper's Religion and Science." 2 (February, 1875): 9. Index.
Comments on John William Draper, *History of the Conflict between Religion and Science*. Royce claims that past ages should not be criticized. They were what they were due to "inflexible laws of social change."

15. "Henry Durant." 2 (February, 1875): 10. Index.
Unsigned. A Eulogy.

16. "The Exercises on the Day of the Funeral." 2, (February, 1875): 10–12. Index.
Unsigned. On the funeral of Durant.

17. "Notes on Exchanges." 2 (February, 1875): 12. Index.
Unsigned. Comments on various student publications received by the *Berkeleyan*.

18. "Turgenieff's 'Liza.'" 2 (March, 1875): 6–7. Index.
Signed.

19. "The Vassar Miscellany and 'Middlemarch.'" 3 (March, 1875): 8–9. Index.
Unsigned. Defends George Eliot against the charge that her work, while good literature, weakens her readers morally.

20. "Irving and his Critics." 2 (March, 1875): 10. Index.
Unsigned. On Mr. Irving, an English actor.

21. "Notes on Exchanges." 2 (March, 1875): 11–12. Index.
    Unsigned. Not all of this item is by Royce. The third paragraph, pp. 11–12, is not.

22. "Truth in Art." 2 (April, 1875): 3–4. Index. Also appeared in the *Oakland Daily News*, 18 (March 2, 1875): 1.
    For description see *1875-5*.

23. "Berkeley Sunsets." 2 (April, 1875): 7. Index.
    Unsigned. Describes various sunsets visible in that area.

24. "Darwin Answered, or Evolution a Myth." 2 (April, 1875): 8. Index.
    Unsigned. Comments on an essay of that name by an unnamed author. Claims that science must educate the public about its discoveries.

25. "T. Hardy's 'Far from the Madding Crowd.'" 2 (April, 1875): 9–10. Index.
    Unsigned. States some general principles in terms of which novels should be evaluated.
    Immediately following this essay, this note appears: "Josh's poem on Chinese lanterns is crowded out." Could this be a reference to some lost artistic effort by Royce?

26. "The Foundation Idea in Poe's Poetry." 2 (April, 1875): 11. Index.
    Unsigned. Strongly critical of Poe.

27. "Notes on Exchanges." 2 (April, 1875): 12–13. Index.
    Unsigned.

28. A resolution. 2 (April, 1875): 13.
    A resolution thanking Daniel C. Gilman for his services to the University of California, adopted on the occasion of his resignation. Royce signed, along with two others, as a member of a committee on resolutions.

29. "Elaine and Ophelia." 2 (May, 1875): 4–5. Index.
    Signed. On a painting by Rosenthal, exhibited in San Francisco.

30. "A Chess Club." 2 (May, 1875): 8. Index.
    Unsigned. Advocates that a chess club be established at the university.

31. "The Aim of Criticism." 2 (May, 1875): 9. Index.
    Unsigned. On controversies between college papers.

32. "The Commencement Appointments." 2 (May, 1875): 10. Index.
    Signed. Criticizes the selection of student speakers for the commencement exercises.

33. "Notes on Exchanges." 2 (May, 1875): 13. Index.
    Unsigned. In part, comments on an item in the *Harvard Advocate* on the teaching of philosophy at Harvard.

34. "The 'Holy Grail' of Tennyson." 2 (June, 1875): 4–6. Index.
    Signed.

35. "A Word about the 'Ideal' in Science and in Art." 2 (June, 1875):
    7. Index.
    Unsigned. On Lewes' *Problems of Life and Mind.*

36. "Draper and 'Religion.'" 2 (June, 1875): 8–9.
    Unsigned. Attributed to Royce because it refers to an earlier
    essay on Draper (*S–14*) in a way that suggests that they are by the
    same author. The attribution is uncertain because the item is not
    mentioned in the General Index.

37. "The Tragic as Conceived by the Ancients and the Moderns." 2
    (June, 1875): 10. Index.
    Unsigned.

38. "Notes on Exchanges." 2 (June, 1875): 13.
    Unsigned. References to earlier notes of this kind suggest that
    they are by the same author.

Publications, 1875–1917

Entries are arranged by year of publication. Within each year, they
are listed alphabetically.

1875

1. "The Aim of Poetry." *Overland Monthly,* 14 (1875): 542–49.
   In part, a discussion of Aristotle's *Poetics.* Royce left California
   for New York, and then Europe, on about June 30, 1875. This and
   item *1875–3* were written before that date. See Royce's letters to
   Daniel C. Gilman of June 14, 1875, and July 11, 1875.

2. "The Intention of the Prometheus Bound of Aeschylus, Being an
   Investigation in the Department of Greek Theology." *Bulletin of the
   University of California,* no. 16 (June, 1875), pp. 113–37.
   Bachelor of Arts thesis, dated April 29, 1875. It was customary to
   "read" theses during commencement week. Royce's was read about
   June 4, 1875.

3. "The Life-Harmony." *Overland Monthly,* 15 (1875): 157–64.
   Discusses the question whether human life develops in a harmonious way, or through a series of sudden changes. Contains references
   to Hegel which are biographically significant.

4. "On a Passage in Sophocles." *Oakland Daily Transcript,* June 10,
   1875, p. 3. Same text also appeared in the *Alameda County Gazette,*
   June 12, 1875.
   The Classical Oration delivered during commencement ceremonies
   at the University of California, on June 9, 1875.

5. "Truth in Art." *Oakland Daily News*, 18 (March 2, 1875): 1. Reprinted in the *Berkeleyan*, S–22.

Oration for the "President's Prize in Oratory," delivered on February 26, 1875, apparently the winning entry. The topic was a common one. The same number of the *Berkeleyan* contains another oration with the same title.

1878

1. "The Circulating Library." *Berkeleyan*, 6 (November, 1878): 222–24.

2. "A Monkish Chronicle." *Berkeleyan*, 6 (December, 1878): 265–80.

Unsigned. Atributed to Royce by Joseph C. Rowell, Royce's contemporary and archivist of the University of California Library, in that library's copy of the *Berkeleyan*. I owe this information to Frank M. Oppenheim, S.J. A copy of this item can be found among the Royce Papers.

3. "Of the Interdependence of the Principles of Knowledge, an Investigation of the Problems of Elementary Epistemology, in Two Chapters, with an Introduction on the Principal Ideas and Problems in Which the Discussion Takes Its Rise." Baltimore, 1878, handwritten.

Doctoral dissertation, presented to the John Hopkins University, dated April 2, 1878. The handwritten original is in the possession of the Johns Hopkins University library. The Harvard University Archives have a typewritten copy, donated to Harvard by Walter Rothman.

4. "Schiller's Ethical Studies." *Journal of Speculative Philosophy*, 12 (1878): 373–92. Reprinted in *FE*.

A study of Kant's influence on Schiller read to the Johns Hopkins Philological Association, in December of 1877. According to his letter to William Torrey Harris, dated January 4, 1878 (*L–7*), he was planning a similar study of Novalis. In his letter to Harris of October 23, 1878 (*L–8*), Royce wrote that the phrase "sobriatur ambulando," on p. 383, should be "solvitur ambulando." The *FE* text is correct.

1880

1. "Natural Rights and Spinoza's Essay on Liberty." *Berkeley Quarterly*, 1 (October, 1880): 312–16. Reprinted in *FE*.

In *FE* it is described as a condensed version of a lecture to the Historico-Political Club, on March 1, 1878, titled "Spinoza's Theory of Religious Liberty in the State." The incomplete text of this lecture can be found in vol. 55 of the Royce Papers. According to Herbert B. Adams, Royce communicated, on March 11, 1878, to the Historical and Political Science Association of Johns Hopkins University an essay titled "The *Tractatus Theologico-Politicus* of

Spinoza." See Herbert B. Adams, "New Methods of Study in History," in *Johns Hopkins University Studies in Historical and Political Science*, 2 (1884): 134.

2. "The Nature of Voluntary Progress." *Berkeley Quarterly*, 1 (July, 1880): 161–89. Reprinted in *FE*.
   On the laws which govern those social changes which are due to human efforts.

3. "Shelley and the Revolution." *The Californian*, 1 (1880): 543–53. Reprinted in *FE*.
   Views Shelley as the "poet of the age of the Revolution."

1881

1. "Before and Since Kant." *Berkeley Quarterly*, 2 (1881): 134–50.
   Views Kant as the synthesizer of the rationalist and empiricist approaches in the philosophy of nature.

2. "The Decay of Earnestness." *The Californian*, 3 (1881): 18–25. Reprinted in *FE*.
   A plea for a return to the study of the ethical aspect of human life. The argument proceeds by means of a discussion of "literary transcendentalism." Vol. 79 of the Royce Papers contains an unfinished revision of this essay.

3. "Doubting and Working." *The Californian*, 3 (1881): 229–37. Reprinted in *FE*. A short excerpt incorporated into *RAP*.
   In *FE* this is described as a revision of an earlier essay titled "The Work of the Truth-Seeker." Royce argues that extensive doubting is a necessary preliminary to the search for truth.

4. "George Eliot as a Religious Teacher." *The Californian*, 3 (1881): 300–10. Reprinted in *FE*.

5. "Kant's Relation to Modern Philosophic Progress." *Journal of Speculative Philosophy*, 15 (1881): 360–81. About eight pages, with extensive changes, were incorporated into *RAP*.
   Read for Royce at the Kant Centennial at Saratoga on July 6, 1881. Develops a program for the future course of philosophy. Royce refers to this essay in the *World and the Individual*, vol. 2, p. vi, as a further stage in his inquiry into the idealistic theory of knowledge, which he began in his doctoral dissertation.

6. " 'Mind-Stuff' and Reality," *Mind*, 6 (1881): 365–77.
   A criticism of W. K. Clifford's doctrine of "mind-stuff." Royce notes that a positive statement of doctrine will follow in a later paper. The paper referred to is "Mind and Reality," *1882–2*.
   For a reply see F. W. Frankland, "Dr. Royce on 'Mind-Stuff' and Reality," *Mind*, 7 (1882): 110–14.

7. "Pessimism and Modern Thought," *Berkeley Quarterly*, 2 (1881): 292–316. Reprinted in *FE*. Most of this essay was incorporated into *RAP*.

Maintains that the goal of human striving is union with the "great whole of conscious life."

8. *Primer of Logical Analysis for the Use of Composition Students.* San Francisco: A. L. Bancroft and Co., 1881, 77 pp. Errata slip inserted.

Royce worked on this book in the summer of 1879, according to his letter to James of January 8, 1880, (*L–17*). In the preface, p. 4, Royce mentions as his sources Sigwart, Lange, Boole, Jevons, and Venn. Royce did not consider the *Primer* a contribution to logic. "Of logic as a philosophic science they [these pages] tell nothing." It is only an attempt to apply the resources of elementary logic to the study of English. In an unpublished essay, "Logic as an English Study," about 1881 (vol. 61, Royce Papers), he argues that logic should be made a part of training in English to teach the student "deliberatness in assertion." The student should obtain "an understanding of the exact meaning of the complex forms of language."

1882

1. "How Beliefs are Made." *The Californian*, 5 (1882): 122–29. Reprinted in *FE*. Most of this paper was incorporated into *RAP*.

Defends the thesis that our own activity is constantly affecting the character of our experience.

2. "Mind and Reality." *Mind*, 7 (1882): 30–54. Most of this paper was incorporated into *RAP*.

The constructive sequel to "'Mind-Stuff' and Reality," *1881–6*. Explains and defends "Berkeley's hypothesis."

1883

1. "The Freedom of Teaching." *Overland Monthly*, n.s. 2 (1883): 235–40.

Defends academic freedom on moral grounds.

2. "Some Recent Studies on Ideas of Motion." *Science*, 2 (1883): 713–17.

Review of S. Stricker, *Studien über die bewegungs Vorstellungen.*

3. "Two Days in Life's Woods." *Overland Monthly*, n.s., 1 (1883): 594–95.

A poem.

1884

1. "After-Images." *Science*, 3 (1884): 321–22.

Comments on Sidney Hodges, "After-Images," *Nineteenth Century*, 14 (1883): 622–38.

2. *Bancroft's First [–Fifth] Reader*, by Charles H. Allen, John Swett, Josiah Royce. San Francisco: A. L. Bancroft & Co., [ᶜ1884].

Several later editions of these readers are known: Indianapolis, Ind.: Indiana School Book Co., [ᶜ1889]; revised under the direction of the Indiana State Board of Education by Annie Klingensmith, Indianapolis, Ind.: Indiana School Book Co., [ᶜ1903]. At least the *First Reader* was, apparently, also published in 1894. These editions, however, do not belong properly to the Royce bibliography.

In a letter to George P. Brett (president of the Macmillan Company, and Royce's publisher at the time) dated February 24, 1904, Royce explains his connection with these readers: He undertook the work in 1882 while an instructor in English, was paid, and has had no connection with them since then. Because the publisher owned the copyright, he himself has "never been consulted as to any later revision of the series" and has "no responsibility whatever for its present form." He claims that his name should not have appeared in the revised editions. In an undated letter to Brett, Royce further notes that he intended to print in a statement about the Indiana Readers, but was unable to do so. Royce's letter to Brett are in the Macmillan Company papers in the New York Public Library. The undated letter can be found in the 1904 file.

Since the readers are compilations, Royce's contribution must have been in the form of editorial advice. In the letter of February 24, he observes that his suggestions often were rejected.

3. Review of Elliott Coues, *Biogen: A Speculation on the Origin and Nature of Life. Science*, 3 (1884): 661–64.

1885

1. *The Religious Aspect of Philosophy: A Critique of the Bases of Conduct and of Faith*. Boston, New York: Houghton, Mifflin & Co., 1885, xix, 484 pp. Reprinted as a Harper Torchbook (New York: Harper & Brothers, 1958, xxiii, 484 pp.).

In the preface, Royce declares that the book incorporates fragments of essays published separately. The manuscript, vols. 1–4 of the Royce Papers, substantiates this. Portions of the text are not written out by hand, but consist of clippings from various periodicals. These fragments are the following:

a. Pages 110–26 are from "Pessimism and Modern Thought," *1881–7* (pp. 162–76 in *FE*).

b. Pages 227–28 are from "Doubting and Working," *1881–3* (p. 342 in *FE*).

c. Pages 252–63 are from "Kant's Relation to Modern Philosophic Progress," *1881–5* (*Journal of Speculative Philosophy*, 15:363–70).

d. Pages 300–304 are from "Mind and Reality," *1882–2* (*Mind*, 7:42–44).

e. Pages 305–6 are from "How Beliefs are Made," *1882–1* (pp. 345–46 in *FE*). This excerpt consists of three separate passages.

f. Pages 306–24 are from "How Beliefs are Made," *1882–1* (pp. 347–63 in *FE*).

g. Pages 338–40 are from "Mind and Reality," *1882–2* (*Mind,* 7:30–31).

h. Pages 340–53 are from "Mind and Reality," *1882–2* (*Mind,* 7:34–41).

i. Pages 355–70 are from "Mind and Reality," *1882–2* (*Mind,* 7:46–53).

In using these clippings, Royce made various changes. Generally, these affect the language rather than the meaning. The passages from "Kant's Relation to Modern Philosophic Progress," however, constitute an important exception. These passages suffered very extensive alterations. Their tendency is to change this essay from an attack upon ontology to a criticism of "certain ontologies."

According to the *Harvard Advocate*, 35 (1883): 13, Royce lectured at Harvard on the "Religious Aspect of Philosophy" in March of 1883. In the preface, p. xiii, he remarks that the book grew out of lectures on religious questions to Harvard students, although "only a small portion of the manuscript of these lectures" is reproduced in the book. Possibly he is referring to the March 1883 lectures. On May 24, 1883, Royce wrote to Horace E. Scudder, of the Houghton, Mifflin Company, asking that Scudder return a manuscript. Apparently Royce had submitted a manuscript to the publisher, but it was rejected. Most likely, this was an early draft of the *Religious Aspect of Philosophy*, which Royce then revised and submitted again. On January 14, 1884, Royce wrote to George B. Coale that his book on religious philosophy "gets shape more and more everyday." Shortly thereafter, according to the *Johns Hopkins University Circulars*, no. 29 (1884), p. 64, on January 31 and February 5, 1884, Royce lectured at Johns Hopkins on the "Religious Aspect of Philosophy." On May 11, 1884, Royce wrote to Daniel C. Gilman that his book was almost finished and that he had submitted the manuscript to the publisher for examination. Writing to Coale on November 1, 1884, Royce declared that his book was completed. The preface of the book is dated January 11, 1885.

In later years, Royce often referred to the *Religious Aspect of Philosophy*, particularly the chapter on "The Possibility of Error." In the *World and the Individual*, vol. 1, p. viii, Royce wrote that his views on certain questions have never varied from those expressed there. In the first of his "Three Lectures on Truth," dating from about 1911–12, p. 17, vol. 85 of the Royce Papers, Royce wrote that his own philosophical idealism is based upon views stated in this early work. According to Royce, this "first book" contains a "theory of truth" which he has adhered to ever since.

2. Review of James Martineau, *Types of Ethical Theory. Nation,* 41 (1885): 304–6.

Unsigned. Attributed to Royce in Poole's.

3. Review of Daniel Greenleaf Thompson, *A System of Psychology.*
Nation, 40 (1885): 343–44.
    Unsigned. Attributed to Royce by Haskell.

4. "The Squatter Riot of '50 in Sacramento: Its Causes and Its Significance." *Overland Monthly,* n.s., 6 (1885): 225–46. Reprinted with
a new introduction in *SGE* as "An Episode of Early California Life:
The Squatter Riot of 1850 in Sacramento."

1886

1. "Abbot's Scientific Theism." *Science,* 7 (1886): 335–38.
    Review of Francis E. Abbot, *Scientific Theism.* Abbot's strongly
worded reply to this review can be found in the preface to the
third edition of *Scientific Theism* (Boston: Little, Brown and Co.,
1888).

2. "Bancroft and Hittell on California." *Nation,* 43 (1886): 99–101.
    Review of Theodore H. Hittell, *History of California,* vol. 2; and
Hubert Howe Bancroft, *History of California,* vol. 4 (vol. 16 in
Bancroft's *History of the Pacific States of North America;* vol. 21 in
Bancroft's *Works*).
    Unsigned. Attributed to Royce in Poole's. In a letter to Henry
L. Oak, one of Bancroft's writers, dated May 31, 1886, Royce writes:
"I hope that my forthcoming review of Hittell's vol. II, and of your
latest. . . ."
    Reviews of other volumes: Bancroft's vols. 2, 3, see *1886–8;* vol. 5,
see *1887–1;* vol. 6, *1889–3.* I have found no signs of reviews of Bancroft's vol. 1 and his vol. 7. For Hittell's vol. 1 see *1886–8;* vols. 3, 4,
see *1898–5.* Hittell's *History of California* consists of four volumes.

3. *California, from the Conquest in 1846 to the Second Vigilance
Committee in San Francisco [1856]: A Study of American Character.*
Boston and New York: Houghton, Mifflin and Co., 1886, xv, 513 pp.
This was vol. 7 of the *American Commonwealths* series, edited by
Horace E. Scudder. A new edition with an introduction by Robert
Glass Cleland (New York: A. A. Knopf, 1948, xxxvii, 394, xv pp.)
was published as a volume in the *Western Americana* series, planned in
connection with California's Centenary Celebrations, 1946–1950, edited
by Robert Glass Cleland and Oscar Lewis. An excerpt, under the
title "The Hanging of a Senora," was published in *Westways,* 28
(1936): 24–25.
    Royce came to write *California* almost by chance. Houghton,
Mifflin and Company had engaged a Mr. Crane for the California
volume of its series, edited by Horace E. Scudder. But Crane died,
and eventually Scudder, who was corresponding with Royce about
the *Religious Aspect of Philosophy,* turned to Royce. This is the
account given by Royce in a letter to Bernard Moses dated September 7, 1883. The same letter makes it probable that Royce accepted

Scudder's offer in September of that year. The manuscript was completed and sent to the publisher by late December of 1885, according to Royce's letter to George B. Coale, dated December 30, 1885.

Royce's motives for accepting the offer are stated in the letter to Moses: "I am tempted, first by the money, then by the affection that I should feel for the task when once I had accepted it, and then by the good that would be done me if I undertook to examine the moral and general significance of just that set of concrete facts, to give my leisure hours to preparing such a book."

Writing to George B. Coale on January 14, 1884, Royce emphasizes the last mentioned motive. "A study of the political life of a growing state is, I find, of great use to a man like me, whose airy studies take him often so far from concrete fact."

The process of writing *California* is well documented in Royce's preface and in a number of letters. Noteworthy here are Royce's letters to Henry L. Oak, one of H. H. Bancroft's collaborators, primarily responsible for Bancroft's volumes on California, in the Henry E. Huntington Library and Art Gallery. Typed copies of some of them are in possession of the Bancroft Library of the University of California. Cleland, in his introduction to the Knopf edition of *California,* quotes extensively from them. Also helpful are Royce's letters to Horace E. Scudder and William Carey Jones in the Bancroft Library and to George B. Coale in the Johns Hopkins University library.

At the time he accepted Scudder's offer, Royce seems to have had no special competence in the history of California. His commitment led him to undertake extensive study of documentary sources. In the summer of 1884, he studied in the library of H. H. Bancroft; early in April of 1885, he examined State and War Department archives in Washington. At least twice, he interviewed Frémont, once before December 9, 1884, and again around July of 1885.

An extended account of the July interview can be found in Royce's letter to Oak of August 8, 1885. According to Cleland, in his introduction to *California,* p. xx, note, copies of several of Royce's letters to Mrs. Frémont and other related materials are in the Bancroft Library of the University of California.

Royce also asked his mother to write an account of the Royce family's journey to California in the gold rush of 1849. This account was edited by Ralph H. Gabriel and published (Sarah Royce, *A Frontier Lady: Recollections of the Gold Rush and Early California* [New Haven: Yale University Press, 1932]).

The writing of *California* involved Royce in a controversy concerning the role of Frémont in the conquest of California. Many of Royce's historical writings develop his side of the controversy. They were written to substantiate the claims made in *California.*

Writings particularly devoted to the Frémont controversy are *1890–3, 1890–4, 1891–6, 1891–10.* Items dealing with California history are *1887–2, 1890–2, 1891–3, 1891–4, 1891–5*. For a list of reviews of books on California history see *1886–2*.

On September 10, 1885, Royce read a paper titled "The Secret History of the Acquisition of California" at the second annual meeting of the American Historical Association at Saratoga. This is described as a chapter of his forthcoming book. A very short abstract can be found in the *Papers of the American Historical Association*, 1 (1885–86): 475. In November of 1885 he lectured on the history of California to Harvard students. These are mentioned in the *Harvard Advocate*, vol. 40 (1885–86), first lecture, November 2, "The Beginning of American Occupation of California," p. 63; second lecture, November 9, "Mining Life in California," p. 64; third lecture, November 16, "Popular Government and Lynch Law in the Mines," p. 79. Probably there were other lectures. The *Boston Evening Transcript*, November 23, 1885, p. 6, states: "Royce will continue his lectures on early California history during this week." The listed titles of these lectures do not correspond to chapter titles in *California*.

4. "Committee on Apparitions and Haunted Houses: Request for Information." *Proceedings of the American Society for Psychical Research*, 1 (July, 1886): 129–31. This item was also printed separately, and this could have been the original form of publication.

In the *Proceedings*, it appears as "Circular No. 6" of the ASPR. It was issued by the commitee, but is numbered in the series of ASPR circulars. It is signed by Royce as chairman, and by Morton Prince, T. W. Higginson, J. C. Ropes, F. E. Abbot, Roland Thaxter, and Woodward Hudson, as members of the committee.

Other items in the *Proceedings* by Royce are *1886–7, 1887–6, 1887–7, 1889–1, 1889–2, 1889–4, 1889–7, 1889–11*.

5. Letter to the Editor. *Overland Monthly*, n.s., 8 (1886): 216.

Correction of a note on p. 429 of *California, 1886–3*. There, he had written that J. S. Hittell dates Meiggs' flight in September 1854. Actually, Hittell dates it correctly, in October 1854. The original note stands in the 1914 reprinting; it is reproduced without comment in the Knopf edition, p. 338, note 46.

6. "Philosophical Questions of the Day." *Science*, 7 (1886): 426.

Notice of Eduard Von Hartmann, *Philosophische fragen der gegenwart*.

7. "Preliminary Report of the Committee on Apparitions and Haunted Houses." *Proceedings of the American Society for Psychical Research*, 1 (July, 1886): 128–29.

Signed by Royce as chairman of the committee. Probably, this is the report given by him at the fourth meeting of the Society, on January 12, 1886, in Boston. For his other writings in the *Proceedings* see *1886–4*.

8. "Two Recent Books upon California History." *Nation*, 42 (1886):
220–22.

Review of Theodore H. Hittell, *History of Clifornia*, vol. 1; and
Hubert Howe Bancroft, *History of California*, vols. 2 and 3 (vols.
14 and 15 in Bancroft's *History of the Pacific States of North
America;* vols. 19 and 20 in Bancroft's *Works*).

Unsigned. Attribution based on style and Royce's letters to Henry
L. Oak. In a letter dated November 12, 1885, Royce wrote that he
had been asked to review Bancroft's vol. 3 for the *Nation*. In his
letter of January 30, 1886, he refers to a *Nation* review which is
"sure to come."

For a list of similar reviews see *1886–2*.

1887

1. "Bancroft's Conquest of California." *Nation*, 44 (1887): 39–40.

Review of Hubert Howe Bancroft, *History of California*, vol. 5
(vol. 17 in Bancroft's *History of the Pacific States of North America;*
vol. 22 in Bancroft's *Works*).

Unsigned. Attributed to Royce in Poole's and by Haskell. For a list
of similar reviews see *1886–2*.

2. Biographical articles on California pioneers in *Appleton's Cyclopae-
dia of American Biography*, James Grant Wilson and John Fiske, eds.
New York: D. Appleton and Co., 1887–89.

In vol. 1 (copyright 1886, issued in 1888, but dated 1887), Royce
is listed as a contributor of "Articles on California Pioneers." All
entries are unsigned and, as far as I know, no author lists exist. In the
absence of relevant letters and manuscripts, it seems impossible to
determine with any assurance what Royce contributed.

Comparison with Royce's *California* suggests that the following
entries could be by Royce:

a. Alvarado, Juan Bautista, p. 61. See *California*, pp. 25–28; pp. 21–24,
Knopf edition.

b. Arce, Francisco, pp. 86–87. See *California*, p. 59; p. 47, Knopf
edition.

c. Bryant, Edwin, p. 421. See *California*, p. 43; p. 35, Knopf edition.

The entries for Sammuel Brannan, p. 359, and William T. Coleman, pp. 686–87, also could be by Royce. Both these men are frequently mentioned in *California*, but there are no definite similarities
between the two texts. There are many other entries for persons who
can be described as California pioneers. Most of them are simply too
brief and factual to allow for comparisons.

3. *The Feud of Oakfield Creek; a Novel of California Life.* Boston
and New York: Houghton, Mifflin and Co., 1887, 483 pp.

According to Royce's letter to George B. Coale of December 30,
1886, most of this novel was written during the summer of 1886.

When the manuscript was sent to the publisher, it was titled *Just Before Nightfall*. Royce described it as follows: "There are two bloody fights, three heroes, two heroines, several villains, and almost no morals in the book." See his letter to Horace E. Scudder, dated September 25, 1886.

4. Letter on Edward Rowland Sill in *A Memorial of Edward Rowland Sill*, published for private circulation, pp. 21–23. Proceedings of a memorial meeting held at Berkeley on April 14, 1887.

The letter is addressed to McChesney and is dated April 6, 1887. It was read at the meeting. While surviving records of courses taken do not substantiate this, Royce has said that Sill was one of his teachers at the University of California. When Royce was teaching English there, he was under Sill's supervision.

5. "Recent Psychical Research." *Nation*, 45 (1887): 116–18.

Review of *Preliminary Report of the Commission Appointed by the University of Pennsylvania to Investigate Modern Spiritualism* and *Proceedings of the Society for Psychical Research* (British).

Unsigned. Attributed to Royce in Poole's and by Haskell.

6. "Report of the Committee on Apparitions and Haunted Houses." *Proceedings of the American Society for Psychical Research*, 1 (December, 1887): 223–29.

Signed by Royce as chairman of the committee. Probably this report was made at the fifth meeting of the Society, on June 15, 1886, in Boston. Royce suggests that the committee change its name to "Committee on Apparitions and Presentiments."

For a list of his writings in the *Proceedings* see *1886–4*.

7. Request for cooperation. *Proceedings of the American Society for Psychical Research*, 1 (December, 1887): 265.

In May of 1887 the Executive Council of the ASPR issued a "Request for Cooperation." Here, the various committees of the ASPR asked the public for help. The request of the Committee on Apparitions and Haunted Houses is signed by Royce as chairman.

For a list of his writings in the *Proceedings* see *1886–4*.

8. Review of Henry Maudsley, *Natural Causes and Supernatural Seemings. Nation*, 44 (1887): 253–54.

Unsigned. Attributed to Royce by Haskell.

9. "Tennyson and Pessimism." *Harvard Monthly*, 3 (1886–87): 127–37. Reprinted in *SGE*.

Occasioned by Tennyson's "Locksley Hall Sixty Years After."

1888

1. "Hallucination of Memory and 'Telepathy.' " *Mind*, 13 (1888): 244–48. Pp. 245–48 are quoted in *1889–11*, pp. 367–70.

Proposes the hypothesis that some reported cases of telepathy can be explained as hallucinations of memory.

1889

1. "Addenda to Cases 24, 28, 36, 56." *Proceedings of the American Society for Psychical Research*, 1 (March, 1889): 527–28.
Unsigned. Supplies additional information on the cases reported in *1889–2* and *1889–11*. For other writings by him in the *Proceedings* see *1886–4*.

2. "Appendix to the Report on Phantasms and Presentiments." *Proceedings of the American Society for Psychical Research*, 1 (March, 1889): 429–515.
Unsigned. Appendix to *1889–11*. Mostly texts of documents received by the committee. Possibly, the arrangement of the material is more the work of Richard Hodgson than of Royce.
For other writings by him in the *Proceedings* see *1886–4*.

3. "Bancroft's California," *Nation*, 48 (1889): 140–42, 164–65.
Review of Hubert Howe Bancroft, *History of California*, vol. 6 (vol. 18 of Bancroft's *History of the Pacific States of North America*; vol. 23 of Bancroft's *Works*).
Unsigned. Attributed to Royce by Haskell. This review refers back to *1887–1*. For a list of similar reviews see *1886–2*.

4. "Comments on the Cases Recorded in the Appendix to the Report of the Committee on Phantasms and Presentiments." *Proceedings of the American Society for Psychical Research*, 1 (March, 1889): 516–26.
Comments on *1889–2*. Signed simply "Josiah Royce." For other writings by him in the *Proceedings* see *1886–4*.

5. "Courses in Ethics in Harvard College." *Ethical Record*, 2 (1889): 138–43.
One of a number of papers on the teaching of ethics in American colleges.

6. "Is there a Philosophy of Evolution?" *Unitarian Review*, 32 (1889): 1–29, 97–113.
Read as "The Fundamental Problem of Recent Philosophy" before the Yale Philosophical Club. Writing to Howison on July 13, 1889, Royce noted that he was invited on "very short notice" and prepared the lecture in haste. It was dictated to a stenographer, corrected, and read as it stood. In *1889–5*, p. 141, he described this as the "substance" of his course on the "Philosophy of Nature" at Harvard.

7. "Note on Two Recently Reported Cases of Pathological and Other Pseudo-Presentiments." *Proceedings of the American Society for Psychical Research*, 1 (March, 1889): 565–67.
Signed. For other writings by him in the *Proceedings* see *1886–4*.

8. "The Practical Value of Philosophy." *Ethical Record*, 2 (1889): 9–22.

An "extemporaneous address" to the convention of Ethical Societies, in Philadelphia, on January 25, 1889. Royce spoke in support of the plan of the Ethical Culture societies to establish a school of philosophy.

9. "Reflections after a Wandering Life in Australasia." *Atlantic Monthly*, 63 (1889): 675–86.

Speculations about the social and political future of Australia and New Zealand, based upon his travels in early 1888. Somewhat autobiographical.

See also *1889–10* and *1891–7*.

10. "Reflections after a Wandering Life in Australasia," Second Paper. *Atlantic Monthly*, 63 (1889): 813–28.

See *1889–9*.

11. "Report of the Committee on Phantasms and Presentiments." *Proceedings of the American Society for Psychical Research*, 1 (March, 1889): 350–428.

Signed. According to the minutes, Royce reported on behalf of the committee at the annual meeting, in Boston, on January 10, 1888. However, the report refers to documents dated as late as December, 1888, so that the date of the report is doubtful.

For other writings by him in the *Proceedings* see *1886–4*.

1890

1. "Dr. Abbot's 'Way Out of Agnosticism.'" *IJE*, 1 (1890–91): 98–113.

Review of Francis Ellingwood Abbot, *The Way Out of Agnosticism*. This review gave rise to the controversy between Abbot and Royce. The Abbot Papers in the Harvard University Archives contain some materials relating to this affair:
a. Abbot's reply to Royce titled "Dr. Royce's 'Professional Warning.'" This copy has a note initialed F.E.A., to the effect that the underscoring was made by Royce.
b. A first proof and a final proof of Royce's reply to Abbot titled "The 'American' and the Hegelian 'Theory of Universals.'" This was intended for the *IJE*, but was not published.
c. Francis Ellingwood Abbot, *Professor Royce's Libel: A Public Appeal for Redress to the Corporation and Overseers of Harvard University*. A pamphlet, dated Boston, October 1, 1891, 48 pp. Another copy is in the New York Public Library. Contains *1891–9*.
d. Francis Ellingwood Abbot, *A Public Remonstrance Addressed to the Board of Overseers of Harvard University: Is not Harvard Responsible for the Conduct of her Professors, as Well as of her*

Students? A pamphlet, dated Boston, February 1, 1892, Another copy is in the New York Public Library.

e. Various letters and memoranda. Among these: numerous letters to Abbot, by various correspondents, supporting him; letter to Abbot from Royce's lawyer, J. B. Warner, dated July 14, 1891; correspondence between Abbott and Felix Adler, editor of the *IJE*.

f. At least two letters from Royce to Abbot, both written, however, before the controversy.

The *Boston Evening Transcript*, October 29, 1891, pp. 1–2, published an account of the affair, including an interview with Royce. See also *1891–2*.

The *Nation*, vol. 53 (1891), published four letters relating to the controversy: C. S. Peirce's, p. 372; William James', pp. 389–90; Joseph B. Warner's, p. 408; Francis E. Abbot's p. 426.

Peirce also expressed his views in a letter to Abbot, in the Houghton Library at Harvard. Royce's letter to Peirce, dated November 18, 1891, explaining his own position, was published in part, see *L–32*. The original is in Houghton.

Royce also reviewed an earlier book by Abbot, see *1886–1*.

2. Editorial contributions to George Hamlin Fitch, "How California Came into the Union," *Century*, n.s., 18 (1890): 775–92. This essay is accompanied by a number of notes signed "Editor."

In 1890–92, the *Century* published a series of papers on the history of California. Besides providing two of these papers (*1890–4, 1891–10*), Royce gave some editorial advice. He suggested changes in the text and provided notes. To what extent Royce is responsible for the series seems impossible to determine. To much of the needed material is, most likely, no longer extant· Other items in this series for which Royce is to some extent responsible are *1891–3, 1891–4, 1891–5*.

In a letter to Robert U. Johnson, dated June 4, 1890, Royce suggested several omissions and provided notes. The documents published in *1890–4*, apparently, were originally included among these notes. Royce's letter to Johnson of June 12, 1890 suggests that Johnson returned the Fitch manuscript to Royce with the request that the documents be published as a separate item. Clearly, the notes published with this essay are much briefer than what Royce must have sent to Johnson originally. It seems impossible to determine the extent to which Royce's notes survive in the printed version.

3. "Frémont." *Atlantic Monthly*, 66 (1890): 548–57.

An attempt to estimate Frémont's public character, written shortly after Frémont's death. For a list of other writings on Frémont see *1886–3*.

4. "Light on the Seizure of California." *Century*, n·s., 18 (1890): 792–94.

Two letters: to Royce from Clements R. Markham, and to Markham from Admiral Lord Alcester. The latter was written to substantiate several claims made in Royce's *California* about the naval capture of California. For other writings on the history of California see *1886–3*.

5. "A Neglected Study." *Harvard Monthly*, 10 (1890): 169–79. Reprinted in *FE*.
Urges the study of English philology.

6. *Professor Josiah Royce before the Harvard Club of Minnesota.* St. Paul: Press of Wm. E. Banning, Jr., 1890. A pamphlet. A copy can be found in the Harvard University Archives. Reprinted in the *Boston Advertiser*, October 8, 1890.
Speech to Harvard alumni on the growth of graduate study and the introduction of the three year college course at Harvard.

7. Review of William MacKintire Salter, *Ethical Religion. Nation*, 50 (1890): 95–96.
Unsigned. Attributed to Royce in Poole's and by Haskell.

1891

1. "Comment on the Foregoing." *IJE*, 1 (1890–91): 497–99.
Comment on "The Moral Aspect of 'Tips' and 'Gratuities,' " by Christine Ladd Franklin, which appeared on pp. 494–97 of the same issue.

2. "Correction from Professor Royce." *Boston Evening Transcript*, October, 30 1891, p. 4.
Letter to the editor correcting the published account of the interview on the Abbot affair which appeared in the *Boston Evening Transcript*, listed in *1890–1*. He spoke about "matters which seem to both of us to be of importance," whereas the published account had it "of no importance." The copy of this issue which I have seen, had it correctly. Possibly, there are several editions.

3. Editorial contributions to "The Official Policy for the Acquisition of California." *Century*, n.s. 19 (1890–91): 928–29. Text of a dispatch from James Buchanan to Thomas O. Larkin, dated October 17, 1845, with an editorial note.
In a letter to Robert U. Johnson, dated August 29, 1890, Royce urged that the dispatch be published and said that the State Department had furnished him with a certified copy. In a letter to Johnson, dated October 19, 1890, Royce wrote that he will send his copy of the dispatch if Johnson should want it. The same letter, however, makes it clear that the *Century* was initiating its own search for documents in Washington. Thus, it could have obtained this on its own.
For a general note on such contributions see *1890–2*.

4. Editorial Contributions to "Sherman and the San Francisco Vigilantes: Unpublished Letters of W. T. Sherman." *Century*, n.s. 21 (1891–92): 296–309. Texts of letters with editorial notes.

That Royce was the editor is made clear by his letter to Robert U. Johnson, dated September 21, 1891, in the Bancroft Library of the University of California and the following four documents in the Century Collection in the New York Public Library:

a. Royce's letter to Johnson dated October 6, 1891;
b. Miss Sherman's letter to Johnson dated October 1, 1891, with marginal comments in Royce's hand;
c. comments by Miss Sherman about Royce's manuscript, with marginal notes in Royce's hand;
d. Royce's letter to Johnson, dated October 7, 1891. In the letter of September 21, Royce suggests that one letter (from Woolo to Sherman) be omitted, and no such letter appears in the published text.

5. Editorial contributions to William T. Coleman, "San Francisco Vigilance Committees." *Century*, n·s., 21 (1891–92): 133–50. This essay is accompanied by several notes signed "Editor."

In a letter to Robert U. Johnson, dated September 21, 1891, Royce wrote that he is returning the proofs of Coleman's article with several notes. For a general note on such contributions see *1890–2*.

6. "The Frémont Legend." *Nation*, 52 (1891): 423–25.

Letter to the editor, dated May 10, 1891. Presents a new document on Frémont's role in the conquest of California. It constitutes Royce's reply to Frémont's own account, published in the *Century*, n.s., 19 (1891): 917–28. The document is the dispatch from George Bancroft to John Drake Sloat, dated October 17, 1845. According to Royce's letter to Horace E. Scudder of April 7, 1891, this was to be his last word in the Frémont controversy. For other writings on Frémont see *1886–3*.

7. "Impressions of Australia." *Scribner's Magazine*, 9 (1891): 75–87.

Based on Royce's travels in Australia in the first half of 1888. In part, speculations about the future course of Australian politics. See also *1889–9* and *1889–10*.

8. "Is There a Science of Education?" *Educational Review*, 1 (1891): 15–25, 121–32.

Written at the invitation of the editor for the first number.

9. "Memorandum of April 13, 1891." In Francis E. Abbot, *Professor Royce's Libel*, see *1890–1*.

Memorandum on the Abbot affair.

10. "Montgomery and Frémont: New Documents on the Bear Flag Affair." *Century*, n.s., 19 (1891): 780–83.

At the request of the editor, Royce summarizes certain documents concerning John B. Montgomery and his relations with Frémont. Frémont's letter to Montgomery of June 16, 1846 is printed entire. For other writings on Frémont see *1886-3*.

11. "A New Study of Psychology." *IJE*, 1 (1890-91): 143-69. Review of William James, *Principles of Psychology*.

12. "Notes on Current Periodical Literature." *IJE*, 1 (1890-91): 499-501.
Comments on current issues of the *Monist, Archiv für Geschichte der Philosophie*, and *Philosophische Studien*.

13. "The Outlook in Ethics." *IJE*, 2 (1891-92): 106-11.
Comments on the more dominant features of current ethical discussion.

14. "Present Ideals of American University Life." *Scribner's Magazine*, 10 (1891): 376-88. Reprinted with the additional title "Certain Tendencies in the Development of the American University," in *American Institute of Instruction, Proceedings of the 62nd Annual Meeting. . .*, (Boston: American Institute of Instruction, 1891), pp. 80-111.
Address delivered to the annual meeting of the Institute, in Bethlehem, New Hampshire, on July 6-9, 1891.

15. Review of John Dewey, *Outlines of a Critical Theory of Ethics*. *IJE*, 1 (1890-91): 503-5.

16. Review of Robert B. Fairbrain, *On the Doctrine of Morality in its Relation to the Grace of Redemption*. *IJE*, 1 (1890-91): 502-3.

17. Review of Herbert Spencer, *Justice: Being Part IV of the Principles of Ethics*. *IJE*, 2 (1891-92): 117-23.

18. "Two Philosophers of the Paradoxical." *Atlantic Monthly*, vol. 67 (1891): "Hegel," pp. 45-60; "Schopenhauer," pp. 161-73.
These two papers are based on the same lectures as is the *Spirit of Modern Philosophy, 1892-7*; see Royce's letters to Horace E. Scudder of September 18, 1890, and November 2, 1890. "Hegel," except for several introductory pages on modern philosophy in general, with slight changes, appears in the *Spirit of Modern Philosophy*, pp. 194-216; "Schopenhauer," with slight changes, on pp. 241-64.

1892

1. "The Implications of Self-Consciousness." *The New World*, 1 (1892): 289-310. Reprinted in *SGE*, with slight changes.
In *SGE*, p. 140, Royce claims to "set forth in brief some of the evidence for an idealistic interpretation of the nature of reality." He also maintains that the argument here is essentially identical with that in the *Religious Aspect of Philosophy, 1885-1*, and the *Spirit of the Modern Philosophy, 1892-7*.

2. "Philosophy." *Harvard Graduates' Magazine*, 1 (1892–93): 115–16.
Report on the work of the Harvard philosophy department, part
of a series of such departmental reports. Most of this one is devoted
to the coming of Hugo Münsterberg to take charge of the work in
experimental psychology.
For other such reports see *1893–5, 1895–4, 1896–4.*

3. "Report on the Recent Literature of Ethics and Related Topics in
America." *IJE*, 2 (1891–92): 378–85.
This report notices the following works:
a. Francis Howe Johnson, *What is Reality?* (pp. 379–80).
b. J. Macbride Sterrett, *Studies in Hegel's Philosophy of Religion*
(pp. 380–81).
c. James Thompson Bixby, *The Crisis in Morals* (pp. 381–83).
d.–g. *Conduct as a Fine Art*, which contains Nicholas Paine Gilman,
The Laws of Daily Conduct and Edward Payson Jackson, *Character Building;* C. C. Everett, *Ethics for Young People;* Julius H.
Seelye, *Duty: A Book for Schools;* Benjamin B. Comegy's, ed.,
A Primer of Ethics (pp. 383–85).
h. Barrett Wendell, *Cotton Mather, The Puritan Priest* (p. 385).
Royce was a member of the editorial committee of the *International Journal of Ethics*. Frequently, his address was given as the
address to which books for review should be sent. This report and
others like it, likely, are the results of such editorial commitments.
For other such reports see *1892–4, 1893–6, 1893–7.*

4. "Report upon the Recent Literature of Ethics and Related Topics
in America." *IJE*, 2 (1891–92): 514–18. Published as the continuation
of *1892–3.*
This report notices the following works:
a. Anonymous, *Calmire* (a novel) (pp. 514–17).
b. Marietta Kies, *The Ethical Principle and its Application In State
Relations* (p.517).
c. James Edward Le Rossignol, *The Ethical Philosophy of Samuel
Clarke* (p. 517).
d. E. Colbert, *Humanity in its Origin and Early Growth* (pp 517–
18).
e. *A Directory of the Charitable and Beneficent Organizations of
Boston etc.* (p. 518).
For a list of other such reports see *1892–3.*

5. Review of Benno Erdmann's *Logische Elementarlehre. Philosophical
Review*, 1 (1892): 547–52. Reprinted in *RLE.*

6. Review of Johann Friedrich Herbert, *A Text-Book in Psychology.
Educational Review*, 4 (1892): 185–91.
This is a review of the English translation by Margaret K. Smith.

7. *The Spirit of Modern Philosophy: An Essay in the Form of Lectures.*
Boston and New York: Houghton, Mifflin and Co., 1892, xv, 519 pp.

Reprinted with an introduction by Ralph Barton Perry (New York: G. Braziller, 1955, xix, 519 pp.). The original edition reproduced (New York: Norton, 1967, xv, 519 pp.). Translated into the Italian by Giuseppe Rensi, *Lo spirito della filosofia moderna*, 2 vols. (Bari: Laterza et Figli, 1910). Translated into Spanish by Vicente P. Quintero, *El espiritu de la filosofia moderna* (Buenos Aires, 1947).

The book grew out of a variety of lectures given mostly to popular audiences over a period of several years. In the preface, p. v, Royce makes it clear that roughly the same lectures were repeated on a number of different occasions. The *Critic* (n.s., 13 [1890]: 136) carried an announcement of one series of these lectures. They were to begin on March 15, 1890, and were to be given in the homes of various women. Probably, this was not the first time these lectures were delivered. In a letter to Horace E. Scudder, dated November 2, 1890, Royce wrote that he planned to repeat several of the lectures in Cambridge in November.

Writing to Scudder on January 25, 1891, Royce stated that he was undecided about the title. He was considering several possibilities —"Representative Modern Thinkers and Problems: A Series of Lectures Introductory to Philosophy"; "A Study in Modern Philosophy, Being a Series of Popular Lectures"; and, an "appeal to humbug," "The Way of Salvation, Being Philosophy for the Fair in Face and Mind." The title finally chosen was used by Royce as early as 1877 in an essay of that name in vol. 55 of the Royce Papers.

In the January 25 letter to Scudder, Royce wrote that he wanted to present the manuscript by June for publication in October. His preface is dated January 1, 1892.

Royce always insisted upon the popular character of the work. In the preface to the *World and the Individual*, vol. 1 p. viii, Royce wrote that in the *Spirit of Modern Philosophy* he had stated his views in a "shape intended for a popular audience." He also makes it clear that the work is not simply a historical study, but is an attempt to show how his own idealism grows out of the history of recent philosophy. Both these aspects are especially emphasized in the preface and in the text of the *Spirit of Modern Philosophy*.

The book contains two appendices which are different in character from the rest of the work. These are titled: "On Kant's Transcendental Deduction of the Categories," and "The Hegelian Theory of Universals."

1893

1. "The Knowledge of Good and Evil." *IJE*, 4 (1893–94): 48–80. Reprinted in *SGE*.

Note on p. 89, *SGE*: "The paper was suggested by one written by Professor Georg Simmel, of Berlin." That paper is titled "Moral Deficiencies as Determining Intellectual Function" (*IJE*, 3 [1892–93]: 490–507). Royce is trying to discover the proper place of the knowledge of evil in man's moral and intellectual life.

2. "Mental Defect and Disorder from the Teacher's Point of View."
Educational Review, 6 (1893): 209–22, 322–31, 449–63.

The tenth lecture of a course of twelve given at Harvard on
"Topics in Psychology of Interest to Teachers" in the early months
of 1893. Vols. 63–66 of the Royce Papers contain manuscripts of
ten of these lectures and proof sheets of the twelfth. They are
described as given at Harvard from February to May 1893. The
titles of the lectures are as follows:

(1) "What is a General Idea?"
(2) "General Ideas and the Theory of Habits"
(3) "The Constituents of a General Idea: The Relations of In-
     tellect, Feeling and Will"
(4) "General Ideas as Products of Imitation: The Psychology of
     Suggestion and the Lessons of Hypnotic Research"
(5) "The Psychology of Imitation; The Place of Authority in
     Education; The Psychology of our Belief in the External
     World; And the Educational Significance of This Portion of
     Psychology"
(6) "Apperception, Attention, and the Theory of an Orderly
     Acquisition of General Ideas"
(7) "Some Imperfections of General Ideas. 'Unconscious' and
     'Segmented' Processes and Ideas"
(8) "The Psychological Theory of Self-Consicousness from the
     Teacher's Point of View"
(9) "On a Due Regard for the Varieties of Individual Tempera-
     ment"
(10) MS missing
(11) "On Some Special Devices for Mental Training"
(12) Proof sheets of *1893–3*.

The lectures were reported extensively in the *Journal of Education*
(Boston) (37 [1893]: 201, 217, 233, 249, 281, 313, 329, 345, 361, 367
[issue of June 15, 1893]; 38 [1893]: 49, 65). These reports summarize
each lecture and list some of the bibliographic material referred to
by the lecturer. In the first eight reports, authorship is indicated in
the following way: "By Professor Josiah Royce [Reported for the
Journal]," in the others, simply by "Professor Josiah Royce." It is
possible that they were prepared by Royce himself, but I have seen
no manuscripts which would support this conjecture. The titles of
the reports, usually in an abbreviated form, correspond to those of
the manuscript.

Royce used at least the same lecture titles on several other occasions. On February 20, 1893, he lectured at the Brooklyn Institute
of Arts and Sciences on "The Psychology of General Ideas from
the Teacher's Point of View." From October 14 to November 11,
1893, he gave a series of five lectures at the Brooklyn Institute with
the general title "Topics in Psychology of Interest to Teachers." The
lecture titles were as follows:

(1) "The Psychology of Imitation from the Teacher's Point of View"
(2) Concluded
(3) "Apperception and the Theory of Orderly Acquisition of Ideas"
(4) "Psychology and the Training of Self-Consciousness"
(5) "On a due Regard for Varieties of Individual Temperament."

3. "On Certain Psychological Aspects of Moral Training." *IJE*, 3 (1892–93): 413–36.
    The twelfth and last lecture of "Topics in Psychology of Interest to Teachers." For a description of the series see *1893-2.*

4. "Phases of Thought and Criticism." *Atlantic,* 71 (1893): 126–29.
    Review of Brother Azarias, *Phases of Thought and Criticism.* Unsigned. Attributed to Royce on stylistic grounds.

5. "Philosophy." *Harvard Graduates' Magazine,* 2 (1893–94): 238–39.
    Report on the Harvard Department of Philosophy for the 1893–94 academic year.
    For a list of other such reports see *1892-2.*

6. "Report on the Recent Literature of Ethics and Related Topics in America." *IJE*, 3 (1892–93): 274–79.
    This report notices the following works:
    a. Matoon Monroe Curtis, *Philosophy and Physical Science* (pp. 274–75).
    b. Joseph Le Conte, *The Relation of Philosophy to Psychology and to Physiology* (p. 275).
    c–d. Herbert Nichols, *The Origin of Pleasure and Pain;* Henry Rutgers Marshall, *Pleasure-Pain and Sensation* (pp. 275–76).
    e. Ferdinand Courtney French, *The Concept of Law in Ethics,* (pp. 276–77).
    f–g. James Gibson Hume, *The Value of a Study of Ethics;* James Gibson Hume, *Political Economy and Ethics* (pp. 277–78).
    h. James McCosh, *Our Moral Nature: Being a Brief System of Ethics* (p. 278).
    i. William Dewitt Hyde, *Practical Ethics* (pp. 278–79).
    For a list of other such reports see *1892-3.*

7. "Report on the Recent Literature of Ethics and Related Topics in America." *IJE*, 3 (1892–93): 527–41.
    This report notices the following books:
    a. George M. Gould, *The Meaning and the Method of Life. A Search for Religion in Biology* (pp. 528–33).
    b. C. M. Williams, *A Review of the Systems of Ethics Founded on the Theory of Evolution* (pp. 533–39). For author's reply see "Principle of Classification of Recent Ethical Writers" (*IJE*, 55 |1893–94|: 238–39). At the bottom of p. 239, there is a comment of several lines on the preceding by Royce.

c. William Mackintire Salter, *First Steps in Philosophy (Physical and Ethical)* (pp. 539–41). Contains a statement of Royce's views on causality. For a list of other such reports see *1892–3.*

8. Review of Bernard Bosanquet, *A History of Aesthetic. The New World*, 2 (1893): 338–42.

9. Review of Theodore F. Wright, *The Human and Its Relations to the Divine. IJE*, 4 (1893–94): 129–30.

10. "Tolstoi and the Unseen Moral Order." In *The First Book of the Author's Club: Liber Scriptorum*, pp. 488–97. New York: Author's Club (of New York), 1893.

All the contributions were written especially for this volume, published to raise funds for the clubhouse. Each essay of each copy is signed in pen and ink by the author. Two hundred and fifty-one copies were printed.

11. "Two Studies of Philosophical Idealism." *Nation*, 57 (1893): 231–33.

Review of Edward Caird, *The Critical Philosophy of Immanuel Kant* and *The Evolution of Religion*.

Unsigned. Attributed to Royce by Haskell.

1894

1. "Can Psychology be Founded upon the Study of Consciousness Alone, or is Physiology Needed for the Purpose?" In *Proceedings of the International Congress of Education of the World's Columbian Exposition*, pp. 687–92. New York: National Educational Association, 1894. A transcript of the discussion which followed is given on p. 692. These proceeding are sometimes bound as vol. 32 (1893) of the *National Educational Association Proceedings*.

Read for Royce by William T. Harris on July 26, 1893, to the Department of Rational Psychology of the Congress.

The question was assigned to him. Since, in Royces' view, it has been answered already in the negative, he will rather attempt to show "why and to what extent" psychology should study man's physical life.

2. "The Case of John Bunyan." *Psychological Review*, 1 (1894): 22–33, 134–51, 230–40. There exist off-prints of this text in pamphlet form. Reprinted in *SGE.* Abstract: *American Psychological Association, Proceedings of the Second Annual Meeting* (New York, 1893), pp. 17–18.

Paper read at the second annual meeting of the Association held on December 27–28, 1893, in New York.

Royce treats Bunyan as an example of a certain kind of mental disorder.

3. "The External World and the Social Consciousness." *Philosophical Review*, 3 (1894): 513–45.

Lecture to the Philosophical Club of Princeton College given on February 2, 1894. Vol. 62 of the Royce Papers contains the manuscript of "The Two-Fold Nature of Knowledge: Imitative and Reflective." It is said to be an altered version of the paper read on August 24, 1893, at the Philosophical Congress at the World's Columbian Exposition. The manuscript has the following note: "MS later mutilated for the paper in the Philos'l Rev. on 'External World & Soc'l Consc.'" This is confirmed by numerous missing pages. It is possible that these missing pages appear in the *Philosophical Review* text. This manuscript, except for the sections with missing pages, was published by Peter Fuss, "The Two-Fold Nature of Knowledge: Imitative and Reflective, An Unpublished Manuscript of Josiah Royce," *P–9*.

4. "The Imitative Functions, and Their Place in Human Nature." *Century*, n.s., 26 (1894): 137–45.

In part, a request for information. Included is a series of questions and an invitation to the public to send their replies to Royce. For another essay on imitation see *1895–5*.

5. "The Problem of Paracelsus," *The New World*, 3 (1894): 89–110. Reprinted in the *Boston Browning Society Papers, 1886–1897* (New York: Macmillan Co., 1897), pp. 221–48. Reprinted in *FE*.

Read before the Boston Browning Society on November 26, 1893. On Browning's *Paracelsus*.

6. Review of Francis H. Bradley, *Appearance and Reality*. *Philosophical Review*, 3 (1894): 212–18.

For further comments on Bradley see the *Conception of God*, *1895–1, 1897–1*, pp. 44, 141, 296, 302; and, especially, the Supplementary Essay of the *World and the Individual.*

7. Review of Redelia Brisbane, *Albert Brisbane: A Mental Biography*. *IJE*, 4 (1893–94): 536–39.

8. Review of Frank Chapman Sharp, *The Aesthetic Element in Morality, and Its Place in a Utilitarian Theory of Morals*. *IJE*, 4 (1893–94): 395–99.

9. "The Student of Philosophy." *Harvard Monthly*, 18 (1894): 87–99.

A sketch of the mental characteristics of those who should not study philosophy.

1895

1. *The Conception of God*. An address before the Philosophical Union by Josiah Royce, with comments thereon by Sidney Edward Mezes, Josiah Le Conte, and George Holmes Howison. Berkeley: Executive

Council of the Union, 1895, 84 pp. Philosophical Union of the University of California, Bulletin no. 15.

Text of a discussion held in the summer of *1895* at Berkeley. For further comments see *1897-3*.

2. Introduction to Anna Boynton Thompson, *The Unity of Fichte's Doctrine of Knowledge*. Boston: Ginn & Co., 1895, pp. ix-xx. Radcliffe College Monographs, no. 7.

3. "Natural Law, Ethics, and Evolution." *IJE*, 5 (1894-95): 489-500. Reprinted in *SGE* with slight changes.

One of a series of papers discussing Thomas H. Huxley's "Evolution and Ethics" (*Popular Science Monthly*, 44 [1893]: 18-35, 178-91). Two other papers on the same topic appeared in *IJE*, 6 (1895-96): James Mark Baldwin, "The Cosmic and the Moral," pp. 93-97; Frances Emily White, "Relation of the Ethical to the Cosmic Process," pp. 97-101.

4. "Philosophy." *Harvard Graduates' Magazine*, 4 (1895-96): 246-47.

Report on the Harvard department of philosophy for 1895-96. For list of other such reports see *1892-2*.

5. "Preliminary Report on Imitation." *Psychological Review*, 2 (1895): 217-35.

Read at the third annual meeting of the American Psychological Association at Princeton, on December 27, 1894. Royce reported on experiments he had been conducting since October 1, 1894, under the "guidance" of H. Münsterberg, dealing with the classification of imitative functions. *Science* refers to this as "A Preliminary Report and Observations on a Research into the Psychology of Imitation." An abstract which appeared in the *Psychological Review* (2 [1895]: 161) is titled "A Preliminary Report on a Research into the Psychology of Imitation."

For another essay on imitation see *1894-4*.

6. Review of Brothers of the Christian Schools, *Elementary Course of Christian Philosophy*. *IJE*, 5 (1894-95): 398-99.

7. Review of William M. Bryant, *A Syllabus of Ethics*. *IJE*, 6 (1895-96): 117-18.

8. Review of John Dewey, *The Study of Ethics: A Syllabus*. *IJE*, 6 (1895-96): 110-13.

9. Review of James H. Hyslop, *The Elements of Ethics*. *IJE*, 6 (1895-96): 113-17.

10. Review of J. Macbridge Sterrett, *The Ethics of Hegel: Translated Selections from his "Rechtsphilosophie."* *IJE*, 5 (1894-95): 257-60.

11. Review of Maurice Thompson, *The Ethics of Literory Art*. *IJE*, 5 (1894-95): 244-47.

12. Review of *Thoughts from the Writings of Rev. John C. Learned.* *IJE*, 5 (1894–95): 270.

13. "Self-Consciousness, Social Consciousness and Nature." *Philosophical Review*, 4 (1895): 465–85, 577–602. Reprinted in *SGE*, with the omission of a reference to *1895–14*, which appears on p. 474 of the *Philosophical Review*.

    A "considerably enlarged" version of a paper read to the Philosophical Club of Brown University, on May 23, 1895. In the *Philosophical Review*, this paper is said to continue the "argument" of *1894–3*.

14. "Some Observations on the Anomalies of Self-Consciousness." *Psychological Review*, 2 (1895): 433–57, 574–84. Reprinted in *SGE*.

    Read to the Medico-Psychological Association of Boston on March 21, 1895.

15. "The Study of Philosophy." *Occident* (University of California), 29 (1895): 50–53.

1896

1. "Browning's Theism." *The New World*, 5 (1896): 401–22. Reprinted in the *Boston Browning Society Papers, 1886–1897* (New York: Macmillan Co., 1897), pp. 7–34.

    Read before the Boston Browning Society in late March of 1896.

2. "Certitudes and Illusions." *Science*, n.s., 3 (1896): 354–55.

    A letter to the editor, dated February 22, 1896. Comments on the treatment of Hegel in J. W. Powell, "Certitudes and Illusions," *Science*, n.s., 3 (1896): 263–71.

3. "Outlines of Psychology; Or, a Study of the Human Mind." In James W. Roosevelt, ed., *In Sickness and in Health*, pp. 171–233. New York: D. Appleton & Co., 1896.

    The *Outlines of Psychology, 1903–3*, is an expansion and reworking of this essay. In its preface, p. v, Royce notes that the present volume was a "popular guide" to hygiene, nursing, and "related topics." His own contribution was an introductory sketch of elementary principles and practical applications of psychology.

4. "Philosophy." *Harvard Graduates' Magazine*, 5 (1896–97): 228–32.

    A report on the Harvard department of philosophy. Royce announces his course in "Advanced Logic" and states that he will begin inquiries about setting up a new course of studies to lead to the doctorate in the "Anthropological and Sociological" sciences.

    For a list of other such reports see *1892–2*.

5. Review of James Mark Baldwin, *Mental Development in the Child and the Race: Methods and Processes.* *Psychological Review*, 3 (1896): 201–11.

1897

1. "Benedict Spinoza." In Charles Dudley Warner, ed., *Library of the World's Best Literature*, 23: 13785–93. New York: R. S. Peale and J. A. Hill, ᶜ1897. Reprinted as the *Warner Library* (New York: Knickerbocker Press for the Warner Library Co., 1917).
 Emphasizes Spinoza's pantheism.

2. "Comment by Professor Royce on Hegel's Social Theory." In James Mark Baldwin, *Social and Ethical Interpretations in Mental Development*, pp. 569–70. New York: Macmillan Co., 1897.
 Extract from a private letter. For another extract from the same letter see *L–2*. There are no indications that Royce consented to publication.

3. *The Conception of God: A Philosophical Discussion Concerning the Nature of the Divine Idea as a Demonstrable Reality*, by Josiah Royce, Joseph Le Conte, George Holmes Howison, and Sidney Edward Mezes. New York: The Macmillan Co.; London: Macmillan & Co., Ltd., 1897, xxxviii, 354 pp. Publications of the Philosophical Union of the University of California, vol. 1, George Holmes Howison, ed.
 Contents:
 (1) "Introduction by the Editor" [Howison]
 (2) "The Conception of God: An Address Before the Philosophical Union," by Royce
 (3) "Worth and Goodness as Marks of the Absolute: A Criticism of Professor Royce's Argument," by Mezes
 (4) "God, And Connected Problems, In the Light of Evolution: With Remarks on Professor Royce's Views," by Le Conte
 (5) "The City of God, And the True God as its Head: Comments on All the Foregoing Theories," by Howison
 (6) "The Absolute and the Individual: A Supplementary Discussion, With Replies to Criticisms," by Royce.
 Parts 1 and 6 were written especially for the second edition. Royce's supplementary discussion is by far the longest contribution, occupying nearly two thirds of the volume. Royce's contributions survive in manuscript, vols. 5 and 6 of the Royce Papers. The manuscript of the supplementary discussion, particularly pp. 65, 65a, 149, of vol. 6, has marginal notes by Howison. Vol. 7 of the Royce Papers contains two undated essays which, with modifications, were used in the supplementary discussion: (1) "The Place of the Will in the Conception of the Absolute" (incomplete); (2) "The Principle of Individuation." The second item, possibly, is a lecture.
 For Royce's reaction to Howison's introduction see his letter to Howison of October 5, 1897. Howison commented on the discussion in "The Real Issue in 'The Conception of God,'" *Philosophical Review*, 7 (1898): 518–22. Royce indicated the relation of the sup-

plementary discussion to the *World and the Individual* in the preface to the *World and the Individual*, vol. 1, p. x.

For the first edition of the *Conception of God* see *1895-1*.

4. "Immanuel Kant." In Charles Dudley Warner, ed., *Library of the World's Best Literature*, 15: 8477-85. New York: R. S. Peale and J. A. Hill, ᶜ1897. Reprinted as the *Warner Library* (New York: Knickerbocker Press for the Warner Library Co., 1917).

For the most part, a description of Kant's character.

5. "Originality and Consciousness." *Harvard Monthly*, 24 (1897): 133-42. Reprinted in *SGE*.

Maintains the view that men are, on the whole, unconscious of the sources of their individuality. In the introduction to the *SGE*, p. xi, Royce suggests that this is due to the "Limitation of Span" which is characteristic of the human type of consciousness.

6. "President Andrews Case." *Boston Evening Transcript*, August 18, 1897, p. 6.

Letter to the editor on the firing of president Andrews of Brown University.

7. "The Problem of Job." *The New World*, 6 (1897): 261-81. Reprinted in *SGE*.

A paper, dealing with the problem of evil, read to a ministerial convention.

8. "Systematic Philosophy in America in the Years 1893, 1894, and 1895." *Archiv für systematische Philosophie*, 3 (1897): 245-66.

9. Review of John Ellis McTaggart, *Studies in the Hegelian Dialectic*. *Philosophical Review*, 6 (1897): 69-76.

10. Review of George Frederick Stout, *Analytic Psychology*. *Mind*, n.s., 6 (1897): 379-99.

Stout's reaction is reported by William James in *Essays in Radical Empiricism* (New York and London: Longmans, Green & Co., 1912), pp. 158, 187. James was the intended reviewer, but passed the book on to Royce. See the letter from James to Flournoy in Robert C. Le Clair, ed., *The Letters of William James and Théodore Flournoy* (Madison, Milwaukee, and London: University of Wisconsin Press, 1966), p. 55.

1898

1. "New Methods at Hingham." *Nation*, 66 (1898): 459.

Letter to the editor, dated June 10, 1898. Royce denies that he is in any way connected with the "New School of Methods" at Hingham. He had consented to give one lecture, but withdrew.

2. "The New Psychology and the Consulting Psychologist." *National Educational Association, Journal of Proceedings and Addresses of the Thirty-Seventh Annual Meeting*, 1898, pp. 554–70. Reprinted in *Forum*, 26 (1898): 80–96.

Presented to the National Council of Education on July 6, 1898. In the minutes of the meeting this paper is titled "The Relation of Psychology in its Various Aspects to Education."

3. "Plato, and His Meaning for European Thought," a biographical and critical introduction to the *Dialogues of Plato*, Benjamin Jowett, trans., pp. vii–xix. New York: D. Appleton and Co., 1898. This edition appears in the *World's Great Books* series.

4. "The Psychology of Invention." *Psychological Review*, 5 (1898): 113–44. Reprinted in the *Scientific American Supplements*, 45 (1898): 18602–3, 18681–83.

Read at the annual meeting of the American Psychological Association at Ithaca, N.Y., on December 28, 1897.

5. Review of Theodore H. Hittell, *History of California*, vols. 3 and 4. *American Historical Review*, 4 (1898–99): 184–86.

For a list of other similar reviews see *1886–2*.

6. Review of Ralph Waldo Trine, *In Tune with the Infinite; Or Fulness of Peace, Power and Plenty. IJE*, 9 (1898–99): 124–26.

7. "The Social Basis of Conscience." *National Educational Association, Journal of Proceedings and Addresses of the Thirty-Seventh Annual Meeting*, 1898, pp. 196–99. Abstract. A transcript of the discussion is given on pp. 199–204.

An address before the National Educational Association given on July 11, in Washington, D.C. It is possible that this was originally the eighth lecture of a series of ten titled "Social Factors in the Development of the Individual Mind." Vols. 69 and 70 of the Royce Papers contain the manuscript of the lectures. Lecture 8, "The Social Basis of Conscience," is missing. The series was given for the Twentieth Century Club of Boston, at Jacob Sleeper Hall of Boston University, beginning on January 15, 1898. A printed syllabus of the lectures was distributed by the club.

8. *Studies of Good and Evil: A Series of Essays upon the Problems of Philosophy and of Life*. New York: D. Appleton and Co., 1898, xvii. 384 pp. Reprinted in an unaltered form (Hamden, Conn.: Archon Books, 1964).

Contents:
(1) "Introduction." Explains the general purpose of the collection and comments upon each paper.
(2) "The Problem of Job," *1897–7*.
(3) "The Case of John Bunyan," *1894–2*.
(4) "Tennyson and Pessimism," *1887–9*.

(5) "The Knowledge of Good and Evil," *1893–1*.
(6) "Natural Law, Ethics, and Evolution," *1895–3*.
(7) "The Implications of Self-Consciousness," *1892–1*.
(8) "Some Observations on the Anomalies of Self-Consciousness," *1895–14*.
(9) "Self-Consciousness, Social Consciousness and Nature," *1895–13*.
(10) "Originality and Consciousness," *1897–5*.
(11) "Meister Eckhart." Previously unpublished. Read to the Plymouth School of Ethics in the summer of 1894.
(12) "An Episode of Early California Life: The Squatter Riot of 1850 in Sacramento," *1885–4*. In *SGE*, most of the original introduction (*Overland Monthly*, n.s., 6: 225–26) is omitted, and a new introduction (*SGE* pp. 298–302) is substituted for it.
(13) "Jean Marie Guyau." Previously unpublished. Prepared for the Cercle Francais of Harvard University. Delivered on March 18, 1896.

1899

1. *The World and the Individual*. 2 vols. New York: Macmillan, 1899. First Series, *The Four Historical Conceptions of Being*, xvii, 588 pp.; Second Series, *Nature, Man, and the Moral Order*, xx, 480 pp. Reprinted with an introduction by John E. Smith (New York: Dover Publications, [ᶜ1959]). The paging of this edition is identical with that of the first, except for the preliminary matter of vol. 1. Translated into Italian by Giuseppe Rensi, *Il Mondo e l'Individuo*, 4 vols. (Bari: Laterza et Figli, 1913–16) (vol. 1, 1913; vol. 2, 1914, vol. 3, 1915; vol. 4, 1916).

The Gifford lectures delivered at the University of Aberdeen. The first series was given between January 11 and February 1, 1899; the second, in January 1900. Royce was appointed Gifford lecturer before June 1897. The appointment was announced in the *Critic*, n.s., 27 (June, 1897): 397. In the Royce Papers, Box F, there are two drafts of "Plan for Gifford Lectures." The first is undated. While it refers to the "Historical Concepts of Being," in other respects it resembles the *Religious Aspect of Philosophy*. For example, Royce was planning a discussion of the "Doctrine of Total Relativity" and the "Possibility of Error." The second draft is dated October 1897.

Of the first series, only one manuscript version is extant (vols. 8–14 of the Royce Papers). According to Royce's remark in the preface to the first series, p. vii, the first series did not require extensive revisions before publication. He notes there, however, that lecture 7 on "The Internal and External Meaning of Ideas" has been enlarged considerably. When sending the manuscript to the publisher, Royce commented in his covering letter to George P. Brett, president of Macmillan Company, dated August 22, 1899: "Should I . . . fail to complete the second course . . . this first course can perfectly well stand upon its legs, as a treatise on general metaphysics."

The supplementary essay, titled "The One, the Many, and the Infinite," published in the first volume, was not a part of the lectures. The completed manuscript was sent to the publisher on September 1, 1899. In the covering letter to George P. Brett, dated September 1, 1899, Royce wrote that the essay is "one of the most serious and important things" that he has ever written or will ever write.

In the preface to the second series (p. v) Royce explained the delay in publishing it as due to revisions which he has had to make. "This revision amounts, in a large portion of the lectures, to a rewriting, and has come to include statements and arguments that I have not previously put into shape at all." This remark is substantiated by the surviving manuscripts. There are three versions of the second series in manuscript form: first draft, vols. 15–18 of the Royce Papers; revised draft, vols. 19–21; final draft, vols. 22–25. All three are undated, and there are no indications whether the first draft is the text presened at Aberdeen.

The first draft contains only nine lectures. Lectures 1, 2, and 10, respectively called "The Recognition of Facts," "The Linkage of Facts," and "The Union of God and Man," of the published text do not appear in the first draft. Lecture 7, "The Place of the Self in Being," numbered 6 in the first draft, underwent extensive revisions before publication. All of these, but especially lecture 2, are dependent upon the supplementary essay of the first series. On the other hand, lectures 3, 4, 5, 6, 8, and 9, numbered as in the published text, show no extensive changes between the first draft and the published text. Respectively, they correspond to lectures 7, 2, 4, 5, 8, and 9 of the first draft. The two lectures of the first draft which do not appear in the published text are lecture 1, "Retrospect and Outlook," and lecture 3, "The Social Origins of the Conception of Natural Law."

The revised draft is much more like the published text. It consists of nine lectures arranged in the same way as they are in the published text. All, except for the first two, are typed. The original numbering of the typed lectures, corresponding to their numbering in the first draft, is crossed out, but still visible. There still is no lecture 10.

The final draft consists of ten lectures. The first nine, except for scattered pages, are typed out. Lecture 10, the lecture not found in the earlier drafts, is written out by hand.

The completed manuscript of the second series was sent to the publisher on August 22, 1901. The preface to the second series is dated September 29, 1901.

In the preface to the first series (p. viii) Royce insists that the view of "the true relations between our finite ideas and the ultimate nature of things" is the same as that of the *Religious Aspect of Philosophy, 1885–1*; the *Spirit of Modern Philosophy, 1892–7*; the *Conception of God, 1895–1, 1897–3*; and "The Implications of Self-Consciousness," *1892–1*. In the last mentioned paper, he uses the device of presenting his own idealism as the outcome of the criticism of other conceptions of being.

In the *Philosophy of Loyalty*, *1908–2*, p. ix, Royce stated that the *World and the Individual* contains the most elaborate statement of his metaphysical views. In the *Problem of Christianity*, *1913–6*, vol. 1, p. x, Royce again singled out the *World and the Individual*. As late as the spring of 1916, Royce was lecturing on this work to his Harvard students. The Johns Hopkins University library has a student's notes for that year titled "Notes of Lectures in Philosophy 9." The second half of the course is called "The Logical Approach to Metaphysics: The World and the Individual." The notebook bears the note: "These reports were made by Ralph W. Brown . . . and placed in the hands of the lecturer himself."

1900

1. "The American University Gymnasium: Its Influence on Academic Life." *Alma Mater*, 17 (February 7, 1900): 135–38.
   Alma Mater was published by Aberdeen University. At Aberdeen, the desirability of building a central athletic facility was under discussion, and Royce was invited to comment on the role of gymnasiums in American Universities.

2. *The Conception of Immortality*. Boston and New York: Houghton, Mifflin and Co., 1900, 91 pp. Reprinted in an identical edition (New York: Greenwood Press, 1968). Reprinted, without the notes, in *RPJR*.
   The Ingersoll Lecture for 1899, delivered at Harvard. Vol. 61 of the Royce Papers contains a manuscript titled "The Conception of Immortality" with the note that it was read at Bryn Mawr and also to the "Free Religious Assoc'n 1889." Some parts of this essay were used for the Ingersoll lecture. For other expressions of his views on immortality see the *Religious Aspect of Philosophy*, *1885–1*, p. 478, and "Immortality," *1907–1*. An undated letter to Howison, written probably in 1886, states his early views especially clearly.

3. "The Pacific Coast, a Psychological Study of Influence." *International Monthly*, 2 (1900): 555–83. Reprinted in *Race Questions*, *1908–3*, as "The Pacific Coast. A Psychological Study of the Relations of Climate and Civilization."
   An "illustrated lecture" given at a special meeting of the National Geographical Society on May 2, 1898.

4. "Professor Everett as a Metaphysician." *The New World*, 9 (1900): 726–41.
   An exposition of the *Science of Thought* by Charles Carroll Everett, written shortly after Everett's death.

5. "The Recent University Movement in America." *Transactions of the Aberdeen Philosophical Society*, 3 (1900): 131–49.
   Communicated to the Society on January 31, 1899, at its invitation, when Royce was Gifford lecturer at Aberdeen.

6. Review of George Frederick Stout, *A Manual of Psychology. IJE,*
10 (1899–1900): 258–61.

7. "Some Characteristic Tendencies of American Civilization." *Transactions of the Aberdeen Philosophical Society,* 3 (1900): 194–217.

Communicated to the Society on January 30, 1900, when Royce was Gifford lecturer at Aberdeen. Deals with the capacity of the United States to assimilate alien populations. Contains some autobiographical passages.

1901

1. Contributions to James Mark Baldwin, *Dictionary of Philosophy and Psychology.* London and New York: Macmillan Co., 1901.

Royce contributed the following entries:
a. "Activity," 1: 13.
b. "Agreement," 1: 27.
c. "All," 1: 33.
d. "Analogy," 1: 41.
e. "Analogy of Experience," 1: 42. A note of five lines.
f. "Apprehension," 1: 63.
g. "Autonomy," 1: 95.
h. "Category," 1: 160–61.
i. "Greek Terminology (considered in relation to Greek philosophy)," 1: 422–30.
j. "Hegel's Terminology (in relation to the Hegelian Philosophy)," 1: 454–65.
k. "History of Philosophy," 1: 480–82. With John Dewey. How far this collaboration extended is unkown.
l. "Individual," 1: 534–37. Reprinted in *RLE.*
m. "Individuality," 1: 539. A note of several lines.
n. "Kant's Terminology (in relation to the *Kantian Philosophy*)," 1: 588–98.
o. "Latin and Scholastic Terminology: with reference principally to the *Patristic* and *Scholastic* philosophy and to *Thomism*," 1: 628–39.

2. "John Fiske: His Work as a Philosophical Writer and Teacher." *Boston Evening Transcript,* July 13, 1901, p. 14. Reprinted with minor changes as "John Fiske as Thinker," *Harvard Graduates' Magazine,* 10 (1901–1902): 23–33.

Written shortly after Fiske's death. Royce addressed the Ethical Society on November 10, 1901, in Philadelphia, and the Brooklyn Institute on December 11, 1901, on John Fiske. This address, in vol. 72 of the Royce Papers, is only slightly dependent upon the printed essay. For further comments on Fiske see *1903–1.*

3. "Joseph Le Conte." *International Monthly,* 4 (1901): 324–34.

Written shortly after Le Conte's death. Contains many recollections of college days, when Royce attended Le Conte's classes.

1902

1. "The Concept of the Infinite." *Hibbert Journal*, 1 (1902): 21–45.
Summarizes several discussions of infinity. He used this concept for metaphysical purposes in the "Supplementary Essay" of the *World and the Individual*.

2. "The Old and the New: A Lesson." *University of California Chronicle*, 2 (1902): 92–103.
Address delivered on June 30, 1902, to the first University Meeting of the summer session of 1902, at the University of California, in Berkeley.

3. "Provincialism: A Plea for Stronger Local Sentiment to Restrain National Heedlessness," *Boston Evening Transcript*, June 14, 1902, p. 32. Reprinted as a pamphlet, *Provincialism: An Address to the Phi Beta Kappa Society of the State University of Iowa* (Iowa City: State University of Iowa, 30 pp.). Reprinted with extensive additions as "Provincialism" in *Race Questions, 1908–3;* this text reprinted in *SPJR.*
Address at the Commencement of the Iowa Alpha chapter of Phi Beta Kappa in Iowa City on June 10, 1902. The student paper, the *Daily Iowan* (1 [June 12, 1902]: 1), carried an account under the headline "Phi Beta Kappa Address; Provincialism. The Cure for Mob Spirit; Professor Josiah Royce of Harvard Discusses International Problems in Scholarly Manner." For another essay on the same topic see *1909–3*

4. "Recent Logical Inquiries and their Psychological Bearings." *Psychological Review*, 9 (1902), pp. 105–133. Reprinted in *RLE.*
Presidential address to the American Psychological Association, probably, given in Chicago on January 1, 1902.

5. Speech at Alumni Banquet. In *Johns Hopkins University Celebration of the 25th Anniversary of the Founding of the University and Inauguration of Ira Remsen L.L.D. as President of the University*, pp. 112–18. Baltimore: Johns Hopkins University Press, 1902.
Royce served as chairman of the banquet. On pp. 120, 128, 132, and 144 are printed his remarks thanking the speaker who has just concluded and introducing the next one. His closing remarks appear on pp. 146–47. The banquet was held on February 22, 1902.

1903

1. Introduction to John Fiske, *Outlines of Cosmic Philosophy*, 4 vols., 1: xxi–cxlix. Boston and New York: Houghton, Mifflin and Co., 1903.
The introduction is dated August 19, 1902. Royce, as the editor,

provided a number of notes. These are scattered throughout the text and are enclosed in brackets. The major ones are listed in the index (4: 387), where they are given the title "Notes mainly relative to advance in science since the writing of *Cosmic Philosophy*."

For additional writings on Fiske see *1901–2*.

2. Letter to Hugo Münsterberg (excerpt). In *The Centenary of the Birth of Ralph Waldo Emerson, as Observed in Concord, May 25, 1903*, The Social Circle in Concord, June, 1903, p. 117.

Royce expresses his pleasure at the success of the fund drive for Emerson Hall at Harvard. The excerpt is quoted by Münsterberg in his address.

3. *Outlines of Psychology: An Elementary Treatise with Some Practical Applications*. New York: The Macmillan Co., 1903, xxvii, 392 pp. Half-title: *Teacher's Professional Library*, Nicholas Murray Butler, ed. Butler's introduction, pp. xxv–xxvii. Italian translation by Umberto Forti, *Lineamenti di Psicologia* (Bari: Laterza et Figli, 1928).

Based upon "Outlines of Psychology," *1896–3*. In a letter to George P. Brett, president of the Macmillan Company, dated October 27, 1901, Royce agreed to revise his earlier piece into a book of some 50,000 words. The preface is dated March 30, 1903.

4. "Pope Leo's Philosophical Movement, and Its Relations to Modern Thought." *Boston Evening Transcript*, July 29, 1903, p. 14. Reprinted in *Review of Catholic Pedagogy* 2 (December 1903): 230–46. Reprinted in *FE*.

Discusses developments in Catholic philosophy initiated by Leo XIII's *Aeterni Patris*.

5. "The Problem of Natural Religion: The Present Position." *International Quarterly* (formerly the *International Monthly*) 7 (1903): 85–107.

Dudleian lecture for 1901–1902 at Harvard, given on March 10, 1902.

6. "What Should Be the Attitude of Teachers of Philosophy Towards Religion?" *IJE*, 13 (1902–1903): 280–85.

Read before the American Philosophical Association meeting in Washington, D.C., on December 30–31, 1902. For a reply see J. Clark Murray, "What Should be the Attitude of Teachers of Philosophy Towards Religion? A Reply," *IJE*, 14 (1903–1904): 353–62.

1904

1. "The Eternal and the Practical." *Philosophical Review*, 13 (1904): 113–42.

Presidential address to the American Philosophical Association, meeting at Princeton, on December 29–31, 1903.

2. "Herbert Spencer and His Contribution to the Concept of Evolution." *International Quarterly* (formerly the *International Monthly*), 9 (1904): 335–65. Reprinted in *Herbert Spencer, 1904–3*.

3. *Herbert Spencer: An Estimate and Review.* New York: Fox, Duffield & Co., 1904, 234 pp.
     Contents:
     (1) "Herbert Spencer and his Contribution to the Concept of Evolution," *1904–2.* On p. 53 of the book, there is a footnote not found in the *International Quarterly.*
     (2) "Herbert Spencer's Educational Theories."
     (3) "Reminiscences of Herbert Spencer," by James Collier.

4. Introduction to L. van Becelaere, O.P., *La Philosophie en Amérique, depuis les origines jusqu'à nos jours, 1607–1900*, pp. ix–xvii. New York: Eclectic Publishing Co., 1904.
     The introduction is in English. Apparently, a different edition was at least planned with the introduction in French, translated by Jean Prével.

5. "The Present Significance of Kant." *Nation*, 78 (1904): 125–26.
     Unsigned. Attributed to Royce by Haskell. Written to commemorate the centenary of Kant's death.

6. "The Sciences of the Ideal." *Science*, n.s., 20 (1904): 449–62. Reprinted in *Congress of Arts and Sciences, Universal Exposition, St. Louis, 1904* (Boston: Houghton, Mifflin Co., 1905), 1: 151–68.
     Address to the Division of Normative Science, given on September 20, 1904. Vol. 72 of the Royce Papers contains an essay titled "Symmetrical and Unsymmetrical Relations in the Exact Sciences," probably written in 1905. This is an elaboration of certain points in the St. Louis paper on the "fundamental relations involved in the exact sciences."

7. "Wie unterscheiden sich gesunde und krankhafte Geisteszüstande beim Kinde." *Pädagogisches Magazin*, 44 (1904): 1–28.
     Translated into German by Chr. Ufer.

1905

1. "Introduction" to Henri Poincaré, *Science and Hypothesis*, trans. George Bruce Halsted, pp. xv–xxxi. New York: Science Press, 1905. Reprinted as the introduction to *Science and Hypothesis* in Henri Poincaré, *The Foundations of Science* (Lancaster, Pa.: The Science Press, 1913), pp. 9–24. Reprinted, with slight omissions, as the introduction to *The Foundations of Science* in *RLE*.

2. "Kant's Doctrine of the Bases of Mathematics." *Journal of Philosophy, Psychology and Scientific Methods*, 2 (1905): 197–207.

Read at a special session to commemorate the centenary of the death of Kant of the annual meeting of the American Philosophical Association, held at Philadelphia, December 28–30, 1904.

3. "The Relation of the Principles of Logic to the Foundations of Geometry." *Transactions of the American Mathematical Society*, 24 (1905): 353–415. Reprinted in *RLE*. An abstract was published in the *Bulletin of the American Mathematical Society*, 2 (1904–1905): 471–72, but it is not known whether this abstract was prepared by Royce.

Paper presented to the Society on April 29, 1905, under the title "The Fundamental Relations of Logical and Geometrical Theory." This paper is an extension of A. B. Kempe, "On the Relation Between the Logical Theory of Classes and the Geometrical Theory of Points," *Proceedings of the London Mathematical Society*, 21 (1890): 147–82. Royce discussed this paper from a different point of view in the *World and the Individual*, 2: 77ff. For the place of this paper in Royce's planned book on logic see *1913–3*. Vol. 75 of the Royce Papers contains a manuscript titled "A Study Towards a Generalization of the O-Relation." This is said to be a supplement to the present paper. The manuscript is undated, and one page is missing.

1906

1. "The Present State of the Question Regarding the First Principles of Theoretical Science." *Proceedings of the American Philosophical Society*, 45 (1906): 82–102.

Paper delivered at the Franklin Bicentenary Celebration, in Philadelphia, on April 18, 1906. It is sometimes referred to as "The Present Position of the Problem of the First Principles of Scientific Theory."

2. "Race Questions and Prejudices." *IJE*, 16 (1905–1906): 265–88. Reprinted in *Race Questions, 1908–3*, and in *SPJR*.

Paper delivered to the Chicago Ethical Society in 1905.

3. Review of James Hervey Hyslop, *Problems of Philosophy. IJE*, 16 (1905–1906): 236–41.

1907

1. "Immortality." *Hibbert Journal*, 5 (1907): 724–44. Reprinted in William James, *1911–4*.

Address to an association of clergymen, given in March of 1906. For other writings on immortality see *1900–2*.

1908

1. "Football and Ideals." *Harvard Illustrated Magazine*, 10 (1908–1909): 40–47.

Described as a "restatement," at the request of the editor, of an earlier essay on physical training, probably, *1908-5*.

2. *The Philosophy of Loyalty*. New York: Macmillan Co., 1908, xii, 409 pp. French translation by Jacqueline Morot-Sir, *Philosophie du loyalisme* (Paris: Editions Montaigne, 1946, 254 pp). Italian translation by Giuseppe Rensi, *La filosofia della fedeltà* (Bari: Laterza et Figli, 1927). Spanish translation by Vincente P. Quintero, *Filosofia de la fidelidad* (Buenos Aires, 1949). First five lectures are reprinted in *SPJR*.

This work grew out of numerous lectures given during 1906 and 1907. Those given at the University of Illinois have been published, see *P-6* and *P-7*. In the form published, the lectures were given at the Lowell Institute in Boston in November and December of 1907. The *Boston Evening Transcript* carried summaries of them: lecture 1, November 19, 1907, p. 4; 2, November 22, p. 5; 3, November 26, p. 12; 4, November 29, p. 11; 5, December 3, p. 4; 6, December 6, p. 12; 7, December 10, p. 10; 8, December 13, p. 12. I have seen nothing showing that these were prepared by Royce; but this is possible, as did happen in the case of the *Problem of Christianity*, *1913-6*.

This is Royce's major work in ethics. He makes it clear, however, that he also has a practical aim, "to win hearts for loyalty." As for his metaphysics, he insists that this has remained unchanged since the *World and the Individual*. The preface is dated March 1, 1908.

3. *Race Questions, Provincialism, and Other American Problems*. New York: Macmillan Co., 1908, xiii, 287 pp. The same text reprinted (Freeport, N. Y.: Books for Libraries Press, 1967).

Contents:
(1) "Preface," dated October 16, 1908.
(2) "Race Questions and Prejudices," *1906-2*.
(3) "Provincialism," *1902-3*.
(4) "On Certain Limitations of the Thoughtful Public in America." Previously unpublished. Originally given as the Founder's Day address at Vassar College, on April 28, 1899. Probably, it was used by him as a stock lecture.
(5) "The Pacific Coast. A Psychological Study of the Relations of Climate and Civilization," *1900-3*.
(6) "Some Relations of Physical Training to the Present Problems of Moral Education in America," n.d., see *1908-5*.

4. Review of I. Woodbridge Riley, *American Philosophy: The Early Schools. Harvard Graduates' Magazine* 16 (1907-1908): 649-51.

5. *Some Relations of Physical Training to the Present Problems of Moral Education in America*. Boston: The Boston Normal School of Gymnastics, [19—]. A pamphlet. Reprinted in *Race Questions, 1908-3*.

An address before the Boston Physical Education Association.

1908–1 refers to this as recent; it is therefore likely that it was published in late 1908.

6. Translations in Benjamin Rand, ed., *Modern Classical Philosophers.* Boston: Houghton Mifflin Co., 1908. Giordano Bruno, "Concerning the Cause, the Principle and the One," pp. 1–23 (with Katharine Royce); Hegel, "The Contrite Consciousness," from the *Phenomenology of Mind*, pp. 614–28, reprinted in J. Loewenberg, ed., *Hegel Selections* (New York: Scribner's, 1929), pp. 79–98. The Hegel excerpt is prefaced by an extended introductory note by Royce.

According to Royce's letter to William T. Harris of December 4, 1892 (*L–12*), Royce was at this time planning to publish a book of translated extracts from the *Phenomenology*, with notes. Possibly, the Hegel excerpt published here dates from this time.

1909

1. "The American College and Life." *Science*, n.s., 29 (1909): 401–407.
Address to the American Association for the Advancement of Science, in Baltimore.

2. "The Problem of Truth in the Light of Recent Discussion." In *Bericht über den III internationalen Kongress für Philosophie*, pp. 62–90. Heidelberg: Carl Winter's Universitatsbuchhandlung, 1909. The discussion which followed is reported on pp. 91–93. Reprinted in *William James (1911–4)* and *RLE*.
Address to the congress which was held at Heidelberg, September 1–5, 1908.

3. "Provincialism Based upon a Study of Early Conditions in California." *Putnam's Magazine*, 7 (1909): 232–40.
For another essay on the same topic see *1902–3*.

4. "The Recent Psychotherapeutic Movement in America." In W. B. Parker, ed., *Psychotherapy: A Course of Readings in Sound Psychology, Sound Medicine, Sound Religion*, vol. 1, no. 1 (1909): 17–36. A summary and notes by the editor follow on pp. 36–41.
Apparently, *Psychotherapy* was first published in 1908 and then reprinted in 1909. Royce's essay appears only in the second version.

5. "What is Vital in Christianity?" *Harvard Theological Review*, 2, (1909): 408–45. Reprinted in *William James (1911–4)* and in Clark S. Northup, William C. Lane, John C. Schwab, eds., *Representative Phi Beta Kappa Orations* (Boston and New York: Houghton Mifflin Co., 1915), pp. 404–41.
Vol. 75 of the Royce Papers contains the first four pages of the manuscript. It is described, by the archivist, as the Phi Beta Kappa address at Vassar College, given on March 8, 1907. This date seems incorrect. In Clark S. Northup, "A Phi Beta Kappa Bibliography,"

The Phi Betta Kappa Key, 3 (1916–19): 305, this is said to be the Vassar Phi Betta Kappa oration for 1909. It is described in this way in *Representative Phi Beta Kappa Orations.* In the *Harvard Theological Review* it is described as three addresses given at Phillips Brooks House, Harvard, on March 18, 25, and April 1, 1909. This description is confirmed by the *Harvard University Gazette* (4, [1908–1909]: 149), where it is further described as part of eight conferences on "The Fundamental Principles of Christianity," given by Francis G. Peabody, Royce, and John W. Platner. In *William James 1911–4,* p. 99n., it is described as "Prepared for a series of addresses to the Young Men's Christian Association of Harvard University in 1909."

1910

1. "Axiom." In James Hastings, ed., *Encyclopaedia of Religion and Ethics,* 2: 279–82. New York: Charles Scribner's Sons, 1910. Reprinted in *RLE,* without the list of literature.

   Other contributions to this encyclopaedia are *1912–1, 1916–6, 1916–7, 1917–1, 1917–3.*

2. "Introductory Word," to Jessie E. Sampter, *The Seekers,* pp. v-xii. New York: Mitchell Kennerley, 1910.

   The Seekers is a record of the meetings of a group of young women in New York City who gathered to discuss religious and literary questions. Sampter, the leader of the group, was apparently a chance social acquaintance of Royce. Royce was impressed by the "practical idealism" shown in the discussions. See Bertha Badt-Strauss, *White Fire: The Life and Works of Jessie Sampter* (New York: The Reconstructionist Press, 1956) p. 17, p. 26.

3. "Loyalty and Insight." *The Simmons Quarterly,* 1 (1910): 4–21. Reprinted in *William James, 1911–4.*

   Commencement address given on June 22, 1910, at Simmons College in Boston.

4. "Minute on the Life and Services of Professor William James," *Harvard University Gazette,* 6 (1910–11): 29–30.

   Unsigned. According to Frank M. Oppenheim's examination of the records of the Harvard Faculty of Arts and Sciences, this minute was prepared by George Herbert Palmer, Royce, and B. Wendell. The minute was placed on the records of the Faculty on October 18, 1910.

5. "The Reality of the Temporal," *IJE,* 20 (1910): 257–71.

   Address to the American Philosophical Association, on December 29, 1909, in New Haven.

6. "A Word of Greeting to William James." *Harvard Graduates' Magazine,* 18 (1909–10): 630–33. Reprinted as "William James' Per-

sonality: An Estimate by a Colleague," in the *Springfield Sunday Republican*, August 28, 1910, p. 20.

Remarks at a dinner in honor of William James, held on January 18 1910. Contains some autobiographical remarks on his first contacts with James.

1911

1. "A Communication Dealing with the Relations Between the Two Institutions." *Yale News*, vol. 34, no. 128, (March 11, 1911). Major portions reprinted as "An Intellectual Contest," *Harvard Graduates' Magazine*, 19 (1910–11): 740–41.

A letter to the editor proposing an intellectual contest between Yale and Harvard. Written in reply to a question by the editor concerning Yale-Harvard relations.

2. "In Honor of Professor Palmer." *Harvard Graduates' Magazine*, 19 (1910–11): 575–78.

Speech at a banquet in honor of George Herbert Palmer, held on February 25, 1911.

3. "James as a Philosopher." *Boston Evening Transcript*, June 29, 1911, p. 13. Reprinted in *Science*, n.s., 34 (1911): 33–45; *Harvard Graduates' Magazine*, 20 (1911–12): 1–18; *William James 1911–4* under the title "William James and the Philosophy of Life." Extensive excerpts were published in a German translation by K. Bornhausen, "James der Philosoph des heutingen Amerika," *Die Christliche Welt*, no. 6 (1913), cols. 121–30.

Phi Beta Kappa oration delivered at Harvard University on June 29, 1911. After the death of William James, Royce received many requests to write about him. He refused all of them. See Royce's letter to Robert U. Johnson September 16, 1910. This address was delivered within a year of James' death.

4. *William James and Other Essays on the Philosophy of Life.* New York: Macmillan Co., 1911, xi, 301 pp.
Contents:
(1) "Preface," dated October 5, 1911.
(2) "William James and the Philosophy of Life," *1911–3*.
(3) "Loyalty and Insight," *1910–3*.
(4) "What is Vital in Christianity?" *1909–5*.
(5) "The Problem of Truth in the Light of Recent Discussion," *1909–2*.
(6) "Immortality," *1907–1*.

1912

1. "Error and Truth." In James Hastings, ed., *Encyclopaedia of Religion and Ethics*, 5: 366–73. New York: Charles Scribner's Sons, 1912. Reprinted in *RLE*.

The *RLE* omits the list of literature. The heading "I. Introduction" was introduced by the editor. Because of this, the sections are numbered differently in the two texts.

2. Introduction to Eugen Kühnemann, *Schiller*, trans. Katharine Royce, 2 vols., 1: vii–ix. Boston and London: Ginn & Co., 1912.
  Royce's introduction is dated April 13, 1912.

3. "On Definitions and Debates." *Journal of Philosophy, Psychology, and Scientific Methods*, 9 (1912): 85–100. Reprinted in *RLE*.
  This is Royce's reaction to a report and discussion of the American Philosophical Association. A committee was formed to select a topic and work out a framework for discussion for the annual meeting to be held at Harvard, December 27–29, 1911. The report of the committee appears in the *Journal of Philosophy, Psychology, and Scientific Methods*, 8 (1911): 701–706; an account of the meeting is given in the same journal, 9 (1912): 101–10. Royce was present at the meeting but does not seem to have taken part in the discussion of the topic. The new realists were heavily represented both on the committee and in the discussions of the meeting. Royce's paper was sent to the editor, F. J. E. Woodbridge, on January 5, 1912. In the covering letter to Woodbridge and another letter to him dated January 20, 1912, Royce explains his reasons for writing the paper.

4. "Prinzipien der Logik." In *Logik*, pp. 61–136. (Tübingen: J. C. B. Mohr (Paul Siebeck), 1912). Vol. 1 of the *Encyclopädie der philosophischen Wissenschaften*, ed. Arnold Ruge. The original English text appears as "The Principles of Logic," in *Logic*, trans. B. Ethel Meyer (London: Macmillan and Co., Ltd., 1913), pp. 67–135. Vol. 1 of the *Encyclopaedia of the Philosophical Sciences*. This text was reprinted in *RLE*. The same text was separately published as *The Principles of Logic* (New York: Wisdom Library, ᶜ1961), 77 pp.
  André-A Devaux ("Bibliographie des traductions d'ouvrages de Royce et des etudes sur l'oeuvre de Royce," *Revue Internationale de Philosophie*, 21 [1967]: 161) lists an Italian translation, "Principii di logica," in *Logica* (Palerme: Remo Sandron, 1914) (vol. 1 of *Enciclopedia delle scienze filosofische*) and a Russian translation, *Printsipy Logiki* (Moscow, 1913). The card catalogue of the Yale University library lists a Chinese translation, *Lo Chih Ti Yuan Li*, 2d ed. (Shanghai, 1947).
  The contents of both the German and the English versions of the *Logik* are as follows:
  (1) "Introduction," A. Ruge
  (2) "The Principles of Logic," W. Windelband
  (3) "The Principles of Logic," J. Royce
  (4) "The Principles of Logic," L. Couturat
  (5) "The Task of Logic," B. Croce
  (6) "The Problems of Logic," F. Enriques
  (7) "The Transformation of the Concept of Consciousness in

Modern Epistemology and its Bearing on Logic," N. Losskij. I have no information about plans for other volumes of the *Encyclopädie*. As far as I know, no other volumes were published.

On the title page of the Widener Library copy (Phil. 5062.18.3) of the German version, there is a note in Royce's hand stating that this essay was written in English in September 1910 and was then sent to Ruge and translated into German by Edmund Schweitzer. On p. 61 of the same copy there is another note by Royce. "By the terms of Royce's contract with Ruge, made in 1909, the German publisher has the copyright of this essay, of which, at the date of this publication (in 1912), no English edition exists. The general idea of Logic as the 'Theory of Order,' as here sketched, has been previously suggested in various of Royce's essays (Cf. World & Indiv; Vol. II, Lectures I & II), but is here more fully outlined than in any previous discussion of Logic by J. R. This paper is thus a programme of a future possible Logic; and, *as* a programme has a place in a fairly extensive plan. The issues discussed have, in J. R.'s opinion, an importance that is greater than the length of the paper indicates."

Vol. 30 of the Royce Papers contains the manuscript of "The Principles of Logic." This appears to be the text published in English. While there are no notes to this effect in the English edition, the text published there is not a retranslation from the German.

5. *The Sources of Religious Insight.* New York: C. Scribner's Sons, 1912, xvi, 297 pp. The Bross Library, vol. 6. The same text was also published in England (Edinburgh: T. & T. Clark, 1912). Also published in paperback in the Scribner Library (New York: Scribner, [1963? ᶜ1940]). The original edition contains a note on the Bross Foundation by John Scholte Nollen, dated March, 1912. The Scribner Library edition omits this note.

The Bross lectures delivered at Lake Forest College, Lake Forest, Illinois, November 13 to 19, 1911. According to his letter to Mrs. Bristol of December 3, 1911, Royce intended to repeat these lectures at the Andover Seminary. Because of his illness, he did not repeat them. According to the *Smith College Monthly* (17 [1909–10]: 488), Royce lectured at Smith College in March and April of 1910, in the series "Modern Philosophy of Life," under the title "Sources of Religious Insight." The connection between these and the Bross lectures is unknown.

On pp. 9–10 of the *Sources of Religious Insight*, Royce observes that here he will not discuss Christianity at any length, because at some future time he will "attempt an application of some of the principles that underlie the present lectures to the special problems which Christianity offers to the student of religion." In a letter to George P. Brett dated January 7, 1912, Royce discusses plans for publishing his study of Christianity and notes that the Bross lectures ignore Christianity because of these plans.

1913

1. "Atonement." *Atlantic Monthly*, 111 (1913): 406–19.
   An excerpt from the *Problem of Christianity, 1913–6*, vol. 1, lect. 6.

2. "The Christian Doctrine of Life." *Hibbert Journal*, 11 (1913): 473–96.
   An excerpt from the *Problem of Christianity, 1913–6*, vol. 1 lect. 7. Most Royce bibliographies list "The Essential Contrast Between Christianity and Buddhism," *Current Opinion*, 55 (1913): 41–42. This is not by Royce, but is an unsigned summary of "The Christian Doctrine of Life," with extensive quotations.

3. "An Extension of the Algebra of Logic." *Journal of Philosophy, Psychology, and Scientific Methods*, 10 (1913): 617–33. List of corrections, p. 672. Reprinted in *RLE* with corrections. *RLE* omits the last paragraph of three lines.
   The list of corrections was prepared by Royce and was printed exactly as he prepared it. It was sent together with a letter to F. J. E. Woodbridge dated November 9, 1913. The letter notes that he is also sending a corrected copy of the *Journal* and that this lists some minor errors not in the list. I have no information as to whether this copy is still extant.
   According to Royce's letter to Woodbridge of September 16, 1913, this paper was to be the first of a series of seven papers, and these were to be part of a book on the "relations between logic and geometry." The seven articles were to be as follows:
   (1) "An Extension of the Algebra of Logic."
   (2) "Kempe's Theory of the Analogies Between the Logical and the Geometrical Relations." A summary of the 1905 paper, "The Relation of the Principles of Logic to the Foundations of Geometry."
   (3) "The Logical Continuum."
   (4) "A New Type of Logical Entities." Royce comments here: "This I suppose to be both a novel and an important contribution."
   (5) "The Transformations of the Logical Continuum, and the Invertible Pair Operation."
   (6) "The Philosophical Significance of the Logical Continuum."
   (7) "What is Vital in Logic?" "Summary & controversial appendix to the whole series."
   Royce proposed to complete the series by Christmas. The Royce Papers contain a considerable number of notes and more or less complete essays on logic. At present, it is impossible to say how much of this material was to be used for this series.

4. "George Fox as a Mystic." *Harvard Theological Review*, 6 (1913): 31–59.

Besides the direct study of Fox, the essay contains extended discussions of mysticism in general.

5. "Primitive Ways of Thinking. With Special Reference to Negation and Classification." *The Open Court*, 27 (1913): 577–98.

Attempts to show how primitive mental processes, particularly tabu and divination, have contributed to the development of more rigorous thinking.

6. *The Problem of Christianity*. 2 vols. New York: Macmillan Co., 1913. Vol. 1, *The Christian Doctrine of Life*, xlvi, 425 pp.; vol. 2, *The Real World and the Christian Ideas*, vi, 442 pp. The same text reprinted (Hamden, Conn.: Archon Books, 1967). Reprinted in a single volume with an introduction by John E. Smith (Chicago & London: University of Chicago Press, 1968, v, 412 pp.). Translated into the Italian by E. Codignola, *Il problema del cristianesimo*, 2 vols. (Florence: Vallecchi, 1924–25).

Lectures delivered before the Lowell Institute in Boston and on the Hibbert Foundation at Manchester College, Oxford. Only the first eight were given in Boston, in November and December of 1912. The *Boston Evening Transcript* published summaries of these lectures: lecture 1, November 19, 1912, p. 13; 2, November 22, p. 15; 3, November 26, p. 16; 4, November 29, p. 13; 5, December 3, p. 2; 6, December 6, p. 7; 7, December 10, p. 11; 8, December 13, p. 12. These summaries were prepared from summaries provided by Royce himself. Vol. 39 of the Royce Papers contains summaries written out in Royce's hand. The *Boston Evening Transcript* summaries follow the manuscripts very closely, the bulk of them being outright quotation. All sixteen lectures were delivered at Oxford. According to the *Oxford University Gazette* (43 [1912–13]: 351, 466), the dates of delivery were January 13, 16, 20, 23, 27, 30, February 3, 6, 10, 13, 17, 20, 24, 27, March 3, 6.

Royce was planning a study of Christianity while writing the *Sources of Religious Insight, 1912–5*. In the preface (vol. 1 p. x) Royce wrote that "in spirit" the *Problem of Christianity* is in "essential harmony" with the "bases of the philosophical idealism" developed in the *World and the Individual* and other works. He makes essentially the same claim in his letter to Mary Whiton Calkins, *1916–2*.

7. "The Second Death." *Atlantic Monthly*, 111 (1913): 242–54.

An excerpt from the *Problem of Christianity, 1913–6*, vol. 1, lecture 5.

8. "Some Psychological Problems Emphasized by Pragmatism." *Popular Science Monthly*, 83 (1913): 394–411.

An address. Royce argues that studies of the psychology of reasoning by some pragmatists suffer because they ignore the discoveries of recent logic.

9. "Some Relations Between Philosophy and Science in the First Half of the Nineteenth Century in Germany." *Science*, n.s., 38 (1913): 567–84. The fourth section is reprinted in *RLE* as "Hypotheses and Leading Ideas."

Paper read before the Pathological Club of the Harvard Medical School, probably in 1913.

1914

1. "Introductory Note" to Federigo Enriques, *Problems of Science*, trans. Katharine Royce, pp. ix-xiii. Chicago: The Open Court Publishing Company, 1914. Reprinted in *RLE*, with some omissions.

2. "The Mechanical, the Historical and the Statistical." *Science*, n.s., 39 (1914): 551–66. Reprinted in *RLE*.

An address to a group of Harvard professors, mostly scientists, called together by Royce to decide whether it would be useful to them to gather regularly to discuss common problems.

3. "A Plea for Provincial Independence in Education; A Letter with Reference to the Report of the Carnegie Foundation for the Advancement of Teaching on Education in Vermont." *Middlebury College Bulletin*, 9 (October, 1914): 3–19.

Royce's letter, dated September 24, 1914, to John M. Thomas, president of Middlebury College in Vermont. Royce is commenting on *A study of Education in Vermont*, Bulletin no. 7 of the Carnegie Foundation for the Advancement of Teaching, New York, 1914. See also *1915-3*.

4. "Professor Royce on His Reviewer." *New Republic*, 1 (1914): 23.

Royce's reply to the review of *War and Insurance* (*1914-5*), which appeared in the *New Republic*, 1 (1914): 26–27.

5. *War and Insurance: An Address Delivered Before the Philosophical Union of the University of California at Its Twenty-Fifth Anniversary at Berkeley California, August 27, 1914*. New York: Macmillan Co., 1914, xlviii, 96 pp. Reprinted, without the introduction and notes, in *SPJR*.

He had intended to discuss the idea of interpretation; but the war broke out, and he abandoned his original plan. According to the preface (p. iv), the address was prepared in August of 1914. Royce always stressed the dependence of his scheme of international insurance on the triadic structure of interpretation. Other writings on insurance are *1914-4* and *1915-5*.

6. "A Word for the Times." *Harvard Graduates' Magazine*, 23 (1914–15): 207–209.

An address given at the beginning of the academic year.

1915

1. "An American Thinker on the War." *Hibbert Journal*, 14 (1915–16): 37–42. Previously printed, with the exception of several paragraphs, in the *London Morning Post*, July 5, 1915. Reprinted as "The Destruction of the Lusitania," in *HGC*.

Extracts from Royce's letter to the editor of the *Hibbert Journal*, L. P. Jacks. The letter gives permission to publish. The *Hibbert Journal* title is the editor's. Other writings on the war are *1915–2, 1916–3, 1916–4, 1916–8*.

2. "Belgium as the Teacher of the Nations. Professor Royce Predicts a New Sense of International Duty and a Rapid Recovery After the War." *New York Times*, December 20, 1915, p. 10. Parts reprinted as "A Hopeful View of the European Situation," *Journal of Education* (Boston), 83 (1916): 92–93.

Part of an address prepared for a group of philosophy teachers gathered in honor of Maurice de Wulf.

3. "The Carnegie Foundation for the Advancement of Teaching and the Case of Middlebury College." *School and Society*, 1 (1915): 145–50.

Address to the organizational meeting of the American Association of University Professors in New York on January 2, 1915 (*School and Society* dates it in 1914, but this is incorrect). It led to the formation of Committee D of the AAUP, on "Limits of Standardization of Institutions, etc.," according to the *Bulletin of the American Association of University Professors*, 2 (April, 1916): 21. In the course of the address, Royce distributed a pamphlet on the case. Most likely, this was *1914–3*.

4. "Introductory Note" to Annie Lyman Sears, *The Drama of the Spiritual Life: A Study of Religious Experience and Ideals*, pp. xv–xxiv. New York: Macmillan Co., 1915.

Dated "Memorial Day," 1915. The author had been a student of his; however, he repudiates the suggestion that the book represents his views.

5. "Professor Josiah Royce of Harvard Advocates Insurance by the Nations of the World." *New York Times*, July 25, 1915, part 4, pp. 2–3. Reprinted as the "Possibility of International Insurance," in *HGC*.

For other writings on insurance see *1914–5*.

1916

1. "Charles Sanders Peirce." *Journal of Philosophy, Psychology, and Scientific Methods*, 13 (1916): 701–709. Fergus Kernan signed as co-author.

For information about the origins and authorship of this essay see W. F. Kernan, "The Peirce Manuscripts and Josiah Royce—A

Memoir Harvard 1915–1916," in *Transactions of the Charles S. Peirce Society*, 1 (1965): 90–95.

2. "Comment by Professor Royce. Extracts from a Letter to Miss Calkins, March 20, 1916." *Philosophical Review*, 25 (1916): 293–96; *Papers in Honor of Josiah Royce* (Offprint of *Philosophical Review* text, with different page numbers), pp. 65–68.

Comments on "The Foundation in Royce's Philosophy for Christian Theism," by Mary Whiton Calkins, *Philosophical Review*, 25 (1916): 282–93; *Papers in Honor of Josiah Royce*, pp. 54–65. Royce especially approves Calkins' account of the relations between his earlier thought and the *Problem of Christianity*. The typewritten original of the letter is in Wellesley (Massachusetts) College library.

3. "Duties of Americans in the Present War." *Boston Evening Transcript*, February 2, 1916, p. 18. Published also as a pamphlet (Boston, 1916). Reprinted in *HGC*.

Address delivered at the Tremont Temple in Boston, on January 30, 1916. The *Boston Evening Transcript* text and the pamphlet show minor differences. The *HGC* text follows that of the pamphlet. The *Boston Evening Transcript* text follows the manuscript in vol. 51 of the Royce Papers. The publisher of the pamphlet is not noted, but on the back cover there is an announcement by the "Citizens League for America and the Allies." Royce is listed as a member.

For other writings on the war see *1915–1*.

4. "The Hope of the Great Community." *Yale Review*, 5 (1916): 269–91. Reprinted in *HGC*, and in *SPJR*.

5. *The Hope of the Great Community*. New York: Macmillan Co., 1916, ix, 136 pp. The same text reprinted (Freeport, N. Y.: Books for Libraries Press, 1967).

Contents:
(1) "Prefatory Note," by Katharine Royce.
(2) "Josiah Royce," a poem by Laura Simmons.
(3) "The Duties of Americans in the Present War," *1916–3*.
(4) "The Destruction of the Lusitania," *1915–1*.
(5) "The Hope of the Great Community," *1916–4*.
(6) "The Possibility of International Insurance," *1915–5*.
(7) "The First Anniversary of the Sinking of the Lusitania, May 7, 1916," *1916–8*.
(8) "Words of Professor Royce at the Walton Hotel at Philadelphia, December 29, 1915," *1916–9*.

According to Katharine Royce, Royce died while this book was in the press.

6. "Mind." In James Hastings, ed., *Encyclopaedia of Religion and Ethics*, 8: 649–57. New York: Charles Scribner's Sons, 1916. Reprinted in *RLE*.

RLE omits the list of literature. For other contributions see *1910–1*.

7. "Monotheism." In James Hastings, ed., *Encyclopaedia of Religion and Ethics*, 8: 817–21. New York: Charles Scribner's Sons, 1916.
For other contributions see *1910–1*.

8. "Professor Royce's 'Lusitania' Speech." *Boston Evening Transcript*, May 8, 1916, p. 13. Reprinted in *HGC* as "The First Anniversary of the Sinking of the Lusitania, May 7, 1916."
Address at the Lusitania Memorial Meeting at the Tremont Temple in Boston, on May 7, 1916. For other writings on the war see *1915–1*.

9. "Words of Professor Royce at the Walton Hotel at Philadelphia, December 29, 1915," *Philosophical Review*, 25 (1916): 507–14; *Papers in Honor of Josiah Royce* (*Philosophical Review* text, with different page numbers), pp. 279–86. Reprinted in *HGC*.
A summary of Royce's address based on notes made by members of the audience. The address was given at a banquet given in Royce's honor at the meeting of the American Philosophical Association in Philadelphia. For the most part, autobiographical.

1917

1. "Negation." In James Hastings, ed., *Encyclopaedia of Religion and Ethics*, 9: 264–71. New York: Charles Scribner's Sons, 1917. Reprinted in *RLE*.
RLE omits the list of literature. For other contributions see *1910–1*.

2. "Nietzsche." *Atlantic Monthly*, 119 (1917): 321–31. With an introductory note by W. Fergus Kernan.
Published, probably due to Kernan's initiative, after Royce's death. Royce claims that Nietzsche is most noteworthy for developing a novel form of "ethical Titanism."

3. "Order." In James Hastings, ed., *Encyclopaedia of Religion and Ethics*, 9: 533–40. New York: Charles Scribner's Sons, 1917. Reprinted in *RLE*.
RLE omits the list of literature. In the *Encyclopaedia*, portions of the text are printed in smaller type, suggesting that these are illustrative. *RLE* uses only one kind of type. For other contributions see *1910–1*.

Posthumous Publications

1. *Fugitive Essays.* Edited by Jacob Loewenberg. Cambridge: Harvard University Press, 1920, 429 pp. Another edition was published by Harvard University Press at the same time. This edition bears the half-title, *Semicentennial Publications of the University of California, 1868–*

1918. It has an additional title page; otherwise, the two are identical. The same text reprinted (Freeport, N. Y.: Books for Libraries Press, 1968).

Contents:

(1) "Editor's Introduction," by Jacob Loewenberg. Contains extended quotations from Royce's diary.
(2) "Schiller's Ethical Studies," *1878–4*.
(3) "Shelley and the Revolution," *1880–3*.
(4) "The Nature of Voluntary Progress," *1880–2*.
(5) "The Practical Significance of Pessimism," 1879. Previously unpublished.
(6) "Pessimism and Modern Thought," *1881–7*.
(7) "Tests of Right and Wrong," 1880. Previously unpublished.
(8) "On Purpose in Thought," 1880. Previously unpublished. Presented to the Metaphysical Club of Johns Hopkins University in late 1880. An abstract appeared in *Johns Hopkins University Circulars*, no. 7, December, 1880, p. 84.
(9) "George Eliot as a Religious Teacher," *1881–4*.
(10) "Natural Rights and Spinoza's Essay on Liberty," 1880. Previously unpublished.
(11) "The Decay of Earnestness," *1881–2*.
(12) "Doubting and Working," *1881–3*.
(13) "How Beliefs are Made," *1882–1*.
(14) "A Neglected Study," *1890–5*.
(15) "The Problem of Paracelsus," *1894–5*.
(16) "Pope Leo's Philosophical Movement and Its Relations to Modern Thought," *1903–4*.

2. *Lectures on Modern Idealism*. Edited by Jacob Loewenberg. New Haven: Yale University Press, 1919, xii, 266 pp. Another edition was published by Yale University Press at the same time. This edition bears the half-tile, *Semicentennial Publications of the University of California, 1868–1918*. It has an additional title page; otherwise, the two are identical. The same text, except for the preliminary matter, was reprinted with a foreword by John E. Smith (New Haven: Yale University Press [1964] xvi, 266 pp.).

Text of the lectures delivered at Johns Hopkins University in Baltimore in late January 1906 under the title "Aspects of Post-Kantian Idealism."

3. *Josiah Royce's Seminar, 1913–1914: As Recorded in the Notebooks of Harry T. Costello*. Edited by Grover Smith. New Brunswick, N. J.: Rutgers University Press, c1963, xxiii, 209 pp.

Costello served as secretary for the seminar. His task was to record the discussions and provide summaries of each session. Generally, the reports of the discussions are very condensed. The seminar for that year is usually called the "Seminary in Comparative Methodology."

4. *The Religious Philosophy of Josiah Royce*. Edited by Stuart Gerry Brown. Syracuse: Syracuse University Press, 1952, 239 pp.
Contents:
   (1) "Introduction: The Religious Philosophy of Josiah Royce," by Stuart Gerry Brown.
   (2) "The Possibility of Error," chapter 11 of *RAP*, with some omissions.
   (3) "Individuality and Freedom," lecture 10 of the *World and the Individual*, vol. 1, with some omissions.
   (4) "The Temporal and the Eternal," lecture 3 of the *World and the Individual*, vol. 2, with some omissions.
   (5) "The Conception of Immortality," the text, except for the notes, of the *Conception of Immortality, 1900–2.*
   (6) "Loyalty and Religion," chapter 8 of the *Philosophy of Loyalty, 1908–2*, with some omissions.
   (7) "The Idea of the Universal Community," lecture 2 of the *Problem of Christianity*, vol. 1, *1913–6*, with some omissions.
   (8) "The Moral Burden of the Individual," lecture 3 of the *Problem of Christianity*, vol. 1, *1913–6.*
   (9) "The Realm of Grace," lecture 4 of the *Problem of Christianity*, vol. 1, *1913–6.*
   (10) "Time and Guilt," lecture 5 of the *Problem of Christianity*, vol. 1, *1913–6.*
   (11) "Atonement," lecture 6 of the *Problem of Christianity*, vol. 1, *1913–6.*

5. *Royce's Logical Essays: Collected Logical Essays of Josiah Royce.* Edited by Daniel S. Robinson. Dubuque, Iowa: Wm. C. Brown Co., ᶜ1951, xvi, 447 pp.
Contents:
   (1) Facsimile of a letter from Daniel Coit Gilman to William Torrey Harris, dated July 18, 1878, introducing Royce to Harris.
   (2) Facsimile of Royce's letter to William Torrey Harris, dated January 4, 1878.
   (3) Facsimile of a postcard from Royce to Harris, dated October 23, 1878.
   (4) "Editor's Preface," by Daniel S. Robinson.
   (5) "Recent Logical Inquiries and Their Psychological Bearings," *1902–4.*
   (6) "The Mechanical, the Historical, and the Statistical," *1914–2.*
   (7) "The Problem of Truth in the Light of Recent Discussion," *1909–2.*
   (8) "Error and Truth," *1912–1*, with some changes.
   (9) "Axiom," *1910–1.*
   (10) "Individual," *1901–1.*
   (11) "Mind," *1916–6.*

(12) "Negation," *1917–1*.
(13) "Order," *1917–3*.
(14) "On Definitions and Debates," *1912–3*.
(15) "Introductory Note to Enrique's Problems of Science," *1914–1*.
(16) "Hypotheses and Leading Ideas," part of *1913–9*.
(17) "Introduction to Poincare's Foundations of Science," *1905–1*, with some omissions.
(18) "Benno Erdmann's Logic," *1892–5*.
(19) "An Extension of the Algebra of Logic," *1913–3*.
(20) "The Principles of Logic," *1912–4*.
(21) "The Relation of the Principles of Logic to the Foundations of Geometry," *1905–3*.

6. "Royce's Urbana Lectures: Lecture I." Edited by Peter Fuss. *Journal of the History of Philosophy*, 5 (1967): 60–78.
   The first of a series of lectures which Royce gave at the University of Illinois in 1907. The material of these lectures was used extensively in the *Philosophy of Loyalty, 1908–2*. See also *P–7*.

7. "Royce's Urbana Lectures: Lecture II," Edited by Peter Fuss. *Journal of the History of Philosophy*, 5 (1967): 269–86.
   The second lecture of a series given by Royce at the University of Illinois, in 1907. See also *P–6*.

8. *The Social Philosophy of Josiah Royce*. Edited by Stuart Gerry Brown. Syracuse: Syracuse University Press, 1950, 220 pp.
   Contents:
   (1) "Introduction: 'From Provincialism to the Great Community,'" by Suart Gerry Brown.
   (2) "Race Questions and Prejudices," *1906–2*.
   (3) "Provincialism," *1902–3*.
   (4) "The Nature and Need of Loyalty," lecture 1 of the *Philosophy of Loyalty, 1908–2*.
   (5) "Individualism," lecture 2 of the *Philosophy of Loyalty, 1908–2*.
   (6) "Loyalty to Loyalty," lecture 3 of the *Philosophy of Loyalty, 1908–2*.
   (7) "Conscience," lecture 4 of the *Philosophy of Loyalty, 1908–2*.
   (8) "Some American Problems in Their Relation to Loyalty," lecture 5 of the *Philosophy of Loyalty, 1908–2*, with some omissions.
   (9) "The Hope of the Great Community," *1916–4*.
   (10) "Address on War and Insurance," the text, except for the introduction and notes of *War and Insurance, 1914–5*.

9. "The Two-Fold Nature of Knowledge: Imitative and Reflective, an Unpublished Manuscript of Josiah Royce." Edited by Peter Fuss. *Journal of the History of Philosophy*, 4 (1966): 326–37.
   For a related essay see *1894–3*.

Published Letters

Listed here are those letters which appeared after Royce's death. Those which were published before this are included in the main listing.

1. To James Mark Baldwin, July 9, 1895. In James Mark Baldwin, *Between Two Wars*, 2: 232–33. Boston: The Stratford Co., 1926.

2. To James Mark Baldwin (excerpts), June 20, 1897. Ibid., pp. 233–35. Other excerpts from this letter were published earlier, see *1897-2*.

3. To H. Wildon Carr, Secretary of the Aristotelian Society, April 26, 1913. In Daniel S. Robinson, *Royce and Hocking: American Idealists.* p. 139. Boston: The Christopher Publishing House, 1968.

4. To George B. Coale (excerpts), December 5, 1881. *Journal of Philosophy*, 36 (1939): 140.

5. To Mrs. Fremont (excerpts), August 20, 1885. In Robert Glass Cleland's introduction to Josiah Royce, *California*, pp. xix-xx. New York: Alfred A. Knopf, 1948.

6. To Daniel Coit Gilman, March 29, 1886. In Fabian Franklin, *The Life of Daniel Coit Gilman*, p. 372. New York: Dodd Mead and Co., 1910.

7. To William Torrey Harris, January 4, 1878. In Daniel S. Robinson, "Josiah Royce's Letters to William Torrey Harris," *The Philosophical Forum*, 13 (1955): 80. Facsimile in *RLE*.

8. To William Torrey Harris (postcard), October 23, 1878. Ibid., p. 82. Facsimile in *RLE*.

9. To William Torrey Harris, August 23, 1881. Ibid., p. 83.

10. To William Torrey Harris, December 28, 1881. Ibid., p. 84.

11. To William Torrey Harris, February 3, 1882. Ibid., p. 84.

12. To William Torrey Harris, December 4, 1892. Ibid., p. 85.

13. To William Torrey Harris, April 15, 1894. Ibid., pp. 85–86.

14. To William Torrey Harris, April 20, 1894. Ibid., p. 86.

15. To William Torrey Harris, May 13, 1894. Ibid., p. 86.

Letters 7–15 are reprinted in Daniel S. Robinson, *Royce and Hocking: American Idealists* (Boston: The Christopher Publishing House, 1968), pp. 127–38.

16. To William James (excerpts), January 14, 1879. In Ralph Barton Perry, *The Thought and Character of William James*, 1: 780–81. Boston, Toronto: Little, Brown and Co., 1935.

17. To William James (excerpts), January 8, 1880. Ibid., 1: 783–85.

18. To William James (excerpts), September 19, 1880. Ibid., 1: 787–89.

19. To William James (excerpts), December 28, 1881. Ibid., 1: 791–92.

20. To William James (excerpts), January 19, 1882. Ibid., 1: 793–94.

21. To William James (excerpts), October 31, 1882. Ibid., 1: 797.

22. To William James (excerpts), May 21, 1888. Ibid., 1: 800–802.

23. To William James (excerpts), October 17, 1892. Ibid., 1: 803–804.

24. To William James (excerpts), March, 1899. Ibid., 2: 729.

25. To William James, February 7, 1900. Ibid., 1: 814.

Extracts from items 22 and 25 are reprinted in Ralph Barton Perry, *The Thought and Character of William James*, Briefer Version (Cambridge: Harvard University Press, 1948); reprinted as a Harper Torchbook (New York: Harper & Row, 1964).

26. To William James (excerpts), September 12, 1900. Ibid., 1: 815–16.

27. To William James (excerpts), [1907]. Ibid., 1: 820–21.

28. To Jacob Loewenberg (facsimile), January 31, 1913. In *The Letters of Western Authors. No. 8: Josiah Royce*, with comment by Benjamin H. Lehman. San Francisco: Book Club of California, 1935.

29. To Florence Sparks Moore, May 3, 1904. In Daniel S. Robinson, *Royce and Hocking: American Idealists*, pp. 140–41. Boston: The Christopher Publishing House, 1968.

30. To Henry L. Oak (excerpts), August 8, 1885. In Robert Glass Cleland's introduction to Josiah Royce, *California*, pp. xviii-xix. New York: Alfred A. Knopf, 1948.

31. To Henry L. Oak (excerpts), September 17, 1885. Ibid., pp. xxvii-xxviii.

32. To Charles S. Peirce (excerpts), November 18, 1891. In James Harry Cotton, *Royce on the Human Self*, pp. 297–300. Cambridge: Harvard University Press, 1954.

33. To Charles S. Peirce (excerpts), June 20, 1902. Ibid., pp. 301–2.

34. To Gertrude Stein, March 27, 1896. In Donald C. Gallup, ed., *The Flowers of Friendship: Letters Written to Gertrude Stein*, pp. 6–7. New York: Alfred A. Knopf, 1953.

Location of Unpublished Letters Cited

To George P. Brett. August 22, 1899; September 1, 1899; October 27, 1901; February 24, 1904; undated [1904]; January 7, 1912. In the Macmillan Co., Papers, New York Public Library.

To Mrs. Bristol. December 3, 1911. In the Yale University library.

To George B. Coale. January 14, 1884; November 1, 1884; December 30, 1885; December 30, 1886. In the Johns Hopkins University library.

To Daniel Coit Gilman. June 14, 1875; July 11, 1875; May 11, 1884. In the Johns Hopkins University library.

To George Holmes Howison. Undated [1886]; July 13, 1889; October 5, 1897. In the Bancroft Library of the University of California.

To Robert U. Johnson. June 4, 1890; June 12, 1890; August 29, 1890; October 19, 1890; September 21, 1891. In the Bancroft Library of the University of California. October 6, 1891; October 7, 1891; September 16, 1910. In the Century Collection in the New York Public Library.

To Bernard Moses. September 7, 1883. In the Bancroft Library of the University of California.

To Henry L. Oak. August 8, 1885; November 12, 1885; January 30, 1886; May 31, 1886. In the Henry E. Huntington Library and Art Gallery. Typewriten copies in the Bancroft Library of the University of California.

To Horace E. Scudder. May 24, 1883; September 25, 1886; November 2, 1890; January 25, 1891; April 7, 1891. In the Bancroft Library of the University of California.

To Frederick J. E. Woodbridge, January 5, 1912; January 20, 1912; September 16, 1913; November 9, 1913. In the Columbia University library.

Additions to the Fordham University Press Edition

1896

3. "A Deplorable Affair." Letter to the editor, *The Cambridge Tribune*, 23 May 1896.
On 16 May 1896, Samuel Epes Turner, a neighbor, was accidentally struck and killed by a wagon while riding his bicycle. Royce claims that it is not enough for those responsible to "deplore" the accident. They must resolve that such things not happen again.

1900

6. Report of an address by Josiah Royce. *Springfield Republican*, 23 August 1900.
Royce gave an address at a dinner to benefit the Ashfield Academy, Ashfield, Mass., organized by Charles Eliot Norton. At the time, the addresses were primarily devoted to attacks on American imperialism. Royce deplored the rise of the mob spirit, stressing the importance of individuality and of small groups taking counsel together.

Index

This index should be supplemented by the Annotated Bibliography by Ignas Skrupskelis (above, p. 1167) and by Royce's extensive use of section headings in the essays and chapters reprinted in these volumes. For help in the preparation of this index, I am grateful to Virginia McDermott and Professor Peter Manicas.

Patriotism: education and, 2:1116;
loyalty and, 2:1155
Paul, Apostle, 2:753, 1006, 1149,
1151, 1153, 1154, 1157
Paul, Jean, 1:302
Peano, Guiseppe, 2:656, 787, 802, 819,
820
Pearson, Karl, 2:671, 672
Peirce, Charles Sanders, 1:10, 16, 453,
461, 502n, 589n; 2:652, 689, 690,
728, 732, 736, 741, 742, 744, 756,
763, 764, 766, 804n
Perception, 2:736, 743, 746, 753
Perry, Ralph Barton, 1:3, 4n, 7n, 8n,
9n; 2:652n, 829
Pessimism, 1:249–72; and
Schopenhauer, 1:267–68
Phenomenological analysis, Husserl
and, 2:661
Philosophy, 2:858, 860, 1020;
comprehension of the meaning of
its own doubts, 1:559; judged,
1:471; systematic scrutiny of
leading ideas, 2:768
Physics, statistical view in, 2:723–26
Plato, 1:276, 288, 304, 310, 311, 328,
329, 347, 368, 369, 371, 381, 406,
472, 473; 2:665, 737, 738, 739, 760,
865
Plotinus, 1:473; 2:881
Poincaré, Henri, 2:670; Royce on,
2:769–84
Polytheism, 1:404
Positivism, 2:683
Posits, 2:653n
Postulates, 1:342; of Kant 1:323–24
Powell, Thomas, 1:3n
Power: conflict and, 2:890; individual
good and, 2:889; Nietzsche and,
2:889
Pragmatism, 2:709, 745, 746, 748,
749, 750, 752, 787, 812, 817, 818,
819, 980, 981, 983, 984, 985, 986,
987, 990, 991, 993, 1000, 1003, 1011,
1060; dialectical method and, 315–
16; modern philosophy and, 2:998
Prejudice, 2:1089–1110
Prometheus, 2:845
Provincialism, 2:953, 954, 1065,
1067–88; meaning of, 2:1069;
modern civilization and, 2:1071–76;
national unity and, 2:1071;
problems of, 2:1084
Puritanism, 1:5, 190; significance for
Royce, 1:5–7
Purpose: experience and, 1:552;
fulfilment of, 1:539; real world as
expression of, 1:604; relative to

idea and object, 1:518, 533

Quantity: intensive and extensive,
2:806–7; new logic and, 2:676;
number-system and, 2:815
Quine, W. V. O., 2:653n

Race questions, 2:1089–1110;
anthrophobia, 2:1108; essential
characteristics of race, 2:1100;
human illusions about race, 2:1110;
present ignorance about racial
types, 2:1107; questioned,
2:1100–1107; race problems caused
by antipathy, 2:1107; race
psychology as a future science,
2:1104; race psychology as
inadequate, 2:1102; self-respect and
degradation of race, 2:1097
Realism, 1:470, 505, 531, 544, 546, 547,
549, 550, 551, 570, 619; abandoned
by Royce, 1:540; new, 2:690
Reck, Andrew J., 1:41n
Relations, 2:788–97; classes and,
2:798, 811; conception of, 2:798;
contrasted with qualities, 2:788;
correspondence, 1:514, 515, 516,
517; defined, 2:788; dyadic, 2:789,
805, 806; epsilon, 2:802; idea and
object, 1:522, 528, 529; impossible
without concept of class, 2:811; of
life, 1:12; logic of, 2:654; logical
properties of, 789–97; necessary to
theory of order, 2:811; polyadic,
2:789, 794; relativism as an eternal
system of, 2:691; symmetry of,
2:790–92, 810; system of functional,
2:808, 809; subsumption, 2:802;
transformation and, 2:809;
transitivity of, 2:791, 795, 802, 804,
809, 810; triadic, 2:796, 805, 806
Religion: anthropological data,
2:1103; creed of absolute religion,
2:1010; differs from morality,
2:1045; dilemma of, 2:1049;
eternally true, 2:1013; guilt and,
2:1032; interpretation, 2:1005;
James on religious experience,
2:1029, 1030; literature of religious
experience, 2:1033–36; loyalty and,
2:994–1013; religious need
presupposes evil, 2:1046; salvation
and, 2:1024, 1032, 1044; salvation
as personal, 2:1030; salvation as
social process, 2:1034; seeks
salvation and communion, 2:1043;